The Information Age

Economy, Society, and Culture

Volume II
The Power of Identity

Para Irene Castells Oliván,
historiadora de utopías

The Power of Identity

Second edition

Manuel Castells

Blackwell Publishing

350 Main Street, Malden, MA 02148-5020, USA
108 Cowley Road, Oxford OX4 1JF, UK
550 Swanston Street, Carlton, Victoria 3053, Australia

First edition published 1997
Second edition published 2004 by Blackwell Publishing Ltd

Library of Congress Cataloging-in-Publication Data

Castells, Manuel.
 The power of identity / by Manuel Castells.–2nd ed.
  p. cm. – (Information age, economy, society, and culture ; v. 2)
 ISBN 1-4051-0713-8
 1. Information society. 2. Social movements. 3. Information technology–Social aspects. 4. Information technology–Political aspects. 5. Identity. I. Title. II. Series: Castells, Manuel. Information age ; v. 2.

 HM851.C37 2003
 303.48'4–dc21

                                        2003006970

A catalogue record for this title is available from the British Library.

Set in 10.5/12pt Sabon
by Kolam Information Services Pvt. Ltd, Pondicherry, India
Printed and bound in the United Kingdom
by MPG Books Ltd, Bodmin, Cornwall

For further information on
Blackwell Publishing, visit our website:
http://www.blackwellpublishing.com

Contents

Figures

Tables

Charts

Preface and Acknowledgments 2003

This is the second volume of the trilogy *The Information Age: Economy, Society, and Culture*. The theme of the analysis presented in the trilogy is the contradictory relationship between a new global social structure – the network society – and resistance to the forms of domination implicit in this social structure. In my observation of social trends in the 1990s it appeared that cultural identity, in its different manifestations, was one of the main anchors of the opposition to the values and interests that had programmed the global networks of wealth, information, and power. Between global networks and cultural identities, the institutions of society, and particularly the nation-state, were shaken in their foundations and challenged in their legitimacy.

I was very careful not to make any predictions, since this is beyond the task of the researcher. Yet, from the vantage point of 2003, it seems that the framework proposed for the understanding of our world at the dawn of the information age may be useful to make sense of some of our current dramas: the rise of religious fundamentalism and of global terror networks; the role of national identity in anchoring societies in a global world; the surge of resistance against unchecked, global capitalism in a multidimensional movement for global justice; the restructuring of states to manage global complexity, evolving toward a new institutional form, the network state, in the age of multilateralism; the efforts by some states to reassert themselves as sovereign actors in spite of living in an interdependent world.

The Power of Identity was finished in November 1996, and published in October 1997. This new edition, completed in April 2003, updates and elaborates the analysis presented years earlier, while keeping the essence of the argument. However, at the time of writing the first edition, the techno-economic transformation of society – which I conceptualized as the rise of the network society – was more apparent than the projects of resistance to this specific form of global network society. Because, in my theoretical approach, societies are always understood in their contradictory and conflictive dynamics, I did identify the embryos of alternative social movements, and the harbingers of the crisis of the nation-state. Yet, equally important in my work is the methodological principle to resist speculation and social forecasting, building theory from observation, within the limits of my knowledge and competence. Thus, although I analyzed religious fundamentalism (particularly Islamic fundamentalism), nationalism, ethnic mobilizations, and anti-globalization movements (such as the Mexican *Zapatistas*) in their opposition to the new global disorder, it was too early to identify fully the profile of some of these social movements, and to draw consequences for the transformation of state institutions in the new international public space.

Nowadays we have evidence to hand that shows the emergence of social movements and political challenges opposed to the one-dimensional logic that dominates the network society in the first stage of its constitution. Here lies the potential usefulness of this new edition: to integrate more fully the analysis of the conflictive processes of resistance and alternative projects of social organization, on the basis of the documented observation of these processes, as they have developed around the turn of the millennium. Accordingly, I have not updated data and references throughout the whole volume. The purpose of the trilogy, and of this volume, is analytical, not documentary. Therefore, there is no point in running after the events for the rest of my life, after having spent 15 years researching and writing this trilogy. Since, for the time being, I have not much to add to my analysis of the crisis of patriarchalism, and to the emergence of the environmental movement, I have kept these two chapters unchanged in this edition. But I have done new research, and furthered my analysis, in those areas that either decisively confirm the analysis presented earlier or require rectification of a key point of the argument. To the first category belong the analysis of social movements against globalization and the study of the crisis of democracy under the conditions of informational politics. Thus, I have added specific analyses of *al-Qaeda*, as a social movement based on religious identity, and of the anti-globalization movement, as a collective social actor that brings together different sources of resistance and aims at proposing alternative projects of social organization; in its own words: another world is possible. Indeed, the network society does not escape the general law of societies throughout history: where there is domination, there is resistance to domination, and contested views and projects of how to organize social life. I have also refined my discussion of the crisis of political legitimacy, which deepened in the last years of the twentieth century in all areas of the world, usually following the lines identified in my analysis, relating this crisis to media politics, to scandal politics, and to the growing contradiction between the globality of issues to be managed and the nation-bounded character of the institutions in charge of their management.

To the second category – that is, the need to re-think the proposed analytical framework – belongs the study of the state in the network society. In the original version of my trilogy I proposed the concept of the network state to designate the adaptive forms that political institutions were taking to respond to the challenges of globalization. It was already clear that nation-states were not about to disappear, and that the role of the state was as central in our world as it has been throughout human history. Yet, it is not the same kind of state as the nation-state built during the modern age, in the same way that this state was also different from other forms of state developed in previous historical periods. I theorized the new form of the state (understood as the set of political institutions) as the network state, made up of a complex network of interactions between nation-states, co-national and supranational institutions, regional and local governments, and even NGOs, as local and global civil society was quickly becoming both a challenger and a partner to the nation-state. In this volume, I go further in the analysis of the global interdependence of political management, domination, and representation, and I try to propose a tentative theoretical construction to think the new historical realities of the state.

As all intellectual products, the second edition of this volume is marked by the social context in which it was conceived and written. This is the context of the open conflict between identity-based challenges, such as Islamic fundamentalism and global networks of terror, and the institutions of uncompromising capitalist globalization, relying on the military might of the last and only superpower. This is also the context in which, in spite of the objective multilateral character of the issues emerging in the global network society, the only relatively autonomous nation-state, the United States, decided to try a last run toward unilateral world domination, wrapped in different ideological arguments, and seasoned with British consent, yet rooted in sheer panic and insecurity when confronted with a truly dangerous, new world that was never on the cards of the strategists and thinkers of the world's dominant elites.

Instead of understanding the new world, and finding new ways of dealing with its issues, the US decided to use its military superiority, based on technological excellence, thus on its advance in the techno-logical revolution, to adapt the world to itself, to its interests, to its ways of thinking and being, rather than the other way round. This was not present in my analysis in the first edition (unlike the violent challenge from fundamentalist terror networks, which was in direct line with my argument as presented in 1996, although I refused to predict anything). In theoretical terms, I studied the deployment of the new social structure, but I paid insufficient attention to the autonomy of agency. Yet, we know in social theory that analysis must bring together the logic of structure and the logic of agency in the formation of social practices. I put this principle at the forefront of my theory, and I tried to implement it by referring to the contradictory logic between the net and the self, between the power of capitalist networks and the power of identity, between corporate globalization and alter-native global movements. Yet I underestimated the capacity of the state, and particularly of the last sovereign nation-state, to ignore the signals of history and go back to asserting the monopoly of violence as its *raison d'être*, sacrificing international legitimacy to a domestic legitimacy built on its role as protector of its citizens and clients. How a unilateral logic can proceed in a multilateral world is a fundamental matter that only experience, and analytical observation of experience, will tell us in the years to come. But, to help the conduct of such an analysis, I have proposed in this volume some theoretical reflections inspired by the observation of the first stages of this fundamental contradiction between the logic of structure and the logic of agency in the construction of our world.

In conducting the revision of this volume, I have continued to benefit from the support of students, colleagues, and academic insti-tutions, whose contribution must be acknowledged as my way of thanking all of them publicly. First of all, my gratitude goes to the research assistants who have helped me with the collection and an-alysis of new data, all of them my doctoral students: Jeff Juris and Rana Tomaira, at the University of California, Berkeley, and Esteve Ollé at the Universitat Oberta de Catalunya, Barcelona.

A number of colleagues have helped with their comments, infor-mation, and suggestions on topics covered in this volume, particularly Alain Touraine, Anthony Giddens, Fernando Calderon, Ruth Car-doso, Vilmar Faria, Emilio de Ipola, Nico Cloete, Johan Muller,

Martin Carnoy, You-tien Hsing, Fernando Henrique Cardoso, Ulrich Beck, Mary Kaldor, Imma Tubella, Peter Evans, Harley Shaiken, Nezar al-Sayyad, Ronald Inglehart, Guy Benveniste, Wayne Baker, John Thompson, Pekka Himanen, Magaly Sanchez, Bish Sanyal, William Mitchell, Douglas Massey, Erkki Tuomioja, Ovsey Shkaratan, and Narcis Serra.

I am also grateful to the following universities, institutions, and foundations which, by their invitation, have provided the opportunity to discuss the ideas presented in this volume in the period of their revision: Center for Higher Education Transformation, South Africa; United Nations Development Programme in Bolivia; United Nations Development Programme in Chile; Oxford University; Institute for Contemporary Arts, London; Ord&Bild Journal, Goteborg and Stockholm; Balie Cultural Center, Amsterdam; Fundacion Marcelino Botin, Madrid; Escuela Superior de Administracion de Empresas (ESADE), Barcelona; Institut Europeu de la Mediterrania, Barcelona; University Humboldt, Berlin; University of Munich; Institute for Social Research, University of Frankfurt; University Bocconi, Milan; Higher School of Economics, Moscow; Massachusetts Institute of Technology; Queen's University, Ontario; University of Michigan; Annenberg School of Communication, University of Southern California, Los Angeles.

I would also like to emphasize the contribution to my research of my new intellectual environment, the Universitat Oberta de Catalunya (UOC) in Barcelona. My arrival here in 2001, recovering the roots of my own identity, constitutes a personal stimulus, and a very good vantage point to develop my analysis of the cultural and political dimensions of the network society. I particularly thank Vice-rector Imma Tubella and Rector Gabriel Ferrate for providing excellent intellectual, material, and personal conditions for this new stage of my research.

I want to reiterate my personal debt to Emma Kiselyova-Castells, who has put up with this endless work on my trilogy for the past decade. To her, I promise this: no more trilogies!

Finally, my doctors, Peter Carroll and James Davis, of the University of California San Francisco Medical Center, deserve a new round of recognition, having cleared me from the grave illness that we all fought together.

I very much hope that the analysis presented in this substantially revised volume will contribute to the understanding of a very troubled world.

April 2003   Barcelona, Spain

The author and publisher gratefully acknowledge the following for permission to reproduce copyright material:

Figure 2.1 "Geographical distribution of Patriot groups in the US by number of groups and paramilitary training sites in each state, 1996," from Southern Poverty Law Center, Klanwatch/Militia Task Force 1996. Reprinted with permission.
Figure 4.1 H-P. Blossfield, "Marriage survival curves for Italy, West Germany, and Sweden: mothers born in 1934–38 and 1949–53," from H-P. Blossfield, *The New Role of Women: Family Formation in Modern Societies* (Westview Press, 1995).
Figure 4.2 I. Alberdi, "Evolution of first marriage in countries of the European Union since 1960," from I. Alberdi (ed.), *Informe sobre la situacion de la familia en España* (Ministerio de Asuntos Sociales, Madrid, 1995).
Figure 4.5 I. Alberdi, "Synthetic index of fertility in European countries since 1960," from I. Alberdi (ed.), *Informe sobre la situacion de la familia en España* (Ministerio de Asuntos Sociales, Madrid, 1995).
Figure 4.10 E. Laumann et al., "Interrelation of different aspects of same-gender sexuality...," from E. Laumann et al., *The Social Organization of Sexuality: Sexual Practices in the United States* (University of Chicago Press, 1994). Reprinted with permission.
Figure 4.14 E. Laumann et al., "Lifetime occurrence of oral sex, by cohort: men and women," from E. Laumann et al., *The Social Organization of Sexuality: Sexual Practices in the United States* (University of Chicago Press, 1994).
Figure 5.1 "General government gross financial liabilities (% of GDP)," from *The Economist Newspaper Limited*, London, January 20, 1996. Reprinted with permission.
Figure 5.2 "Labour costs in manufacturing, 1994 ($ per hour)," from *The Economist Newspaper Limited*, London, January 27, 1996. Reprinted with permission.
Figure 6.2 T. Fackler and T-M. Lin, "Average number of corruption stories per periodical in US, 1890–1992," from T. Fackler and T-M. Lin, "Political corruption and presidential elections, 1929–1992," from *The Journal of Politics*, 57 (4): 971–93 (1995). Reprinted with permission.

Every effort has been made to trace all the copyright holders, but if any has been inadvertently overlooked, the publisher will be pleased to make the necessary arrangement at the first opportunity.

Acknowledgments
1996

The ideas and analyses presented in this volume have grown out of 25 years of study which I have conducted on social movements and political processes in various areas of the world, although they are now re-elaborated and integrated in a broader theory of the information age, as presented in the three volumes of this book. A number of academic institutions were essential environments for the development of my work in this specific area of inquiry. Foremost among them was the Centre d'Étude des Mouvements Sociaux, École des Hautes Études en Sciences Sociales, Paris, founded and directed by Alain Touraine, where I was a researcher between 1965 and 1979. Other research institutions that helped my work on social movements and politics were: Centro Interdisciplinario de Desarrollo Urbano, Universidad Catolica de Chile; Instituto de Investigaciones Sociales, Universidad Nacional Autonoma de Mexico; Center for Urban Studies, University of Hong Kong; Instituto de Sociologia de Nuevas Tecnologias, Universidad Autonoma de Madrid; Faculty of Social Sciences, Hitotsubashi University, Tokyo.

The final elaboration and writing of the material presented here took place in the 1990s in what has been, since 1979, my intellectual home, the University of California at Berkeley. Many of the ideas were discussed and refined in my graduate seminar on "Sociology of the Information Society." For this, I thank my students, a constant source of inspiration for and criticism of my work. This volume has benefited from exceptional research assistance by Sandra Moog, a sociology graduate student at Berkeley, and a future outstanding scholar. Additional valuable research assistance was provided by

Lan-chih Po, a doctoral student in city and regional planning, also at Berkeley. As with the other volumes of this book, Emma Kiselyova considerably helped my research by facilitating access to languages that I do not know, as well as by assessing and commenting on various sections of the volume.

Several colleagues read drafts of the whole volume, or of specific chapters, and commented extensively, helping me to correct some mistakes and to tighten up the analysis, although I obviously take full responsibility for the final interpretation. My gratitude goes to: Ira Katznelson, Ida Susser, Alain Touraine, Anthony Giddens, Martin Carnoy, Stephen Cohen, Alejandra Moreno Toscano, Roberto Laserna, Fernando Calderon, Rula Sadik, You-tien Hsing, Shujiro Yazawa, Chu-joe Hsia, Nancy Whittier, Barbara Epstein, David Hooson, Irene Castells, Eva Serra, Tim Duane, and Elsie Harper-Anderson. I wish to express my special thanks to John Davey, Blackwell's editorial director, who provided his expert insight, as well as careful suggestions on substance in several key sections of the volume.

This is to say that, as with the other volumes of this book, the process of thinking and writing is largely a collective endeavor, albeit ultimately assumed in the solitude of authorship.

November 1996   Berkeley, California

Our World, our Lives

Lift up your faces, you have a piercing need
For this bright morning dawning for you.
History, despite its wrenching pain,
Cannot be unlived, and if faced
With courage, need not be lived again.

Lift up your eyes upon
This day breaking for you,
Give birth again
To the dream.
Maya Angelou, "On the Pulse of Morning"[1]

Our world, and our lives, are being shaped by the conflicting trends of globalization and identity. The information technology revolution, and the restructuring of capitalism, have induced a new form of society, the network society. It is characterized by the globalization of strategically decisive economic activities. By the networking form of organization. By the flexibility and instability of work, and the individualization of labor. By a culture of real virtuality constructed by a pervasive, interconnected, and diversified media system. And by the transformation of the material foundations of life, space and time, through the constitution of a space of flows and of timeless time, as expressions of dominant activities and controlling elites. This new

1 Poem on the inauguration of the US President, January 22, 1993.

form of social organization, in its pervasive globality, is diffusing throughout the world, as industrial capitalism and its twin enemy, industrial statism, did in the twentieth century, shaking institutions, transforming cultures, creating wealth and inducing poverty, spurring greed, innovation, and hope, while simultaneously imposing hardship and instilling despair. It is indeed, brave or not, a new world.

But this is not the whole story. Along with the technological revolution, the transformation of capitalism, and the demise of statism, we have experienced, in the past twenty-five years, the widespread surge of powerful expressions of collective identity that challenge globalization and cosmopolitanism on behalf of cultural singularity and people's control over their lives and environment. These expressions are multiple, highly diversified, following the contours of each culture, and of historical sources of formation of each identity. They include proactive movements, aiming at transforming human relationships at their most fundamental level, such as feminism and environmentalism. But they also include a whole array of reactive movements that build trenches of resistance on behalf of God, nation, ethnicity, family, locality, that is, the fundamental categories of millennial existence now threatened under the combined, contradictory assault of techno-economic forces and transformative social movements. Caught between these opposing trends, the nation-state is called into question, drawing into its crisis the very notion of political democracy, predicated upon the historical construction of a sovereign, representative nation-state. More often than not, new, powerful technological media, such as worldwide, interactive telecommunication networks, are used by various contenders, amplifying and sharpening their struggle, as, for instance, when the Internet becomes an instrument for international environmentalists, Mexican *Zapatistas*, or American militia, responding in kind to computerized globalization of financial markets and information processing.

This is the world explored in this volume, focusing primarily on social movements and politics, as they result from the interplay between technology-induced globalization, the power of identity (gender, religious, national, ethnic, territorial, socio-biological), and the institutions of the state. In inviting the reader to this intellectual journey through the landscapes of contemporary social struggles and political conflicts, I will start with a few remarks that may help the voyage.

This is not a book about books. Thus, I will not discuss existing theories on each topic, or cite every possible source on the issues presented here. Indeed, it would be pretentious to attempt setting, even superficially, the scholarly record on the whole realm of themes covered in this book. The sources and authors that I do use for each topic are materials that I consider relevant to construct the hypotheses I am proposing on each theme, as well as on the meaning of these analyses for a broader theory of social change in the network society. Readers interested in bibliography, and in critical evaluations of such a bibliography, should consult the many available good textbooks on each matter.

The method I have followed aims at communicating theory by analyzing practice, in successive waves of observation of social movements in various cultural and institutional contexts. Thus, empirical analysis is mainly used as a communication device, and as a method of disciplining my theoretical discourse, of making it difficult, if not impossible, to say something that observed collective action rejects in practice. However, I have tried to provide a few empirical elements, within the space constraints of this volume, to make my interpretation plausible, and to allow the reader to judge for her/himself.

There is in this book a deliberate obsession with multiculturalism, with scanning the planet, in its diverse social and political manifestations. This approach stems from my view that the process of techno-economic globalization shaping our world is being challenged, and will eventually be transformed, from a multiplicity of sources, according to different cultures, histories, and geographies. Thus, moving thematically between the United States, Western Europe, Russia, Mexico, Bolivia, the Islamic world, China and Japan, as I do in this volume, has the specific purpose of using the same analytical framework to understand very different social processes that are, nonetheless, interrelated in their meaning. I would also like, within the obvious limits of my knowledge and experience, to break the ethnocentric approach still dominating much social science at the very moment when our societies have become globally interconnected and culturally intertwined.

One word about theory. The sociological theory informing this book is diluted for your convenience in the presentation of themes in each chapter. It is also blended with empirical analysis as far as it could be done. Only when it is unavoidable will I submit the reader to a brief theoretical excursus, since for me social theory is a tool to understand the world, not an end for intellectual self-enjoyment. I shall try, in the conclusion to this volume, to tighten up the analysis in a more formal, systematic manner, bringing together the various threads woven in each chapter. However, since the book focuses on social movements, and since there is a great deal of disagreement on the meaning of the concept, I advance my definition of social movements as being: purposive collective actions whose outcome, in victory as in defeat, transforms the values and institutions of society.

Since there is no sense of history other than the history we sense, *from an analytical perspective* there are no "good" and "bad," progressive and regressive social movements. They are all symptoms of who we are, and avenues of our transformation, since transformation may equally lead to a whole range of heavens, hells, or heavenly hells. This is not an incidental remark, since processes of social change in our world often take forms of fanaticism and violence that we do not usually associate with positive social change. And yet, this is our world, this is us, in our contradictory plurality, and this is what we have to understand, if necessarily to face it, and to overcome it. As for the meaning of *this* and *us*, please dare to read on.

1

Communal Heavens: Identity and Meaning in the Network Society

The capital is established near Zhong Mountain;
The palaces and thresholds are brilliant and shining;
The forests and gardens are fragrant and flourishing;
Epidendrums and cassia complement each other in beauty.
The forbidden palace is magnificent;
Buildings and pavilions a hundred stories high.
Halls and gates are beautiful and lustrous;
Bells and chimes sound musically.
The towers reach up to the sky;
Upon altars sacrificial animals are burned.
Cleansed and purified,
We fast and bathe.
We are respectful and devout in worship,
Dignified and serene in prayer.
Supplicating with fervor,
Each seeks happiness and joy.
The uncivilized and border people offer tribute,
And all the barbarians are submissive.
No matter how vast the territory,
All will be eventually under our rule.

Hong Xiuquan

Such were the words of the "Imperially Written Tale of a Thousand Words," composed by Hong Xiuquan, the guide and prophet of the Taiping Rebellion, after establishing his heavenly kingdom in Nanjing in 1853.[1]

---

1 Cited by Spence (1996: 190–1).

The insurgency of Taiping Tao (Way of Great Peace) aimed at creating a communal, neo-Christian fundamentalist kingdom in China. The kingdom was organized, for more than a decade, in conformity with the revelation of the Bible that, by his own account, Hong Xiuquan received from his elder brother, Jesus Christ, after being initiated into Christianity by evangelical missionaries. Between 1845 and 1864, Hong's prayers, teachings, and armies shook up China, and the world, as they interfered with the growing foreign control of the Middle Kingdom. The Taiping Kingdom perished, as it lived, in blood and fire, taking the lives of 20 million Chinese. It longed to establish an earthly paradise by fighting the demons that had taken over China, so that "all people may live together in perpetual joy, until at last they are raised to Heaven to greet their Father."[2] It was a time of crisis for state bureaucracies and moral traditions, of globalization of trade, of profitable drug traffic, of rapid industrialization spreading in the world, of religious missions, of impoverished peasants, of the shaking of families and communities, of local bandits and international armies, of the diffusion of printing and mass illiteracy, a time of uncertainty and hopelessness, of identity crisis. It was another time. Or was it?

The Construction of Identity

Identity is people's source of meaning and experience. As Calhoun writes:

> We know of no people without names, no languages or cultures in which some manner of distinctions between self and other, we and they, are not made ... Self-knowledge – always a construction no matter how much it feels like a discovery – is never altogether separable from claims to be known in specific ways by others.[3]

By identity, as it refers to social actors, I understand the process of construction of meaning on the basis of a cultural attribute, or a related set of cultural attributes, that is given priority over other sources of meaning. For a given individual, or for a collective actor, there may be a plurality of identities. Yet, such a plurality is a source of stress and contradiction in both self-representation and social action. This is because identity must be distinguished from what, traditionally, sociologists have called roles, and role-sets. Roles (for example, to be a worker, a mother, a neighbor, a socialist militant, a union member, a basketball player, a churchgoer, and a smoker, at the

2   Spence (1996: 172).
3   Calhoun (1994: 9–10).

same time) are defined by norms structured by the institutions and organizations of society. Their relative weight in influencing people's behavior depends upon negotiations and arrangements between individuals and these institutions and organizations. Identities are sources of meaning for the actors themselves, and by themselves, constructed through a process of individuation.[4]

Although, as I will argue below, identities can also be originated from dominant institutions, they become identities only when and if social actors internalize them, and construct their meaning around this internalization. To be sure, some self-definitions can also coincide with social roles, for instance when to be a father is the most important self-definition from the point of view of the actor. Yet, identities are stronger sources of meaning than roles because of the process of self-construction and individuation that they involve. In simple terms, identities organize the meaning, while roles organize the functions. I define *meaning* as the symbolic identification by a social actor of the purpose of her/his action. I also propose the idea that, *in the network society*, for reasons that I will develop below, for most social actors, meaning is organized around a primary identity (that is an identity that frames the others), which is self-sustaining across time and space. While this approach is close to Erikson's formulation of identity, my focus here will be primarily on collective, rather than on individual, identity. However, individualism (different from individual identity) may also be a form of "collective identity," as analyzed in Lasch's "culture of narcissism."[5]

It is easy to agree on the fact that, from a sociological perspective, all identities are constructed. The real issue is how, from what, by whom, and for what. The construction of identities uses building materials from history, from geography, from biology, from productive and reproductive institutions, from collective memory and from personal fantasies, from power apparatuses and religious revelations. But individuals, social groups, and societies process all these materials, and rearrange their meaning, according to social determinations and cultural projects that are rooted in their social structure, and in their space/time framework. I propose, as a hypothesis, that, in general terms, who constructs collective identity, and for what, largely determines the symbolic content of this identity, and its meaning for those identifying with it or placing themselves outside of it. Since the social construction of identity always takes place in a context marked by power relationships, I propose a distinction between three forms and origins of identity building:

4 Giddens (1991).
5 Lasch (1980).

- *Legitimizing identity*: introduced by the dominant institutions of society to extend and rationalize their domination *vis à vis* social actors, a theme that is at the heart of Sennett's theory of authority and domination,[6] but also fits with various theories of nationalism.[7]
- *Resistance identity*: generated by those actors who are in positions/conditions devalued and/or stigmatized by the logic of domination, thus building trenches of resistance and survival on the basis of principles different from, or opposed to, those permeating the institutions of society, as Calhoun proposes when explaining the emergence of identity politics.[8]
- *Project identity*: when social actors, on the basis of whatever cultural materials are available to them, build a new identity that redefines their position in society and, by so doing, seek the transformation of overall social structure. This is the case, for instance, when feminism moves out of the trenches of resistance of women's identity and women's rights, to challenge patriarchalism, thus the patriarchal family, and thus the entire structure of production, reproduction, sexuality, and personality on which societies have been historically based.

Naturally, identities that start as resistance may induce projects, and may also, along the course of history, become dominant in the institutions of society, thus becoming legitimizing identities to rationalize their domination. Indeed, the dynamics of identities along this sequence shows that, from the point of view of social theory, no identity can be an essence, and no identity has, *per se*, progressive or regressive value outside its historical context. A different, and very important matter, is the benefits of each identity for the people who belong.

In my view, each type of identity-building process leads to a different outcome in constituting society. *Legitimizing identity generates a civil society*; that is, a set of organizations and institutions, as well as a series of structured and organized social actors, which reproduce, albeit sometimes in a conflictive manner, the identity that rationalizes the sources of structural domination. This statement may come as a surprise to some readers, since civil society generally suggests a positive connotation of democratic social change. However, this is in fact the original conception of civil society, as formulated by Gramsci, the intellectual father of this ambiguous concept. Indeed, in Gramsci's

6 Sennett (1980).
7 Anderson (1983); Gellner (1983).
8 Calhoun (1994: 17).

conception, civil society is formed by a series of "apparatuses," such as the Church(es), unions, parties, cooperatives, civic associations, and so on, which, on the one hand, prolong the dynamics of the state, but, on the other hand, are deeply rooted among people.[9] It is precisely this dual character of civil society that makes it a privileged terrain of political change by making it possible to seize the state without launching a direct, violent assault. The conquest of the state by the forces of change (let's say the forces of socialism, in Gramsci's ideology) present in civil society is made possible exactly because of the continuity between civil society's institutions and the power apparatuses of the state, organized around a similar identity (citizenship, democracy, the politicization of social change, the confinement of power to the state and its ramifications, and the like). Where Gramsci and de Tocqueville see democracy and civility, Foucault and Sennett, and before them Horkheimer and Marcuse, see internalized domination and legitimation of an over-imposed, undifferentiated, normalizing identity.

The second type of identity-building, *identity for resistance*, leads to the formation of *communes*, or *communities*, in Etzioni's formulation.[10] This may be the most important type of identity-building in our society. It constructs forms of collective resistance against otherwise unbearable oppression, usually on the basis of identities that were, apparently, clearly defined by history, geography, or biology, making it easier to essentialize the boundaries of resistance. For instance, ethnically based nationalism, as Scheff proposes, often "arises out of a sense of alienation, on the one hand, and resentment against unfair exclusion, whether political, economic or social."[11] Religious fundamentalism, territorial communities, nationalist self-affirmation, or even the pride of self-denigration, inverting the terms of oppressive discourse (as in the "queer culture" of some tendencies in the gay movement), are all expressions of what I name *the exclusion of the excluders by the excluded*. That is, the building of defensive identity in the terms of dominant institutions/ideologies, reversing the value judgment while reinforcing the boundary. In such a case, the issue arises of the reciprocal communicability between these excluded/exclusionary identities. The answer to this question, which can only be empirical and historical, determines whether societies remain as societies or else fragment into a constellation of tribes, sometimes euphemistically renamed communities.

9   Buci-Glucksman (1978).
10   Etzioni (1993).
11   Scheff (1994: 281).

The third process of constructing identity, that is *project identity*, produces *subjects*, as defined by Alain Touraine:

> I name subject the desire of being an individual, of creating a personal history, of giving meaning to the whole realm of experiences of individual life...The transformation of individuals into subjects results from the necessary combination of two affirmations: that of individuals against communities, and that of individuals against the market.[12]

Subjects are not individuals, even if they are made by and in individuals. They are the collective social actor through which individuals reach holistic meaning in their experience.[13] In this case, the building of identity is a project of a different life, perhaps on the basis of an oppressed identity, but expanding toward the transformation of society as the prolongation of this project of identity, as in the above-mentioned example of a post-patriarchal society, liberating women, men, and children, through the realization of women's identity. Or, in a very different perspective, the final reconciliation of all human beings as believers, brothers and sisters, under the guidance of God's law, be it Allah or Jesus, as a result of the religious conversion of godless, anti-family, materialist societies, otherwise unable to fufill human needs and God's design.

How, and by whom, different types of identities are constructed, and with what outcomes, cannot be addressed in general, abstract terms: it is a matter of social context. Identity politics, as Zaretsky writes, "must be situated historically."[14] Thus, our discussion must refer to a specific context, the rise of the network society. The dynamics of identity in this context can be better understood by contrasting it with Giddens's characterization of identity in "late modernity," a historical period which, I believe, is an era reaching its end – by which I do not mean to suggest that we are in some way reaching the "end of history" as posited in some postmodern vagaries. In a powerful theorization, whose main lines I share, Giddens states that "self-identity is not a distinctive trait possessed by the individual. It is the self as reflexively understood by the person in terms of her/his biography." Indeed, "to be a human being is to know...both what one is doing and why one is doing it...In the context of post-traditional order, the self becomes a reflexive project."[15]

12   Touraine (1995a: 29–30); my translation.
13   Touraine (1992).
14   Zaretsky (1994: 198).
15   Giddens (1991: 53, 35, 32).

How does "late modernity" impact this reflexive project? In Giddens's terms,

> one of the distinctive features of modernity is an increasing interconnection between the two extremes of extensionality and intentionality: globalising influences on the one hand and personal dispositions on the other... The more tradition loses its hold, and the more daily life is reconstituted in terms of the dialectical interplay of the local and the global, the more individuals are forced to negotiate lifestyle choices among a diversity of options... Reflexively organized life-planning... becomes a central feature of the structuring of self-identity."[16]

While agreeing with Giddens's theoretical characterization of identity-building in the period of "late modernity," I argue, on the basis of analyses presented in volume I of this trilogy, that the rise of the network society calls into question the processes of the construction of identity during that period, thus inducing new forms of social change. This is because the network society is based on the systemic disjunction between the local and the global for most individuals and social groups. And, I will add, by the separation in different time–space frames between power and experience (volume I, chapters 6 and 7). Therefore, reflexive life-planning becomes impossible, except for the elite inhabiting the timeless space of flows of global networks and their ancillary locales. And the building of intimacy on the basis of trust requires a redefinition of identity fully autonomous *vis à vis* the networking logic of dominant institutions and organizations.

Under such new conditions, civil societies shrink and disarticulate because there is no longer continuity between the logic of power-making in the global network and the logic of association and representation in specific societies and cultures. The search for meaning takes place then in the reconstruction of defensive identities around communal principles. Most of social action becomes organized in the opposition between unidentified flows and secluded identities. As for the emergence of project identities, it still happens, or may happen, depending on societies. But, I propose the hypothesis that the constitution of subjects, at the heart of the process of social change, takes a different route to the one we knew during modernity, and late modernity: namely, *subjects, if and when constructed, are not built any longer on the basis of civil societies, which are in the process of disintegration, but as prolongation of communal resistance.* While in modernity (early or late) project identity was constituted from civil society (as in the case of socialism on the basis of the labor

16   Giddens (1991: 1, 5).

movement), in the network society, project identity, if it develops at all, grows from communal resistance. This is the actual meaning of the new primacy of identity politics in the network society. The analysis of processes, conditions, and outcomes of the transformation of communal resistance into transformative subjects is the precise realm for a theory of social change in the information age.

Having reached a tentative formulation of my hypotheses, it would be against the methodological principles of this book to go any further down the path of abstract theorizing that could quickly divert into bibliographical commentary. I shall try to suggest the precise implications of my analysis by focusing on a number of key processes in the construction of collective identity selected by their particular relevance to the process of social change in the network society. I will start with *religious fundamentalism*, both in its Islamic and Christian versions, although this does not imply that other religions (for example, Hinduism, Buddhism, Judaism) are less important or less prone to fundamentalism. I shall continue with *nationalism*, considering, after some overview of the issue, two very different, but significant processes: the role of nationalism in the disintegration of the Soviet Union, and in post-Soviet republics; and the formation and re-emergence of Catalan nationalism. I will then turn to *ethnic identity*, focusing on contemporary African American identity. And I will end by considering, briefly, *territorial identity*, on the basis of my observation of urban movements and local communities around the world. In conclusion, I shall try a succinct synthesis of major lines of inquiry that will emerge from examining various contemporary processes of the (re)construction of identity on the basis of communal resistance.

God's Heavens: Religious Fundamentalism and Cultural Identity

It is an attribute of society, and I would dare to say of human nature if such an entity were to exist, to find solace and refuge in religion. The fear of death, the pain of life, need God, and faith in God, whichever of God's manifestations, for people just to go on. Indeed, outside us God would become homeless.

Religious fundamentalism is something else. And I contend that this "something else" is a most important source of constructing identity in the network society for reasons that will become clearer, I hope, in the following pages. As for its actual content, experiences, opinions, history, and theories are so diverse as to defy synthesis. Fortunately, the American Academy of Arts and Sciences undertook, in the late

1980s, a major comparative project aimed at observing fundamental-isms in various social and institutional contexts.[17] Thus, we know that "fundamentalists are always reactive, reactionary,"[18] and that:

> fundamentalists are selective. They may well consider that they are adopting the whole of the pure past, but their energies go into employing those features which will best reinforce their identity, keep their move-ment together, build defenses around its boundaries, and keep others at a distance... Fundamentalists fight under God – in the case of theistic religion – or under the signs of some transcendent reference.[19]

To be more precise, I believe, to be consistent with the collection of essays gathered in the "Fundamentalism Observed" Project, in defin-ing *fundamentalism*, in my own understanding, as *the construction of collective identity under the identification of individual behavior and society's institutions to the norms derived from God's law, interpreted by a definite authority that intermediates between God and humanity.* Thus, as Marty writes, "It is impossible for fundamentalists to argue or settle anything with people who do not share their commitment to an authority, whether it be an inerrant Bible, an infallible Pope, the *Shari'a* codes in Islam, or the implications of *halacha* in Judaism."[20]

Religious fundamentalism has, of course, existed throughout the whole of human history, but it appears to be surprisingly strong and influential as a source of identity in this new millennium. Why so? My analyses of Islamic fundamentalism, and of Christian fundamental-ism, in this section, will try to propose some clues to understand one of the most defining trends in the making of our historical epoch.[21]

Umma *versus* Jahiliya: *Islamic fundamentalism*

The only way to accede to modernity is by our own path, that which has been traced for us by our religion, our history and our civilization.
Rached Gannouchi[22]

The 1970s, the birthdate of the information technology revolution in Silicon Valley, and the starting-point of global capitalist restructuring, had a different meaning for the Muslim world: it marked the begin-

17   Marty and Appleby (1991).
18   Marty (1988: 20).
19   Marty and Appleby (1991: ix–x).
20   Marty (1988: 22).
21   See also Misztal and Shupe (1992a).
22   Rached Gannouchi, interview with *Jeune Afrique*, July 1990. Gannouchi is a leading intellectual in the Tunisian Islamist movement.

ning of the fourteenth century of the *Hegira*, a period of Islamic revival, purification, and strengthening, as at the onset of each new century. Indeed, in the next two decades an authentic cultural/religious revolution spread throughout Muslim lands, sometimes victorious, as in Iran, sometimes subdued, as in Egypt, sometimes triggering civil war, as in Algeria, sometimes formally acknowledged in the institutions of the state, as in the Sudan or Bangladesh, most times establishing an uneasy coexistence with a formally Islamic nation-state, fully integrated in global capitalism, as in Saudi Arabia, Indonesia, or Morocco. Overall, the cultural identity and political fate of almost a billion people were being fought for in the mosques and in the wards of Muslim cities, crowded by accelerated urbanization, and disintegrated by failed modernization. Islamic fundamentalism, as a reconstructed identity, and as a political project, is at the center of a most decisive process, largely conditioning the world's future.[23]

But, what is Islamic fundamentalism? Islam, in Arabic, means state of submission, and a Muslim is one who has submitted to Allah. Thus, according to the definition of fundamentalism I presented above, it would appear that all Islam is fundamentalist: societies, and their state institutions, must be organized around uncontested religious principles. However, a number of distinguished scholars[24] argue that, while the primacy of religious principles as formulated in the Qur'ān is common to all of Islam, Islamic societies and institutions are also based on multivocal interpretation. Furthermore, in most traditional Islamic societies, the pre-eminence of religious principles over political authority was purely formal. Indeed, the *shari'a* (divine law, formed by the Qur'ān and the Hadiths) relates in classic Arabic language to the verb *shara'a*, to walk toward a source. Thus, for most Muslims, *shari'a* is not an invariable, rigid command, but a guide to walk toward God, with the adaptations required by each historical and social context.[25] In contrast to this openness of Islam, Islamic fundamentalism implies the fusion of *shari'a* with *fiqh*, or interpretation and application by jurists and authorities, under the absolute domination of *shari'a*. Naturally, the actual meaning depends on the process of interpretation, and on who interprets. Thus, there is a wide range of variation between conservative fundamentalism, such as the one represented by the House of Saud, and radical fundamentalism, as elaborated in the writings of al-Mawdudi or Sayyid Qtub in the 1950s and 1960s.[26]

23 Hiro (1989); Balta (1991); Sisk (1992); Choueri (1993); Juergensmeyer (1993); Dekmejian (1995).
24 See, for example, Bassam Tibi (1988, 1992a); al-Azmeh (1993); Farhad Khosrokhavar (1995), among others.
25 Garaudy (1990).
26 Carre (1984); Choueri (1993).

There are also considerable differences between the Shia tradition, the one inspiring Khomeini, and the Sunni tradition, which constitutes the faith for about 85 percent of Muslims, including revolutionary movements such as Algeria's *Front Islamique de Salvation* (FIS), or Egypt's *Takfir wal-Hijrah*. Yet, in the vision of writers who constitute Islamist thought from the end of the nineteenth century, such as Persia's Jamal ad-Din al-Afghani, and into the twentieth century, such as Egypt's Hassan al-Banna and Sayyid Qtub, India's Ali al-Nadawi, or Pakistan's Sayyid Abul al-Mawdudi, the history of Islam is reconstructed to show the perennial submission of state to religion.[27] For a Muslim, the fundamental attachment is not to the *watan* (homeland), but to the *umma*, or community of believers, all made equal in their submission to Allah. This universal confraternity supersedes the institutions of the nation-state, which is seen as a source of division among believers.[28] In the writing of Sayyid Qtub, probably the most influential writer on Islamic fundamentalism among radical Islamists:

> the ties of ideology and faith are stronger than the ties of fervent patriotic feelings that relate to a region or a territory. Thus false differentiation between Muslims on a territorial basis is nothing but an expression of the campaigns against the Orient, and an expression of the Zionist imperialism that must be exterminated . . . the homeland is not the land but the group of believers or the whole Islamic "umma."[29]

For the *umma* to live, and expand, until embracing the whole of humanity, it has to accomplish a godly task: to undertake, anew, the fight against *Jahiliya* (the state of ignorance of God, or of lack of observance of God's teachings), into which societies have fallen again. To regenerate humanity, Islamization must proceed first in the Muslim societies that have secularized and departed from the strict obedience of God's law, then in the entire world. This process must start with a spiritual rebirth based on *al-sirat al-mustaqin* (straight path), modeled after the community organized by the Prophet Muhammad in Medina. Yet, to overcome impious forces, it may be necessary to proceed through *jihad* (struggle on behalf of Islam) against the infidels, which may include, in extreme cases, the resort to holy war. In the Shia tradition, martyrdom, re-enacting Imam Ali's sacrifice in 681, is indeed at the heart of religious purity. But the whole of Islam shares

27 Hiro (1989); al-Azmeh (1993); Choueri (1993); Dekmejian (1995).
28 Oumlil (1992).
29 Qtub (n.d./1970s)

the praise for the necessary sacrifices implied by the call of God (*al-da'wah*). As stated by Hassan al-Banna, the founder and leader of Muslim Brotherhood, assassinated in 1949: "The Qur'ān is our constitution, the Prophet is our Guide; death for the glory of Allah is our greatest ambition."[30] The ultimate goal of all human actions must be the establishment of God's law over the whole of humankind, thus ending the current opposition between *Dar al-Islam* (the Muslim world), and *Dar al-Harb* (the non-Muslim world).

In this cultural/religious/political framework, Islamic identity is constructed on the basis of a double deconstruction: by the social actors, and by the institutions of society. Social actors must deconstruct themselves as subjects, be it as individuals, as members of an ethnic group, or as citizens of a nation. In addition, women must submit to their guardian men, as they are encouraged to fulfill themselves primarily in the framework of the family: "Men are the protectors and maintainers of women, because God has given the one more (strength) than the other, and because they support them from their means."[31] As Bassam Tibi writes, "Habermas' principle of subjectivity is a heresy for Islamic fundamentalists."[32] Only in the *umma* can the individual be fully himself/herself, as part of the confraternity of believers, a basic equalizing mechanism that provides mutual support, solidarity, and shared meaning. On the other hand, the nation-state itself must negate its identity: *al-dawla islamiiyya* (the Islamic state), based on the *shari'a*, takes precedence over the nation-state (*al-dawla qawmiyya*). This proposition is particularly effective in the Middle East, a region where, according to Tibi, "the nation-state is alien and is virtually imposed on its parts... The political culture of secular nationalism is not only a novelty in the Middle East, but also remains on the surface of involved societies."[33] Indeed, as Lawrence writes, "Islam is not merely a religion. It is a religion and more. It encompasses both the spiritual and the political, the private and the political domain... Nationalism becomes the most despised front edge of secularism because it demands the state act as an obedience-context ... in true Islam, according to Qtub, 'Nationalism is belief, homeland is *dar al-islam*, the rules are God, and the constitution is the Qur'ān.'"[34]

---

30   Cited by Hiro (1989: 63).
31   Qur'ān, surāh IV, v. 34 (trans. Abdullah Yusuf Ali, 1988). See Hiro (1989: 202); Delcroix (1995); Gerami (1996).
32   Tibi (1992b: 8).
33   Tibi (1992b: 5).
34   Lawrence (1989: 216).

However, and this is essential, Islamic fundamentalism is not a traditionalist movement. For all the efforts of exegesis to root Islamic identity in history and the holy texts, Islamists proceeded, for the sake of social resistance and political insurgency, with a reconstruction of cultural identity that is in fact hypermodern.[35] As al-Azmeh writes: "The politicization of the sacred, the sacralization of politics, and the transformation of Islamic pseudo-legal institutes into 'social devotions', are all means of realizing the politics of the authentic ego, a politics of identity, and therefore the means for the very formation, indeed the invention, of this identity."[36]

But, if Islamism (although rooted in the writings of nineteenth-century Islamic reformers and revivalists, such as al-Afghani) is essentially a contemporary identity, why now? Why has it exploded in the past two decades, after being repeatedly subdued by nationalism in the post-colonial period, as exemplified by the repression of the Muslim Brothers in Egypt and Syria (including the execution of Qtub in 1966), the rise of Sukarno in Indonesia or of the *Front de Libération Nationale* in Algeria?[37]

For Tibi, "the rise of Islamic fundamentalism in the Middle East is inter-related with the exposure of this part of the world of Islam, which perceives itself as a collective entity, to the processes of globalization, to nationalism and the nation-state as globalized principles of organization."[38] Indeed, the explosion of Islamic movements seems to be related to both the disruption of traditional societies (including the undermining of the power of traditional clergy), and to the failure of the nation-state, created by nationalist movements, to accomplish modernization, develop the economy, and/or to distribute the benefits of economic growth among the population at large. Thus, Islamic identity is (re)constructed by fundamentalists in opposition to capitalism, to socialism, and to nationalism, Arab or otherwise, which are, in their view, all failing ideologies of the post-colonial order.

A case in point is, of course, Iran.[39] The Shah's White Revolution, launched in 1963, was a most ambitious attempt to modernize the economy and society, with the support of the United States, and with the deliberate project of linking up with new global capitalism in the making. So doing, it undermined the basic structures of traditional society, from agriculture to the calendar. Indeed, a major conflict

35 Gole (1995).
36 Al-Azmeh (1993: 31).
37 Piscatori (1986); Moen and Gustafson (1992); Tibi (1992a); Burgat and Dowell (1993); Juergensmeyer (1993); Dekmejian (1995).
38 Tibi (1992b: 7).
39 Hiro (1989); Bakhash (1990); Esposito (1990); Khosrokhavar (1995).

between the Shah and the *ulemas* concerned control over time, when, on April 24, 1976, the Shah changed the Islamic calendar to the pre-Islamic Achemenian dynasty calendar. When Khomeini landed in Tehran on February 1, 1979, to lead the revolution, he returned as the representative of Imam Nacoste, Lord of Time (*wali al-zaman*) to assert the pre-eminence of religious principles. The Islamic revolution opposed simultaneously the institution of monarchy (Khomeini: "Islam is fundamentally opposed to the whole notion of monarchy");[40] the nation-state (article 10 of the new Iranian Constitution: "All Muslims form a single nation"); and modernization as an expression of Westernization (article 43 of the Iranian Constitution asserts the "prohibition of extravagance and wastefulness in all matters related to the economy, including consumption, investment, production, distribution, and services"). The power of the *ulemas*, the main targets of the Shah's institutional reforms, became enshrined as the intermediary between the *shari'a* and society. The radicalization of the Islamic regime, after Iraq's attack in 1980 and the atrocious war that followed, led to the purification of society, and the setting up of special religious judges to repress impious acts, such as "adultery, homosexuality, gambling, hypocrisy, sympathy for atheists and hypocrites, and treason."[41] There followed thousands of imprisonments, flagellations, and executions, on different grounds. The cycle of terror, particularly aimed at leftist critics and Marxist guerrillas, closed the circle of fundamentalist logic in Iran.

What are the social bases of fundamentalism? In Iran, where other revolutionary forces participated in the long, hard-fought mobilizations to topple the Pahlavis' bloody dictatorship, the leaders were the clerics, and mosques were the sites of revolutionary committees that organized popular insurgency. As for the social actors, the strength of the movement was in Tehran and other large cities, particularly among the students, intellectuals, bazaar merchants, and artisans. When the movement came onto the streets, it was joined by the masses of recent rural immigrants that populated Tehran's sprawling shanty towns in the 1970s, after the modernization of agriculture expelled them from their villages.

Islamists in Algeria and Tunisia seem to present a similar social profile, according to some scattered data: support for the FIS originated in a heterogeneous group of educated intellectuals, university teachers, and low-level civil servants, joined by small merchants and artisans. However, these movements, which took place in the 1980s,

40   Hiro (1989: 161).
41   Official documents reported in the press, quoted by Hiro (1989: 190).

also had their social roots in rural exodus. Thus, a survey in Tunisia found that 48 percent of fathers of militants were illiterate, as they migrated to the cities in the 1970s, from impoverished rural areas. The militants themselves were young: in Tunisia, the average age of 72 militants sentenced in a major trial in 1987 was 32 years.[42] In Egypt, Islamism is predominant among university students (most student unions have been under Islamic fundamentalist leadership since the mid-1980s), and receives support from government employees, particularly teachers, with a growing influence in the police and the army.[43]

The social roots of radical fundamentalism appear to derive from the combination of successful state-led modernization in the 1950s and 1960s and the failure of economic modernization in most Muslim countries during the 1970s and 1980s, as their economies could not adapt to the new conditions of global competition and technological revolution in the latter period. Thus, a young, urban population, with a high level of education as a result of the first wave of modernization, was frustrated in its expectations, as the economy faltered and new forms of cultural dependency settled in. It was joined in its discontent by impoverished masses expelled from rural areas to cities by the unbalanced modernization of agriculture. As Kepel writes,

> From the outset the Islamist movement was two-pronged. First, it embraced the younger generation in the cities, a class created by the postwar demographic explosion in the Third World and the resultant mass exodus in the countryside. Though poverty-stricken, these young urbanites had access to literacy and some education. Second, it included the traditional God-fearing bourgeoisie, the descendants of mercantile families from the bazaars and souks who had been thrust aside during the process of decolonization. In addition to this devout middle class, there were also doctors, engineers, and businessmen who had gone away to work in the conservative oil-exporting nations and had rapidly become wealthy while being kept outside the traditional circles of political power.[44]

This social mixture was made explosive by the crisis of the nation-state, whose employees, including military personnel, suffered declining living standards, and lost faith in the nationalist project. The crisis of legitimacy of the nation-state was the result of its widespread corruption, inefficiency, dependency upon foreign powers, and, in the Middle East, repeated military humiliation by Israel, followed

42   Data reported by Burgat and Dowell (1993).
43   Hiro (1989); Dekmejian (1995).
44   Kepel (2002: 6).

by accommodation with the Zionist enemy. The construction of contemporary Islamic identity proceeds as a reaction against unreachable modernization (be it capitalist or socialist), the evil consequences of globalization, and the collapse of the post-colonial nationalist project. This is why the differential development of fundamentalism in the Muslim world seems to be linked to variations in the capacity of the nation-state to integrate in its project both the urban masses, through economic welfare, and the Muslim clergy, through official sanction of their religious power under the aegis of the state, as had been the case in the Ummayyad caliphate or the Ottoman Empire.[45] Thus, while Saudi Arabia is formally an Islamic monarchy, the *ulemas* are on the payroll of the House of Saud, which succeeded in being, at the same time, guardian of the holy sites and guardian of Western oil.

Indonesia and Malaysia seemed, for some time, to be able to integrate Islamist pressures within their authoritarian nation-states by ensuring fast economic growth, thus providing some promising prospects for their subjects. However, after the economic crisis of 1997, and the resignation of Suharto, Indonesia discovered the importance of Islamic parties in politics and in society. The growth of a radical, fundamentalist organization, *Jamaah Islamiyah*, led by Abu Bakar Bashir, with suspected ties to *al-Qaeda*, underscored the fragility of state control in Muslim societies when the shocks of globalization reduced the capacity of social integration through economic growth. Thus, early in the twenty-first century, Indonesia appeared to be rejoining other Muslim societies, in which failed modernization contributed to the crisis of nationalism and to the rise of Islamism.

The nationalist projects of Egypt, Algeria, and Tunisia, some of the most Westernized Muslim countries, collapsed by and large in the 1980s, thus ushering in social tensions that were predominantly captured by Islamists under moderate (Muslim Brotherhood), radical (*Jamaah Islamiyah*), or democratic-radical versions (Algeria's FIS).[46] The challenge of Hamas to the proto-Palestinian state constituted around the leadership of Yasser Arafat may constitute one of the most dramatic schisms between Arab nationalism (of which the Palestinian movement is the epitome) and radical Islamic fundamentalism. It is, of course, ironic that the Israeli Mossad helped in the creation of Hamas, at its outset, as a way of undermining the OLP's authority and legitimacy.

When Islamist electoral victories, such as in Algeria in December 1991, were made void by military repression, widespread violence

45   Balta (1991).
46   Sisk (1992).

and civil war ensued.[47] Even in the most Westernized Muslim country, Turkey, Kemal Atatürk's secular, nationalist heritage came under historical challenge when, in the elections of 1995, Islamists became the country's first political force, relying on the vote of radicalized intellectuals and the urban poor, and formed the government in 1996, before being barred from open political competition under pressure from the nationalist armed forces. Yet, with a revamped political label, and a more moderate program, the Turkish Islamists again became the first party in the elections of November 2002. In an ironic twist of history, pressure from the European Union on Turkey to become a full democracy led the armed forces to authorize the coming to power of an elected government dominated by the Islamic party. It remains to be seen whether Islamists in Turkey can coexist with the principle of secularism, one of the pillars of European democratic states.

Political Islamism, and Islamic fundamentalist identity, expanded in a variety of social and institutional contexts, always related to the dynamics of social exclusion and/or the crisis of the nation-state. Thus, social segregation, discrimination, and unemployment among French youth of Maghrebian origin, among young Turks born in Germany, among Pakistanis in Britain, or among African Americans, induces the emergence of a new Islamic identity among disaffected youth, in a dramatic transference of radical Islamism to the socially excluded areas of advanced capitalist societies.[48] On the other hand, the collapse of the Soviet state triggered the emergence of Islamic movements in the Caucasus and Central Asia, and even the formation of an Islamic Revival Party in Russia, threatening to realize the fears of a spread of Islamic revolutions in Afghanistan and Iran into the former Soviet republics. The war in Chechnya, enacted both on behalf of ethno-nationalism and of Islam, with the support of Saudi Arabia, Pakistan, and bin Laden, became a fundamental feature of politics in post-communist Russia.[49]

Through a variety of political processes, depending upon the dynamics of each nation-state, and the form of global articulation of each economy, an Islamic fundamentalist project emerged in all Muslim societies, and among Muslim minorities in non-Muslim societies. A new identity is being constructed, not by returning to tradition, but by working on traditional materials in the formation of a new godly, communal world, where deprived masses and disaffected

47   Nair (1996).
48   Luecke (1993); Kepel (1995).
49   Mikulsky (1992).

intellectuals may reconstruct meaning in a global alternative to the exclusionary global order.[50]

However, political Islamism is confronted with a fundamental contradiction because, as Lawrence writes, "Sunni Islamic fundamentalists want to take over the system [of the nation-state] rather than overthrow it. Fundamentalists can only succeed by adapting to what they oppose."[51] This is what Kepel observed empirically in his thorough and influential analysis of political Islamism in the 1990s, based on his observation of several countries. After studying various processes that ended in repression or cooptation, or a combination of both, he concluded, against the common wisdom, that Islamism in fact failed as a political force in most of the Muslim countries. And, he argues, it is precisely because of this failure that radical and terrorist groups emerged as a desperate alternative to impose their utopia by the violent means of a global revolutionary vanguard, in a twisted historical echo of the early times of communism.[52]

Furthermore, as Khosrokhavar writes:

> When the project of constituting individuals fully participating in modernity reveals its absurdity in the actual experience of everyday life, violence becomes the only form of self-affirmation of the new subject... The neo-community becomes then a necro-community. The exclusion from modernity takes a religious meaning: thus, self-immolation becomes the way to fight against exclusion.[53]

In the final analysis, in assessing the impact of radical Islamism on power relationships, it all depends on what we characterize as failure or success. If, by success, in a long tradition of state-centered political analysis, we mean seizing state power, then, by the turn of the millennium, Islamic fundamentalism fell short of its expectations. Even in Iran, the only successful Islamic revolution, there has been an increasing separation between the institutions of the state and the religious power of the ayatollahs, as Iran engaged in a contradictory, yet significant, process of democratization and modernization. However, if the historical outcome of an ideology is not measured in votes or in ministries, or even in organized popular support, but in its capacity to change minds, to challenge dominant values, and to alter global power relationships, then the jury is still out on the actual effects of Islamic fundamentalism as a social movement, as opposed to its expression as a political force.

50 Tibi (1992a, b); Gole (1995).
51 Lawrence (1989: 226).
52 Kepel (2002).
53 Khosrokhavar (1995: 249–50); my translation.

In at least some influential currents of Islamic fundamentalism, political participation in the institutions of the democratic state is contradictory to the principles of Islam that should rule Muslim societies. Thus, al-Zhawahiri, the senior leader of *al-Qaeda*, in his book *The Bitter Harvest*, writes that: "to subscribe to democracy is to subscribe to the idea of granting the right of legislation to someone other than God. The person who endorses this idea is an infidel since anyone who legislates for the people has appointed himself a God and anyone who subscribes to this legislator has taken him to be God."[54] Islamic fundamentalism, in its essence, does not recognize the authority of the state, does not submit God's will to votes and political participation. This is why the measure of its success or failure relates to the battle for minds rather than to the fight over the institutions of the state. Therefore, I will pause here on the study of Islamism as a cultural/religious identity and resume its analysis as a social movement against the dominant global order in the next chapter.

Regardless of our judgment on the matter, what has to be reckoned with is that, through the negation of cultural exclusion, even in the extreme form of self-sacrifice, a new Islamic identity has emerged in a new historical attempt to build the *umma*, the communal heaven for true believers.

God save me! American Christian fundamentalism

We have come into an electronic dark age, in which the new pagan hordes, with all the power of technology at their command, are on the verge of obliterating the last strongholds of civilized humanity. A vision of death lies before us. As we leave the shores of Christian western man behind, only a dark and turbulent sea of despair stretches endlessly ahead . . . unless we fight!

Francis Schaeffer, *Time for Anger*[55]

Christian fundamentalism is a perennial feature of American history, from the ideas of post-revolutionary federalists, like Timothy Dwight and Jedidiah Morse, to the pre-millennial eschatology of Pat Robertson, through the 1900 revivalists, such as Dwight L. Moody, and the 1970s reconstructionists inspired by Rousas J. Rushdoony.[56] A society relentlessly at the frontier of social change and individual mobility is bound to doubt periodically the benefits of modernity and seculariza-

---

54 Al-Zhawahiri (1999: n.p.).
55 Schaeffer (1982: 122). Francis Schaeffer is one of the leading inspirations of contemporary American Christian fundamentalism. His *Christian Manifesto*, published in 1981, shortly after his death, was the most influential pamphlet in the 1980s' anti-abortion movement in America.
56 Marsden (1980); Ammerman (1987); Misztal and Shupe (1992b); Wilcox (1992).

tion, yearning for the security of traditional values and institutions rooted in God's eternal truth. Indeed, the very term "fundamentalism," widely used around the world, originated in America, in reference to a series of ten volumes entitled *The Fundamentals*, privately published by two businessmen brothers between 1910 and 1915, to collect holy texts edited by conservative evangelical theologians at the turn of the century. While fundamentalist influence has varied in different historical periods, it has never faded away. In the 1980s and 1990s it certainly surged. While the disintegration of Jerry Falwell's Moral Majority in 1989 led some observers to announce the decline of fundamentalism (parallel to the end of the Communist Satan whose opposition was a major source of legitimacy and funding for fundamentalists), it quickly became obvious that it was the crisis of an organization, and of a political ploy, rather than that of fundamentalist identity.[57] In the 1990s, in the wake of Bill Clinton's presidential victory in 1992, fundamentalism came to the forefront of the political scene, this time in the form of the Christian Coalition, led by Pat Robertson and Ralph Reed, claiming 1.5 million organized members, and marshaling considerable political influence among the Republican electorate. Furthermore, the ideas and world vision of fundamentalists seemed to find considerable echo in *fin-de-siècle* America. For instance, according to a Gallup poll on a national sample in 1979, one in three adults declared that they had had an experience of religious conversion; almost half of them believed that the Bible was inerrant; and more than 80 percent thought that Jesus Christ was divine.[58] To be sure, America has always been, and still is, a very religious society, much more so, for instance, than Western Europe or Japan. But, this religious sentiment seems increasingly to take a revivalist tone, drifting toward a powerful fundamentalist current. According to Simpson:

> fundamentalism, in its original sense, is a set of Christian beliefs and experiences that include (1) subscription to the verbal, plenary inspiration of the Bible and its inerrancy; (2) individual salvation through and acceptance of Christ as a personal Saviour (being born-again) on account of Christ's efficacious, substitutionary atonement for sin in his death and resurrection; (3) the expectation of Christ's premillennial return to earth from heaven; (4) the endorsement of such Protestant orthodox Christian doctrines as the Virgin birth and the trinity.[59]

---

57 Lawton (1989); Moen (1992); Wilcox (1992).
58 Lienesch (1993: 1).
59 Simpson (1992: 26).

Yet, Christian fundamentalism is such a wide, diversified trend that it defies a simple definition cutting across the cleavages between pentecostal and charismatic evangelicals, pre-millennial or post-millennial, pietists and activists. Fortunately, we can rely on an excellent, well-documented, scholarly synthesis of American fundamentalist writings and doctrines by Michael Lienesch, on the basis of which, and with the support of other sources that confirm, in general terms, his record and arguments, I will attempt to reconstruct the main traits of Christian fundamentalist identity.[60]

As Lienesch writes, "at the center of Christian conservative thinking, shaping its sense of the self, lies the concept of Conversion, the act of faith and forgiveness through which sinners are brought from sin into a state of everlasting salvation."[61] Through the personal experience of being born again, the whole personality is reconstructed, and becomes "the starting place for constructing a sense not only of autonomy and identity, but also of social order and political purpose."[62] The linkage between personality and society goes through the reconstruction of the family, the central institution of society, which used to be the refuge against a harsh, hostile world, and is now crumbling in our society. This "fortress of Christian life" has to be reconstructed by asserting patriarchalism, that is the sanctity of marriage (excluding divorce and adultery) and, above all, the authority of men over women (as established in biblical literalism: Genesis 1; Ephesians 5, 22–3), and the strict obedience of children, if necessary enforced by spanking. Indeed, children are born in sin: "it is of great benefit to the parent when he realizes that it is natural for his child to have desire for evil."[63] Thus, it is essential for the family to educate children in the fear of God and in respect for parental authority, and to count on the full support of a Christian education in school. As an obvious consequence of this vision, public schools become the battleground between good and evil, between the Christian family and the institutions of secularism.

A bounty of earthly rewards awaits the Christian who dares to stand up for these principles, and chooses God's plans over his/her own, imperfect, life planning. To start with, a great sex life in marriage. Best-selling authors Tim and Beverly La Haye propose their sex manual as "fully biblical and highly practical,"[64] and show, with the

---

60   Zeskind (1986); Jelen (1989, 1991); Barron and Shupe (1992); Lienesch (1993); Riesebrodt (1993); Hicks (1994).
61   Lienesch (1993: 23).
62   Lienesch (1993: 23).
63   Beverly La Haye, quoted in Lienesch (1993: 78).
64   Quoted in Lienesch (1993: 56).

support of illustrations, all the joys of sexuality that, once sanctified and channeled toward procreation, are in strict accordance with Christianity. Under such conditions, men can be men again: instead of current "Christianettes," men should look and act like men, another Christian tradition: "Jesus was not sissified."[65] Indeed, the channeling of male aggressive sexuality in a fulfilling marriage is essential for society, both for the control of violence, and because it is the source of the "Protestant work ethic," and thus of economic productivity. In this view, sexual sublimation is the foundation of civilization. As for women, they are biologically determined to be mothers, and to be the emotional complement of rational men (as per Phyllis Schlafly). Their submission will help them to achieve a sense of self-esteem. It is through sacrifice that women assert their identity as independent from men. Thus, as Beverly La Haye writes, "Don't be afraid to give, and give, and give."[66] The result will be the salvation of the family, "this little commonwealth, the foundation on which all of society stands."[67]

With salvation guaranteed, as long as a Christian strictly observes the Bible, and with a stable patriarchal family as a solid footing for life, business will also be good, provided that government does not interfere with the economy, leaves the undeserving poor alone, and brings taxes within reasonable limits (at about 10 percent of income). Indeed, Christian fundamentalists do not seem to be bothered by the contradiction between being moral theocratists and economic libertarians.[68] Furthermore, God will help the good Christian in his business life: after all he has to provide for the family. A living proof is offered, by his own account, by the very leader of the Christian Coalition, Pat Robertson, a noted tele-evangelist. After his conversion, armed with his newborn self-assurance, he went to his business: "God has sent me here to buy your television station," and he offered a sum, based on "God's figure": "The Lord spoke: 'Don't go over two and a half million.'"[69] Overall, it turned out to be an excellent deal, for which Pat Robertson weekly thanked God in his "700 Club" television show.

Yet, the Christian way cannot be fulfilled individually because institutions of society, and particularly government, the media, and the public school system, are controlled by humanists of various origins, associated, in different fundamentalist versions, with com-

65   Edwin L. Cole, quoted in Lienesch (1993: 63).
66   Beverly La Haye, quoted in Lienesch (1993: 77).
67   Lienesch (1993: 77).
68   Hicks (1994).
69   Reported by Pat Robertson and quoted in Lienesch (1993: 40).

munists, bankers, heretics, and Jews. The most insidious and dangerous enemies are feminists and homosexuals because they are the ones undermining the family, the main source of social stability, Christian life, and personal fulfillment. (Phyllis Schlafly referred to "the disease called women's liberation.")[70] The fight against abortion symbolizes all the struggles to preserve family, life, and Christianity, bridging over to other Christian denominations. This is why the pro-life movement is the most militant and influential expression of Christian fundamentalism in America.

The struggle must be intensified, and the necessary political compromises with institutional politics must be achieved, because time is becoming short. The "end of times" is approaching, and we must repent, and clean up our society, to be ready for Jesus Christ's Second Coming, which will open a new era, a new millennium of unprecedented peace and prosperity. Yet, there is a dangerous passage because we will have to go through the atrocious Battle of Armageddon, originating in the Middle East, then expanding to the whole world. Israel, and the New Israel (America), will finally prevail over their enemies, but at a terrible cost, and only counting on the capacity of our society to regenerate. This is why the transformation of society (through grassroots Christian politics), and the regeneration of the self (through a pious, family life), are both necessary and complementary.

Who are the contemporary American fundamentalists? Clyde Wilcox provides some interesting data on the demographic characteristics of evangelicals, as compared to the whole population, in 1988.[71] Taking into account the characteristics of the doctrinal evangelicals, it would seem that they are less educated, poorer, more influential among housewives, more often residents of the South, significantly more religious, and 100 percent of them consider the Bible to be inerrant (as compared to 27 percent for the population at large). According to other sources,[72] the recent expansion of Christian fundamentalism is particularly strong in the suburbs of the new South, South West, and Southern California, among lower-middle class and service workers, recently migrated to the new suburbs of fast-expanding metropolitan areas. This prompts Lienesch to hypothesize that they may represent "the first modernized generation of traditional people of recent immigration maintaining rural values in a secular urban society."[73] However, it appears that values, beliefs, and

70 Quoted by Lienesch (1993: 71).
71 Wilcox (1992).
72 Cited by Lienesch (1993).
73 Lienesch (1993: 10).

political stands are more important than demographic, occupational, or residential characteristics in spurring Christian fundamentalism. After reviewing a substantial body of available evidence on the matter, Wilcox concludes that "the data demonstrate that the best predictors of support for the Christian Right are religious identities, doctrines, behaviors, affiliations, and political beliefs."[74] Fundamentalism does not appear to be a rationalization of class interests or territorial positioning. Rather, it acts on the political process in the defense of moral, Christian values.[75] It is, as most fundamentalisms in history, a reactive movement, aiming to construct social and personal identity on the basis of images of the past and project them into a utopian future, to overcome unbearable present times.

But a reaction to what? What is unbearable? The most immediate sources of Christian fundamentalism seem to be twofold: the threat of globalization, and the crisis of patriarchalism. As Misztal and Shupe write, "the dynamics of globalization have promoted the dynamics of fundamentalism in a dialectical fashion."[76] Lechner elaborates further the reasons for this dialectic:

> In the process of globalization societies have become institutionalized as global facts. As organizations, they operate in secular terms; in their relations, they follow secular rules; hardly any religious tradition attributes transcendent significance to worldly societies in their present form...By the standards of most religious traditions, institutionalized societalism amounts to idolatry. But this means that life within society also has become a challenge for traditional religion...Precisely because global order is an institutionalized normative order it is plausible that there emerges some search for an "ultimate" foundation, for some transcendent reality beyond this world in relation to which the latter could be more clearly defined.[77]

Furthermore, while the communist threat provided ground for identification between the interests of the US government, Christianity, and America as the chosen nation, the collapse of the Soviet Union, and the emergence of a new global order, create a threatening uncertainty over the control of America's destiny. A recurrent theme of Christian fundamentalism in the US at the turn of the millennium is opposition to the control of the country by a "world government," superseding the US federal government (which it believes complicit in this development), enacted by the United Nations, the International

74   Wilcox (1992: 223).
75   Jelen (1991).
76   Misztal and Shupe (1992a: 8).
77   Lechner (1991: 276–7).

Monetary Fund, and the World Trade Organization, among other international bodies. In some eschatological writings, this new "world government" is assimilated to the Anti-Christ, and its symbols, including the microchip, are the Mark of the Beast that announces the "end of times." The construction of Christian fundamentalist identity seems to be an attempt to reassert control over life, and over the country, in direct response to the uncontrollable processes of globalization that are increasingly sensed in the economy and in the media.

Yet probably the most important source of Christian fundamentalism in the 1980s and 1990s was the reaction against the challenge to patriarchalism, issued from the 1960s' revolts, and expressed in women's, lesbian, and gay movements.[78] Furthermore, the battle is not just ideological. The American patriarchal family is indeed in crisis, according to all indicators of divorce, separation, violence in the family, children born out of wedlock, delayed marriages, shrinking motherhood, single lifestyles, gay and lesbian couples, and the widespread rejection of patriarchal authority (see chapter 4). There is an obvious reaction by men to defend their privileges, which are better suited to divine legitimacy, after their diminishing role as sole breadwinners undermined the material and ideological bases of patriarchalism. But there is something else, shared by men, women, and children. A deep-seated fear of the unknown, particularly frightening when the unknown concerns the basis of everyday, personal life. Unable to live under secular patriarchalism, but terrified of solitude and uncertainty in a wildly competitive, individualistic society, where family, as a myth and a reality, represented the only safe haven, many men, women, and children pray God to return them to the state of innocence where they could be content with benevolent patriarchalism under God's rules. And by praying together they become able to live together again. This is why American Christian fundamentalism is deeply marked by the characteristics of American culture, by its familistic individualism, by its pragmatism, and by the personalized relationship to God, and to God's design, as a methodology for solving personal problems in an increasingly unpredictable and uncontrollable life. As if the fundamental prayer were to receive from God's mercy the restoration of the lost American Way of Life in exchange for the sinner's commitment to repentance and Christian testimony.

78   Lamberts-Bendroth (1993).

Nations and Nationalisms in the Age of Globalization: Imagined Communities or Communal Images?

Only when all of us – all of us – recover our memory, will we be able, we and them, to stop being nationalists.

Rubert de Ventos, *Nacionalismos*[79]

The age of globalization is also the age of nationalist resurgence, expressed both in the challenge to established nation-states and in the widespread (re)construction of identity on the basis of nationality, always affirmed against the alien. This historical trend has surprised some observers, after nationalism had been declared deceased by a triple death: the globalization of the economy and the internationalization of political institutions; the universalism of a largely shared culture, diffused by electronic media, education, literacy, urbanization, and modernization; and the scholarly assault on the very concept of nations, declared to be "imagined communities"[80] in the mild version of anti-nationalist theory, or even "arbitrary historical inventions" in Gellner's forceful formulation,[81] arising from elite-dominated nationalist movements in their way to build the modern nation-state. Indeed, for Gellner, "nationalisms are simply those tribalisms, or for that matter any other kind of groups, which through luck, effort or circumstance succeed in becoming an effective force under modern circumstances."[82]

Success means, both for Gellner and for Hobsbawm,[83] the construction of a modern, sovereign nation-state. Thus, in this view, nationalist movements, as rationalizers of interests of a certain elite, invent a national identity which, if successful, is enshrined by the nation-state, and then diffused by propaganda among its subjects, to the point that "nationals" will then become ready to die for their nation. Hobsbawm does accept the historical evidence of nationalism that emerged from the bottom up (from sharing linguistic, territorial, ethnic, religious, and historical political attributes), but he labels it "proto-nationalism," since only when the nation-state is constituted do nations and nationalism come into existence, either as an expression of this nation-state or as a challenge to it on behalf of a future state. The explosion of nationalisms at this turn of the millennium, in

79   Rubert de Ventos (1994: 241); my translation.
80   Anderson (1983).
81   Gellner (1983: 56).
82   Gellner (1983: 87).
83   Hobsbawm (1992).

close relationship to the weakening of existing nation-states, does not fit well into this theoretical model that assimilates nations and nationalism to the emergence and consolidation of the modern nation-state after the French Revolution, which operated in much of the world as its founding mold. Never mind. For Hobsbawm, this apparent resurgence is in fact the historical product of unsolved national problems, created in the territorial restructuring of Europe between 1918 and 1921.[84]

However, as David Hooson writes, in his introduction to the global survey he edited, *Geography and National Identity*:

> the last half of the twentieth century will go down in history as a new age of rampant and proliferating nationalisms of a more durable nature than the dreadful but now banished tyrannies which have also characterized our century...The urge to express one's identity, and to have it recognized tangibly by others, is increasingly contagious and has to be recognized as an elemental force even in the shrunken, apparently homogenizing, high-tech world of the end of the twentieth century. [85]

And, as Eley and Suny write, in the introduction to their most insightful reader, *Becoming National*:

> Does the stress on subjectivity and consciousness rule out any "objective" basis for the existence of nationality? Clearly, such a radically subjectivist view would be absurd. Most successful nationalisms presume some prior community of territory, language, or culture, which provide the raw material for the intellectual project of nationality. Yet, those prior communities should not be "naturalized", as if they had always existed in some essential way, or have simply prefigured a history yet to come.. (Culture is more often not what people share, but what they choose to fight over.)[86]

In my view, the incongruence between some social theory and contemporary practice comes from the fact that nationalism, and nations, have a life of their own, independent of statehood, albeit embedded in cultural constructs and political projects. However attractive the influential notion of "imagined communities" may be, it is either obvious or empirically inadequate. Obvious for a social scientist if it is to say that all feelings of belonging, all worshipping of icons, is culturally constructed. Nations would not be an exception to this. The opposition between "real" and "imagined" communities is of

84 Hobsbawm (1992: 173–202).
85 Hooson (1994b: 2–3).
86 Eley and Suny (1996: 9).

little analytical use beyond the laudable effort at demystifying ideologies of essentialist nationalism *à la* Michelet. But if the meaning of the statement is, as it is explicit in Gellner's theory, that nations are pure ideological artifacts, constructed through arbitrary manipulation of historical myths by intellectuals for the interests of social and economic elites, then the historical record seems to belie such an excessive deconstructionism.[87] To be sure, ethnicity, religion, language, territory, *per se*, do not suffice to build nations, and induce nationalism. Shared experience does: both the United States and Japan are countries of strong national identity, and most of their nationals do feel, and express, strong patriotic feelings. Yet Japan is one of the most ethnically homogeneous nations on earth, and the United States one of the most ethnically heterogeneous. But in both cases there is a shared history and a shared project, and their historical narratives build on an experience, socially, ethnically, territorially, and genderly diversified, but common to the people of each country on many grounds. Other nations, and nationalisms, did not reach modern nation-statehood (for example, Scotland, Catalonia, Quebec, Kurdistan, Palestine), and yet they display, and some have displayed for several centuries, a strong cultural/territorial identity that expresses itself as a national character.

Thus, four major analytical points must be emphasized when discussing contemporary nationalism with regard to social theories of nationalism. First, contemporary nationalism may or may not be oriented toward the construction of a sovereign nation-state, and thus nations are, historically and analytically, entities independent of the state.[88] Secondly, nations, and nation-states, are not historically limited to the modern nation-state as constituted in Europe in the two hundred years following the French Revolution. Current political experience seems to reject the idea that nationalism is exclusively linked to the period of formation of the modern nation-state, with its climax in the nineteenth century, replicated in the decolonization process of the mid-twentieth century by the import of the Western nation-state into the Third World.[89] To assert so, as it has become fashionable, is simply Euro-centrism, as argued by Chatterjee.[90] As Panarin writes:

87   Moser (1985); Smith (1986); Johnston et al. (1988); Touraine (1988); Perez-Argote (1989); Chatterjee (1993); Blas Guerrero (1994); Hooson (1994b); Rubert de Ventos (1994); Eley and Suny (1996).
88   Keating (1995).
89   Badie (1992).
90   Chatterjee (1993).

> The misunderstanding of the century was the confusion of self-determination of people with the self-determination of nation. The mechanical transference of certain West European principles to the soil of non-European cultures often spawns monsters. One of these monsters was the concept of national sovereignty transplanted to non-European soil ... The syncretism of the concept of nation in the political lexicon of Europe prevents Europeans from making extremely important differentiations touching on the "sovereignty of people", "national sovereignty", and "rights of an ethnos."[91]

Indeed, Panarin's analysis is vindicated by the development of nationalist movements in many areas of the world, following a wide variety of cultural orientations and political projects, toward the end of the twentieth century.

Thirdly, nationalism is not necessarily an elite phenomenon, and, in fact, nationalism nowadays is more often than not a reaction against the global elites. To be sure, as in all social movements, the leadership tends to be more educated and literate (or computer literate in our time) than the popular masses that mobilize around nationalist goals, but this does not reduce the appeal and significance of nationalism to the manipulation of the masses by elites for the self-interest of these elites. As Smith writes, with obvious regret:

> Through a community of history and destiny, memories may be kept alive and actions retain their glory. For only in the chain of generations of those who share an historic and quasi-familial bond, can individuals hope to achieve a sense of immortality in eras of purely terrestrial horizons. In this sense, the formation of nations and the rise of ethnic nationalisms appears more like the institutionalization of "surrogate religion" than a political ideology, and therefore far more durable and potent than we care to admit.[92]

Fourthly, because contemporary nationalism is more reactive than proactive, it tends to be more cultural than political, and thus more oriented toward the defense of an already institutionalized culture than toward the construction or defense of a state. When new political institutions are created, or recreated, they are defensive trenches of identity, rather than launching platforms of political sovereignty. This is why I think that a more appropriate point of theoretical departure for understanding contemporary nationalism is Kosaku Yoshino's analysis of cultural nationalism in Japan:

91   Panarin (1994/1996: 37).
92   Smith (1989/1996: 125).

Cultural nationalism aims to regenerate the national community by creating, preserving, or strengthening a people's cultural identity when it is felt to be lacking or threatened. The cultural nationalist regards the nation as a product of its unique history and culture, and as a collective solidarity endowed with unique attributes. In short, cultural nationalism is concerned with the distinctiveness of the cultural community as the essence of a nation.[93]

Thus, nationalism is constructed by social action and reaction, both by elites and by the masses, as Hobsbawm argues, countering Gellner's emphasis on "high culture" as the exclusive origin of nationalism. But, against Hobsbawm's or Anderson's views, nationalism as a source of identity cannot be reduced to a particular historical period and to the exclusive workings of the modern nation-state. To reduce nations and nationalisms to the process of construction of the nation-state makes it impossible to explain the simultaneous rise of postmodern nationalism and decline of the modern state.

Rubert de Ventos, in an updated, refined version of Deutsch's classical perspective,[94] has suggested a more complex theory that sees the emergence of national identity through the historical interaction of four series of factors: *primary factors*, such as ethnicity, territory, language, religion, and the like; *generative factors*, such as the development of communications and technology, the formation of cities, the emergence of modern armies and centralized monarchies; *induced factors*, such as the codification of language in official grammars, the growth of bureaucracies, and the establishment of a national education system; and *reactive factors*, that is the defense of identities oppressed and interests subdued by a dominant social group or institutional apparatus, triggering the search for alternative identities in the collective memory of people.[95] Which factors play which role in the formation of each nationalism, and of each nation, depends on historical contexts, on the materials available to collective memory, and on the interaction between conflicting power strategies. Thus, nationalism is indeed culturally, and politically, constructed, but what really matters, both theoretically and practically, is, as for all identities, how, from what, by whom, and for what it is constructed.

At this turn of the millennium, the explosion of nationalisms, some of them deconstructing multinational states, others constructing pluri-national entities, is not associated with the formation of classical, sovereign, modern states. Rather, nationalism appears to be a

---

93   Yoshino (1992: 1).
94   Deutsch (1953); Rubert de Ventos (1994).
95   Rubert de Ventos (1994: 139–200).

major force behind the constitution of quasi-states; that is, political entities of shared sovereignty, either in stepped-up federalism (as in the Canadian (re)constitution in process, or in the "nation of nationalities," proclaimed in the Spanish Constitution of 1978, and widely expanded in its practice in the 1990s); or in international multilateralism (as in the European Union, or in the renegotiation of the Commonwealth of Independent States of ex-Soviet republics). Centralized nation-states resisting this trend of nationalist movements in search of quasi-statehood as a new historical reality (for example, Indonesia, Nigeria, Sri Lanka, even India) may well fall victim to this fatal error of assimilating the nation to the state, as a state as strong as Pakistan realized after the secession of Bangladesh.

In order to explore the complexity of the (re)construction of national identity in our new historical context, I will briefly elaborate on two cases that represent the two poles of the dialectic I am proposing as characteristic of this period: the deconstruction of a centralized, multinational state, the former Soviet Union, and the subsequent formation of what I consider to be quasi-nation-states; and the national quasi-state emerging in Catalonia through the dual movement of federalism in Spain and of confederalism in the European Union. After illustrating the analysis with these two case studies, I shall offer some hints on the new historical avenues of nationalism as a renewed source of collective identity.

Nations against the state: the breakup of the Soviet Union and the Commonwealth of Impossible States (Sojuz Nevozmoznykh Gosudarstv)

The Russian people of the cities and villages, half-savage beasts, stupid, almost frightening, will die to make room for a new human race.
Maxim Gorki, "On the Russian peasantry"[96]

The revolt of constituent nations against the Soviet state was a major factor, albeit not the only one, in the surprising collapse of the Soviet Union, as argued by Helene Carrere d'Encausse and Ronald Grigor Suny,[97] among other scholars. I shall analyze (in volume III) the complex intertwining of economic, technological, political, and national identity elements that, *together*, explain one of the most extraordinary developments in history, as the Russian Revolutions both opened and

---

96   1922, in *SSR vnutrennie protivorechiia*, Tchalidze Publications, 1987: 128, as cited by Carrere d'Encausse (1993: 173).
97   Carrere d'Encausse (1993); Suny (1993).

closed the political span of the twentieth century. Yet, while discussing the formation of national identity, and its new contours from the 1990s, it is essential to refer to the Soviet experience, and its aftermath, because it is a privileged terrain for observing the interplay between nations and the state, two entities that, in my view, are historically and analytically distinct. Indeed, the nationalist revolt against the Soviet Union was particularly significant because it was one of the few modern states explicitly built as a pluri-national state, with nationalities affirmed both for individuals (every Soviet citizen had an ascribed nationality written in his/her passport), and in the territorial administration of the Soviet Union.

The Soviet state was organized in a complex system of 15 federal republics, to which were added autonomous republics within the federal republics, territories (*krai*), and autonomous native districts (*okrag*), each republic comprising also several provinces (*oblasti*). Each federal republic, as well as autonomous republics within the federal republics, was based on a territorial nationality principle. This institutional construction was not a simple fiction. Certainly, autonomous nationalist expressions in contradiction to the will of the Soviet Communist party were ruthlessly repressed, particularly during the Stalinist period, and millions of Ukrainians, Estonians, Latvians, Lithuanians, Volga Germans, Crimean Tatars, Chechens, Mesketyans, Ingushi, Balkars, Karachai, and Kalmyks were deported to Siberia and Central Asia to prevent their cooperation with German invaders, or with other potential enemies, or simply to clear land for strategic projects of the state. But so were millions of Russians, for a variety of reasons, often randomly assigned. Yet, the reality of nationality-based administrations went beyond token appointments of national elites to leading positions in the republics' administration.[98] Policies of nativization (*korenizatsiya*) were supported by Lenin and Stalin until the 1930s, and renewed in the 1960s. They encouraged native languages and customs, implemented "affirmative action" programs, favoring recruitment and promotion of non-Russian nationalities in the state and party apparatuses of the republics, as well as in educational institutions, and fostered the development of national cultural elites, naturally on the condition of their subservience to Soviet power. As Suny writes:

> Lost in the powerful nationalist rhetoric is any sense of the degree to which the long and difficult years of Communist party rule actually continued the "making of nations" of the pre-revolutionary period ... It

thereby increased ethnic solidarity and national consciousness in the non-Russian republics, even as it frustrated full articulation of a national agenda by requiring conformity to an imposed political order.[99]

The reasons for this apparent openness to national self-determination (enshrined in the Soviet Constitution in the right of republics to secede from the Union) lie deep in the history and strategy of the Soviet state.[100] Soviet pluri-national federalism was the result of a compromise following intense political and ideological debates during the revolutionary period. Originally, the Bolshevik position, in line with classical Marxist thought, denied the relevance of nationality as a significant criterion in building the new state: proletarian internationalism was intended to supersede "artificial," or "secondary," national differences between the working classes, manipulated into inter-ethnic bloody confrontations by imperialist interests, as shown by World War I. But in January 1918, the urgency of finding military alliances in the civil war, and in the resistance against foreign invasion, convinced Lenin of the need for support from nationalist forces outside Russia, particularly in the Ukraine, after observing the vitality of national consciousness. The Third All-Russian Congress of Soviets adopted the "Declaration of the Rights of Working and Exploited People," transforming the ruins of the Russian Empire into "the fraternal union of Soviet Republics of Russia freely meeting on an internal basis." To this "internal federalization" of Russia, the Bolsheviks added, in April, the call for "external federalization" of other nations, explicitly naming the people of Poland, the Ukraine, Crimea, Transcaucasia, Turkestan, Kirghiz, "and others."[101]

The critical debate concerned the principle under which national identity would be recognized in the new federal state. The Bundists, and other socialist tendencies, wanted national cultures recognized throughout the whole structure of the state, without distinguishing them territorially, since the goal of the revolution was precisely to transcend ancestral bondings of ethnicity and territory on behalf of new, class-based, socialist universalism. To this view, Lenin and Stalin opposed the principle of territoriality as the basis for nationhood. The result was the multilayered national structure of the Soviet state: national identity was recognized in the institutions of governance. However, in application of the principle of democratic centralism, this diversity of territorial subjects would be under the control of the

---

99   Suny (1993: 101, 130).
100   Pipes (1954); Conquest (1967); Carrere d'Encausse (1987); Suny (1993); Slezkine (1994).
101   Singh (1982: 61).

dominant apparatuses of the Soviet Communist party, and of the Soviet state. Thus, the Soviet Union was constructed around a dual identity: on the one hand, ethnic/national identities (including Russian); on the other, Soviet identity as the foundation of the new society. *Sovetskii narod* (the Soviet people) would be the new cultural identity to be achieved in the historical horizon of Communist construction.

There were also strategic reasons for the conversion of proletarian internationalists into territorial nationalists. A. M. Salmin has proposed an interesting model for interpreting the Leninist–Stalinist strategy underlying Soviet federalism.[102] The Soviet Union was a centralized, but flexible institutional system whose structure should remain open and adaptive to receive new countries as members of the Union, as the cause of communism would advance throughout the world. Five concentric circles were designed as both security areas and waves of expansion of the Soviet state as vanguard of the revolution. The first was Russia, and its satellite republics, organized in the RSFSR. Paradoxically, Russia, and the Russian Federation, was the only republic with no autonomous Communist party, no President of the republican Supreme Soviet, and with the least developed republican institutions: it was the exclusive domain of the Soviet Communist party. To make this bastion safer, Russia did not have land borders with the potentially aggressive capitalist world. Thus, around Russia, Soviet republics were organized, in the outlying borders of the Soviet Union, so that they would eventually protect, at the same time, Soviet power and their national independence. This is why some ethnically based areas, such as Azerbaijan, became Soviet republics because they were bordering the outside world, while others, equally distinctive in their ethnic composition, like Chechnya, were kept in the Russian Federation because they were geographically closer to the core. The third ring of Soviet geopolitics was constituted by people's democracies under Soviet military power: this was originally the case for Khoresm, Bukhara, Mongolia, and Tannu-Tura, and became the precedent for the incorporation of Eastern Europe after World War II. The fourth circle would be formed by distant socialist countries, such as, years later, Cuba, North Korea, and Vietnam. China was never considered to be a part of this category because of deep distrust of future Chinese power. Finally, allied progressive governments and revolutionary movements around the world constituted the fifth circle, and their potential would depend on keeping a balance between their internationalism (meaning their pro-Soviet stand) and

102   Salmin (1992).

their national representativeness. It was this constant tension between the class-based universalism of communist utopia and geopolitical interests based on the ethnic/national concerns of potential allies that determined the schizophrenia of Soviet policy toward the national question.

The result of these contradictions throughout the tormented history of the Soviet Union was an incoherent patchwork of people, nationalities, and state institutions.[103] The more than one hundred nationalities and ethnic groups of the Soviet Union were dispatched all along its immense geography, according to geopolitical strategies, collective punishments and rewards, and individual caprice. Thus, Armenian-populated Nagorno-Karabaj was included by Stalin in Azerbaijan to please Turkey by putting its ancestral enemies under Azeri control (Azeris are a Turkic people); Volga Germans ended up in Kazakhstan, in whose northern territory they are now the driving economic force, supported by German subsidies to keep them out of Germany; Cossack settlements proliferated in Siberia and in the Far East; Ossetians were split between Russia (North) and Georgia (South), while Ingushis were distributed between Chechnya, North Ossetia, and Georgia; Crimea, taken by Russia from the Tatars in 1783, and from where the Tatars were deported by Stalin during World War II, was transferred by Khrushchev (himself a Ukrainian) to the Ukraine in 1954 to commemorate 300 years of Russian–Ukrainian friendship, reportedly after a night of heavy drinking. Furthermore, Russians were sent all over the territory of the Soviet Union, most often as skilled workers or willing pioneers, sometimes as rulers, sometimes as exiles. Thus, when the Soviet Union disintegrated, the principle of territorial nationality trapped tens of millions of suddenly "foreign nationals" inside the newly independent republics. The problem seems to be particularly acute for the 25 million Russians living outside the new Russian frontiers.

One of the greatest paradoxes of Soviet federalism is that Russia was probably the most discriminated of nationalities. The Russian Federation had much less political autonomy from the central Soviet state than any other republic. Analysis by regional economists showed that, in general terms, there was a net transfer of wealth, resources, and skills from Russia to the other republics (Siberia, which is the most ethnically Russian area of the Russian Federation, was the fundamental source of exports, and thus of hard currency for the Soviet Union).[104] As for national identity, it was Russian history,

---

103   Kozlov (1988); Suny (1993); Slezkine (1994).
104   Granberg and Spehl (1989); Granberg (1993).

religion, and traditional identity that became the main target of Soviet cultural repression, as documented in the 1980s by Russian writers and intellectuals, such as Likhachev, Belov, Astafiev, Rasputin, Solukhin, and Zalygin.[105] After all, the new Soviet identity had to be built on the ruins of the historical Russian identity, with some tactical exceptions during World War II, when Stalin needed to mobilize everything against the Germans, including Alexander Nevsky's memory. Thus, while there was indeed a policy of russification of culture throughout the Soviet Union (indeed, contradictory to the parallel trend of *korenizatsiya*), and ethnic Russians kept control of party, army, and KGB (but Stalin was Georgian, and Khrushchev was Ukrainian), Russian identity as a national identity was repressed to a much greater extent than other nationalities, some of which were in fact symbolically revived for the sake of pluri-national federalism.

This paradoxical constitution of the Soviet state expressed itself in the revolt against the Soviet Union, using the breathing space provided by Gorbachev's *glasnost*. The Baltic republics, forcefully annexed in 1940 in defiance of international law, were the first to claim their right to self-determination. But they were closely followed by a strong Russian nationalist movement that was in fact the most potent mobilizing force against the Soviet state. It was the merger of the struggle for democracy, and the recovery of Russian national identity under Yeltsin's leadership in 1989–91, that created the conditions for the demise of Soviet communism and the breakup of the Soviet Union.[106] Indeed, the first democratic election of the head of state in Russian history, with the election of Yeltsin on June 12, 1991, marked the beginning of the new Russia and, with it, the end of the Soviet Union. It was Russia's traditional flag that led the resistance to the Communist coup in August 1991. And it was Yeltsin's strategy of dismantling the Soviet state, by concentrating power and resources in the republican institutions, that led to the agreement with other republics, first of all with the Ukraine and Belarus, in December 1991, to end the Soviet Union, and to transform the ex-Soviet republics into sovereign states, loosely confederated in the Commonwealth of Independent States (*Sojuz Nezavisimykh Gosudarstv*). The assault on the Soviet state was not conducted only by nationalist movements: it linked up with democrats' demands, and with the interests of political elites in a number of republics, carving their own turf among the ruins of a crumbling empire. But it took a nationalist form, and received popular support on behalf of the nation. The

---

105   Carrere d'Encausse (1993: ch. 9).
106   Castells (1992b); Carrere d'Encausse (1993).

interesting matter is that nationalism was much less active in the most ethnically distinctive republics (for example, in Central Asia) than in the Baltic states, and in Russia.[107]

The first years of existence of this new conglomerate of independent states revealed the fragility of their construction, as well as the durability of historically rooted nationalities, across the borders inherited from the disintegration of the Soviet Union.[108] Russia's most intractable problem became the war in Chechnya. The Baltic republics practiced discrimination against their Russian population, inducing new inter-ethnic strife. The Ukraine saw the peaceful revolt of the Russian majority in Crimea against Ukrainian rule, and continued to experience the tension between strong nationalist sentiment in western Ukraine, and pan-Slavic feelings in eastern Ukraine. Moldova was torn between its historical Romanian identity and the Russian character of its eastern population that tried to create the Republic of Dniester. Georgia exploded in a bloody confrontation between its multiple nationalities (Georgians, Abkhazians, Armenians, Ossetians, Adzharis, Meshketians, Russians). Azerbaijan continued to fight intermittently with Armenia over Nagorno-Karabaj, and induced pogroms against Armenians in Baku. And the Muslim republics of Central Asia were torn between their historic links with Russia and the perspective of joining the Islamic fundamentalist whirlwind spinning from Iran and Afghanistan. As a result, Tajikistan suffered a fullscale civil war, and other republics Islamized their institutions and education to integrate radical Islamism before it was too late. Thus, the historical record seems to show that artificial, half-hearted, acknowledgment of the national question by Marxism–Leninism not only did not solve historical conflicts, but actually made them more virulent.[109] Reflecting on this extraordinary episode, and on its aftermath in the 1990s, several key issues of theoretical relevance deserve commentary.

First of all, one of the most powerful states in the history of humankind was not able, after 74 years, to create a new national identity. *Sovetskii narod* was not a myth, in spite of what Carrere d'Encausse says.[110] It did have some reality in the minds and lives of the generations born in the Soviet Union, in the reality of people making families with people from other nationalities, and living and working throughout the whole Soviet territory. Resistance against the Nazi juggernaut rallied people around the Soviet flag. After the

107   Carrere d'Encausse (1993); Starovoytova (1994).
108   Hooson (1994b); Lyday (1994); Stebelsky (1994); Khazanov (1995).
109   Twinning (1993); Panarin (1994); Khazanov (1995).
110   Carrere d'Encausse (1993: 234).

Stalinist terror subsided, in the late 1950s, and when material conditions improved, in the 1960s, a certain pride in being part of a superpower nation did develop. And, in spite of widespread cynicism and withdrawal, the ideology of equality and human solidarity took root in the Soviet citizenry, so that, overall, a new Soviet identity started to emerge. However, it was so fragile, and so dependent on the lack of information about the real situation of the country and of the world, that it did not resist the shocks of economic stagnation and the learning of the truth. In the 1980s, Russians who dared to proclaim themselves as "Soviet citizens" were derided as *Sovoks* by their compatriots. While *sovetskii narod* was not necessarily a failing identity project, it disintegrated before it could settle in the minds and lives of the people of the Soviet Union. Thus, the Soviet experience belies the theory according to which the state can construct national identity by itself. The most powerful state, using the most comprehensive ideological apparatus in history for more than seven decades, failed in recombining historical materials and projected myths into the making of a new identity. Communities may be imagined, but not necessarily believed.

Secondly, the formal acknowledgment of national identities in the territorial administration of the Soviet state, as well as policies of "nativization," did not succeed in integrating these nationalities into the Soviet system, with one significant exception: the Muslim republics of Central Asia, precisely those that were most distinctive from the dominant Slavic culture. These republics were so dependent on central power for their daily survival that only in the last moments of the disintegration of the Soviet Union did their elites dare to lead the drive for independence. In the rest of the Soviet Union, national identities could not find themselves expressed in the artificially constructed institutions of Soviet federalism. A case in point is Georgia, a multi-ethnic puzzle constructed on the basis of an historic kingdom. Georgians represent about 70 percent of the 5.5 million population. They generally belong to the Georgian Orthodox Church. But they had to coexist with Ossetians, primarily Russian Orthodox, whose population is split between North Ossetia Autonomous Republic (in Russia) and South Ossetia Autonomous Oblast (in Georgia). In the north-western corner of Georgia, the Abkhaz, a Sunni Muslim Turkic people, number only about 80,000, but they constituted 17 percent of the Abkhaz Autonomous Soviet Socialist Republic, created inside Georgia as a counterpoint to Georgian nationalism. It did succeed: in the 1990s, the Abkhaz, with support from Russia, fought to obtain quasi-independence in their territory, in spite of being a minority of the population. Georgia's second autonomous republic, Adzharia, is also Sunni Muslim, but from ethnic Georgians, thus supporting Georgia, while seeking their autonomy. Muslim Ingushis are in conflict with Ossetians in the border areas between Georgia, Ossetia, and Chechnya-Ingushetia. In addition, Meshketian Turks, deported by Stalin, are returning to Georgia, and Turkey has expressed its willingness to protect them, inducing distrust in Georgia's Armenian population. The net result of this territorially entangled history was that, in 1990–91, when Gamsakhurdia led a radical Georgian nationalist movement, and proclaimed independence without considering the interests of Georgia's national minorities, and without respecting civil liberties, he triggered a civil war (in which he died), both between his forces and Georgian democrats, and between Georgian forces, Abkhazians, and Ossetians. The intervention of Russia, and the pacifying role of Shevernadze, elected president in 1991 as a last resort to save the country, brought an unstable peace to the region, only to see neighboring Chechnya explode in an atrocious, protracted, debilitating guerrilla war. Thus, the failure of integrating national identities into the Soviet Union did not come from their recognition, but from the fact that their artificial institutionalization, following a bureaucratic and geopolitical logic, did not pay attention to the actual history and cultural/religious identity of each national community, and their geographical specificity. This is what authorizes Suny to speak of "the revenge of the past,"[111] and David Hooson to write:

> The question of identity is clearly the most insistent to have surfaced after the long freeze [in the former Soviet Union]. But it is not enough to treat it as a purely ethnic or cultural question. What is involved here is a re-search for the real regions of cultures, economies *and* environment which mean something (or in some cases everything) to the peoples who inhabit them. The process of crystallization of these regions, beyond the bald and flawed "Republic" boundaries of today, promises to be long and painful but inevitable and ultimately right.[112]

Thirdly, the ideological emptiness created by the failure of Marxism–Leninism to actually indoctrinate the masses was replaced, in the 1980s, when people were able to express themselves, by the only source of identity that was kept in the collective memory: *national identity*. This is why most anti-Soviet mobilizations, including democratic movements, were carried under the respective national flag. It is true, as it has been argued, and as I have argued, that political elites, in Russia, and in the federal republics, utilized nationalism as the

111 Suny (1993).
112 Hooson (1994a: 140).

ultimate weapon against failing communist ideology, to undermine the Soviet state, and seize power in the institutions of each republic.[113] However, the elites used this strategy because it was effective, because nationalist ideology resonated more in people's minds than abstract appeals to democracy, or to the virtues of the market, often assimilated to speculation in people's personal experience. Thus, the resurgence of nationalism cannot be explained by political manipulation: rather, its use by the elites is a proof of the resilience and vitality of national identity as a mobilizing principle. When, after 74 years of endless repetition of official socialist ideology, people discovered that the king was naked, the reconstruction of their identity could only take place around basic institutions of their collective memory: family, community, the rural past, sometimes religion, and, above all, the nation. But the nation was not meant as the equivalent of statehood and officialdom, but as personal self-identification in this now confusing world: I am Ukrainian, I am Russian, I am Armenian, became the rallying cry, the perennial foundation from which to reconstruct life in collectivity. This is why the Soviet experience is a testimony to the perdurability of nations beyond, and despite, the state.

Perhaps the greatest paradox of all is that when, at the end of this historical *parcours*, new nation-states emerged to assert their suppressed identities, *it is unlikely that they could really function as fully sovereign states*. This is, first of all, because of the intertwining of a mosaic of nationalities and historical identities within the current boundaries of independent states.[114] The most obvious issue refers to the 25 million Russians living under a different flag. But the Russian Federation (although currently populated by 82 percent of ethnic Russians) is also made up of 60 different ethnic/national groups, some of which are sitting on top of a wealth of natural and mineral resources, as in Sakha-Yakutia, or Tatarstan. As for the other republics, besides the illustrative case of Georgia, Kazakhs are only a minority in Kazakhstan; Tajikistan has 62 percent of Tajiks, and 24 percent Uzbeks; Kyrgyz make up only 52 percent of Kyrgyzstan's population; Uzbekistan has 72 percent of Uzbeks, and a wide diversity of different nationalities; 14 percent of Moldova's residents are Ukrainian, and 13 percent Russian. Ukrainians account for only 73 percent of the Ukraine's population. Latvians are 52 percent of Latvia, and Estonians 62 percent of Estonia. Thus, any strict defin-

---

113   Castells (1992b); Hobsbawm (1994).
114   Twinning (1993); Hooson (1994b).

ition of national interests around the institutionally dominant nationality would lead to intractable conflicts in the whole Eurasian continent, as Shevernadze conceded, explaining his willingness to cooperate with Russia, after his initial hostility. Furthermore, the interpenetration of the economies, and the sharing of infrastructure, from the electrical grid to pipelines and water supply, make the disentanglement of the territories of the former Soviet Union extremely costly, and put a decisive premium on cooperation. More so in a process of multilateral integration in the global economy that requires inter-regional linkages to operate efficiently. Naturally, the deep-seated fears of a new form of Russian imperialism will loom large in the future evolution of these new states. This is why there will be no reconstruction of the Soviet Union, regardless of who is in power in Russia. Yet, the full recognition of national identity cannot be expressed in the full independence of the new states, *precisely because of the strength of identities that cut across state borders.* This is why I propose, as the most likely, and indeed promising future, the notion of the Commonwealth of Inseparable States (*Sojuz Nerazdelimykh Gosudarstv*); that is, of a web of institutions flexible and dynamic enough to articulate the autonomy of national identity and the sharing of political instrumentality in the context of the global economy. Otherwise, the affirmation of sheer state power over a fragmented map of historical identities will be a caricature of nineteenth-century European nationalism: it will lead in fact to a Commonwealth of Impossible States (*Sojuz Nevozmoznykh Gosudarstv*).

Nations without a state: Catalunya

The State must be fundamentally differentiated from the Nation because the State is a political organization, an independent power externally, a supreme power internally, with material forces in manpower and money to maintain its independence and authority. We cannot identify the one with the other, as it was usual, even by Catalan patriots themselves who were speaking or writing of a Catalan nation in the sense of an independent Catalan state ... Catalunya continued to be Catalunya after centuries of having lost its self-government. Thus, we have reached a clear, distinct idea of nationality, the concept of a primary, fundamental social unit, destined to be in the world society, in Humanity, what man is for the civil society.

Enric Prat de la Riba, *La nacionalitat catalana*[115]

---

115   Originally published 1906; this edition 1978: 49–50.

If the analysis of the Soviet Union shows the possibility of states, however powerful, failing to produce nations, the experience of Catalonia (or *Catalunya*, in Catalan) allows us to reflect on the conditions under which nations exist, and (re)construct themselves over history, without a nation-state, and without searching to establish one.[116] Indeed, as stated by the current president, and national leader of *Catalunya* in the last quarter of the twentieth century, Jordi Pujol: "*Catalunya* is a nation without a state. We belong to the Spanish state, but we do not have secessionist ambitions. This must be clearly affirmed... The case of *Catalunya* is peculiar: we have our own language, and culture, we are a nation without a state."[117] To clarify this statement, and to elaborate on its broader, analytical implications, a brief historical review is necessary. Since not every reader is familiar with Catalonian history, I shall put forward, succinctly, the historical elements that authorize one to speak of the continuity of *Catalunya* as a materially lived, distinctive, national reality, of which the persistence of its language, and its contemporary widespread use against all odds, is a powerful indicator.[118]

Catalunya's official birthday as a nation is generally dated to 988, when Count Borrell finally severed links with the remnants of the Carolingian Empire that, around 800, had taken the lands and inhabitants of this southern frontier of the empire under its protection to counteract the threat from Arab invaders to Occitania. By the end of the ninth century, Count Guifrè el Pelòs, who had fought successfully against Arab domination, received from the French king the counties of Barcelona, Urgell, Cerdanya-Conflent, and Girona. His heirs became counts in their own right, without needing to be appointed by the French kings, assuring the hegemony of the Casal de Barcelona over the borderlands that would be called *Catalunya* in the twelfth century. Thus, while most of Christian Spain was engaged in the "Reconquest" against the Arabs for eight centuries, building in the process the kingdom of Castile and Leon, *Catalunya*, after a period of Arab domination in the eighth and ninth centuries, evolved from its Carolingian origins to become, between the early thirteenth and mid-fifteenth centuries, a Mediterranean empire. It extended to Mallorca (1229), Valencia (1238), Sicily (1282), part of Greece, with Athens (1303), Sardinia

116   Keating (1995).
117   1986; quoted in Pi (1996: 254).
118   For historical sources, see the compendium of Catalan history in Vilar (1987–90); and the special issue of *L'Avenc: Revista d'Historia* (1996). See also Vicens Vives and Llorens (1958); Vicens Vives (1959); Vilar (1964); Jutglar (1966); Sole-Tura (1967); McDonogh (1986); Rovira i Virgili (1988); Azevedo (1991); Garcia-Ramon and Nogue-Font (1994); Keating (1995); Salrach (1996).

(1323), and Naples (1442), including, as well, French territories beyond the Pyrénées, particularly Roussillon and Cerdagne.

Although *Catalunya* had a significant rural hinterland, it was primarily a commercial empire, governed by the alliance of nobility and urban merchant elites, along lines similar to those of the merchant republics of northern Italy. Concerned with the military power of Castile, the prudent Catalans accepted the merger proposed by the kingdom of Aragon in 1137. It was only in the late fifteenth century, after the voluntary merger with proto-imperial Castile, through the marriage of Fernando, king of *Catalunya*, Valencia and Aragon, with Isabel, queen of Castile, that *Catalunya* ceased to be a sovereign political entity. The marriage of the two nations was supposed to respect language, customs, and institutions, as well as sharing wealth. Yet, the power and wealth of the Spanish Crown and of its landowning nobility, as well as the influence of the fundamentalist Church built around the Counter-Reformation, steered the historical course in a different direction, subjugating non-Castilian peoples, in Europe, and in the Iberian peninsula, as well as in America. *Catalunya*, as the rest of Europe, was excluded from commerce with the American colonies, a major source of wealth in the Spanish kingdom. It reacted by developing its own consumer goods industry and by trading in its regional environment, triggering a process of incipient industrialization and capital accumulation from the second half of the sixteenth century. In the meantime Castile, after crushing, in 1520–23, the free Castilian cities (*Comunidades*) where an artisan class and a proto-bourgeoisie were emerging, went on to build a *rentier* economy to finance a warrior-theocratic state with proceeds from its American colonies and from heavy taxation on its subjects.

The clash of culture and institutions accelerated in the seventeenth century when Philip IV, in need of additional fiscal revenues, tightened up centralism, leading to the insurrection of both Portugal and *Catalunya* (where the Revolt of the Reapers took place) in 1640. Portugal, with the support of England, regained its independence. *Catalunya* was defeated, and most of its freedoms were taken away. Again, between 1705 and 1714, *Catalunya* fought for its autonomy, supporting the cause of the Austrians against Philip V, from the Bourbon dynasty, in the Spanish War of Succession. It is a mark of the Catalan character that its defeat, and the entry of Philip V's armies into Barcelona on September 11, 1714, is now celebrated as *Catalunya*'s national day. *Catalunya* lost all its political institutions of self-government, established since the Middle Ages: the municipal government based on democratic councils, the parliament, the Catalan sovereign government (*Generalitat*). The new institutions, established by the *Decreto de nueva planta*, issued by Philip V, concentrated authority in the hands of the military commander, or General Captain of *Catalunya*.

There followed a long period of outright institutional and cultural repression by central powers, which, as documented by historians, deliberately aimed at the gradual elimination of the Catalan language, which was first banned in the administration, then in commercial transactions, and, finally, in the schools, reducing its practice to the domains of family and Church.[119] Again, Catalans reacted by closing themselves off from state matters, and going back to work, reportedly just two days after the occupation of Barcelona, in a concerted action. Thus, *Catalunya* industrialized by the end of the eighteenth century, and was, for more than a century, the only truly industrial area of Spain.

The economic strength of the Catalan bourgeoisie, and the relatively high educational and cultural level of the society at large, contrasted throughout the nineteenth century with its political marginality. Then, when trade policies from Madrid began to threaten the still fragile Catalan industry, which required protectionism, a strong Catalan nationalist movement developed from the late nineteenth century, inspired by articulate ideologues, such as pragmatic nationalist Enric Prat de la Riba, or the federalists Valenti Almirall and Francesc Pi i Margall, sung by national poets, such as Joan Maragall, chronicled by historians, such as Rovira i Virgili, and supported by the work of philologists, such as Pompeu Fabra, who codified the modern Catalan language in the twentieth century. Yet, the Madrid political class never really accepted the alliance with Catalan nationalists, not even with the Lliga Regionalista, a clearly conservative party, probably the first modern political party in Spain, created in 1901 as a reaction to the control of elections by local bosses (*caciques*) on behalf of the central government. On the other hand, the growth of a powerful working-class movement, mainly anarcho-syndicalist, in *Catalunya* in the first third of the twentieth century, pushed Catalan nationalists, by and large dominated by their conservative wing until the 1920s, to rely on Madrid's protection against workers' demands, and threats of social revolution.[120]

However, in 1931, when the Republic was proclaimed in Spain, the left-wing republicans (*Esquerra republicana de Catalunya*) were able to establish a bridge between the Catalan working class, the petty bourgeoisie, and the nationalist ideals, and they became the dominant force in Catalan nationalism. Under the leadership of Lluis Com-

119   Ferrer i Girones (1985).
120   Sole-Tura (1967).

panys, a labor lawyer elected president of the restored *Generalitat*, *Esquerra* made a Spain-wide alliance with the Spanish Republicans, the Socialists, the Communists, and the labor unions (Anarchists, and Socialists). In 1932, under popular pressure expressed in a referendum, the Spanish government approved a Statute of Autonomy that re-stated liberties, self-government, and cultural/linguistic autonomy to *Catalunya*. Indeed, the satisfaction of nationalist demands from *Catalunya* and the Basque Country by the Spanish Republic was one of the most powerful triggers of the military insurrection that provoked the 1936–9 Civil War. Consequently, after the Civil War, the systematic repression of Catalan institutions, language, culture, identity, and political leaders (starting with the execution of Companys in 1940, after being delivered to Franco by the Gestapo) became a distinctive mark of Franco's dictatorship. It included the deliberate elimination of Catalan-speaking teachers from schools, in order to make the teaching of Catalan impossible. In a corresponding movement, nationalism became a rallying cry for the anti-Franco forces in *Catalunya*, as it was in the Basque Country, to the point that all democratic political forces, from Christian Democrats and Liberals to Socialists and Communists, were Catalan nationalists as well. This meant, for instance, that all political parties in *Catalunya*, both during the anti-Franco resistance and since the establishment of Spanish democracy in 1977, were and are Catalan, not Spanish, although they are federated in most cases with similar parties in Spain, while keeping their autonomy as parties (for example, the Catalan Socialist Party is linked to the Spanish PSOE; the Unified Socialist Party of *Catalunya* to the Communists, and so on).

In 1978, Article 2 of the new Spanish Constitution declared Spain a "nation of nationalities," and, in 1979, the Statute of Autonomy of *Catalunya* provided the institutional basis for Catalan autonomy, within the framework of Spain, including the declaration of official bilingualism, with Catalan being enshrined as "*Catalunya's* own language." In the regional elections of *Catalunya*, the Catalan nationalist coalition (*Convergencia i Unio*), led by *Catalunya's* contemporary leader, an educated, cosmopolitan, medical doctor of modest background, Jordi Pujol, obtained a majority five consecutive times, still being in power in 2003. The *Generalitat* (Catalan government) was strengthened, and became a dynamic institution, pursuing autonomous policies on all fronts, including the international arena. In the 1990s, Jordi Pujol was the president of the Association of European Regions. The city of Barcelona mobilized on its own, led by another charismatic figure, Catalan Socialist mayor Pasqual Maragall, a professor of urban economics, and the grandson of *Catalunya's* national poet. Barcelona projected itself into the world, skillfully using the 1992 Summer Olympic Games to emerge internationally as a major metropolitan center, linking historical identity with informational modernity. In the 1990s, the Catalan Nationalist party came to play a major role in Spanish politics. The inability of either the Socialist party (in 1993) or the Conservative *Partido Popular* (in 1996) to win a majority of seats in the Spanish general elections made Jordi Pujol the indispensable partner of any governing parliamentary coalition. He supported the Socialists first, the Conservatives later – at a price. *Catalunya* received the management of 30 percent of its income taxes, as well as exclusive competence in education (which is conducted in Catalan, at all levels), health, environment, communications, tourism, culture, social services, and most police functions. Thus, slowly, but surely, *Catalunya*, together with the Basque Country, was forcing Spain to become, unwillingly, a highly decentralized federal state, as the other regions claimed the same level of autonomy and resources that Catalans and Basques have obtained.

However, in the Catalan elections of 1999, the Catalan Nationalist party maintained a slim majority in parliament, which required its alliance in *Catalunya* with the conservative *Partido Popular* (PP). In addition, in 2000, the PP won an absolute majority in the Spanish election, freeing itself from dependence on the support of Catalan Nationalists in the Spanish Parliament. Then, the PP, and particularly its leader, Aznar, revealed its true centralist nature, and reversed the process of devolution of power to *Catalunya* and to the Basque Country. As a result, tensions ran high in the Basque Country, where the governing nationalist party threatened to engage in a process seeking sovereignty. In *Catalunya*, the Nationalist party distanced itself from the Conservatives; and in 2003 all Catalan parties, except the PP, demanded a new Statute of Autonomy, enhancing Catalan self-government. So, as of mid-2003, months before a new election in *Catalunya*, the question of Catalan autonomy, and the debate on the extent of Spanish federalism, are again at the forefront of Spanish politics. And yet, with the exception of a small, democratic, and peaceful pro-independence movement, mainly supported by young intellectuals, the Catalans, and the Catalan nationalist coalition, reject the idea of separatism, claiming they simply need institutions to exist as a nation, not to become a sovereign nation-state.[121]

What, then, is this Catalan nation, which is able to survive centuries of denial, and yet to refrain from entering the cycle of building a state

121   Keating (1995).

against another nation, Spain, which also became part of *Catalunya*'s historical identity? For Prat de la Riba, probably the most lucid ideologist of conservative Catalan nationalism in its formative stage, "*Catalunya* is the long chain of generations, united by the Catalan language and tradition, that succeed each other in the territory where we live."[122] Jordi Pujol also insists on the language as the foundation of Catalan identity, and so do most observers: "The identity of *Catalunya* is, to a very large extent, linguistic and cultural. *Catalunya* has never claimed ethnic or religious specificity, nor has insisted on geography, or being strictly political. There are many components of our identity, but language and culture are its backbone."[123] Indeed, *Catalunya* was, for more than two thousand years, a land of passage and migrations, between various European and Mediterranean peoples, thus forging its sovereign institutions in interaction with several cultures, from which it became clearly differentiated by the beginning of the twelfth century, when the name *Catalunya* appears for the first time.[124] According to the leading French historian of *Catalunya*, Pierre Vilar, what made Catalans distinctive as a people, from an early time (as early as the thirteenth and fourteenth centuries), was the language, clearly distinct from Spanish or French, with a developed literature already in the thirteenth century, exemplified in the writings of Raimon Llull (1235–1315), using the *Catalanesc*, which evolved from Latin in parallel with Provençal and Spanish.

Language as identity became particularly relevant in the last half of the twentieth century when a traditionally low birth rate among Catalans in modern times, coupled with the differential industrialization of *Catalunya*, led to massive migration from impoverished Southern Spain, thus submerging Catalan speakers, still fighting against the prohibition of their language, with wave after wave of Spanish-speaking workers, who set up their life and families in *Catalunya*, particularly in the Barcelona suburbs. Thus, after *Catalunya* recovered its autonomy under the 1978 Spanish Constitution, in 1983 the Catalan Parliament voted unanimously a "Law of Linguistic Normalization," introducing teaching in Catalan in all public schools and universities, as well as the Catalan language in the administration, in public places, streets and roads, and in public television.[125] The explicit policy was to achieve, over time, the full integration of the non-Catalan population into Catalan culture, so as to avoid the creation of cultural ghettos that would fracture the society probably along class lines.

122 Prat de la Riba (1894), cited by Sole-Tura (1967: 187); my translation.
123 Pujol (1995), quoted in Pi (1996: 176); my translation.
124 Salrach (1996).
125 Puiggene i Riera et al. (1991).

So, in this strategy, the state is used to reinforce/produce the nation, without claiming sovereignty from the Spanish state.

Why is language so important in the definition of Catalan identity? One answer is historical: it is, over hundreds of years, what has been the sign of identification of being Catalan, together with democratic political institutions of self-government when they were not suppressed. Although Catalan nationalists define as a Catalan whoever lives and works in *Catalunya*, they also add "and wants to be a Catalan." And the sign of "wanting to be" is speaking the language, or trying to (in fact, "trying to" is even better because it is a real sign of willingness to be). Another answer is political: it is the easiest way to expand, and reproduce, the Catalan population without resorting to criteria of territorial sovereignty that would then necessarily collide with the territoriality of the Spanish state. Yet, an additional, and more fundamental, answer may be linked to what language represents, as a system of codes, crystallizing historically a cultural configuration that allows for symbolic sharing without worshipping of icons other than those emerging in the communication of everyday life. It may well be that nations without states are organized around linguistic communities – an idea on which I will elaborate below – although, obviously, a common language does not make a nation. Latin American nations would certainly object to this approach, as would the UK and the US. But, for the moment, let us stay in *Catalunya*.

I hope that, after this historical review, it can be conceded that it is not an invented identity. For over a thousand years at least, a given human community, mainly organized around language, but with a great deal of territorial continuity as well, and with a tradition of indigenous political democracy and self-government, has identified itself as a nation, in different contexts, against different adversaries, being part of different states, having its own state, searching for autonomy without challenging the Spanish state, integrating immigrants, enduring humiliation (indeed, commemorating it every year), and yet existing as *Catalunya*. An effort has been made by some analysts to identify Catalanism with the historical aspirations of a frustrated industrial bourgeoisie asphyxiated by a pre-capitalist, bureaucratic Spanish monarchy.[126] This was certainly a major element present in the Catalanist movement of the late nineteenth century, and in the formation of the Lliga.[127] But class analysis cannot account for the continuity of explicit discourse of Catalan identity throughout

126   Jutglar (1966).
127   Sole-Tura (1967).

history, in spite of all the efforts of Spanish centralism to eradicate it. Prat de la Riba denied that *Catalunya* was reducible to class interests, and he was right, although his Lliga was primarily a bourgeois party.[128]

Catalanism has often been associated with nineteenth-century romanticism, but it was also connected to the modernist movement of the turn of the century, oriented toward Europe and the international movement of ideas, and away from traditional Spanish regenerationism, searching for a new source of transcendent values after the loss of the remnants of empire in 1898. A cultural community, organized around language and a shared history, *Catalunya* is not an imagined entity, but a constantly renewed historical product, even if nationalist movements construct/reconstruct their icons of self-identification with codes specific to each historical context, and relative to their political projects.

A decisive characterization of Catalan nationalism concerns its relationship to the nation-state.[129] Declaring *Catalunya* at the same time European, Mediterranean, and Hispanic, Catalan nationalists, while rejecting separatism from Spain, search for a new kind of state. It would be a state of variable geometry, bringing together respect for the historically inherited Spanish state with the growing autonomy of Catalan institutions in conducting public affairs, and the integration of both Spain and *Catalunya* in a broader entity, Europe, which translates not only into the European Union, but into various networks of regional and municipal governments, as well as of civic associations, that multiply horizontal relationships throughout Europe under the tenuous shell of modern nation-states. This is not simply the clever tactics of the present. It comes from the centuries-old, pro-European standing of Catalan elites, in contrast with the splendid cultural isolationism practiced by most Castilian elites in most historical periods. It is explicit also in the thinking of some of the most universal Catalan writers or philosophers, such as Josep Ferrater Mora, who could write in 1960: "The catalanization of *Catalunya* may be the last historical opportunity to make Catalans 'good Spaniards', and to make Spaniards 'good Europeans.'"[130] This is because only a Spain that could accept its plural identity – *Catalunya* being one of its most distinctive – could be fully open to a democratic, tolerant Europe. And, for this to happen, Catalans have first to feel at home within the territorial sovereignty of the Spanish state, being able to think, and speak, in Catalan, thus creating their

128 Prat de le Riba (1906).
129 Keating (1995); Pi (1996); Trias (1996).
130 Ferrater Mora (1960: 120).

commune within a broader network. This differentiation between cultural identity and the power of the state, between the undisputed sovereignty of apparatuses and the networking of power-sharing institutions, is an historical innovation in relation to most processes of construction of nation-states, solidly planted in historically shaky soil. It seems to relate better than traditional notions of sovereignty to a society based on flexibility and adaptability, to a global economy, to the networking of media, to the variation and interpenetration of cultures. By not searching for a new state but fighting to preserve their nation, Catalans may have come full circle to their origins as people of borderless trade, cultural/linguistic identity, and flexible government institutions, all features that seem to characterize the information age.

Nations of the information age

Our excursus at the two opposite extremes of Europe yields some knowledge of the new significance of nations and nationalism as a source of meaning in the information age. For the sake of clarity, I shall define nations, in line with the arguments and elaborations presented above, as *cultural communes constructed in people's minds and collective memory by the sharing of history and political projects*. How much history must be shared for a collectivity to become a nation varies with contexts and periods, as are also variable the ingredients that predispose the formation of such communes. Thus, Catalan nationality was distilled over a thousand years of sharing, while the United States of America forged a very strong national identity, in spite of, or because of, its multi-ethnicity, in a mere two centuries. What is essential is the historical distinction between nations and states, which only came to merge, and not for all nations, in the modern age. Thus, from the vantage point of our perspective at the turn of the millennium, we know of nations without states (for example, Catalonia, the Basque Country, Scotland, and Quebec), of states without nations (Singapore, Taiwan, and South Africa), of pluri-national states (the former Soviet Union, Belgium, Spain, and the United Kingdom), of uni-national states (Japan), of shared-nation states (South Korea and North Korea), and of nations sharing states (Swedes in Sweden and Finland, Irish in Ireland and the United Kingdom, maybe Serbs, Croats, and Bosnian Muslims in a future Bosnia-Herzegovina).

What is clear is that citizenship does not equate with nationality, at least exclusive nationality, as Catalans feel Catalan first of all; yet, at the same time, most declare themselves Spanish, and even

"European," as well. So, the assimilation of nations and states to the composite nation-state, beyond a given historical context, is simply contradicted by observation when the record is constructed over the long haul and in a global perspective. It seems that the rationalist reaction (Marxist or otherwise) against German idealism (Herder, Fichte), and against French nationalistic hagiography (Michelet, Renan), obscured the understanding of the "national question," thus inducing bewilderment when confronted with the power and influence of nationalism at the end of the twentieth century.

Two phenomena, as illustrated in this section, appear to be characteristic of the current historical period: first, the disintegration of plurinational states that try to remain fully sovereign or to deny the plurality of their national constituents. This was the case of the former Soviet Union, of the former Yugoslavia, of the former Ethiopia, of Czechoslovakia, and maybe it could be the case, in the future, of Sri Lanka, India, Indonesia, Nigeria, and other countries. The result of this disintegration is the formation of *quasi-nation-states*. They are nation-states because they receive the attributes of sovereignty on the basis of a historically constituted national identity (for example, the Ukraine). But they are "quasi" because the entangled set of relationships with their historical matrix forces them to share sovereignty with either their former state or a broader configuration (for example, the CIS, Eastern European republics associated with the European Union). Secondly, we observe the development of nations that stop at the threshold of statehood, but force their parent state to adapt, and cede sovereignty, as in the case of *Catalunya*, the Basque Country, Flanders, Wallonie, Scotland, Quebec, and, potentially, Kurdistan, Kashmir, Punjab, and East Timor. I label these entities *national quasi-states* because they are not fully fledged states, but win a share of political autonomy on the basis of their national identity.

The attributes that reinforce national identity in this historical period vary, although, in all cases, they presuppose the sharing of history over time. However, *I would make the hypothesis that language, and particularly a fully developed language, is a fundamental attribute of self-recognition, and of the establishment of an invisible national boundary less arbitrary than territoriality, and less exclusive than ethnicity.* This is, in an historical perspective, because language provides the linkage between the private and the public sphere, and between the past and the present, regardless of the actual acknowledgment of a cultural community by the institutions of the state. And it is not because Fichte used this argument to build pan-German nationalism that the historical record should be discarded. But there is also a powerful reason for the emergence of language-based nationalism in our societies. If nationalism is, most often, a reaction against a threatened autonomous identity, then, in a world submitted to cultural homogenization by the ideology of modernization and the power of global media, language, as the direct expression of culture, becomes the trench of cultural resistance, the last bastion of self-control, the refuge of identifiable meaning. Thus, after all, nations do not seem to be "imagined communities" constructed at the service of power apparatuses. Rather, they are produced through the labors of shared history, and then spoken in the images of communal languages whose first word is *we*, the second is *us*, and, unfortunately, the third is *them*.

Ethnic Unbonding: Race, Class, and Identity in the Network Society

See you 100 Black Men... See you jailed. See you caged. See you tamed. See you pain. See you fronting. See you lamping. See you want. See you need. See you dissed. See you Blood. See you Crip. See you Brother. See you sober. See you loved. See you peace. See you home. See you listen. See you love. See you on it. See you faithful. See you chumped. See you challenged. See you change. See you. See you. See you... I definitely wanna be you.
> Peter J. Harris, "Praisesong for the Anonymous Brothers"[131]

Do *you* want, as well? Really? Ethnicity has been a fundamental source of meaning and recognition throughout human history. It is a founding structure of social differentiation, and social recognition, as well as of discrimination, in many contemporary societies, from the United States to Sub-Saharan Africa. It has been, and it is, the basis for uprisings in search of social justice, as for Mexican Indians in Chiapas in 1994, as well as the irrational rationale for ethnic cleansing, as practiced by Bosnian Serbs in 1994. And it is, to a large extent, the cultural basis that induces networking and trust-based transactions in the new business world, from Chinese business networks (volume I, chapter 3) to the ethnic "tribes" that determine success in the new global economy. Indeed, as Cornel West writes: "In this age of globalization, with its impressive scientific and technological innovations in information, communication, and applied biology, a focus on the lingering effects of racism seems outdated and antiquated... Yet race – in the coded language of welfare reform, immigration policy, criminal punishment, affirmative action, and suburban privatization – remains a central signifier in the political

131   From Wideman and Preston (1995: xxi).

debate."[132] However, if race and ethnicity are central – to America, as to other societies' dynamics – their manifestations seem to be deeply altered by current societal trends.[133] I contend that while race matters, probably more than ever as a source of oppression and discrimination,[134] ethnicity is being specified as a source of meaning and identity, to be melted not with other ethnicities, but under broader principles of cultural self-definition, such as religion, nation, and gender. To convey the arguments in support of this hypothesis I shall discuss, briefly, the evolution of African American identity in the United States.

The contemporary condition of African Americans has been transformed in the past three decades by a fundamental phenomenon: their profound division along class lines, as shown in the pioneering work of William Julius Wilson,[135] the implications of which shattered for ever the way America sees African Americans, and, even more importantly, the way African Americans see themselves. Supported by a stream of research in the past decade, Wilson's thesis, and its development, points to a dramatic polarization among African Americans. On the one hand, spurred by the civil rights movement of the 1960s, particularly thanks to affirmative action programs, a large, well-educated, and relatively comfortable African American middle class has emerged, making significant inroads into the political power structure, from mayoral offices to chairmanship of the Joint Chiefs of Staff, and, to some extent, in the corporate world. Thus, about a third of African Americans are now part of the American middle class, although men, unlike women, still make much less money than their white counterparts.

On the other hand, about a third of African Americans, comprising 45 percent of African American children at or below the poverty level, are much worse off now than they were in the 1960s. Wilson, joined by other researchers, such as Blakely and Goldsmith, or Gans, attributes the formation of this "underclass" to the combined effect of an unbalanced information economy, of spatial segregation, and of misled public policy. The growth of an information economy emphasizes education, and reduces the availability of stable manual jobs, disadvantaging blacks at the entry level of the job market. Middle-class blacks escape the inner city, leaving behind, entrapped, the masses of the urban poor. To close the circle, the new black political elite finds support among the urban poor voters, but only as long as

132   West (1996: 107–8).
133   Appiah and Gates (1995).
134   Wieviorka (1993); C.West (1993).
135   Wilson (1987).

they can deliver social programs, which is a function of how worri-some, morally and politically, urban poor are for the white majority. Thus, new black political leadership is based on its ability to be the intermediary between the corporate world, the political establish-ment, and the ghettoized, unpredictable poor.

Between these two groups, the final third of African Americans strives not to fall into the poverty hell, hanging onto service jobs, disproportionately in the public sector, and to educational and voca-tional training programs that provide some skills to survive in a deindustrializing economy.[136] The punishment for those who do not succeed is increasingly atrocious. Among poorly educated, central-city, black male residents in 1992, barely one-third held full-time jobs. And even among those who do work, 15 percent are below the poverty line. The average net worth of assets of the poorest fifth of blacks in 1995 was exactly zero. One-third of poor black households lives in substandard housing, meaning, among other criteria, "to show evidence of rats." The ratio of urban crime rate over suburban crime rate has grown from 1.2 to 1.6 between 1973 and 1992. And, of course, inner-city residents are those who suffer most from these crimes.

Furthermore, the poor male black population is subjected to mas-sive incarceration, or lives under the control of the penal system (awaiting trial, probation). While blacks are about 12 percent of the American population, in the 1990s they accounted for more than 50 percent of prison inmates.[137] The overall incarceration rate for black Americans in 1990 was 1,860 per 100,000, that is 6.4 times higher than for whites. And, yes, African Americans are better educated, but in 1993 23,000 black men received a college diploma, while 2.3 million were incarcerated.[138] If we add all persons under supervision of the penal system in America in 1996, we reach 5.4 million people. Blacks represented 53 percent of inmates in 1991.[139] The ratios of incarceration and surveillance are much higher among poor blacks, and staggering among young black males. In cities such as Washing-ton, DC, for age groups 18–30, the majority of black males are in prison or on probation. Women, and families, have to adjust to this situation. The notorious argument of the absent male in the poor African American family has to account for the fact that many poor men spend considerable periods of their life in prison, so

136   Wilson (1987); Blakely and Goldsmith (1993); Carnoy (1994); Wacquant (1994); Gans (1995); Hochschild (1995); Gates (1996).
137   Tonry (1995: 59).
138   Gates (1996: 25).
139   See volume III, chapter 2.

that women have to be prepared to raise children by themselves, or to give birth on their own responsibility.

These are well-known facts, whose social roots in the new techno-logical and economic context I shall try to analyze in volume III. But I am concerned, at this point in my analysis, with the consequences of such a deep class divide on the transformation of African American identity. To comprehend this transformation since the 1960s, we must go back to the historical roots of this identity: as Cornel West argues, blacks in America are precisely African and American. Their identity was constituted as kidnapped, enslaved people under the freest society of the time. Thus, to conciliate the obvious contradiction between the ideals of freedom, and the highly productive, slavery-based economy, America had to deny the humanity of blacks because only non-humans could be denied freedom in a society constituted on the principle that "all men are born equal." As Cornel West writes: "This unrelenting assault on black humanity produced the fundamen-tal condition of black culture – that of *black invisibility* and *nameless-ness*."[140] Thus, black culture, following Cornel West's analysis, had to learn to cope with its negation without falling into self-annihilation. It did. From songs to art, from communal churches to brotherhood, black society emerged with a deep sense of collective meaning, not lost during the massive rural exodus to the Northern ghettos, trans-lated into extraordinary creativity in art, music, and literature, and into a powerful, multifaceted political movement, whose dreams and potential were personified by Martin Luther King Jr in the 1960s.

Yet, the fundamental divide introduced among blacks by the partial success of the civil rights movement has transformed this cultural landscape. But, how exactly? At first sight, it would seem that the black middle class, building on its relative economic affluence and political influence, could be assimilated into the mainstream, consti-tuting itself under a new identity, as African Americans, moving toward a position similar to that of Italian Americans, or Chinese Americans. After all, Chinese Americans were highly discriminated against for most of California's history, yet they have reached in recent years a rather respected social status. Thus, in this perspective, African Americans could become another, distinctive segment in the multi-ethnic quilt of American society. While, on the other hand, the "underclass" would become more poor than black.

Yet, this thesis of a dual cultural evolution does not seem to hold when checked against available data. Jennifer Hochschild's powerful

---

140   West (1996: 80).

study of the cultural transformation of blacks and whites in their relationship to the "American Dream" of equal opportunity and individual mobility shows exactly the contrary.[141] Middle-class blacks are precisely those who feel bitter about the frustrated illusion of the American Dream, and feel most discriminated against by the permanence of racism, while a majority of whites feel that blacks are being unduly favored by affirmative action policies, and complain about reverse discrimination. On the other hand, poor blacks, while fully conscious of racism, seem to believe in the American Dream to a greater extent than middle-class blacks, and, in any case, are more fatalistic and/or individualistic about their fate (it always was like this), although a temporal perspective in the evolution of opinion polls seems to indicate that poor blacks, too, are losing whatever faith in the system they had. Still, the major fact that clearly stands out from Hochschild's effort to bring to the analysis a wealth of empirical data is that, by and large, affluent African Americans do not feel welcome in mainstream society. Indeed, they are not. Not only racial hostility among whites continues to be pervasive, but gains by middle-class black males still leave them way behind whites in education, occupation, and income, as shown by Martin Carnoy.[142]

So, race matters a lot.[143] But, at the same time, the class divide among blacks has created such fundamentally different living conditions that there is growing hostility among the poor against those former brothers who left them out.[144] Most middle-class blacks strive to get ahead not only from the reality of the ghetto, but from the stigma that the echoes from the dying ghetto project on them through their skin. They do so, particularly, by insulating their children from the poor black communities (moving to suburbs, integrating them into white-dominated private schools), while, at the same time, re-inventing an African American identity that revives the themes of the past, African or American, while keeping silent on the plight of the present.

In a parallel move, end-of-millennium ghettos developed a new culture, formed out of affliction, rage, and individual reaction against collective exclusion, where blackness matters less than the situations of exclusion that create new sources of bonding, for instance, territorial gangs, started in the streets, and consolidated in and from the prisons.[145] Rap, not jazz, emerged from this culture. This new culture

141 Hochschild (1995).
142 Carnoy (1994).
143 West (1996).
144 Hochschild (1995); Gates (1996).
145 Sanchez Jankowski (1991).

expresses identity, as well, and it is also rooted in black history, and in the venerable American tradition of racism and racial oppression, but it incorporates new elements: the police and penal system as central institutions, the criminal economy as a shop floor, the schools as contested terrain, churches as islands of conciliation, mother-centered families, rundown environments, gang-based social organization, violence as a way of life. These are the themes of new black art and literature emerging from the new ghetto experience.[146] But it is not the same identity, by any means, as the identity emerging in middle-class African-America through the careful reconstruction of the humanity of the race.

Yet, even accepting their cultural split, both sets of identities face what appear to be insuperable difficulties in their constitution. This is, for affluent African Americans, because of the following contradiction:[147] they feel the rejection of institutional racism, so that they can only integrate into the American mainstream as leaders of their kin, as the "Talented Tenth" that Du Bois, the leading black intellectual at the turn of the century, considered to be the necessary saviors of "the negro race," as for all races.[148] But the social, economic, and cultural divide between the "Talented Tenth" and a significant, growing proportion of black America is such that they would have to deny themselves, and their children, accomplishing such a role, to become part of a pluri-class, multiracial coalition of progressive social change. In their superb little book debating this question, Henry Louis Gates Jr and Cornel West seem to think, on the one hand, that there is no other alternative, and yet, they do have reasonable doubts of the feasibility of such an option. Gates: "The real crisis of black leadership is that the very idea of black leadership is in crisis."[149] West:

> Since a multi-racial alliance of progressive middlers, liberal slices of the corporate elite, and subversive energy from below is the only vehicle by which some form of radical democratic accountability can redistribute resources and wealth and restructure the economy and government so that all benefit, the significant secondary efforts of the black Talented Tenth alone in the twenty-first century will be woefully inadequate and thoroughly frustrating.[150]

---

146 Wideman and Preston (1995); Giroux (1996).
147 Hochschild (1995).
148 Gates and West (1996: 133).
149 Gates (1996: 38).
150 West (1996: 110).

Indeed, Du Bois himself left America for Ghana in 1961 because, he said, "I just cannot take any more of this country's treatment . . . Chin up, and fight on, but realize that American Negroes can't win."[151]

Will this failure of full integration efforts lead to a revival of black separatism in America? Could this be the new basis for identity, in direct line with the radical 1960s' movements, as exemplified by the Black Panthers? It would seem so, at least among the militant youth, if we were to pay attention to the renewed cult of Malcolm X, the growing influence of Farrakhan's Nation of Islam, or, even more so, the extraordinary impact of the 1995 "Million Men March" in Washington, DC, built around atonement, morality, and black male pride. Yet, these new manifestations of cultural–political identity reveal further cleavages among African Americans, and they are actually organized around principles of self-identification that are not ethnic but religious (Islam, black churches), and strongly gendered (male pride, male responsibility, subordination of females). The impact of the "Million Men March," and its foreseeable development in the future, cuts across class lines, but shrinks the gender basis of African American identity, and blurs the lines between religious, racial, and class self-identification. In other words, it was not based on identity but on the reflection of a disappearing identity. How can it be that, while society is reminding blacks every minute that they are black (thus, a different, stigmatized human kind, coming in a long journey from non-humanity), blacks themselves are living so many different lives, so as not to be able to share, and, instead, become increasingly violent toward each other? A yearning for the lost community began to emerge in black America in the 1990s – because perhaps the deepest wound inflicted on African Americans in the preceding decade had been the gradual loss of collective identity, leading to individual drifting, while still bearing a collective stigma.

This is not a necessary process. Socio-political movements such as Jesse Jackson's "Rainbow Coalition," among others, continue to try hard to bring together black churches, minorities, communities, unions, and women, under a common banner to fight politically for social justice and racial equality. Yet this is a process of building a political identity that only if fully successful in the long term could create a collective, cultural identity that would be necessarily new for both whites and blacks, if it is to overcome racism while maintaining historical, cultural differences. Cornel West, while acknowledging a "hope not hopeless but unhopeful," calls for "radical democracy" to transcend both racial divisions and black nationalism.[152] But in the

151   Gates and West (1996: 111).
152   West (1996: 112).

ghetto trenches, and in the corporate boardrooms, historical African American identity is being fragmented, and individualized, without yet being integrated into a multiracial, open society.

Thus, I formulate the hypothesis that ethnicity does not provide the basis for communal heavens in the network society because it is based on primary bonds that lose significance, when cut from their historical context, as a basis for reconstruction of meaning in a world of flows and networks, of recombination of images, and reassignment of meaning. Ethnic materials are integrated into cultural communes that are more powerful, and more broadly defined than ethnicity, such as religion or nationalism, as statements of cultural autonomy in a world of symbols. Or else, ethnicity becomes the foundation for defensive trenches, then territorialized in local communities, or even gangs, defending their turf. Between cultural communes and self-defense territorial units, ethnic roots are twisted, divided, reprocessed, mixed, differentially stigmatized, or rewarded, according to a new logic of informationalization/globalization of cultures and economies that makes symbolic composites out of blurred identities. Race matters, but it hardly constructs meaning any longer.

Territorial Identities: The Local Community

One of the oldest debates in urban sociology refers to the loss of community as a result of urbanization first, and of suburbanization later. Empirical research some time ago, most notably by Claude Fischer and by Barry Wellman,[153] seems to have put to rest the simplistic notion of a systematic co-variation between space and culture. People socialize and interact in their local environment, be it in the village, in the city, or in the suburb, and they build social networks among their neighbors. On the other hand, locally based identities intersect with other sources of meaning and social recognition, in a highly diversified pattern that allows for alternative interpretations. So, where, in recent years, Etzioni sees the revival of community to a large extent on a local basis, Putnam watches the disintegration of the Tocquevillian vision of an intense civil society in America, with membership and activity in voluntary associations dropping substantially in the 1980s.[154] Reports from other areas of the world are equally conflicting in their estimates. However, I do not think it would be inaccurate to say that local environments, *per se*, do

153   Wellman (1979); Fischer (1982).
154   Etzioni (1993); Putnam (1995).

not induce a specific pattern of behavior, or, for that matter, a distinctive identity. Yet, what communalist authors would argue, and what is consistent with my own cross-cultural observation, is that people resist the process of individualization and social atomization, and tend to cluster in community organizations that, over time, generate a feeling of belonging, and ultimately, in many cases, a communal, cultural identity. I introduce the hypothesis that, for this to happen, a process of social mobilization is necessary. That is, people must engage in urban movements (not quite revolutionary), through which common interests are discovered, and defended, life is shared somehow, and new meaning may be produced.

I know something about this subject, having spent a decade of my life studying urban social movements around the world.[155] Summarizing my findings, as well as the relevant literature, I proposed that urban movements (processes of purposive social mobilization, organized in a given territory, oriented toward urban-related goals) were focused on three main sets of goals: urban demands on living conditions and collective consumption; the affirmation of local cultural identity; and the conquest of local political autonomy and citizen participation. Different movements combined these three sets of goals in various proportions, and the outcomes of their efforts were equally diversified. Yet, in many instances, regardless of the explicit achievements of the movement, its very existence produced meaning, not only for the movement's participants, but for the community at large. And not only during the lifespan of the movement (usually brief), but in the collective memory of the locality. Indeed, I argued, and I argue, that this production of meaning is an essential component of cities, throughout history, as the built environment, and its meaning, is constructed through a conflictive process between the interests and values of opposing social actors.

I added something else, referring to the historical moment of my observation (the late 1970s and early 1980s), but projecting my view toward the future: urban movements were becoming critical sources of resistance to the one-sided logic of capitalism, statism, and informationalism. This was, essentially, because the failure of proactive movements and politics (for example, the labor movement, political parties) to counter economic exploitation, cultural domination, and political oppression had left people with no other choice but either to surrender or to react on the basis of the most immediate source of self-recognition and autonomous organization: their locality. Thus, so emerged the paradox of increasingly local politics in a world struc-

155   Castells (1983).

tured by increasingly global processes. There was production of meaning and identity: my neighborhood, my community, my city, my school, my tree, my river, my beach, my chapel, my peace, my environment. But it was a defensive identity, an identity of retrenchment of the known against the unpredictability of the unknown and uncontrollable. Suddenly defenseless against a global whirlwind, people stuck to themselves: whatever they had, and whatever they were, became their identity. I wrote in 1983:

> Urban movements do address the real issues of our time, although neither on the scale nor terms that are adequate to the task. And yet they do not have any choice since they are the last reaction to the domination and renewed exploitation that submerges our world. But they are more than a last symbolic stand and a desperate cry: they are symptoms of our own contradictions, and therefore potentially capable of superseding these contradictions ... They do produce new historical meaning – in the twilight zone of pretending to build within the walls of a local community a new society they know unattainable. And they do so by nurturing the embryos of tomorrow's social movements within the local utopias that urban movements have constructed in order never to surrender to barbarism."[156]

What has happened since then? The empirical answer is, of course, extraordinarily diverse, particularly if we look across cultures and areas of the world.[157] I would, however, venture, for the sake of the analysis, to synthesize urban movements' main trajectories in the 1980s and 1990s under four headings.

First, in many cases, urban movements, and their discourses, actors, and organizations, have been integrated into the structure and practice of local government, either directly or indirectly, through a diversified system of citizen participation, and community development. This trend, while liquidating urban movements as sources of alternative social change, has considerably reinforced local government, and introduced the possibility of the local state as a significant instance of reconstruction of political control and social meaning. I will return to this fundamental development in chapter 5, when analyzing the overall transformation of the state.

Secondly, local communities, and their organizations, have indeed nurtured the grass roots of a widespread, and influential, environmental movement, particularly in middle-class neighborhoods, and in the suburbs, exurbia, and urbanized countryside (see chapter 3).

156   Castells (1983: 331).
157   Massolo (1992); Fisher and Kling (1993); Calderon (1995); Judge et al. (1995); Tanaka (1995); Borja and Castells (1997); Hsia (1996); Yazawa (1997).

However, these movements are often defensive and reactive, focusing on the strictest conservation of their space and immediate environment, as exemplified, in the United States, by the "not in my backyard" attitude, mixing in the same rejection toxic waste, nuclear plants, public housing projects, prisons, and mobile home settlements. I will make a major distinction, which I will develop in chapter 3 when analyzing the environmental movement, between the search for controlling space (a defensive reaction), and the search for controlling time; that is, for the preservation of nature, and of the planet, for future generations, in the very long term, thus adopting cosmological time, and rejecting the instant time approach of instrumentalist development. Identities emerging from these two perspectives are quite different, as defensive spaces lead to collective individualism, and offensive timing opens up the reconciliation between culture and nature, thus introducing a new, holistic philosophy of life.

Thirdly, a vast number of poor communities around the world have engaged in collective survival, as with the communal kitchens that flourished in Santiago de Chile or Lima during the 1980s. Be it in squatter settlements in Latin America, in American inner cities, or in working-class neighborhoods in Asian cities, communities have built their own "welfare states" (in the absence of responsible public policies) on the basis of networks of solidarity and reciprocity, often around churches, or supported by internationally funded non-governmental organizations (NGOs), sometimes with the help of leftist intellectuals. These organized, local communities have played, and continue to play, a major role in the daily survival of a significant proportion of the world's urban population, on the threshold of famine and epidemic. This trend was illustrated, for instance, by the experience of community associations organized by the Catholic Church in São Paulo in the 1980s,[158] and by internationally sponsored NGOs in Bogota in the 1990s.[159] In most of these cases, a communal identity does emerge, although very often it is absorbed into a religious faith, to the point that I would risk the hypothesis that this kind of communalism is, essentially, a religious commune, linked to the consciousness of being the exploited and/or the excluded. Thus, people organizing in poor local communities may feel revitalized, and acknowledged as human beings, by and through religious deliverance.

Fourthly, there is a darker side of the story, concerning the evolution of urban movements, particularly in segregated urban areas, a trend that I foresaw some time ago:

158   Cardoso de Leite (1983); Gohn (1991).
159   Espinosa and Useche (1992).

If urban movements' appeals are not heard, if the new political avenues remain closed, if the new central social movements (feminism, new labor, self-management, alternative communication) do not develop fully, then the urban movements – reactive utopias that tried to illuminate the path they could not walk – will return, but this time as urban shadows eager to destroy the closed walls of their captive city.[160]

Fortunately, the failure was not total, and the diversified expression of organized local communities did provide avenues of reform, survival, and self-identification, in spite of the lack of major social movements able to articulate change in the new society emerging in the past two decades. Yet, harsh policies of economic adjustment in the 1980s, a widespread crisis of political legitimacy, and the exclusionary impact of the space of flows over the space of places (see volume I), took their toll on social life and organization in poor local communities. In American cities, gangs emerged as a major form of association, work, and identity for hundreds of thousands of youths. Indeed, as Sanchez Jankowski has shown in his first-hand, comprehensive study of gangs,[161] they play a structuring role in many areas, which explains the ambiguous feeling of local residents toward them, partly fearful, yet partly feeling able to relate to the gang society better than to mainstream institutions, which are usually present only in their repressive manifestation. Gangs, or their functional equivalent, are not, by any means, an American graffito. The *pandillas* in most Latin American cities are a key element of sociability in poor neighborhoods, and so are they in Jakarta, in Bangkok, in Manila, in Mantes-la-Jolie (Paris), or in Meseta de Orcasitas (Madrid). Gangs are, however, an old story in many societies, particularly in America (remember William White's *Street Corner Society*). Yet there was something new in the gangs of the 1990s, characterizing the construction of identity as the twisted mirror of informational culture. It is what Magaly Sanchez and Yves Pedrazzini, on the basis of their study of the *malandros* (bad boys) of Caracas, call the *culture of urgency*.[162] It is a culture of the immediate end of life, not of its negation, but of its celebration. Thus, everything has to be tried, felt, experimented, accomplished, before it is too late, since there is no tomorrow. Is this really so different from the culture of consumerist narcissism *à la* Lasch? Have the bad boys of Caracas, or elsewhere, understood faster than the rest of us what our new society is all about? Is the new gang identity the culture of communal hyper-individualism? Individualism because, in a pattern of immediate gratification, only the

160   Castells (1983: 327).
161   Sanchez Jankowski (1991).
162   Sanchez and Pedrazzini (1996).

individual can be a proper accounting unit. Communalism because, for this hyper-individualism to be an identity – that is, to be socialized as value not just as senseless consumption – it needs a milieu of appreciation and reciprocal support: a commune, as in White's times. But, unlike White's, this commune is ready to explode at any time, it is a commune of the end of time, it is a commune of timeless time, characterizing the network society. And it exists, and explodes, territorially. Local cultures of urgency are the reverse expression of global timelessness.

Thus, local communities, constructed through collective action and preserved through collective memory, are specific sources of identities. But these identities, in most cases, are defensive reactions against the impositions of global disorder and uncontrollable, fast-paced change. They do build havens, but not heavens.

Conclusion: The Cultural Communes of the Information Age

The transformation of our culture and our society would have to happen at a number of levels. If it occurred only in the minds of individuals (as to some degree it already has), it would be powerless. If it came only from the initiative of the state, it would be tyrannical. Personal transformation among large numbers is essential, and it must not only be a transformation of consciousness but must also involve individual action. But individuals need the nurture of groups that carry a moral tradition reinforcing their own aspirations.

Robert Bellah et al., *Habits of the Heart*[163]

Our intellectual journey through communal landscapes provides some preliminary answers to the questions raised at the beginning of this chapter on the construction of identity in the network society.

For those social actors excluded from or resisting the individualization of identity attached to life in the global networks of power and wealth, cultural communes of religious, national, or territorial foundation seem to provide the main alternative for the construction of meaning in our society. These cultural communes are characterized by three main features. They appear as reactions to prevailing social trends, which are resisted on behalf of autonomous sources of meaning. They are, at the outset, defensive identities that function as refuge and solidarity, to protect against a hostile, outside world. They are culturally constituted; that is, organized around a specific set of values

163   Bellah et al. (1985: 286).

whose meaning and sharing are marked by specific codes of self-identification: the community of believers, the icons of nationalism, the geography of locality.

Ethnicity, while being a fundamental feature of our societies, especially as a source of discrimination and stigma, may not induce communes on its own. Rather, it is likely to be processed by religion, nation, and locality, whose specificity it tends to reinforce.

The constitution of these cultural communes is not arbitrary. It works on raw materials from history, geography, language, and environment. So, they are constructed, but materially constructed, around reactions and projects historically/geographically determined.

Religious fundamentalism, cultural nationalism, territorial communes are, by and large, defensive reactions. Reactions against three fundamental threats, perceived in all societies, by the majority of humankind, at this turn of the millennium. Reaction against globalization, which dissolves the autonomy of institutions, organizations, and communication systems where people live. Reaction against networking and flexibility, which blur the boundaries of membership and involvement, individualize social relationships of production, and induce the structural instability of work, space, and time. And reaction against the crisis of the patriarchal family, at the roots of the transformation of mechanisms of security-building, socialization, sexuality, and, therefore, of personality systems. When the world becomes too large to be controlled, social actors aim to shrink it back to their size and reach. When networks dissolve time and space, people anchor themselves in places, and recall their historic memory. When the patriarchal sustainment of personality breaks down, people affirm the transcendent value of family and community, as God's will.

These defensive reactions become sources of meaning and identity by constructing new cultural codes out of historical materials. Because the new processes of domination to which people react are embedded in information flows, the building of autonomy has to rely on reverse information flows. God, nation, family, and community will provide unbreakable, eternal codes, around which a counter-offensive will be mounted against the culture of real virtuality. Eternal truth cannot be virtualized. It is embodied in us. Thus, against the informationalization of culture, bodies are informationalized. That is, individuals bear their gods in their heart. They do not reason, they believe. They are the bodily manifestation of God's eternal values, and as such, they cannot be dissolved, lost in the whirlwind of information flows and cross-organizational networks. This is why language, and communal images, are so essential to restore communication between the autonomized bodies, escaping the domination of a-historical flows, yet trying to restore new patterns of meaningful communication among the believers.

This form of identity-building revolves essentially around the principle of *resistance identity*, as defined at the beginning of this chapter. *Legitimizing identity* seems to have entered a fundamental crisis because of the fast disintegration of civil society inherited from the industrial era, and because of the fading away of the nation-state, the main source of legitimacy (see chapter 5). Indeed, cultural communes organizing the new resistance emerge as sources of identity by breaking away from civil societies and state institutions from which they originate, as in the case of Islamic fundamentalism breaking away from economic modernization (Iran), and/or from Arab states' nationalism; or with nationalist movements, challenging the nation-state and the state institutions of societies where they come into existence. This negation of civil societies and political institutions where cultural communes emerge leads to the closing of the boundaries of the commune. In contrast to pluralistic, differentiated civil societies, cultural communes display little internal differentiation. Indeed, their strength, and their ability to provide refuge, solace, certainty, and protection, comes precisely from their communal character, from their collective responsibility, canceling individual projects. Thus, in the first stage of reaction, the (re)construction of meaning by defensive identities breaks away from the institutions of society, and promises to rebuild from the bottom up, while retrenching themselves in a communal heaven.

It is possible that from such communes, new subjects – that is, collective agents of social transformation – may emerge, thus constructing new meaning around *project identity*. Indeed, I would argue that, given the structural crisis of civil society and the nation-state, this may be the main potential source of social change in the network society. As for how and why these new proactive subjects could be formed from these reactive, cultural communes, this will be the core of my analysis of social movements in the network society to be elaborated throughout this volume.

But we can already say something on the basis of the observations and discussions presented in this chapter. The emergence of project identities of different kinds is not an historical necessity. It may well be that cultural resistance will remain enclosed in the boundaries of communes. If this is the case, and where and when this is the case, communalism will close the circle of its latent fundamentalism on its own components, inducing a process that might transform communal heavens into heavenly hells.

2

The Other Face of the Earth: Social Movements against the New Global Order

Your problem is the same as many people have. It relates to the social and economic doctrine known as "neo-liberalism." This is a meta-theoretical problem. I am telling you. You start from the assumption that "neo-liberalism" is a doctrine. And by you I refer to all those with schemes as rigid and square as their head. You think that "neo-liberalism" is a capitalist doctrine to confront economic crises that capitalism charges are caused by "populism." Well, in fact "neo-classicism" is not a theory to explain crises or to confront them. It is the crisis itself, made theory and economic doctrine! This is to say that "neo-liberalism" does not have the slightest coherence, neither has plans nor historical perspective. I mean, it's pure theoretical shit.

Durito, talking to Subcomandante Marcos in the Lacandon Forest, 1994[1]

---

1 *Durito* is a common character in the writings of Subcomandante Marcos, the *Zapatista* spokesperson. He is a beetle, but a very clever one: indeed, he is Marcos's intellectual adviser. The problem is: he always fears being crushed by the too numerous guerrillas around him, so he begs Marcos to keep the movement small. This text by *Durito* is cited from *Ejercito Zapatista de Liberacion Nacional*/Subcomandante Marcos (1995: 58–9); my translation, with *Durito*'s benevolence.

Globalization, Informationalization, and Social Movements[2]

Globalization and informationalization, enacted by networks of wealth, technology, and power, are transforming our world. They are enhancing our productive capacity, cultural creativity, and communication potential. At the same time, they are disfranchising societies. As institutions of state and organizations of civil society are based on culture, history, and geography, the sudden acceleration of the historical tempo, and the abstraction of power in a web of computers, are disintegrating existing mechanisms of social control and political representation. With the exception of a small elite of *globapolitans* (half beings, half flows), people all over the world resent the loss of control over their lives, over their environment, over their jobs, over their economies, over their governments, over their countries, and, ultimately, over the fate of the Earth. Thus, following an old law of social evolution, resistance confronts domination, empowerment reacts against powerlessness, and alternative projects challenge the logic embedded in the new global order, increasingly sensed as disorder by people around the planet. However, these reactions and mobilizations, as is often the case in history, come in unusual formats and proceed in unexpected ways. This chapter, and the next one, explore these ways.

To broaden the empirical scope of my inquiry, while keeping its analytical focus, I will compare five movements that explicitly oppose the new global, social and/or cultural order, coming from extremely different cultural, economic, and institutional contexts, through sharply contrasting ideologies: the *Zapatistas* in Chiapas, Mexico; the American militia; *Aum Shinrikyo*, a Japanese cult; *al-Qaeda*, a global terrorist network; and the movement for global justice, popularly known as the anti-globalization movement.

In the next chapter I will analyze the environmental movement, arguably the most comprehensive, influential movement of our time. In its own way, and through the creative cacophony of its multiple voices, environmentalism also challenges global ecological disorder, indeed the risk of eco-suicide, brought about by uncontrolled global development, and by the unleashing of unprecedented technological

2   This chapter has benefited from valuable intellectual exchanges at the International Seminar on Globalization and Social Movements organized by the International Sociological Association's Research Committee on Social Movements, held at Santa Cruz, California, April 16–19, 1996. I thank the organizers of the seminar, Barbara Epstein and Louis Maheu, for their kind invitation.

forces without checking their social and environmental sustainability. But its cultural and political specificity, and its character as a pro-active, rather than reactive, social movement, suggest a separate analytical treatment for the environmental movement, as distinct from defensive movements built around the trenches of resistance from specific identities and/or specific interests.

Before proceeding into the heart of the matter, let me introduce three brief methodological remarks that are necessary for understanding the analyses to be presented in the following pages.[3]

First, *social movements* must be understood in their own terms: namely, *they are what they say they are*. Their practices (and foremost their discursive practices) are their self-definition. This approach takes us away from the hazardous task of interpreting the "true" conscious-ness of movements, as if they could only exist by revealing the "real" structural contradictions. As if, in order to come to life, they would necessarily have to bear these contradictions, as they bear their weapons and brandish their flags. A different, and necessary, research operation is to establish the relationship between the movements, as defined by their practice, their values, and their discourse, and the social processes to which they seem to be associated: for example, globaliza-tion, informationalization, the crisis of representative democracy, and the dominance of symbolic politics in the space of media. In my analysis I will try to conduct both operations: the characterization of each movement, in terms of its own specific dynamics; and its interaction with the broader processes that induce its existence, and become modi fied by this very existence. The importance I give to the movement's discourse will be reflected in my writing. When presenting and analyz-ing the movements, I will follow very closely their own *words*, not just ideas, as recorded in documents on which I have worked. However, in order to spare the reader from the minute details of reference citation, I have opted for giving generic references to the materials from which the discourses have been obtained, leaving the interested reader to find in these materials the precise words reported in my writing.

Secondly, social movements may be socially conservative, socially revolutionary, or both, or none. After all, we now have concluded (I hope for ever) that there is no predetermined directionality in social evolution, that the only sense of history is the history we sense. Therefore, from an analytical perspective, there are no "bad" and "good" social movements. They are all symptoms of our societies,

3   For a theoretical discussion of social movements directly relevant to the inquiry presented here, see Castells (1983); Dalton and Kuechler (1990); Epstein (1991); Riechmann and Fernandez Buey (1994); Calderon (1995); Dubet and Wieviorka (1995); Maheu (1995); Melucci (1995); Touraine (1995a); Touraine et al. (1996); Yazawa (1997).

and all impact on social structures, with variable intensities and outcomes that must be established by research. Thus, I like the *Zapatistas*, I dislike the American militia, and I am horrified by *Aum Shinrikyo* and *al-Qaeda*. Yet, they are all, as I will argue, meaningful signs of new social conflicts, and embryos of social resistance and, in some cases, social change. Only by scanning with an open mind the new historical landscape will we be able to find shining paths, dark abysses, and muddled breakthroughs into the new society emerging from current crises.

Thirdly, to put some order into a mass of disparate material on the social movements to be examined in this and following chapters, I find it useful to categorize them in terms of Alain Touraine's classic typology that defines a social movement by three principles: the movement's *identity*, the movement's *adversary*, and the movement's vision or social model, which I call *societal* goal.[4] In my personal adaptation (which I believe to be consistent with Touraine's theory), *identity* refers to the self-definition of the movement of what it is, on behalf of whom it speaks. *Adversary* refers to the movement's principal enemy, as explicitly identified by the movement. *Societal goal* refers to the movement's vision of the kind of social order, or social organization, it would wish to attain in the historical horizon of its collective action.

Having clarified our point of departure, let us set off on this voyage to the other face of the Earth, the one refusing globalization for the sake of capital and informationalization for the sake of technology. And where dreams of the past, and nightmares of the future, inhabit a chaotic world of passion, generosity, prejudice, fear, fantasy, violence, flawed strategies, and lucky strikes. Humanity, after all.

The movements I have selected to understand insurgency against globalization are extremely different in their identity, in their goals, in their ideology, and in their relationship to society.[5] This is precisely the interest of the comparison because they are similar, however, in their explicit opposition to the new global order, identified as the enemy in their discourse and in their practice. And all of them have had significant impacts on their societies, directly or indirectly. And on the world at large. The *Zapatistas* have already transformed Mexico, inducing a crisis in the corrupt politics and unjust economy prevailing in Mexico, while putting forward proposals for democratic reconstruction that are

4   Touraine (1965, 1966). Touraine's formulation in fact uses a slightly different terminology, in French: *principe d'identité*; *principe d'opposition*; *principe de totalité*. I decided that it would be clearer for an international audience to use more plain words to say the same thing, at the risk of losing the authentic French flavor.
5   This comparative analysis is based on a joint study with Shujiro Yazawa and Emma Kiselyova, conducted in 1995. For a first elaboration of this study, see Castells et al. (1996).

being widely debated in Mexico, and throughout the world. The American militia, the most militant component of a broader socio-political movement self-identified as *The Patriots* (or *False Patriots*, as their critics call them), has much deeper roots in American society than are usually acknowledged, and may produce unpredictable, significant outcomes in America's tense political scene, as I will argue below. *Aum Shinrikyo*, while remaining a marginal cult in Japanese society, dominated media attention and public debate for more than a year (in 1995–6), and it acted as a symptom of unseen injuries, and unfolding dramas, behind the curtains of Japanese serenity. *Al-Qaeda*, with its related Islamic organizations around the world, has dramatically altered the geopolitical balance and the psychological framework in the United States, and in the world at large. And the movement for global justice has challenged the inevitability of market-led globalization, inducing a major debate in societies and institutions in most countries about alternative forms of global economy and social organization.

The point I am trying to make by bringing together these different, powerful insurgencies, is precisely the diversity of sources of resistance to the new global order. Along with the reminder that the neoliberal illusion of the end of history is over, as historically specific societies take their revenge against their domination by global flows.

Mexico's *Zapatistas*: The First Informational Guerrilla Movement[6]

The Movimiento Civil Zapatista is a movement that opposes social solidarity to organized crime from the power of money and government.
Manifesto of *Movimiento Civil Zapatista*, August 1995

6 The analysis of the *Zapatista* movement presented here is greatly indebted, as is often the case in this book, to contributions by two women. Professor Alejandra Moreno Toscano, a distinguished urban historian at the Universidad Nacional Autonoma de Mexico, and a former Secretary of Social Welfare of Mexico DF, was deputy to Manuel Camacho, the President's representative, during the critical period of negotiations between the Mexican government and the *Zapatistas* in the first months of 1994. She provided me with documents, opinion, and insights, and decisively helped my understanding of the overall process of Mexican politics in 1994–96. For her analysis (the most intelligent approach that I have read), see Moreno Toscano (1996). Secondly, Maria Elena Martinez Torres, one of my doctoral students at Berkeley, was a thorough observer of Chiapas peasantry. During our intellectual interaction, she provided me with her own analyses (Martinez Torres, 1994, 1996). Naturally, I bear exclusive responsibility for the interpretation, and possible mistakes, in the conclusions presented in this book. Additional sources used on the *Zapatista* movement are: Garcia de Leon (1985); Arquilla and Rondfeldt (1993); Collier and Lowery Quaratiello (1994); *Ejercito Zapatista de Liberacion Nacional* (1994, 1995); Trejo Delarbre (1994a, b); Collier (1995); Hernandez Navarro (1995); Nash et al. (1995); Rojas (1995); Rondfeldt (1995); Tello Diaz (1995); Woldenberg (1995).

The novelty in Mexico's political history was the inversion of the control process against the powers that be, on the basis of alternative communication...The newness in Chiapas' political war was the emergence of various senders of information that interpreted events in very different ways.

The flow of public information reaching society, through the media, and through new technological means, was much greater than what conventional communication strategies could control. Marcos gave his opinion, the Church gave its opinion, and independent journalists, NGOs, and intellectuals, from the forest, from Ciudad de Mexico, from the world's financial and political capitals, all gave their own opinion. These alternative opinions, made possible by open media, or by closed media that felt the pinch from open media, called into question forms of construction of "the truth", and induced, within the political regime as well, a variety of opinions. The view from power became fragmented.

Moreno Toscano, *Turbulencia politica*, p. 82

Mexico, the nation that generated the prototype of social revolution of the 20th century, is now the scene of a prototype transnational social netwar of the 21st century.

Rondfeldt, Rand Corporation, 1995

On January 1, 1994, the first day of the North American Free Trade Agreement (NAFTA), about 3,000 men and women, organized in the *Ejercito Zapatista de Liberacion Nacional*, lightly armed, took control of the main municipalities adjacent to the Lacandon Forest, in the Southern Mexican state of Chiapas: San Cristobal de las Casas, Altamirano, Ocosingo and Las Margaritas. Most of them were Indians from various ethnic groups, although there were also *mestizos*, and some of their leaders, and particularly their spokesperson, Subcomandante Marcos, were urban intellectuals. The leaders had their faces hidden behind ski masks. When the Mexican Army dispatched reinforcements, the guerrillas withdrew to the rainforest in good order. However, several dozen of them as well as civilians, and a number of soldiers and policemen, died in the confrontation or were summarily executed by soldiers in the aftermath.

The impact of the uprising in Mexico, and the widespread sympathy that the *Zapatistas*' cause immediately inspired in the country, and in the world, convinced the Mexican president, Carlos Salinas de Gortari, to negotiate. On January 12, Salinas announced a unilateral ceasefire, and appointed as his "peace representative," Manuel Camacho, a respected Mexican politician, once considered his likely successor, who had just resigned from government after his presidential hopes were frustrated by Salinas. Manuel Camacho, and his trusted intellectual adviser, Alejandra Moreno Toscano, traveled to Chiapas, met with the influential Catholic Bishop Samuel Ruiz, and were able to engage in serious peace talks with the *Zapatistas*, who quickly acknowledged the sincerity of the dialogue, although they remained justifiably wary of potential repression and/or manipulation. Camacho read to the insurgents a text in *tzotzil*, also broadcast in *tzeltal* and *chol*: the first time ever a leading Mexican official had acknowledged Indian languages. On January 27, an agreement was signed, establishing a ceasefire, freeing prisoners on both sides, and engaging in a process of negotiation on a broad agenda of political reform, Indian rights, and social demands.

Who are the Zapatistas?

Who were these insurgents, unknown until then to the rest of the world, in spite of two decades of widespread peasant mobilizations in the communities of Chiapas and Oaxaca? They were peasants, most of them Indians, *tzeltales, tzotziles,* and *choles*, generally from the communities established since the 1940s in the Lacandon rainforest on the Guatemalan border. These communities were created with government support in order to find a way out of the social crisis created by the expulsion of *acasillados* (landless peasants working for landowners) from the *fincas* (farms), and ranches, owned by middle and large landowners, generally *mestizos.*

For centuries, Indians and peasants have been abused by colonizers, bureaucrats, and settlers. And for decades they have been kept in constant insecurity, as the status of their settlements constantly changed, in accordance with the interests of government and landowners. In 1972, President Echeverria decided to create the "bioreserve" of Montes Azul, and to return most of the forest to 66 families of the original Lacandon tribe, thus ordering the relocation of 4,000 families that had resettled in this area, after their expulsion from their original communities. Behind the Lacandon tribes and the sudden love of nature, there were the interests of the forestry company Cofolasa, supported by the government development corporation, NAFINSA, which received logging rights. Most settlers refused to relocate, and began a 20-year struggle for their right to land, which was still lingering on when Salinas assumed the Presidency in 1988. Salinas finally accepted the rights of some colonists, but restricted his generosity to those few supporting the PRI (*Partido Revolucionario Institucional*), the government party. In 1992, a new decree abolished the legal rights of the Indian communities that had resettled for the second time. This time the pretext was the Rio Conference on the Environment, and the need to protect the rainforest. Cattle feeding in the area was also curtailed in order to help Chiapas ranchers, competing with cattle smuggling from Guatemala.

The final blow to the fragile economy of peasant communities came when Mexican liberalization policies in the 1990s, in preparation for NAFTA, ended restrictions on imports of corn, and eliminated protection on the price of coffee. The local economy, based on forestry, cattle, coffee, and corn, was dismantled. Furthermore, the status of communal land became uncertain after Salinas's reform of the historic article 27 of the Mexican Constitution, which ended communal possession of agricultural property by the villagers (*ejidos*), in favor of full commercialization of individual property, another measure directly related to Mexico's alignment with privatization in accordance with NAFTA. In 1992 and 1993, peasants mobilized peacefully against these policies. But when their powerful march of Xi' Nich, which brought thousands of peasants from Palenque to Ciudad de Mexico, received no response, they changed tactics. By the middle of 1993, in most communities of Lacandon, corn was not planted, coffee was left on the bushes, children withdrew from schools, and cattle were sold to buy weapons. The headline of the insurgents' Manifesto on January 1, 1994 read: "*Hoy decimos* BASTA!" ("Today, we say ENOUGH!")

These peasant communities, mostly Indian, joined by other settlements from the Los Altos area, were not alone in the social struggles they had undertaken since the early 1970s. They were supported, and to some extent organized, by the Catholic Church, under the initiative of the bishop of San Cristobal de las Casas, Samuel Ruiz, who was somewhat associated with liberation theology. Not only did the priests support and legitimize Indian claims, but they also helped to form hundreds of cadres of peasant unions. These cadres shared membership of the Church and of the unions. There were over one hundred *tuhuneles* (aides of priests), and over one thousand catechists, who provided the backbone of the movement, which developed in the form of peasant unions, each one of them based in a community (*ejido*). Strong religious feeling among Indian peasants was reinforced by education, information, and support from the Church, leading to frequent conflicts between the local Church, on the one hand, and Chiapas ranchers and Chiapas PRI apparatus, on the other hand.

Yet, while the Church was decisive in educating, organizing, and mobilizing Indian peasant communities for many years, Samuel Ruiz and his aides strongly opposed armed struggle and were not among the insurgents, contrary to accusations by Chiapas ranchers. The cadres who organized the armed insurrection came, for the most part, from the Indian communities themselves, particularly from the ranks of young men and women who had grown up in the new climate of economic distress and social struggle. Other cadres came from Maoist groups formed in urban Mexico (particularly in Ciudad de Mexico and in Monterrey) in the 1970s, in the aftermath of the student movement of 1968 crushed in the Tlatelolco massacre. The *Fuerzas de Liberacion Nacional* seem to have been active in the area for a long time, although accounts diverge on this point. In any case, whatever the origin, it seems that, after a series of setbacks in urban areas, a few revolutionaries, men and women, undertook the long march of establishing their credibility among the most oppressed sectors of the country, through patient work and daily sharing of their hardship and struggles.

Marcos seems to have been one of these militants, coming to the region in the early 1980s, according to government sources, after completing studies in sociology and communication in Mexico and Paris, and teaching social sciences in one of the best universities in Mexico DF.[7] He is clearly a very learned intellectual, who speaks several languages, writes well, is extraordinarily imaginative, has a wonderful sense of humor, and is at ease in his relationship with the media.

These revolutionary intellectuals, because of their honesty and dedication, were welcomed by the priests and, for a long time, in spite of ideological differences, they worked together in organizing peasant communities, and in supporting their struggles. It was only after 1992, when promises of reforms continued to go unfulfilled, and when the situation in the Lacandon communities become more dire because of the overall process of economic modernization in Mexico, that *Zapatista* militants set up their own structure and initiated preparations for guerrilla warfare.

In May 1993 a first skirmish with the army took place, but the Mexican government downplayed the incident to avoid problems in the ratification of NAFTA by the US Congress. It should, however, be emphasized that the leadership of the *Zapatistas* is genuinely peasant, and mainly Indian. Marcos, and other urban militants, could not act

---

7   The Mexican government claims to have identified Subcomandante Marcos and the main leaders of the *Zapatistas*, and its claim appears to be plausible. It has been widely reported in the media. However, since the *Zapatistas* are still insurgents at the time of writing, I do not feel it is proper to accept these claims as a matter of fact.

on their own.[8] The process of deliberation, as well as negotiation with the government, consisted of lengthy procedures with the full participation of the communities. This was critical since, once a decision had been made, the whole community had to follow the common decision, to the extent that, in a few instances, villagers were expelled because of their refusal to participate in the uprising. Yet, during the two and a half years of open insurgency, the overwhelming majority of Lacandon communities, and a majority of Indians in Chiapas, showed their support for the insurgents, following them to the forest when the army took over their villages in February 1995.

The value structure of the Zapatistas: identity, adversaries, and goals

The deep causes of the rebellion are obvious. *But what are the insurgents' demands, goals, and values? How do they see themselves and how do they identify their enemy?* On the one hand, they place themselves in historical continuity with five hundred years of struggle against colonization and oppression. Indeed, the turning point of the peasant movement was the massive demonstration in San Cristobal de las Casas on October 12, 1992, protesting against the fifth centenary of the Spanish conquest of America by destroying the statue of Chiapas' conqueror, Diego de Mazariegos. On the other hand, they see the reincarnation of this oppression in the current form of the new global order: NAFTA, and the liberalizing reforms undertaken by President Salinas, which fail to include peasants and Indians in the modernization process. The changes in the historic article 27 of the Mexican Constitution, which had given formal satisfaction to the demands of agrarian revolutionaries championed by Emiliano Zapata, became the symbol of the exclusion of peasant communities by the new order of free traders.

To this critique, shared by the whole movement, Marcos and others added their own challenge to the new global order: the projection of the socialist revolutionary dream beyond the end of communism and the demise of guerrilla movements in Central America. As Marcos wrote with irony:

> There is nothing to fight for any longer. Socialism is dead. Long life to conformism, to reform, to modernity, to capitalism and to all kind of cruel etceteras. Let's be reasonable. That nothing happens in the city, or in the countryside, that everything continues the same. Socialism is

8 Moreno Toscano (1996).

dead. Long life to capital. Radio, press, and television repeat it. Some socialists, now reasonably repentant, also repeat the same.[9]

Thus, the *Zapatistas*' opposition to the new global order is twofold: they fight against the exclusionary consequences of economic modernization, but they also challenge the inevitability of a new geopolitical order under which capitalism becomes universally accepted.

The insurgents affirm their Indian pride, and fight for the recognition of Indian rights in the Mexican Constitution. However, it does not seem that the defense of ethnic identity is a dominant element in the movement. Indeed, the Lacandon communities have been created by forced resettlement which broke up original identities from different communities and brought them together as peasants. Furthermore, it seems that, as Collier writes,

> Ethnic identity once *divided* indigenous communities from one another in the Chiapas central highlands. Recent events underscore a transformation: now, in the wake of the Zapatista rebellion, peoples of diverse indigenous background are emphasizing what they share with one another in revindication of economic, social, and political exploitation.[10]

Thus, this new Indian identity was constructed through their struggle, and came to include various ethnic groups: "What is common to us is the land that gave us life and struggle."[11]

The *Zapatistas* are not subversives, but legitimate rebels. They are *Mexican patriots*, up in arms against new forms of foreign domination by American imperialism. And they are *democrats*, appealing to article 39 of the Mexican Constitution which proclaims "the right of the people to alter or modify its form of government." Thus, they call upon Mexicans to support democracy, ending *de facto* rule of one-party government based on electoral fraud. This call, coming from Chiapas, the Mexican state with the largest vote for PRI candidates,

9   EZLN (1994: 61); my translation.
10   Collier (1995: 1); a similar argument is put forward by Martinez Torres (1994). In the Manifesto issued by the *Zapatistas* over the Internet in November 1995, to commemorate the twelfth anniversary of the founding of their organization, they strongly emphasized their character as a Mexican movement for justice and democracy, beyond the defense of Indian identity: "The country we want, we want for all Mexicans, and not only for the Indians. The Democracy, Liberty, and Justice we want, we want for all Mexicans, and not only for the Indians. We do not want to separate from the Mexican Nation, we want to be part of it, we want to be accepted as equal, as persons with dignity, as human beings ... Here we are brothers, the dead of always. Dying again, but now to live" (EZLN, *Comunicado* on Internet, 17 November 1995; my translation).
11   *Zapatista* declaration, January 25, 1994; cited by Moreno Toscano (1996: 92).

traditionally imposed by local *caciques*, elicited a strong echo in the urban middle-class sectors of a Mexican society craving freedom, and tired of systemic corruption. That the uprising took place precisely in the year of the presidential election, and in an election that was supposed to liberalize the PRI's hold on the state, is a sign of the tactical ability of the *Zapatistas*, and it was a major factor in protecting them from outright repression. President Salinas wanted to establish his legacy as both economic modernizer and political liberalizer, not only for his place in history, but for his next job: his candidacy to become the first secretary general of the newly constituted World Trade Organization, precisely the institution articulating the new world economic order. Under these circumstances, a Harvard-educated economist could hardly launch all-out military repression against a genuine peasant, Indian movement fighting against social exclusion.

The communication strategy of the Zapatistas: the Internet and the media

The success of the *Zapatistas* was largely due to their communication strategy, to the point that they can be called the *first informational guerrilla movement*. They created a media event in order to diffuse their message, while desperately trying not to be brought into a bloody war. There were, of course, real deaths, and real weapons, and Marcos, and his comrades, were ready to die. Yet, actual warfare was not their strategy. The *Zapatistas* used arms to make a statement, then parlayed the possibility of their sacrifice in front of the world media to force a negotiation and advance a number of reasonable demands which, as opinion polls seem to indicate, found widespread support in Mexican society at large.[12] Autonomous communication was a paramount objective for the *Zapatistas*:

> When the bombs were falling over the mountains south of San Cristobal, when our combatants were resisting attacks from federal troops, when the air smelled with powder and blood, the "Comite Clandestino Revolucionario Indigena del EZLN" called and told me, more or less: We must say our word and be heard. If we do not do it now, others will take our voice and lies will come out from our mouth without us wanting it. Look for a way to speak our word to those who would like to listen.[13]

12   According to a poll conducted on December 8 and 9, 1994, 59 percent of Mexico City residents had a "good opinion" of the *Zapatistas*, and 78 percent thought that their demands were justified (published in the newspaper *Reforma*, December 11, 1994).
13   Marcos, February 11, 1994; cited by Moreno Toscano (1996: 90).

The *Zapatistas'* ability to communicate with the world, and with Mexican society, and to capture the imagination of people and of intellectuals, propelled a local, weak insurgent group to the forefront of world politics. In this sense Marcos was essential. He did not have organizational control of a movement that was rooted in the Indian communities, and he did not show any signs of being a great military strategist, although he was wise in ordering retreat every time the army was to engage them. But he was extraordinarily able in establishing a communication bridge with the media, through his well-constructed writings, and by his *mise-en-scène* (the mask, the pipe, the setting of the interviews), somehow serendipitously found, as in the case of the mask that played such an important role in popularizing the revolutionaries' image: all over the world, everybody could become *Zapatista* by wearing a mask. Furthermore (although this may be an over-theorization), masks are a recurrent ritual in pre-Colombian Mexican Indian cultures, so that rebellion, equalization of faces, and historical flashback played into each other in a most innovative theatrics of revolution.

Essential in this strategy was the *Zapatistas'* use of telecommunications, videos, and of computer-mediated communication, both to diffuse their message from Chiapas to the world (although probably not transmitted from the forest), and to organize a worldwide network of solidarity groups that literally encircled the repressive intentions of the Mexican government; for instance, during the army invasion of insurgent areas on February 9, 1995. It is interesting to underline that at the origins of the *Zapatistas'* use of the Internet are two developments of the 1990s: the creation of *La Neta*, an alternative computer communication network in Mexico and Chiapas; and its use by women's groups (particularly by "*De mujer a mujer*") to link up Chiapas' NGOs with other Mexican women, as well as with women's networks in the US. *La Neta*[14] originated in the link-up in 1989–93 between Mexican NGOs, supported by the Catholic Church, and the Institute for Global Communication in San Francisco, supported by skilled computer experts donating their time and expertise to good causes. In 1994, with the help of a grant from the Ford Foundation, *La Neta* was able to establish a node in Mexico with a private Internet provider. In 1993 *La Neta* had been established in Chiapas, with the purpose of getting local NGOs on line, including the Center for Human Rights "Bartolome de las Casas,"

---

14   It seems necessary to clarify the multiple meaning of *La Neta* for non-Mexican readers. Besides being the figurative Spanish feminine of The Net, *la neta* is Mexican slang for "the real story."

and a dozen other organizations, which came to play a major role in informing the world during the *Zapatista* uprising. Extensive use of the Internet allowed the *Zapatistas* to diffuse information and their call throughout the world instantly, and to create a network of support groups which helped to produce a movement of international public opinion that made it literally impossible for the Mexican government to use repression on a large scale. Images and information from and around the *Zapatistas* acted powerfully on the Mexican economy and politics. As Martinez Torres writes:

> Ex-President Salinas created a "bubble economy" which for several years permitted the illusion of prosperity based on a massive inflow of speculative investments in high-interest government bonds, that via a spiraling trade deficit and debt allowed the middle and working classes to enjoy for a while a multitude of imported consumer goods. Yet, as easy as it was to lure investors in, any loss of investor confidence could potentially spiral into panic and run on Mexican bonds, with the possibility of causing a collapse of the system. In effect, the Mexican economy [in 1994] was an enormous confidence game. Since confidence is basically created by manipulation of information it can be destroyed in exactly the same way. In the new world order where information is the most valuable commodity, that same information can be much more powerful than bullets.[15]

This was the key to the *Zapatistas'* success. Not that they deliberately sabotaged the economy. But they were protected by their relentless media connection, and by their worldwide, Internet-based alliances, from outright repression, forcing negotiation and raising the issue of social exclusion and political corruption to the eyes and ears of public opinion worldwide.

Indeed, experts of the Rand Corporation concur with this analysis,[16] having forecast the eventuality of *Zapatista*-type "netwars" since 1993: "The revolutionary forces of the future may consist increasingly of widespread multi-organizational networks that have no particular national identity, claim to arise from civil society, and include aggressive groups and individuals who are keenly adept at using advanced technology for communications, as well as munitions."[17] The *Zapatistas* seem to have realized the worst nightmares of the experts of the new global order.

---

15   Martinez Torres (1996: 5).
16   Rondfeldt (1995).
17   Arquilla and Rondfeldt (1993).

The contradictory relationship between social movement and political institution

However, while the impact of the *Zapatistas*' demands shook up the Mexican political system, and even the Mexican economy, they became entangled in their own contradictory relationship to the political system. On the one hand, the *Zapatistas* called for the democratization of the political system, reinforcing similar demands being made within Mexican society. But they were never able to make the meaning of their political project precise, besides the obvious condemnation of electoral fraud. In the meantime, the PRI had been irreversibly shaken, divided into groups that were literally killing each other. The presidential elections of August 1994 were reasonably clean, giving Zedillo, an obscure PRI candidate brought into the limelight by accidental circumstances, a triumph fueled by fear of the unknown. Ironically, political reforms in the election process, partly as a result of *Zapatista* pressure, contributed to the legitimacy of the election, after the agreement on January 27, 1994 between all presidential candidates. The leftist opposition party, whose leader had been rebuffed by the *Zapatistas*, suffered electorally for having sought Marcos's support.

In August 1994, the *Zapatistas* called a National Democratic Convention in a site of the Lacandon Forest that they named Aguascalientes, the name of the historic site where, in 1915, revolutionary leaders (Villa, Zapata, Orozco) met to establish the Revolutionary Convention. In spite of massive participation from grassroots organizations, leftist parties, intellectuals, and media, Aguascalientes exhausted itself in the symbolism of the event, this ephemeral gathering being unable to translate the new *Zapatista* language into conventional, leftist politics. Thus, in May 1995, in the midst of protracted negotiations with the government in San Andres Larrainzar, the *Zapatistas* organized a popular consultation on the possibility of becoming a civilian political force. In spite of the obvious difficulties (they were still an insurgent organization), almost 2 million people participated in the consultation throughout Mexico, supporting the proposal in their vast majority. Thus, in January 1996, to commemorate two years of their uprising, the *Zapatistas* decided to transform themselves into a political party, seeking full participation in the political process. They also decided, however, to keep their weapons until an agreement could be reached with the government on all points of contention.

In January 1996 an important agreement on a future constitutional acknowledgment of Indian rights was reached, but negotiations concerning political reform and economic matters ultimately failed. A difficult issue seemed to be the claim by the Indian communities to keep ownership of their land, including their underground resources, a demand adamantly rejected by the Mexican government since it is widely believed that Chiapas is rich in hydrocarbons below ground. The hope for political reform, which came with the end of the PRI regime and the election of President Fox, faded away very soon, as far as the *Zapatistas* are concerned. Thus, the future potential of the *Zapatista* movement and its transformation into a political force remain uncertain.

Yet, regardless of the *Zapatistas'* fate, their insurgency did change Mexico, challenging the one-sided logic of modernization, character-istic of the new global order. Acting on the powerful contradictions existing inside the PRI between modernizers and the interests of a corrupt party apparatus, the debate triggered by the *Zapatistas* helped considerably to break PRI's hold on Mexico. The Mexican economy, buoyant and euphoric in 1993, was exposed in all its weakness, prompting US critics of NAFTA to claim vindication. An absent actor in the current Latin American modernization processes, the Indian peasantry (about 10 percent of the Mexican population) sud-denly came to life. A constitutional reform acknowledged the pluri-cultural character of Mexico, and gave new rights to the Indians, including the publication of textbooks in 30 Indian languages to be used in public schools. Health and education services improved in many Indian communities, and limited self-government was in the process of implementation.

The affirmation of Indian cultural identity, albeit in a reconstructed manner, was connected to their revolt against outrageous abuse. But their fight for dignity was decisively helped by religious affiliation expressed in the deep current of populist Catholicism in Latin Amer-ica, as well as by the last stand of the Marxist left in Mexico. That this left, built on the idea of the proletariat fighting for socialism with its guns, was transformed into an Indian, peasant movement of the excluded fighting for democracy, on behalf of constitutional rights, via the Internet and the mass media, shows the depth of the trans-formation of liberation avenues in Latin America. It also shows that the new global order induces multiple local disorder, caused by his-torically rooted sources of resistance to the logic of global capital flows. Chiapas Indians fighting against NAFTA by means of their alliance with ex-Maoist militants and liberation theologists are a distinctive expression of the old search for social justice under new historical conditions.

Up in Arms against the New World Order: The American Militia and the Patriot Movement[18]

In brief, the New World Order is a utopian system in which the US economy (along with the economy of every other nation) will be "globalized"; the wage levels of all US and European workers will be brought down to those of workers in the Third World; national boundaries will for all practical purposes cease to exist; an increased flow of Third World immigrants into the United States and Europe will have produced a non-White majority everywhere in the formerly White areas of the world; an elite consisting of international financiers, the masters of mass media, and managers of multinational corporations will call the shots; and the United Nations peacekeeping forces will be used to keep anyone from opting out of the system.

William Pierce, *National Vanguard*[19]

The Internet was one of the major reasons the militia movement expanded faster than any hate group in history. The militia's lack of an organized center was more than made up for by the instant communication and rumor potential of this new medium. Any militia member in remote Montana who had a computer and a modem could be part of an entire worldwide network that shared his or her thoughts, aspirations, organizing strategies and fears – a global family.

Kenneth Stern, *A Force upon the Plain*, p. 228

The blast of a truck loaded with fertilizer-based explosives in Oklahoma City on April 19, 1995 not only blew up a federal government

18   The main source of information on the American militia and the "Patriots" is the Southern Poverty Law Center, headquartered in Montgomery, Alabama. This remarkable organization has displayed extraordinary courage and effectiveness in protecting citizens against hate groups in America since its foundation in 1979. As part of its program, it has established a Klanwatch/ Militia Task Force which provides accurate information and analysis to understand and counteract new and old, anti-government and anti-people extremist groups. For most recent information, used in my analysis, see Klanwatch/Militia Task Force (1996, subsequently cited as KMTF). A well-documented account of the American militia in the 1990s is Stern (1996). I have also used the excellent analysis provided by my doctoral student Matthew Zook on militia groups and the Internet in 1996 (Zook, 1996). Additional sources specifically used in the analysis presented in this chapter are: Anti-Defamation League (1994, 1995); Armond (1995); Armstrong (1995); Bennett (1995); Berlet and Lyons (1995); *Broadcasting and Cable* (1995); *Business Week* (1995d); Coalition for Human Dignity (1995); J. Cooper (1995); *Gallup Poll Monthly* (1995); Heard (1995); Helvarg (1995); Ivins (1995); Jordan (1995); Maxwell and Tapia (1995); *The Nation* (1995); *The New Republic* (1995); *The New York Times Sunday* (1995a, b); Orr (1995); Pollith (1995); *The Progressive* (1995); Ross (1995); Sheps (1995); *Time* (1995); WEPIN Store (1995); Dees and Corcoran (1996); Winerip (1996).
19   Quote from White supremacist William Pierce's article in the March 1994 issue of his journal *National Vanguard*, cited by KMTF (1996: 37). Pierce is head of the National Alliance and author of the best-selling novel *The Turner Diaries*.

building, killing 169 people, but it also exposed a powerful undercurrent in American society, until then relegated to traditional hate groups and political marginality. Timothy McVeigh, convicted as the terrorist who did the bombing, and later executed, used to carry with him William Pierce's novel about an underground cell, *The Patriots*, that bombs a federal building: McVeigh reportedly called Pierce's private number hours before the actual Oklahoma bombing. McVeigh, and his army buddy, and co-conspirator in the bombing, Terry Nichols, were found to be loosely related to the Michigan Militia. The bombing occurred on the second anniversary of the Waco assault, in which most members of the Davidian cult, and their children, were killed in a siege by federal agents, an event denounced, as a rallying cry, by militia groups all around the United States.[20]

The militia groups are not terrorist, but some of their members may well be, organized in a different, but ideologically related form of movement, the "underground patriots." These are constituted on the basis of autonomous, clandestine cells, which set up their own targets in accordance with views pervasive throughout the movement. In 1994–6 a number of bombings, bank robberies, railroad sabotage, and other violent acts are believed to have been committed by such groups, and the intensity and lethality of their actions are increasing. Tons of explosives have been stolen from commercial sites, and stocks of military weaponry, including Stinger portable missiles, have disappeared from military arsenals. Attempts to develop bacteriological weapons have been discovered. And tens of thousands of "Patriots" around the United States are armed with war weapons, and undergo regular training in guerrilla tactics.[21]

The militia are the most militant, and organized, wing of a much broader, self-proclaimed "Patriot movement,"[22] whose ideological galaxy encompasses established, extreme conservative organizations, such as the John Birch Society; a whole array of traditional, white supremacist, neo-nazi, and anti-semitic groups, including the KuKlux Klan, and the Posse Comitatus; fanatic religious groups such as Christian Identity, an anti-semitic sect emanating from Victorian England's British Israelism; anti-federal government groups, such as the Counties' Rights movement, Wise Use anti-environmental

---

20   The Texas Militia issued the following appeal a few days before April 19, 1995, the second anniversary of the Waco incident: "All able-bodied citizens are to assemble with their arms to celebrate their right to keep and bear arms and to assemble as militias in defense of the Republic" (cited in the editorial of *The Nation*, 1995: 656).
21   KMTF (1996).
22   KMTF (1996); Stern (1996).

coalition, the National Taxpayers' Union, and defenders of "Common Law" courts. The Patriots' galaxy also extends, in loose forms, to the powerful Christian Coalition, as well as to a number of militant "Right to Life" groups, and counts on the sympathy of many members of the National Rifle Association, and pro-gun advocates. The direct appeal of the Patriots may reach to as many as 5 million people in America, according to well-informed sources,[23] although the very character of the movement, with its blurred boundaries, and the lack of organized membership, makes an accurate statistical estimate impossible. Still, its influence can be counted in millions, not thousands, of supporters.

What these disparate groups, formerly unrelated, came to share in the 1990s, and what broadens their appeal, is their common, declared enemy: the US federal government, as representative of the "New World Order," being set up against the will of American citizens. According to views pervasive throughout the Patriot movement, this "New World Order," aimed at destroying American sovereignty, is enacted by a conspiracy of global financial interests and global bureaucrats that have captured the US federal government. At the core of this new system are the World Trade Organization, the Trilateral Commission, the International Monetary Fund, and, above all, the United Nations, whose "peacekeeping forces" are seen as an international, mercenary army, spearheaded by Hong Kong policemen and Gurkha units, ready to suppress people's sovereignty.

Four events seemed to confirm this conspiracy for the Patriots: the passing of NAFTA in 1993; the approval by Clinton of the Brady Bill in 1994, establishing limited controls on the sale of some types of automatic weapons; the siege of white supremacist Randy Weaver in Idaho, resulting in the killing of his wife by the FBI, in 1992; and the tragic siege of Waco, leading to the death of David Koresh and his followers in 1993. A paranoid reading of these events led to the conviction that the government was proceeding to disarm citizens, to subdue them later, submitting Americans to surveillance from hidden cameras, and black helicopters, and implanting biochips in the newborn.

To this global threat, to jobs, to privacy, to liberty, to the American way of life, they oppose the Bible and the original American Constitution, expunged of its Amendments. In accordance with these texts, both received from God, they affirm the sovereignty of citizens and its direct expression in county governments, not acknowledging the authority of federal government, its laws, its courts, as well as the

23   Berlet and Lyons (1995); KMTF (1996); Winerip (1996).

validity of the Federal Reserve Bank. The choice is dramatic. In the words of the Militia of Montana, created in February 1994, and an organizational inspiration for the whole movement: "Join the Army and Serve the UN or Join America and Serve the Militia" (motto on the world wide web home page of the Montana Militia). Federal agents, particularly those from the Bureau of Alcohol, Tobacco, and Firearms, are considered to be in the frontline of the repression against Americans on behalf of the emerging world government. This, in the view of the militia, justifies making federal agents potential targets of the movement. Thus, as popular broadcaster Gordon Liddy put it in one of his talk shows: "They've got a big target [on their chest]: ATF. Don't shoot at that because they've got a vest on underneath that. Head shots, head shots. Kill the sons of bitches!"[24]

In some segments of this highly diverse Patriot movement there is also a powerful mythology rooted in eschatological views of the world and End of Times prophecies (see chapter 1). Following the Book of Revelations, chapter 13, preachers such as tele-evangelist Pat Robertson, the leader of the Christian Coalition, remind Christians that they may be asked to submit to the satanic "Mark of the Beast," variously identified as new codes on paper money, supermarket bar codes, or microchip technology.[25] Resisting the new global, ungodly order, coming at the End of Times, is seen as a Christian duty and an American citizen's right. Yet, the sinister colorfulness of the movement's mythology sometimes obscures its profile, and actually downplays its political and social significance. This is why it is important to pay attention to the diversity of the movement, while still emphasizing its underlying commonality.

The militias and the Patriots: a multi-thematic information network

Militias, self-organized citizens armed to defend their country, religion, and freedom, are institutions that played an important role during the first century of America's existence.[26] The state militias were replaced by state national guards in 1900. However, in the 1990s, starting with the Montana Militia, right-wing populist groups have formed "unorganized militias," using some legal ambiguity in federal laws to circumvent the legal prohibition on the forming of military units outside government control.

24 Stern (1996: 221).
25 Berlet and Lyons (1995).
26 Whisker (1992); J. Cooper (1995).

The most distinctive feature of militia groups is that they are armed, sometimes with war weapons, and are structured in a military-style chain of command. By the end of 1995, KMTF could count 441 active militias in all 50 states, with paramilitary training sites in at least 23 states (see figure 2.1). Numbers of militia members are difficult to estimate. Berlet and Lyons ventured to evaluate them, in 1995, at between 15,000 and 40,000.[27] By all accounts they are growing rapidly. There is no national organization. Each state's militia is independent, and there are sometimes several, unrelated militia groups in the same state: 33 in Ohio, with about 1,000 members, and hundreds of thousands of sympathizers, according to police sources.[28] The Militia of Montana is the founding example, but the largest is the Michigan Militia, with several thousand active members. Their ideology, beyond the common opposition to the new world order and to the federal government, is highly diversified. Their membership is overwhelmingly white, Christian, and predominantly male. They certainly include a significant number of racists, anti-semites, and sexists among their ranks. Yet, most militia groups do not define themselves as racist or sexist, and some of them (for instance the Michigan Militia) make an explicit anti-racist statement in their propaganda. In Zook's analysis of militia pages on the world wide web, focusing on 11 of the most popular militia, seven of the home pages made anti-racist statements, four made no mention of race, and none contained overt racism.[29] Two pages took anti-sexist stands, two welcomed women, and the others did not mention sex. Indeed, the Michigan Militia refused to support the "Montana freemen," during their 1996 siege in a ranch, because they were racist. And one of the militia home pages "E Pluribus Unum," part of the Ohio Militia, is run by an African-American Christian fundamentalist couple. To be sure, these statements could be faked, but given the importance of Internet posting to contact new members, it would be inconsistent to misrepresent the ideology on which new recruits are attracted. It seems that the militia and the Patriots, while including traditional racist, anti-semitic, hate groups, have a much broader ideological constituency, and this is exactly one of the reasons for their new success. Namely, their ability to reach out across the ideological spectrum to unite all sources of disaffection against the federal government. As KMTF's report says:

27   Berlet and Lyons (1995).
28   Winerip (1996).
29   Zook (1996).

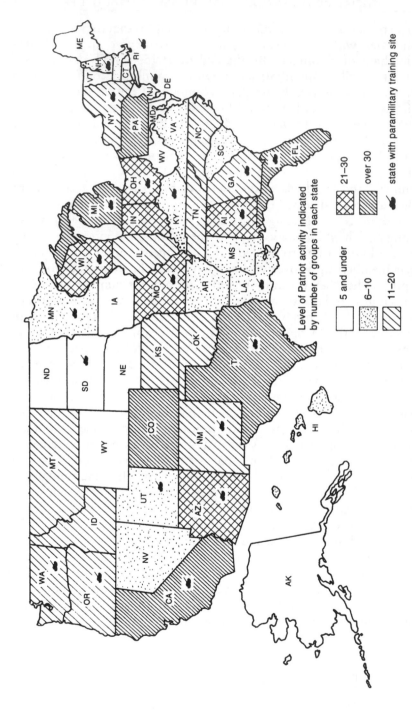

Figure 2.1 Geographical distribution of Patriot groups in the US by number of groups and paramilitary training sites in each state, 1996

Source: Southern Poverty Law Center, Klanwatch/Militia Task Force, Montgomery, Alabama, 1996

Unlike their factious white supremacist predecessors, Patriots have been able to bridge minor ideological differences in favor of a broad unity on the anti-government agenda. As a result, they have created the most inviting insurgent force in recent history, home to a wide variety of anti-government groups whose organizational roles may differ dramatically.[30]

Two fast-expanding components of the Patriot movement are the Counties' Rights movement, and the "Common Law" courts. The first is a militant wing of the Wise Use coalition, which has growing influence in the Western states. The coalition opposes environmental regulation enforced by the federal government and appeals to the "customs and culture" of logging, mining, and grazing on public land. Land-use zoning is equated with socialism, and management of the ecosystem is considered to be a part of the new world order.[31] Consequently, the movement asserts the right of county sheriffs to arrest federal land managers, which prompted a number of violent incidents. People and communities are urged to acknowledge exclusively the authority of their elected officials at the municipal and county level, rejecting the federal government's right to legislate on their property. Seventy counties have passed Wise Use ordinances claiming local control over public land, and violent actions have intimidated environmentalists and federal land managers from New Mexico and Nevada to northern Idaho and Washington.

Common Law courts have been established in 40 states, supported by an array of books and videos that claim to provide a legal basis for people to reject the judicial system, setting up their own "judges," "trials," and "juries." They have even established a national "Supreme Court of Common Law" with 23 justices, based on the Bible and on their own interpretation of law. Common Law followers declare themselves "sovereign," that is freemen, and refuse accordingly to pay taxes and social security, to comply with driving licensing, and to submit to all other government controls not contemplated in the original American legal body. To protect their sovereignty, and retaliate against public officials, they often file commercial liens against targeted public officials and judges, creating a nightmarish confusion in a number of county courts. As an extension of the Common Law movement, a rapidly expanding network of people, from Montana to California, refuse the authority of the Federal Reserve Bank to print money, and they issue their own bank documents, including cashier checks, with such good reproduction technology that they have often

30   KMTF (1996: 14).
31   Helvarg (1995).

been cashed, prompting a number of arrests for forgery and fraud. These practices are making the Common Law movement the most confrontational of all the Patriot groups, and were at the root of the three-month stand-off between "freemen" and the FBI in a ranch in Jordan, Montana, in 1996.

Such a diverse, almost chaotic, movement cannot have a stable organization, or even a coordinating authority. Yet, the homogeneity of its core world vision and, particularly, its identification of a common enemy are remarkable. This is because linkages between groups and individuals do exist, but they are carried out through the media (radio, mainly), through books, pamphlets, speaking tours, and alternative press, by fax, and, mainly, through the Internet.[32] According to KMTF, "the computer is the most vital piece of equipment in the Patriot movement's arsenal."[33] On the Internet there are numerous militia bulletin board systems, home pages, and chat groups; for instance, the Usenet group MAM, established in 1995.

Several reasons have been proposed for the widespread use of the Internet by militiamen. One is that, as Stern writes, the "Internet was the perfect culture in which to grow the virus of conspiracy theory. Messages appeared on the screen with no easy way to separate junk from credible... For conspiracy enthusiasts like militia members, unverified statements from cyberspace reaffirmed their set conclusions by providing an endless stream of additional 'evidence.'"[34] Also, the frontier spirit characteristic of the Internet fits well with the freemen expressing themselves, and making their statements, without mediation or government control. More importantly, the network structure of the Internet reproduces exactly the autonomous, spontaneous networking of militia groups, and of the Patriots at large, without boundaries, and without definite plan, but sharing a purpose, a feeling, and, most of all, an enemy. It is mainly on the Internet (backed up by fax and direct mailing) that the movement thrives and organizes itself.

It was through the Associated Electronic Network News, organized by the Thompsons in Indianapolis, that a conspiracy theory was diffused according to which the Oklahoma bombing was a provocation by the federal government similar to Hitler's arson of the Reichstag in order to crack down on the militia. Other bulletin board systems, such as the "Paul Revere Net," link up groups around the country, exchange information, circulate rumors, and coordinate actions. For example, confidential reports inform browsers that

32   KMTF (1996); Stern (1996); Zook (1996).
33   KMTF (1996: 16).
34   Stern (1996: 228).

Gorbachev, after giving a speech in California saying that "we are now entering the new world order," went on to hide in a Southern California naval base to oversee the dismantling of America's armed forces in preparation for the arrival of the new world order's army. Indeed, its arrival took place in May 1996, when a permanent base was established in New Mexico to train hundreds of German pilots in cooperation with the US Air Force. Or so thought the thousands of callers that submerged the Pentagon's switchboard after CNN reported the opening of such a base.

Radio talk shows are also important. Rush Limbaugh's audience of 20 million on 600 stations around the country was an instrument of political influence without parallel in 1990s' America. While he is not a militia supporter, his themes ("femi-nazis," "eco-wacos") resonate in the movement. Other popular radio programs are more directly in tune with the Patriots: Gordon Liddy's call-in show, or *The Intelligence Report*, hosted by white supremacist Mark Koernke. Alternative cable channels, broadcasting similar topics to similar audiences, include National Empowerment Television, Jones Intercable, and Time–Warner-owned Paragon Cable in Florida, which features *Race&Reason*, an anti-semitic, racist show. A myriad of newspapers and bulletins, such as Washington, DC's *Spotlight*, or the white supremacist tract *The Turner Diaries*, add to a highly decentralized, extensive network of alternative media. This network diffuses targeted information, airs people's resentment, publicizes right, extremist ideas, spreads rumors of conspiracies, and purveys the eschatological mythology that has become the cultural background for turn-of-millennium right-wing populism. Thus, while the FBI looks in vain for proof of an organized conspiracy to overturn the government by force, the actual conspiracy, with no names (or multiple names), and with no organization (or hundreds of them), flows in the information networks, feeding paranoia, connecting anger, and maybe spilling blood.

The Patriots' banners

In spite of its diversity, the Patriot movement, with the militia at its forefront, does share some common goals, beliefs, and foes. It is this set of values and purposes that constructs a world vision and, ultimately, defines the movement itself. There is an underlying, simple, but powerful view of the world and society, which is expressed in different forms in the Patriot movement. According to this vision, America is divided into two kinds of people: producers and parasites. Producers, working people, are oppressed between two layers of parasites:

corrupt government officials, wealthy corporate elites, and bankers, at the top; and stupid and lazy people, undeserving of the welfare they receive of society, at the bottom. The situation is being made worse by the current process of globalization, steered by the United Nations and international financial institutions, on behalf of corporate elites and government bureaucracies, which threatens to transform ordinary people into mere slaves of a worldwide plantation-like economy. God will prevail, but for this citizens must take up their guns to fight for "the future of America itself."[35] From this world vision emerges a specific set of targets for the movement, which organize its practice.

First of all, the militia, and the Patriots in general, are an extreme libertarian movement (and, in this sense, very different from traditional Nazis or fascists who call for a strong state). Their enemy is the federal government. In their view, the basic units of society are the individual, the family, and the local community. Beyond that immediate level of face-to-face acknowledgment, government is only tolerated as the direct expression of the citizens' will; for example, county governments, with elected officials who can be known and controlled on a personal basis. Higher levels of government are suspected, and the federal government is denounced outright as illegitimate, as having usurped citizens' rights and manipulated the Constitution to overstep the original mandate of the founding fathers of America. For militiamen, Thomas Jefferson and Patrick Henry are the heroes, and Alexander Hamilton the obvious villain. This rejection of the legitimacy of federal government expresses itself in very concrete, powerful attitudes and actions: rejection of federal taxes, refusal of environmental regulation and land-use planning, sovereignty of Common Law courts, jury nullification (namely deciding as jurors in court cases not in accordance with the law but according to their consciences), preeminence of county governments over higher authorities, and hatred of federal law-enforcement agencies. At the limit, the movement calls for civil disobedience against the government, backing it up, if and when necessary, with the guns of "natural law"-abiding citizens.

While the federal government and its enforcement agencies are the immediate enemies, and the immediate cause of the mobilization of the Patriots, a more ominous threat looms on the horizon: the new world order. The new world order, a notion popularized by teleevangelist Pat Robertson, extrapolating from Bush's post-Cold War end-of-history ideology, implies that the federal government is actively working toward the goal of one world government in collaboration with Russia (particularly with Gorbachev, considered to be a

35   M. Cooper (1995).

key strategist in the plot). This project is supposedly being carried out by the intermediary of international organizations: the United Nations, the new World Trade Organization, and the International Monetary Fund. The placement of American military troops under the command of the United Nations, and the signing of NAFTA, are considered but the first steps toward such a new order, often explicitly associated with the coming of the information age. The actual impact on the American people is seen as their economic impoverishment for the benefit of multinational corporations and banks, and their political disfranchisement for the sake of global political bureaucracies.

Together with these localist, libertarian strands, a third major theme runs through the movement: a backlash against feminists (not against women as long as they remain in their traditional role), gays, and minorities (as beneficiaries of government protection). There is one clearly predominant characteristic in the Patriot movement: in a large majority, they are white, heterosexual males. The "Angry White Males" (actually the name of one Patriot organization) seem to have come together in this mixture of reactions to economic deprivation, reaffirmation of traditional values and privileges, and cultural backlash. Traditional national and family values (that is, patriarchalism) are affirmed against what are considered to be excessive privileges accorded by society to gender, cultural, and ethnic minorities, as exemplified by affirmative action and anti-discrimination legislation. While this theme does connect with a much older rejection of racial equality by white supremacist groups and anti-immigrant coalitions, it is new in its comprehensiveness, particularly because of the explicit rejection of women's rights, and in its hostile targeting of liberal values diffused by the mainstream media.

A fourth theme present in most of the movement is the intolerant affirmation of the superiority of Christian values, so linking up closely with the Christian fundamentalist movement, analyzed in chapter 1. Most Patriots seem to subscribe to the pretension that Christian values and rituals, as interpreted by their defenders, must be enforced through the institutions of society; for example, mandatory prayer in public schools and the screening of libraries and the media to censor what would be considered anti-Christian or anti-family values. The widespread anti-abortion movement, with fanatic assassins at its fringes, is its most notorious organizational instrument. Christian fundamentalism seems to be pervasive throughout the whole movement. It might seem paradoxical, this connection between an extreme libertarian movement, such as the militia, and Christian fundamentalism, a movement that aims at theocracy and therefore would seek government imposition of moral and religious values on its citizens.

However, this is only a contradiction on the historical horizon, since in turn-of-the-millennium America both fundamentalists and libertarians converge on the destruction of a federal government that is perceived as being apart from both God and The People.

Guns and Bibles could well be the movement's motto.[36] Guns were the rallying point around which the militia came together in 1994 in response to the Brady Bill. A vast coalition was formed against this, and subsequent attempts at gun control. Around the powerful lobby of the National Rifle Association, controlling many votes in Congress, coalesced rural folks around the country, gun-shop owners, extreme libertarians, and militia groups, to make the defense of the constitutional right to bear arms the last line of defense for America as it ought to be. Guns equal freedom. The Wild West rides again, on the streets of Los Angeles as on Michigan farms. Two of the deepest features of American culture, its rugged individualism and its mistrust of despotic governments, from which many immigrants escape to come to America, provide the seal of authenticity to the resistance against threats generated by the informationalization of society, the globalization of the economy, and the professionalization of politics.

Who are the Patriots?

A component of the movement is certainly made up of disaffected farmers in the Midwest and in the West, supported by a miscellaneous cast of small town societies, from coffee-shop owners to traditionalist pastors. But it would be inaccurate to consider that the appeal of the movement is limited to a rural world phased out by technological modernization. There are no demographic data on the movement's composition, but a simple look at the geographical distribution of the militia (figure 2.1) shows its territorial, thus social, diversity. The groups of states with the highest numbers of militia activity include such diverse areas as Pennsylvania, Michigan, Florida, Texas, Colorado, and California, more or less following the most populous states (minus New York, plus Colorado), but this is precisely the point: militia seem to be where people are, all over the country, not just in Montana. If we consider the Christian Coalition to be a part of the movement, then Patriots are present in the suburbs of most large metropolitan areas (there are about 1.5 million members of the Christian Coalition). Some militia groups, for instance in New Hampshire, and in California, seem to recruit among computer professionals. Thus, it does not seem that the Patriots are a class-based, or territori-

36   Maxwell and Tapia (1995).

ally specific, movement. Rather, they are, fundamentally, a cultural and political movement, defenders of the traditions of the country against cosmopolitan values, and of self-rule of local people against the imposition of global order.

However, if class is not relevant in the composition of the movement, it is relevant in the identification of its enemies. Corporate elites; bankers; the wealthy, powerful, and arrogant big firms, and their lawyers; and scientists and researchers, are their enemies. Not as a class, but as representatives of an un-American world order. Indeed, the ideology is not anti-capitalist, but is, rather, an ideology in defense of free capitalism, opposed to a corporate manifestation of state capitalism that appears to be close to socialism. Thus, a class analysis of the Patriots does not seem to address the essence of the movement. It is a political insurgency that cuts across class lines and regional differentiation. And it relates to the social and political evolution of American society at large.

The militia, the Patriots, and American society

Right-wing populism is hardly a novelty in the United States; indeed, it is a phenomenon that has played an important role in American politics throughout the country's history.[37] Furthermore, angry popular reactions to economic distress have occurred in both America and Europe in different forms, from classic fascism and Nazism to the xenophobic and ultra-nationalist movements of recent years. One of the conditions that can help explain the fast spread of the militia, besides the Internet, is growing economic hardship and social inequality in America. Men's average income has deteriorated substantially in the past two decades, particularly during the 1980s. Families are barely maintaining the living standards of a quarter of a century ago by putting in the contribution of two wage earners instead of one. On the other hand, the top 1 percent of households increased its average income from $327,000 to about $567,000 between 1976 and 1993, while average family income remains at about $31,000. CEOs' pay is 190 times higher than that of their average worker.[38] For the American worker and small entrepreneur, the age of globalization and informationalization has been the age of a relative, and often an absolute, decline in their standard of living, reversing the historical trend of the improvement of each generation's material well-being over that of previous generations. Occasionally, the culture of the new

37   Lipset and Raab (1978).
38   *The New York Times* (1995).

global rich adds insult to injury. For instance, Montana, the seedbed of the new militia, is also one of the favorite destinations of the new billionaires, fond of acquiring thousands of acres of pristine land to build ranches from which to run their global networks. Ranchers in the area resented these moves.[39]

Furthermore, at the moment when the traditional family becomes indispensable as an instrument of both financial and psychological security, it has been falling apart, in the wake of the gender war ignited by the resistance of patriarchalism to women's rights (see chapter 4). Cultural challenges to sexism and to heterosexual orthodoxy confuse masculinity. In addition, a new wave of immigration, this time from Latin America and Asia, and the growing multi-ethnicity of America, although in continuity with the country's history, add to the feeling of loss of control. The shifts from agriculture and manufacturing to services, and from goods handling to information processing, undermine acquired skills and work subcultures. And the end of the Cold War, with the collapse of communism, eliminates the easy indentification of the external enemy, hampering the chances of bringing America together in a common cause. The age of information becomes the age of confusion, and thus the age of fundamental affirmation of traditional values and uncompromising rights. Bureaucratic, and sometimes violent, reactions by law-enforcement agencies to various forms of protest deepen the anger, sharpen the feelings, and seem to justify the call to arms, bringing the new American militia in direct confrontation with the emerging global order.

The Lamas of Apocalypse: Japan's *Aum Shinrikyo*[40]

The final goal of body techniques that Aum tries to develop by yoga and austerity is a mode of communication without any medium. Communication can be obtained by having resonance with others' bodies without relying on consciousness of identity as self, without using the medium of language.

Masachi Osawa, Gendai, October 1995[41]

---

39   Stevens (1995).
40   The analysis of *Aum Shinrikyo* presented here essentially reproduces the contribution to our joint study, and article, by Shujiro Yazawa, who conducted most of the research on *Aum*, although I also studied the movement, in cooperation with Yazawa, in Tokyo in 1995. Sources directly used in the analysis, besides reports in newspapers and magazines, are Aoyama (1991); Asahara (1994, 1995); *Vajrayana Sacca* (1994); Drew (1995); Fujita (1995); *Mainichi Shinbun* (1995); Miyadai (1995); Nakazawa et al. (1995); Ohama (1995); Osawa (1995); Shimazono (1995); Yazawa (1997).
41   Translated by Yazawa.

On March 20, 1995, an attack with sarin gas in three different trains on the Tokyo subway killed 12 people, injured over 5,000, and shook the foundations of the apparently stable Japanese society. The police, using information from a similar incident which had occurred in Matsumoto in June 1994, determined that the attack had been carried out by members of *Aum Shinrikyo*, a religious cult at the core of a network of business activities, political organizations, and paramilitary units. The ultimate goal of *Aum Shinrikyo*, according to its own discourse, was to survive the coming apocalypse, to save Japan, and eventually the world, from the war of extermination that would inevitably result from the competing efforts by Japanese corporations and American imperialism to establish a new world order and a united world government. To overcome Armageddon, *Aum* would prepare a new kind of human being, rooted in spirituality and self-improvement through meditation and exercise. Yet, to face the aggression of world-powers-that-be, *Aum* had to defend itself by taking up the challenge of new weapons of extermination. The challenge came quickly indeed. The cult's founder and guru, Shoko Asahara, was arrested and put on trial (probably to be sentenced to death), along with the most prominent members of the cult. The cult itself continues to exist, albeit with a reduced constituency.

The debate over the origins, development, and goals of *Aum* went on for months in the Japanese media. It prompted fundamental questions about the actual state of Japanese society. How could such acts be possible in one of the wealthiest, least unequal, safest, most ethnically homogeneous, and most culturally integrated societies in the world? Especially striking for the public was the fact that the cult had recruited particularly among scientists and engineers from some of the best Japanese universities. Coming in a period of political uncertainty, after the crisis of the LDP, Japan's governing party for almost five decades, the apparently senseless act was seen as a symptom. But a symptom of what? To understand a very complex development, with fundamental, but not so obvious, implications, we must reconstruct the evolution of the cult, starting with the biography of its founder, who played a crucial role in this development.

Asahara and the development of Aum Shinrikyo

Asahara was born blind in a poor family in Kumamoto Prefecture. He attended a special school for the blind, and, after completing his studies there, prepared for admission examinations to Tokyo University. His explicit project was to become Prime Minister. After failing the exams, he opened a pharmacy and specialized in the sale of traditional Chinese medicine. Some of these medicines were of questionable use, and his lack of a license eventually led to his arrest. After marrying and having a child, in 1977 he shifted his interest to religion. He educated himself in Sento, and tried to develop a spiritual health care method based on Taoism. The decisive change in his life came when he joined the Agon cult, a religious group preaching perfection through the practice of austerity.[42] Meditation, physical exercise, yoga, and esoteric Buddhism were essential practices of the group. Asahara combined Agon's teaching with his own ideas about creating a new religious world. In 1984, he opened a yoga school in Shibuya, Tokyo. At the same time, he established *Aum* as a corporation (*Aum* is a Sanskrit word meaning "deep wisdom"). He developed his yoga school's reputation by making claims in the media about his own supernatural powers, as shown by his ability to float in the air (a claim he backed up with photos showing himself in action, a first venture in special visual effects, which signaled *Aum*'s future emphasis on media technology).

Stating that God had ordered him to build a utopia with a few elected ones, in 1985 the yoga master became a religious leader, and instructed his disciples at the school in search of perfection through the hard practice of austerity. In 1986 Asahara created the formal religious cult *Aum Shinsen*, with about 350 members. Most of them were inducted as priests, unlike other cults where only a small minority of members can devote themselves fully to the practice of austerity and meditation. This high ratio of priesthood was very important for the future of *Aum*, since it had to find substantial means of financial support for such a large number of priests. Thus, *Aum* requested donations of all assets from its recruits (sometimes by force), charged for teaching and training seminars, and invested in various businesses. Among these business activities, it created a very profitable commercial chain of stores (*Mahaposha*), selling personal computers at discount price, and specializing in the distribution of pirated software. With the profits from these computer stores, *Aum* financed a number of eating and drinking outlets, and other miscellaneous businesses. In 1987, the name was changed to *Aum Shinrikyo* (the Japanese word for "truth"). A year later, as a step to utopia, *Aum* built its headquarters in a village in the foothills of Mount Fuji. In spite of some resistance from the authorities, it finally obtained recognition as a non-profit, tax-exempt, religious corporation.

Having consolidated *Aum*'s position, and with the support of about 10,000 members, Asahara decided to enter politics in order to trans-

---

42 Austerity implies strenuous physical exercise and privation of food and bodily pleasure as a regular form of existence.

form society. In 1990, he and 25 other *Aum* members ran for Congress but obtained almost no votes. They claimed that their votes had been stolen. This political disappointment was a turning point for the ideology of *Aum*, which abandoned its attempts to participate in the political process. Future efforts would be directed toward confrontation with government. Shortly afterwards, an attempt to build a new hall for the cult in Naminomura was fiercely opposed by local residents, and, after a few incidents, *Aum* members were arrested. The media echoed rumors of kidnapping and extortions of former cult members. When a group of victims of *Aum* formed an association, their lawyer disappeared. The cult went into a paranoiac frenzy, feeling harassed by police, government, and the media.

In this context, Asahara started to emphasize the eschatological line of thinking that had been present in the cult's themes from its inception. Asahara, referring to the prophecies of Nostradamus, predicted that, around the year 2000, nuclear war between the US and the USSR would break out, and that, as a result, 90 percent of urban dwellers would die. Thus, the very best should prepare themselves to survive the disaster. To do so, hard physical exercise, austerity, and meditation, following the teachings of Asahara, would be needed in order to create a superhuman race. *Aum*'s meditation halls would be the birth places of a new civilization after Armageddon. Yet spiritual perfection would not be enough. The enemy would use all kinds of new weapons: nuclear, chemical, bacteriological. Therefore, *Aum*, as the last chance for humankind's survival, should be prepared for this terrible warfare at the End of Times. Consequently, *Aum* established several companies to buy and process materials for the development of chemical and biological weapons. It imported one helicopter and several armored vehicles, bought on Russia's black market, and started to learn how to design and produce high-technology weapons, including laser-guided guns.[43]

In a logical development, in 1994, *Aum* decided to become a counter-state. It formed ministries and bureaux, mirroring the structure of the Japanese state, and appointed members to each ministry and agency, to constitute a shadow government, with Asahara at the top of this holy counter-state. The role of this organization would be to lead the cult and the few elected survivors in the final battle against the forces of evil, namely the united world government (dominated by multinational corporations) and its direct agents: American imperialists and Japanese police. In June 1994, a first experiment with nerve gas was carried out in Matsumoto, killing seven people. Police investigations of the cult,

43   Drew (1995).

and reports in the media, prompted the sense among cult members that confrontation was inevitable, and that the first episodes leading to the prophecy were taking place. The attack on Tokyo's subway, a few months later, propelled the cult, Japan, and maybe the world, into a new era of messianic critique potentially backed by weapons of mass extermination.

Aum's beliefs and methodology

The beliefs and teachings of *Aum Shinrikyo* are complex, and have been changing somewhat throughout the cult's evolution. Yet it is possible to reconstruct the essence of its vision and practice on the basis of available documents and reports. At the root of its purpose and method, *Aum* stresses the notion of deliverance (*gedatsu*), that is, according to Osawa, one of *Aum*'s best observers:

> Dissolving the integrity of the body as individual to overcome the locality of the body. Believers must transcend the boundary between the body and its external world by differentiating the body endlessly. By continual exercise, it is possible to reach the point where the body can be felt as fluid, gas, or wave of energy. The body tries to integrate itself as individual because we have self consciousness in the inner side of the integrated body. It is this inner side of the body that organizes the self. Therefore, to disintegrate our bodies to the extent that we feel our bodies as fluid or gas, means the disorganization of ourselves. This is deliverance.[44]

Deliverance means true freedom and happiness. Indeed, humans have lost their selves and become impure. The real world is in fact an illusion, and life as usually lived by people is full of burdens and pains. Realizing and accepting this harsh reality enables one to face death in truth. To reach this truth, through deliverance, *Aum* developed a technology of meditation and austerity (*Mahayana*), with precise indicators of the stage of perfection achieved by every believer at various stages.

However, for most followers, deliverance is uncertain at best. Thus, two additional elements provide coherence to *Aum*'s method and vision: on the one hand, faith in the guru's superpowers, guaranteeing salvation after a certain stage of perfection is achieved; on the other hand, a sense of urgency derived from the coming catastrophic crisis of civilization. In *Aum*'s view, there is a direct link between the end of the world and the salvation of believers, who are preparing for the

44   Osawa (1995).

apocalypse by acquiring supernatural powers. In this sense, *Aum* is at the same time a mystical cult and a practical corporation, which aimed to provide survival training for doomsday 2000 – at a price.

Aum *and Japanese society*

Most *Aum* priests were young university graduates. In 1995, 47.5 percent of its priests were in their twenties, and 28 percent in their thirties; 40 percent were women. Indeed, an explicit goal of *Aum* was "to solve gender differences" by changing "the inner world of gender." In the absence of a powerful feminist movement in Japan (as yet), *Aum* gained some influence among college-educated women frustrated by an extremely patriarchal society. A high proportion of the men were graduates in the natural sciences from distinguished universities.[45] *Aum*'s appeal to highly educated youth came as a shock to the Japanese public.

According to Yazawa,[46] this appeal can be better understood by the alienation of Japanese youth, in the aftermath of the defeat of the powerful Japanese social movements of the 1960s. Instead of transformative social values, the "Information Society" was promised. But this promise fell short of cultural innovation and spiritual fulfillment. In a society with no mobilized social challengers, and without values of cultural transformation, a new generation has grown up since the 1970s in material affluence, but without spiritual meaning. It was seduced at the same time by technology and esotericism. Many *Aum* believers were people who could not find a place for their desires for change and meaningfulness in the bureaucratized structure of schools, administrations, and corporations, and were revolting against traditional, authoritarian family structures. They had no purpose in their lives, and not even enough physical space to express themselves in the congested conurbation of Japanese cities. The only thing left for them was their own bodies. For many of these young people, their desire was to live in a different world by using science and technology to help their bodies transcend natural and social limits. In Yazawa's concept, theirs was a desire based on the "informationalization of the body," meaning the transformation of human physical potential by the power of ideas, beliefs, and meditation. This is where *Aum*'s methodology of deliverance fitted particularly well. The promise of deliverance was that people could feel themselves and others at the same time. Community and belonging were restored, but as an

45   *Mainichi Shinbun* (1995).
46   Castells et al. (1996); Yazawa (1997).

expression of the self, through perfection and control of the body's own limits, not as a result of external imposition, enabling communication without a medium by directly connecting to other bodies. This new form of communication was only considered to be possible among bodies that had already overcome their locality. Asahara's body, by having already escaped from his body's locality, would be the catalyst to induce the deliverance of others. As a result, a virtual community of communicating bodies was gradually formed, with Asahara as the sole center of this community.[47]

Some of these ideas and practices are not unusual in yoga and in Tibetan Buddhism. What was specific to *Aum*'s version of disembodied communication through yoga and meditation was, on the one hand, its technological implementation (for instance, through the extensive use of training videos and of electronic stimulating devices), and, on the other hand, its political instrumentation. In some instances, experiments were carried out by means of electronic helmets attached to the followers' heads, to enable them to receive communication waves directly from the guru's brain (a little technological push to the theory of disembodied communication). Asahara's ideas developed finally into the identity of his self or "true self," in which the selves of all disciples were to be ultimately dissolved. Communication channels with the outside world were closed off, as it was declared the enemy, heading toward Armageddon. The inside network was structured in a hierarchical organization, in which communication came from the top, with no horizontal channels of communication among the believers. In this view, the outside world was unreal, and the virtual reality generated by a combination of technology and yoga techniques was the real world. The outside, unreal world was evolving toward its apocalypse. The inner, virtual reality, internally communicated world was the fundamental reality, preparing itself for salvation.

In the latest stage of the discourse of *Aum*, a more precise social prediction took shape: future social change would be caused by a cycle of economic recession, then depression, followed by war and death. Natural disasters and economic depression would overtake Japan in the last years of the millennium. The reason: increased competition from other Asian countries using their comparative advantage of lower labor costs. To answer this challenge, Japan would develop its military industry and try to impose its will on Asia, in the interests of Japanese corporations striving to create a world government under the control of multinational corporations. In response,

47   Osawa (1995).

the United States would enter the war against Japan to protect its Asian vassals, and to advance its own project of world government. The war would linger on, and all kinds of high-technology weapons would be used. This would be a war of extermination, which could lead to the end of humankind. In this account, *Aum*'s vision reflected, in a distorted and schematic way, the fears of Japanese society about losing its competitive edge in the world economy, about a potential conflict with the United States, and about the catastrophic consequences of uncontrolled new technologies.

What distinguished *Aum* was its response to these threats. To be ready for such a war, and to survive it (as in some popular science fiction movies of the 1990s), would require both the rebirth of spirituality and the mastery of advanced weapons technology, particularly biological, chemical, and laser-guided weapons. As mentioned above, *Aum* did indeed try to acquire these weapons and hire scientists able to develop them in the United States, Israel, and Russia. While pursuing spiritual perfection, and uniting its members in a collective, spiritual body, *Aum* equipped itself to fight the war of survival, and declared such a war in advance, against the supporters of the united world government looming on the horizon.

In a distorted way, *Aum*'s fears and ideas were similar to those found in many of the youth subcultures of Japan. According to Shinji Miyadai, two perceptions of the world could be found among them.[48] The first one was that of an "endless everyday life" without purpose, goals, or happiness. The second was that of possible commonality only in the case of a nuclear war that would force the survivors to unite. By building on both ideas – that is, by finding happiness in the inner self and preparing for the post-nuclear war commune – *Aum* directly connected with these expressions of cultural despair from youth alienated in an over-organized society. In this sense, *Aum* was not an act of collective madness, but the hyperbolic, amplified manifestation of educated rebels, manipulated by a messianic guru at the crossroads between meditation and electronics, business and spirituality, informational politics and high-tech warfare. *Aum* appears to have been a horror caricature of the Japanese Information Society, mirroring its government structure, its corporate behavior, and its worship of advanced technology mixed with traditional spiritualism. Perhaps the reason Japan became obsessed with *Aum* was because of the recognition of how truly Japanese this close-up vision of apocalypse was.

48   Miyadai (1995).

Al-Qaeda, 9/11, and Beyond: Global Terror in the Name of God

Our duty, which we have fulfilled, is to incite the "umma" to take up a holy war in the name of God against America, Israel, and their allies... It is time for the Muslim people to realize... that the countries of the region have no sovereignty. Our enemies move about freely and merrily in our seas, land, and air. They hit without asking permission from anyone... I say that there are two sides in the conflict: the international crusade movement allied with Jewish Zionism and led by America, Britain, and Israel. And the other side is the Muslim world. It is unacceptable in such a conflict that he commits an aggression, enters my land and holy places, and robs the oil of the Muslims and then when he is confronted with any form of resistance from the Muslims he says: these are terrorists. This is either sheer stupidity, or assuming that others are stupid. We believe that it is our legitimate duty to resist this occupation with all the strength we have got and punish the enemy with the same means that it uses against us.
Osama bin Laden, interview on Al Jazeera News Network, September 20, 2001 (translated from Arabic)

The horror that made New York's twin towers into Ground Zero, murdering 3,000 people and shattering the lives of countless others, surged from the depth of our world's untreated contradictions. The magnitude of the event, arguably ushering in a new geopolitics, and a new public consciousness, obscures an understanding of it. From simplistic denunciations of timeless fanaticism, to interested rehearsals of pre-conceived, ideological arguments, rational analysis of this most important phenomenon seems to be another victim of terror, buried under the climate of revengeful hysteria that came to dominate the American scene, and the wave of primitive anti-Americanism that swept much of the world after the war in Afghanistan.

We do have considerable information, albeit most often from tainted sources, on the process that led to 9/11, about its actors, their motivations, and the not-always-clear web of interests surrounding them.[49] But to understand this continuing process, we must bring

---

49   There is an abundant literature on *al-Qaeda*, related Islamic groups, and the events that led to 9/11, most of it in the form of journalistic books and investigative reporting. There is also a plethora of media reports, which I will not cite unless I find it necessary to refer to specific information. Since most of this is in the public domain, and I do not pretend to add any new information, I have constructed my own analysis by combining different sources, without specifically referring to the

these materials together in a coherent interpretive framework, using the standard methodology for the study of social movements. Indeed, the global Islamic networks, symbolically represented by al-Qaeda, constitute a special type of social movement, by which I understand: purposive collective action aimed at changing the dominant values and institutions of society on behalf of the values and interests that are meaningful for the actors of the movement. This is why, in accordance with the method presented in the introduction to this chapter, I will start with the characterization of the goals and values of al-Qaeda, in its own discourse, as this self-definition is what attracts its followers, and provides meaning for them. I will then detail the sequential development of al-Qaeda's actions over time, and identify the actors involved in the global fundamentalist networks, their supporting social bases (there are several), their forms of organization, their strategies, and their relationship to institutions in different contexts, and particularly to the state. Only after reconstructing the actual profile of the movement will we be able to relate it to the sources of its existence; that is, to the cultural, social, and political contradictions characterizing the global, network society.

One preliminary remark before undertaking our analysis. *The movement is in fact a very complex set of organizations and actors, which is not reducible to al-Qaeda.* I am not referring to Islamic fundamentalism or to the Islamist political movements around the

---

source used for each particular point, except in the case of actual quotes. This note should serve as a generic source not to the countless bibliographical sources that are available, but only to those that I found particularly useful. As of the end of 2002, the best-documented account of al-Qaeda is Gunaratna (2002), based on the direct interviewing of about 200 terrorists (according to the author), and on reports from Western intelligence services, as well as on original al-Qaeda documentary sources. Among the academic analyses of Islamism and religious fundamentalism that I found particularly rigorous and challenging, regardless of my own interpretation of the matter, are the studies by Lawrence (1989) and by Kepel (2000, consulted again in the 2002 American edition). An important contribution on the dynamics of religious terrorism is Juergensmeyer (2000). A clear analysis of the inner logic of al-Qaeda can be found in Abdel Majed (2001). On the historical/cultural relationship between the West and Islam, I continue to refer primarily to Said, particularly to his classic *Orientalism* (1979). The definitive strategic and organizational analysis of al-Qaeda, and other networks of opposition to global power, is by Arquilla and Rondfeldt (2001). Good documentary sources on financial networks supporting al-Qaeda, along with insightful analysis, can be found in Brisard and Dasquie (consulted in the updated American edition, 2002). On the Taliban, Pakistan, and Central Asia, a thorough analysis is provided by Rashid (2001). Bergen (2001) contributes a first-hand, perceptive report that sheds new light on some of the issues and facts. Jacquard (2002) documents the international connections of al-Qaeda, and provides some hints on its efforts to obtain weapons of mass destruction. The best account of the events that led to 9/11 is the investigative report by the team of *Der Spiegel*, Stefan Aust and Cordt Schnibben (2002). The references indicated are just a few selected windows on what has become the cottage industry of reporting, analysis, ideological statements, and geomilitary strategic studies of the global networks of terror. I have been able to consult a number of documents in Arabic thanks to valuable research assistance from Rana Tomaira, doctoral candidate at the University of California, Berkeley.

world. Islamic fundamentalism is a cultural construction based on the proclaimed primacy of religious identity. Political Islamism is a political ideology, based on this form of religious identity, which aims to seize power in the nation-state of a given society, as a necessary step in the process of building the *umma* of true believers throughout the world. The movement symbolically represented by *al-Qaeda*, and partly organized around it, is a different kind of movement. It is indeed based on Islamic fundamentalism, but it is explicitly global in the definition of its adversary, in its organization, in its support basis, and in its tactics. It is built around the definition of the adversary, rather than on a definition of its identity principle. It goes on the attack against the Crusaders, to free Muslim lands from the disbelievers, be it the Soviets in Afghanistan, the Americans in Saudi Arabia, or, down the line, the Jews in Palestine. And because it recognizes the United States as the power center of the West, and of the world's capitalist order, it wages war against the United States, everywhere, "from the heights of Moctezuma to the sands of Tripoli."[50] That a social movement, without significant support from any state, dared to confront the greatest superpower in history, around the planet, including on American soil, makes it a very special kind of social movement, regardless of the suicidal/murderous character of its enterprise.

As I will show, defined in this specific way, *al-Qaeda*, and Osama bin Laden, form only one component of the movement, but they are the symbol, the role models, and the main nodes of a vast, diversified network of terrorist groups, some of which are rooted in Islamist movements, but many of which are largely autonomous cells, or country-specific Islamic organizations. They are all inspired by a common hatred of the adversary, and a common belief in the goodness of martyrdom on behalf of Islam, as freely interpreted by each of the components of the movement. I will analyze in detail below the novelty, and dynamism, of this organizational structure, but from the outset I want to delimit the object of our study in this chapter. It is neither Islamic fundamentalism nor political Islamism, but the fundamentalist, terrorist, global network built around the World Islamic Front for the Jihad Against the Jews and the Crusaders (*al-Jabbah al-Islamiyyah al-'Alamiyyha Li-Qital al-Yahud Wal-Salibiyyin*) formed on February 23, 1998. It was established by Osama bin Laden and his *al-Qaeda* network; Muhammad Rabi' al-Zhawahiri, on behalf of the Egyptian Islamic *Jihad*; Shayyakh Mir Hamzah, representing the *Jamiat-ul-Ulema-e-Pakistan*; Fazlul Rahman, from the Jihad Move-

---

50   These words are from the anthem of the US Marine Corps.

ment of Bangladesh, and a number of undisclosed signatories. I use this formal event to identify more precisely the movement I will analyze, but the complexity of the movement goes far beyond the actors that came together on that date and in that form. It is an evolving network whose origins can be traced to the CIA-financed training camps for the anti-Soviet *mujahedeen* in Pakistan, and whose ramifications in the early twenty-first century extend to at least 65 countries and to numerous autonomous groups and factions of Islamic political movements. It is a global terror network, enacting global *jihad* against the global power of the United States and its allies, as well as against any power that oppresses Muslims, be it Russia, India, or the Philippines. Yet, to understand it, we must start with the values and beliefs that root the ardent desire of martyrdom in the hearts of thousands of young Muslims around the world.

The goals and values of al-Qaeda

The ultimate goal of *al-Qaeda* is no different from other Islamic fundamentalist movements (see chapter 1). It is the construction of the *umma*, or worldwide community of the believers, transcending the boundaries of nation-states. Muslim societies should be ruled according to the *shari'a*, that is the Qur'ān and the Hadiths, interpreted, as literally as possible, by the religious leaders of each land. The Taliban regime in Afghanistan came closest to the Islamic ideals espoused by bin Laden and his followers. Indeed, bin Laden acknowledged Mullah Mohammed Omar as Commander of the Faithful, having the right to wear the Cloak of the Prophet, Afghanistan's holiest relic. Bin Laden saw Afghanistan as the Medina of the twenty-first century, from where the reconquest of Mecca could be prepared.

The interpretation of Islam by *al-Qaeda*'s main leaders, bin Laden and al-Zhawahiri, was influenced by the fact that they were both Salafis. While associated with the strictly orthodox Wahhabism, predominant in Saudi Arabia, Salafism emphasizes the multi-ethnicity and multinational character of Islam. It is an integrist version of Islam that places accordance to the divine law, expressed in the *Salafi Dawah* (the Call of the Salafis) as the only guide for people's behavior and for the organization of society. Thus, in proclaiming the establishment of the World Islamic Front, on February 23, 1998, Osama bin Laden prefaced the pronouncement:

> Praise be to God, who revealed the Book, controls the clouds, defeats factionalism, and says in His Book: "But when the forbidden months

are past, then fight and slay the pagans wherever you find them, seize them, beleaguer them, and lie in wait for them in every stratagem [of war]"; and peace be upon our Prophet Muhammad bin-'Abdallah, who said: "I have been sent with the sword between my hands to ensure that no one but God is worshipped, God who put my livelihood under the shadow of my spear and who inflicts humiliation and scorn on those who disobey my orders."[51]

However, *what is distinctive to the identity principle on which al-Qaeda was built is the territorial expression of religious identity.* For bin Laden, the defense of Islam starts with the defense of the holy sites of Islam, Mecca, Medina, Jerusalem, occupied by the Christians and the Jews. Indeed, the presence of American troops in Saudi Arabia in the aftermath of the first Gulf War is what prompted bin Laden's split with the Saudi monarchy, and the beginning of his conspiracy against Western interests. The territoriality of Islam is a fundamental principle of *al-Qaeda*'s beliefs. It is the profanation of the holy sites, more than anything else, that justifies *jihad*, as in the time of the Muslim mobilization against the Crusaders. An important document of *al-Qaeda* states: "When the enemy enters that land of the Muslims, *jihad* becomes individually obligatory, according to all the jurists, *mufassirin* and *muhaddithin*,"[52] echoing bin Laden's "Declaration of Jihad on the Americans Occupying the Country of the Two Sacred Places," on August 23, 1996: "The Muslims have realized that they are the main target of the aggression of the coalition of the Jews and of the Crusaders... The latest of these assaults is the greatest disaster since the death of the Prophet Muhammad (Peace be upon him) – that is the occupation of the country of the two sacred mosques – the home ground of Islam."[53] Therefore, as stated by bin Laden in February 1998, "It is a duty now on every tribe in the Arabian peninsula to fight, *jihad*, the cause of Allah and to cleanse the land from those occupiers."[54] However, the principle of territoriality does not refer to the territory of the nation-state, a pagan institution, but to the inviolability of the holy sites, and of the Muslim land, any land where Muslims live. It is the territory as expression of the *umma*, of the community of believers. It is the domain of God, not the space of the state.

Bin Laden and *al-Qaeda* are not preoccupied with the kind of Islamic society they want to build. And even less with the accuracy

51   Quoted by Gunaratna (2002: 88).
52   Quoted by Gunaratna (2002: 87).
53   Quoted by Bergen (2001: 93–4).
54   Quoted by Gunaratna (2002: 91).

of their reading of Islamic teachings. In their view, everything needed to live according to God's will is already written in the Book (in spite of the fact that of the 6,666 verses of the Qur'ān less than 300 refer to institutional rules). The reason for this simplified view of Islam is that they are pragmatic militants; they know that their immediate task is to engage in a most difficult struggle against a powerful, multi-faceted enemy. So, the process is more important than the ultimate outcome, a goal that is distant in time. Because the liberation of Muslim lands cannot be accomplished only in these lands, it is necessary to attack the enemy at its core, striking in all lands and in all forms, until forcing the withdrawal of the occupier. Ultimately, the Muslim lands will be freed, as was accomplished centuries ago against the Crusaders. This territorialized religious identity is a resistance identity, not a project identity. It does not propose a program for society, or for humankind, because *Jahiliya* has taken over the whole world, including Muslim societies, so that a new holy war has to be waged, fulfilling anew the pledge contained in the Hadith of the Prophet Muhammad on his deathbed: "If Allah wills and I live, God willing I will expel the Jews and the Christians from Arabia."[55]

But this resistance identity has an offensive, global projection due to the nature of the adversary. The characterization of this adversary, the source of all evil for contemporary, fundamentalist Islam, is what defines the specificity of *al-Qaeda*. Who is this adversary?

The political regimes of Muslim countries are oppressing Muslims, either because they are secular regimes or because, as in the case of Saudi Arabia, they have become subordinates of the Western powers, and particularly of the United States. But they are not the real enemy. They may be targeted as pawns of the Crusaders, but fighters of Islam must concentrate their struggle on the sources of oppression. Zionism is the enemy because it occupies Jerusalem, oppresses the Palestinians, and threatens the Arabs. States around the world oppress, exploit, and kill Muslims:

> to the extent that the Muslims' blood has become the cheapest in the eyes of the "world", and their wealth has become a loot, in the hands of their enemies. Their blood was spilled in Palestine and Iraq. The horrifying pictures of the massacre of Qana, Lebanon, are still fresh in our memories. Massacres in Tajikistan, Burma, Kashmir, Assam, the Philippines, Fatani, Ogaden, Somalia, Eritrea, Chechnya, and Bosnia have taken place, massacres that sent shivers through the body, and shake the conscience. All of this – and the world watched and heard, and not only did they not respond to the atrocities, but also, under a

---

55 Quoted by Bergen (2001: 94).

> clear conspiracy – between the USA and its allies, under the cover of the iniquitous "United Nations" – the dispossessed people were even prevented from obtaining arms to defend themselves. The people of Islam awakened, and realised that they were the main target for the aggression of the Zionist–Crusader alliance.[56]

There is a profound feeling of injustice, of humiliation, in these paragraphs, and in similar texts. There is compassion for the suffering of millions of Muslims, and this suffering is perceived to be inherent in their marginalization by the powers-that-be, ultimately the Western powers. Hence the mockery that, in the views of bin Laden, represents the discourse in terms of "human rights"which comes from the same powers that ignore the humanity of Muslims. Observers could certainly object to the inadequate factual basis of this excessive perception. But, when understanding a social movement, what is objective is the perception of the actors who constitute this movement. And *al-Qaeda*'s militants are clearly enraged by the oppression and humiliation that they observe in the Muslim world, even if many of them are members of the affluent elites of this world, a familiar occurrence in the history of social movements, as young idealists born into the social elites embrace revolutionary causes to fight against perceived injustice.

In *al-Qaeda*'s definition of goals, regimes oppressing Muslims around the world should be overthrown, including the Saudi monarchy which allowed the holy sites to be in the hands of Crusaders. This would pave the way to build a true Islamic society. *But the real threat for Muslims is the worldwide conspiracy against Islam, led by the United States*. Traitor Muslim regimes, and secular oppressive regimes, rely, ultimately, on the Crusader–Zionist power, represented by the United States, and its surrogate state, Israel. And because bin Laden and *al-Qaeda* went through the experience of defeating a world superpower, the Soviet Union, in Afghanistan, and since they believed that this defeat brought down the Soviet empire, they undertook the struggle against the United States, now identified as the enemy, with the conviction that they could ultimately force its withdrawal from Muslims lands, which could then be freed from their apostate rulers.

Thus, in *al-Qaeda*'s case, the strategic goals of the movement become more important than the values around which the movement was constructed. The "struggle on behalf of Islam"(the literal meaning of the word *jihad*) mutated in the practice of the movement into the use of Islam on behalf of the struggle. The most important

---

56   Bin Laden (1996), quoted by Gunaratna (2002: 90).

expression of this switch of goals is the relevance of martyrdom in the practice of *al-Qaeda*. Martyrdom, as a valued practice, provides *al-Qaeda* with the most effective weapon (humans as weapons), and the most intimidating tactics: there is no negotiation, no surrender, no way out, other than annihilation of the enemy, or the *mujahedeen*'s own grateful death. These specific goals of the movement define its tactics, its organization, its evolution.

The evolving process of al-Qaeda's struggle

The formation of *al-Qaeda*'s network, and the development of its struggle, went through six distinct stages between the early 1980s and the early years of the twenty-first century. The first stage was linked to the resistance to the Soviet occupation of Afghanistan in 1979. The resistance was organized by the CIA, the ISI (Pakistani Intelligence Service), and the Saudi Intelligence Service. The CIA provided money, weapons (including Stinger missiles), and decided the general strategy, allowing the Pakistanis, and the Afghan warlords, direction of operations on the ground. Saudi Arabia financed the war effort and set up the connection with the Muslim volunteers who joined the struggle from all over the world (indeed, the Saudi Airline offered 75 percent discount tickets to volunteers going to Pakistan to fight *jihad* – one way ticket). Bin Laden was an essential part of this connection: first, because he initiated the financing with his family's money, and led by example in joining the struggle personally; secondly, because he actually worked for Prince Turki ibn Faisal ibn Abdelaziz, the head of the Saudi intelligence service, and coordinated his actions with his sponsors in the Saudi government. While the Arab volunteers played a secondary role in the operations against the Soviets (although they participated in combat), they received training and indoctrination in the Afghan refugee and fighters camps in Pakistan. The original matrix of *al-Qaeda* networks was created in these camps, the so-called Arab Afghans. Thus, while it is inexact to say that bin Laden was an agent of the CIA, it was with CIA support that these camps and the subsequent networks of *mujahedeen* were constituted. It is fair to say that the last war of the Cold War period engendered the first global war of the information age: the network war launched by the Islamic networks of terror against the United States, in a process of radicalization that was emboldened by the defeat of the Soviets in Afghanistan.

The second stage of the struggle enacted by these networks was not global but local. Militants trained in the Afghan camps, and returning to their countries, linked up with Islamic fundamentalist movements that were engaged in a political–military battle against their own national governments. This was particularly the case in Algeria and in Egypt (see chapter 1). These movements by and large failed in transforming their political support into an effective assault on state power. The weaker they became, the greater the orientation of the most radical groups toward terror as a form of struggle, as was particularly the case with GIA in Algeria and with Islamic *Jihad* in Egypt.

At about the same time, in the context of the Gulf War, bin Laden joined the Saudi Islamic dissidents in the critique of the Saudi regime, whom they accused of betraying the principles of Islam by allowing the occupation of the holy land of Arabia by American troops. However, in sharp contrast with other countries, Islamic fundamentalists did not engage in open struggle against the Saudi monarchy, in spite of their denunciation of the Saudi rulers, and in spite of the fact that they were severely repressed, and some of them executed. The terrorist attacks in Saudi Arabia were concentrated on US troops and US installations. The Saudi authorities managed the repression of these activities by themselves and did not let the US interfere in the conflict. Although reliable information is not public on this matter, it is plausible to think that the Saudi elite was (and is) itself split on its relationship with the fundamentalist movements, as was demonstrated by their support of the Taliban until the US attack on Afghanistan. Thus, *al-Qaeda* refrained from targeting the Saudi regime, and the Saudi elite kept the channels of communication open with bin Laden. On the other hand, *al-Qaeda* supported, with money, weapons, and volunteers, the struggles of Muslims around the work, particularly in Bosnia, Chechnya, Kashmir, and the Philippines.

The third stage, occurring at different times in different areas of the world, witnessed the beginning of the direct attack by *al-Qaeda*, and related networks, against symbols of American power and interest. The first one, full of premonition, was the bombing of New York's World Trade Center in 1993. Attacks against US installations in Saudi Arabia, as well as isolated events in other areas of the world, were also part of this open declaration of war against the United States. But the most significant of these attacks took place in Somalia, in cooperation with Somali warlords, with the killing, in 1993, of a group of US special forces soldiers who could be isolated and decimated, their bodies then dragged through the streets of Mogadishu, in full exposure to the global media. This humiliating defeat prompted the US to leave Somalia to avoid further involvement in a war that was perceived by the Clinton Administration to be of minimal interest to national security. It was the Somalia episode that convinced bin Laden that victory against the US was possible, if only the price Americans had to pay with their own lives could be increased sharply. As we know, this was a gross underestimation of American determination once confronted with a direct threat.

The fourth stage concentrated on supporting movements in countries where a power base could be achieved by truly Islamic fundamentalist forces. This was the case in the Sudan, where bin Laden established his base in 1992 after fleeing Saudi Arabia, helping with funding, and global networking, in exchange for a support base, including training camps and financial institutions. It was, above all, the case in Afghanistan, with the support of the Taliban, as an alternative to the warlords who had brought destruction and death to the whole country. The support of the successful Taliban campaign reproduced to some extent the alliance against the Soviets. It was spearheaded by the Pakistani ISI, financed by the Saudis, and fully supported by bin Laden, providing the legitimacy of his personal support, his financial backing, and the help of *al-Qaeda* cadres. As for the US, documents from reliable sources[57] indicate the more or less tacit consent of the US administration to Taliban power until 1999, from a conviction that it was the way to bring order to the country, and in the hope of improving the chances of building the strategic pipeline to export Central Asian gas and oil through Afghanistan.[58] Bin Laden made Afghanistan the key node of his global *jihad*, and this is why he praised Mullah Omar as a saint, and linked his fate to the fate of the Taliban. Here again, bin Laden's calculation was that the US would never engage in anything resembling the Vietnam War. He was right, but did not realize that technology and military organization had nothing to do with the conditions under which the Vietnam War – or, for that matter, the Soviet war in Afghanistan – had been fought.

The fifth stage came in 1998 when, faced with increasing pressure from the US on the Saudis and the Sudanese to deliver bin Laden, *al-Qaeda* moved toward open confrontation with the superpower, and bombed the US embassies in Nairobi and Dar es Salaam; then, escalating their offensive, in 2000 they gravely damaged the *USS Cole* in Aden (a direct act of war on a powerful ship); and, ultimately, attacked the heart of the US on Sepember 11, 2001. This stage can be seen as the beginning of the network war between *al-Qaeda*, and its associated organizations, and the US and its allies.

---

57   Brisard and Dasquie (2002).
58   Rashid (2001).

The sixth stage is open-ended at the time of writing. It refers to the US-led counter-offensive that destroyed the Taliban regime in Afghanistan, obliterated the basis of *al-Qaeda* in that country, and launched a global manhunt for *al-Qaeda* cadres and leaders, which, in spite of superficial accounts to the contrary, yielded considerable results. At the time of writing, no one really knows the fate of bin Laden, although some information points to the possibility of his survival but in very poor health, reducing him largely to a symbolic role rather than the commander of the network. Al-Zhawahiri, second in command to bin Laden, Shaikh Mohammed, chief of operations of *al-Qaeda*, and a number of other cadres, were still at large, but thousands of activists, including experienced military leaders and organizers have been killed or are prisoners of the US and its allies. And yet, *al-Qaeda* does not seem to have been entirely destroyed because of its global networking structure, to which I will refer below. Furthermore, many associated networks in a number of countries, including the US, and particularly in Pakistan and South-east Asia, seem capable of operating along similar lines of thought and action. It is plausible that, without addressing the structural causes and social bases that engendered *al-Qaeda*, this network war could continue for years to come, in a series of actions and reactions of unpredictable consequences.

Throughout these developments, the Palestinian struggle remained as a separate issue. While *al-Qaeda* squarely places Israel and the Jews as the enemy, indistinguishable from the United States, its support for the Palestinian cause is essentially symbolic. This is partly because the Palestinians have their own resources, from Saudi Arabia among other sources, and enough fighters and martyrs of their own, but also partly because the mainstream of the Palestinian liberation movement is a nationalist movement aimed at the construction of a nation-state, not exactly *al-Qaeda*'s goal. While there are certainly common features between *al-Qaeda* and Palestinian organizations such as Hamas and Islamic *Jihad*, there seems to be a division of labor according to which the Palestinians fight Israel, country-based Islamic movements fight their oppressing states, as is the case with the Chechens in Russia or the Kashmiri in India, while *al-Qaeda* and its associated networks take on the US on a global stage. Nor did the confrontation between the US and Iraq dovetail with these networks, even though bin Laden repeatedly used the plight of Iraqi children as proof of the violation of the human rights of Muslims by the West, and the US claimed, without proof, the links between Saddam Hussein and *al-Qaeda* as a reason to attack Iraq. The profoundly nationalist and lay character of Saddam Hussein's regime, and its savage repression of Shiite Muslims, explains the considerable distance between *al-Qaeda* and Iraq, in spite of unreliable reports to the contrary. However, in the event of a general conflagration in the Middle East, after the war in Iraq, with radicalization of the struggle in Palestine and Israel, and possible conflict with Hezbollah and Syria, it is likely that *al-Qaeda* would time and coordinate its actions in the context of generalized war against Israel and the US – indeed, this is the horizon it is aiming for.

This summarizes *al-Qaeda*'s goals and sequence of actions. But who are the actors engaged in *al-Qaeda*? What are the bases of The Base?[59]

The mujahedeen *and their support bases*

In characterizing the actors involved in the Islamic global network of terror, it is necessary to differentiate between *al-Qaeda* and its con- nected networks. It is also essential to distinguish the militants them- selves from the groups that support them, and from the constituencies that the movement aspires to influence and mobilize.

Let us start with the critical characterization: who are the members of *al-Qaeda*? The first, and essential, feature is that they come from a multiplicity of ethnic and national backgrounds, even if bin Laden himself, and the original leadership of *al-Qaeda*, are Arabs. If we take as an indicator the composition of the 055 Brigade, the all-*al-Qaeda* unit that fought to the end in Afghanistan, alongside the Taliban, it included Arabs (Saudis, Egyptians, Yemenis, Jordanians, Palestinians, Sudanese, Algerians, Moroccans, Tunisians, Libyans, Lebanese), as well as Pakistanis, Bangladeshis, Chechens, Tajiks, Uzbeks, Kyrgiz, Kazaks, Filipinos, Malaysians, Indonesians, Chinese, and even a few Americans, including a very white one. Furthermore, European Muslims, and Muslims based in Europe, particularly in Germany, the UK, Spain, and France, were critical in setting up the *al-Qaeda* infrastructure that prepared for 9/11. This is without considering the multiple nodes that radical Islamic groups have developed in their own countries, such as the Moro Liberation Front and *Abbu Sayyaf* in the Philippines or *Jamaah Islamiyah* in Indonesia. Al-Qaeda, strictly speaking, is a multi-ethnic, multinational network, united around the values and goals that I analyzed above.

It is in fact no surprise that the multiplicity of the ethnic/national backgrounds does not impede the common goal of protecting the holy sites in the Arabian peninsula, and Jerusalem, as these are the places

59 *Al-Qaeda in Arabic means "The Base."*

of pilgrimage and prayers for Muslims throughout the whole world: Islam is a global community spiritually oriented toward highly localized holy sites – literally in the direction of the daily prayers. This is why, if these holy sites have been, in the views of the faithful, sullied by the presence of disbelievers, the prayers cannot reach God. Only if we understand this process of materialized, spiritual communication can we sense the fundamental wound felt by the fundamentalists.

How did these actors from such diverse origins come into contact and ultimately form *al-Qaeda*? As mentioned above, the original nucleus was formed in the Pakistani camps where Muslim volunteers came from all over to help the Afghan *mujahedeen* fight the Soviets. The personal bonds, common ideology, and shared worldview of *al-Qaeda* were formed in these camps, and in the hard battles that these *mujahedeen* fought together against the Soviets. When the Soviets were forced to withdraw from Afghanistan, these volunteers continued to fight for the liberation of Muslim lands, of all lands. Many continued to fight in Afghanistan alongside the Taliban which, with the support of Pakistan and Saudi Arabia, opposed the factions that had seized power in Kabul. The Taliban (Islamic students, many of them trained in the *madrassas* – Islamic schools – in Pakistan) opposed the other factions for a variety of reasons: most of the warlords were not ethnically *pashtun* (as were most of the Taliban, and the Pakistanis of the border regions); some of the factions in power in Kabul were pro-Iranian Shiites, while the Taliban, like bin Laden, were Sunnis; many of the Afghan factions were led by mercenary warlords; all were more interested in squeezing the people than in defending Islamic principles; and most were opposed to Pakistani and Saudi influence. Thus, the CIA supported Pakistan and Saudi Arabia in their support of the *mujahedeen*, and later on, of the Taliban. When the CIA disengaged itself from Afghanistan, without further interest once the Soviet Union's influence ended, Pakistan and Saudi Arabia used the Taliban to control Afghanistan.

The fighters trained in the camps spread themselves around the Muslim world, constituting, for instance, the main nucleus of radical Islamic guerrillas in Algeria and Egypt, and connecting with revolutionary Islamic groups in the Philippines, in Yemen, in the Sudan, in Indonesia, in Bosnia, and other countries. Bin Laden returned to Saudi Arabia but, after his split with the Saudi regime (see below), established himself in the Sudan, then in Afghanistan, and began the struggle against the US in New York (the 1993 bombing of the World Trade Center), Saudi Arabia, Somalia, East Africa, Yemen, and beyond. Using his money and, more importantly, his charisma, and his leadership, bin Laden kept together a network of the veterans of the Afghan camps, and used this network to recruit and train a new generation of fighters, reproducing what they had learned from their Pakistani/Afghan experience. This original network, and its offspring, is the essential collective actor that constituted *al-Qaeda* and its expanded global network. This is why it is multi-ethnic and multi-national. This is also why it is such a special actor. It is not a class, or an ethnic group, or a national group, or a regional group, or the expression of a revolt against economic exploitation. It is certainly a group based on religious identity, but with no specific social attach-ment, except for the shared experience of the first religious war in Afghanistan. It is what in other fields of social science we conceptual-ize as a "community of practice," the practice in this case being *jihad*, with the compliments of the CIA and its allied secret services.

Who are the people, from multiple origins, participating in these special "communities of practice"? Naturally, we have no reliable statistics on *al-Qaeda*'s composition; what could come close to it, the list of prisoners in Guantanamo and other places, is off limits, since most of the prisoners are secretly detained by the US authorities. But we have some elements to draw a hypothetical sketch of the socio-demographic characteristics and biographies of at least a seg-ment of *al-Qaeda*, starting with those involved in the 9/11 attacks. They were all male and young, in their twenties and early thirties, the oldest being the leader, Mohammed Atta who was 34. This seems to have been the case for most of the activists, although some of the top leaders, for example, al-Zhawahiri, are of bin Laden's generation (born in Riyadh in 1957). Bin Laden often refers to the young fighters of Islam who will strike fear in the hearts of the enemy: "The cru-saders have agreed to devour us and the nations of the world have placed us before judgment, and we have no one left for us, after God, but the youth that have not been burdened by life's filth."[60] Although this reliance on young people is a typical feature of armed militant groups, it also indicates the frame of mind and determination of young idealists ready to die, and very often looking forward to martyrdom.

Focusing on the 9/11 suicidal group, the multi-ethnicity of *al-Qaeda* is somewhat reduced: 15 of the 19 were born in Saudi Arabia, two in the United Arab Emirates, one in Lebanon and one (the leader) in Egypt. The first circle of support was more diversified: out of five identified, two were Algerian French, one Yemeni, one Moroccan, and one Moroccan German; all Arab (meaning, essentially, from Arabic-speaking countries). Thus, while the overall network is

60   Osama bin Laden, Al Jazeera News Network, September 20, 2001.

multi-ethnic and multinational, the core group and trusted activists seem to come from the Arabian peninsula and Egypt; in fact, the original components of the *al-Qaeda* network, constituted around bin Laden (a Saudi of Yemeni origin) and al-Zhawahiri (an Egyptian). This indicates another important feature: personal knowledge, sometimes through family ties, or tribal allegiances in the case of Arabia, is crucial to be admitted to the core of the network, where central planning of major operations takes place, and from where the fatwas are issued.

Interestingly, there are very few Palestinians associated with *al-Qaeda*. It would seem that, while the liberation of Palestine, and the destruction of Israel, are among the goals of *al-Qaeda*, bin Laden always considered that Palestinian nationalism was not a true Islamic movement, and could easily be pacified by an accommodation with Israel on a future Palestinian state. On the other hand, Chechens, Afghans, Kashmiris, and Pakistanis worked closely with bin Laden and his Arab militants, but they were supposed to take care of the liberation of their own land, as potential bases for *al-Qaeda*, while the elite group of *al-Qaeda*, mainly built around its Arab nucleus, would confront the US in the rest of the world. A critical connection here is the European Arab and Muslim minorities, in which Islamic movements of various origins have acquired a sizable influence, providing a recruiting ground for *al-Qaeda*, as illustrated by a number of incidents in which Arabs living in, or citizens of, the UK, Germany, France, and Spain have played a significant role in the strategy of global terror.

In sum, while multi-ethnicity is a characteristic of the overall network of networks around *al-Qaeda*, there seems to be a specialization of tasks by origin and location: those engaged in territorial liberation struggles, for example Chechens, are essentially dedicated to their task on the ground, fighting against Russia, and being helped by *al-Qaeda*, with cadres, supplies, and money, more than they contribute to the network. The core of *al-Qaeda* is built around personal ties of trust, and this means, essentially, Arabs from the Arab peninsula and Egypt. And the Arab and Muslim diaspora in Europe and the United States is targeted as a potential supplier of activists with greater capacity to operate in the heart of the enemy's territory. Thus, ethnicity and nationality become subsumed in the strategic goals of organizing and operating the network: being from Arabia is not significant in itself, what counts is being related to some personal network that can be trusted. Once again we find that *al-Qaeda*'s logic revolves around the long-term strategy of facing, and ultimately destroying, a mighty adversary – which happens to be the Great Satan.

A significant number of *al-Qaeda*'s cadres who are known come from well-to-do families and are highly educated. The core group of 9/11 attackers was made up of graduate engineering students from Hamburg's Technical University, an engineering school with a very good reputation. The leader of the group, Mohammed Atta, studied architecture and urban planning in the School. Indeed, one of his open grievances against the West concerned the destruction of traditional architecture, and traditional cities, by the process of market-led urbanization. He abhorred modern structures, and skyscrapers, a perfect ideological fit for the mission he was assigned to accomplish. Muhammad Rabi' al-Zhawahiri, undoubtedly *al-Qaeda*'s leader after bin Laden, is a physician and comes from a very respected intellectual family in Egypt: his grandfather was sheikh of the Al-Azhar mosque, his father was a professor of medicine, and his mother was the daughter of the president of the University of Cairo.

The military commanders of *al-Qaeda* also have an elite pedigree. Before being arrested in September 1998, Ali Mohammed was for several years the leading military trainer for *al-Qaeda*. Born in Alexandria, Egypt, he went to the military academy in Cairo, reaching the grade of major in the Egyptian army, while also graduating in psychology from the University of Alexandria. While being secretly a member of Egyptian *Jihad*, he emigrated to the US, became a US citizen, and became an instructor in the US Army Special Warfare Center at Fort Bragg. After leaving the army, he alternated between training Islamist militants, including bin Laden's bodyguards, and unknown missions in the Middle East, allegedly on behalf of American intelligence services. In the UK, another key *al-Qaeda* member, Anas al-Liby, who lived in Manchester until 1999, was a highly skilled computer expert, who trained *al-Qaeda* members in surveillance techniques. The list could go on.

It appears that the cadres of the terrorist network are highly educated professionals, which, in the Middle East, means almost necessarily that they come from affluent families. Their family background includes businessmen, professionals (doctors, lawyers), and intellectuals. These young men grew up in modernity, in the age of informationalization and globalization. They traveled to the West, many were deeply immersed in Europe or in the United States, in some cases they married Western women, and they related naturally, and peacefully, to their personal environment in the West. In addition, as mentioned above, some of them were actually born in, or became citizens of, Western countries. They could have had a cozy professional life, as many professionals of the Middle East do, both in the West, and in the Westernized sectors of their Muslim societies. Therefore, they were not revolting against their social exclusion. Indeed, they were, to some extent, part of the excluders in terms of their class origins. While compassion for impoverished Muslims around the world is an important theme of their ideology, there is no direct connection between these militants and the poor of the world. They hope, and expect, that the masses will one day rise up against their masters. Indeed, this is their strategic hope. But not as exploited, but as true Muslims, in search of an Islamic world in which wealth will be shared according to God's timeless principles.

The social origins of the *al-Qaeda* leadership and cadres are not an expression of the popular classes. They are, by and large, professionals, usually from the technical, scientific, and medical professions. They are familiar with advanced technology, and they use it skillfully to the benefit of their cause. They are not traditionalists in this sense. They are hypermodernists. They propose an alternative path of social development, around a different set of principles, in direct contradiction with the rules and logic of capitalist globalization and modernization based on Western values. In their militant opposition they are in fact powerfully supported by a number of wealthy people and prosperous business groups from the Middle East, particularly from the Arabian peninsula. Thus, rather than being a movement of the socially excluded against the capitalist global order, it is a self-righteous affirmation of the religious values of a segment of the Muslim intelligentsia, supported by a fraction of Middle Eastern business groups. "It is *not* the economy, stupid!" It is all about values and contradictory paths of modernity. But why do these business groups play with fire, destroying the world from which they exact their high profits? And how can these alternative paths of modernity lead to the celebration of mass murder as the right course of action on behalf of Islam? To answer these two essential questions, it will be useful to reflect on the personal trajectory of the charismatic leader of *al-Qaeda*, Osama bin Laden.

The young lion of the global jihad: Osama bin Laden[61]

So much has been written about Osama bin Laden in the media, and in mass-market books, that there is no point in repeating his biography here. Instead, I will highlight the moments and events in his personal trajectory that give meaning to the formation, orientation, and practice of *al-Qaeda*.

---

61   Osama in Arabic means "young lion."

If *al-Qaeda*'s cadres are often from affluent families, bin Laden was a member of the business oligarchy of Saudi Arabia. The assets of the bin Laden family's group are estimated to be at least US $5 billion, in a diversified pattern of investment beyond its original empire in construction and public works. Osama himself was a well-trained professional, who graduated in economics and public administration from the elite Abdul Aziz University in Jeddah. He also worked in the family's construction business, specializing (interestingly enough) in demolition work.

The family connection is extremely important not only to understanding Osama's evolution, but also as a window into the contradictory nature of the Saudi elite. Osama's father, Mohammed, a self-made immigrant entrepreneur from Yemen, was named Minister of Construction Works by King Faisal, in recognition of his help in the power struggle to win the crown. Bin Laden's company received the commission to restore and maintain the holy sites of Mecca and Medina, and was also in charge of the reconstruction project of the Grand Mosque of Jerusalem. Thus, the priority given by Osama to the integrity of the Muslim holy sites is for him a very concrete experience, having grown up in Medina, and having prayed frequently in the three holy sites, a rare privilege for a Muslim. Furthermore, Osama's father, who died in a plane crash when he was ten years old, was a very religious man, and for Osama he remained a role model; Osama was convinced that his father would have approved of his practice of *jihad*. Through the family connection, Osama had access to the royal family, and to the heights of Saudi power, cooperating directly from 1980 with Prince Turki ibn Faisal ibn Abdelaziz, the head of the Saudi intelligence service. In other words, Osama bin Laden was a member of the Saudi economic and political elite, and worked with the intelligence service until the early 1990s at least, having helped the Saudi intelligence service to organize the anti-communist *jihad* in South Yemen, after he returned from the war in Afghanistan in February 1989.

The ideological influences he received at university were also meaningful, as we shall see in the personal connection between the texts of Islamism and his coming into the practice of *jihad*. While a university student he came into contact with the Muslim Brotherhood, and with two of its most influential teachers of Islamic studies. One of them was Muhammad Qtub, the brother of perhaps the most significant Islamist, Sayyid Qtub, executed in Egypt in 1966, and an icon of the Islamist movement (see chapter 1). The other was Abdullah Azzam, a Palestinian theologian, doctor in Islamic jusriprudence from Cairo's al-Azhar University, who, in 1980, moved to Pakistan, and preached the need to help the *mujahedeen* to expel the Soviets from Afghanistan and the infidels from all Muslim lands. He wrote a well-publicized pamphlet, "Defending Muslim Territory is the Most Important Duty," and undertook the project himself, traveling around the world, raising funds for the Muslim volunteers to fight in Afghanistan, and organizing a base in Pakistan for those responding to the call. Under the control of the ISI, the Pakistani secret service, in 1984 Azzam organized the Afghan Service Bureau, or MAK, which was the organizational platform to train and mobilize the Arabs and other Muslim volunteers to fight the Soviets. Osama bin Laden joined his intellectual and political mentor, Azzam, and helped to finance MAK with his own funds and his connection to Saudi Arabia. In fact, bin Laden heard the call to liberate Afghanistan even earlier than Azzam, having traveled in 1979 to Pakistan, before returning to Saudi Arabia to raise funds and support, which he personally managed in Pakistan, building camps, roads, and bunkers, training fighters, and ultimately leading them personally into battle.

In the process, bin Laden came close to the most radical, Egyptian faction of MAK, and supported its strategy to expand *jihad* beyond Afghanistan, engaging in terrorism, as the only workable tactics to confront an enemy even more powerful than the Soviet Union. Azzam opposed the move, advising that they concentrate first on making Afghanistan an Islamic country (even after the withdrawal of the Soviets there was still a pro-Soviet government in power), and rejecting terrorism for both moral and tactical reasons. In November 1989, Azzam and his two sons were assassinated, probably by the Egyptian faction of MAK. Although the circumstances of the killing are still unclear, and while Osama continued to refer to the teachings of Azzam as his guide, Gunaratna, one the leading analysts on *al-Qaeda*, writes that Osama "sanctioned, if not condoned the murder,"[62] in order to free *al-Qaeda* from the strict following of Azzam's principles and advice. At any rate, after Azzam's death, Osama bin Laden became the unchallenged leader of MAK, and of the whole support network, and started to build the foundations of the global offensive strategy that was suggested in the writings of Qtub. The episode (regardless of responsibility for the killing) reveals in bin Laden a special mixture of spirituality and faith with a ruthless determination in implementing the will of God in the practice of the struggle, a mixture that appears to have become a feature of *al-Qaeda*.

62   Gunaratna (2002: 23).

The turning point of bin Laden's struggle came in February 1991 when he publicly opposed the presence of American troops in Saudi Arabia after the end of the Gulf War. In a fatwa issued by *al-Qaeda* in August 1996, bin Laden explained why he was convinced in 1991 that the Saudi monarchy had to be overthrown: "Ignoring the divine shari'ah law; depriving people of their legitimate rights; allowing the Americans to occupy the land of the two Holy Places; imprisonment, unjustly, of the sincere scholars ... Through this course of action the regime has torn off its legitimacy," and he went on to denounce the profanation of the holy places through ungodly practices and the occupation by infidels:

> Manmade laws are put forward permitting what has been forbidden by Allah such as usury (*riba*) and other matters. Banks dealing with usury are competing for land with the two Holy Places and declaring war against Allah by disobeying His order... All this taking place in the vicinity of the Holy Mosque in the Holy Land... There is no more important duty than pushing the Americans out of the holy land.[63]

Breaking with his homeland and with the Saudi elite, which he and his father had loyally served throughout their lives, was the definitive gesture by which bin Laden confronted the Saudi fundamentalist Wahhabite regime with its contradictory double role as Guardian of the Holy Sites and Guardian of Western oil. It cost him his Saudi citizenship, and his assets were seized. However, his family, while formally breaking with him, continued to see him, visiting him in the Sudan, and perhaps continued to provide financial support for him. This family bond, critical for self-esteem in Arab culture, has been a source of strength for bin Laden, and for many of his followers.

Bin Laden went back to Pakistan in April 1991 to organize terrorism against foreigners in Saudi Arabia, and everywhere his networks could strike, now strengthened by the support of Saudi dissidents who acknowledged him as the leader of their resistance. Then he moved to the Sudan, at the invitation of Hasan al-Turabi, the spiritual guide of the National Islamic Front, which seized power in 1989. With the support of the Sudan, bin Laden joined forces with the remnants of Egyptian Islamic terrorist groups, organized training camps in the Sudan, and called upon the network of Islamic militants that he had built around *al-Qaeda* and the MAK during the first Afghan War. It is estimated that over 1,000 fighters responded to the call. He invested

63   Quoted by Gunaratna (2002: 28–9).

the money he could save (around $ 50 million) in the Sudan, and through the informal money markets of the Middle East, making substantial profits which made him financially independent of any state support.

In the following years, bin Laden and his associates master-minded and executed a series of bombings and assassinations in various countries, as mentioned above. For some time, many of these actions were attributed to different sources by Middle Eastern governments, and American intelligence services, partly because of lack of accurate information, and partly because they were fearful of the publicity that could benefit bin Laden. Nonetheless, word came out, particularly after the bombing of the US embassies in Kenya and Tanzania in 1998, and made bin Laden, at the same time, public enemy number one for the US and a mythical hero for thousands of disaffected Muslim youth. Bin Laden ceased to be just an organizer, and a financier, and became the charismatic leader of the radical Islamic global networks. He built on his prestige in the Afghan War, as the *mujahedeen* recognized his sincere devotion to the cause, and his willingness to share their life and death, coming from one of the most privileged family backgrounds in Arabia. His uncompromising attitude, his willingness to confront anyone standing in the way of his religious principles, including the revered House of Saud, and the American superpower, induced both respect and admiration. Bin Laden, the person, became Osama, the myth. The power of the myth attracted capital and labor to his enterprise. His networks of terror received the support of thousands of would-be young martyrs, while also benefiting from the funding provided by rich families and business groups of the Middle East in one of the most intriguing, and politically significant, ploys of the new geopolitics of the twenty-first century.

From bin Laden to bin Mahfouz: financial networks, Islamic networks, terrorist networks

Before and after 9/11, several reports have documented the extent to which a number of Saudis and rich Middle Eastern families and business groups have financed Islamic NGOs and Islamist fundamentalist groups around the world for a long period of time. The use of these funds to support activities linked to *al-Qaeda* has also been shown in some cases. Although many of these allegations are still under investigation, there are enough facts to assert the existence of a hidden relationship between financial institutions linked to the Saudi elite and the complex infrastructure that represents the lifeline of *al-Qaeda* and its global associates. In bringing these facts into our analytical picture we must keep a distance from two equal and opposite dangers: on the one hand, the potential fabrication and manipulation of information by Western and Israeli secret services to discredit, and ultimately criminalize, Islamic solidarity organizations around the world; on the other hand, the conspiracy theories that proliferate in the minds of an unsettled public opinion, seeing bin Laden and *al-Qaeda* as puppets of an Arab-American conspiracy that went out of control. So let us recall these facts, first of all, without going into the details that are widely published, and can be found in the sources cited.[64]

There are well-known connections between Islamic banks and financial institutions and Islamic charities and Islamic organizations around the world. This is a widespread practice, common to similar funding networks in other religions or cultures. In many instances, this funding comes from the management of *zakat* funds. *Zakat* is the religious tax in Saudi Arabia and other Islamic countries that requires anyone (person, business, or institution) buying financial assets to donate money to charitable causes. This has been an important source of finance for organizations, such as the International Islamic Relief Organization (IIRO), which has sponsored humanitarian programs worldwide, as well as self-help projects, and NGOs with a focus on Muslim populations. In a number of instances, local groups in the IIRO, and other similar organizations, have been connected to Islamic fundamentalist militants, and sometimes to the activities of individuals or groups related to *al-Qaeda*. This does not mean that the IIRO is part of *al-Qaeda*, as some intelligence services would have it. But it does mean that it is a useful channel to provide, indirectly, the funds needed by militants engaged in the struggle on behalf of Islam.

A second series of observations refers to the creation and support of Islamic international organizations by the Saudi regime, in its policy of diffusing Wahhabism throughout the world, particularly to counter the Shiite influence, and to fight in the defense of Muslim lands. The most significant example is the Muslim World League, created in 1962, and supported by Aramco (the leading oil company in the world and at that time an Arab-American company) and a consortium of Islamic banks. In cases where a major political strategy was at stake, as in Afghanistan or in South Yemen, the Saudi intelligence service intervened directly, in coordination with the financial support effort. The 4,000 or so princes of the royal family are expected to give generously to Islamic organizations which support Wahhabism, and,

---

64 On financial networks, see Brisard and Dasquie (2002).

more generally, to those organizations furthering the Islamic cause. The support was channeled by a network of financial institutions, at the heart of which were two banks: DMI, founded in 1981 by Mohammed al-Faisal, brother of the head of the Saudi secret service; and Dalla-al-Baraka, established in 1982 by Saleh Abdullah Kamel, who was Inspector General of Finance of the Saudi government. Some of the financial institutions in this network seem to have been used by bin Laden and his organizations's to channel and manage *al-Qaeda*'s own funds. For instance, Kamel was president of the Albaraka Bank-Sudan, and a major shareholder of the Tadamon Bank of Sudan, itself a major partner in the Al-Shamal Islamic Bank of Sudan, considered by the US government to have been the main financial institution used by bin Laden to finance his base in the Sudan.

Thirdly, Saudi families and companies established, particularly after the oil boom of the 1970s, a series of financial intermediaries to invest around the world, sometimes in dubious business practices, usually in association with Western banks, most notably the Bank of America. The most important case was the Bank of Credit and Commerce International (BCCI), created in 1972 by a Pakistani Shiite businessman, in association with several prominent business and political leaders from Kuwait, the United Arab Emirates, and Saudi Arabia, and the Bank of America. The BCCI, based in Luxembourg and the Cayman Islands, engaged in schemes of money-laundering and tax evasion, with ramifications in the United States, Panama, and Colombia (it was allegedly used by the narco-traffickers, particularly Pablo Escobar). After an international audit, it was finally liquidated by American and European authorities in July 1991. A number of connections have been established between the BCCI and the funding of Islamic organizations of different kinds, but the main connection seems to be to the shadowy world of money-laundering and unregulated financial deals where all the money is good, regardless of its origin.

There is, however, a more meaningful, personal connection between the BCCI, the Saudi financial elite, and Islamic networks through the most important figure on this stage of passions, interests, and ideologies: Khalid bin Mahfouz, in 2002 under house arrest in a hospital in Taif, Saudi Arabia. A member of the most influential family in the financial world of Saudi Arabia, he succeeded his father at the head of the bank that his father created in 1950, the National Commercial Bank (NCB), the first in Saudi Arabia, and the bank that manages the investments of the royal family. The bin Mahfouz family assets are estimated at about US$ 1.7 billion. He was a top executive in the BCCI, but survived the crisis by agreeing to a settlement payment of $ 245 million. At the helm of a vast, diversified business group, which includes at least 70 companies around the world, he sat on the boards of major Saudi and international corporations, including the Council of Aramco, by appointment of King Fahd. His family was close to the bin Laden family, as the two families come originally from the same province in South Yemen, Hadramauth. Indeed, Khalid bin Mahfouz's sister is one of the four wives of Osama bin Laden.

In 1998, after the bombing of the US embassies in Africa, the CIA charged the NCB with funding, in tens of millions of dollars, charity organizations with ties to Osama bin Laden. The Saudi government conducted its own investigation, leading to the dismissal and arrest of bin Mahfouz. Also, the Saudi government bought 50 percent of NCB shares, still leaving 36 percent to the bin Mahfouz family, including 10 percent for Khalid himself.

The financial connections get even murkier, and lean dangerously toward the fiction thriller or the stuff rejoiced in by conspiracy theorists, when we consider the connections of the bin Mahfouz and bin Laden families in the United States, and particularly in the land where America and Arabia meet around the shared networks of the oil industry: Texas. Abdullah Taha Bakhsh was the representative of the bin Laden family in the United States between 1976 and 1982. He currently represents Khalid bin Mahfouz's interests in Investcorp. Investcorp, located in Bahrain, and a subsidiary of holding companies in Luxembourg and the Cayman Islands, brings together the investment interests of several leading members of the Arab oil elite, including former oil ministers of Kuwait and Saudi Arabia. Investcorp counts on the association of Chase Manhattan Bank, and among its associates are several of the Saudi business players that were involved in the BCCI affair, including Bakhsh, Mohammed al-Zalil, and Bakr Mohammed bin Laden. Mohammed al-Zalil's company in Saudi Arabia has Khalid bin Mahfouz as the main shareholder. Al-Zalil also manages a network of 20 banks that includes the Tadamon Islamic Bank, whose Sudanese subsidiary was identified as managing Osama bin Laden's funds. As for Bakr Mohammed bin Laden, he is the older brother of Osama, and the head of the bin Laden group. The bin Laden group, together with the bin Mahfouz group, created a network of subsidiaries, including the Saudi Investment Company, managed by another brother of Osama. The Saudi Investment Company is the parent company of yet another network of investment companies registered in the Bahamas, the Cayman Islands, and Ireland. All the above-mentioned companies, working in a global investment environment, have, naturally, deep connections in the US economy, and partnerships with US companies. Thus, in 1987,

Abdullah Taha Bakhsh, the former representative of the bin Laden group, and at that time a partner and representative of Khalid bin Mahfouz, came to the rescue of a small Texas oil company, Harken, which was in need of recapitalization. He took an 11.5 percent share and helped to restructure the company. The director of Harken Energy Corporation at that time was a certain George W. Bush.

In 2002, various reports from official US sources point, albeit in a contradictory way, to contacts between Saudi-backed agents and the attackers of 9/11. Thus, in November 2002 a draft report by the Joint Congressional Committee on 9/11 found, among other links, that two of the hijackers, Khalid al-Midhar and Nawaq Alzhami, living in San Diego at the time, were meeting with Omar al-Bayoumi and Ossama Bassnan, each one of whom was receiving financial support from the wife of the Saudi Ambassador to the US, a Saudi princess daughter of King Faisal. Naturally, she was totally unaware that her charitable donations to a family in need would end up indirectly helping the terrorists. But it is precisely this web of indirect connections that is significant. The Congressional Committee faulted the CIA and the FBI for not investigating thoroughly these contacts, as well as other potential links to Saudi personalities and organizations. Indeed, al-Midhar and Alzhami had been identified by the CIA as operatives of *al-Qaeda* in January 2001, in spite of which they could enter the United States legally under their own names in August 2001.[65]

What should we make of this tangled web of interests and strategies by so many different actors? The story is not so complicated, in fact, if we stick with analysis and leave aside speculation. Let us recall some meaningful historical antecedents. The Saud dynasty was created on a religious foundation, Wahhabism, going back to the mid-eighteenth century, when a religious fundamentalist, Muhammad bin Abd al-Wahhab, persecuted for his intepretation of the Qu'rān, arrived in the oasis of the al-Saud tribe. Muhammad bin Saud followed Wahhab's teachings, and put his sword at Wahhab's service (or Wahhab's teachings at the service of his sword – it usually works both ways). He conquered Arabia, and his descendants carried on a secular struggle, against other tribes, other people, then against Turkey, until they brought Mecca and Medina under their control in 1924–5. Muhammad bin Saud's great great grandson, Abd al-Aziz, helped by the British, created the Saudi Arabian Kingdom in 1932. The unification of the tribes of the Arabian peninsula came under the double aegis of

---

65   Reported by *The New York Times* on November 23, 2002: David Johnston and James Risen "9/11 report says Saudi Arabia links went unexamined. Draft of Congressional finding says agents didn't pursue leads on Saudi funds," pp. A1 and A9.

the religious authority of the Wahhabite *ulemas* and the absolute political–military authority of the House of Saud. There can be no distinction. Cultural/religious legitimacy is as determinant in ruling societies as sheer force or the persuasion of sharing in privileges. The Saudi kingdom was, and is, a religious fundamentalist monarchy. But oil was discovered in 1938, and changed forever the Arabian land. Concessions to American companies sealed the bond between Saudis and Americans. It became a tripartite regime: Wahhabism, the House of Saud, and Aramco (the American-dominated monopoly of Saudi oil which became Saudi Aramco, with Saudi majority, in 1988). This was an indissoluble triangle of power and wealth, skillfully managed by the Saudi elite – when necessary, replacing the king, as they did in 1964, displacing the incompetent Saud in favor of the sophisticated Faisal, with the help, among others, of the bin Laden family.

The dual character of the House of Saud, paying obeisance at the same time to the *ulemas* and to the US, in order to keep the power that provided wealth, was not a hypocritical manipulation. The Saudi elite is Wahhabist, and it continued to enforce Islamic law, supported by the large majority of its subjects, while accommodating Western ways and interests. So, unlike Mossadeqh in Iran, they were loyal managers of the Western oil from which they derived their wealth. But they also had to be loyal guardians of the holy sites, from which they derived their legitimacy, not only in Arabia but throughout the Muslim world – as epitomized by the *hadj* (the pilgrimage to Mecca that all Muslims must do at least once in their lives).

Therefore, they used their wealth to play the global financial markets, which they quickly understood very well, having sent their brightest sons to study in the best Western universities. But they also used this wealth to help development in Islamic countries, and among Islamic populations, around the world. This strategy was directed, as in the case of the United States foreign projection, in several inter-related dimensions: helping economic and social development in Islamic countries, bringing them under the sphere of Saudi economic influence; providing relief for the needy; and supporting Islamic movements that would advance the power and influence of Islam, particularly along the teachings of Wahhabism – as was the case with the Taliban.

In this fully coherent strategy, the borderline between supporting Islamism and supporting the struggle of the *mujahedeen* was definitively crossed in Afghanistan. When the dynamics of this struggle went on to confront Western interests, including the United States, it was difficult to reverse the machinery that had been triggered in the past – except for dismissing, in 2001, the legendary chief of the secret service, Prince Turki ibn Faisal ibn Abdelaziz. Furthermore, while the Saudi government clearly understood the need to make a clean break with bin Laden, given his hostility and his alliance with Saudi dissidents, it was careful not to align itself completely with the US against the fundamentalist networks. The memory was still fresh in their minds of November 1979, the first year of the new Hegira, when an officer of the Saudi National Guard and several hundred followers occupied the Grand Mosque of Mecca, and fought Saudi troops for several weeks, denouncing the abandonment of the Qu'rān's teaching by the Saudi monarchy. After the end of the occupation, all the rebels and their accomplices were beheaded, except one. He was precisely the one whom the Saudis suspected of providing the plans of Mecca to the assailants. He was one of the few people with access to such documents: Mahrous bin Laden, brother of Osama, nowadays still in charge of family business in Medina.

Thus, to appease the deep resentment among true Wahhabites, the Saudi government has had to balance its US connections with its continuing support of Islamic causes around the world, including, of course, the financing of Palestinian resistance. Even when the Saudi regime decided that the ties with bin Laden had become too dangerous, in the aftermath of the bombing of the US embassies, it continued to support the Taliban, which was another way of supporting bin Laden.

Furthermore, the Saudi elite is not unified on this matter. What the government does is not necessarily what other members of the royal family or of the business elite do. For many of them, the support of Islamism, including the militant networks without a name, is a religious duty. Given the web of family, tribal, political, and financial connections among the few thousand members of the Saudi elite, repression of these initiatives is unlikely, on the fundamental condition that the Saudi regime is not targeted itself – something that bin Laden was careful not to do, concentrating his attacks on Arab soil to the American presence in the holy land.

Therefore, there is a deep empathy between the defense of the Wahhabite Saudi regime and the worldwide Islamic networks from which *al-Qaeda* and the terrorist networks developed. This is not the traditional form of state-sponsored terrorism because the Saudis have never encouraged terror against the United States (they did it against Russia; for example, Chechens), and tried, unsuccessfully, to rein in bin Laden, until he escaped their control. Yet there is a critical connection between the Wahhabite kingdom and the networks of Islamic martyrs: the paramount affirmation of Islamic principles, sharing the belief in the power of identity.

Networking and media politics: the organization, tactics, and strategy of al-Qaeda

How can a relatively small group of militants, however determined, confront the most powerful state in history without the active support of other states? Bin Laden and his followers believe the answer is that God is with them. But, just in case, they built a new form of organization, and developed tactics and an overall strategy appropriate to the conditions of what has become known as asymmetrical confrontation. On the one hand, all the military power the world can master. On the other hand, a total disregard for human life, starting with the fighter's life, and a reliance on surprise, unpredictability, and global networking.

Networking is critical. It means that *al-Qaeda* has a core leadership (bin Laden and, in the event of his death, al-Zhawahiri and others will follow), but it does not have a command and control structure. It provides training and indoctrination to the true believers who answer the call, after careful screening. Then, in most cases, they return to their roots, and engage in militant tactics in their own countries. They keep in touch with the leadership of *al-Qaeda*, but, by and large, they are on their own, they improvise, they find the resources, and take their own initiatives. After all, the fighting principle is very simple: strike as hard as you can, anytime and anywhere you can, the enemy being, first of all, the US government and American companies and citizens, but also all Westerners, and the symbolic points of connection between Muslim societies and the disbelievers: airports, multi-national corporate facilities, transportation lanes, global tourism centers, and the daily life of any society engaged in the struggle against Muslims (for example, Afghanistan, Chechnya, Kashmir, the Philippines).

After the command center of *al-Qaeda* in Afghanistan was destroyed in 2001, networking with local struggles became increasingly important. Nation-specific organizations fight against the states that oppress true Muslims in their own countries, while being ready to launch strikes against the US and other enemies throughout the globe. The South-east Asian network of *al-Qaeda*, and its inter-related organizations, was probably the most significant in 2002–3. It was initiated in the early 1990s, with careful preparation by bin Laden, on the basis of the Indonesian, Filipino, and Malaysian Islamists who responded to the call in Afghanistan. Bin Laden sent his brother-in-law, Muhammad Jamal Khalifa to the Philippines to set up a mutual support connection with the two Muslim separatist organizations in

Mindanao, the Moro Islamic Front and *Abbu Sayyaf*. The Moro Front opened its camps to *al-Qaeda* recruits from around the world, therefore diversifying the training ground from Afghanistan. Camp Palestine was mainly for Arabs, while Camp Vietnam and Camp Hudaibie were for South-east Asians. In the 1990s, about 1,500 Indonesians went through these camps, and most of them are assumed to have returned to Indonesia. The main radical Islamic Indonesian movement is *Jamaah Islamiyah*, whose project is the establishment of an Islamic state throughout South-east Asia. Its leader is the respected *ulema* Abu Bakar Bashir. Its main operative is Riudan Isamuddin, known as Hambali, a student leader in Indonesia, who joined *al-Qaeda* in Afghanistan and returned to Indonesia to set up a militant, terrorist network. He is accused of having masterminded the Bali bombing in 2002. The South-east Asian *al-Qaeda* cells were among the most active in the late 1990s. Bin Laden organized a cell in Manila, led by two of the militants involved in the 1993 bombing of the World Trade Center, Ramzi Yousef and Khalid Shaikh Mohammed. In 1994, they planned, from Manila, the bombing of 11 US airliners over the Pacific, but the plot was discovered by an accidental explosion in Yousef's Manila flat. From the Philippines and Indonesia, *al-Qaeda*-related groups planned attacks on US interests in Malaysia and Singapore, but they were prevented by efficient police action in those countries. However, with the dismantling of the Afghan and Pakistani bases of action, *al-Qaeda*'s South-east Asian networks, particularly in Indonesia, the largest Muslim country in the world, became critical sources of both local opposition and global *jihad*.

A similar trend was evident in Chechnya, where the secular, ethnic-national struggle of Chechen nationalists against Russia became an Islamic struggle, and received strong backing in money, training, and weapons from *al-Qaeda*. For bin Laden, the Chechen struggle was simply a continuation of the fight against the Russians in Afghanistan, and for some time, Saudis, Pakistanis, and the CIA seemed to concur. Thus, in the context of an all-out struggle between Islamic networks and the dominant world powers, Chechen fighters, on behalf of Islam, took their battle to Moscow, with the mass terrorist attack on a Moscow theater in October 2002, an attack made even more tragic by the use of gas by the Russian commandos who stormed the theater, killing 120 of the people who had been taken hostage. Thus, while the Chechen conflict goes back to the nineteenth century, the connection with the *al-Qaeda* network intensified it, and transformed it into another node of the global network of terror against the oppressors of the Muslims. It is this dual character of local struggles and global networking that is the essence of *al-Qaeda*'s strategy in the post-Afghanistan war situation.

The strategy is characterized by a relentless attack, anytime, anywhere, on all objectives that represent the powers-that-be (Christians, including Russians, Jews, and any other oppressors of the Muslim people, e.g. India and eventually China). Targets of opportunity may happen anytime, anywhere. Campaigns are easily launched, though not necessarily coordinated, by tapes and statements released to the media, and particularly to the global, independent Muslim network, Al Jazeera, the alternative to CNN. There is also a strictly *al-Qaeda* network, separate from the organizations that receive support and training from *al-Qaeda*. This is a network financed by bin Laden's resources, and commanded by the *al-Qaeda* core leadership. They are the select ones, hand-picked by bin Laden while he was the operational leader (he is probably very ill at the time of writing in 2002: dialysis problems are more lethal than American smart bombs).

But even *al-Qaeda* cells are largely autonomous in their initiatives. They are provided with resources, and given general instructions, and a field of action, but they are left to their own basic instinct and planning strategy. Only some decisive actions are centrally planned, as was the case with 9/11. But even in this case, many of the operations of the plan were left to the field commanders, and only a few (maybe only Atta) knew the overall plan from the start. These are the traditional cell-organization tactics of all revolutionary movements in history. But *al-Qaeda*'s organization adds a few twists: autonomy is much greater because there is a simplicity of goals, and because the mystical character of the organization, entirely devoted to God's will, minimizes problems of discipline. Also, communications are enhanced by advanced infrastructure in communication technologies. Naturally, the Internet has been widely used, particularly with e-mails using encryption technology (PGP, available on line for free downloading). But satellite-based mobile phones have made global contact easy, on the basis of pre-agreed cyphers. However, in spite of governments' emphasis on the importance of the Internet (finding a new pretext to control free communication on the Internet), the most important contacts have been personal, and the critical messages hand delivered. For this, what is really decisive is the global network of air transport, which brings anyone in potential contact with anyone else by means of a flight, provided he has the proper visas. Interestingly enough, *al-Qaeda* decided not to use the vast market of falsified visas and passports, relying instead on an assumption of the incompetence of US surveillance agencies. They were right: only a few of the would-be terrorists had any trouble securing a regular US visa under their real names and with their own passports. An additional feature of this terror network is that their main activists, those who ultimately come into direct contact with the enemy, are supposed to die. So, no fear of cracking under torture, no turncoats, and no information other than the traces of a lost life. Of course, there is always the chance that, at the last minute, one of them changes his mind. This is why they live and work in groups, and this is why only at the very last minute are the details of the plan revealed. Moreover, many of the militants of the centrally planned attacks have personal bonds to others in the group: they are family, they are friends, they have studied together, rediscovered Islam together. This is a close-knit circle that becomes a node in a network of close-knit circles around the world.

The implications of this networking organization are huge.[66] How can states fight networks? They can bomb some operational bases, and some headquarters (as they did in Afghanistan), but they cannot bomb Hamburg, where 9/11 was actually prepared. It is not possible to bomb a network, only its nodes, in a very long, and costly, world-wide strategy which always has to deal with the self-reproducing and reconfiguring capacities of the network. Mobile global networks versus the nation-bound state is indeed an asymmetrical conflict: networks have a decisive advantage. States do try to build global state-networks. However, this state-networking increases their puni-tive capacity (they can bomb more places) but not their effectiveness all that much: nodes still proliferate in many different points, mixing with the population, striking when and where they seem fit, in an endless spiral of violence.

On the basis of this organizational flexibility, Islamic global net-works rely on two main tactics of action. The first one is terror: to inflict damage anywhere, anytime in such a way that people and institutions from the United States, and the states that support them, live in fear. Their expectation is that over time this becomes unten-able. It is a matter of pursuing the struggle long enough. Terror should be expanded as much as possible, but also diversified, according to circumstances and the capabilities of the fighters. Naturally, chemical and biological weapons are a major tool of intimidation. Small nu-clear bombs could be used down the line. But this is not so easy, so tactics have to be simplified. Using commercial airplanes as bombs was much simpler and more efficient than acquiring and firing mis-siles. Other downsized tactics are to be expected. *Al-Qaeda* suicidal activists have a problem-solving, engineering mentality. After all,

66 Arquilla and Rondfeldt (2001).

quite a few are professional engineers and medical doctors. Once the problem is defined, the proper solution depends on conditions and resources. Expect the unexpected because it is so obvious that nobody thought of it – at least no one in positions of power, although fiction writers had depicted scenarios similar to 9/11 years earlier.

The second tactic is media politics. Ultimately, the action is geared toward human minds, toward transforming consciousness. The media, local and global, are the means of communication through which the public mind is formed. Therefore, action has to be media oriented, it has to be spectacular, provide good footage, so that the whole world can see it: like a Hollywood movie because this is what has trained the human mind in our times. But there is no need to sign or claim the actions – this is the ultimate mistake of US and Western analysts. *Al-Qaeda* only claims its actions much later, when no information can be given away as a result of the claim. And it does not do so because it is not necessary. It has no copyright on terror on behalf of Islam. Anything, anywhere that hits the enemy will be welcome by the oppressed Muslim masses. These minds, the minds of true Muslims, are the real target for *al-Qaeda*. For Westerners, *al-Qaeda* aims at the heart, not the mind. Not for them to understand, but to fear. And fear is even more frightening when it comes from unseen sources. Media as a way of communicating with the Muslims of the world is the essential weapon for *al-Qaeda* because they follow the secular, anarchist tradition of exemplary action, practiced by Russian, French, Italian, and Spanish anarchists: to strike in the heart of the enemy as a way of showing its weakness, to shatter the myth of its invincibility, to shake off fear from the minds and wills of the young lions of Islam. Every major terror act in America is a victory of the will of God over the greatest power on Earth. As sad as this image was, when Muslim youth were dancing in the streets of cities around the world, after watching New York exploding, *al-Qaeda* knew that its tactics were right, in their particular distorted vision of the world.

There is more. Exemplary action, in the anarchist tradition, or in the terrorist nationalist tradition, is also a provocative act. It is hoped that, by infuriating the enemy, it will engage in an unreasonable response that will then inflame the rotten world, so that a purified civilization will emerge from the ashes. As a destructive strategy it has worked in history: World War I was triggered by a single assassin in Sarajevo. This is exactly what Hamas or Islamic *Jihad* are doing in Israel, or what *al-Qaeda* is doing in the world. US policy toward Iraq, a bystander in the conflict, seems to show that the strategy indeed works.

In the final analysis, *al-Qaeda* oscillates between two blueprints. The first one, to which they held until 2001, can be labeled the Somalia Syndrome. America and Americans are not ready to die, unlike the warriors of Islam for whom martyrdom is an ardent desire. Thus, a few spectacular killings, like those of the US soldiers in Somalia, will force them to retreat, as they did in Vietnam or in Somalia for that matter. But after the 2001 campaign in Afghanistan, *al-Qaeda*, having barely survived the US retaliation, and after seeing the Taliban disintegrate and its Pakistani supporters run for cover, changed its mind and its tactics. Terror would become truly global, and would strike at opportunity targets. The network became much looser, but the media conveyed an indirect channel of communication to share the struggle. Finding ways to use weapons of mass destruction was given special emphasis, but was by no means the only objective because the real target was the awakening of the Muslim masses, and this required their full participation. Thus, uprisings in Muslim countries and attacks on Western symbols were more feasible and more educational. Yet the ultimate weapon in *al-Qaeda*'s mind is God's will. This is why there is no doubt about the outcome of the struggle, and this is why the struggle will go on, endlessly. Because in this case the power of identity is the power of God.

9/11 and beyond: death or birth of a networked, global, fundamentalist movement?

The horror and the symbolism of 9/11 struck the minds and hearts of the world. Suddenly, America discovered its vulnerability. And in a few days, the feeling of business euphoria, technological innovation, and personal freedom that characterized the first years of the information age in the wealthy countries and the affluent classes, turned to an obsession with security, suspicion, and control.

The actual implementation of the 9/11 plot was revealing of the nature of the emerging confrontation between the identity-based, revolutionary vanguards and the institutions and organizations of the nation-state, still imprinted with the mentality and routine of the industrial era and Cold War geopolitics. The suicidal group of *al-Qaeda* that infiltrated the United States executed with few mistakes a very simple plan, aimed at inflicting maximum damage in human lives and, more importantly, in media-conveyed humiliation of the imperial power of the United States, thus potentially freeing the Muslim masses from their feeling of powerlessness. It could have been even more symbolically powerful (the destruction of the White House?) except for the heroic struggle of the passengers of flight UA

93 which aborted the targeting of the last human missile. The cold, methodical execution of the plan for over two years, without leaks or mishaps, and without hesitation in the long path toward self-destruction, is proof of the organizational capacity, ruthless determination, and psychological motivation of *al-Qaeda* members. They even showed how global terrorism can be a shoestring operation, using under US$ 300,000, and still wiring back to headquarters, before boarding their fatal flights, the remaining $12,000.

In strictly financial terms, it is obvious that this kind of war can outlast the high-tech wars fought with thousands of smart missiles at US$ 1 million a piece. But the plan could work only because it was based on the assumption that the enemy "is stupid," in one of the statements of Ramzi bin al-Shibh, one *al-Qaeda*'s leaders (subsequently captured in Pakistan by an enemy who was learning the lesson). If we take this statement in the sense of organizational intelligence, it was proved right. The endless list of inexplicable mistakes that US security agencies committed all along the process leading to 9/11 has been fully documented and exposed. They can be linked to a number of inter-related factors, including complacency in the feeling of absolute power, and total reliance on technology, rather than on human intelligence, in obtaining and processing information, for reasons that are at the same time ideological (the American – and modern – belief that technology can solve everything) and financial (it is so much cheaper to pay for computers or use, as a byproduct, the armed forces' electronic toys, than to invest in well-paid, well-trained intelligence officers). Therefore, lack of coordination between agencies, bureaucratic routine, and disdain for foreign sources of information (e.g. accurate reports from the French intelligence services were ignored) left the US in the dark about a plot that was not in fact fully concealed.

But there is something even more important: security agencies were (and are) still the product of a nation-state engaged in potential war against other nation-states, and during the Cold War against the mighty Soviet empire. The organizational logic and mind frame of these would-be warring states was very similar; so was their understanding, and their strategies of penetration and, sometimes, of bargaining – for instance, one of the reasons there was no terrorism in the United States and very little in the Soviet Union during the Cold War period was the understanding between the two superpowers that they should restrain their subrogate organizations (be it Palestinians or Mossad) from engaging in terrorism in their territories. When confronted with a new kind of enemy, the US security system proved unable to prevent a devastating attack, and when it reacted, with full force, it did so on the old terms; that is, finding localized targets that could be dealt with by military technology. The Afghanistan war, rapidly won by American technology and special forces, seemed to prove the accuracy of the strategy. Thus, the determination to disarm Iraq, at the price of a costly war if necessary, and beyond Iraq to confront the "axis of evil," an axis of variable geometry, remained rooted in the conviction that the only real danger could come from state-supported terrorism. This is in contradiction with the analysis of *al-Qaeda* I have presented here, based on the documentation that is available. While losing its support base in Afghanistan was a major setback for the fundamentalist networks, it did not in itself eliminate their operational capacity. And of course, the Iraqi connection has not been proven, and the US motivation to attack Iraq seemed to derive more from its policy of preventive action against the designated "rogue states" than aimed at confronting *al-Qaeda*. Only after 9/11 did the US, and other Western states, fully realize the nature of the conflict, and moved slowly toward networking among themselves, including acting jointly to control the financial networks and the sources of funding that are the lifeline of terrorist activities. So doing, they stepped up the transformation of the nation-state into a new form of state, the network state, whose analysis I will present below in this volume, and in volume III of this trilogy.

At the time of writing, in early 2003, *al-Qaeda* seems to have been seriously diminished in its operational capacity. And most of its sponsors have stopped their support, rightly fearful of the irate reaction of a wounded superpower. However, a number of similar groups, representing similar actors in several countries, seem to be taking up various forms of terrorist activities, aimed at US and Western interests and symbols, in Kuwait, in Bali, in Yemen, in Pakistan, in the Philippines, in Moscow, in Jordan, and, for the first time, striking Israeli civilians in Mombassa. And the tense alert continues in the United States, where people at the end of 2002 were still as shaken and afraid as they were at the end of 2001, according to national opinion polls. It may well be that the power and resources of *al-Qaeda* have been overestimated, as most European intelligence services think. It is highly possible that *al-Qaeda* benefited from a spectacular "lucky strike" on 9/11, taking advantage of the lack of preparedness of the US security system. Yet global networks of terror, based on the perceived need of defending identity and following God's will, can be reconstituted and reconfigured with relative ease, as long as the sources from which they emerge continue to flow. Because what *al-Qaeda* has demonstrated is the organizational and operational possibility of confronting the power of major nation-states on the basis of flexible networking, media-oriented politics, and asymmetrical confrontation strategy, by using knowledge, advanced technology, and possibly weapons of mass destruction. This implies the acceptance of human sacrifice, both for the perpetrators and their victims. A sacrifice that is perceived as a religious duty to save mankind from its moral corruption, and the Muslim masses from the continuing humiliation and oppression inflicted upon them by the new Crusaders.

But what is this humiliation? How can we sense this oppression? The social exclusion of a great number of people on the planet, in economic and technological terms, is easily observed, as I will argue and document in volume III. But, whatever the future derivation of the conflict enacted by global fundamentalist networks will be, this is not the immediate cause of *al-Qaeda* or of related terrorist groups. The Taliban were recruited in the *madrassas* of refugee camps, but *al-Qaeda* cadres, as I explained above, are mainly from well-to-do social origins. What is common to both groups is the depth, and simplicity, of their religious beliefs, and the conviction that their own countries live in sin, and have been corrupted by the infidels. In analyzing the development of this resistance identity we cannot refer only to the indirect effects of socio-economic exclusion. It has to be related to the cultural and institutional transformation induced by globalization. The constitution of a global techno-economic system as the operational framework for all societies, led the nation-states, during the last years of the twentieth century, to either adapt or lead the process of globalization, since their positioning in the global networks of capital, technology, information, and communication was essential to keep, expand, or negotiate their power. Paying obeisance to the logic of global networks, be it financial markets, CNN-like media, world technology centers, and international networks of state institutions, meant for many nation-states, including those in the Muslim world, distancing themselves from their traditional constituencies and support bases. Some, like the Saudi regime, tried skillfully to preserve the traditional symbols of culture and religious orthodoxy. But it was too obviously a facade, as the *ulemas* could easily be exposed as bureaucrats on the payroll of the monarchy. To be modern, and therefore accepted, came to be tantamount to renouncing the codes and values that were meaningful for people at large, and particularly for the traditional elites. It also implied the acceptance of a global, cosmopolitan culture that, by and large, was identified with Americanization – even in France. In the case of Muslim culture, traditionally vilified in the colonial metropolises, marginalization of traditional values came with a twist of blame for their obscurantism, often symbolized by the submission of women under Islam, according to Western standards. This personally felt humiliation is rooted in the ethnocentric, racist representation of Arabs and Muslims in the West under the ideological characterization of "Orientalism." As Edward Said writes:

> Along with all other peoples variously designated as backward, degenerate, uncivilized, and retarded, the Orientals were viewed in a framework constructed out of biological determinism and moral-political admonishment. The Oriental was linked thus to elements in the Western society (delinquents, the insane, women, the poor) having in common an identity best described as lamentably alien. Orientals were rarely seen or looked at; they were seen through, analyzed not as citizens, or even people, but as problems to be solved or confined or – as the colonial powers openly coveted their territory – taken over... Since the Oriental was a member of a subject race, he had to be subjected: it was that simple.[67]

Therefore, for most poor Muslims, living their local lives, the appeal of fundamentalism had to come together with social and economic reform: this was the project of political fundamentalism that failed when confronted with the direct repression of the nation-states. But for those Muslim elites living in contact with the global, dominant networks, the choice was between becoming culturally Western or being downgraded in their social and cultural status. This was particularly poignant for the young generation whose members were technologically and intellectually very modern, yet found no meaning for their lives in values that were strange to their experience. An experience that was demeaned as oriental. This sector of alienated youth was the nurturing milieu of fundamentalist, terrorist networks. Their ability to link up with the aspirations of the dispossessed Muslim masses of the world is still a matter of project rather than an observable phenomenon. However, in the event, it would be a connection between the revolt against socio-economic irrelevance and the resistance of identity against Western cultural domination that could alter the course of history, by opposing to the global networks of wealth and technology, the global networks of belief and terror.

67   Said (1979: 207).

"No Globalization without Representation!":
The Anti-globalization Movement[68]

The shutting down of the meeting of the World Trade Organization in Seattle on November 30, 1999, as a result of the action of tens of thousands of demonstrators, signaled the coming of age of a major social movement that opposes, on a global scale, the values and interests shaping the current globalization process. Social struggles, which explicitly reject unfettered, capitalist globalization, had been taking place for over a decade, including riots against IMF-inspired austerity policies in various developing countries,[69] as well as identity-based insurgencies which called for global resistance against global domination, particularly the *Zapatista* insurgency that I analyzed above. But the demonstrations in Seattle struck the public mind around the world, via their impact on the global media, bringing to everybody's attention the fact that globalization was not a natural process, but a political decision. Furthermore, the Seattle protesters submitted to public debate their view that the specific ways in which the globalization process was taking place were shaped by the power-ful economic and ideological interests of a dominant, global elite. It was not globalization *per se* that most activists were opposing, but this specific brand of globalization. Indeed, as soon as the media

---

68   There is a growing literature on the anti-globalization movement, and an even larger body of sources related to the debates and projects emerging from the movement. The references that follow refer to the movement itself, and not to the content of its proposals and critics. I indicate simply a few sources that have been important in framing my analysis, as well as following the activities of the movement in the media and on the Internet. The main source, and a source that will become a fundamental work on the movement, is the dissertation by Jeff Juris, a doctoral candidate in Anthropology at the University of California, Berkeley, still in progress in 2003 ("Transnational activism and the cultural logic of networking"). I am deeply grateful to him for his willingness to share his work and ideas with me, beyond my role in supervising his disserta-tion. I must emphasize that, while sharing much of the analysis, we do have substantive disagree-ments on the characterization of the movement, as well as in our value judgments, which means that the analysis presented here, while informed by our discussions, is my exclusive responsibility. An excellent collection on social movements opposing global institutions is O'Brien et al. (2000). On the so-called IMF-riots, see Walton and Seddon (1994). On the crisis of globalization in Latin America, and the mobilization of social movements against the crisis, see Calderon (2003). On indigenous movements, with particular emphasis on Ecuador, see Chiriboga (2003). On the emergence of a global civil society, see the best reference book to date: Anheier et al. (2001). For information and analysis on the movement itself, see Cockburn (2000), Danaher and Burbach (2001), Welton and Wolf (2001), Galdon (2002), Klein and Levy (2002), Monereo and Riera (2002), Negri et al. (2002), Starhawk (2002), and Ziegler (2002). On the practice of networking and its implications, see Arquilla and Rondfeldt (2001). On the role of global media in shaping public consciousness, see Volkmer (1999).
69   Walton and Seddon (1994).

coined the label "anti-globalization" to characterize the movement, most social actors engaged in the movement rejected that name, proposing instead that they be designated as the movement for global justice, or anti-capitalist globalization movement, or anti-corporate globalization movement, or a variety of alternative names in which each one of the many faces of this movement felt best represented. Why I have chosen to keep the media label in the title of this section has to do with analytical reasons which will, I hope, become clear after I have conducted my analysis.

The Seattle demonstrations were followed by a series of similar demonstrations, some of them smaller, others much larger, in various sites around the planet, always following a similar pattern of action and always targeting a major meeting of some of the political institutions managing globalization: the April 16, 2000 meeting of the IMF/World Bank in Washington, DC; the US Republican Party National Convention in Philadelphia and Democratic Party Convention in Los Angeles in the summer of 2000; the IMF/World Bank meeting in Prague on September 26, 2000; the Nice summit of the European Union on December 6, 2000; the Summit of the Americas in Quebec City on April 20, 2001; the European Union summit in Gothenburg on June 14, 2001; the World Bank meeting in Barcelona on June 25, 2001 (in spite of the cancellation of the meeting which was transferred to cyberspace); the G-8 meeting in Genoa on July 19, 2001; the Barcelona European Union summit on March 16, 2002, and the Seville European Union summit on June 15, 2002; and a number of smaller but powerful demonstrations around similar summits in Brussels, in Durban, in Fortaleza, in Monterrey, in Quito, in Montreal, in São Paulo, in Johannesburg, in Florence, as well as, by the time this volume is published, a number of other sites of other meetings, including Copenhagen, Athens, Miami, and Cancun. Furthermore, the informal annual gathering of the global elite around the World Economic Forum, usually meeting in Davos, was targeted with demonstrations in Zurich, as well as in New York (in 2002 when the meeting moved there), while a much larger meeting began to take place annually in Porto Alegre around the World Social Forum, which would meet at exactly the same time as the World Economic Forum to debate its own alternatives to the proposals being discussed by the global elites.

This mirror effect of the anti-globalization movement *vis à vis* the times and spaces of the institutions managing globalization clearly indicates what the movement is: a deliberate attempt to establish the control of society over its institutions after the failure of traditional democratic controls under the conditions of globalization of wealth, information, and power. This is what is well expressed in the most popular slogan of the Seattle demonstrators, "No globalization without representation," in a historical transposition of the rallying cry of American patriots in their fight for independence, "No taxation without representation." However, the anti-globalization movement is highly diverse, and to some extent contradictory in its constituencies and in its messages, and its composition and expression vary from context to context. This is why its characterization requires careful analysis, which, following my general method for the study of social movements, will look sequentially at its actors, its goals, its organizational forms, its practices of struggle, and its relationship with the institutions of society. Before embarking on this study, however, there are three points that we must keep in mind.

First, the movement is composed of such deep contrasts that we have to argue, and demonstrate, why there is a movement instead of a coalition of movements and social actors. I do think there is a movement, but a very specific kind of movement. Let me say this before elaborating the concept below: it is a network movement, in which the unit is the network. Secondly, it is a global movement, and its global nature represents a qualitative transformation *vis à vis* the struggles against capitalist globalization that have taken place around the world, occasionally triggering solidarity from other sites of struggle, but not existing globally together in real time. Third, what this movement affirms by its existence, regardless of its content and future evolution, is the oldest rule in the dynamics of human societies: where there is domination, there is resistance to domination; where new forms of domination emerge, new forms of resistance ultimately surge to act upon the specific patterns of domination. Therefore, the deployment of a global, network society, characterized by the structural dominance of specific interests and values, politically enforced and managed, ultimately came to be met by the resistance of a global, networked social movement whose components, strategies, and values I will now turn to analyze.

"El pueblo desunido jamas sera vencido": the diversity of the anti-globalization movement

Reflecting on the characteristics of new social movements in 2002, social anthropologist Ruth Cardoso reversed the traditional motto of the Latin American left, proposing that the strength of the new social movements came particularly from their internal diversity: "the people, disunited, will never be defeated."[70] Beyond the language

70 Cardoso (2002).

effect of this paradox, I think it can be documented that the internal cacophony of the anti-globalization movement, made up of diverse and even contradictory components, is indeed what makes it, collect-ively, a source of challenge to capitalist globalization. Because it is this diversity that broadens the basis of the opposition in an otherwise seemingly impossible union of interests and ideologies: "teamster and turtles," as it was said of the Seattle convergence between one of the most conservative trade unions in the world and the defenders of endangered species, both threatened by the liberalization of trade. What are these diverse components? Who are the actors who have converged in the anti-globalization movement? The empirical answer is rather complicated because it is necessary to differentiate between the participants in the mass actions around the events and gatherings of the institutions of global governance, and the social movements against globalization taking place in specific locales or connected in a global network of debate and protest.

Let us start with the demonstrators at the symbolic events around the meetings of the global elites. In Seattle, the major contingent in terms of numbers, although by no means the most belligerent, was made up of labor union workers, organized by the King County Labor Council, around an alliance between the machinist workers unions of AFL-CIO and the teamsters. The militant International Longshore and Warehouse Union, still proud of its history of communist leader-ship in the 1930s, organized strikes in the West Coast ports, demanding the release of the demonstrators arrested in Seattle. There were also numerous environmental groups, from the most militant, such as Earth First! and Rainforest Action Network, to the moderate constituencies of the Sierra Club and Greenpeace. The main force in the demonstration was organized by a coalition formed around the Direct Action Network, whose core was formed by Art&Revolution, a self-styled anarchist grouping of artists and theater groups which emerged from the 1996 demonstrations against the Democratic Convention in Chicago. An activist group advocating non-violent protest, the Ruckus Society, trained the demonstrators in civil disobedience tactics. Teach-ins were organized by Global Exchange, a coalition against the social and environmental con-sequences of free trade, and the International Forum on Globaliza-tion, a network of intellectuals proposing alternative policies for globalization. Indigenous people and peasants from around the world were also present, partly through the initiative of the People for Global Action (PGA) which organized a West Coast Caravan to Seattle from across the Americas. French farmers, led by the charis-matic Jose Bove, were also present, carrying with them an abundance of illegally imported French cheese. Violent protesters from various origins were mainly organized by the Black Block, which was to be a constant presence in future demonstrations. Dressed in military camouflage, black attire, including bandanas and hoods, Black Block followers tend to be anarchists, and deliberately attack commercial property and police forces as symbols of oppression and alienation. What is significant is that in Seattle, and in other demonstrations (for instance, in Barcelona, according to my own observation) they are joined by local youths with little political ideology, but a potential of rage against "the system." Women were present in large numbers, and individual women played a leadership role, although only a few formal women's organizations were among the organizers of the demonstration.

This original configuration of the participants in the protests changed over time and depending upon context. Labor participation substantially decreased in the United States, but dramatically increased in Western Europe and in Latin America. The women's component of the movement increased its visibility through the World March of Women, started by the Women Federation of Quebec in 1998, with its first major march in 2000. Indigenous movements and land demands movements, from India and Latin America, as well as farmers from France and other developed countries, increased their coordination around the PGA network, perhaps the network that most explicitly targeted the connection between South and North. In Italy, the tradition of the autonomous movements of the radical left in the 1970s was revived (and theorized by Toni Negri, one of the major intellectual figures of the movement) around the Ya Basta/Tute Bianche movement which practices direct action in a non-violent, but confrontational, theatrical form. In Spain, the Movement for Global Resistance, mainly centered around Barcelona, and largely inspired by the anarchist tradition, provided one of the largest contingents of demonstrators around Europe. The Black Block anarchist and autonomous groups, not hesitating to engage in violent actions, gained militancy and influence in Europe.

At the same time, the global debate on globalization found its most eventful expression in the World Social Forum, which has gathered in Porto Alegre, annually, since 2001, and which in 2002 began to organize regional social forums, in Florence, in Quito, in Hyderabad, and in cities around the world. These gatherings of tens of thousands of activists, soon followed by thousands of journalists, provided a platform for debate and expression of all political ideologies, NGOs, social movements, intellectuals, groups, and individuals, from the old and new left, from various continents, and with various agendas. The notion that there were places where the thinking could be diverse, away from the orthodoxy of the Washington consensus, and where there was, according to the *Zapatista* expression, "a world where all the worlds can fit," represented an extraordinary liberation for many in a world that had come to believe in the inevitability of a stark choice between the domination of the present and the struggles of the past.

So, the main components of the movement, as they emerge from an observation of the symbolic events that epitomize the movement's action, are: critics of the social and environmental consequences of a globalization based on free trade and dominated by the interests of capitalist corporations; proponents of the regulation of global financial markets; NGOs in solidarity with the poor of the world, including proponents of the cancellation of the foreign debt of poor countries; religious groups; humanitarian NGOs; workers, and their trade unions, defending their jobs, benefits, and working conditions; farmers and peasants refusing to accept the consequences of free-trade agreements; peasant movements around the world, and their solidarity networks; indigenous people's movements and their solidarity networks; environmental movements; women's movements; revolutionary artists; anarchists and autonomous groups from different ideologies and traditions; young people in violent revolt against their societies; political parties of the old left, both from the mainstream (communists, left socialists) and from the radical left (Trotskyites); critical, independent intellectuals, such as the members of the ATTAC movement, and the International Forum on Globalization.

The mere presentation of this list shows the diversity of the movement, and also that values and goals, rather than specific social characteristics, are the defining elements of the movement. However, if we take into consideration the participants in the major events, demonstrators and militants tend to be young, middle class, and, overwhelmingly, from industrialized countries, particularly from Western Europe and North America. Although, when the World Social Forum meets in Porto Alegre, in Quito, or in Hyderabad, then there is wide participation from social movements in the global South, such as the Ecuadoran CONAIE, the Brazilian MST, the *Zapatistas*, the Indian Karnataka Farmers Movement, and a broad array of left-wing groups and critical intellectuals. Furthermore, there is a distinction to be made between the participants in the symbolic protests of the movement, around the meetings of the institutions of global governance, and the participants in the social struggles against globalization. There are two layers of the movement, and, in analytical terms, they have to be differentiated and related at the same time.

I will illustrate this point by briefly considering the powerful indigenous movement in Ecuador.[71]

The Confederacion de Nacionalidades Indigenas de Ecuador (CONAIE) was formed in 1986 by an alliance between the peoples of the Amazon and those of the highlands. It started as a way of preserving their lands and identities, particularly opposing the oil exploration process of American companies. For this they sought the support of international environmental networks, such as the Rainforest Action Network. They also mobilized against ethnic discrimination and the situation of marginality and poverty that characterized the indigenous populations of Ecuador. Ultimately, they opposed the IMF-inspired, neo-liberal policies of the Ecuadoran government, in the context of adapting Ecuador to the globalization process. In the 1990s and particularly in 2000 and 2001, they led four powerful non-violent uprisings that ultimately forced the resignation of the president, and led, in November 2002, to the election of a populist president, Gutierrez, supported by Pachakutik, the political party that emerged from the indigenous movement. The CONAIE organizations linked up with other indigenous movements in Latin America, and were represented in major forums and events of the anti-globalization movement, particularly in Quebec and in the Porto Alegre World Social Forum. They hosted in Quito, in October 2002, the regional World Social Forum for Latin America. They used the Internet both to maintain their own communication channels, and to coordinate and interact with other social movements against globalization in Latin America and around the world. Thus, what started as a resistance identity movement, shifted gradually from the defense of the indigenous people to an alternative project of globalization, or "globalization from below" as the CONAIE leaders put it, linking up both with indigenous movements and with the broader current of alternative globalization militants. They were the leading force in building a "Social Continental Alliance" in Latin America which brought together social movements from various countries in a project of "Alternative Integration," explicitly opposing the ALCA project proposed by the US Administration in the Quebec 2000 Americas Summit to create a free-trade area in the whole continent.

The anti-globalization movement therefore cannot be reduced to the major demonstrations played out by young activists from developed countries. It is made up of a plurality of social struggles from around the world. These struggles are inter-related and communicated through a combination of Internet networks, media diffusion,

71   Chiriboga (2003).

discussion forums, and convergence in protest events that move around the globe, from Washington to Quito, and from Durban to Geneva. While indigenous movements, farmers, squatters, and labor militants are present in fewer numbers in the global media events, because of the limits on their ability to travel, they are increasingly relevant in the movement as a whole. Accordingly, the social base of the anti-globalization movement is being extended to all sectors of society that are hurt by globalization and are mobilized against globalization. What is significant is the combination of multiple local sources of global opposition to unfettered globalization. What is also significant is the extraordinary social, ethnic, ideological, and political diversity of the actors in the movement. Thus, rather than differentiating the Northern and Southern versions of the movement, we must emphasize its global networking as its main feature. And, rather than concentrating on the characteristics of the actors in order to understand the logic of the movement, we can find the source for the existence of the movement in the values and goals of these actors.

The values and goals of the movement against globalization

It should be clear by now that the internal diversity of the movement forbids a simple, unified characterization of its values and goals. Furthermore, what started as a convergence from multiple sources (environmentalism, labor rights, social rights, solidarity against poverty, indigenous rights, women's rights, and the like), in opposing a process of globalization perceived as unjust, has paved the way for heated debates on what kind of society the movement should put forward to replace the current system. Neo-liberalism is indeed the recognizable common enemy, and this was an original contribution from the *Zapatistas*. However, the meaning of neo-liberalism is not the same for everybody: probably a majority of the movement identifies it with capitalism, but the so-called reformist wing is not necessarily anti-capitalist. After all, the subtitle of the Lugano Report authored by Susan George, one of the main spokespersons for the movement, calls for the survival of capitalism.

Overall, there is first a cleavage between those in the movement seeking institutional reform, and globalization with a human face, and those opposing capitalism, or at least the corporate capitalism that is its current and only incarnation. ATTAC focused on the effort to implement the Tobin tax as a way of regulating financial markets and avoiding major economic disruption. This goal had more symbolic than technical value, and even the symbol was somewhat lost when

Tobin himself rejected the idea, shortly before his death. But even within those opposing capitalism, there are sharply confrontational views, as an increasingly influential current, mainly organized around the People's Global Action network, can be characterized as anarchist or neo-anarchist, in their explicit rejection of all structures of authority, and in their criticism of the cooptation of the movement by the reformist intellectuals and political forces of the traditional left. Indeed, the remnants of the Marxist left, in disarray in the 1990s, found in the anti-globalization movement both a perceived confirmation of their views and a space for activism and political influence. While this is clearly a misreading of the dynamics and characteristics of the anti-globalization movement, it adds to the internal diversity of the movement, and to the contradictory expression of the values present in it. However, since there is no central command structure, and no one needs permission to be active in this highly diversified, pervasive movement, its contradictory nature is a source of strength, rather than of weakness, as would have been the case in traditional socio-political organizations. Divisions and differences add new support because many social actors recognize themselves in at least one of the facets of the movement, and do not feel themselves subject to the pressure or discipline of those factions with whom they disagree. Nonetheless, trying to provide a synthesis of the foundations of the movement in terms of its values, observation of its practice and its debates can yield four main characterizations:

1   Each component of the movement has its own set of values, and its own agenda, be it the defense of indigenous identity or the preservation of protectionism for French agricultural products. But each of these agendas is affirmed in opposition to the current globalization process, dominated by asymmetrical liberalization that fits the interests of corporate capitalism.

2   A large part of the movement mobilizes for institutional reform of the current process of globalization: "another world is possible" as the most popular slogan of the World Social Forum states. Here, the emphasis is on "possible" rather than on "another."

3   A significant, and growing, current of the movement, loosely organized around PGA networks, challenges capitalism outright. An articulate position within this anti-capitalist movement is explicitly anarchist and proposes a new form of socio-political organization around the practice of grassrooted networking. For the neo-anarchists, the Internet and other forms of networking are not just an organizational tool but an emergent form of a self-managed society. Another world is possible, but for these

views, the emphasis is on "another," and the possibility can only emerge through the radicalization of the struggle.

4   But if, in spite of these sharp contradictions, which may well lead to distinct networks of action, there is still a movement, it is because what truly characterizes the anti-globalization movement is what gave rise to it in the first place: the radical critique of the mechanisms of political representation in the institutions of global governance. At first sight, the critique would not appear to be justified. After all, the international institutions and meetings that are the targets of protest are made up of governments, most of them democratically elected governments. This is in fact the argument put forward by these institutions to dismiss the protests as undemocratic. Yet, if the anti-globalization movement has such a broad appeal, and has struck the public mind throughout the world well beyond its militant ranks, it must be addressing a deeply felt democratic deficit. Between the act of voting every four years for the lesser evil of two restricted options, and the outcome of a process of complex decision-making among a plurality of governmental actors taking into consideration the structurally dominant interests of private corporations, there is an increasing gap, made even greater by a lack of transparency and by citizen distrust of the political class. Thus, the glue that binds the anti-globalization movement together, in the mind if not in organization, is the shared project toward alternative forms of democratic representation and governance. It is not a movement against globalization, but a movement for democratic globalization, for a system of governance that would fit democratic ideals in the new context of decision-making that has emerged in a global, network society.

Networking as a political way of being

Networking, and particularly Internet-based networking, is of the essence in the anti-globalization movement. The numerous struggles, actions, and organizations that opposed neo-liberal policies in the 1990s ultimately converged in a network of networks by means of electronic communication. The coordination of initiatives and the discussions that led to Seattle were considerably helped by the use of the Internet, as were the subsequent mobilizations and calls to arms for each of the global events that take place periodically. By using the Internet, the movement did not need a centralized, command structure invested with authority and decision-making power. Different groups would call on different messages, and present their views, and their conflicts, to everybody via the Net. Coordination meetings took place prior to each event, usually in the same place as the event, and the counter-event, were due to happen. Yet most of these meetings were limited to the sharing of logistics, and physically separating the different components of the demonstration, so that those ready to use violent confrontation would have their own space of action. In other words, the diversity of tactics and ideologies in the movement was expressed in spatial and organizational separation, and then networked communication around the shared goals assured the overall effectiveness of the movement.

E-mailing lists, chat rooms, forums, and the posting of information and statements, made the Internet the permanent *agora* of the movement, and made a wide debate possible without the disruption of antagonistic meetings leading to sharp confrontations. The movement could be coordinated and diversified at the same time, and anyone wanting to say something could do so by posting her message and engaging in personalized, networked debate. It must be emphasized that the use of the Internet is not restricted to the militants of developed countries. As Chiriboga has demonstrated, the organizations of indigenous people in Latin America have used the Internet as an essential organizing and mobilizing tool, following the pioneer experience of the *Zapatista* solidarity movement.[72] It is through the Internet that relatively isolated movements have succeeded in building their networks of global solidarity and support, and have been able to post their information in real time, becoming less vulnerable to repression in their localities.

The experience of mobilizing and organizing around the Internet has led some militants to propose the network as a potential form for a future democratic society, in which people keep their autonomy, and make their collective decisions through debates and votes without the intermediation of professional politicians. While this is, for the time being, a political utopia, it is worth while considering it with regard to the history of political institutions. Mass political parties, which characterized the political left of the industrial era, were modeled upon the experience of mass social movements, such as the labor movement or the peasant movement, with their organization in chapters, local committees, and delegated, federal structure. Thus, the organizational forms and principles of political practice in a period of formation of a new social structure configure the experience of the future representatives of these movements in the institutions of society. Should the militants of the anti-globalization movement ultimately constitute the new forces of political change in the institutions of society (through forms such as green parties, identity-based alliances,

72   Chiriboga (2003)

human rights coalitions, or other expressions still to be discovered) their networking practice would most likely be transferred to the emerging political institutions. While these developments are clearly still in the process of social experimentation, what is analytically important is to underline that networking, and particularly Internet-based networking, is not just an instrument of organization and struggle, it is a new form of social interaction, mobilization, and decision-making. It is a new political culture: networking means no center, thus no central authority. It means an instant relationship between the local and the global, so that the movement can think locally, rooted in its identity and interests, and act globally, where the sources of power are. It also means that all nodes in the network can and may contribute to the goals of the network, thus strengthening it by its relentless expansion. But it also means that dysfunctional nodes that block the overall dynamics of the network can easily be switched off or bypassed, thus overcoming the traditional ailments of social movements so often engaged in self-destruction through factionalism.

The contradictory diversity of the anti-globalization movement would make it an impossible collective actor, except under the conditions of its existence as a network. This is why the movement is the network, it is a network movement, and this is clearly distinct from being a network of movements. The added value of the anti-globalization movement is its capacity to operate as a unit in its diversity, but it is a unit of variable geometry, made possible by the changing integration of its goals and components, through a self-evolving network. However, this is not a purely electronic network. The network connects localities, and it also connects places that become symbolic sites of events and counter-events. The networking is both face to face and electronic, and it relates both to web sites and to geographical sites. These physical sites are made from two geographies: the geography of experience and the geography of power. Sites of experience where the actors of the movement live and find their meaning. Sites of power where the institutions of global governance meet for the shared enjoyment of their domination, dotting the planet with their self-defined time and space. Thus, through networking, sites of experience become trenches of resistance, and sites of power come under spatial siege from the counterpowers-that-be.

An informational movement: the theatrical tactics of anti-globalization militants

If the *Zapatistas* were the first informational guerrillas, in the terms defined above, the anti-globalization movement generalized this strategy to a whole array of convergent struggles against the capitalist global order. The real targets of the militants' mobilization are the minds of people around the world. It is by changing minds that they expect to put pressure on the institutions of governance and, ultimately, bring democracy and alternative social values to these institutions. But we live in an information age in which people tend to form their opinions on the basis of the images and sounds processed by the media. Therefore, the movement acts on this process of formation/information of the public mind by two main channels. On the one hand, by introducing new messages into the mainstream media. On the other hand, by creating an alternative media system to reach people through horizontal networks of communication, escaping the control of corporate media. To influence the media it is necessary to speak the language of the media, and particularly the language of television.[73] This is the origin of the idea of transforming global events of power-making into global events of power-unmaking, by converging on the times and spaces covered by the media as expressions of the globalization process, and then subverting the content of these events by creating counter-messages, conveyed by the interfering presence of militant protests. But mere presence is not enough to make it news or to be in the news. Some action is required that can be reported, such as blocking access to the sites of the meetings (Seattle), or trapping the attendees in their meeting place (Prague). In all cases, this is bound to prompt police action, and once the police are sent in, violence usually ensues. Moreover, some components of the movement, the Black Block particularly, consider violent confrontation to be part of the educational process for society to wake up, so that the movement has come to accept that different constituencies lead to different forms of action, and they must coexist.

Violence has a contradictory effect on the movement. On the one hand, it guarantees media coverage. On the other hand, it portrays the image of the movement as a violent movement, and may alienate the silent majority of the population. Thus, in some instances (Barcelona, June 2001; Genoa, July 2001) the police, probably under political orders, sent in agents provocateurs to induce violence. Most participants in the protest, however, do not condone violence, but many practice non-violent civil disobedience, often in a theatrical manner, such as the Italian Tute Bianche (White Overall) who, completely dressed in white, advance toward police lines under white plastic shields. Street theater, clowns, puppets, music, dancing, and a carnival-like atmosphere are a constant expression of the movement,

73   Volkmer (1999).

picking up on the line of action pioneered by the British Reclaim the Streets group and the American Art&Revolution movement. Feasting and street celebration are the expression of an alternative project of life and meaning, substituting the joy of creativity and the sharing of public space for the seclusion and distance of the bureaucracies of governance. It also projects an image of goodness to society at large, and attracts participants to the pleasure of a multi-dimensional happening, in the language of the youth culture to which many of the participants belong. Thus, public celebration is a goal in itself for the movement, the value of enjoyment, but it is also a form of communication to the media, providing interesting footage and sound bites that can be easily channeled into the usual language of news as entertainment.

At the same time as the movement acts on the mainstream media, it has also developed its own medium of communication. A key element is the Indymedia network, an independent, multimedia group that formed spontaneously around the Seattle demonstration and has continued its activity around events. It is largely based on the Internet, with news reporting and billboard posting open to anyone. But it also functions as a reporting agency, providing accurate information about the actual events, often obscured by the authorities and unreported by the media. It is characterized by courageous, on-the-spot reporting, often facing violent repression. Groups loosely connected to the Indymedia network also make films, and photos, and provide a continuing audiovisual account of the movement, which is then diffused throughout the global network. It is through this dual communication system with people around the world that the movement acts on the most powerful lever of social change: people's minds and wills.

The movement in context: social change and institutional change

As with all major social movements, the outcome of the anti-globalization movement is not easy to assess. While some of the international meetings have been seriously disrupted, and particularly the WTO meeting in Seattle, largely due to the surprise effect of a movement that had been underestimated in its appeal, most functions of global governance have been able to proceed, within barricaded buildings, behind police lines, and even (as in Genoa) with air-missile defense systems on board warships. To be sure, an image has been created of increasing seclusion and social distance between the institutions of power and active civil society. But, by and large, writing at the end of 2002, it is difficult to detect a major change in the policies managing globalization *vis à vis* its original liberal matrix. And yet, there are changes. There are changes in the attitude and language of some of the governing institutions, which seem to be ready at least to listen to the "respectable" components of the movement, particularly to the religious groups and mainstream NGOs that voiced the need for reform and global solidarity. Some governments, for instance the French government under Jospin and the Belgian government, have attended the World Social Forum, as have United Nations agencies, such as the International Labor Office. In meetings of the global elite, they have made room for NGOs and alternative social actors, and have invited intellectual critics to express their views. Most of this is a change of discourse rather than of policy option, but it does indicate a deeper trend: the process of globalization is subject to public debate. It is no longer assumed to be a natural process, resulting from the inner logic of technology and the market. The need for the political management of globalization is now widely recognized, although the values and goals informing this management are still, by and large, what the movement labels as "corporate values."

The key distinction to be made in the relationship between the movement and political institutions of society is contextual. The anti-globalization movement, while being indeed global, has a very uneven level of penetration and mobilization throughout the world. It is basically absent in China, unless the anti-foreign values position of Falun Gong is considered the functional equivalent of the movement – an analysis that I would not follow. It has also a very weak existence in Muslim countries where Islamic fundamentalism plays, in my opinion, an oppositional role to the global order. Indeed, the WTO meeting in Dhofar took place without protest because of the ability of authoritarian countries to close the borders to external would-be protesters: it may become a pattern for future meetings. In the most impoverished continent, Africa, only in developed South Africa is there a recognizable anti-globalization movement. And much of Asia, including Japan, is still untouched by the protest, although Malaysian environmental activists were among the pioneers of the movement. Moreover, while the US was the most active setting for the movement in 1999–2000, after 9/11 an iron curtain came down over the movement, as the majority of the population embraced the politics of fear and appeared to be ready to go to war against anyone likely to shatter the historical feeling of homeland security. The demonstration against the World Economic Forum in New York in January 2002 was limited to a few thousand demonstrators wary of confronting the very popular New York police. Anti-war demonstrations in America seemed to revitalize the movement in the Fall of 2002, but the anti-globalization movement had become clearly subordinated to the dynamics of the war on terror. At the same time, the movement expanded in Europe, and was energized in Latin America by the social movements in Argentina, and by political victories of allied parties in Ecuador and, particularly, in Brazil, thus challenging the Washington consensus that had dominated the 1990s in Latin America.

This contextual differentiation of the anti-globalization movement stresses its global character. It is not a sum of nationally bound struggles. It is a global network of opposition to the values and interests embedded in the globalization process. Therefore, its nodes grow and shrink alternately, depending on the conditions under which each society relates to globalization and its political manifestations. It is the network that maintains the vitality of the movement even when some of its nodes decline. However, the fact that major authoritarian societies (China), or semi-authoritarian systems (Russia), see limited action by the movement seems to indicate that the movement's main nodes need the context of an open society in order to be active. Perhaps this combination between powerful nodes rooted in open societies, and networks that reach out through a planet in which most people suffer oppression and poverty, is the distinctive trend of the movement as a social movement challenging globalization on behalf of the whole of humankind.

This is why I ultimately consider it accurate to identify the movement by the name of what it opposes rather than by an adjective describing its ideology, since its values are clearly diverse and even contradictory. It is a movement that says "no" on behalf of humankind, including in this negation those who are still voiceless. From this rejection appears the possibility of a different world whose principles and historical horizon are a function of the debate that the anti-globalization movement has prompted with its struggles.

The Meaning of Insurgencies against the New Global Order

After analyzing five movements against globalization, in their practices, in their discourses, and in their contexts, I will venture their comparison, seeking to draw conclusions for the broader analysis of social change in the network society. I will use my adaptation of Alain Touraine's typology as a way of reading the movements in relation to the same analytical categories. Seen from this perspective, the movements analyzed here coincide in the identification of their adversary: it is the new global order designated by the *Zapatistas* as the conjunction of American imperialism and corrupt, illegitimate PRI government in NAFTA; incarnated by international institutions, most notably the United Nations, and the US federal government in the view of American militia; for *Aum* the global threat comes from a unified world government representing the interests of multinational corporations, US imperialism and Japanese police; for *al-Qaeda*, the global order is dominated by the Crusaders, the alliance of Christians and Jews imposing their values and interests through violence, militarily led by the United States; for the anti-globalization movement, the adversary is global corporate capitalism, and the undemocratic institutions of global governance that support the interests of the corporations. Thus, the five movements are primarily organized around their opposition to an adversary that is, by and large, the same: the agents and institutions of a new global, capitalist order, seeking to establish a world power that will subdue the sovereignty of all countries and all people.

To such an enemy, each movement opposes a different principle of identity, reflecting the sharp contrasts between the five movements: in the case of the *Zapatistas*, they see themselves as Indians and oppressed Mexicans fighting for their dignity, their rights, their land, and the Mexican nation, but they also call for global solidarity, and see themselves as the vanguard of a much broader coalition against globalization. In the case of the militia, they see themselves as American citizens fighting for their sovereignty, and for their liberties, as expressed in the original, godly American Constitution. While it might seem surprising to list an American nationalist movement alongside *al-Qaeda*, in fact in the days following 9/11 several websites related to the Patriot movement in the United States expressed their sympathy for an attack on the symbols of corporate capitalism, although regretting the American victims. To a large extent, American Patriots are related to Christian fundamentalism, so that there is a common cultural code of religious fundamentalism with Islamic movements. For *Aum*, their identity principle is more complex: it is in fact their individual identity, expressed in their bodies, although such bodies share each other in the guru's mind – it is the combination of physical individuality and reconstructed spiritual community. For *al-Qaeda*, the identity is clearly defined: they are true Muslims, engaged in *jihad* to save the world, and particularly the Muslim world, from *Jahiliya*. However, the anti-globalization movement does not have a single identity. Its specificity is precisely that it brings together multiple identities that join the common struggle against corporate, undemocratic globalization.

In four cases, there is an appeal to authenticity in their identity principle, but with different manifestations: an historically rooted, broad community (the Indians of Mexico, as part of the Mexican population, as part of other indigenous people, and as part of the peoples of the world); local communities of free citizens; a spiritual community of individuals freed from dependence on their bodies; and the worldwide community of true believers in Allah. The multiple identity of the anti-globalization movement refers implicitly to the people of the world, to their human rights, to their social rights, but also to the conservation of nature and to the defense of specific cultural identities, so that what is really important in the case of the anti-globalization movement is that it is a network of identities and interests. For all movements, their identities are based on cultural specificity and on a desire for control over their own destiny. And they are opposed to the global adversary on behalf of a higher societal goal, which in all cases leads to integration between their specific identity and the well-being of society at large: Mexico, America, surviving humankind, the *umma* of believers, global democracy. Yet, this integration is sought through the fulfillment of different values for each movement: social justice and democracy for all Mexicans; individual freedom from government domination for all American citizens; transcendence of materiality through spiritual liberation in the case of *Aum*; the law of God as the foundation of societies around the planet; participatory democracy and global justice as the guiding principle for new, democratic institutions of global governance. These societal goals, however, are not the strongest element in four of the five movements: they are primarily identity-based mobilizations in reaction to a clearly identified adversary. They are reactive, and defensive, rather than purveyors of a societal project, even if they do propose visions of an alternative society. On the other hand, the anti-globalization movement, although essentially organized around a common opposition to corporate globalization, does emphasize the project for alternative globalization. This alternative, however, concerns mainly the claim for global democratic institutions. The projects for different forms of globalization do exist, but they diverge among the different components of the movement. Thus, the anti-globalization movement transformed itself from a multiple identity, resistance movement into a movement organized around the political project of global democracy, with various models of society to be debated in this new democratic space. Chart 2.1 lists the elements defining each movement.

The powerful impact of each of these movements has come, to a large extent, from their media presence and from their effective use of

Chart 2.1   Structure of values and beliefs of insurgent movements against globalization

Movement	Identity	Adversary	Goal
Zapatistas	Oppressed, excluded Indians/ Mexicans	Global capitalism (NAFTA), illegal PRI government	Dignity, democracy, land
American militia	Original American citizens	New world order, US federal government	Liberty and sovereignty of citizens and local communities
Aum Shinrikyo	Spiritual community of delivered bodies of believers	United world government, Japanese police	Survival of apocalypse
al-Qaeda	True Muslims	Global power of the Christians and Jews	Humankind as *umma*, societies ruled by *shari'a*
Anti-globalization movement	Multiple identities	Global corporate capitalism	Global democracy

information technology. Media attention is sought, or found, by performing in the Russian, Catalan, or French anarchist tradition, briefly revived in May 1968, of *l'action exemplaire*: a spectacular action is undertaken which, by its powerful appeal, even through sacrifice, calls people's attention to the movement's claims, and is ultimately intended to wake up the masses, manipulated by propaganda and subdued by repression. Forcing a debate on their claims, and inducing people to participate, movements expect to put pressure on governments and institutions, reversing the course of submission to the new world order.

This is why weapons are essential in four of the five movements, not as a goal, but as a sign of freedom, and as an event-triggering device, attracting media attention. This media-oriented strategy was particularly explicit, and skillfully executed, in the case of the *Zapatistas*, who tried carefully to minimize violence and to work via the media and the Internet to reach out to the world. But the paramilitary theatrics of the militia, and the deliberate exploitation of violent tactics, or the threat of it, to attract media attention are also a key component of American Patriots. Even *Aum*, distrustful of the media, did pay considerable attention to debates on television, and to press reports, dedicating some of its best members to such tasks. And its gas attacks seem to have had the dual purpose of verifying the doomsday prophecy and of diffusing their warning throughout the world, through the media. Of course, *al-Qaeda*'s extreme violence targets the most powerful symbols of global power: the World Trade Center, the Pentagon, Western ships crossing Muslim waters, as well as the symbols of degenerate Western culture, e.g. disco bars in Bali, tourist resorts in Africa. It would seem that the new protest movements cast their messages and project their claims in the form of symbolic politics characteristic of informational society (see chapter 6). Their media skills are fundamental fighting tools, while their manifestos and their weapons are means to create an event worth reporting.

New communication technologies are fundamental to the existence of these movements: indeed, they are their organizational infrastructure. Without the Internet, fax, and alternative media, the Patriots would not have been an influential network, but a disconnected, powerless series of reactions. Without the communication capacity enabling the *Zapatistas* to reach urban Mexico, and the world, in real time, they might have remained an isolated, localized guerrilla force, as others still fighting in Latin America. *Aum* did not make much use of the Internet, simply because the Internet was hardly present in Japan in the early 1990s. But they did extensively use fax, and video, and computers, as crucial tools in building a highly controlled, yet decentralized organizational network. Besides, they were attempting a technological breakthrough by developing electronically stimulated, direct communication from brain to brain. The revolutionary cells of the information age are built on flows of electrons. *Al-Qaeda* used the Internet less than the US government pretends – in an obvious pretext to justify censorship of the Internet. But, of course, e-mail was one of the means of communication, and mobile, satellite phones are essential in the communications of terror networks. And the Internet is of the essence in the anti-globalization movement, as a mobilizing medium, as a form of organization and debate, and as a blueprint for the grassrooted, open, democratic society that the militants oppose to the seclusion and isolation of global corporate institutions.

Alongside their similarity, the five movements also display profound differences, linked to their historical/cultural origins, and to the specific dynamics of their societies. A sharp distinction must be drawn between the articulate political project of the *Zapatistas*, the confusion and paranoia of most militia groups, and the apocalyptic logic of *Aum*. This also relates to the difference between the eschatological component in both the militia and *Aum*, and the absence of such views of the End of Time in the *Zapatistas*. *Al-Qaeda* is culturally specific, but not country-specific, and the same can be said of the anti-globalization movement. In fact, both *al-Qaeda* and the anti-globalization movement are global networks from their starting-point, aiming at a global adversary, and purporting a global project. Therefore, they seem to represent a qualitative shift in the development of social movements against the new global order. What started as local trenches of resistance transformed into a global social movement. In fact, the three localized movements had different fates. Both the American militia and *Aum* could not sustain their existence when confronted with a major, violent crisis. After the Oklahoma bombing, enacted by sympathizers of the militia, the appeal of the Patriot movement, in its formalized organization, faded away, although its themes and constituencies are still alive in the United States. Although *Aum* has survived the trial of its guru, it has been so stigmatized that it is no longer able to cultivate its fatal attraction among Japanese youth. However, the causes of alienation among Japanese youth are still current, so that other specific expressions of this alienation are to be expected. The most interesting transformative process concerns the *Zapatistas*. Even if, at the time of writing, they are still confined in their stronghold of Chiapas, without having received satisfaction for their most important demands, their initial call for a global uprising against globalization has been widely answered. They are indeed considered by most anti-globalization militants as the harbingers of the movement, and their themes and forms of organization (their practice as an informational guerrilla movement) have become the foundation of the indigenous movements in Latin America and of the anti-globalization movement around the world. What the Afghan camps were for *al-Qaeda*, the *Zapatistas'* solidarity meetings were for a number of militants and organizations of the anti-globalization movement. This is a clear expression of the transformation of a resistance identity into a project identity, in a development that I will analyze later in this volume.

Thus, new social movements, in their diversity, react against globalization, and against its political agents, and act upon the continuing process of informationalization by changing the cultural codes at the root of new social institutions. In this sense, they surge from the depths of historically exhausted social forms, but decisively affect, in a complex pattern, society in the making.

Conclusion: The Challenge to Globalization

The social movements I have analyzed in this chapter are very different. And yet, under different forms, reflecting their diverse social and cultural roots, they all challenge current processes of globalization, on behalf of their constructed identities, in some instances claiming to represent the interests of their country, or of humankind, as well.

The movements I have studied, in this and other chapters of this volume, are not the only ones opposing the social, economic, cultural, and environmental consequences of globalization. In other areas of the world, for instance in Europe, similar challenges rise against capitalist restructuring, and against the imposition of new rules in the name of global competition, on the basis of the labor movement, and of farmers' movements, such as the one led by Jose Bove in France. Some of these movements, like that led by Jose Bove, have linked up with the anti-globalization movement. Some have not, but they also aim at a deliberate opposition to the processes of one-sided globalization, often identified with the policies of the European Union. In China, Falun Gong can be identified as a force of opposition against the social consequences of modernization and globalization in China, building on traditional Chinese values and practices to preserve health and well-being against the destitution being brought to many by the Chinese brand of communist-led, global capitalism. In Argentina, the social movements prompted by the financial crisis of 2001–2 opposed both the global economic order and the national political order, forcing a change of regime, and bringing new social actors into the public space, in a process that looms large in the transformation of South America.[74] In Europe, in 2002, populist movements, generally related to fear and xenophobia, have blurred the political scene, as I will analyze later in this volume.

After a decade of development of a new, global economy and of the decline of the nation-state in its transition to institutions of global governance, societies around the world have claimed their right to assert control over the emerging institutions. What started as resistance, based on identity, and preservation of the economic status quo, evolved into a multiplicity of projects, in which cultural identity, economic interests, and political strategies have combined in an in-

74   Calderon (2003).

creasingly complex pattern: the canvas of social movements in the network society. These movements, spreading throughout the world, have ended the neo-liberal fantasy of creating a new global economy independent of society by escaping into computer networks. The grand exclusionary scheme (explicit or implicit) of concentrating information, production, and markets in a valuable segment of the population, disposing of the rest in different forms, more or less humane according to each society's temper, has triggered, in Touraine's expression, a *"grand refus."*[75] But the transformation of this rejection into the reconstruction of new forms of social control over new forms of capitalism, globalized and informationalized, requires the processing of social movements' demands by the political system and the institutions of the state. The ability, or inability, of the state to cope with the conflicting logics of global capitalism, identity-based social movements, defensive movements of workers and consumers, and alternative projects of globalization, will largely condition the society of the twenty-first century. Yet, before examining the dynamics of the state in the information age, we must analyze the development of different kinds of powerful social movements that are proactive rather than reactive: environmentalism and feminism.

75   Touraine et al. (1996).

3

The Greening of the Self: The Environmental Movement

The Green approach to politics is a kind of celebration. We recognize that each of us is part of the world's problems, and we are also part of the solution. The dangers and potentials for healing are not just outside us. We begin to work exactly where we are. There is no need to wait until conditions become ideal. We can simplify our lives and live in ways that affirm ecological and human values. Better conditions will come because we have begun... It can therefore be said that the primary goal of Green politics is an inner revolution, "the greening of the self."

Petra Kelly, *Thinking Green*[1]

If we are to appraise social movements by their historical productivity, namely, by their impact on cultural values and society's institutions, the environmental movement has earned a distinctive place in the landscape of human adventure. At this turn of the millennium, 80 percent of Americans, and over two-thirds of Europeans, consider themselves environmentalists; parties and candidates can hardly be elected to office without "greening" their platform; governments and international institutions alike multiply programs, special agencies, and legislation to protect nature, improve the quality of life and, ultimately, save the Earth in the long term and ourselves in the short term. Corporations, including some notorious polluters, have included environmentalism in their public relations agenda, as well as

---

1 *In Essays by Petra Kelly (1947–1992)* (Kelly, 1994: 39–40). In this quote, she refers to Joanna Macy's "the greening of the self" (Macy, 1991).

among their most promising new markets. And throughout the globe, the old, simplistic opposition between development for the poor and conservation for the rich has been transformed into a multilayered debate over the actual content of sustainable development for each country, city, and region.

To be sure, most of our fundamental problems concerning the environment remain, since their treatment requires a transformation of modes of production and consumption, as well as of our social organization and personal lives. Global warming looms as a lethal threat, the rainforest still burns, toxic chemicals are deeply into the food chain, a sea of poverty denies life, and governments play games with people's health, as exemplified by Major's madness with British cows. Yet, the fact that all these issues, and many others, are in the public debate, and that a growing awareness has emerged of their interdependent, global character, creates the foundation for their treatment, and, maybe, for a reorientation of institutions and policies toward an environmentally responsible socio-economic system. The multifaceted environmental movement that emerged from the late 1960s in most of the world, with its strong points in the United States and Northern Europe, is to a large extent at the root of a dramatic reversal in the ways in which we think about the relationship between economy, society, and nature, thus giving rise to a new culture.[2]

It is somewhat arbitrary, however, to speak of the environmental movement since it is so diverse in its composition, and varies so much in its expressions from country to country, and between cultures. Thus, before assessing its transformative potential, I will attempt a typological differentiation of various components of environmentalism, and use examples for each type, to bring the argument down to earth. Then, I shall proceed to a broader elaboration on the relationship between environmentalists' themes and fundamental dimensions on which structural transformation takes place in our society: the struggles over the role of science and technology, over the control of space and time, and over the construction of new identities. Having characterized the environmental movements in their social diversity and in their cultural sharing, I shall analyze their means and ways of acting on society at large, thus exploring the issue of their institutionalization, and their relationship to the state. Finally, consideration will be given to the growing linkage between environmental movements and social struggles, both locally and globally, along the increasingly popular perspective of environmental justice.

2   For an overview of the environmental movement, see (among other sources) Holliman (1990); Gottlieb (1993); Kaminiecki (1993); Shabecoff (1993); Dalton (1994); Alley et al. (1995); Diani (1995); Brulle (1996); Wapner (1996).

The Creative Cacophony of Environmentalism: A Typology

Collective action, politics, and discourses grouped under the name of environmentalism are so diverse as to challenge the idea of a movement. And, yet, I argue that it is precisely this cacophony of theory and practice that characterizes environmentalism as a new form of decentralized, multiform, network-oriented, pervasive social movement. Besides, as I will try to show, there are some fundamental themes that run across most, if not all, environmentally related collective action. However, for the sake of clarity, it seems helpful to proceed in the analysis of this movement on the basis of one distinction and one typology.

The distinction is between environmentalism and ecology. By *environmentalism* I refer to all forms of collective behavior that, in their discourse and in their practice, aim at correcting destructive forms of relationship between human action and its natural environment, in opposition to the prevailing structural and institutional logic. By *ecology*, in my sociological approach, I understand a set of beliefs, theories, and projects that consider humankind as a component of a broader ecosystem and wish to maintain the system's balance in a dynamic, evolutionary perspective. In my view, environmentalism is ecology in practice, and ecology is environmentalism in theory, but in the following pages I will restrict the use of the term "ecology" to explicit, conscious manifestations of this holistic, evolutionary perspective.

As for the typology, I shall again call upon Alain Touraine's useful characterization of social movements, as presented in chapter 2, to differentiate five major varieties of environmental movement, *as they have manifested themselves in observed practices* in the past two decades, at international level. I suggest that this typology has general value, although most of the examples are drawn from North American and German experiences because they are the most developed environmental movements in the world, and because I had easier access to this information. Please accept the usual disclaimer about the inevitable reductionism of this and all typologies, which I hope will be compensated for by examples that will bring the flesh and blood of actual movements into this somewhat abstract characterization.

To undertake our brief journey across the kaleidoscope of environmentalism by means of the proposed typology, you need a map. Chart 3.1 provides it, and requires some explanation. Each type is defined, analytically, by a specific combination of the three characteristics defining a social movement: *identity*, *adversary*, and *goal*. For each type, I identify the precise content of the three characteristics, resulting from observation, using several sources, to which I refer.

Chart 3.1   Typology of environmental movements

Type (Example)	Identity	Adversary	Goal
Conservation of nature (Group of Ten, USA)	Nature lovers	Uncontrolled development	Wilderness
Defense of own space (Not in my Back Yard)	Local community	Polluters	Quality of life/health
Counter-culture, deep ecology (Earth First!, ecofeminism)	The green self	Industrialism, technocracy, and patriarchalism	Ecotopia
Save the planet (Greenpeace)	Internationalist eco-warriors	Unfettered global development	Sustainability
Green politics (*Die Grünen*)	Concerned citizens	Political establishment	Counter-power

Accordingly, I give a name to each type, and provide examples of movements that best fit each type. Naturally, in any given movement or organization there may be a mixture of characteristics, but I select, for analytical purposes, those movements that seem to be closer to the ideal type in their actual practice and discourse. In addition to Chart 3.1, I will give a brief description of each of the examples that illustrate the five types, so that distinct voices of the movement can be heard through its cacophony.

The *conservation of nature*, under its different forms, was at the origin of the environmentalist movement in America, as enacted by organizations such as the Sierra Club (founded in San Francisco in 1891 by John Muir), the Audubon Society, or the Wilderness Society.[3] In the early 1980s, old and new mainstream environmental organizations came together in an alliance, known as the Group of Ten, which included, besides the above-cited organizations, the National Parks and Conservation Association, the National Wildlife Federation, the Natural Resources Defense Council, Izaak Walton League, Defenders

3   Allen (1987); Scarce (1990); Gottlieb (1993); Shabecoff (1993).

of Wildlife, Environmental Defense Fund, and the Environmental Policy Institute. In spite of differences in approach and in their specific field of intervention, what brings these organizations together, with many others created along similar lines, is their pragmatic defense of conservationist causes through the institutional system. In the words of Michael McCloskey, Sierra Club Chairman, their approach can be characterized as "muddling through": "We come out of a mountaineering tradition where you first decide that you're going to climb the mountain. You have a notion of a general route, but you find handholds and the footholds as you go along and you have to adapt and keep changing."[4] Their summit to be climbed is the preservation of wilderness, in its different forms, within reasonable parameters of what can be achieved in the present economic and institutional system. Their adversaries are uncontrolled development, and unresponsive bureaucracies such as the US Bureau of Reclamation, not caring to protect our natural preserve. They define themselves as nature lovers, and appeal to this feeling in all of us, regardless of social differences. They work through and by the institutions, very often using lobbying with great skill and political muscle. They rely on widespread popular support, as well as on donations from well-wishing, wealthy elites, and from corporations. Some organizations, such as the Sierra Club, are very large (about 600,000 members) and are organized in local branches, whose actions and ideologies vary considerably, and do not always fit the image of "mainstream environmentalism."

Most others, such as the Environmental Defense Fund, focus on lobbying, analyzing, and diffusing information. They often practice coalition politics, but they are careful not to be carried away from their environmental focus, distrusting radical ideologies and spectacular action out of step with the majority of public opinion. However, it would be a mistake to oppose mainstream conservationists to the true, radical environmentalists. For instance, one of the historic leaders of the Sierra Club, David Brower, became a source of inspiration for radical environmentalists. Reciprocally, Dave Foreman, from Earth First!, was, in 1996, on the Board of Directors of the Sierra Club. There is a great deal of osmosis in the relationships between conservationists and radical ecologists, as ideologies tend to take second place to their shared concern about the relentless, multiform destruction of nature. This, in spite of sharp debates and conflicts within a large, diversified movement.

The *mobilization of local communities in defense of their space*, against the intrusion of undesirable uses, constitutes the fastest-

4   Quoted in Scarce (1990: 15).

growing form of environmental action, and the one that perhaps most directly links people's immediate concerns to broader issues of environmental deterioration.[5] Often labeled, somewhat maliciously, the *"Not in my Back Yard" movement*, it developed in the United States first of all under the form of the toxics movement, which originated in 1978 during the infamous Love Canal incident of industrial toxic waste dumping in Niagara Falls, New York. Lois Gibbs, the homeowner who gained notoriety because of her fight to defend the health of her son, as well as the value of her home, went on to establish, in 1981, the Citizens' Clearinghouse for Hazardous Wastes. According to Clearinghouse figures, in 1984 there were 600 local groups fighting against toxic dumping in the United States, which increased to 4,687 in 1988. Over time, communities mobilized also against freeway construction, excessive development, and the location of hazardous facilities in their proximity. While the movement is local, it is not necessarily localistic, since it often affirms residents' right to quality of life in opposition to business or bureaucratic interests. To be sure, life in society is made up of trade-offs among people themselves, as residents, workers, consumers, commuters, and travelers. But what is questioned by these movements is, on the one hand, the bias of location of undesirable materials or activities toward low-income communities and areas inhabited by minorities, and, on the other, a lack of transparency and participation in decision-making about the uses of space. Thus, citizens call for extended local democracy, for responsible city planning, and for fairness in sharing the burdens of urban/industrial development, while avoiding exposure to hazardous dumping or utilities. As Epstein concludes in her analysis of the movement:

> The demand of the toxics/environmental justice movement for a state that has more power to regulate corporations, a state that is accountable to the public rather than the corporations, seems entirely appropriate, and possibly a basis for a broader demand that state power over corporations be reasserted and expanded, and that state power be exercised on behalf of public welfare and especially the welfare of those who are most vulnerable.[6]

In other instances, in middle-class suburbs, residents' mobilizations have been more focused on preserving the status quo against non-desired development. Yet, regardless of their class content, all forms of protest have aimed at establishing control over the living environment on behalf of the local community, and, in this sense, defensive

5   Gottlieb (1993); Szasz (1994); Epstein (1995).
6   Epstein (1995: 20).

local mobilizations are certainly a major component of the broader environmental movement.

Environmentalism has also nurtured some of the *counter-cultures* that sprang from the 1960s' and 1970s' movements. By counter-culture, I understand the deliberate attempt to live according to norms different, and to some extent contradictory, from those institutionally enforced by society, and to oppose those institutions on the ground of alternative principles and beliefs. Some of the most powerful counter-cultural currents in our societies express themselves in the form of abiding only by the laws of nature, and thus affirming the priority of respect for nature over any other human institution. This is why I think it makes sense to include under the notion of counter-cultural environmentalism expressions as apparently distinct as radical environmentalists (such as Earth First! or the Sea Shepherds), the animal liberation movement, and ecofeminism.[7] In fact, in spite of their diversity and lack of coordination, most of these movements share the ideas of "deep ecology" thinkers, as represented, for instance, by Norwegian writer Arne Naess. According to Arne Naess and George Sessions, the basic principles of "deep ecology" are:

(1) The well-being and flourishing of human and non-human Life on Earth have value in themselves. These values are independent of the usefulness of the non-human world for human purposes. (2) Richness and diversity of life forms contribute to the realization of these values and are also values in themselves. (3) Humans have no right to reduce this richness and diversity except to satisfy vital needs. (4) The flourishing of human life and cultures is compatible with a substantial decrease of the human population. The flourishing of non-human life requires such a decrease. (5) Present human interference with the non-human world is excessive, and the situation is rapidly worsening. (6) Policies must therefore be changed. These policies affect basic economic, technological, and ideological structures. The resulting state of affairs will be deeply different from the present. (7) The ideological change is mainly that of appreciating life quality (dwelling in situations of inherent value) rather than adhering to an increasingly high standard of living. There will be profound awareness of the difference between big and great. (8) Those who subscribe to the foregoing points have an obligation directly or indirectly to try to implement the necessary changes.[8]

To respond to such an obligation, in the late 1970s a number of radical ecologists, led by David Foreman, an ex-Marine turned

---

7   For sources, see Adler (1979); Spretnak (1982); Manes (1990); Scarce (1990); Davis (1991); Dobson (1991); Epstein (1991); Moog (1995).
8   Naess and Sessions (1984), reproduced in Davis (1991: 157–8).

eco-warrior, created in New Mexico and Arizona *Earth First!*, an uncompromising movement that engaged in civil disobedience and even "ecotage" against dam construction, logging, and other aggressions against nature, thus facing prosecution and jail. The movement, and a number of other organizations which followed suit, were completely decentralized, formed by autonomous "tribes," which would meet periodically, according to the rites and times of Native American Indians, and decide their own actions. Deep ecology was the ideological foundation of the movement, and it figures prominently in *The Earth First! Reader*, published with a foreword by David Foreman.[9] But equally influential, if not more so, was Abbey's novel *The Monkey Wrench Gang*, about a counter-cultural group of eco-guerrillas, who became role models for many radical ecologists. Indeed, "monkey wrenching" became a synonym for eco-sabotage. In the 1990s, the animal liberation movement, focusing on outright opposition to experimentation with animals, seems to be the most militant wing of ecological fundamentalism.

Ecofeminism is clearly distant from the "macho-tactics" of some of these movements. And yet, ecofeminists share the principle of absolute respect for nature as the foundation of liberation from both patriarchalism and industrialism. They see women as victims of the same patriarchal violence that is inflicted upon nature. And so, the restoration of natural rights is inseparable from women's liberation. In the words of Judith Plant:

> Historically, women have had no real power in the outside world, no place in decision-making. Intellectual life, the work of the mind, has traditionally not been accessible to women. Women have been generally passive, as has been nature. Today, however, ecology speaks for the earth, for the "other" in human/environmental relations. And ecofeminism, by speaking for the original others, seeks to understand the interconnected roots of all domination, and ways to resist to change.[10]

Some ecofeminists were also inspired by Carolyn Merchant's controversial historical reconstruction, going back to prehistoric, natural societies, free of male domination, a matriarchal Golden Age, where there was harmony between nature and culture, and where both men and women worshipped nature in the form of the goddess.[11] There has also been, particularly during the 1970s, an interesting connection between environmentalism, spiritual feminism, and neo-paganism,

9   Davis (1991).
10   Plant (1991:101).
11   Merchant (1980); see also Spretnak (1982); Moog (1995).

sometimes expressed in ecofeminist and non-violent direct action militancy by witches belonging to the craft.[12] Thus, through a variety of forms, from eco-guerrilla tactics, to spiritualism, going through deep ecology and ecofeminism, radical ecologists link up environmental action and cultural revolution, broadening the scope of an all-encompassing environmental movement, in their construction of *ecotopia*.

Greenpeace is the world's largest environmental organization, and probably the one that has most popularized global environmental issues, by its media-oriented, non-violent direct action.[13] Founded in Vancouver in 1971, around an anti-nuclear protest off the coast of Alaska, and later headquartered in Amsterdam, it has grown into a transnational, networked organization which, in 1994, had 6 million members worldwide and annual revenues in excess of $100 million. Its highly distinctive profile as an environmental movement derives from three major components. First, a sense of urgency regarding the imminent demise of life on the planet, inspired by a North American Indian legend: "When the earth is sick and the animals have disappeared, there will come a tribe of peoples from all creeds, colours and cultures who believe in deeds not words and who will restore the Earth to its former beauty. The tribe will be called 'Warriors of Rainbow.'"[14] Secondly, a Quaker-inspired attitude of bearing witness, both as a principle for action, and as a strategy of communication. Thirdly, a business-like, pragmatic attitude, largely influenced by Greenpeace's historic leader and chairman of the board, David McTaggart, "to get things done." No time for philosophical discussions: key issues must be identified by using knowledge and investigative techniques throughout the planet; specific campaigns must be organized on visible targets; spectacular actions geared toward media attention will follow, thus raising a given issue in the public eye, and forcing companies, governments, and international institutions to take action or face further unwanted publicity.

Greenpeace is at the same time a highly centralized organization, and a globally decentralized network. It is controlled by a council of country's representatives, a small executive board, and regional trustees for North America, Latin America, Europe, and the Pacific. Its resources are organized in campaigns, each one of them subdivided by issues. In the mid-1990s, major campaigns involved toxic substances, energy and the atmosphere, nuclear issues, and ocean/terrestrial ecology. Offices in

12   Adler (1979); Epstein (1991).
13   Hunter (1979); Eyerman and Jamison (1989); DeMont (1991); Horton (1991); Ostertag (1991); Melchett (1995); Wapner (1995, 1996).
14   Greenpeace Environmental Fund, cited in Eyerman and Jamison (1989: 110).

30 countries in the world serve to coordinate global campaigns, and raise funds and support, on a national/local basis, but most of the action aims at a global impact since the main environmental problems are global. Greenpeace sees as its adversary a model of development characterized by a lack of concern for its consequences on life on the planet. Accordingly, it mobilizes to enforce the principle of environmental sustainability as the over-arching truth to which all other policies and activities must be subordinated. Because of the importance of their mission, the "rainbow warriors" are not inclined to engage in debates with other environmental groups, and do not indulge in counter-culture, regardless of individual variation in the attitudes of their huge membership. They are resolutely internationalists, and see the nation-state as the major obstacle to accomplishing control over currently unfettered, destructive development. They are at war against an eco-suicidal model of development, and they aim to deliver immediate results on each front of action, from converting the German refrigeration industry to "green-freeze" technology, thus helping to protect the ozone layer, to influencing the restriction of whaling, and the creation of a whale sanctuary in Antarctica. The "rainbow warriors" are at the crossroads of science for life, global networking, communication technology, and intergenerational solidarity.

Green politics does not appear, at first sight, to be a type of movement by itself but, rather, a specific strategy, namely entering the realm of electoral politics on behalf of environmentalism. Yet, a close up of the most important example of green politics, *Die Grünen*, clearly shows that, originally, it was not politics as usual.[15] The German Green party, constituted on January 13, 1980, on the basis of a coalition of grassroots movements, is not strictly speaking an environmental movement, even if it has probably been more effective in advancing the environmental cause in Germany than any other European movement in its country. The major force underlying its formation was the Citizen Initiatives of the late 1970s, mainly organized around the peace and anti-nuclear mobilizations. It uniquely brought together veterans of the 1960s' movements with feminists who discovered themselves as such by reflecting precisely on the sexism of 1960s' revolutionaries, and with youth and educated middle classes concerned with peace, nuclear power, the environment (the forest disease, *waldsterben*), the state of the world, individual freedom, and grassroots democracy.

15   See, among an ocean of sources on the German Green party, Langguth (1984); Hulsberg (1988); Wiesenthal (1993); Scharf (1994); and, particularly, Poguntke (1993) and Frankland (1995).

The creation and rapid success of the Greens (they entered the national parliament in 1983) stemmed from very exceptional circumstances. First of all, there were no real political vehicles for social protest in Germany beyond the three main parties which had alternated in power, and even formed a coalition in the 1960s: in 1976, over 99 percent of the vote went to the three parties (Christian Democrats, Social Democrats, and Liberals). Thus, there was a potential disaffected vote, particularly among the young, waiting for the chance to express itself. Financial political scandals (the Flick affair) had rocked the reputation of all political parties and suggested their reliance on industry's contributions. Furthermore, what political scientists call the "political opportunity structure" supported the strategy of forming a party, and keeping unity among its constituents: among other elements, significant government funds were made available to the movement, and the German electoral law which requires at least 5 percent of the national vote to enter parliament disciplined the otherwise fractious Greens.

Most Green voters were young, students, teachers, or members of other categories not involved in industrial production, either unemployed (but supported by the government) or working for the government. Their agenda included ecology, peace, the defense of liberties, the protection of minorities and immigrants, feminism, and participatory democracy. Two-thirds of Green party leaders were active participants in various social movements in the 1980s. Indeed, *Die Grünen* presented themselves, in Petra Kelly's words, as an "anti-party party," aimed at "politics based on a new understanding of power, a 'counter-power' that is natural and common to all, to be shared by all, and used by all for all."[16] Accordingly, they rotated representatives elected to office, and took most of the decisions in assemblies, following the anarchist tradition that inspired the Greens more than the Greens would accept.

The acid test of real politics by and large dissolved these experiments after a few years, particularly after the 1990 electoral débâcle, mainly explained by the Greens' total misunderstanding of the relevance of German unification, in an attitude consistent with their opposition to nationalism. The latent conflict between the *realos* (pragmatic leaders trying to advance the Green agenda through institutions) and the *fundis* (loyal to the basic principles of grassroots democracy and ecologism) exploded into the open in 1991, leaving an alliance of centrists and pragmatics in control of the party. Reoriented, and reorganized, the German Green party recovered its

16   Kelly (1994: 37).

strength in the 1990s, entered Parliament again, and won strong positions in regional and local governments, particularly in Berlin, Frankfurt, Bremen, and Hamburg, sometimes governing in alliance with the Social Democrats. Yet, it was not the same party. That is, it had indeed become a political party. Besides, this party no longer had the monopoly on environmental agenda since the Social Democrats, and even the Liberals, became much more open to new ideas put forward by the social movements. Furthermore, Germany in the 1990s was a very different country. There was no danger of war, but of economic decay. Widespread youth unemployment and the retrenchment of the welfare state became more pressing issues for the "greying" green voters than cultural revolution. The murder of Petra Kelly in 1992, probably by her male companion, who then committed suicide, struck a dramatic chord, suggesting the limits of escaping society in everyday life while leaving untouched fundamental economic, political, and psychological structures. However, through green politics, the Green party became consolidated as the consistent left of *fin-de-siècle* Germany, and the 1970s' rebellious generation still kept most of their values when ageing, and transmitted them to their children through the way they lived their lives. Thus, a very different Germany emerged from the green politics experiment, both culturally and politically. But the impossibility of integrating party and movement without inducing either totalitarianism (Leninism) or reformism at the expense of the movement (social democracy), received another historical confirmation of the iron law of social change.

The Meaning of Greening: Societal Issues and the Ecologists' Challenge

The conservation of nature, the search for environmental quality, and an ecological approach to life are nineteenth-century ideas that, in their distinct expression, remained for a long time confined to the enlightened elites of dominant countries.[17] Often they were the preserve of a gentry overwhelmed by industrialization, as in the origins of the Audubon Society in the United States. In other instances, a communal, utopian component was the nest of early political ecologists, as in the case of Kropotkin, who linked for ever anarchism and ecology, in a tradition best represented in our time by Murray Bookchin. But in all cases, and for almost a century, it remained a restricted

17   Bramwell (1989, 1994).

intellectual trend, aimed primarily at influencing the consciousness of powerful individuals, who would foster conservationist legislation or donate their wealth to the good cause of nature. Even when social alliances were forged (for example, between Robert Marshall and Catherine Bauer in the United States in the 1930s), their policy outcome was packaged in a way that economic and social welfare concerns were paramount.[18] Although there were influential, courageous pioneers, such as Alice Hamilton and Rachel Carson in the United States, it was only in the late 1960s that, in the United States, in Germany, in Western Europe, then rapidly diffusing to the entire world, North and South, West and East, a mass movement emerged, both at the grass roots and in public opinion.

Why was this so? Why did ecological ideas suddenly catch fire in the planet's dried prairies of senselessness? I propose the hypothesis that there is a direct correspondence between the themes put forward by the environmental movement and the fundamental dimensions of the new social structure, the network society, emerging from the 1970s onwards: science and technology as the basic means and goals of economy and society; the transformation of space; the transformation of time; and the domination of cultural identity by abstract, global flows of wealth, power, and information, constructing real virtuality through media networks. To be sure, in the chaotic universe of environmentalism we can find all these themes and, at the same time, none of them in specific cases. However, I contend that there is an implicit, coherent ecological discourse which cuts across various political orientations and social origins within the movement, and which provides the framework from which different themes are emphasized at different moments and for different purposes.[19] There are, naturally, sharp conflicts and strong disagreements in and between components of the environmental movement. Yet, these disagreements are more frequently about tactics, priorities, and language, than about the basic thrust in linking up the defense of specific environments to new human values. At the risk of oversimplification, I will synthesize the main lines of discourse present in the environmental movement in four major themes.

First, *an ambiguous, deep connection with science and technology.* As Bramwell writes: "the development of Green ideas was the revolt of science against science that occurred towards the end of the 19th

18   Gottlieb (1993).
19   For evidence of the presence, and relevance, of these themes in the environmental movements of several countries, see Dickens (1990); Dobson (1990); Scarce (1990); Epstein (1991); Zisk (1992); Coleman and Coleman (1993); Gottlieb (1993); Shabecoff (1993); Bramwell (1994); Porrit (1994); Riechmann and Fernandez Buey (1994); Moog (1995).

century in Europe and North America."[20] This revolt intensified and diffused, in the 1970s, simultaneously with the information technology revolution, and with the extraordinary development of biological knowledge through computer modeling that took place in the aftermath. Indeed, science and technology play a fundamental, albeit contradictory, role in the environmental movement. On the one hand, there is a profound distrust of the goodness of advanced technology, leading in some extreme manifestations to neo-Luddite ideologies, as represented by Kirkpatrick Sale. On the other hand, the movement largely relies on gathering, analyzing, interpreting, and diffusing scientific information about the interaction between manmade artifacts and the environment, sometimes with a high degree of sophistication. Major environmental organizations usually have scientists on their staff, and in most countries there is a tight connection between scientists and academics and environmental activists.

Environmentalism is a science-based movement. Sometimes it is bad science, but it nonetheless pretends to know what happens to nature, and to humans, revealing the truth hidden by vested interests of industrialism, capitalism, technocracy, and bureaucracy. While criticizing the domination of life by science, ecologists use science to oppose science on behalf of life. The principle advocated is not the negation of knowledge, but superior knowledge: the wisdom of a holistic vision, able to reach beyond piecemeal approaches and short-sighted strategies geared toward the satisfaction of basic instincts. In this sense, environmentalism aims to retake social control over the products of the human mind before science and technology take on a life of their own, with machines finally imposing their will on us, and on nature, humankind's ancestral fear.

Struggles over structural transformation are tantamount to fighting for historical redefinition of the two fundamental, material expressions of society: space and time. And, indeed, *control over space, and the emphasis on locality,* form another major, recurrent theme of various components of the environmental movement. I proposed, in volume I, chapter 6, the idea of a fundamental opposition emerging in the network society between two spatial logics: the space of flows and the space of places. The space of flows organizes the simultaneity of social practices at a distance, by means of telecommunications and information systems. The space of places privileges social interaction and institutional organization on the basis of physical contiguity. What is distinctive of the new social structure, the network society, is that most dominant processes, concentrating power, wealth, and

20   Bramwell (1994: vii).

information, are organized in the space of flows. Most human experience, and meaning, are still locally based. The disjunction between the two spatial logics is a fundamental mechanism of domination in our societies because it shifts the core economic, symbolic, and political processes away from the realm where social meaning can be constructed and political control can be exercised. Thus, the emphasis of ecologists on locality, and on the control by people of their living spaces, is a challenge to a basic lever of the new power system. Even in the most defensive expressions, such as in the struggles labeled "Not in my Back Yard," to assert the priority of local living over the uses of a given space by "outside interests," such as companies dumping toxic waste or airports extending their runways, bears the profound meaning of denying abstract priorities of technical or economic interests over the actual experience of actual uses by actual people.

What is challenged by environmental localism is the loss of connection between these different functions and interests under the principle of mediated representation by abstract, technical rationality exercised by uncontrolled business interests and unaccountable technocracies. Thus, the logic of the argument develops into yearning for small-scale government, privileging the local community and citizen participation: *grass-roots democracy is the political model implicit in most ecological movements*. In the most elaborated alternatives, the control over space, the assertion of place as source of meaning, and the emphasis on local government are linked up to the self-management ideals of the anarchist tradition, including small-scale production, and an emphasis on self-sufficiency, which lead to assumed austerity, the critique of conspicuous consumption, and the substitution of the use value of life for the exchange value of money. To be sure, people protesting against toxic dumping in their neighborhood are not anarchists, and few of them would actually be ready to transform the entire fabric of their lives as they are. But the internal logic of the argument, the connection between the defense of one's place against the imperatives of the space of flows, and the strengthening of economic and political bases of locality, allow for the sudden identification of some of these linkages in the public awareness when a symbolic event takes place (such as the building of a nuclear power plant). So are created the conditions for a convergence between the problems of everyday life and the projects for an alternative society: this is how social movements are made.

Alongside space, *control over time is at stake in the network society, and the environmental movement is probably the most important actor in projecting a new, revolutionary temporality*. This matter is as important as complex, and requires slow-pace elaboration. In volume I, chapter 7, I proposed a distinction (on the basis of current debates in sociology and history, as well as of Leibniz's and Innis's philosophies of time and space) between three forms of temporality: clock time, timeless time, and glacial time. *Clock time*, characteristic of industrialism, for both capitalism and statism, was/ is characterized by the chronological sequencing of events, and by the discipline of human behavior to a predetermined schedule, creating scarcity of experience out of institutionalized measurement. *Timeless time*, characterizing dominant processes in our societies, occurs when the characteristics of a given context, namely, the informational paradigm and the network society, induce systemic perturbation in the sequential order of phenomena performed in that context. This perturbation may take the form of compressing the occurrence of phenomena, aiming at instantaneity (as in "instant wars" or split-second financial transactions), or else by introducing random discontinuity in the sequence (as in the hypertext of integrated, electronic media communication). Elimination of sequencing creates undifferentiated timing, thus annihilating time. In our societies, most dominant, core processes are structured in timeless time, yet most people are dominated by and through clock time.

There is still another form of time, as conceived and proposed in social practice: *glacial time*. In Lash and Urry's original formulation, the notion of glacial time implies that "the relation between humans and nature is very long-term and evolutionary. It moves back out of immediate human history and forwards into a wholly unspecifiable future."[21] Developing their elaboration, I propose the idea that the environmental movement is precisely characterized by the project of introducing a "glacial time" perspective in our temporality, in terms of both consciousness and policy. Ecological thinking considers interaction between all forms of matter in an evolutionary perspective. The idea of limiting the use of resources to renewable resources, central to environmentalism, is predicated precisely on the notion that alteration of basic balances in the planet, and in the universe, may, *over time*, undo a delicate ecological equilibrium, with catastrophic consequences. The holistic notion of integration between humans and nature, as presented in "deep ecology" writers, does not refer to a naïve worshipping of pristine natural landscapes, but to the fundamental consideration that the relevant unit of experience is not each individual or, for that matter, historically existing human communities. To merge ourselves with our cosmological self we need first to change the notion of time, to feel "glacial time" running

21   Lash and Urry (1994: 243).

through our lives, to sense the energy of stars flowing in our blood, and to assume the rivers of our thoughts endlessly merging in the boundless oceans of multiformed living matter. In very direct, personal terms, glacial time means to measure our life by the life of our children, and of the children of the children of our children. Thus, managing our lives and institutions for them, as much as for us, is not a New Age cult, but old-fashioned care-taking of our descendants, that is of our own flesh and blood. To propose sustainable development as intergenerational solidarity brings together healthy selfishness and systemic thinking in an evolutionary perspective. The anti-nuclear movement, one of the most potent sources of the environmental movement, based its radical critique of nuclear power on the long-term effects of radioactive waste, besides immediate safety problems, thus bridging to the safety of generations thousands of years from us. To some extent, interest in the preservation of and respect for indigenous cultures extends backwards the concern for all forms of human existence coming from different times, and affirming that we are them, and they are us.

It is this *unity of the species, then of matter as a whole, and of its spatiotemporal evolution*, that is called upon implicitly by the environmental movement, and explicitly by deep ecologist and ecofeminist thinkers.[22] The material expression unifying different claims and themes of environmentalism is their alternative temporality, demanding the assumption by society's institutions of the slow-pace evolution of our species in its environment, with no end to our cosmological being, as long as the universe keeps expanding from the moment/place of its shared beginning. Beyond the time-bounded shores of subdued clock time, still experienced by most people in the world, the historical struggle over new temporality takes place between the annihilation of time in the recurrent flows of computer networks, and the realization of glacial time in the conscious assumption of our cosmological self.

Through these fundamental struggles over the appropriation of science, space, and time, ecologists induce *the creation of a new identity*, a biological identity, *a culture of the human species as a component of nature*. This socio-biological identity does not imply denial of historical cultures. Ecologists bear respect for folk cultures, and indulge in cultural authenticity from various traditions. Yet, their objective enemy is state nationalism. This is because the nation-state, by definition, is bound to assert its power over a given territory. Thus, it breaks the unity of humankind, as well as the interrelation between

22   Diamond and Orenstein (1990); McLaughlin (1993).

territories, undermining the sharing of our global ecosystem. In the words of David McTaggart, the historic leader of Greenpeace International: "The biggest threat we must address is nationalism. In the next century we are going to be faced with issues which simply cannot be addressed on a nation-by-nation basis. What we are trying to do is work together internationally, despite centuries of nationalist prejudice."[23] In what is only an apparent contradiction, ecologists are, at the same time, localists and globalists: globalists in the management of time, localists in the defense of space. Evolutionary thinking and policy require a global perspective. People's harmony with their environment starts in their local community.

This *new identity as a species*, which is a socio-biological identity, can be easily superimposed on multifaceted, historical traditions, languages, and cultural symbols, but it will hardly mix with state-nationalist identity. Thus, to some extent, environmentalism supersedes the opposition between the culture of real virtuality, underlying global flows of wealth and power, and the expression of fundamentalist cultural or religious identities. It is the only global identity put forward on behalf of all human beings, regardless of their specific social, historical, or gender attachments, or of their religious faith. However, since most people do not live their lives cosmologically, and the assumption of our shared nature with mosquitoes still poses some tactical problems, the critical matter for the influence of new ecological culture is its ability to weave threads of singular cultures into a human hypertext, made out of historical diversity and biological commonality. I call this culture *green culture* (why invent another term when millions of people already call it this), and I define it in Petra Kelly's terms: "We must learn to think and act from our hearts, to recognize the interconnectedness of all living creatures, and to respect the value of each thread in the vast web of life. This is a spiritual perspective, and it is the foundation of all Green politics... Green politics requires us to be both tender and subversive."[24] The tenderness of subversion, the subversion of tenderness: we are a long way from the instrumentalist perspective that has dominated the industrial era, in both its capitalist and statist versions. And we are in direct contradiction with the dissolution of meaning in the flows of faceless power that constitute the network society. Green culture, as proposed in and by a multifaceted environmental movement, is the antidote to the culture of real virtuality characterizing dominant processes in our societies.

23 Interview in Ostertag (1991: 33).
24 Kelly (1994: 37).

Thus, the science of life versus life under science; local control over places versus an uncontrollable space of flows; realization of glacial time versus annihilation of time, and continued slavery to clock time; green culture versus real virtuality. These are the fundamental challenges of the environmental movement to the dominant structures of the network society. And this is why it addresses the issues that people perceive vaguely as being the stuff of which their new lives are made. It remains the fact that, between this "fierce green fire" and people's hearths, the tenements of society stand tall, forcing environmentalism to a long march through the institutions from which, as with all social movements, it does not emerge unscathed.

Environmentalism in Action: Reaching Minds, Taming Capital, Courting the State, Tap-dancing with the Media

Much of the success of the environmental movement comes from the fact that, more than any other social force, it has been able to best adapt to the conditions of communication and mobilization in the new technological paradigm.[25] Although much of the movement relies on grassroots organizations, environmental action works on the basis of media events. By creating events that call media attention, environmentalists are able to reach a much broader audience than their direct constituency. Furthermore, the constant presence of environmental themes in the media has lent them a legitimacy higher than that of any other cause. Media orientation is obvious in the cases of global environmental activism such as Greenpeace, whose entire logic is geared toward creating events to mobilize public opinion on specific issues in order to put pressure on the powers-that-be. But it is also the daily staple of environmental struggles at the local level. Local TV news, radio, and newspapers are the voice of environmentalists, to the point that corporations and politicians often complain that it is the media rather than ecologists who are responsible for environmental mobilization.

The symbiotic relationship between the media and environmentalism stems from several sources. First of all, the non-violent, direct action tactics, which permeated the movement from the early 1970s, provided good reporting material, particularly when news requires fresh images. Many environmental activists have imaginatively practiced the traditional French anarchist tactics of *l'action exemplaire*,

---

25   See Epstein (1991); Horton (1991); Ostertag (1991); Costain and Costain (1992); Gottlieb (1993); Kanagy et al. (1994).

a spectacular act that strikes minds, provokes debate, and induces mobilization. Self-sacrifice, such as enduring arrests and jail, risking their lives in the ocean, chaining themselves to trees, using their bodies as blocking devices against undesirable construction or evil convoys, disrupting official ceremonies, and so many other direct actions, coupled with self-restraint and manifest non-violence, introduce a witness-bearing attitude that restores trust and enhances ethical values in an age of widespread cynicism. Secondly, the legitimacy of the issues raised by environmentalists, directly connecting to the basic humanistic values cherished by most people, and often distant from partisan politics, provided a good terrain for the media to assume the role of the voice of the people, thus increasing their own legitimacy, and making journalists feel good about it. Furthermore, in local news, the reporting of health hazards or the environmental disruption of people's lives brings home systemic problems in a more powerful way than any traditional ideological discourses. Often, environmentalists themselves feed the media with precious images that say more than a thick report. Thus, American environmental groups have distributed video cameras to grassroots groups around the world, from Connecticut to Amazonia, for them to film explicit violations of environmental laws, then using the technological infrastructure of the group to process, and diffuse, accusatory images.

Environmentalists have also been at the cutting edge of new communication technologies as organizing and mobilizing tools, particularly in the use of the Internet.[26] For instance, a coalition of environmental groups in the United States, Canada, and Chile, formed around Friends of the Earth, the Sierra Club, Greenpeace, Defenders of Wildlife, the Canadian Environmental Law Association, and others, mobilized against approval of the North American Free Trade Agreement (NAFTA) because of the lack of sufficient environmental protection provisions in it. They used the Internet to coordinate action and information, and they built a permanent network that draws the battle lines of transnational environmental action in the Americas. World wide web sites are rallying points for environmentalists around the world, as, for example, the sites established in 1996 by organizations such as Conservation International and Rainforest Action Network to defend the cause of indigenous people in tropical forests. Food First, a California-based organization, has linked up with a network of environmental groups in developing countries, connecting environmental and poverty issues. Thus, through the Net, it was able to coordinate its action with Global South, a

26   Bartz (1996).

Thailand-based organization that provides the environmental perspective of newly industrializing Asia. Through these networks, grassroots groups around the world become suddenly able to act globally, at the level at which major problems are created. It seems that a computer-literate elite is emerging as the global, coordinating core of grassroots environmental action groups around the world, a phenomenon not entirely dissimilar to the role played by artisan printers and journalists at the beginning of the labor movement, orienting, through information to which they had access, the illiterate masses that formed the working class of early industrialization.

Environmentalism is not merely a consciousness-raising movement. Since its beginnings, it has focused on making a difference in legislation and governance. Indeed, the core of environmental organizations (such as the so-called Group of Ten in the United States) gears its efforts to lobby for legislation, and to support, or oppose, political candidates on the basis of their stand on certain issues. Even nontraditional, action-oriented organizations, such as Greenpeace, have increasingly shifted their focus to put pressure on governments, and on international institutions, to obtain laws, decisions, and the implementation of decisions on specific issues. Similarly, at the local and regional levels, environmentalists have campaigned for new forms of city and regional planning, for public health measures, for control of excessive development. It is this pragmatism, this issue-oriented attitude, that has given environmentalism an edge over traditional politics: people feel that they can make a difference right here and now, without mediation or delay. There is no distinction between means and goals.

In some countries, particularly in Europe, environmentalists have entered political competition, running candidates for office, with mixed success.[27] Evidence shows that green parties do much better in local elections, where there is still a direct link between the movement and its political representatives. They also perform relatively well in international elections – for example, the elections to the European Parliament – because, being an institution that holds only symbolic power, citizens feel comfortable about seeing their principles represented, with little cost in losing influence in decision-making. In national politics, political scientists have shown that the chances for green parties are influenced less by people's environmental beliefs than by specific institutional structures framing the opportunities for political competition.[28] In a nutshell, the greater the accessibility of

27   Poguntke (1993); Dalton (1994); Diani (1995); Richardson and Rootes (1995).
28   Richardson and Rootes (1995).

environmental themes and/or a protest vote to mainstream parties, the lower the chances for the Greens; the greater the chances of a symbolic vote, without consequences for holding office, the better the performance by Green candidates. Indeed, it seems that Germany was the exception, not the rule, in the development of green politics, as I argued above.

Overall, it seems that there is a worldwide trend toward the greening of mainstream politics, albeit often in a very pale green, together with the sustained autonomy of the environmental movement. As for the movement itself, its relationship to politics increasingly mixes lobbying, targeted campaigning for or against candidates, and influencing voters through issue-oriented mobilizations. Through these diverse tactics, environmentalism has become a major public opinion force with which parties and candidates have to reckon in many countries. On the other hand, most environmental organizations have become largely institutionalized; that is, they have accepted the need to act in the framework of existing institutions, and within the rules of productivism and a global, market economy. Thus, cooperation with large corporations has become the rule rather than the exception. Corporations often fund a variety of environmental activities, and have become extremely aware of green self-presentation, to the point that environmental themes are now standard images in corporate advertising. But not all is manipulation. Corporations around the world have also been influenced by environmentalism, and have tried to adapt their processes and their products to new legislation, new tastes, and new values, naturally trying to make a profit out of it at the same time. However, because the actual production units in our economy are no longer individual corporations, but transnational networks made up of various components (see volume I, chapter 3), environmental transgression has been decentralized to small business, and to newly industrializing countries, thus modifying the geography and topology of environmental action in the coming years.

Overall, with the extraordinary growth of environmental consciousness, influence, and organization, the movement has become increasingly diversified, socially and thematically, reaching from the corporate boardrooms to the fringe alleys of counter-cultures, passing through city halls and parliamentary houses. In the process, themes have been distorted, and in some cases manipulated. But this is the mark of any major social movement. Environmentalism is indeed a major social movement of our time, as it reaches out to a variety of social causes under the comprehensive banner of environmental justice.

Environmental Justice: Ecologists' New Frontier

Since the 1960s environmentalism has not been solely concerned with watching birds, saving forests, and cleaning the air. Campaigns against toxic waste dumping, consumers' rights, anti-nuclear protests, pacifism, feminism, and a number of other issues have merged with the defense of nature to root the movement in a wide landscape of rights and claims. Even counter-cultural trends, such as New Age meditation and neo-paganism, mingled with other components of the environmental movement in the 1970s and 1980s.

At the turn of the millennium, while some major issues, such as peace and anti-nuclear protest, have receded into the background, partly because of the success of protests, partly because of the end of the Cold War, a variety of social issues have come to be a part of an increasingly diversified movement.[29] Poor communities and ethnic minorities have mobilized against being the target of environmental discrimination, subjected more often than the population at large to toxic substances, pollution, health hazards, and degradation of their living quarters. Workers have revolted against the source of occupational injuries, old and new, from chemical poisoning to computer-induced stress. Women's groups have shown that, being more often than not the managers of everyday family life, they are the ones who suffer most directly the consequences of pollution, of deteriorating public facilities, and of uncontrolled development.

Homelessness is a major cause of declining quality of urban life. And, throughout the world, poverty has been shown, again and again, to be a cause of environmental degradation, from the burning of forests, to pollution of rivers, lakes, and oceans, to rampaging epidemics. Indeed, in many industrializing countries, particularly in Latin America, environmental groups have blossomed, and have linked up with human rights groups, women's groups, and non-governmental organizations, forming powerful coalitions that go beyond, but do not ignore, institutional politics.[30] Thus, the concept of environmental justice, as an all-encompassing notion that affirms the use value of life, of all forms of life, against the interests of wealth, power, and technology, is gradually capturing minds and policies, as the environmental movement enters a new stage of development.

At first sight, it would seem to be opportunistic tactics. Given the success and legitimacy of the environmental label, less popular causes

29   Gottlieb (1993: 207–320); Szasz (1994); Epstein (1995); Brulle (1996).
30   Athanasiou (1996); Borja and Castells (1997).

wrap themselves in new ideologies to win support and attract attention. And, indeed, some of the conservative, nature groupings of the
environmental movement have grown wary of an excessively broad
embrace that might take the movement away from its focus. After all,
labor unions have fought for occupational health legislation since the
onset of industrialization, and poverty is, and was, a major issue in its
own right, without having to paint its sinister darkness in green. Yet,
what is happening in environmentalism goes beyond tactics. The
ecological approach to life, to the economy, and to the institutions
of society emphasizes the holistic character of all forms of matter, and
of all information processing. Thus, the more we know, the more we
sense the possibilities of our technology, and the more we realize the
gigantic, dangerous gap between our enhanced productive capacities,
and our primitive, unconscious, and ultimately destructive social
organization. This is the objective thread that weaves the growing
connectedness of social revolts, local and global, defensive and offensive, issue-oriented and value-oriented, emerging in and around the
environmental movement. This is not to say that a new international
of good-intentioned, generous citizens has emerged. Yet. As shown in
this volume, old and new cleavages of class, gender, ethnicity, religion,
and territoriality are at work in dividing and subdividing issues,
conflicts, and projects. But this is to say that embryonic connections
between grassroots movements and symbol-oriented mobilizations on
behalf of environmental justice bear the mark of alternative projects.
These projects hint at superseding the exhausted social movements of
industrial society, to resume, under historically appropriate forms, the
old dialectics between domination and resistance, between *realpolitik*
and utopia, between cynicism and hope.

4

The End of Patriarchalism: Social Movements, Family, and Sexuality in the Information Age

---

If all who have begged help
From me in this world,
All the holy innocents,
Broken wives, and cripples,
The imprisoned, the suicidal –
If they had sent me one kopeck
I should have become "richer
Than all Egypt"...
But they did not send me kopecks,
Instead they shared with me their strength,
And so nothing in the world
Is stronger than I,
And I can bear anything, even this.
Anna Akhmatova, Selected Poems[1]

Patriarchalism is a founding structure of all contemporary societies. It is characterized by the institutionally enforced authority of males over females and their children in the family unit. For this authority to be exercised, patriarchalism must permeate the entire organization of society, from production and consumption to politics, law, and

---

1   Akhmatova (1985: 84).

culture. Interpersonal relationships, and thus personality, are marked, as well, by domination and violence originating from the culture and institutions of patriarchalism. Yet, it is analytically, and politically, essential not to forget the rooting of patriarchalism in the family structure, and in the socio-biological reproduction of the species, as historically (culturally) framed. Without the patriarchal family, patriarchalism would be exposed as sheer domination, and thus eventually overrun by the uprising of the "half of the heaven" historically kept under submission.

The patriarchal family, the cornerstone of patriarchalism, is being challenged at this turn of the millennium by the inseparably related processes of the transformation of women's work and the transformation of women's consciousness. Driving forces behind these processes are the rise of an informational, global economy, technological changes in the reproduction of the human species, and the powerful surge of women's struggles, and of a multifaceted feminist movement, three trends that have developed since the late 1960s. The massive incorporation of women into *paid* work increased women's bargaining power *vis-à-vis* men, and undermined the legitimacy of men's domination as providers of the family. Besides, it put an unbearable burden on women's lives by their daily, quadruple shift (paid work, homemaking, child rearing, and night shift for the husband). Contraception first, *in vitro* fertilization later, and genetic manipulation looming on the horizon, are giving women, and society, growing control over the timing and frequency of child bearing.

As for women's struggles, they did not wait until this turn of the millennium to manifest themselves. They have characterized the entire span of human experience, albeit in a diversity of forms, most often absent from history books and from the written record altogether.[2] I have argued that many historical, and contemporary, urban struggles were, in fact, women's movements dealing with the demands and management of everyday life.[3] And feminism as such has an old history, as exemplified by the suffragists in the United States. Yet, I think it is fair to say that only since the last quarter of the twentieth century have we witnessed what amounts to a mass insurrection of women against their oppression throughout the world, albeit with different intensity depending on culture and country. The impact of such movements has been felt deeply in the institutions of society, and, more fundamentally, in the consciousness of women. In industrialized countries, a large majority of women consider

2   Rowbotham (1974).
3   Castells (1983).

themselves equal to men, entitled to their rights, and to women's control over their bodies and their lives. Such a consciousness is rapidly extending throughout the planet. This is the most important revolution because it goes to the roots of society and to the heart of who we are.[4] And it is irreversible. To say so does not mean that problems of discrimination, oppression, and abuse of women, and of their children, have disappeared, or even substantially diminished in their intensity. In fact, while legal discrimination has been somewhat curtailed, and the labor market place shows equalizing trends as women's education soars, interpersonal violence and psychological abuse are widespread, precisely because of male anger, individual and collective, in losing power. This is not, and will not be, a velvet revolution. The human landscape of women's liberation and men's defense of their privileges is littered with corpses of broken lives, as is the case with all true revolutions. Nonetheless, in spite of the sharpness of conflict, the transformation of women's consciousness, and of societal values in most societies, in three decades, is staggering, and it yields fundamental consequences for the entire human experience, from political power to the structure of personality.

I argue that the process that summarizes and concentrates this transformation is the undoing of the patriarchal family. If the patriarchal family crumbles, the whole system of patriarchalism, gradually but surely, and the whole of our lives, will be transformed. This is a scary perspective, and not only for men. This is why the challenge to patriarchalism is one of the most powerful factors presently inducing fundamentalist movements aimed at restoring the patriarchal order, as those studied in the previous chapters of this volume. Their backlash could indeed alter current processes of cultural change, since no history is pre-scripted. Yet, current indicators point to a substantial decline of traditional forms of patriarchal family. I will start my analysis by focusing on some of these indicators. Not that statistics, by themselves, can tell the story of the crisis of patriarchalism. But when changes are so widespread as to be reflected in national and comparative statistics, we can safely assume the depth and speed of these changes.

Then, we still have to account for the timing of this transformation. Why now? Feminist ideas have been present at least for a century, if not longer, albeit in their specific historical translation. Why did they catch fire in our time? I propose the hypothesis that the reason lies in a combination of four elements: first, the transformation of the economy, and of the labor market, in close association with the opening of

4   Mitchell (1966).

educational opportunities to women.[5] Thus, I will try to present some of the data displaying such a transformation, linking them to the characteristics of the informational, global economy, and of the network enterprise, as presented in volume I. Secondly, there is the technological transformation in biology, pharmacology, and medicine that has allowed a growing control over child bearing, and over the reproduction of the human species, as argued in volume I, chapter 7. Thirdly, against this background of economic and technological transformation, patriarchalism has been impacted by the development of the feminist movement, in the aftermath of the 1960s' social movements. Not that feminism was a distinctive component of these movements. In fact, it started afterwards, in the late 1960s and/or early 1970s, among women who had been part of the movements, as a reaction to the sexism, and even abuse (see below), that they had had to suffer in the movements. But the context of social movement formation, with its emphasis on the "personal as political," and with its multidimensional themes, freed the possibility of thinking away from the instrumental avenues of male-dominated movements (such as the labor movement, or revolutionary politics), and toward a more experimental approach to the actual sources of oppression as felt, before they could be tamed by the discourse of rationality. The fourth element inducing the challenge to patriarchalism is the rapid diffusion of ideas in a globalized culture, and in an interrelated world, where people and experience travel and mingle, quickly weaving a hyperquilt of women's voices throughout most of the planet. Thus, after surveying the transformation of women's work, I will analyze the formation of a highly diversified feminist movement, and the debates emerging from the collective experience of constructing/reconstructing women's identity.

The impact of social movements, and particularly of feminism, on gender relations triggered a powerful shock wave: the calling into question of heterosexuality as the norm. For lesbians, separation from men as the subjects of their oppression was the logical, if not inevitable, consequence of their view of male domination as the source of women's plight. For gay men, the questioning of the traditional family, and the conflictive relationships between men and women, provided an opening to explore other forms of interpersonal relationships, including new forms of families, gay families. For all, sexual liberation, without institutional limits, became the new frontier of self-expression. Not in the homophobic image of endless cruising, but in the affirmation of the self, and in the experimentation with

5   Saltzman-Chafetz (1995).

sexuality and love. The impact of gay and lesbian movements on patriarchalism is, of course, devastating. Not that forms of interpersonal domination cease to exist. Domination, as exploitation, always renews itself in history. But patriarchalism, as it has probably existed since the dawn of human times (Carolyn Merchant notwithstanding), is definitively shaken by the undermining of the heterosexual norm. Thus, I will explore the origins and horizon of gay and lesbian movements, bridging from San Francisco to Taipei, to emphasize the growing cultural and geographical diversity of these movements.

Finally, I will address the issue of the transformation of personality in our society, as it results from the transformation of family structure and of sexual norms, since I think it can be argued that families constitute the basic socialization mechanism, and sexuality has something to do with personality. This is how the interaction between structural change and social movements – that is, between the network society and the power of identity – transforms us.

The Crisis of the Patriarchal Family

By the crisis of the patriarchal family I refer to the weakening of a model of family based on the stable exercise of authority/domination over the whole family by the adult male head of the family. It is possible to find indicators of such a crisis in most societies, particularly in the most developed countries. It is not obvious to use very rough statistical indicators as evidence of a feature, patriarchalism, that is political, cultural, and psychological. Yet, since a population's behavior and structure usually evolve at a very slow pace, the observation of sizable trends affecting the structure and dynamics of the patriarchal family in comparative national statistics are, in my view, a powerful sign of change, and, I argue, of crisis of previously stable patriarchal patterns. I will summarize the argument before proceeding with a quick statistical scan.

The dissolution of households of married couples, by divorce or separation, is a first indicator of disaffection with a model of family that relied on the long-term commitment of family members. To be sure, there can be (and this is the rule, in fact) successive patriarchalism: the reproduction of the same model with different partners. However, structures of domination (and mechanisms of trust) are undermined by the experience, both for women and for children, often caught in conflicting loyalties. Furthermore, with increasing frequency, the dissolution of married households leads to the formation of single households and/or single-parent households, in this case ending patriarchal authority in the family, even if the structures of domination reproduce mentally in the new household.

Secondly, the increasing frequency of marital crises, and the growing difficulty of making marriage, work, and life compatible, seem to be associated with two other powerful trends: delaying coupling; and setting up partnerships without marriage. Here, again, the lack of legal sanction weakens patriarchal authority, both institutionally and psychologically.

Thirdly, as a result of these different tendencies, together with demographic factors, such as the aging of the population, and the difference in mortality rates between sexes, an increasing variety of household structures emerges, thus diluting the prevalence of the classic nuclear family model (first time married couples and their children), and undermining its social reproduction. Single households, and single-parent households, proliferate.

Fourthly, under the conditions of family instability, and with the increasing autonomy of women in their reproductive behavior, the crisis of the patriarchal family extends into the crisis of social patterns of population replacement.[6] On the one hand, an increasing proportion of children are born out of wedlock, and are usually kept by their mothers (although unmarried couples jointly parenting a child are also part of the statistic). Thus, biological reproduction is assured, but outside traditional family structure. On the other hand, women, with heightened consciousness and facing hardship, limit the number of children they give birth to, and delay their first child. Ultimately, in some small circles, whose size seems to be increasing, women give birth to children for themselves, or adopt children alone.

Altogether, these trends, reinforcing each other, call into question the structure and values of the patriarchal family. It is not necessarily the end of the family, since other family arrangements are being experimented with, and may in the end reconstruct how we live with each other, and how we procreate and educate in different, maybe better, ways.[7] But the trends that I mention point to the end of the family as we have known it until now. Not just the nuclear family (a modern artifact), but the family based on patriarchal domination that has been the rule for millennia.

Let us have a look at some basic statistics. I will emphasize here a comparative approach, while reserving a more systematic overview of

6   In the European Union in 1995 the birth rate was the lowest in peacetime in the twentieth century: there were only 290,000 more births than deaths. In Germany and Italy, there were more deaths than births. Eastern Europe's population declined even further, particularly in Russia (*The Economist*, November 19, 1996).
7   Stacey (1990).

the crisis of the patriarchal family in the United States, where the process seems to be more advanced, in a later section of this chapter.[8] While the trends indicated are most pronounced in developed countries, there is a general change in the same direction in much of the world. Thus, I will rely to a large extent on the report elaborated in 1995 by the Population Council on the transformation of families in the world,[9] which I will complement with various sources, as cited. I will focus on the 1970–95 period for reasons presented above in this chapter.

Table 4.1 shows, with one exception, a significant increase in the crude rate of divorce for selected countries: more than doubling in the UK, France, Canada, and Mexico between 1971 and 1990. The less pronounced increases in the US (still +26 percent) and in the USSR (+29 percent) over the period are due to the fact that they had the highest rates in 1971. Interestingly enough, the one Muslim country that I selected for purposes of comparison displays a decrease in the divorce rate (probably reflecting trends toward the Islamization of society), although it is still higher, in 1990, than that of Italy, Mexico, or Japan.

Table 4.2 shows the divorce rates per 100 marriages for selected, highly industrialized countries. There is a discrepancy between the levels of divorce for each country, but there is a general upward trend between 1970 and 1980, and between 1980 and 1990, again with the exception of the United States in 1990, partly because almost 55 percent of marriages ended in divorce in this country in 1990. *De facto* separations are not included in the statistics, nor are the rates of the ending of cohabitation. However, we know, through survey research, that cohabitation households are more likely to separate than married couples,[10] and that separations correlate with the rate of divorce, thus actually increasing the overall number, and proportion, of termination of households.[11] A global survey of divorce patterns found that a growing proportion of divorces involve couples with young children, thus increasing the likelihood that marital dissolution will lead to single parenthood.[12] Figure 4.1 shows the decreasing rate of marriage survival between older and younger cohorts of women for Italy, West Germany, and Sweden.[13]

---

8   See United Nations (1970–95, 1995); Saboulin and Thave (1993); Valdes and Gomariz (1993); Cho and Yada (1994); OECD (1994b); Alberdi (1995); Bruce et al. (1995); De Vos (1995); Mason and Jensen (1995).
9   Bruce et al. (1995).
10   Bruce et al. (1995).
11   Alberdi (1995).
12   Goode (1993).
13   Blossfeld (1995).

Table 4.1   Rate of change in crude divorce rate in selected countries,
1971–90

Country	1971	1990	Rate of change 1971–90	
			Rate	%
Canada	1.38	2.94	1.56	113
France	0.93	1.86	0.93	100
Italy	0.32	0.48	0.16	50
Japan	0.99	1.27	0.28	28
UK	1.41	2.88	1.47	104
USA	3.72	4.70	0.98	26
USSR	2.63	3.39	0.76	29
Mexico	0.21	0.54	0.33	157
Egypt	2.09	1.42	−0.67	−32

Source: UN, Demographic Yearbook (1970–1995)

Table 4.2   Trends in divorce rates per 100 marriages in developed
countries

Country	1970	1980	1990
Canada	18.6	32.8	38.3
Czechoslovakia	21.8	26.6	32.0[a]
Denmark	25.1	39.3	44.0
England and Wales	16.2	39.3	41.7[a]
France	12.0	22.2	31.5[a]
Greece	5.0	10.0	12.0
Hungary	25.0	29.4	31.0
Italy	5.0	3.2	8.0
Netherlands	11.0	25.7	28.1
Sweden	23.4	42.2	44.1
United States	42.3	58.9	54.8[b]
(former) West Germany	12.2	22.7	29.2

Note: Rates shown are a synthetic index calculated by summing duration-
specific divorce rates in each year. (Original source incorrectly identifies rates as
"per 1,000 marriages.")
[a]   1989
[b]   1985
Source: Monnier, Alain and de Guibert-Lantoine, Catherine (1993) "La
conjoncture démographique: l'Europe et les pays développés d'outre-mer,"
Population 48(4):1043–67
Compiled and elaborated by Bruce et al. (1995)

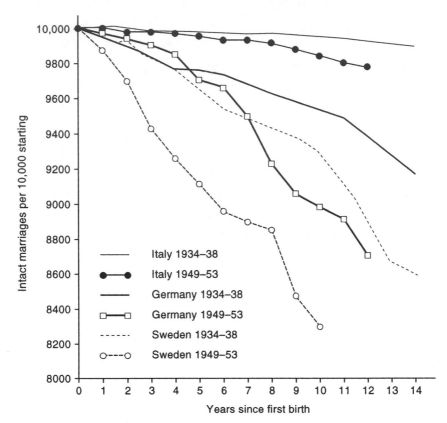

Figure 4.1 Marriage survival curves for Italy, West Germany, and
Sweden: mothers born in 1934–38 and 1949–53
Source: Blossfeld (1995)

This trend is by no means limited to industrialized countries. Table
4.3, for selected developing countries, displays rates of dissolution,
for different causes, of first marriages for women aged 40–49: with
the exception of Tunisia, it oscillates between 22.8 percent and 49.5
percent, with a peak of 60.8 percent in Ghana.

Since the 1990s in Europe the number of divorces *vis-à-vis* marriages has stabilized, but this is mainly due to a reduction in the
number of marriages since 1960, so that overall the number, and
proportion, of dual-parent married households has decreased substantially.[14] Figure 4.2 displays the general trend toward the reduction
of first marriages in countries of the European Union, and figure 4.3

14   Alberdi (1995).

Table 4.3 Percentage of first marriages dissolved through separation, divorce, or death among women aged 40–49 in less-developed countries

Region/country	Date	%
Asia		
Indonesia	1987	37.3
Sri Lanka	1987	25.6
Thailand	1987	24.8
Latin America/Caribbean		
Colombia	1986	32.5
Dominican Republic	1986	49.5
Ecuador	1987	28.9
Mexico	1987	25.5
Peru	1986	26.1
Middle East/North Africa		
Egypt	1989	22.8
Morocco	1987	31.2
Tunisia	1988	11.1
Sub-Saharan Africa		
Ghana	1988	60.8
Kenya	1989	24.2
Senegal	1986	42.3
Sudan	1989/90	28.2

Sources: United Nations (1987), table 47 in *Fertility Behaviour in the Context of Development: Evidence from the World Fertility Survey* (New York: United Nations), and tabulations from demographic and health surveys
Compiled and elaborated by Bruce et al. (1995)

presents the evolution of crude marriage rates for selected countries in different areas of the world. With the exception of Mexico and Germany, there is a decline over the 20-year period, with a significant drop in Japan.

The delay in the age of marriage is also a quasi-universal trend, and a particularly important one in the case of young women. Table 4.4 shows the percentage of women aged 20–24 who have never married. The later dates are very diverse, so it is difficult to compare, but, with the exception of Ghana and Senegal, between one-third and two-thirds of young women are unmarried; with the exception of Spain and Sri Lanka, the proportion of unmarried women aged 20–24 has increased since 1970. Worldwide, the proportion of married women

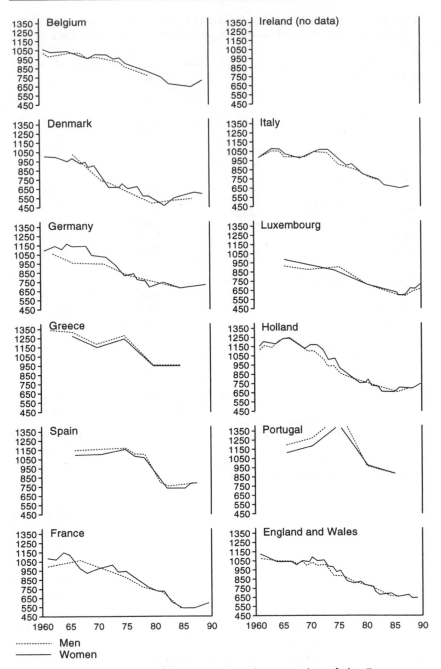

Figure 4.2   Evolution of first marriage in countries of the European
Union since 1960   *Source*: Alberdi (1995)

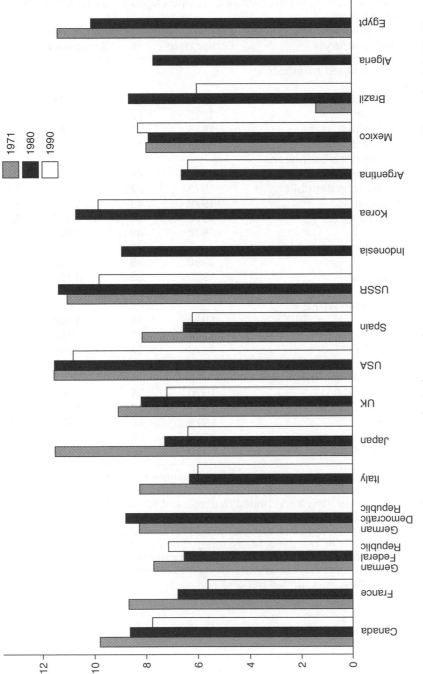

Figure 4.3 Crude marriage rates in selected countries   *Source:* United Nations, *Demographic Yearbook* (1970–95)

Table 4.4 Trends in percentage of women aged 20–24 who have never been married

Region/country	Earlier date	%	Later date	%
Less-developed countries				
Asia				
Indonesia	1976	20	1987	36
Pakistan	1975	22	1990/91	39
Sri Lanka	1975	61	1987	58
Thailand	1975	42	1987	48
Latin America/Caribbean				
Colombia	1976	44	1986	39
Dominican Republic	1975	27	1986	39
Ecuador	1979	43	1987	41
Mexico	1976	34	1987	42
Peru	1978	49	1986	56
Middle East/North Africa				
Egypt	1980	36	1989	40
Morocco	1980	36	1987	56
Tunisia	1978	57	1988	64
Sub-Saharan Africa				
Ghana	1980	15	1988	23
Kenya	1978	21	1989	32
Senegal	1978	14	1986	23
Developed countries				
Czechoslovakia	1970	35	1980	33
Austria	1971	45	1980	57
France	1970	46	1980	52
Spain	1970	68	1981	59
United States	1970	36	1980	51

Sources: Less-developed countries: United Nations (1987), table 43 in *Fertility Behaviour in the Context of Development: Evidence from the World Fertility Survey* (New York: United Nations), and Westoff, Charles F., Blanc, Ann K. and Nyblade, Laura (1994) *Marriage and Entry into Parenthood* (Demographic and Health Surveys Comparative Studies no. 10. Calverton, Maryland: Macro International Inc.); *developed countries*: compiled by the United Nations Statistical Division for: United Nations (1995) *The World's Women 1970–1995: Trends and Statistics* (New York: United Nations)
Compiled and elaborated by Bruce et al. (1995)

aged 15 and older declined from 61 percent in 1970 to 56 percent in 1985.[15]

An increasing proportion of children are born out of wedlock in developed countries (table 4.5), and the most important observation concerns the trend: in the United States, the proportion jumped from 5.4 percent of all births in 1970 to 28 percent in 1990. The phenomenon is ethnically differentiated: it reaches 70.3 percent for African American women in the age group 15–34 (figure 4.4). In Scandinavian countries non-marital child bearing in the 1990s accounted for about 50 percent of all child bearing.[16]

As a result of both separations and single motherhood, the proportion of single-parent households with dependent children (usually female-headed) increased between the early 1970s and the mid-1980s in developed countries (table 4.6), and the upward trend continued in the 1990s in the US (see below). For developing countries, a similar trend can be detected on the basis of statistics on households headed by women *de jure*. Table 4.7 shows an overall upward trend in the proportion of female-headed households between the mid-1970s and the mid/late-1980s (with some exceptions, e.g. Indonesia), with Brazil showing over 20 percent of its households in this category in 1989, up from 14 percent in 1980.

Bringing together various indicators of household formation, Lesthaeghe constructed table 4.8 for OECD countries, whose data contrast northern Europe and North America with southern Europe, where traditional family structures resist better. Even so, excepting Ireland and Switzerland, the proportion of one-parent households with children in the mid-1980s represented between 10 percent and 32 percent of all households.

Table 4.9 shows the percentage of single households for selected countries in the early 1990s. It deserves a close look: with the exception of southern Europe, it oscillates between 20 percent and 39.6 percent of all households, with 26.9 percent for the UK, 24.5 percent for the US, 22.3 percent for Japan, 28.0 percent for France, and 34.2 percent for Germany. Obviously, most of these households are formed by single elderly, and thus the aging of the population accounts for a good part of the phenomenon. Still, the fact that between one-fifth and over one-third of households are single does call into question the pervasiveness of the patriarchal way of life. Incidentally, the resistance of traditional patriarchal families in Italy and Spain takes its toll: women counteract by not having children, so that both countries are the lowest in the world in fertility rate, way

15   United Nations (1991).
16   Alberdi (1995); Bruce et al. (1995).

Table 4.5 Non-marital births as a percentage of all births by region (country averages)

Region/country (no. of countries)	1970	1980	1990
Developed countries			
Canada	n.a.	13.2	21.1[a]
Eastern Europe (6)	7.1	9.0	12.9
Northern Europe (6)	8.8	19.5	33.3
Southern Europe (5)	4.1	5.4	8.7
Western Europe (6)	5.6	8.3	16.3
Japan	1.0[b]	1.0[c]	1.0[d]
Oceania (2)	9.0[b]	13.4[c]	20.2[e]
United States	5.4[b]	14.2[c]	28.0
(former) USSR (14)	8.2	8.8	11.2
Less-developed countries			
Africa (12)	n.a.	4.8[f]	n.a.
Asia (13)	n.a.	0.9[f]	n.a.
Latin America/Caribbean (13)	n.a.	6.5[f]	n.a.

n.a. = not available.
[a] 1989 [b] 1965 [c] 1975
[d] 1988 [e] 1985 [f] 1975–1980 (average)
Sources: *Eastern, Northern, Southern, and Western Europe, (former) USSR, and Canada*: Council of Europe (1993) *Recent Demographic Developments in Europe and North America, 1992* (Strasbourg: Council of Europe Press); *USA, Oceania, and Japan*: United Nations (1992) *Patterns of Fertility in Low Fertility Settings* (New York: United Nations), and US Department of Health and Human Services (1993) *Monthly Vital Statistics Report* 42(3) supplement; *less-developed countries*: United Nations (1987) *Fertility Behaviour in the Context of Development* (New York: United Nations)
Compiled and elaborated by Bruce et al. (1995)

below the replacement rate for the population (1.2 for Italy, 1.3 for Spain).[17] In addition, in Spain the age of emancipation is also the highest in Europe: 27 years for women, 29 for men. Widespread youth unemployment and an acute housing crisis contribute to keeping the traditional family together, at the cost of creating fewer families, and stopping the reproduction of Spaniards.[18]

This is, in fact, the most obvious consequence of the crisis of the patriarchal family: the precipitous decline of fertility rates in developed countries, below the rate of replacement of their population (see figure 4.5 for European countries). In Japan, the total fertility rate

17 Alberdi (1995).
18 Leal et al. (1996).

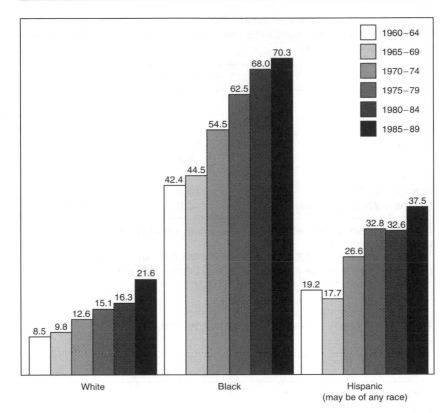

Figure 4.4 Percentage of women (15–34 years) with first birth occur ing before first marriage, by race and ethnic origin, in US, 1960–89
Source: US Bureau of the Census (1992a)

has been below replacement level since 1975, reaching 1.54 in 1990.[19] In the US, the total fertility rate has declined sharply in the past three decades, from its high historical point in the late 1950s, to reach a level below the replacement rate during the 1970s and 1980s, until stabilizing in the early 1990s at about the replacement level of 2.1. The number of births, however, increased because of the arrival of the baby boomer cohorts to procreation age (figure 4.6). Table 4.10 displays the total fertility rate by main regions of the world, with projections up to the mid-1990s. It has declined overall in the past two decades, and in the more developed regions has slipped below the replacement rate, and stays there. It should be noticed, however, that this is not an iron rule of population. Anna Cabre has shown the

19   Tsuya and Mason (1995).

Table 4.6 Trends in single-parent households as a percentage of all households with dependent children and at least one resident parent in developed countries

Country	Early 1970s	Mid-1980s
Australia	9.2	14.9
France	9.5	10.2
Japan	3.6	4.1
Sweden	15.0	17.0
United Kingdom	8.0	14.3
United States	13.0	23.9
(former) USSR	10.0	20.0
(former) West Germany	8.0	11.4

Note: Single-parent households are households with dependent children and one resident parent.
Source: Burns, Ailsa (1992) "Mother-headed families: an international perspective and the case of Australia," *Social Policy Report* 6(1)
Compiled and elaborated by Bruce et al. (1995)

Table 4.7 Trends in percentage of households headed by women *de jure*

Region/country	Earlier date	%	Later date	%
Demographic survey data				
Asia				
Indonesia	1976	15.5	1987	13.6
Sri Lanka	1975	15.7	1987	17.8
Thailand	1975	12.5	1987	20.8
Latin America/Caribbean				
Colombia	1976	17.5	1986	18.4
Dominican Republic	1975	20.7	1986	25.7
Ecuador	1979	15.0	1987	14.6
Mexico	1976	13.5	1987	13.3
Peru[a]	1977/78	14.7	1986	19.5
Trinidad and Tobago	1977	22.6	1987	28.6
Middle East/North Africa				
Morocco	1979/80	11.5	1987	17.3
Sub-Saharan Africa				
Ghana	1960	22.0	1987	29.0
Sudan	1978/79	16.7	1989/90	12.6

Table 4.7 contd

Region/country	Earlier date	%	Later date	%
Census data				
Asia				
Hong Kong	1971	23.5	1991	25.7
Indonesia	1971	16.3	1980	14.2
Japan	1980	15.2	1990	17.0
Korea	1980	14.7	1990	15.7
Philippines	1970	10.8	1990	11.3
Latin America/Caribbean				
Brazil	1980	14.4	1989	20.1
Costa Rica	1984	17.5	1992	20.0
Panama	1980	21.5	1990	22.3
Peru	1981	22.1	1991	17.3
Uruguay	1975	21.0	1985	23.0
Venezuela	1981	21.8	1990	21.3
Sub-Saharan Africa				
Burkina Faso	1975	5.1	1985	9.7
Cameroon	1976	13.8	1987	18.5
Mali	1976	15.1	1987	14.0

Note: de jure = "usual" household headship.
[a] de facto = headship on day of interview.
Sources: Demographic surveys: Ghana: Lloyd, Cynthia B. and Gage Brandon, Anastasia J. (1993) "Women's role in maintaining households: family welfare and sexual inequality in Ghana," *Population Studies* 47(1): 115–31. Ecuador: Ono-Osaku, Keiko and Themme, A.R. (1993) "Cooperative analysis of recent changes in households in Latin America," in IUSSP *Proceedings of Conference on the Americas, Vera Cruz*; all other countries: Ayad, Mohamed et al. (1994) *Demographic Characteristics of Households* (Demographic and Health Surveys Comparative Studies no. 14. Calverton, Maryland: Macro International Inc.); censuses: United Nations (1995) *The World's Women 1970–1995: Trends and Statistics* (New York: United Nations)
Compiled and elaborated by Bruce et al. (1995)

relationship between the recuperation of the fertility rate in Scandinavia in the 1980s and the generous social policy, and tolerance of society, in this privileged area of the world.[20] This is exactly why over 50 percent of children were conceived in an extra-marital relationship. Under conditions of psychological and material support, and not being penalized in their jobs, Scandinavian women went back to

20   Cabre (1990); Cabre and Domingo (1992).

Table 4.8 Indicators of recent changes in family and household formation: selected Western countries, 1975–90

Region and country	Women 20–24 in cohabitation, c. 1985–90 (%)	Extramarital births, c. 1988 (%)	Rise in extramarital births, 1975–88 (%)	One-parent households with children c. 1985 (%)
Scandinavia				
Iceland	–	52	19	–
Sweden	44	52	19	32
Denmark	43	45	23	26
Norway	28	34	23	23
Finland	26	19	9	15
Northern Europe				
Netherlands	23	11	8	19
United Kingdom	24	25	16	14
France	24	26	18	10
West Germany	18	10	4	13
Austria	–	23	8	15
Switzerland	–	6	2	9
Luxembourg	–	12	8	18
Belgium	18	10	7	15
Ireland	4	13	8	7
Southern Europe				
Portugal	7	14	7	–
Spain	3	8	6	11
Italy	3	6	3	16
Greece	1	2	1	–
Malta	–	2	1	–
Cyprus	–	1	0	–
North America				
United States	8	26	12	28
Canada	15	21	14	26
Oceania				
Australia	6	19	7	15
New Zealand	12	25	9	–

Sources: Council of Europe (various issues); European Values Studies, 1990 Round; Moors and van Nimwegen (1990); United Nations (various years, 1990); personal communications from Larry Bumpass (United States), Peter McDonald, Lincoln Day (Australia), Thomas Burch (Canada), Ian Pool (New Zealand).
Compiled by Lesthaeghe (1995)

Table 4.9 Percentage of one-person households over total number of households for selected countries, 1990–93

Country	Year	Total households (000s)	One-person households (000s)	%
Germany[a]	1993	36,230	12,379	34.2
Belgium	1992	3,969	1,050	26.5
Denmark[b]	1993	2,324	820	35.3
France	1992	22,230	6,230	28.0
Greece	1992	3,567	692	19.4
Great Britain	1992	23,097	6,219	26.9
Ireland	1991	1,029	208	20.2
Italy	1992	19,862	4,305	21.7
Luxembourg	1992	144	34	23.6
Netherlands	1992	6,206	1,867	30.1
Portugal	1992	3,186	399	12.5
Spain	1992	11,708	1,396	11.9
Estimates				
Finland	1993	2,120	716	33.8
Austria	1993	3,058	852	27.9
Sweden	1990	3,830	1,515	39.6
US	1993	96,391	23,642	24.5
Japan	1993	41,826	9,320	22.3

[a]   Data from microcensus, April 1993.
[b]   Data for Faeroe and Greenland not included.
Source: Statistisches Bundesamt (1995) *Statistisches Jahrbuch 1995 fuer das Ausland* (Wiesbaden: Metzer and Poeschel)

having children, and their countries displayed in the 1980s the highest fertility rate in Europe. However, the recent picture is not so rosy. Constraints on the Scandinavian welfare state reduced the amount of support, and, accordingly, in the early 1990s Scandinavian fertility rates stabilized, at replacement rate levels.[21] Also, in a number of countries, particularly in the United States, the total fertility rate is being pushed up by their immigrant population, thus inducing multi-ethnicity and multiculturalism. One of the most important socio-cultural differences might be the preservation of patriarchalism among ethnic minority immigrant communities in contrast to the disintegration of traditional families among native ethnic groups (black and white) in industrialized societies. This trend is, of course,

21   Alberdi (1995).

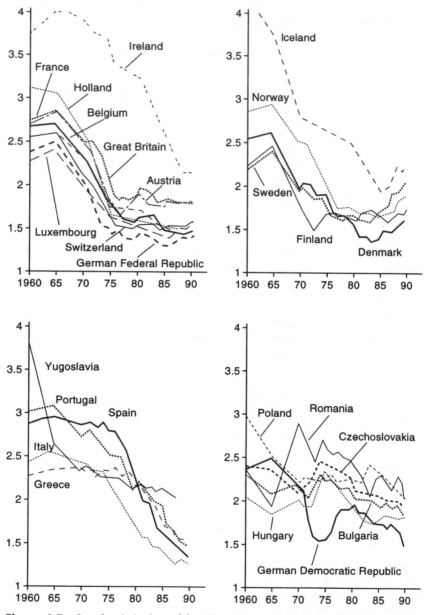

Figure 4.5 Synthetic index of fertility in European countries since 1960
Source: Alberdi (1995)

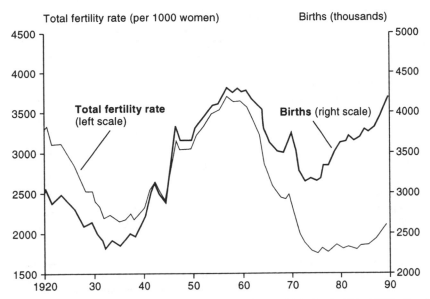

Figure 4.6 Total fertility rate and number of births in US, 1920–90
(total fertility rate = number of children that women would have by the
end of their child-bearing years based on age-specific birth rates of a
single year)
Source: US Bureau of the Census (1992a)

self-reproducing, even accounting for a reduction in the birth rate of
immigrant minorities as soon as they improve their economy and their
education.

Overall, it seems that in most developed countries, with the major
exceptions of Japan and Spain, the patriarchal family is in the process
of becoming a minority form in the way people live. In the United
States, only about one-quarter of all households in the 1990s fitted the
ideal type of a married couple with children (see below). If we add the
qualification "with the couple's children," the proportion drops. Certainly, not all is women's liberation. Demographic structure has something to do with it: another one-quarter of households in the US are
one-person households, and the majority of them are elderly people,
mainly women outliving their husbands. Yet, a statistical study conducted by Antonella Pinelli on the variables conditioning new demographic behavior in Europe concludes that:

> we see that marital instability, cohabitation, and extramarital births are
> taking place where there is a high-value on non-material aspects of the
> quality of life, and where women enjoy economic independence and

Table 4.10   Total fertility rate by main regions of the world

	1970–75	1980–85	1990–95[a]
World	4.4	3.5	3.3
More-developed regions	2.2	2.0	1.9
Less-developed regions	5.4	4.1	3.6
Africa	6.5	6.3	6.0
Asia	5.1	3.5	3.2
Europe	2.2	1.9	1.7
Americas	3.6	3.1	–
Latin	–	–	3.1
Northern	–	–	2.0
Oceania	3.2	2.7	2.5
USSR	2.4	2.4	2.3

[a]   1990–95 as projections.
Sources: United Nations, *World Population Prospects*, estimates as assessed in 1984; United Nations, *World Population at the Turn of the Century* (1989), p. 9; United Nations Population Fund, *The State of World Population: Choices and Responsibilities* (1994)

> relatively great political power. The conditions for women should be emphasized. Divorce, cohabitation, and extramarital fertility are the most widespread where women enjoy economic independence and are in a position to face the possibility of being a single mother without becoming, for this reason, a social subject at risk.[22]

Her conclusions must be corrected, however, by the observation that this is only part of the story. Children born out of wedlock in the United States result as much from poverty and lack of education as from women's self-affirmation. Nonetheless, the general trend, as shown in a few statistical illustrations, is toward the weakening and potential dissolution of traditional family forms of unchallenged patriarchal domination, with wife and children clustering around the husband/father.

In developing countries similar trends are at work in the urban areas, but national statistics, overwhelmed by traditional rural societies (particularly in Africa and Asia), downplay the phenomenon, in spite of which we still have been able to detect some traces. The Spanish exception is fundamentally linked to youth unemployment, and to a serious housing shortage that precludes the formation of new households in the largest metropolitan areas.[23] As for Japan, cultural

22   Pinelli (1995: 88).
23   Leal et al. (1996).

trends, such as the shame of non-marital births, help to consolidate patriarchalism, although recent trends seem to be eroding patriarchal ideology and women's relegation to the secondary labor market.[24] But my hypothesis about Japanese exceptionalism in preserving the patriarchal structure concerns mainly the absence of a significant feminist movement. Since such a movement began to grow in the 1990s, I dare to forecast that in this matter, as in many others, Japanese uniqueness is to some extent a function of time. Without denying the cultural specificity of Japan, the forces at work, in the structure of society and in the minds of women, are such that Japan too will have to reckon with the challenge to patriarchalism from Japanese working women.[25]

If current trends continue to expand throughout the world, and I contend they will, families as we have known them will become, in a number of societies, an historical relic not too long in the historical horizon. And the fabric of our lives will have been transformed, as we already feel, sometimes painfully, the tremors of this transformation. Let us now turn to analyze the underlying trends at the root of this crisis and, it is to be hoped, at the source of new forms of togetherness between women, children, pets, and even men.

Women at Work

Work, family, and labor markets were deeply transformed in the last quarter of the twentieth century by the massive incorporation of women to *paid labor*, in most cases outside their home.[26] Worldwide, 854 million women were economically active in 1990, accounting for 32.1 percent of the global labor force. Among women aged 15 years and over, 41 percent were economically active.[27] In OECD countries, the average labor force participation rate for women rose from 48.3 percent in 1973 to 61.6 percent in 1993, while for men it declined from 88.2 percent to 81.3 percent (see table 4.11). In the United States, women's labor participation rate went up from 51.1 percent in 1973 to 70.5 percent in 1994. Growth rates of employment for 1973–93 also indicate a general upward trend for women (reversed in some European countries in the 1990s), and a positive differential *vis-à-vis* men (table 4.12). Similar trends can be observed worldwide.

---

24   Tsuya and Mason (1995).
25   Gelb and Lief-Palley (1994).
26   Kahne and Giele (1992); Mason and Jensen (1995).
27   United Nations (1995).

Table 4.11 Labor force participation rates by sex (%)

	Men						Women					
	1973	1979	1983	1992	1993	1994[a]	1973	1979	1983	1992	1993	1994[a]
Australia	91.1	87.6	85.9	85.3	85.0	84.9	47.7	50.3	52.1	62.3	62.3	63.2
Austria	83.0	81.6	82.2	80.7	80.8	..	48.5	49.1	49.7	58.0	58.9	..
Belgium	83.2	79.3	76.8	72.6			41.3	46.3	48.7	54.1		
Canada	86.1	86.3	84.7	78.9	78.3		47.2	55.5	60.0	65.1	65.3	
Denmark	89.6	89.6	87.6	88.0	86.0		61.9	69.9	74.2	79.0	78.3	
Finland	80.0	82.2	82.0	78.5	77.6	77.1	63.6	68.9	72.7	70.7	70.0	69.8
France	85.2	82.6	78.4	74.7	74.5		50.1	54.2	54.3	58.8	59.0	
Germany	89.6	84.9	82.6	79.0	78.6		50.3	52.2	52.5	61.3	61.4	
Greece	83.2	79.0	80.0	73.0	73.7		32.1	32.8	40.4	42.7	43.6	
Ireland[b]	92.3	88.7	87.1	81.9			34.1	35.2	37.8	39.9		
Italy	85.1	82.6	80.7	79.1	74.8		33.7	38.7	40.3	46.5	43.3	
Japan	90.1	89.2	89.1	89.7	90.2	90.1	54.0	54.7	57.2	62.0	61.8	61.8
Luxembourg[b]	93.1	88.9	85.1	77.7			35.9	39.8	41.7	44.8		
Netherlands	85.6	79.0	77.3	80.8			29.2	33.4	40.3	55.5		
New Zealand	89.2	87.3	84.7	83.0	83.3		39.2	45.0	45.7	63.2	63.2	
Norway	86.5	89.2	87.2	82.6	82.0	82.3	50.6	61.7	65.5	70.9	70.8	71.3
Portugal[c]		90.9	86.9	82.3	82.5	82.8		57.3	56.7	60.6	61.3	62.2
Spain	92.9	83.1	80.2	75.1	74.5	73.9	33.4	32.6	33.2	42.0	42.8	43.9
Sweden	88.1	87.9	85.9	81.8	79.3	78.1	62.6	72.8	76.6	77.7	75.7	74.6
Switzerland	100.0	94.6	93.5	93.7	92.5	91.0	54.1	53.0	55.2	58.5	57.9	56.9
United Kingdom	93.0	90.5	87.5	84.5	83.3	81.8	53.2	58.0	57.2	64.8	64.7	64.5
United States	86.2	85.7	84.6	85.3	84.9	85.4	51.1	58.9	61.8	69.0	69.0	70.5
North America	86.2	85.8	84.6	84.6	84.2		50.7	58.6	61.6	68.6	68.7	
OECD Europe[d]	88.7	84.8	82.3	79.2	80.1		44.7	48.6	49.8	56.9	60.6	
Total OECD[d]	88.2	85.9	84.3	82.9	81.3		48.3	53.1	55.1	61.9	61.6	

[a] Secretariat estimates.   [b] 1991 instead of 1992 for Ireland and Luxembourg.
[c] Labor force data include a significant number of persons aged less than 15 years.   [d] Above countries only.
Source: OECD *Employment Outlook* (1995)

Table 4.12 Total employment by sex (average annual growth rates in percentages)

	Men						Women					
	1973–75	1975–79	1979–83	1983–91	1992	1993	1973–75	1975–79	1979–83	1983–91	1992	1993
Australia	-0.3	0.6	-0.1	1.5[d]	-0.3	0.0	2.0	1.7	2.0	3.9[d]	0.6	0.8
Austria	-1.1	0.8	0.9	0.7	0.8	:	-1.2	1.0	0.8	2.1	3.3	:
Belgium	-0.4	-0.4	-1.8	0.0	-1.1	:	0.8	0.9	0.2	2.0	0.5	:
Canada	1.9	1.8	-0.6	1.1	-1.2	1.2	4.7	4.5	2.6	2.8	-0.4	1.1
Denmark	-1.8	0.7[b]	-1.7	0.9	:	:	-0.5	3.6[b]	0.9	1.4	:	:
Finland	0.7	-0.6[b]	0.9	-0.5	-7.6	-5.9	2.0	-0.0[b]	1.9	-0.1	-6.5	-6.3
France	-0.4	-0.2	-0.7	-0.1	-1.2	:	0.8	1.6	0.7	1.4	0.5	:
Germany	-2.5	0.3	-0.5	0.8[e]	-0.3	:	-1.0	0.9	-0.0	2.0[e]	1.7	:
Greece	-0.5	0.8	0.6	0.1	:	:	1.6	1.1	4.1	0.7	:	:
Ireland	-0.2	1.5	-1.4	-0.5	:	:	1.6	2.0	1.9	1.1	:	:
Italy	0.6	-0.1	0.0	0.1	-1.1	:[h]	2.4	2.7	1.3	1.6	0.3	:[h]
Japan	0.5	0.7	0.8	1.1	1.1	0.6	-1.7	2.0	1.7	1.7	1.0	-0.3
Luxembourg	1.0	-0.7	-0.7	2.3[f]	:	:	4.6	1.5	1.8	3.3[f]	:	:
Netherlands	-1.5	0.3	-0.8	2.1	1.3	:	2.9	2.7	4.0	5.3	3.2	:
New Zealand	2.1	0.2	-0.3	-1.0[d]	0.4	:	5.2	2.7	0.8	1.3[d]	0.6	:
Norway	0.9	1.1	-0.2	-0.4	-0.5	-0.5	2.9	4.4	1.8	1.4	-0.1	0.5
Portugal	-1.3[a]	0.3	0.4[c]	1.0	[g]	-2.8	-1.5[a]	0.9	1.1[c]	3.0	[g]	-1.2
Spain	-0.2	-1.7[b]	-1.8	0.8	-3.2	-5.4	-1.5	-1.3[b]	-1.7	3.0	0.3	-2.4
Sweden	1.0	-0.3	-0.6	0.1[c]	-5.1	-7.9	4.2	2.0	1.3	0.9[c]	-3.5	-6.2
Switzerland	-2.8	-0.5	0.8	0.8	-2.1	-2.5	-1.9	0.6	2.0	1.6	-2.4	-2.5
United Kingdom	-1.0	-0.2	-2.3	0.4	-3.3	-2.8	1.5	1.2	-1.0	2.3	-1.0	-1.3
United States	-0.6	2.5	-0.3	1.3	0.3	1.3	2.0	5.0	1.7	2.4	0.9	1.5
North America	-0.4	2.4	-0.4	1.2	0.2	1.3	2.2	4.9	1.8	2.4	0.8	1.5
OECD Europe[i]	-0.8	-0.2	-0.8	0.4	-2.0	:	1.2	1.4	0.5	2.0	-0.3	:
Total OECD[i]	-0.4	0.9	-0.3	0.9	-1.4	:	1.0	2.8	1.2	2.2	-0.1	:

a Break in series between 1973 and 1974.
b Break in series between 1975 and 1976.
c Break in series between 1982 and 1983.
d Break in series between 1985 and 1986.
e Break in series between 1986 and 1987.
f Data refer to 1983–90.
g Break in series between 1991 and 1992.
h Break in series between 1992 and 1993.
i Above countries only.

Source: OECD Employment Outlook (1995).

Switching to the United Nations' statistical categorization of "economic activity rate" (whose percentages are lower than those of labor force participation), tables 4.13 and 4.14 show a similar upward trend for women's economic activity rate, with the partial exception of Russia which already had a high level in 1970.

The massive entry of women into the paid labor force is due, on the one hand, to the informationalization, networking, and globalization of the economy; on the other hand, to the gendered segmentation of the labor market taking advantage of the specific social conditions of women to enhance productivity, management control, and ultimately profits.[28] Let us look at some statistical indicators.[29]

When analyzing the transformation of employment structure in the informational economy (volume I, chapter 4), I showed the growth of service employment, and, within services, the strategic role played by two distinctive categories of services: business services, and social services, characteristic of the informational economy, as forecasted by early theorists of postindustrialism. Figure 4.7 displays the convergence between growth of services and of female employment in 1980–90. Figure 4.8a shows the concentration of women in service employment in different areas of the world. However, it should be noticed that, in most of the world, the majority of labor is still agricultural (but not for long), and therefore, most women still work in agriculture: 80 percent of economically active women in sub-Saharan Africa, and 60 percent in southern Asia. Worldwide, about half of economically active women are in services.[30] The proportion is much higher in most developed countries, and has been increasing over time, to reach about 85 percent of the female labor force in the US and the UK. However, the most significant aspect is in which kind of services women work. As shown in table 4.15, in most developed countries, the bulk of female employment is in social services and personal services. However, if we calculate the rate of increase of each type of service in total female employment for the 1973–93 period (table 4.16), we observe a spectacular increase in business services, followed at some distance by social/personal services. Trade and restaurant employment is the least dynamic segment in the evolution of women's employment in advanced countries. Thus, there is a direct correspondence between the type of services linked to informationalization of the economy and the expansion of women's employment in

28 Kahne and Giele (1992); Rubin and Riney (1994).
29 See Blumstein and Schwartz (1983); Cobble (1993); OECD (1993–95, 1994a, b, 1995); Mason and Jensen (1995); United Nations (1995).
30 United Nations (1991).

Table 4.13 Economic activity rates, 1970–90

			1970	1975	1980	1985	1990
OECD							
Canada	(15+)	Total	40.9(71)	44.6(76)			
		Men	53.3	55.6			
		Women	28.4	33.8			
France	(15+)	Total	42.0(71)	42.6	43.3	43.4(86)	44.8
		Men	55.2	55.1	54.4	52.6	51.6
		Women	29.4	30.5	32.7	34.6	38.2
Germany	(14+)	Total	43.9	43.4	44.9		49.6
		Men	59.2	57.1	58.4		60.8
		Women	30.0	30.9	32.6		39.2
Italy	(14+)	Total	36.6	35.4	40.2	41.1	42.0
		Men	54.7	52.2	55.2	54.6	54.3
		Women	19.3	19.4	26.0	28.2	30.3
Japan	(15+)	Total	51.0	48.6	48.4	51.5	51.7
		Men	63.4	62.3	60.2	63.6	62.4
		Women	39.1	35.2	36.8	39.8	41.3
UK	(16+)	Total	42.5		47.3(81)		50.3
		Men	51.7		59.4		58.4
		Women	33.0		35.8		42.6
USA	(16+)	Total	41.8	44.5	49.1		
		Men	53.9	55.6	56.8		
		Women	30.2	33.9	41.8		44.4(92)
Russian	(16+)	Total	48.4		51.7(79)		50.2
Federation		Men	52.1		55.7		55.0
		Women	45.3		48.1		45.8
Asia							
China	(15+)	Total			52.3(82)		
		Men			57.3		
		Women	44.25		47.0		
India	(15+)	Total	32.9(71)				37.5(91)
		Men	52.5				51.6
		Women	11.9				22.3
Indonesia	(15+)	Total	34.9(71)		35.5		
		Men	47.3		48.1		
		Women	22.8		23.5		
Korea	(15+)	Total	33.0	38.5	37.9		
		Men	42.8	46.9	46.3		
		Women	23.2	30.0	29.3		
Latin America							
Argentina	(14+)	Total	38.5		38.5	37.5	38.1
		Men	57.9		55.1	55.3	55.4
		Women	19.4		22.0	19.9	21.0
Mexico	(12+)	Total	26.9	27.6	33.0		29.6
		Men	43.6	42.9	48.2		46.2
		Women	10.2	12.0	18.2		13.6

Table 4.13   contd

			1970	1975	1980	1985	1990
Brazil	(10+)	Total	31.7			36.3	41.9
		Men	10.5			53.1	56.3
		Women	13.1			19.8	27.9
Africa							
Algeria	(6+)	Total	21.7(66)				23.6
		Men	42.2				42.4
		Women	1.8				4.4
Nigeria	(14+)	Total					30.3
		Men					40.7
		Women					19.7
Middle East							
Egypt	(6+)	Total	27.9(71)	30.2(76)			31.6
		Men	51.2	54.1			49.3
		Women	4.2	5.5			13.5

Note: Economic activity rate = economically active population/total population.
Source: ILO, *Yearbook of Labour Statistics* (1970–94)

Table 4.14   Growth of women's economic activity rate, 1970–90

	1970	1990	Growth (%)
France	29.4	38.2	29.9
Germany	30.0	39.2	30.7
Italy	19.3	30.3	57.0
Japan	39.1	41.3	5.6
UK	33.0	42.6	29.1
USA	30.2	44.4	47.0
Russia	45.3	45.8	1.1
India	11.9	22.3	87.4
Argentina	19.4	21.0	8.2
Mexico	10.2	13.6	33.3
Brazil	13.1	27.9	113.0
Algeria	1.8	4.4	144.4
Egypt	4.2	13.5	221.4

Note: Economic activity rate = economically active population/total population.
Source: ILO, *Yearbook of Labour Statistics* (1970–94)

advanced countries. A similar conclusion results from observing the changing evolution of female employment by occupation between 1980 and 1989 in selected OECD countries (table 4.17). Overall,

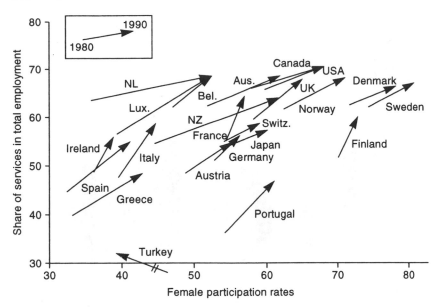

Figure 4.7 Growth in service sector employment and in female participation rates, 1980–90 (Aus., Australia; Bel., Belgium; Lux., Luxembourg; NL, Netherlands; NZ, New Zealand; Switz., Switzerland)
Source: OECD (1994b), Statistical Annex, tables A and D

professional/technical and administrative/managerial categories have grown faster than others, although clerical workers still account, in general, for the largest group of women workers. Women are not being relegated to the lowest skilled service jobs: they are employed across the entire skills structure, and the growth of women's jobs is higher at the upper end of the occupational structure. This is exactly why there is discrimination: because they perform similarly qualified jobs at lower pay, with greater job insecurity, and with lower chances of careers to the top.

Globalization has also played a major part in involving women in the labor force around the world. The electronics industry, internationalized since the late 1960s, recruited mainly among young, unskilled women in Asia.[31] The US *maquiladoras* in northern Mexico rely heavily on female labor. And the newly industrialized economies have brought into paid work underpaid women at almost all levels of the occupational structure.[32] At the same time, a substantial share of

31   Salaff (1981, 1988).
32   Standing (1990).

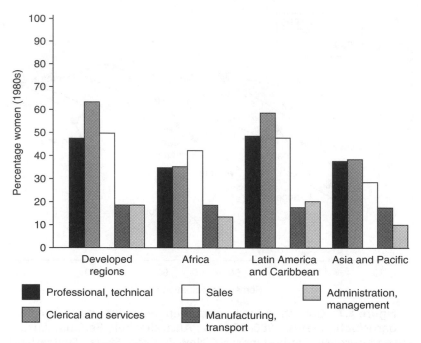

Figure 4.8a   Women as a percentage of the labor force by type
of employment

Source: Prepared by the Statistical Office of the United Nations Secretariat (1991)
from International Labour Office, *Yearbook of Labour Statistics* (various years)

urban employment for women in developing countries remains in the
informal sector, particularly in providing food and services for metropolitan dwellers.[33]

Why women? First, because, in contrast with the misleading statements printed in the media, overall there has been sustained job
creation in the world in the past three decades, with the exception
of Europe (see volume I, chapter 4). But, even in Europe, women's
labor participation has increased while men's has declined. So,
women's entry into the labor force is not just a response to labor
demand. Also, women's unemployment is not always higher than for
men: in 1994 it was lower than men's in the United States (6 percent *v.*
6.2 percent), and in Canada (9.8 percent *v.* 10.7 percent); and it was
much lower than men's in 1993 in the United Kingdom (7.5 percent *v.*
12.4 percent). On the other hand, it was slightly higher in Japan and

33   Portes et al. (1989).

Figure 4.8b   Married couple families with wives in the labor force, in US, 1960–90 (data for 1983 not available)
Source: US Bureau of the Census (1992a)

Spain, and significantly higher in France and Italy. Thus, the increase in women's labor participation rate goes on independently of their differential in unemployment *vis-à-vis* men, and of the growth of labor demand.

If labor demand, in purely quantitative terms, does not explain calling upon women, their appeal for employers must be explained by other characteristics. I think it is well established in the literature that it is the social gendering of women's work that makes them, as a whole, an attractive labor pool.[34] This has certainly nothing to do with biological characteristics: women have proved that they can be firefighters and dockers around the world, and strenuous factory work by women marked industrialization from its beginning. Nor, for that matter, has young women's employment in electronics anything to do with the myth of their fingers' dexterity, but with the social acceptance of wasting their eyes in 10 years through microscopic assembly. Anthropologists have documented how, at the outset of women's employment in electronic factories in South-east Asia, there was a pattern of patriarchal authority extending from the family

34   Spitz (1988); Kahne and Giele (1992); OECD (1994b).

Table 4.15 Female service employment by activities and rank of information intensity of total employment (%), 1973–93

| | | *1* | *2* | *2* | *3* | *(Rank of information intensity)* | |
		Financing, insurance, real estate, and business services	*Community, social, and personal services*	*Transport, storage, and communications*	*Wholesale and retail trade, restaurants, and hotels*	*Activities not adequately defined*	*Total*
Canada	1975	11.2	40.2	4.0	25.8		81.2
	1983	12.1	40.9	4.2	25.4		82.6
	1993	13.6	43.9	3.7	24.8		86.0
USA	1973	9.1	41.5	3.5	23.9		78.0
	1983	11.9	41.9	3.3	24.5		81.6
	1993	12.6	46.6	3.5	22.7		85.3
Japan	1973	3.4	22.0	2.0	24.7	0.2	52.3
	1983	6.9	24.1	1.9	27.1	0.2	60.3
	1993	9.4	26.9	2.5	27.5	0.4	66.7
Germany	1973						
	1983	8.2	34.2	3.3	22.5		68.2
	1993	10.3	38.4	3.6	22.4		74.6
Italy	1977	1.7	31.0	1.8	18.8		53.3
	1983	3.1	34.6	2.0	21.0		60.6
	1993	8.1	36.4	2.7	22.6		69.8
UK	1973	7.4	36.0	2.8	24.7		70.7
	1983	9.8	42.2	2.8	25.0	0.1	79.9
	1993						84.9
Spain	1977	2.1	28.2	1.5	24.4		56.3
	1983	3.0	35.8	1.7	24.4		64.9
	1993	6.3	41.8	2.2	26.9		77.2

Source: OECD, *Labour Force Statistics* (1995)

Table 4.16 Rates of growth for each category of female service
employment as a percentage of total female employment, 1973–1993[a]

Country	Business services (%)	Social and personal services (%)	Transportation, storage, and communication (%)	Trade, hotels, and restaurants (%)
USA	38.5	12.2	0	−5.0
Japan	176.5	22.2	25	1.3
Germany (1983–93)	25.6	12.3	9	−0.4
Italy (1977–93)	376.5	17.4	50	−3.9
UK	32.4	17.2	0	1.2
Spain (1977–93)	200.0	48.2	47	10.2

[a] Unless dates for calculations are otherwise indicated.
Source: Elaboration on data from table 4.15

household into the factory, under agreement between factory managers and the paterfamilias.[35]

Neither, it seems, is the reason for hiring women to do with their
lack of unionization. The causality seems to work the other way
around: women are not unionized because they are often employed
in sectors where there is little or no unionization, such as private
business services or electronics manufacturing. Even so, women constitute 37 percent of union members in the United States, 39 percent
in Canada, 51 percent in Sweden, and 30 percent in Africa, on
average.[36] Garment workers in the United States and in Spain,
women in the Mexican *maquiladoras*, and teachers and nurses
throughout the world have mobilized in defense of their demands,
with greater vehemence than male-dominated steel or chemical
workers' unions in recent times. The supposed submissiveness
of women workers is an enduring myth whose fallacy managers
have come to realize, at their cost.[37] So, what are the main factors
inducing the explosion of women's employment?

The first, and most obvious, factor concerns the possibility of
paying less for similar work. With the expansion of universal education, including college education, particularly in most developed
countries, women came to constitute a pool of skills that was immediately tapped by employers. Women's wage differential *vis-à-vis* men
persists throughout the world, while, as we have seen, in most

35 Salaff (1981).
36 United Nations (1991).
37 Cobble (1993).

Table 4.17 Distribution of female employment by occupation,[a] 1980 and 1989 (%)

Country [b,c]	Professional, technical, and related	Administrative and managerial	Clerical and related	Sales workers	Service workers	Agriculture and related	Production and related
Belgium							
1983	25.9	1.4	24.4	13.7	18.6	2.8	13.2
1988	28.2	1.4	27.3	14.6	14.4	2.1	11.6
Index (1983 = 100)	118.0	113.0	122.0	116.0	84.0	86.0	95.0
Canada							
1980	19.1	5.4	34.5	10.0	18.3	2.8	9.9
1989	20.9	10.7	30.5	9.9	17.0	2.2	8.9
Index (1980 = 100)	143.0	185.0	114.0	123.0	122.0	98.0	113.0
Finland							
1980	19.8	1.4	21.8	8.6	22.3	10.5	15.5
1989	31.2	1.9	22.7	11.5	16.2	6.5	10.0
Index (1980 = 100)	172.0	147.0	113.0	145.0	79.0	66.0	70.0
Germany							
1980	14.1	1.3	30.7	12.9	16.3	6.9	15.9
1986	16.2	1.5	29.8	12.8	16.1	5.5	13.3
Index (1980 = 100)	118.0	115.0	99.0	102.0	102.0	83.0	86.0
Greece							
1981	10.7	0.7	12.9	9.0	9.7	41.6	15.5
1989	14.4	0.8	14.6	10.8	11.5	34.0	13.9
Index (1981 = 100)	156.0	130.0	131.0	138.0	137.0	95.0	104.0

Table 4.17 contd

Country[b,c]	Professional, technical, and related	Administrative and managerial	Clerical and related	Sales workers	Service workers	Agriculture and related	Production and related
Japan							
1980	9.6	0.5	23.1	14.3	12.7	13.1	26.5
1989	11.4	0.8	26.4	14.4	11.4	8.8	26.5
Index (1980 = 100)	173.0	132.0	116.0	104.0	77.0	116.0	250.0
Norway							
1980	23.6	2.2	19.2	12.8	24.9	5.9	11.2
1989	28.3	3.5	19.8	12.4	22.3	3.9	9.4
Index (1980 = 100)	141.0	188.0	121.0	114.0	106.0	78.0	99.0
Spain							
1980	8.7	0.2	13.2	15.4	25.6	18.2	18.7
1989	15.2	0.4	18.2	15.4	25.2	11.1	14.4
Index (1980 = 100)	202.0	280.0	160.0	116.0	114.0	70.0	89.0
Sweden							
1980	30.6	0.8	21.6	8.7	22.8	3.0	12.4
1989	42.0	n.a.	21.9	9.3	13.2	1.8	11.7
Index (1980 = 100)	154.0	n.a.	114.0	120.0	65.0	66.0	106.0
United States							
1980	16.8	6.9	35.1	6.8	19.5	1.2	13.8
1989	18.1	11.1	27.8	13.1	17.7	1.1	11.1
Index (1980 = 100)	136.0	202.0	99.0	243.0	115.0	115.0	101.0

a   Major groups of the International Standard Classification of Occupations (ISCO).
b   Not all countries publish data according to ISCO. Countries in which occupational classification systems have changed during the relevant period are omitted.
c   The index indicates the growth in total numbers employed in the occupation over the decade.
Source: ILO, Yearbook of Labour Statistics (various years)

advanced countries differences in occupational profile are small. In the US, women earned 60–65 percent of men's earnings in the 1960s, and their share improved somewhat to 72 percent in 1991, but the main reason for this was the decline in men's real wages.[38] In the UK, women's earnings were 69.5 percent of men's in the mid-1980s. They were 73.6 percent in Germany in 1991, up from 72 percent in 1980. For France, the corresponding figures are 80.8 percent, up from 79 percent. Women's average wage is 43 percent of men's in Japan, 51 percent in Korea, 56 percent in Singapore, 70 percent in Hong Kong, and varies in a wide range between 44 percent and 77 percent in Latin America.[39]

I want to emphasize that, in most cases, women are not being deskilled, or reduced to menial jobs, but quite the opposite. They are often promoted to multi-skilled jobs that require initiative, and education, as new technologies demand an autonomous labor force able to adapt, and reprogram its own tasks, as in the case studies of insurance and banking that I summarized in volume I, chapter 4. This is in fact the second major reason for hiring women, at a bargain price: their relational skills, increasingly necessary in an informational economy where the administration of things takes second place to the management of people. In this sense, there is an extension of the gendered division of labor between male's traditional production and female's traditional home-making, and social-making, under patriarchalism. It just happens that the new economy increasingly requires the skills that were confined to the private domain of relational work to be brought to the forefront of the management and processing of information and people.

But there is something else that I believe is probably the most important factor in inducing the expansion of women's employment: their flexibility as workers.[40] Indeed, women account for the bulk of part-time employment and temporary employment, and for a still small but growing share of self-employment (tables 4.18 and 4.19). Relating this observation to the analyses presented in volume I, chapters 3 and 4, concerning the networking of economic activity, and the flexibilization of work as major features of the informational economy, it seems reasonable to argue that there is a fit between women's working flexibility, in schedules, time, and entry and exit to and from the labor market, and the needs of the new economy.[41] This fit is also a gendered condition. Since women's work has traditionally been

38   Kim (1993).
39   United Nations (1995).
40   Susser (1997).
41   Thurman and Trah (1990); Duffy and Pupo (1992).

Table 4.18 Size and composition of part-time employment, 1973–94 (%)

| | Part-time employment as a proportion of employment | | | | | | | | | | | |
| | Men | | | | | | Women | | | | | |
	1973	1979	1983	1992	1993	1994	1973	1979	1983	1992	1993	1994
Australia	3.7	5.2	6.2	10.6	10.3	10.9	28.2	35.2	36.4	43.3	42.3	42.6
Austria	1.4	1.5	1.5	1.6	1.7	..	15.6	18.0	20.0	20.5	22.8	..
Belgium	1.0	1.0	2.0	2.1	2.3	2.5	10.2	16.5	19.7	28.1	28.5	28.3
Canada	4.7	5.7	7.6	9.3	9.8	9.5	19.4	23.2	26.1	25.8	26.2	26.1
Denmark	..	5.2	6.6	10.1	11.0	..	..	46.3	44.7	36.7	37.3	..
Finland	..	3.2	4.5	5.5	6.2	6.0	..	10.6	12.5	10.4	11.1	11.2
France	1.7	2.4	2.5	3.6	4.1	4.6	12.9	17.0	20.1	24.5	26.3	27.8
Germany[a]	1.8	1.5	1.7	2.6	2.9	..	24.4	27.6	30.0	30.7	32.0	..
Greece	..	..	3.7	2.8	2.6	3.1	..	..	12.1	8.4	7.6	8.0
Iceland	..	..	..	9.2	9.9	..	..	..	..	49.8	47.5	..
Ireland	3.7	2.1	2.7	3.9	4.8	..	..	13.1	15.5	18.6	21.3	..
Italy	6.8	3.0	2.4	2.8	2.5	2.8	14.0	10.6	9.4	11.5	11.0	12.4
Japan	1.0	7.5	7.3	10.6	11.4	11.7	25.1	27.8	29.8	34.8	35.2	35.7
Luxembourg	..	1.0	1.0	1.2	1.0	..	18.4	17.1	17.0	16.5	18.3	..
Mexico[b]	..	..	..	18.7	19.6	..	..	..	..	36.1	36.6	..
Netherlands[c]	4.6	5.5	7.2	13.3	13.6	14.7	..	44.0	50.1	62.1	63.0	64.8
New Zealand	8.6	4.9	5.0	10.3	9.7	9.7	24.6	29.1	31.4	35.9	35.7	36.6
Norway[d]	..	10.6	11.5	9.8	9.8	9.5	47.8	51.7	54.9	47.1	47.6	46.5
Portugal	..	2.5	..	4.1	4.5	4.7	..	16.5	..	11.3	11.1	12.1
Spain	..	..	..	2.0	2.4	2.6	..	..	..	13.7	14.8	15.2
Sweden[e]	..	5.4	6.3	8.4	9.1	9.7	..	46.0	45.9	41.3	41.4	41.0
Switzerland	..	..	..	8.3	8.6	8.8	..	..	..	53.7	54.1	55.4
Turkey	..	..	..	11.3	17.9	..	..	..	..	37.0	40.4	..
United Kingdom	2.3	1.9	3.3	6.2	6.6	7.1	39.1	39.0	42.4	43.5	43.8	44.3
United States[f]	8.6	9.0	10.8	10.8	10.9	11.5	26.8	26.7	28.1	25.4	25.3	27.7

Continued

Table 4.18 contd

	Part-time employment as a proportion of employment						Women's share in part-time employment					
	1973	1979	1983	1992	1993	1994	1973	1979	1983	1992	1993	1994
Australia	11.9	15.9	17.5	24.5	23.9	24.4	79.4	78.7	78.0	75.0	75.3	74.2
Austria	6.4	7.6	8.4	9.0	10.1	..	85.8	87.8	88.4	89.6	89.7	..
Belgium	3.8	6.0	8.1	12.4	12.8	12.8	82.4	88.9	84.0	89.7	89.3	88.1
Canada	9.7	12.5	15.4	16.7	17.2	17.0	68.4	72.1	71.3	69.7	68.9	69.4
Denmark	..	22.7	23.8	22.5	23.3	..	..	86.9	84.7	75.8	74.9	..
Finland	..	6.7	8.3	7.9	8.6	8.5	..	74.7	71.7	64.3	63.1	63.6
France	5.9	8.1	9.6	12.5	13.7	14.9	82.3	82.1	84.3	83.7	83.3	82.7
Germany[a]	10.1	11.4	12.6	14.4	15.1	..	89.0	91.6	91.9	89.3	88.6	..
Greece	..	..	6.5	4.8	4.3	4.8	..	..	61.2	61.3	61.6	58.9
Iceland	..	..	..	27.8	27.3	..	..	..	..	82.1	80.4	..
Ireland	..	5.1	6.6	9.1	10.8	..	..	71.2	71.6	72.5	71.7	71.1
Italy	6.4	5.3	4.6	5.8	5.4	6.2	58.3	61.4	64.8	68.8	70.5	67.5
Japan	13.9	15.4	16.2	20.5	21.1	21.4	70.0	70.1	72.9	69.3	67.7	..
Luxembourg	5.8	5.8	6.3	6.9	7.3	..	87.5	87.5	88.9	88.9	91.2	..
Mexico[b]	..	..	..	24.0	24.9	..	..	..	..	46.3	46.1	..
Netherlands[c]	..	16.6	21.4	32.5	33.4	35.0	..	76.4	77.3	75.2	75.7	75.1
New Zealand	11.2	13.9	15.3	21.6	21.2	21.6	72.3	77.7	79.8	73.3	74.2	74.9
Norway[d]	23.0	27.3	29.6	26.9	27.1	26.5	76.4	77.0	77.3	80.1	80.5	80.6
Portugal	..	7.8	..	7.3	7.4	8.0	..	80.4	..	68.2	66.3	67.1
Spain	..	..	..	5.8	6.6	6.9	..	..	..	77.0	75.6	74.9
Sweden[e]	..	23.6	24.8	24.3	24.9	24.9	..	87.5	86.6	82.3	81.3	80.1
Switzerland	..	..	..	27.8	28.1	28.9	..	..	..	83.1	82.5	82.7
Turkey	..	..	..	19.3	24.8	..	..	..	..	59.3	50.2	..
United Kingdom	16.0	16.4	19.4	22.8	23.3	23.8	90.9	92.8	89.8	84.9	84.5	83.6
United States[f]	15.6	16.4	18.4	17.5	17.5	18.9	66.0	68.0	66.8	66.4	66.2	67.3

a Up to 1990 data refer to Western Germany; thereafter, they refer to the whole of Germany.
b 1991 instead of 1992.   c Break in series after 1985.   d Break in series after 1992.   e Break in series after 1986 and after 1992.   Break in series after 1987.
f Break in series after 1993.

Source: OECD, *Employment Outlook* (1995)

Table 4.19 Share of self-employment in total employment, by sex and activity (%)

| | All non-agricultural activities | | | | Service activities (1990) both sexes | | | |
| | Share of female employment | | Share of male employment | | Wholesale and retail trade, restaurants, and hotels (ISIC 6) | Transport, storage, and communications (ISIC 7) | Financing, insurance, real estate, and business services (ISIC 8) | Community, social, and personal services (ISIC 9) |
	1979	1990	1979	1990				
Australia	10.0	9.6	13.9	14.4	15.5	14.5	14.0	6.6
Austria	..	..	..	..	13.7	3.6	10.0	5.0
Belgium	8.8	10.3	12.6	16.7	36.0	5.5	21.7	8.2
Canada	6.0	6.4	7.2	8.3	7.2	6.4	10.4	8.5
Denmark	..	2.8	..	10.4	13.3	6.9	9.6	3.2
Finland	4.2	5.6	7.9	11.5	16.0	11.2	10.5	4.0
France	..	5.5	..	11.9	19.2	4.8	9.2	5.3
Germany	4.8	5.4	9.4	9.7	15.7	6.6	17.1	5.5
Greece	25.7	15.4	34.0	32.7	48.0	25.5	35.9	9.4
Ireland	..	6.1	..	16.8	24.4	13.7	13.6	6.8
Italy	12.8	15.1	21.7	25.8	45.8	14.1	8.9	15.5
Japan	12.9	9.3	14.6	12.1	15.0	4.8	8.1	12.0
Luxembourg	..	5.8	..	7.9	17.5	3.8	7.0	3.7
Netherlands	..	7.3	..	9.6	13.4	3.3	11.9	7.8
New Zealand	..	11.8	..	24.0	18.2	11.1	19.2	9.6
Norway	3.4	3.6	8.9	8.8	7.5	9.3	6.7	4.4
Portugal	..	12.3	..	18.3	38.3	8.6	13.7	4.6
Spain	12.5	13.9	17.1	19.2	34.0	26.8	13.7	6.0
Sweden	6.2	3.9	2.5	10.1	13.6	8.8	11.6	3.7
United Kingdom	3.2	7.0	9.0	16.6	15.9	10.5	14.2	7.8
United States	4.9	5.9	8.7	8.7	8.5	4.6	11.4	7.3

Source: OECD, *Employment Outlook* (1991), table 2.12; (1992) tables 4.A.2 and 4.A.8.

considered as complementary to men's earnings in the family, and since women are still responsible for their household and, above all, for the rearing of their children, work flexibility fits, as well, the survival strategies of coping with both worlds on the edge of a nervous breakdown.[42] Indeed, in the European Union (as everywhere else), marriage and children are the most important factors in inducing women's part-time employment (figure 4.9). Thus, the type of worker required by the informational, networked economy fits the survival interests of women who, under the conditions of patriarchalism, seek to make compatible work and family, with little help from their husbands.

This process of full incorporation of women into the labor market, and into paid work, has important consequences for the family. The first is that more often than not a woman's financial contribution becomes decisive for the household budget. Thus, female bargaining power in the household increases significantly. Under strict patriarchalism, women's domination by men was, to start with, a living matter: home-making was their job. Thus, rebellion against patriarchal authority could be only extreme, often leading to marginality. With women bringing pay home, and with men in many countries (for instance in the United States) seeing their real pay-checks decline, matters of disagreement could be discussed without necessarily escalating to all-out patriarchal repression. Furthermore, the ideology of patriarchalism legitimizing domination on the basis of the family provider's privilege was decisively undermined. Why could husbands not help at home if both members of the couple were equally absent for long hours, and if both were equally contributing to the family budget? The questions became more pressing with the increasing difficulty for women of assuming paid work, home work, child rearing, and management of husbands, while society was still organized on the assumption of the vanishing full-time housewife. With no proper child care, no planning of the spatial connection between residence, jobs, and services, and deteriorating social services,[43] women were confronted with their reality: their beloved husbands/fathers were taking advantage of them. And since their work outside the home opened their world, and broadened their social networks and their experience, often marked by sisterhood against daily harshness, they started to ask questions of themselves, and to give their answers to their daughters. The soil was ready for the seeding of feminist ideas that were *simultaneously* germinating in the fields of cultural social movements.

42   Michelson (1985).
43   Servon and Castells (1996).

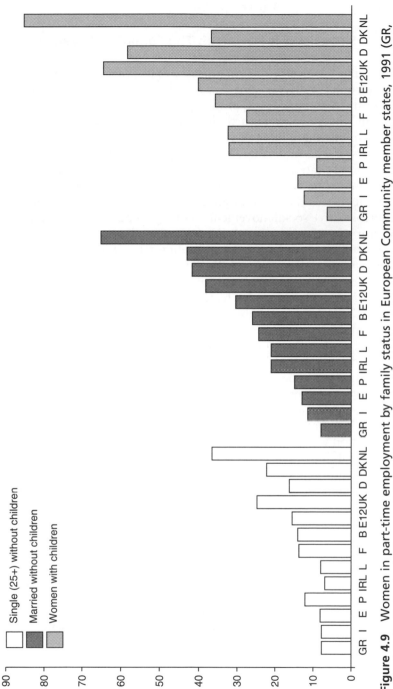

Figure 4.9 Women in part-time employment by family status in European Community member states, 1991 (GR, Greece; I, Italy; E, Spain; P, Portugal; IRL, Ireland; L, Luxembourg; F, France; B, Belgium; E12, average of member states; UK, United Kingdom; D, Germany; DK, Denmark; NL, Netherlands)

Source: European Commission, *Employment in Europe* (1993)

Sisterhood is Powerful: The Feminist Movement

The feminist movement, as manifested in its practice and discourses, is extraordinarily diverse. Its richness and depth increase as we analyze its contours in a global, comparative perspective, and as feminist historians and theoreticians unearth the hidden record of women's resistance and feminist thinking.[44] I will limit the analysis presented here to the contemporary feminist movement that surged in the late 1960s, first in the United States, then in Europe in the early 1970s, and diffused throughout the world in the next two decades. I will also focus on those features that are common to the movement, and that make it a transformative social movement challenging patriarchalism, while accounting for the diversity of women's struggles and the multiculturalism of their expression. As a preliminary, working definition of feminism, as understood here, I will follow Jane Mansbridge in broadly defining feminism as "the commitment to ending male domination."[45] I also concur with her view of feminism as a "discursively created movement." This does not imply that feminism is just discourse, or that the feminist debate, as expressed in the writings of various women, theorists and academics, is the primordial manifestation of feminism. What I contend, in line with Mansbridge and others,[46] is that the essence of feminism, as practiced and as narrated, is the (re)definition of woman's identity: sometimes by affirming equality between men and women, thus de-gendering biological/cultural differences; in other instances, on the contrary, as affirming the essential specificity of women, often in association with stating the superiority of women's ways as sources of human fulfillment; or else, claiming the necessity to depart from men's world, and recreate life, and sexuality, in sisterhood. *In all cases, through equality, difference, or separation, what is negated is woman's identity as defined by men, and as enshrined in the patriarchal family.* As Mansbridge writes:

> This discursively created movement is the entity that inspires movement activists and is the entity to which they feel accountable... This kind of accountability is an accountability through identity... It requires thinking of the collective as a worthy identity and oneself as part of that identity. Feminist identities are usually achieved, not given... Today, feminist identities are created and reinforced when feminists get together, act together, and read what other feminists have written. Talking and acting creates street theory and gives it meaning. Reading

44 Rowbotham (1974, 1992); Kolodny (1984); Spivak (1990); Massolo (1992).
45 Mansbridge (1995: 29).
46 Butler (1990); Chodorow (1994); Whittier (1995).

keeps one in touch and continues to make one think. Both experiences, of personal transformation and continuing interaction, make feminists "internally accountable" to the feminist movement.[47]

Thus, a fundamental commonality underlies the diversity of feminism: the historical effort, individual as well as collective, formal and informal, to redefine womanhood in direct opposition to patriarchalism.

To assess such an effort, and to propose a grounded typology of feminist movements, I will recall, succinctly, the trajectory of feminist movements in the past three decades. To simplify the argument, I will focus mainly on its place of rebirth, the United States, and I will try to correct the potential ethnocentrism of this approach with brief observations on other areas of the world, followed by a commentary on feminism in a comparative perspective.

American feminism: a discontinuous continuity [48]

American feminism has a long history in a country with a short history. From the official birth of organized feminism in 1848 at a village chapel in Seneca Falls, New York, American feminists undertook a protracted struggle in defense of women's rights to education, work, and political power, culminating in the conquest of their right to vote in 1920. Then, afterwards, for almost half a century, feminism was kept in the backstage of the American scene. Not that women ceased to fight.[49] In one of the most noted expressions of women's struggles, the 1955 bus boycott in Montgomery, Alabama, which arguably ushered in the civil rights movement in the South, and changed American history for ever, was enacted predominantly by African American women organizing their communities.[50] Yet, an explicitly feminist mass movement surged only in and from the 1960s' social movements, both from their human rights component, and from their counter-cultural, revolutionary tendencies.[51] On the one hand, in the wake of the work of John F. Kennedy's Presidential Commission on the Status of Women, in 1963, and of the approval of

---

47   Mansbridge (1995: 29).
48   For an excellent analysis of the evolution and transformation of the American feminist *movement* in the past three decades, see Whittier (1995); for an overview of feminist *organizations* in America, see Ferree and Martin (1995); for a well-organized and usefully commented collection of American feminist *discourses* since the 1960s, see Schneir (1994). Other sources used in my analysis are specifically cited in the text.
49   Rupp and Taylor (1987).
50   Barnett (1995).
51   Evans (1979).

Title VII of the 1964 Civil Rights Act concerning women's rights, a group of influential women, headed by writer Betty Friedan, created the National Organization of Women (NOW) on October 29, 1966. NOW would become the most comprehensive national organization in defense of women's rights, and over the following three decades it demonstrated extraordinary political skill and perdurability, in spite of recurrent ideological and organizational crises. It came to epitomize the so-called liberal feminism, focusing on equal rights for women in all spheres of social, economic, and institutional life.

Around the same time, women participating in various radical social movements, and particularly in SDS (Students for a Democratic Society), started to organize separately as a reaction against pervasive sexism and male domination in revolutionary organizations that led not only to the personal abuse of women, but to the ridiculing of feminist positions as bourgeois and counter-revolutionary. What started in December 1965 as a workshop on "Women in the Movement" in the SDS Convention, and became articulated as Women's Liberation in a 1967 convention at Ann Arbor, Michigan, generated a flurry of autonomous women's groups, most of which split from male-dominated revolutionary politics, giving birth to radical feminism. In these founding moments it is fair to say that the feminist movement was ideologically split between its liberal and radical components. Whereas NOW's first statement of purpose started by saying "We, MEN AND WOMEN [capitals in the original] who hereby constitute ourselves as the National Organization for Women, believe that the time has come for a new movement toward a fully equal partnership of the sexes, as part of the world-wide revolution of human rights now taking place within and beyond our national borders,"[52] the 1969 Redstockings Manifesto, which propelled radical feminism in New York, asserted: "We identify the agents of our oppression as men. Male supremacy is the oldest, most basic form of domination. All other forms of exploitation and oppression (racism, capitalism, imperialism etc.) are extensions of male supremacy; men dominate women, a few men dominate the rest."[53]

Liberal feminism centered its goals on obtaining equal rights for women, including the adoption of a constitutional amendment, which, after being approved by Congress, failed to obtain the required ratification by two-thirds of the states, being finally defeated in 1982. Yet, the significance of this amendment was more symbolic than anything else, since the real battles for equality were won in federal and state

52 Reproduced in Schneir (1994: 96).
53 Reproduced in Schneir (1994: 127).

legislation, and in the courts, from the right to equal pay for equal work to reproductive rights, including the right of access to all occupations and institutions. These impressive achievements, in less than two decades, were obtained by skillful political lobbying, media campaigns, and support for women candidates or pro-women candidates in their bids for public office. Particularly important was the presence in the media of women journalists who were either feminists or supportive of feminist causes. A number of somewhat feminist commercial publications, most notably *Ms Magazine* founded in 1972, were also instrumental in reaching out to American women beyond organized feminist circles.

Radical feminists, while participating actively in equal rights campaigns, and particularly in the mobilizations to obtain and defend reproductive rights, focused on *consciousness raising* (CR), through the organization of women-only CR groups, and the building of institutions of a women's autonomous culture. Defense of women against male violence (anti-rape campaigns, self-defense training, shelters for battered women, psychological counseling for abused women) provided a direct link between women's immediate concerns and the ideological critique of patriarchalism in action. Within the radical stream, lesbian feminists (one of whose first public political demonstrations, the "Lavender Menace," appeared in the Second Congress to Unite Women, in May 1970 in New York) quickly became a source of dedicated activism, cultural creativity, and theoretical innovation. The relentless growth and widespread influence of lesbian feminism in the feminist movement was to become both a major force and a major challenge for the women's movement, which had to face its own internal prejudice about forms of sexuality, and to confront the dilemma of where (or whether) to draw the line for women's liberation.

For a while, socialist feminists tried to associate the radical feminist challenge to broader issues of anti-capitalist movements, linking up when necessary with the political left, and engaging in an enriching debate with Marxist theory. Some of them worked in the labor unions. For instance, in 1972 a Coalition of Labor Union Women was formed. However, in the 1990s the fading away of socialist organizations, and of socialism as a historical point of reference, as well as the declining influence of Marxist theory, lessened the impact of socialist feminism, which remained by and large confined to academia.[54]

---

54 For an analysis of the rise and fall of one of the most dynamic and influential socialist feminist organizations, the Chicago Women's Liberation Union (CWLU), see Strobel (1995).

However, the distinction between liberal and radical feminism was blurred in the practice of the movement, and in the ideology of individual feminists from the mid-1970s onwards. Several factors contributed to the overcoming of ideological cleavages in a feminist movement that kept its diversity, and featured vibrant debates as well as internecine fights, but established bridges and coalitions among its components.[55] On the one hand, as Zillah Eisenstein pointed out,[56] the issues to be tackled by liberal feminism, namely equal rights and the de-gendering of social categories, involved such a level of institutional transformation that patriarchalism would be ultimately called into question, even within the most restrained strategy of being practical about achieving gender equality. Secondly, the anti-feminist backlash of the 1980s, supported by the Republican adminis-tration that governed America in 1980–92, prompted an alliance between different strings of the movement, which, regardless of their lifestyles and political beliefs, found each other together in the mobilizations to defend women's reproductive rights or in the build-ing of women's institutions to provide services and assert cultural autonomy. Thirdly, most radical feminist organizations had faded away by the late 1970s, with their founders personally exhausted, and their local utopias confronting daily battles with "really existing patriarchalism."

Yet, since most radical feminists never gave up on their basic values, they found refuge in the established organizations of liberal feminism, and in the enclaves that feminism managed to build within main-stream institutions, particularly in academia (women's studies pro-grams), in non-profit foundations, and in women's caucuses of professional associations. These organizations and institutions were in need of militant support in their increasingly difficult task, when they began to move beyond the most obvious abuses of human rights into more controversial spheres, such as reproductive choice, sexual liberation, and the advancement of women in men's various citadels. Indeed, it can be argued that the presence of liberal organizations helped radical feminism to survive as a movement, whereas most men-based counter-cultural movements originating in the 1960s, with the major exception of ecologists, all but faded away, or were ideologically subdued during the 1980s. As a result of this multi-layered process, liberalism and radicalism, in their different brands, became interwoven in their practice, and in the minds of most women

---

55   Ferree and Hess (1994); Ferree and Martin (1995); Mansbridge (1995); Spalter-Roth and Schreiber (1995); Whittier (1995).
56   Eisenstein (1981/1993).

supporting feminist causes and values. Even lesbianism became an accepted component of the movement, although still attached to some kind of tactical rejection within mainstream feminism (Betty Friedan opposed it), as exemplified by the tensions within NOW in the late 1980s after the "confession" of bisexuality by NOW's president Patricia Ireland.

Other distinctions became more relevant for the feminist movement, as it developed, diversified, and reached out, at least in their minds, to the majority of American women, between the mid-1970s and the mid-1990s. On the one hand, there were important distinctions in the kind of feminist *organizations*. On the other hand, there were substantial differences between what Nancy Whittier calls "political generations" within the feminist *movement*.[57]

In terms of organizations, Spalter-Roth and Schreiber[58] propose an empirically grounded, useful typology that differentiates between:

1   National membership organizations demanding equal rights, such as NOW or the Coalition of Labor Union Women, founded in 1972. They tried deliberately to avoid feminist language while advancing the cause of women in all domains of society, thus sacrificing principles for effectiveness in increasing women's participation in male-dominated institutions. Spalter-Roth and Schreiber conclude that "despite the hopes of organizations' leaders who wished to appeal to both liberals and radicals, the use of politically palatable language obscured relations of domination and subordination. Their efforts may have failed to raise the consciousness of the very women these organizations hoped to represent and empower."[59]

2   Direct service providers, such as the Displaced Homemakers Network, and the National Coalition against Domestic Violence. These are predominantly networks of local groups receiving support from government and corporations for their programs. Their main problem is the contradiction between assisting women and empowering them: usually, the urgency of the problem takes precedence over the long-term goals of consciousness raising and political self-organizing.

3   Staff-run and expert-based pro-women organizations, such as the Women's Legal Defense Fund, the Institute for Women Policy Research, the Center for Women Policy Studies, the Fund for Feminist Majority (supporting women in political institutions), the National Institute for Women of Color, or the National Committee for Pay

57   Whittier (1995).
58   Spalter-Roth and Schreiber (1995: 106–8).
59   Spalter-Roth and Schreiber (1995: 119).

Equity. The challenge for this type of organization is to broaden the range of their issues as more women are brought into the movement's sphere of influence, and as feminist themes become increasingly diversified, ethnically, socially, and culturally.

Beyond mainstream organizations, there is a myriad of local organizations of the women's community, many of them originally linked to radical feminism, then evolving along a great variety of trajectories. Alternative women's health clinics, credit unions, training centers, bookstores, restaurants, day-care centers, centers to prevent violence against women and to cope with its injuries, theater groups, music groups, writers' clubs, artists' studios, and a whole range of cultural expressions, went through ups and downs and, usually, when they survived they did so by downplaying their ideological character and becoming more integrated in society at large. They are, in the broader sense, feminist organizations that, in their diversity and with their flexibility, have provided the networks of support, the experience, and the discursive materials for a women's culture to emerge, thus undermining patriarchalism in its most powerful site: women's minds.

The other major distinction to be introduced in understanding the evolution of American feminism is Whittier's concept of political generations and micro-cohorts. In her insightful sociological study of the evolution of American radical feminism over three decades, she shows both the continuity of feminism, and the discontinuity of feminist styles between the early 1970s, the 1980s, and the 1990s:

Political generations are important to social movement continuity in three ways. First, the collective identity of a political generation remains consistent over time, as it has for women who participated in the feminist movement of the 1970s. Second, even when protest declines a social movement continues to have an impact if a generation of movement veterans carry its key elements into societal institutions and other social movements. Institutions and innovations established by activists within these other settings serve not only as agents of change themselves but also as resources for the resurgence of a future wave of mobilization. Third, a social movement changes as new participants enter the movement and redefine its collective identity. The continual entry of micro-cohorts at regular intervals produces gradual changes. Each micro-cohort constructs a collective identity that is shaped by its context, and therefore activists who enter during movement resurgence, growth, peak and decline differ from each other. Despite the gradual shifts that occur continually within social movements, there are clearly sharper changes at certain points. At these times, a series of micro-cohorts converge into one political generation, as their similar-

ities to each other outweigh their differences from a distinct set of
incoming micro-cohorts that make up a second political generation...The passing of social movements from one political generation
to another thus becomes key to movement survival over the long haul.[60]

Whittier shows, on the basis of her case study of Columbus, Ohio, as
well as by reviewing evidence from secondary sources, the persistence
and renewal of feminist movement, including radical feminism, over
three decades, from the 1960s to the 1990s. She is supported in her
argument by a number of other sources.[61] It seems that the "post-
feminist age" was an interested manipulation of some short-term
trends, excessively highlighted in the media.[62] But Whittier also
emphasizes, convincingly, the profound transformation of radical
feminism, leading sometimes to considerable difficulty in the understanding between generations: "Newcomers to the women's movement are mobilizing for feminist goals in different ways from
longtime activists, who sometimes see their successors' efforts as apol-
itical or misdirected...Newcomers constructed a different model of
themselves as feminists."[63] As a result of these sharp differences,

> it is painful for longtime feminists to see newer entrants to the move-
> ment dismissing their dearly held beliefs or changing organizations they
> struggled to form. Recent debates within the feminist community ex-
> acerbate many women's feelings that they and their beliefs are vulner-
> able to attack. In the "sex wars" in particular, lesbian practitioners of
> sadomasochism, along with heterosexual women and others, argued
> that women should have the right to act freely on any sexual desires,
> and accused those who taught otherwise of being anti-sex, "vanilla", or
> puritanical.[64]

The main differences between feminist political generations do not
seem to be related to the old divide between liberals and radicals,
since Whittier concurs in her observation with the blurring of such an
ideological definition in the collective action of the movement when
confronted with a powerful patriarchal backlash. It seems that three
different issues, somewhat interrelated, interfere with communication
between veterans and newcomers in the radical feminist movement.
The first concerns the growing importance of lesbianism in the feminist movement. Not that it was absent from radical feminism in

60   Whittier (1995: 254–6).
61   Buechler (1990); Staggenborg (1991); Ferree and Hess (1994); Ferree and Martin (1995).
62   Faludi (1991); Schneir (1994).
63   Whittier (1995: 243).
64   Whittier (1995: 239).

earlier times, or that it is opposed by radical feminists. But the lifestyles of lesbians, and their emphasis on breaking the mold of heterosexual families, as well as the tactical problems in reaching out to mainstream women from the trenches of a movement with a lesbian heart, made the non-lesbian component of radical feminism increasingly uneasy about lesbian visibility. The second, and much sharper split, concerns the importance given to sexual expression in all its forms by the new generations of feminists. This includes, for instance, the breaking of the "classic" feminist dress code that used to avoid the traps of femininity, to emphasize sexiness and self-expression in women's self-presentation. It also extends to the acceptance of all manifestations of women's sexuality, including bisexuality, and experimentation. The third split is in fact the consequence of the two others. More assured of themselves, and more sharply separatist in their cultural and political values, younger radical feminists, and particularly lesbians, are more open than radical feminists were previously to cooperate with men's social movements, and to relate to men's organizations precisely because they feel less threatened by such alliances since they have already constructed their autonomy, often through separatism. The main point of alliance is between lesbians and gay men (for instance in Queer Nation), who share the oppression of homophobia, and meet in their defense of sexual liberation, and in their critique of the heterosexual/patriarchal family. However, Whittier also reports that old and new radical feminists share fundamental values and meet each other in the same struggles.

Other internal tensions in the feminist movement originate precisely from its expansion into the whole range of classes and ethnic groups in America.[65] While the 1960s' pioneers who rediscovered feminism were overwhelmingly white, middle class, and highly educated, in the next three decades feminist themes linked up with the struggles that African American women, Latinas, and other ethnic minorities have traditionally carried out in their communities. Women workers, both through labor unions and through autonomous women workers' organizations, mobilized in defense of their demands, using to their advantage the new context of legitimacy for women's struggles. There followed an increasing diversification of the women's movement, and a certain vagueness in their feminist self-definition. Yet, according to opinion polls, from the mid-1980s most women related positively to feminist themes and causes, precisely because feminism did not become associated with any particular ideological stand.[66] Feminism became the common word

65   Morgen (1988); Matthews (1989); Blum (1991); Barnett (1995); Pardo (1995).
66   Stacey (1990); Whittier (1995).

(and banner) for the whole range of sources of women's oppression as women, to which each woman, or category of women, would attach her personal or collective claim, and label.

Thus, through a variety of practices and self-identifications, women from different origins and with different goals, but sharing a common source of oppression which defined women from outside themselves, constructed a new, collective identity: this is in fact what made possible the transition from women's struggles to a feminist movement. As Whittier writes: "I propose to define the women's movement in terms of the collective identity associated with it rather than in terms of its formal organizations... What makes these organizations, networks, and individuals part of a social movement is their shared allegiance to a set of beliefs, practices, and ways of identifying oneself that constitute feminist collective identity."[67]

Are these questions and answers, inspired by the American experience, relevant to feminism in other cultures and countries? Can women's issues, and women's struggles, be generally related to feminism? How collective is this collective identity when women are seen in a global perspective?

Is feminism global?

To advance a tentative answer to such a fundamental question, even superficially, we must distinguish various areas of the world. In the case of Western Europe, Canada, and Australia, it seems apparent that a widespread, diverse, multifaceted feminist movement is active, and growing, albeit with different intensities and characteristics. In Britain, for instance, after a decline in the early 1980s, largely motivated by the neo-conservative assault prompted by Thatcherism, feminist ideas, and the cause of women, permeated throughout society.[68] As in the United States, on the one hand, women fought for equality, and engaged in self-empowerment in work, social services, legislation, and politics. On the other hand, cultural feminism and lesbianism emphasized women's specificity, and built alternative women's organizations. The emphasis on singular identities gives the impression of fragmentation in the movement. Yet, as Gabriele Griffin writes:

> It is the case that many women's groups give themselves titles which specify certain identities... This identification provides the impetus for their activism. On one level, feminist activism based on identity politics

---

67   Whittier (1995: 23–4).
68   Brown (1992); Campbell (1992); Griffin (1995); Hester et al. (1995).

leads to the fragmentation which many feminists regard as typical for the current political climate, and which is supposed to be in direct contrast to the homogeneity, common purpose and mass mobilization of the Women's (Liberation) Movement, all with capital letters. The latter seems to me to be a myth, a nostalgic retrospective view of some golden age feminism that probably never was. Single issue or single identity feminist organizations such as are common in the 1990s may have the drawback of overly localized politics but their very specificity can also be a guarantee for expertise and impact, for maximum, clearly defined effort within a specific arena.[69]

Thus, single-issue organizations may work on a multiplicity of women's issues, and women may participate in different organizations. It is this intertwining and networking of individuals, organizations, and campaigns that characterizes a vital, flexible, and diverse feminist movement.

Throughout Europe, in every single country, there is a pervasive presence of feminism, both in the institutions of society, and in a constellation of feminist groups, organizations, and initiatives, which feed each other, debate with each other (sometimes sharply), and keep inducing a relentless flow of demands, pressures, and ideas on women's condition, women's issues, and women's culture. By and large, feminism, as in the United States, and in Britain, has fragmented, and no single organization or institution can pretend to speak on women's behalf. Instead, there is a transversal line cutting across the entire society that emphasizes women's interests, and women's values, from professional caucuses to cultural expressions, and political parties, many of which have established a minimum percentage of women among their leadership (usually the norm, rarely fulfilled, is set at 25 percent of leaders and deputies, so that women are "only" 50 percent under-represented).

Ex-statist societies present a peculiar situation.[70] On the one hand, statist countries helped/forced the full incorporation of women into paid work, opened up educational opportunities, and set up a widespread network of social services and child care, although abortion was banned for a long time, and contraception was not available. Women's organizations were present in all spheres of society, albeit under the total control of the Communist party. On the other hand, sexism was pervasive, and patriarchalism paramount in society, institutions, and politics. As a result, a generation of very strong women grew up, feeling their potential, yet having to fight their way every day

69   Griffin (1995: 4).
70   Funk and Mueller (1993).

to accomplish some of this potential. After the disintegration of Soviet-style communism, feminism as an organized movement is weak, and, until now, limited to a few circles of Westernized intellectuals, while the old-style, patronizing organizations are fading away. Yet, women's presence in the public sphere is increasing dramatically. In Russia, for instance, the Women's Party, although rather conservative in its position and membership, received about 8 percent of the vote in the 1995 parliamentary elections, while a number of women were in the way of becoming key political figures. There is a widespread feeling in Russian society that women could play a decisive role in rejuvenating leadership in Russian politics. In 1996, for the first time in Russian history, a woman was elected Governor of Koryakiya Territory. Furthermore, the new generation of women, educated in the values of equality, and with room to express themselves personally and politically, seem to be ready to crystallize their individual autonomy in collective identity and collective action. It is easy to predict a major development of the women's movement in Eastern Europe, *under their own cultural and political forms of expression*.

In industrialized Asia, patriarchalism still reigns, barely challenged. This is particularly stunning in Japan, a society with a high rate of women's participation in the labor force, a highly educated female population, and a powerful string of social movements in the 1960s. Still, pressure from women's groups, and from the Socialist party, led to legislation to limit work discrimination for women in 1986.[71] But, overall, feminism is limited to academic circles, and professional women still suffer blatant discrimination. Structural features are fully present in Japan to unleash a powerful feminist critique, but the absence of such a critique on a scale large enough to impact society until now, clearly demonstrates that social specificity (in this case the strength of the Japanese patriarchal family, and men's fulfillment of their duties as patriarchs, in general) determines the actual development of a movement, regardless of structural sources of discontent. Korean women are even more subdued than Japanese women, although embryos of a feminist movement have appeared recently.[72] China is still on the edge of the contradictory statist model of supporting the rights of the "half of heaven," while keeping them under the control of the "half of hell." However, the development of a powerful feminist movement in Taiwan since the late 1980s belies the

71   Gelb and Lief-Palley (1994).
72   Po (1996).

notion of the necessity of women's submission under the patriarchal tradition of Confucianism (see below).[73]

Throughout the so-called developing world, the situation is complex, indeed contradictory.[74] Feminism as an autonomous ideological or political expression is clearly the preserve of a small minority of intellectual and professional women, although their presence in the media amplifies their impact well beyond their numbers. Additionally, in a number of countries, particularly in Asia, women leaders have become towering figures in the politics of their countries (in India, Pakistan, Bangladesh, the Philippines, Burma, maybe in Indonesia in a not too distant future), and they have come to represent the rallying symbols for democracy and development. While femaleness does not guarantee womanhood, and most women politicians operate within the framework of patriarchal politics, their impact as role models, particularly for young women, and for the breaking of society's taboos, cannot be neglected.

The most important development, however, from the 1980s onwards, is the extraordinary rise of grassroots organizations, overwhelmingly enacted and led by women, in the metropolitan areas of the developing world. They were spurred by the simultaneous processes of urban explosion, economic crisis, and austerity policies, which left people, and particularly women, with the simple dilemma of fight or perish. Together with the growing employment of women, both in the new industries and in the urban informal economy, it has indeed transformed the condition, organization, and consciousness of women, as has been shown, for instance, by the studies conducted by Ruth Cardoso de Leite and Maria da Gloria Gohn in Brazil, Alejandra Massolo in Mexico, and Helena Useche in Colombia.[75] From these collective efforts not only have grassroots organizations developed and impacted on policies and institutions, but a new collective identity, as empowered women, has emerged. Thus, Alejandra Massolo, concluding her analysis of women-based urban social movements in Ciudad de Mexico, wrote:

> Women's subjectivity of experiences of struggle is a revealing dimension of the process of social construction of new collective identities through urban conflicts. Urban movements of the 1970s and 1980s made visible, and distinguishable, the unusual collective identity of segments of popular classes. Women were part of the social production

---

73   Po (1996).
74   Kahne and Giele (1992); Massolo (1992); Caipora Women's Group (1993); Jaquette (1994); Kuppers (1994); Blumberg et al. (1995).
75   Cardoso de Leite (1983); Gohn (1991); Espinosa and Useche (1992); Massolo (1992).

of this new collective identity – from their daily territorial bases, transformed into bases for their collective action. They gave to the process of constructing collective identity the mark of plural motivations, meanings, and expectations from the feminine gender, a complex set of meanings found in the urban movements, even when gender issues are not explicit, and when their membership is mixed and men are in the leadership.[76]

It is this massive presence of women in the collective action of grass-roots movements around the world, and their explicit self-identification as collective actors, that is transforming women's consciousness and social roles, even in the absence of an articulate feminist ideology.

However, while feminism is present in many countries, and women's struggles/organizations are exploding all over the world, *the feminist movement displays very different shapes and orientations, depending upon the cultural, institutional, and political contexts in which it arises.* For instance, feminism in *Britain* was marked, from its inception in the late 1960s, by a close relationship with the trade unions, the Labour party, the socialist left, and, moreover, the welfare state.[77] It was more explicitly political – that is, geared toward the state – than American feminism, and more directly connected to the daily problems of working women. Yet, because of its proximity to left politics and to the labor movement, it suffered, during the 1970s, from debilitating internal fights with and between different brands of socialist and radical feminists. For instance, the popular "Wages for Housework" campaign of 1973 was criticized by some feminists because of its implicit acceptance of women's subordinate status at home, potentially inducing them to stay in their domestic enclosures. This contradictory linkage to labor and to socialist politics affected the movement itself. As Rowbotham wrote:

> There is probably some truth in the argument that the emphasis on trade-union support – much stronger in Britain than in many other women's liberation movements – influenced the terms in which the call for abortion was presented. Fusty trades council rooms are not the most commodious sites for learned perorations on the multiplicity of female desire. But . . . I think it is more likely to be partly because of an evasion within the women's liberation movement itself. The movement sought to avoid counterposing heterosexuality and lesbianism, but in the process the scope of sexual self-definition narrowed and any discussion of heterosexual pleasure went into defensive retreat.[78]

76 Massolo (1992: 338); my translation.
77 Rowbotham (1989).
78 Rowbotham (1989: 81).

Partly as a result of this reluctance to face its diversity, and to drift away from the strategic rationality of traditional politics, British feminism was weakened by the 1980s' Thatcherite juggernaut. Yet, as soon as a new generation of feminists felt free of the old attachments of party politics and labor allegiance, feminism resurged in the 1990s, not only as cultural feminism, and lesbianism, but in a multiplicity of expressions that include, but not in an hegemonic position, socialist feminism and institutionalized feminism.

Spanish feminism was even more obviously marked by the political context in which it was born, the democratic movement against Franco's dictatorship in the mid-1970s.[79] Most women's organizations were linked to anti-Franquist, semi-clandestine opposition, such as the Communist party influenced *Asociacion de Mujeres Democratas* (a political association) and the *Asociaciones de Amas de Casa* (Housewives Associations, territorially organized). Every political tendency, particularly from the revolutionary left, had "its" women's "mass organization." In *Catalunya* and in the Basque Country, women's organizations, and feminists, also had their own organizations, reflecting the national cleavages in Spanish politics. Toward the end of Franquism, in 1974–77, autonomous feminist collectives started to appear in the climate of cultural and political liberation that characterized Spain in the 1970s. One of the most innovative and influential was the Madrid-based *Frente de Liberacion de la Mujer.* Its membership was limited (less than one hundred women), but it focused its activity on impacting the media, using its network of women journalists, thus winning popularity for women's demands and discourses. It focused on abortion rights, divorce (both unlawful in Spain at that point), and free expression of women's sexuality, including lesbianism. It was mainly influenced by cultural feminism, and by the French/Italian ideas of *feminisme de la difference*, but it also participated in the political struggles pro-democracy, alongside communist and socialist women's organizations. However, with the establishment of democracy in Spain in 1977, and with the coming to power of the Socialist party in 1982, autonomous feminist movements all but disappeared, precisely because of their success at the institutional and political level. Divorce was legalized in 1981, and abortion, with restrictions, in 1984. The Socialist party promoted an

79 My understanding of Spanish feminism comes from direct, personal experience and observation, as well as from conversations with a number of women who played a significant role in the movement. I want to thank the women from whom I learned most, particularly Marina Subirats, Françoise Sabbah, Marisa Goi, Matilde Fernandez, Carlota Bustelo, Carmen Martinez-Ten, Cristina Alberdi, and Carmen Romero. Naturally, responsibility for the analysis and information presented here is exclusively mine.

Instituto de la Mujer, within the government, which acted as a lobby of feminists *vis-à-vis* the government itself. Many feminist activists, and particularly those from the *Frente de Liberacion de la Mujer*, joined the Socialist party, and occupied leadership positions in parliament, in the administration, and, to a lesser extent, in the cabinet. A leading socialist feminist, from the labor union movement, Matilde Fernandez, was appointed Minister of Social Affairs, and exercised her influence and strong will in strengthening women's causes in the second half of the Socialist regime. She was replaced as minister in 1993 by Cristina Alberdi, another veteran of the feminist movement, and a prestigious jurist. Carmen Romero, the country's first lady, and a socialist militant of long date, alongside her husband Felipe Gonzalez, was elected to parliament, and played a major role in modifying the party's traditional sexism. For instance, a rule was approved in the party's statutes reserving 25 percent of leadership positions to women (a promise that remained unfulfilled, although women's numbers did increase in the leadership of both party and government).

Thus, on the one hand, feminism did have a major impact on improving Spanish women's legal, social, and economic condition, as well as in facilitating the entry of Spanish women to prominent positions in politics, business, and society at large. Attitudes of traditional machismo were dramatically eroded in the new generations.[80] On the other hand, the feminist movement practically disappeared as an autonomous movement, emptied of its cadres and entirely focused on institutional reform. There was little room left for lesbian feminism, and for an emphasis on difference and sexuality. Yet, the new tolerance won in Spanish society helped the growth of a new, more culturally oriented feminism in the 1990s, closer to current feminist trends in Britain or France, and distant from traditional politics, except in the Basque Country where it kept self-damaging links with the radical Basque separatist movement. Thus, Spanish feminism exemplifies the potential of using politics and institutions to improve women's status, as well as the difficulty of remaining an autonomous social movement under conditions of successful institutionalization.

Our last exploration of variations of feminism, according to the broader social context in which the movement develops, takes us to *Italy*, the site of what was, arguably, the most potent and innovative mass feminist movement in the whole of Europe during the 1970s.[81] As Bianca Beccalli writes: "From the historical survey of

---

80   Alonso Zaldivar and Castells (1992).
81   My understanding of the Italian feminist movement comes, to a large extent, from my friendship and conversations with Laura Balbo, as well as from personal observation of social

Italian feminism, two themes emerge clearly: the close association between feminism and the Left, and the particular significance of the intertwining of equality and difference."[82] Indeed, contemporary Italian feminism emerged, like most other feminist movements in the West, from the powerful social movements that shook Italy in the late 1960s and early 1970s. But, unlike its counterparts, the Italian feminist movement included an influential current within the Italian trade unions, and was welcome in, and supported by, the Italian Communist party, the largest Communist party outside the Communist world, and Italy's largest membership party. Thus, Italian feminists succeeded in popularizing their themes, as feminists, among large sectors of women, including working-class women, during the 1970s. Economic demands and demands for equality were interwoven with women's liberation, the critique of patriarchalism, and the subversion of authority in the family as in society.

However, relationships between feminists and the left, and particularly with the revolutionary left, were not easy. Indeed, in December 1975, the *servizio d'ordine* (self-appointed marshals) of *Lotta Continua*, the largest and most radical extreme-left organization, insisted on protecting the demonstration of *Lotta Continua*'s women in Rome, and when women refused their protection, they beat them up, prompting the secession of women from the organization, and the dissolution of *Lotta Continua* itself a few months later. The increasing autonomy of the Communist-inspired organization *Unione delle Donne Italiane* (UDI) *vis-à-vis* the party led ultimately to the self-dissolution of the UDI in 1978. Yet, overall, there were many linkages between women organizing, labor unions, and left political parties (except socialists), and a great deal of receptivity among party and union leaders to women's issues, and even to feminist discourses. This close cooperation resulted in some of the most advanced legislation on working women in the whole of Europe, as well as in the legalization of divorce (by a 1974 Referendum), and of abortion. For a long period, in the 1970s, this political collaboration went hand in hand with the proliferation of women's collectives which raised issues of women's autonomy, women's cultural difference, sexuality, and lesbianism, as separate trends, yet interacting with the world of politics and class struggle. And yet

---

movements in Milan, Turin, Venice, Rome, and Naples throughout the 1970s. For a more recent analysis, see the excellent overview of the movement by Bianca Beccalli (1994). On the formative stage of the movement, and its development during the 1970s, see Ergas (1985) and Birnbaum (1986).

82   Beccalli (1994: 109).

by the end of the decade [1970s] feminism was in decline; and the beginning of the 1980s saw it virtually disappear as a movement. It lost its visibility in political struggles and grew ever more fragmented and out of touch, as feminist activists increasingly committed their energies to private projects and experiences, whether of an individual or communal nature. Thus it was that the "new" feminist movement, following the example of other "new social movements" of the 1970s, evolved into just another form of lifestyle politics.[83]

Why was this so? Here, I will not put Beccalli's words into my own interpretation, although I do not think I contradict her account. On the one hand, Italian women conquered substantial legal and economic reforms, entered massively the labor force and educational institutions, undermining sexism and, more importantly, the traditional power exercised by the Catholic Church over their lives. Thus, the open, clear battles in which the left, the unions, and women could easily converge were won, although the victory was not always exploited to its utmost, as in the Law on Equality that, as Beccalli argues, stopped way short of its British model.

At the same time, the close connection between the women's movement and the left prompted the crisis of political feminism together with the crisis of the left itself. The revolutionary left, living in a Marxist/Maoist fantasy (elaborated with remarkable intelligence and imagination, thus making artificial paradises even more artificial), disintegrated in the second half of the 1970s. The labor movement, while not having to confront a neo-conservative backlash as in Britain or the United States, was faced in the 1980s with the new realities of globalization and technological change, and had to accept the constraints of Italian capitalism's international interdependence. The networking economy, which actually took Emilia Romagna as its model, made Italian small firms dynamic and competitive, yet at the price of decisively undermining union bargaining power concentrated in large factories and the public sector. The Communist party was brushed aside from its power bid by an anti-Communist front led by the Socialist party. And the Socialist party used the levers of power to illegally finance itself to buy its dream of *sorpasso* (that is, overtaking the Communists in the popular vote): the justice system caught up with the Socialists before they could reach the Communists who, in the meantime, had ceased to be Communists, and had joined the Socialist International.

It is hardly surprising that Italian feminists, as political as they were, went home. That is, not to their husbands'/fathers' homes,

83   Beccalli (1994: 86).

but to the House of Women, to a diverse and vital women's culture which, by the late 1980s, had reinvented feminism, emphasizing *differenzia* without forgetting *egalita*. Luce Irigaray and Adrienne Rich replaced Marx, Mao, and Alexandra Kollontai, as the intellectual points of reference. Yet, new feminist collectives continued in the 1990s to link up feminist discourse and women's demands, particularly in the local governments controlled by the left. One of the most innovative and active campaigns concerned the reorganization of time, from working time to the opening hours of stores and public services, to make flexible schedules adapted to women's multiple lives. In the 1990s, in spite of the political threat from Berlusconi and the neo-fascists, calling for the restoration of traditional family values, the coming to power of a center-left coalition, including the now Socialist, ex-Communist *Partito Democratico di Sinistra* in 1996, opened the way for a renewal of institutional innovation. This time, on the basis of a decentralized, autonomous feminist movement that had learned the lessons of "dancing with the wolves."

Thus, feminism, and women's struggles, go up and down throughout the whole landscape of human experience at this turn of the millennium, always resurfacing, under new forms, and increasingly linking up with other sources of resistance to domination, while maintaining the tension between political institutionalization and cultural autonomy. The contexts in which feminism develops shape the movement in an array of forms and discourses. And, yet, I contend that an essential (yes, I said essential) nucleus of values and goals constituting identitie(s) permeates across the cultural polyphony of feminism.

Feminism: an inducive polyphony[84]

The strength and vitality of the feminist movement lies in its diversity, in its adaptability to cultures and ages. Thus, trying to find the nucleus of fundamental opposition and essential transformation that is shared across movements, we must first acknowledge this diversity. To read meaningfully through this diversity, I propose a typology of feminist movements based, on the one hand, on observation, as referred to in

---

84   In assessing the main themes of the feminist movement I do not pretend to give justice to the richness of the feminist debate, nor can I survey, even if I knew it, the full range of theories and positions that are now available for an in-depth understanding of women's sources of oppression and avenues of liberation. My analytical synthesis here is geared toward the theoretical purpose of this book: to interpret the interaction between social movements claiming the primacy of identity, and the network society, as the new structure of domination in the information age. If this disclaimer sounds defensive, it is.

the cited sources; and, on the other hand, on Touraine's categorization of social movements, as presented in chapter 2. The use of this typology is analytical, not descriptive. It cannot render the multi-faceted profile of feminism across countries and cultures. As all typologies, it is reductionist, a particularly unhappy circumstance concerning women's practices, since women have reacted, rightfully, against their constant cataloguing and labeling in their history as objects, rather than subjects. Furthermore, specific feminist movements, and individual women in the movements, often cut across these and other categories, mixing identities, adversaries, and goals in the self-definition of their experience and struggle. Besides, some of the categories may represent a very small segment of the feminist movement, although I consider them analytically relevant. Yet, overall, I believe it may be useful to consider the distinctions presented in Chart 4.1 as a way to begin with the diversity of feminist movements in a necessary step to investigate their commonality.

Under these types I have included, at the same time, collective actions and individual discourses which are debated in and around feminism. This is because, as stated above, feminism does not exhaust itself in militant struggles. It is also, and sometimes fundamentally, a discourse: a discourse subverting women's place in man's history, thus transforming the historically dominant relationship between space and time, as suggested by Irigaray:

> The gods, God, first create space ... God would be time itself, exterior izing itself in its action in space, in places ... Which would be inverted in sexual difference? Where the feminine is experienced as space, but often with connotations of the abyss and night ... while the masculine is experienced as time. The transition to a new age requires a change in our perception and conception of space-time, the inhabiting of places, and of containers, or envelopes of identity.[85]

This transition, and this change, are being operated through an array of women's insurgencies, some of which are presented in Chart 4.1, the content of which I will try to clarify by my commentary.

The *defense of women's rights* is the bottom line of feminism. Indeed, all other forms include this basic affirmation of women as human beings, not as dolls, objects, things, or animals, in the terms of classic feminist critique. In this sense, feminism is indeed an extension of the human rights movement. This movement comes in two versions, liberal and socialist, although this inclusion as variants of one

---

85   Irigaray (1984/1993: 7).

Chart 4.1 Analytical typology of feminist movements

Type	Identity	Adversary	Goal
Women's rights (liberal, socialist)	Women as human beings	Patriarchal state and/or patriarchal capitalism	Equal rights (includes reproductive rights)
Cultural feminism	Women's commune	Patriarchal institutions and values	Cultural autonomy
Essentialist feminism (spiritualism, ecofeminism)	Female way of being	Male way of being	Matriarchal freedom
Lesbian feminism	Sexual/cultural sisterhood	Patriarchal heterosexuality	Abolition of gender through separatism
Women' specific identities (ethnic, national, self-defined: e.g. black lesbian feminist)	Self-constructed identity	Cultural domination	Degendered multi-culturalism
Practical feminism (workers, community self-defense, motherhood etc.)	Exploited/ abused women/ homemakers	Patriarchal capitalism	Survival/dignity

type may be surprising given their sharp ideological opposition. Indeed, they are different, but in terms of identity they both assert women's rights as equal to men. They differ in their analysis of the roots of patriarchalism, and in their belief, or disbelief, in the possibility of reforming capitalism and operating within the rules of liberal democracy while fulfilling the ultimate goals of equality. Both include economic rights and reproductive rights in women's rights. And both consider the winning of these rights as the movement's goals, although they may diverge sharply in tactical emphases and language. Socialist feminists see the struggle against patriarchalism as necessarily linked to the supersession of capitalism, while liberal feminism approaches socio-economic transformation with a more skeptical view, focusing on advancing the cause of women independently of other goals.

Cultural feminism is based on the attempt to build alternative women's institutions, spaces of freedom, in the midst of patriarchal society, whose institutions and values are seen as the adversary. It is sometimes associated with the "feminism of difference," although it does not imply essentialism. It starts with the double affirmation that women are different, mainly because of their differential history, and that in any case they can only rebuild their identity, and find their own ways, by constructing their own commune. In many cases this implies the will of separation from men, or at least from men-dominated institutions. But it does not lead necessarily to lesbianism or to separatism from males. It aims at building cultural autonomy as a basis of resistance, thus inspiring women's demands on the basis of alternative values, such as non-competitiveness, non-violence, cooperation, and multidimensionality of the human experience, leading to a new women's identity, and women's culture, which could induce cultural transformation in society at large.

The "consciousness raising" movement, at the origins of radical feminism, was linked to cultural feminism, and induced a whole network of women's organizations and institutions that became spaces of freedom, protection, support, and unfettered communication among women: women's bookstores, health clinics, women's cooperatives. While these organizations were providing services to women, and became organizing tools for a variety of women's rights mobilizations, they also generated and diffused an alternative culture, which established the specificity of women's values.

Essentialist feminism goes a step further, and proclaims, simultaneously, women's essential difference from men, rooted in biology and/ or history, and the moral/cultural superiority of womanhood as a way of life. In Fuss's formulation, "essentialism can be located in appeals to a pure or original femininity, a female essence, outside the boundaries of the social and thereby untainted (though perhaps repressed) by a patriarchal order."[86] For instance, for Luce Irigaray, an articulate

86   Fuss (1989: 2).

and influential voice of essentialist feminism, "by our lips we are women."[87]

> How can I say it? That we are women from the start. That we don't have to be turned into women by them, labeled by them, made holy and profaned by them. That that has always happened, without their efforts. And that their history, their stories, constitute the locus of our displacement... Their properties are our exile. Their enclosures, the death of our love. Their words, the gag upon our lips... Let's hurry and invent our own phrases. So that everywhere and always we can continue to embrace... Our strength lies in the very weakness of our resistance. For a long time now they have appreciated what our suppleness is worth for their own embraces and impressions. Why not enjoy ourselves? Rather than letting ourselves be subjected to their branding. Rather than being fixed, stabilized, immobilized. Separated... We can do without models, standards, or examples. Let's never give ourselves orders, commands or prohibitions. Let our imperatives be only appeals to move, to be moved, together. Let's never lay down the law to each other, or moralize, or make war.[88]

Liberation is "making each woman 'conscious' of the fact that what she has felt in her personal experience is a condition shared by all women, thus allowing that experience to be politicized."[89] By accepting the specificity of their bodies women are not captured in biology, but, on the contrary, escape from their definition by men that has ignored their true nature. In a masculine order, women will be permanently annihilated because they are characterized from outside their primordial, bodily experience: their bodies have been reinterpreted, and their experience reformulated by men.[90] Only by reconstructing their identity on the basis of their biological and cultural specificity can women become themselves.

For instance, the revival of Italian feminism in the early 1980s was somewhat marked by the affirmation of women's difference, and the primacy given to the reconstruction of women's identity on the basis of their biological/cultural specificity, as expressed in the highly popular *"Piu donne che uomini"* pamphlet published by the Women's Bookstore in Milan. It tried to address the inability of women to act in the public sphere by emphasizing the necessity of women working

87   Irigaray (1977/1985: 210).
88   Irigaray (1977/1985: 215–17).
89   Irigaray (1977/1985: 164).
90   Fuss (1989).

on their own personality, largely determined by their biological specificity. It found a wide echo among Italian women.[91]

Another stream of essentialism links womanhood to history and culture, and claims the myth of a matriarchal golden age when women's values, and the worshipping of the goddess, assured social harmony.[92] Spiritualism and ecofeminism are also among the most powerful manifestations of essentialism, bringing together biology and history, nature and culture, in the affirmation of a new age constructed around women's values and their merger with nature.[93]

Essentialism has come under spirited attack in the feminist movement, both on political grounds, and from opposing intellectual perspectives. Politically, it is argued,[94] that essentializing differences between men and women plays into the hands of traditional values of patriarchalism, and justifies keeping women in their private domain, necessarily in an inferior position. Intellectually, materialist feminists, such as Christine Delphy and Monique Wittig, consider anatomical sex as socially constructed.[95] For them, gender does not create oppression; rather, oppression creates gender. Womanhood is a man's category, and the only liberation consists in degendering society, canceling the dichotomy man/woman.

Yet, the affirmation of women's irreducible specificity, and the proposal to rebuild society around women's values, does have an undeniable appeal among women, and feminists, while it provides the linkage to the powerful trends of spiritualism and radical ecologism characteristic of the information age.

Lesbian feminism has been the fastest growing, and most militant, component of the feminist movements in developed countries (and not only in the United States) in the past decade, organized in a number of collectives, as well as in caucuses and tendencies within broader feminist movements. It can certainly not be assimilated to a particular sexual orientation. Adrienne Rich proposes the notion of a "lesbian continuum," to include a broad spectrum of women's experiences, marked by their oppression from, and resistance to, the inseparable institutions of patriarchy and compulsory heterosexuality.[96] Indeed, the 1970 Manifesto of American Radicalesbians, started with the following statement: "What is a lesbian? A lesbian is the

---

91 Beccalli (1994).
92 Merchant (1980).
93 Spretnak (1982); Epstein (1991).
94 Beccalli (1994).
95 Delphy (1984); Wittig (1992).
96 Rich (1980/1993).

rage of all women condensed to the point of explosion."[97] From this perspective, lesbianism, as women's radical, self-conscious separation from males as sources of their oppression, is the discourse/practice of liberation. This explains the success of elective lesbianism for many women, as the way to express their autonomy *vis-à-vis* men's world in an uncompromising form. In Monique Wittig's words:

> The refusal to become (or to remain) heterosexual always meant to refuse to become a man or a woman, consciously or not. For a lesbian this goes further than the refusal of the role "woman". It is the refusal of the economic, ideological, and political power of a man... We are escapees of our class in the same way as the American runaway slaves were escaping slavery and becoming free. For us this is an absolute necessity; our survival demands that we contribute all our strength to the destruction of the class of women within which men appropriate women. *This can be accomplished only by the destruction of hetero-sexuality* as a social system which is based on the oppression of women by men and which produces the doctrine of the difference between sexes to justify this oppression.[98]

Because heterosexuality is the paramount adversary, lesbian feminism finds in the gay men's movement a potential, if ambivalent, ally (see below).

Increasingly, the feminist movement is being fragmented into a *multiplicity of feminist identities* that constitute the primary definition for many feminists. As I argued above, this is not a source of weakness but of strength in a society characterized by flexible networks and variable alliances in the dynamics of social conflicts and power struggles. These identities are self-constructed, even if they often use ethnicity, and sometimes nationality, as boundary making. Black feminism, Mexican American feminism, Japanese feminism, black lesbian feminism, but also sadomasochist lesbian feminism, or territorial/ethnic self-definitions, such as the Southall Black Sisters in England,[99] are but examples of endless possibilities of self-defined identities through which women see themselves in movement.[100] So doing, they oppose the standardization of feminism, which they see as a new form of cultural domination, not alien to the patriarchal logic of overimposing officialdom to the actual diversity of women's experiences. In some instance, self-identity starts with a pseudonym, as in the case of black feminist writer bell hooks: "I chose the name bell

97   Reproduced in Schneir (1994: 162).
98   Wittig (1992: 13–20); my italics.
99   Griffin (1995: 79).
100 Whittier (1995); Jarrett-Macauley (1996).

hooks because it was a family name, because it had a strong sound. Throughout childhood, this name was used to speak to the memory of a strong woman, a woman who spoke her mind... Claiming this name was a way to link my voice to an ancestral legacy of women speaking – of woman power." [101] Thus, the self-construction of identity is not the expression of an essence, but a power stake through which women as they are mobilize for women as they want to be. Claiming identity is power-making.

I have deliberately chosen a controversial term, *practical feminists*, to refer to the widest and deepest stream of women's struggles in today's world, particularly in the developing world, but also among working-class women and community organizations in industrialized countries. Of course, all feminists are practical, in the sense that they all undermine everyday, in many different ways, the foundations of patriarchalism, be it by fighting for women's rights or by demystifying patriarchal discourses. But, it may also be that many women are feminist in practice, while not acknowledging the label or even having a clear consciousness of opposing patriarchalism. Thus, the question arises: *can feminism exist without feminist consciousness?* Aren't the struggles and organizations of women throughout the world, for their families (meaning, mainly, their children), their lives, their work, their shelter, their health, *their dignity*, feminism in practice? Frankly, I am hesitant on this point, and my work on Latin American grass roots, and readings on other areas of the world, only deepens my ambivalence, so that the best I can do is to convey it. [102]

On the one hand, I stand by the classic norm of "no class without class consciousness," and by the fundamental methodological principle of defining social movements by the values and goals they express themselves. From this perspective, the overwhelming majority of women's struggles and organizations, in the developing world and beyond, do not express a feminist consciousness, and, more importantly, do not explicitly oppose patriarchalism and male domination, either in their discourse or in the goals of their movements. Issues of cultural feminism, of lesbian feminism, or of sexual liberation, are rarely present among common women's movements, although not absent, as the revealing experience of the Taiwanese lesbian movement shows (see below). Yet, overall, developing countries' explicit feminism is still, by and large, elitist. This would leave us with a rather fundamental split between feminism and women's struggles

101   hooks (1989: 161).
102   This issue has been discussed by some feminist historians. My category of "practical feminism" is close to what they call "social feminism"; see Offen (1988); Cott (1989).

that would also have a North/South connotation. Indeed, the 1995 United Nations Women's Forum in Beijing showed some evidence of this split, amplified and highlighted by some interested parties, namely the "Crusade of the Half Moon" formed by the Vatican and Islamists, fighting hand in hand against feminism and women's reproductive rights.

On the other hand, through their collective action, women around the world are linking their struggle, and their oppression, to their everyday lives. They see the transformation of their condition in the family as connected to their intervention in the public sphere. Let us listen to the words of a woman in a Bogota shanty, as recorded by Helena Useche, in her women's stories reported from the trenches of activist social research:

> In recent years, women have made themselves noticed, and now men respect us. Just because of the fact that the compaero does not see the woman just at home, cooking, washing, ironing, but he also sees her as a compaera, contributing financially also. Because now it is very rare to see the husband telling the wife: I work and you stay home. Then, here there are the solutions we provide to our problems, such as building gardens, helping other women, making them aware of people's condition. Before, women were uninterested in all this. Now, we are concerned not only with being mothers, but with knowing how to be properly so.[103]

Is this feminism? Maybe the issue is one of cultural translation. Not between languages or continents, but between experiences. Maybe the parallel development of women's struggles and organizations, and feminist discourses and debates, is simply a stage in the historical development of a movement, whose fully fledged, global existence may result from the interaction and *reciprocal transformation* of both components.

If feminism is so diverse as to possibly include even women in movements who do not call themselves feminists, or would even object to the term, does it make sense to keep the word (after all invented by a man, Charles Fourier), or even to claim the existence of a feminist movement? I believe so, nonetheless, because of a major theoretical reason: in all types of feminism, as presented in Chart 4.1, *the fundamental task of the movement, through struggles and discourses, is to de/re/construct woman's identity by degendering the institutions of society.* Women's rights are claimed on behalf of women as subjects autonomous from men, and from the roles they

103   Espinosa and Useche (1992: 48); my translation.

are assigned under patriarchalism. Cultural feminism builds the women's community to raise consciousness, and reconstruct personality. Essentialist feminism affirms woman's irreducible specificity, and proclaims her autonomous, superior values. Lesbian feminism, by rejecting heterosexuality, voids of meaning the sexual division of existence, underlying both manhood and womanhood. Women's multiple identities redefine ways of being on the basis of their actual experience, either lived or fantasized. And women's struggles for survival and dignity empower women, thus subverting the patriarchalized woman, precisely defined by her submission. Under different forms, and through different paths, feminism dilutes the patriarchal dichotomy man/woman as it manifests itself in social institutions and in social practice. So doing, feminism constructs not one but many identities, each one of which, by their autonomous existence, seizes micro-powers in the world wide web of life experiences.

The Power of Love: Lesbian and Gay Liberation Movements[104]

Any theory of cultural/political creation that treats lesbian existence as a marginal or less "natural" phenomenon, as mere "sexual preference" or as the mirror image of either heterosexual or male homosexual relations is profoundly weakened thereby...A feminist critique of compulsory heterosexual orientation for women is long overdue.
   Adrienne Rich, "Compulsory heterosexuality and lesbian existence,"
p. 229

Our movement may have begun as the struggle of a minority but what we should now be trying to "liberate" is an aspect of the personal lives of all people – sexual expression.
   John D'Emilio, "Capitalism and gay identity," p. 474

Patriarchalism requires compulsory heterosexuality. Civilization, as historically known, is based on taboos and sexual repression.

---

104 The analysis presented here does not include the study of gay and lesbian *issues* and *values*, nor their relationship to social institutions. It is focused on lesbian and gay *movements*, and on their impact on patriarchalism through sexual liberation. In order to be specific, I will use two case studies, one for each movement. On the one hand, I will discuss the emergence of a powerful lesbian movement in Taipei, in the 1990s, in interaction with the feminist movement, and with the gay movement. This is a deliberate effort to move away from North American and Western European scenes of lesbian liberation, and to emphasize the increasing influence of lesbianism on cultures as patriarchal as the Chinese culture. On the other hand, I will succinctly analyze the

Sexuality, as Foucault argued, is socially constructed.[105] The regulation of desire underlies social institutions, thus channeling transgression and organizing domination. There is an endless spiral of desire, repression, sublimation, transgression, and punishment, accounting for much of human passion, accomplishment, and failure, when the epics of history are observed from the hidden side of experience. This coherent system of domination, which links the corridors of power to the pulse of the libido through mothering, fathering, and the family, does have a weak link: the heterosexual assumption. If this assumption is challenged, the whole system crumbles: the linkage between controlled sex and reproduction of the species is called into question; sisterhood, and then women's revolt, become possible, by undoing the gendered division of sexual labor that splits women; and male bonding threatens manhood, thus undermining the cultural coherence of men-dominated institutions.

While historical accounts show permissiveness for male homosexuality in some cultures, particularly in classical Greece,[106] lesbianism has been severely repressed throughout most of human experience, not in spite but because of resistance to heterosexuality. As Adrienne Rich writes:

> The fact is that women in every culture and throughout history have undertaken the task of independent, non-heterosexual, woman-connected existence, to the extent made possible by their context, often in the belief that they were the "only ones" ever to have done so. They have undertaken it even though few women have been in an economic position to resist marriage altogether, and even though the attacks against unmarried women have ranged from aspersion and mockery to deliberate gynocide, including the burning and torturing of millions of widows and spinsters during the witch persecutions of the fifteenth, sixteenth, and seventeenth centuries in Europe.[107]

---

formation and development of the gay community in San Francisco, arguably one of the most powerful and visible gay communities/movements in the world. My presentation of the lesbian movement in Taipei primarily relies on an excellent study by my Berkeley doctoral student Lan-chih Po, who is also an active militant in the feminist movement in Taipei (Po, 1996). I have also used for my understanding of Taipei's scene, besides my personal knowledge, my Taiwan connection. For this, I am grateful to You-tien Hsing, and to Chu-joe Hsia. As for San Francisco, I have relied on the fieldwork study I conducted in the early 1980s, with the cooperation of Karen Murphy (Castells and Murphy, 1982; Castells, 1983: 138–72), adding some observations on recent developments. There is really no place here for a review of the abundant, relevant literature on gay and lesbian issues. For a scholarly overview of this bibliography in the English language, see the excellent *Lesbian and Gay Studies Reader*, edited by Abelove et al. (1993).

105　Foucault (1976, 1984a, b).
106　Halperin et al. (1990).
107　Rich (1980/1993: 230).

Male homosexuality was generally confined in time and space by "knowingly ignoring" adolescent impulses or hidden expressions in specific contexts (for example, in the religious orders of the Catholic Church). Because men kept their gender, class, and race privileges, repression of homosexuality was/is highly socially selective. Yet, the norm, the fundamental norm of patriarchalism was, and is, life organized around the heterosexual family, occasionally allowing the private expression of same-sex desire for men, as long as it could be kept in the back alleys of society.

While resistance to compulsory heterosexuality has existed in all times and cultures, it is only in the past three decades that social movements in defense of lesbian and gay rights, and affirming sexual freedom, have spurred throughout the world, starting in the United States in 1969–70, then in Europe and, thereafter, over much of the planet. Why in this period? There seem to be some common factors, and some specific elements for each of these two distinct movements, explaining the timing and circumstances of their development.

Lesbianism is, in fact, a component of the feminist movement, as I proposed above, although lesbians often seek alliances with gay men in fighting cultural domination from heterosexual women. Once the feminist critique of gendered institutions eroded patriarchal orthodoxy, the calling into question of sexual norms was the logical line of development for those sectors of the feminist movement which wanted to express their identity in all dimensions. Furthermore, the identification of men as the source of the oppression of women made their emotional and sexual partnership with their "class enemies" increasingly difficult for women, thus favoring the expression of the latent lesbianism existing in many women.

As for gay men, their coming into a movement seems to have been induced by three concurrent factors: the insurgent climate of the 1960s' movements in which self-expression and the questioning of authority made it possible to think and act the unthinkable, thus "coming out of the closet"; the impact of feminism on patriarchalism, calling into question the category of woman, and therefore, of man, since they can only exist in their dichotomy; and the ferocity of repression by a homophobic society which radicalized even those gay men who simply wanted an accommodation.[108]

In my view, there were three additional factors in inducing the extraordinary development of both gay and lesbian liberation movements in America and elsewhere. One is structural: the formation of an advanced informational economy in the largest metropolitan areas

108   D'Emilio (1983).

led to a diversified, innovative labor market and flexible business networks, and created new kinds of jobs, at all levels of skills, independent of the large-scale organizations where individual behavior could be more easily regulated. The second factor refers to the popularity of sexual liberation as a theme of the 1960s' movements. For instance, having been a close witness of the 1968 May movement in Paris (I was assistant professor of sociology in the Nanterre campus where the movement started), I can say that sexual liberation and self-expression were *the* paramount goals of the radical student movement: in fact, the movement started as a joint protest by males and females to obtain free access to their university's dormitories. Around the banner of sexual liberation, which also sustained the daily morale of the movement, both in France and in the United States, the utopian wish of freeing desire was the driving force of the 1960s, the rallying cry around which a whole generation felt the possibility of a different life. But sexual liberation, if it is to be liberation, has no limits. Thus, the liberation of sexuality led to rejecting the diktat of heterosexuality and, in many cases, to the abolition of all limits to desire, opening up the exploration of transgression, for instance in the fast-growing, and ideologically articulate, sadomasochist movement.

The third factor that, in my view, induced, in parallel, lesbian and gay movements, is more controversial. It refers to the separation, physical and psychological, created among both men and women by the feminist challenge to patriarchalism. By this I do not mean that women became lesbians and men became gay because they were quarreling with their heterosexual partners. Indeed, homosexuality has its own existence and pattern of development independently from heterosexuality. Yet, the profound cleavage introduced by the joint effect of the feminist challenge and the inability of most men to cope with the ending of their privileges, reinforced the likelihood of same-sex support networks and friendships, creating a milieu where all kinds of desires could be more easily expressed.

Finally, while sexual liberation is at the heart of gay and lesbian movements, *gayness and lesbianism cannot be defined as sexual preferences. They are, fundamentally, identities*, and in fact two distinct identities: lesbian, and gay men. As such identities, they are not given; they do not originate from some form of biological determination. While biological predispositions do exist, most homosexual desire is mixed with other impulses and feelings (see figure 4.10), so that actual behavior, the boundaries of social interaction, and self-identity, are culturally, socially, and politically constructed. As for the specifics of this political process of constructing identity, I now turn to the case studies of the lesbian movement in Taipei, and of the gay community in San Francisco.

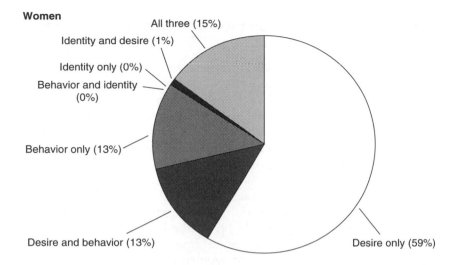

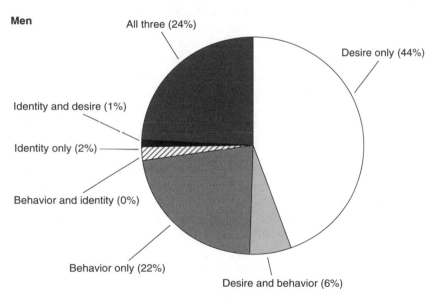

Figure 4.10 Interrelation of different aspects of same-gender sexuality: for 150 women (8.6% of the total 1,749) who report any adult same-gender sexuality; for 143 men (10.1% of the total 1,410) who report any adult same-gender sexuality

Source: Laumann et al. (1994)

Feminism, lesbianism, and sexual liberation movements in Taipei[109]

In Taipei, as in most of the world, the lesbian movement emerged as a component of the feminist movement, and remained so, although in the 1990s it acted in close alliance with an equally powerful gay men's liberation movement. The fact that such a movement, with widespread influence among young women in Taipei, took place in a quasi-authoritarian political context, and amidst a deeply patriarchal culture, shows the breaking of traditional molds by global trends of identity politics.

Taiwan's feminist movement started in 1972, under the initiative of a pioneer intellectual woman, Hsiu-lien Lu who, returning to Taipei after completing her master's degree in the United States, created a women's group, set up "protection hot-lines," and founded the Pioneer Publishing Company to print women-related books. Lu's "new feminism" echoed closely the classic themes of liberal feminism, combined with the idea of modernization in the labor market, challenging sex discrimination, and the confinement of women in certain roles: "Women should first be human, and then women"; "women should walk out of the kitchen"; "sex discrimination against women should be removed and women's potential developed." At the same time, she emphasized the genuine Chinese character of her movement, and opposed some of the values of Western feminism, such as eliminating gender differences, or rejecting feminine dressing. For Lu, "women should be like they are."

In the late 1970s, feminists joined the political opposition movement, and after the 1979 Kaoshiung riot, they were repressed, and Lu was imprisoned. The organized movement could not survive repression, but women's networks did, so that a second wave of feminism developed in the early 1980s. In 1982, a small group of women created *Awakening* magazine, a monthly, to voice women's opinions, and to press for women's rights. In January 1987 hundreds of women took to the streets of Taipei to protest against the sex industry in the city. In 1987, after the lifting of the martial law that had subdued Taiwan's opposition for decades, the Awakening Foundation was formally established: it went on to become the coordinating instance

109   My analysis of Taipei's lesbian movement closely follows the study by Lan-chih Po (1996). In addition to her observations, she also relies partially on the papers (in Chinese) of a Conference on "New Maps of Desire: Literature, Culture, and Sexual Orientation" organized on April 20, 1996 at National Taiwan University, Taipei, and on the special issue of *Awakening* magazine (1995: no. 158–61) on relationships between feminism and lesbianism.

of Taiwan's women's struggles, mixing liberal themes, radical causes, and support for a whole array of women's initiatives. In a largely spontaneous movement, in the late 1980s, numerous women's groups were formed, such as associations of divorced women, housewives, groups to rescue young people from prostitution, and the like. The media started to report the activities of these groups, increasing their visibility, and attracting a growing number of women, particularly among the educated and professional groups in Taipei.

With the beginning of democratic political life in the 1990s (indeed, the democratic opposition conquered the municipality of Taipei in the local elections), a diversified culturally oriented social movement emerged in Taipei. The women's movement both grew in numbers and influence, and became internally differentiated between its struggle for women's rights, its defense of women workers, and the expression of new women's identities, including lesbianism. University campuses were literally taken by feminism. In May 1995, the chairwoman of the "women's studies group" in National Taiwan University (Taiwan's premier university) was elected as chairperson of the student body, displacing both the government's party candidate, and the political opposition students. The support found by the feminist movement, outside the university, among women, particularly married women, of the new Taiwanese society prompted a series of debates, particularly around the notion of family, on the occasion of the revision of the "family law" in the Taiwanese parliament.

It was in this context of cultural effervescence and rise of feminist ideas that a number of young radical feminists started to introduce the lesbian debate in Taipei. The "Axis Collective" diffused ideas from radical feminists and lesbian theorists, such as Audre Lorde, Adrienne Rich, Gayle Rubin, and Christine Delphy, and translated some of their texts into Chinese. Following Lorde's notion of the "erotic as power," a new field of identity politics, centered on women's body and sexuality, was created. Alongside the rise of women's groups on campuses, the first explicitly lesbian group was formed in Taiwan in 1990: "Between Us (*wo-men-chih-chien*)."

On May 22, 1994, an "anti-sexual harassment parade" was organized by feminists in the streets of Taipei, with about 800 women, mainly students, marching from their campuses to the center of the city. During the march, Ho, a feminist scholar who had advanced the discourse of sexual liberation, improvised a slogan: "I want sexual orgasm, I don't want sexual harassment!" which was enthusiastically repeated by participants in the march, and sounded loudly in the streets of a shocked patriarchal Taipei. It made the headlines of most newspapers. The publicity of this incident raised a fundamental debate within the feminist movement. When the movement was winning legitimacy and acceptance, improving women's condition and asserting gender equality, many feminists felt that it was embarrassing, and potentially destructive, to identify feminism with sexual liberation in public opinion. Moreover, some feminists also argued that sexual liberation in the West was a trap for women, and in fact worked to the advantage of men. They suggested, instead, fighting for the "right to autonomy of the body." Ho and other feminists, related to the lesbian movement, argued for the need for a feminist approach to sexual liberation, seeking at the same time the emancipation of women and that of women's sexuality. In their view, sexual liberation is the radical way of challenging patriarchal culture, manifested in the control over a woman's body. The sexual liberation women's movement, including, but not exclusively, a strong lesbian component, went into action. In 1995, the women's studies groups in Taiwan University, mobilizing to elect their candidate to the student government, began showing pornographic movies in the women's dormitories. Simultaneously, a "women's erotic pioneering festival" was organized in different campuses. The activities of these women, most of them very young, were highly publicized in the media, shocked Taipei's society, and created considerable concern among feminist leaders, inducing a sharp, sometimes acrimonious, debate within feminism.

It is in this context of both feminist awakening and sexual liberation that lesbian and gay men's groups proliferated, breaking a deep-seated taboo in Chinese culture. Furthermore, in the 1990s, the traditional marginality of homosexuals in Taiwan had been reinforced, and rationalized, by the stigma of AIDS. And yet, after the creation of the lesbian group "Between Us," there followed an explosion of both lesbian and gay collectives, most of them on university campuses: lesbian groups such as "Between Us," ALN, "Lambda" (Taiwan University), and "I Bao"; gay men's groups such as "Gay Chat" (Taiwan University), "NCA," and "Speak Out." Other groups joined forces between lesbians and gays: "Queer Workshop," "We Can" (Chin-hua University), DV8 (She-shin College), "Quist" (Chong-yung University), and so on. These groups created a homosexual community. They "collectively came out," and linked sexuality, enjoyment, and politics, rediscovering that "the personal is political." Bars were critical for information, networking, education, and, ultimately, for the production of gay and lesbian culture. As Po writes: "Just like pubs for the making of British working class, gay bars play important roles for the formation of urban gay/lesbian communities in Taipei."[110]

110   Po (1996: 20).

Yet, in the information age, in which Taiwan is fully immersed, gays and lesbians are not limited to bars in their networking. They extensively use the Internet, and message boards, as forms of contact, communication, and interaction. They have also created "alternative media," particularly through a number of gay/lesbian underground radio stations. In addition, in 1996 two gay/lesbian programs were broadcast on mainstream radio stations in Taipei.

Beyond communication, networking, and self-expression, the lesbian movement, in close political alliance with the gay movement, has been active in a number of campaigns, social protests, and political demands. Particularly significant was the mobilization around AIDS policy. On the one hand, feminists, lesbians, and gay men took to the streets to protest against the incrimination of gay men by government policies as responsible for the epidemic. On the other hand, since heterosexual women are the fastest growing group of HIV infected in Asia, the feminist group "Awakening" took up the issue as a woman's survival matter. Indeed, in Taiwan, the largest group of HIV-infected women are housewives, defenseless victims of their husbands' prostitution habits. Women's groups in Taiwan acted on the contradiction of policies to prevent the spread of AIDS: how could women escape infection from their husbands if they could not have control over their sexual lives? By bringing down to earth the issues of sexual liberation, and showing women that they were facing deadly sexual oppression, the anti-AIDS movement built by feminists, lesbians, and gay men together introduced a fundamental challenge to the patriarchal structure of sexual domination.

A second major line of action by lesbian and gay movements in an extremely patriarchal society was the fight against traditional stigma and invisibility in the public image. Gay men had to fight the stigma of abnormality. Lesbians had to fight invisibility. For both, coming out in the public sphere became a paramount goal to achieve social existence. Cultural activities were essential to that end. A 1992 film festival of "queer cinema" was the starting-point of public, collective self-affirmation. Lesbian and gay audiences packed several movie theaters, and the films were introduced with debates on "queer theory." Incidentally, Taiwanese and Hong Kong activists have creatively translated into Chinese the term "queer" by "*tong-chii*," meaning "comrade," so that "comrade" does not refer any longer to communist fraternity but to "queer" identity. Starting with the film festival, a number of cultural activities, always communal and festive, substantially modified the perception of lesbian and gay culture in Taiwan to the point that, in 1996, the movement felt strong enough to mark St Valentine's Day by voting for the top ten "gay/lesbian idols" among prominent figures of entertainment, society, and politics (to be sure, not all of the chosen were enchanted by their popularity among gays and lesbians).

Thirdly, and not surprisingly, the lesbian and gay movements have been seeking control over public space, symbolized by their struggle around Taipei's New Park, which they vowed to "take back." The park, near the Presidential Hall, had become a "queer space," a major site for gathering and cruising for the gay community. In 1996, the new democratic municipal administration was planning the renewal of Taipei, including its parks. Fearful of being deprived of their "liberated space," lesbians and gays requested participation in the design project, as heavy users of the park, and organized themselves in the "Comrade Space Front Line" network, demanding free use of the park for their activities during daytime to escape their status as "the community in the darkness."

With the growing influence and militancy of lesbians, a series of conflicts emerged between them and the feminist movement at large. The major one concerned the revision of family law in the parliament. Lesbians criticized the proposal by women's groups because it assumed the norm of the heterosexual family, ignoring the rights of homosexuals. Thus, lesbians and gay men *mobilized actively for the legal sanction of same-sex marriage*, a fundamental issue, present in most lesbian/gay movements around the world, and on which I will elaborate below. The conflict stimulated thinking and debate in the feminist movement, particularly in the mainstream Awakening Foundation. Lesbians criticized the hypocrisy of feminist slogans, such as "women love women," as expressions of solidarity, while ignoring the sexual dimension of this love. Lesbians in 1996 were in the open within the feminist movement, and argued vehemently for their specific rights to be acknowledged, and defended, as a legitimate part of the women's movement.

Several elements deserve emphasis in this narrative of the lesbian movement in Taipei. It shattered the preconception of the solidity of patriarchalism, and heterosexuality, in cultures inspired by Confucianism. It was an extension of the feminist movement, while linking up at the same time with the gay liberation movement in a united front for the defense of rights to sexuality in all its forms. It joined the mobilization against AIDS, relating it to the consequences of housewives' sexual submission. It bridged the cutting-edge theoretical debates on feminism and lesbianism in the world with specific adaptations to Chinese culture and to Taiwan's social institutions in the 1990s. It used a whole range of cultural expressions to "come out collectively" in the midst of public attention. It made extensive use of the Internet, and of alternative means of communication, such as pirate broadcasting. It linked up with urban social movements and political struggles at the local level. And it deepened the critique of the patriarchal family, engaging in a legal and cultural battle to advance the notion of same-sex marriages, and non-heterosexual families. I will elaborate on these matters when summing up the relationship between lesbian and gay movements and their challenge to patriarchalism.

Spaces of freedom: the gay community in San Francisco[111]

The American gay liberation movement is generally considered to have as its starting-point the Stonewall Revolt in New York's Greenwich Village on June 27, 1969, when hundreds of gays fought the police for three days in reaction to yet another brutal raid on The Stonewall, a gay bar. Thereafter, the movement grew with extraordinary speed, particularly in the major metropolitan areas, as gays came out of the closet, individually and collectively. In 1969 there were about 50 organizations nationwide; in 1973 the number had jumped to over 800. While New York and Los Angeles, because of their size, became home to the largest gay populations, San Francisco was the site of the formation of a visible, organized, and politicized gay community, which went on in the next two decades to transform the city in its space, its culture, and its politics. By my calculations (necessarily tentative, since, fortunately, there is no statistical recording of sexual preference), around 1980, the gay and lesbian population could account for about 17 percent of the city's adult residents (two-thirds of them gay men), and in important local elections, because of their high turn-out rate, they may have represented around 30 percent of voters. In the 1990s, in spite of decimation by the AIDS epidemics in the mid-1980s, the gay and lesbian populations in San Francisco increased, mainly because of an increase in lesbians, continuing gay immigration, and the consolidation of stable same-sex partnerships. More significantly, gays settled predominantly in certain areas of the city, forming authentic communes, in which residences, businesses, real estate, bars, restaurants, movie theaters, cultural centers, community-based associations, street gatherings and celebrations wove a fabric of social life and cultural autonomy: a space of freedom.

---

111   For sources and methods for my study of San Francisco's gay community, see Castells (1983), particularly the Methodological Appendix, pp. 355–62.

On the basis of this space, gays and lesbians organized politically, and came to exercise considerable influence in the San Francisco local government, including the mandatory recruitment of gays and lesbians by the police department, to make up at least 10 percent of the force. This spatial concentration of gay populations is indeed a mark of the gay culture in most cities, although since the 1990s, with greater social tolerance and many more openly gay people, they have diffused into most American metropolitan geography, to the great fear of homophobic conservatives.

The reason for this geographic concentration in the formative stage of gay culture is twofold: visibility and protection. As Harry Britt, a political leader of San Francisco's gays, told me in an interview years ago: "When gays are spatially scattered, they are not gay, because they are invisible." The fundamental liberating act for gays was/is "to come out," to publicly express their identity and their sexuality, then to resocialize themselves. But how is it possible to be openly gay in the middle of a hostile and violent society increasingly insecure about its fundamental values of virility and patriarchalism? And how can one learn a new behavior, a new code, and a new culture, in a world where sexuality is implicit in everybody's presentation of self and where the general assumption is heterosexuality? In order to express themselves, gays have always met together – in modern times in night bars and coded places. When they became conscious enough and strong enough to "come out" collectively, they earmarked places where they could be safe together and could invent new lives. The territorial boundaries of their selected places became the basis for the building of autonomous institutions, and the creation of cultural autonomy. Levine has shown the systematic patterning of spatial concentrations of gays in American cities during the 1970s.[112] While he and others used the term "ghetto," gay militants speak of "liberated zones": and there is indeed a major difference between ghettos and gay areas since the latter are usually deliberately constructed by gay people to create their own city, in the framework of the broader urban society.

Why San Francisco? An instant city, a settlement for adventurers attracted by gold and freedom, San Francisco was always a place of tolerant moral standards. The Barbary Coast was a meeting point for sailors, travelers, transients, dreamers, crooks, entrepreneurs, rebels, and deviants – a milieu of casual encounters and few social rules where the borderline between the normal and the abnormal was blurred. Yet, in the 1920s, the city decided to become respectable,

112   Levine (1979).

emerging as the cultural capital of the American West, and growing up gracefully under the authoritative shadow of the Catholic Church, relying on the support of its Irish and Italian working-class legions. With the reform movement reaching City Hall and the police in the 1930s, "deviants" were repressed and forced into hiding. Thus, the pioneer origins of San Francisco as a free city are not enough to explain its destiny as the setting for gay liberation.

The major turning point was World War II. San Francisco was the main port for the Pacific front. About 1.6 million young men and women passed through the city: alone, uprooted, living on the edge of death and suffering, and sharing it most of the time with people of their own sex, many of them discovered, or elected, their homosexuality. And many were dishonorably discharged from the Navy, and disembarked in San Francisco. Rather than going home to Iowa bearing the stigma, they stayed in the city, joined by thousands of other gay people at the end of the war. They met in bars, and they built networks of support and sharing. A gay culture started to emerge from the late 1940s. The transition from the bars to the streets had to wait, however, for more than a decade, when alternative lifestyles flourished in San Francisco, with the beatnik generation, and around literary circles networked in the City Lights bookstore, with Ginsberg, Kerouac, and the Black Mountain poets, among others. This culture concentrated spatially in the old Italian North Beach area, near the red-light tourist zone of Broadway. Gays were fully accepted in this tolerant, experimental ambience. When the media focused on the beatnik culture, they emphasized the widespread presence of homosexuality as a proof of its deviance. So doing, they publicized San Francisco as a gay Mecca, attracting thousands of gays from around America. City Hall responded with repression, leading to the formation, in 1964, of the Society of Individual Rights, which defended gays, in connection with the Tavern Guild, a business association of gay and bohemian bar owners fighting against police harassment.

Then, in the late 1960s, the hippy culture, the social movements that took place in the San Francisco Bay Area, particularly in Berkeley/Oakland, and the emergence of the gay liberation movement throughout America, induced a qualitative change in the development of San Francisco's gay community, building on the strength of historically established networks. In 1971, for the first time, the California gay movement was strong enough to organize a march on the capital, Sacramento, in support of gay rights. In the 1970s, in San Francisco a gay community flourished in certain neighborhoods, particularly in the Castro area, buying or renting homes in a rundown, traditional working-class district, which came to be rehabilitated by gay house-holds, gay realtors, and gay renovation companies. Gay-owned busi-nesses also settled in the area. From scattered locations, following bars and counter-cultural areas, gays were able, by the 1970s, to concentrate on a neighborhood that they could call theirs. Figure 4.11 shows the expansion of gay residential areas in San Francisco between 1950 and 1980 on the basis of my fieldwork research.

Yet, the building of the gay community was not purely spontan-eous. It was also the result of deliberate political action, particularly under the impulse of the historic leader of San Francisco's gay com-munity, Harvey Milk. A graduate of the State University of New York at Albany, he was not able to teach after being discharged from the Navy because of homosexuality. Like thousands of gays, he migrated to San Francisco in 1969. After leaving a job as a financial analyst, he opened a photography business, Castro Camera, on Castro Street. He conceived a plan for gays to evolve from community, to business, to power. He called for "gays to buy gay," so that Castro would be more than a cruising place, but a space owned by gays, lived by gays, and enjoyed by gays. Then, if gays could buy gay, and live as gays, they could also vote gay. In 1973, he ran for supervisor (council member) of the city of San Francisco, explicitly as a gay candidate. He did well, but was not elected. He went back to work on building a political basis, strengthening gays' political clubs, linking up with the Demo-cratic party, and broadening his program to address issues of local urban policies, such as the control of real estate speculation.

A political event changed his destiny. In 1975, a liberal California Senator, George Moscone, was elected mayor of San Francisco by a narrow margin. To secure the support of the by then strong gay community, Moscone appointed Harvey Milk to an important post in the local administration. For the first time an openly gay leader became a city official. Around the same time, the powerful neighbor-hood movement in San Francisco obtained a reform of the electoral law, establishing elections to the city council (Board of Supervisors) by local districts, instead of voting in the city at large. Then, on the basis of the territory that the gay community had conquered in the Castro area, which became an electoral district, Harvey Milk was elected supervisor in 1977. From his new platform, he mobilized gay power around the city, and around the state. In 1978 a conservative proposition was put in the ballot to California voters to ban homo-sexuals from teaching in public schools. The voters rejected it by 58 percent of the vote in California, 75 percent in San Francisco. Harvey Milk, with skillful media performance, was the leader of the cam-paign. In April 1978, the Board of Supervisors approved a very liberal

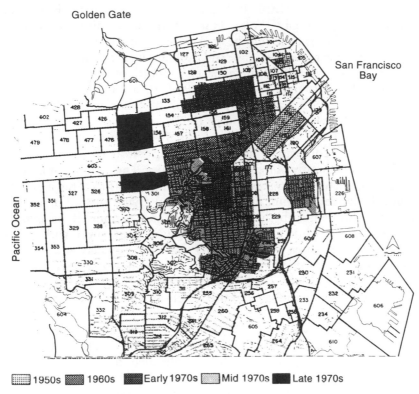

Golden Gate

San Francisco
Bay

Pacific Ocean

▦ 1950s ▦ 1960s ▰ Early 1970s ▱ Mid 1970s ■ Late 1970s

Figure 4.11   Gay residential areas in San Francisco
Source: Castells (1983)

Gay Rights Ordinance. At the same time, two lesbian leaders, Del
Martin and Phyllis Lyon, holding City Hall Posts, received from the
city of San Francisco a certificate of honor for their civic services –
including support for lesbians – and for their 25 years of living
together.

These, and other gay breakthroughs, were more than the homophobic culture could take. On November 27, 1978, a conservative
city supervisor, Dan White, an ex-policeman who had campaigned
against tolerance toward "sexual deviants," shot and killed mayor
George Moscone and supervisor Harvey Milk in their offices at City
Hall. He later surrendered to his former colleagues in the police
department. The mourning of Moscone and Milk was one of the
most impressive political demonstrations ever seen in San Francisco:
20,000 people marched with candles, in silence, after listening to
speakers who called on the movement to pursue the struggle in the

way shown by Harvey Milk. It did. The new mayor, Dianne Feinstein, appointed another gay leader, Harry Britt, a socialist, to replace Harvey Milk in his post, and he was subsequently elected supervisor.

Over the next decade, gay and lesbian leaders increased their representation on the 11-member city Board of Supervisors, and although they lost one election, in 1992, to a conservative mayor, they again became a major component of the coalition that helped to elect Willie Brown, a veteran Black Democratic leader, mayor of San Francisco in 1996. An anecdote of the 1996 campaign reveals the state of mental confusion of the homophobic culture in San Francisco, lost in the uncertainty of long cherished values. The incumbent mayor, an ex-police chief, may have lost his re-election bid after a major political blunder. Trailing in the polls, and trying to find a way to ingratiate himself with the gay audience, he let himself be photographed naked, while giving an interview in his shower with radio journalists in the same attire. The backlash from both gay and straight offended voters doomed his chances. The new mayor renewed the by then two decades old commitment from the city to respect and enhance gay rights, and gay culture, celebrated in parades and festivities several times in the year.

However, the gay community of the 1990s was not the same as the one formed in the 1970s because in the early 1980s AIDS struck.[113] In the next 15 years, about 15,000 people died from AIDS in San Francisco, and several more thousands were diagnosed as infected with the HIV virus. The reaction of the gay community was remarkable, as San Francisco became a model for the entire world in self-organization, prevention, and political action geared toward controlling the AIDS epidemics, a danger for humankind. I believe it is accurate to say that the most important gay movement of the 1980s and 1990s was the gay component of the anti-AIDS movement, in its different manifestations, from health clinics to militant groups such as ACT UP! In San Francisco, the first effort was directed toward helping the ill, and preventing the spread of the disease. A large-scale effort for the education of the community was undertaken, with safe-sex procedures taught and diffused. After a few years, the results were spectacular. In the 1990s, in San Francisco, and in California, the incidence of new cases of AIDS was much greater in the heterosexual population, as a result of drug use, prostitution, and infection of women by careless men, while the gay population, more educated

113   For a discussion of the relationship between the gay movement, the fight against AIDS, and society's reactions, see Coates et al. (1988); Mass (1990); Heller (1992); Price and Hsu (1992); Herek and Greene (1995); Lloyd and Kuselewickz (1995).

and better organized, saw a significant decline in new infections. The care of the ill was organized at all levels, with San Francisco General Hospital becoming the first hospital to establish a permanent AIDS section, and a whole network of volunteers provided help and comfort to people in the hospital and at home. Militant pressures to step up research efforts, and to obtain accelerated approval of experimental drugs as they became available, yielded significant results. The University of California at San Francisco Hospital became one of the leading centers in AIDS-related research. In a broader perspective, the 1996 worldwide AIDS Conference in Vancouver announced potential breakthroughs in controlling the disease and, maybe, in diminishing its lethality in the future.

But perhaps the most important effort by the gay community, in San Francisco and elsewhere, was the cultural battle to demystify AIDS, to remove the stigma, and to convince the world that it was not produced by homosexuality or, for that matter, by sexuality. Contact networks, including sexual contact, but comprising many other forms, were the lethal messengers, not homosexuality.[114] And the disconnection of these networks, thus controlling the epidemics, was not a matter of confinement but of education, organization, and responsibility, supported both by public health institutions and civic consciousness. That the gay community, starting in San Francisco, could win this uphill battle was a decisive contribution to humankind. Not least because a new crime against humanity was avoided, when the movement successfully fought back the calls for detection and confinement of HIV carriers. What was fundamentally at stake was the ability of the world to look AIDS directly into its horrifying eyes, and to face the epidemics in terms of the virus(es) as it (they) is (are), not in terms of our prejudices and nightmares. We came very close, in the world at large, to considering AIDS as a deserved divine punishment against New Sodom, thus not taking the necessary measures to prevent an even greater spread of the disease until it may have been too late to control it at all. That we did not, that societies learned in time that AIDS was not a homosexual disease, and that the sources and vehicles of its spread had to be fought in society at large was, to a large extent, the work of the gay-community based, anti-AIDS movement, with its pioneers (many of them on their way to death) in the liberated city of San Francisco.

Not unrelated to the AIDS epidemic, another major trend took place in the 1990s in the San Francisco gay community. Patterns of sexual interaction became more stable, partly a sign of the aging and

114   Castells (1992c).

maturation of some segments of the community, partly as a way of channeling sexuality into safer patterns of love. The yearning for same-sex families became one of the most powerful cultural trends among gays and, even more so, among lesbians. The comfort of a durable, monogamous relationship became a predominant model among middle-aged gays and lesbians. Consequently, a new movement sprouted out from the gay community to obtain the institutional recognition of such stable relationships as families. Thus, certificates of partnership were sought from local and state governments, with this recognition carrying the entitlement to spousal benefits. Furthermore, the legalization of same-sex marriages became a major demand of the movement, taking conservatives at their word in promoting family values, and extending the value of the family to non-traditional, non-heterosexual forms of love, sharing, and child rearing. What started as a movement of sexual liberation came full circle to haunt the patriarchal family by attacking its heterosexual roots, and subverting its exclusive appropriation of family values.

Since any action brings a reaction, the relative taming of sexuality in new gay and lesbian families induced, in parallel, the development of sexual minority cultures (both heterosexual and homosexual), such as the sadomasochist movement, and voluntary sex-slave networks, a significant phenomenon in the San Francisco scene, particularly in the South of Market area, although I identified the importance of this cultural/personal revolt in my fieldwork 20 years ago. Sadomasochists, whose culture includes some very articulate intellectuals, criticize mainstream gays for trying to define new norms of the "socially acceptable," thus reproducing the logic of domination that oppressed gays and lesbians throughout history. For sadomasochists the journey has no end. Thus, controlled violence, accepted humiliation, slave auctions, painful pleasure, leather dress, Nazi emblems, chains and whips, are more than sexual stimuli. They are cultural expressions of the need to destroy whatever moral values straight society has left them with since these values have traditionally been used to stigmatize and repress homosexuality, and sexuality. The considerable embarrassment that this cultural minority causes to most gays and lesbians is the symptom that they do address an important, if difficult, issue.

Left to itself, in its cultural ghetto, the gay community is unlikely to accomplish the sexual revolution and the subversion of patriarchalism that are, implicitly, the goals of the movement, even if they are not supported by the growing segment of male elites that consume rather than produce the gay movement. Strategic alliances with lesbians, and with the feminist movement at large, seem to be a necessary condition for the fulfillment of gay liberation. Yet, gays are men, and their socialization as men, and the privileges they enjoy, particularly if they are white and middle class, limit their fully fledged incorporation into an anti-patriarchal alliance. This is why in San Francisco there is a growing split between a radically oriented gay and lesbian alliance, and a respectable gay elite that has established itself as an interest group to defend gay rights as a tolerated minority within the institutions of patriarchalism. Yet, if this diversity can be expressed within a broader movement that allows people freedom to chose whom they love, in contradiction with the heterosexual norm, it is because Harvey Milk, and other pioneers, built a free commune once upon a time in the West.

Summing up: sexual identity and the patriarchal family

Lesbian and gay movements are not simply movements in defense of basic human rights to choose whom and how to love. They are also powerful expressions of sexual identity, and therefore of sexual liberation. This is why they challenge some of the millennial foundations on which societies were built historically: sexual repression and compulsory heterosexuality.

When lesbians, in an institutional environment as repressive and patriarchal as the Chinese culture in Taipei, are able to openly express their sexuality, and to claim the inclusion of same-sex marriages in the family code, a fundamental breach has been opened in the institutional scaffolding constructed to control desire. If the gay community is able to overcome ignorant stigmatization, and to help prevent the plague of AIDS, it means that societies have become able to extract themselves from their darkness, and to look into the whole diversity of human experience, without prejudice and without violence. And if presidential electoral campaigns in America have unwillingly to reckon with the debate on gay rights, it means that the social movements' challenge to heterosexuality cannot be ignored or purely repressed any longer. Yet the forces of transformation unleashed by sexual identity movements can hardly be confined within the limits of simple tolerance and respect for human rights. They bring into motion a corrosive critique of sexual normalization and of the patriarchal family. Their challenge is particularly frightening for patriarchalism because it comes at an historical time when biological research and medical technology allow the disassociation between heterosexuality, patriarchalism, and the reproduction of the species. Same-sex families, which will not give up rearing children, are the most open expression of this possibility.

On the other hand, the blurring of sexual boundaries, decoupling family, sexuality, love, gender, and power, introduces a fundamental cultural critique to the world as we have known it. This is why the future development of sexual liberation movements will not be easy. By shifting from the defense of human rights to the reconstruction of sexuality, family, and personality, they touch the nerve centers of repression and civilization, and they will be responded to in kind. There is a stormy horizon ahead for the gay and lesbian movements, and AIDS will not be the only hideous face of anti-sexual backlash. Yet, if the experience of the past has any indicative value, the power of identity seems to become magic when touched by the power of love.

Family, Sexuality, and Personality in the Crisis of Patriarchalism[115]

In the separating and divorcing society, the nuclear family generates a diversity of new kin ties associated, for example, with the so-called recombinant families. However, the nature of these ties changes as they are subject to greater negotiation than before. Kinship relations often used to be taken for granted on the basis of trust; now trust has to be negotiated and bargained for, and commitment is as much an issue as in sexual relationships.

Anthony Giddens, *The Transformation of Intimacy*, p. 96

The incredibly shrinking family

The crisis of patriarchalism, induced by the interaction between informational capitalism and feminist and sexual identity social movements, manifests itself in the increasing diversity of partnership arrangements among people to share their lives and raise children. I will illustrate this point by using American data to simplify the argument. I do not imply, however, that all countries and cultures will follow this path. Yet, if the social, economic, and technological trends underlying the crisis of patriarchalism are present around the world, it is plausible that most societies will have to reconstruct, or replace, their patriarchal institutions under the specific conditions of their culture and history. The following discussion, empirically based

115   Data reported in this section are from the US Bureau of the Census and from *The World Almanac and Book of Facts* (1996), unless referred to otherwise. US Bureau of the Census publications used to retrieve these data are: US Department of Commerce, Economics and Statistics Administration, Bureau of the Census (1989, 1991, 1992a–d).

on American trends, aims at identifying social mechanisms connecting the crisis of the patriarchal family, and the transformation of sexual identity, to the social redefinition of family life, thus of personality systems.

What is at issue is not the disappearance of the family but its profound diversification, and the change in its power system. Indeed, most people continue to marry: 90 percent of Americans do over their lifetime. When they divorce, 60 percent of women and 75 percent of men remarry, on average within three years. And gays and lesbians are fighting for their right to legal marriage. Yet, later marriages, frequency of cohabitation, and high rates of divorce (stabilized at about half of all marriages), and of separation, combine to produce an increasingly diverse profile of family and non-family life (figures 4.12a and 4.12b summarize its broad trends for 1960–90 and for 1970–95). The so-called "non-family households" doubled between 1960 and 1995, increasing from 15 percent of all households to 29 percent of households, naturally including single elderly, and thus reflecting a demographic trend, as well as a cultural change. Women account for two-thirds of single-households. More significantly, the archetypical category "married couples with children" dropped from 44.2 percent of households in 1960 to 25.5 percent in 1995. Thus, the "model" of the patriarchal nuclear family is the reality for just over one-quarter of American households. Stacey quotes sources indicating that if we consider the most traditional version of patriarchalism, meaning the married couple with children in which the only breadwinner is the male, and the wife is a full-time homemaker, the proportion drops to 7 percent of all households.[116]

The life of children has been transformed. As figure 4.13 shows, over one-quarter of children did not live with two parents in 1990, in contrast to less than 13 percent in 1960. Furthermore, according to a US Bureau of the Census study, in 1991 the proportion of children living with their two biological parents was only 50.8 percent.[117] Other sources also estimate that "nearly 50 percent of all children do not live with both of their genetic parents."[118] Adoptions have substantially increased over the past two decades, and 20,000 babies have been born from *in vitro* fertilization.[119] The *trends*, all pointing in the same direction of the fading away of the patriarchal nuclear family, are what really matters: the proportion of children living with a lone parent doubled between 1970 and 1990, reaching 25 percent of

116   Stacey (1990: 28).
117   US Bureau of the Census (1994).
118   Buss (1994: 168).
119   Reigot and Spina (1996: 238).

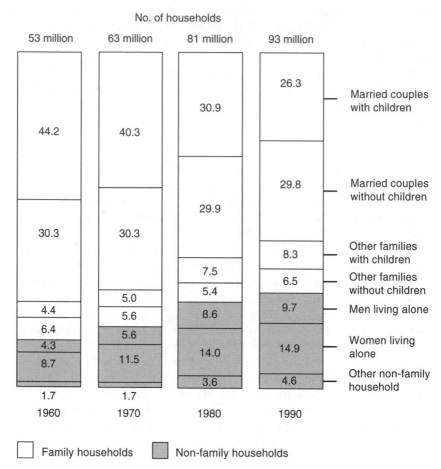

Figure 4.12a   Household composition in US, 1960–90 (%)
(children = own children under 18)
Source: US Bureau of the Census (1992a)

all children. Among these children, the proportion living with a never-married mother increased from 7 percent in 1970 to 31 percent in 1990. One-parent female-headed households with children increased by 90.5 percent in the 1970s, and by an additional 21.2 percent in the 1980s. One-parent male-headed households with children, while accounting only for 3.1 percent of all households in 1990, are growing even faster: by 80.6 percent in 1970s, and by 87.2 percent in the 1980s. Female-headed families without a husband present grew from 11 percent of all families in 1970 to 18 percent in 1994. The percentage of

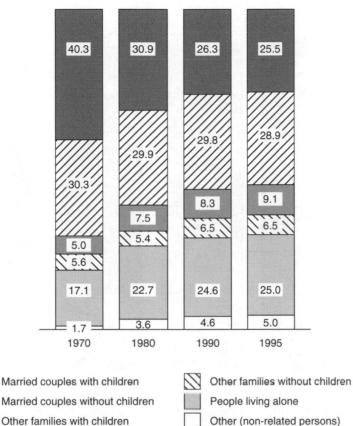

▨	Married couples with children	◩ Other families without children
▨	Married couples without children	▨ People living alone
▨	Other families with children	☐ Other (non-related persons)

Figure 4.12b Household composition in US, 1970–95 (%)
Source: US Bureau of the Census (1996)

children living only with their mother doubled between 1970 and 1994, from 11 to 22 percent, while the proportion of children living only with their father trebled in the same period, going from 1 to 3 percent.

New profiles of living arrangements multiply.[120] In 1980, there were 4 million recombinant families (including children from a previous marriage); in 1990, 5 million. In 1992, one-quarter of single women over 18 had children; in 1993, there were 3.5 million unmarried couples, of which 35 percent had children in the household; the number of unmarried fathers with children doubled from 1980 to 1992; 1 million children were living with their grandparents

120   Reigot and Spina (1996).

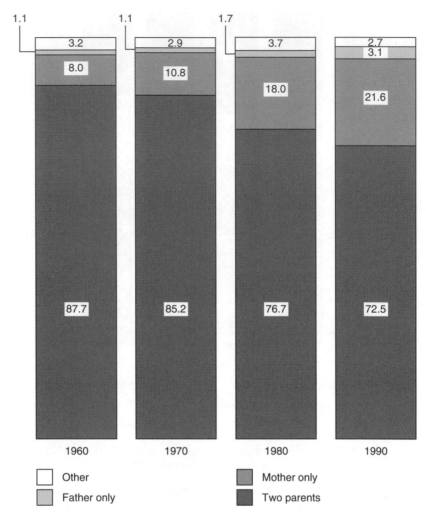

Figure 4.13 Living arrangements of children under the age of 18, by
presence of parent, in US, 1960–90 (% distribution)
Source: US Bureau of the Census (1992a)

in 1990 (10 percent up from 1960), out of a total of 3.5 million
children sharing their household with a grandparent. Marriages pre-
ceded by cohabitation increased from 8 percent in the late 1960s to 49
percent in the mid-1980s, and half of cohabitating couples have
children.[121] Furthermore, with the massive entry of women into the
paid labor force, and their indispensable role in providing for the

121   Coleman and Ganong (1993: 113).

family, few children can enjoy their mother's or father's full-time care. In 1990, both husband and wife worked outside the home in about 70 percent of married couple families, and 58 percent of mothers with young children worked outside the home. Child care is a major problem for families, and was performed in their home by relatives or neighbors for two-thirds of children,[122] to which we should add unregistered home helpers. Poor women, unable to pay for child care, are faced with the choice of separating from their children or giving up work, then falling into the welfare trap that may lead eventually to their children being taken away from them.[123]

There are few reliable estimates on same-sex households and families. One of the few is by Gonsioreck and Weinrich, according to whom an estimated 10 percent of the American male population are gay, and between 6 and 7 percent of the female population are lesbian.[124] They estimate that about 20 percent of the gay male population were married once, and that between 20 and 50 percent of them had children. Lesbians are often mothers, many of them from previous heterosexual marriages. A very wide range evaluation puts the figure of children living with their lesbian mothers at between 1.5 and 3.3 million. The number of children living with either gay or lesbian parents is estimated at between 4 and 6 million.[125] Among non-family households, the fastest growth is in the category "other non-family households," which increased from 1.7 percent of total households in 1970 to 5 percent in 1995. In this group are, according to the US census, roommates, friends, and unrelated individuals. In fact, this category would include both heterosexual and homosexual couples in cohabitation without children.

In the mid-1990s, according to Harvard University's estimates of household formation to the year 2000, as a percentage of total households, married couples with children were expected to decline further, from 31.5 percent in 1980 to 23.4 percent in 2000, while single-person households were projected to increase from 22.6 percent to 26.6 percent in 2000, statistically overtaking the household type of married couples with children.[126] Lone parents would increase

122   Farnsworth Riche (1996).
123   Susser (1991).
124   Gonsioreck and Weinrich (1991). The 10 percent threshold of homosexuality for the population at large is a demographic myth inspired by a superficial reading of the half-century old Kinsey Report (in fact reporting on American white males). As Laumann et al. (1994) suggest, with a strong empirical basis, there is no clear boundary of homosexuality that can be traced back to some distinctive biological impulse. The extent of homosexual behavior, in its different manifestations, evolves according to cultural norms and social contexts. For a discussion of the matter, see Laumann et al. (1994: 283–320).
125   Reigot and Spina (1996: 116).
126   Masnick and Ardle (1994); Masnick and Kim (1995).

slightly from 7.7 to 8.7 percent. Married couples without children would become the most numerous, but not predominant, household type, remaining at about 29.5 percent of all households, an effect of the longer survival of both spouses, together with the replacement of these formerly married couples with children by a more diversified array of household forms. Indeed, what they called "other households," comprising miscellaneous living arrangements, were projected to increase their share from 8.8 percent in 1980 to 11.8 percent in 2000. Overall, in the Harvard University estimates and projections, while in 1960 three-quarters of all US households were formed by married couples, and non-family households accounted for only 15 percent of households, in the year 2000, married couples would account for about 53 percent, and non-family households would increase their share to 38 percent. What emerges from this statistical overview is a picture of diversification, of moving boundaries in people's partnerships, with a large and increasing proportion of children being socialized under family forms that were marginal, or even unthinkable, only three decades ago, an instant by the standards of historical time.[127]

So, what are these new arrangements? How do people live now, in and outside the family, on the borderlines of patriarchalism? We know something about it, after pioneer research by Stacey, Reigot and Spina, Susser, and others.[128] As Stacey writes:

> women and men have been creatively remaking American family life during the past three decades of post-industrial upheaval. Out of the ashes and residue of the modern family they have drawn on a diverse, often incongruous array of cultural, political, economic, and ideological resources, fashioning these resources into new gender and kinship strategies to cope with post-industrial challenges, burdens and opportunities.[129]

Similar conclusions are reached in the qualitative study by Reigot and Spina on new forms of families.[130] There is no new prevailing type of family emerging; diversity is the rule. But some elements seem to be

---

127 According to data cited by Ehrenreich (1983: 20), in 1957, 53 percent of Americans believed that unmarried people were "sick," "immoral," or "neurotic," and only 37 percent viewed them "neutrally." By 1976, only 33 percent had negative attitudes toward the unmarried, and 15 percent looked favorably upon people who remained single.
128 Stacey (1990); Susser (1991, 1996); Reigot and Spina (1996); see also Bartholet (1990); Gonsioreck and Weinrich (1991); Brubaker (1993); Rubin and Riney (1994); Fitzpatrick and Vangelisti (1995).
129 Stacey (1990: 16).
130 Reigot and Spina (1996).

critical in the new arrangements: *networks of support, increasing female-centeredness, a succession of partners and patterns throughout the life-cycle.* Networks of support, often between members of families of divorced couples are a new, important form of sociability and burden-sharing, particularly when children have to be shared and supported between the two parents after they both form new households. Thus, a study of middle-class divorced couples in the San Francisco suburbs found one-third of them sustaining kinship ties with former spouses and their relatives.[131] Women's support networks are critical for single mothers, as well as for full-time working mothers, according to the case studies reported by Reigot and Spina, and by Susser, as well as by Coleman and Ganong.[132] Indeed, as Stacey writes "if there is a family crisis, it is a male family crisis."[133] Furthermore, since most people keep trying to form families in spite of disappointments or misfits, step-parent families and a succession of partnerships become the norm. Because of both life experience and the complexity of households, arrangements within the family, including the distribution of roles and responsibilities, no longer adjust to tradition: they must be negotiated. Thus Coleman and Ganong, after observing widespread family disruption, conclude: "Does this mean the end of the family? No. It does mean, however, that many of us will be living in new, more complex families. In these new families, roles, rules and responsibilities may have to be negotiated rather than taken for granted as is typical in more traditional families."[134]

So, patriarchalism in the family is altogether eliminated in the case of the growing proportion of female-headed households, and seriously challenged in most other families, because of the negotiations and conditions requested by women and children in the household. Additionally, another growing proportion of households, maybe soon reaching almost 40 percent, relates to non-family households, thus voiding the meaning of the patriarchal family as an institution in much of the practice of society, in spite of its towering presence as a powerful myth.

Under such conditions, what happens to the socialization of children, underlying the reproduction of gender division in society, and thus the reproduction of patriarchalism itself?

131 Cited in Stacey (1990: 254).
132 Coleman and Ganong (1993); Reigot and Spina (1996); Susser (1996).
133 Stacey (1990: 269).
134 Coleman and Ganong (1993: 127).

The reproduction of mothering under the non-reproduction of patriarchalism

There is no place within the limits of this chapter to enter the detail of a complex, diversified, and controversial empirical record, most of which is hidden in the clinical files of child psychologists, on the transformation of family socialization in the new family environment. But, I think a number of hypotheses can be advanced, on the basis of the classic work by feminist psychoanalyst Nancy Chodorow. In her *Reproduction of Mothering*, Chodorow proposed a simple, elegant, and powerful psychoanalytical model of the production/reproduction of gender, a model that she refined and complemented in her later writings.[135] Although her theory is controversial, and psychoanalysis is certainly not the only possible approach to understanding personality changes in the crisis of patriarchalism, it provides, in my view, a useful starting-point to theorize these changes. Let me first summarize Chodorow's analytical model in her own words, then elaborate on the implications of this model for personality and gender under the conditions of the crisis of patriarchalism. Following Chodorow, the reproduction of mothering is central to the reproduction of gender. It happens through a social-structurally induced psychological process, which is not the product of either biology or institutional role-training. In her words:

> Women, as mothers, produce daughters with mothering capacities and the desire to mother. These capacities and needs are built into and grow out of the mother–daughter relationship itself. By contrast, women as mothers (and men as not-mothers) produce sons whose nurturant capacities and needs have been systematically curtailed and repressed. This prepares men for their affective later family role and for their primary participation in the impersonal, extra-familial world of work and public life. The sexual and familial division of labor in which women mother and are more involved in interpersonal, affective relationships than men, produces in daughters and sons a division of psychological capacities which leads them to reproduce this sexual and familial division of labor... Women have primary responsibility for child care in families and outside them; women by and large want to mother, and get gratification for their mothering; and with all the conflicts and contradictions, women have succeeded at mothering.[136]

135 Chodorow (1989, 1994).
136 Chodorow (1978: 7).

This model of reproduction has an extraordinary impact on sexuality, and therefore on personality and family life: "Because women mother, the development of heterosexual object-choice differ for men and women."[137] Boys retain their mother as their primary love object in their boyhood, and, because of the fundamental taboo, they have to go through the classic process of separation, and resolution of their oedipus complex, by repressing their attachment to the mother. When becoming adults, men are ready to find a primary relationship with someone *like* their mother (Chodorow's italics). Things are different for girls:

> Because her first love object is a woman, a girl, in order to attain her *proper heterosexual orientation*,[138] must transfer her primary object-choice to her father and men...For girls, as for boys, mothers are primary love objects. As a result, the structural inner object setting of female heterosexuality differs from that of males. When a girl's father does become an important primary person, it is in the context of a bisexual relational triangle...For girls, then, there is no absolute change of object, nor exclusive attachment to their fathers...The implications of this are two-fold. First, the nature of the heterosexual relationship differs for boys and girls. Most women emerge from their oedipus complex oriented to their father and men as primary *erotic* objects, but it is clear that men tend to remain *emotionally* secondary, or at most emotionally equal, compared to the primacy and exclusivity of an oedipal boy's tie to his mother and women. Second...women, according to Deutsch, experience heterosexual relationships in a triangular context, in which men are not exclusive objects for them. The implication of her statement is confirmed by cross-cultural examination of family structure and relations between the sexes, which suggests that conjugal closeness is the exception and not the rule.[139]

Indeed, men tend to fall in love romantically, while women, because of their economic dependence and their women-oriented affective system, engage *vis-à-vis* men in a more complex calculation, in which access to resources is paramount,[140] according to the

---

137   Chodorow (1978: 191).
138   Adrienne Rich (1980) criticized Chodorow for not emphasizing the potential lesbian inclination of many women, in line with her theory. In my view, this criticism is unfair because Rich's "lesbian continuum" takes place within the context of institutionalized heterosexuality. What Chodorow explains is how the uninterrupted mother/daughter link is channeled toward the institutions of heterosexual marriage, from where it is also originates. It is essential for the psychoanalyst, and for the sociologist, to keep a distance between analysis and advocacy.
139   Chodorow (1978: 192–3).
140   Of course, the world's literature, as our personal experience, is full of examples of women abandoning everything in pursuit of romance. I would argue, however, that this is a manifestation of the ideological domination of the patriarchal model, and rarely resists the actual experience of the relationship. This is why it makes good material for novels!

cross-cultural study by Buss on strategies of human mating.[141] But let us pursue Chodorow's logic:

> [Women] while they are likely to become and remain erotically hetero-sexual [Castells: albeit with more and more exceptions to the rule], they are encouraged both by men's difficulties with love and by their own relational history with their mothers to look elsewhere for love and emotional gratification. One way that women fulfill these needs is through the creation and maintenance of important personal relations with other women... However, deep affective relationships to women are hard to come by on a routine, daily, ongoing basis for many women. Lesbian relationships do tend to recreate mother-daughters, but most women are heterosexual... There is a second alternative... Given the triangular situation and emotional asymmetry of her own parenting, a woman's relation to a man *requires* on the level of psychic structure a third person, since it was originally established in a trian-gle... Then, a child completes the relational triangle for a woman [142]

Indeed, "women come to want and need primary relationships to chil-dren."[143] For men, again, it is different, because of their primordial attachment to their mother, and, later on, to their mother-like figure: "For men, by contrast, the heterosexual relationship alone recreates the early bond to their mother; *a child interrupts it* [my italics]. Men, more-over do not define themselves in relationships, and have come to suppress relational capacities and repress relational needs. This prepares them to participate in the affect-denying world of alienated work, but not to fulfill women's needs for intimacy and primary relationships."[144] Thus, "men's lack of emotional availability and women's less exclusive heterosexual commitment help ensure women's mothering." Ultimately,

> institutionalized features of family structure and the social relations of reproduction reproduce themselves. A psychoanalytical investigation shows that women's mothering capacities and commitments, and the general psychological capacities and wants which are the basis of women's emotions work, are built developmentally into feminine per-sonality. Because women are themselves mothered by women, they grow up with the relational capacities and needs, and psychological definition of self in relationships, which commits them to mothering. Men, because they are mothered by women, do not. Women mother daughters who, when they become women, mother.[145]

141 Buss (1994).
142 Chodorow (1978: 201).
143 Chodorow (1978: 203).
144 Chodorow (1978: 207).
145 Chodorow (1978: 209).

Chodorow's model has been assailed, notably by lesbian theorists and materialist feminists, and unfairly accused of downplaying homosexuality, of fixing patriarchalism, and of predetermining individual behavior. In fact, it is not so. Chodorow herself has made clear her views: "I claim – against generalization – that men and women love in as many ways as there are men and women."[146] And she has refined her analysis by emphasizing that "differentiation is not distinctness and separateness, but a particular way of being connected to others."[147] The problem for women, she argues, and I concur, is not to claim their female identity, but their identification with an identity that has been socially devalued under patriarchalism. What Chodorow analyzes is not an eternal, biological process of male/female specificity, but a fundamental mechanism of reproduction of gender, and hence of identity, sexuality, and personality, *under the conditions of patriarchalism and heterosexuality*, as she has made clear repeatedly.

My question, then, is whether this institutional/psychoanalytical model can help us in understanding what happens when the patriarchal family disintegrates. Let me try to link up my observations on new forms of families and living arrangements with Chodorow's theory.[148] Under the classic, now fading, patriarchal/heterosexual condition, heterosexual women relate primarily to four kinds of objects: children as the object of their mothering; women's networks as their primary emotional support; men as erotic objects; and men as providers of the family. Under current conditions, for most families and women, the fourth object has been canceled as the exclusive provider. Women do pay a dear price, in working time, and in poverty, for their economic independence and for their indispensable role as family providers, but, by and large, the economic basis of family patriarchalism has been eroded, since most men also need women's income to reach decent living standards. As men were already secondary as assets of emotional support, this leaves them, primarily, with their role as erotic objects, a dwindling source of interest for women in a time of widespread development of women's support networks (including expressions of affection in a "lesbian continuum"), and given women's focus on combining their mothering with their working lives.

---

146 Chodorow (1994: 71).
147 Chodorow (1989: 107).
148 I should remind the reader that Chodorow is primarily a psychoanalyst, focused on developing theory *on the basis of clinical evidence*. Therefore, this use of her cautious, psychoanalytical approach to construct my sweeping sociological generalizations goes far beyond her usual boundaries, and is undertaken, naturally, under my exclusive responsibility.

Thus, the first living arrangement resulting from the crisis of patriarchalism, corresponding to the logic of Chodorow's model, is the formation of mother/children families, relying on the support of women's networks. These "women/children's communes" experience, from time to time, the visit of men, for heterosexual women, in a pattern of successive partnerships that leave behind additional children and further reasons for separatism. When mothers age, daughters mother, reproducing the system. Then, mothers become grandmothers, reinforcing the support networks, both *vis-à-vis* their daughters and grandchildren, and *vis-à-vis* the daughters and children of their networked households. This is not a separatist model, but a rather self-sufficient women-centered model, where men come and go. The main problem for the woman-centered model, as Barbara Ehrenreich pointed out years ago,[149] is its weak economic basis. Child-care, social services, and women's education and job opportunities are the missing links for this model to become a largely self-sufficient women's commune on a societal scale.

The situation for men, while being more socially privileged, is more complicated personally.[150] With the decline of their economic bargaining power, they usually cannot enforce discipline in the family any longer by withholding resources. Unless they engage in egalitarian parenting, they cannot alter the basic mechanisms by which their daughters are produced as mothers and they are produced as desirers of women/mothers *for themselves*. Thus, they continue to seek after *the* woman, as their object of love, not only erotic but emotional, as well as their safety blanket, and, not forgetting, their useful domestic worker. With fewer children, women working, men earning less and in less secure jobs, and with feminist ideas floating around, men face a number of options, none of which is the reproduction of the patriarchal family, if this analysis is correct.

The first is *separation*, "the flight from commitment,"[151] and, indeed, we observe such a trend in the statistics. Consumerist narcissism may help, particularly in the younger years. Yet, men do not do well in networking, solidarity, and relational skills, a feature that is also explained by Chodorow's theory. Male bonding is indeed a usual practice in traditional patriarchal societies. But, as I remember from my Spanish experience (old and recent), "men only" social gatherings are based on the assumption of family/female support waiting at

---

149   Ehrenreich (1983).
150   Ehrenreich (1983); Astrachan (1986); Keen (1991).
151   Ehrenreich (1983).

home. It is only on a stable structure of domination satisfying basic affective needs that men can then play together, generally talking about, boasting about, and parading for women. The men's *peas*[152] become silent and depressing when women disappear, suddenly transformed into drinking mortuaries of male power. Indeed, in most societies, single men have poorer health, lower longevity, and higher suicide and depression rates than married men. The contrary is true for women who divorce or separate, in spite of frequent, but short post-divorce depressions.

A second alternative is *gayness*. Indeed, it seems that gayness is expanding among men whose biological predispositions allow both forms of sexual expression, but that, under circumstances of privileged patriarchalism, may have chosen to abstain from the homosexual stigma. Gayness increases the chances of support networks, of which men are usually deprived. It also makes easier egalitarian, or negotiated, partnerships, since social norms do not assign dominant roles in the couple. Thus, gay families may be the experimental milieux of everyday life's egalitarianism.

Yet, for most men, the most acceptable, stable, long-term solution is to *renegotiate the heterosexual family contract*. This includes domestic work sharing, economic partnership, sexual partnership, and, above everything else, *full sharing of parenting*. This latter condition is critical for men because only under such circumstances can the "Chodorow effect" be altered, and women could be produced not only as mothers, but as men-desiring women, and men could be raised not just as women-lovers, but as children's fathers. Indeed, unless this mechanism is reversed, the simple reform of economic and power arrangements in the family cannot last as a satisfactory condition for men because, as they are still yearning for *the* woman as *their* exclusive love object, and they are decreasingly needed by women, their conditional surrender in the reformed nuclear family is structurally filled with resentment. Thus, beyond individual bargaining in the reformed family, the future possibility for reconstructing viable heterosexual families lies in the subversion of gender through the revolution of parenting, as Chodorow suggested in the first place. Without going into another round of statistical detail, let me just say that, while

---

152 The *pea* is a medieval Spanish institution, originally for men only, and still male dominated, which brought/brings together the youth of the village or neighborhood around the preparation of the annual religious/folk festivity of the village. It serves as a socializing network for drinking and enjoying together the annual round, as in the most famous *peas*, those of Pamplona's San Fermines. The word *pea* means solid rock. The *peas* are the rocks of male bonding.

considerable progress has been made in this direction,[153] egalitarian parenting has still a long way to go, and its growth is slower than the rise of separatism for both men and women.

The main victims of this cultural transition are children, as they have become increasingly neglected under current conditions of family crisis. Their situation may even worsen, either because women stay with their children under difficult material conditions, or because women, looking for autonomy and personal survival, begin to neglect their children the way men do. Since support from the welfare state is dwindling, men and women are left to themselves in handling their children's problems, while losing control over their lives. The dramatic increase in child abuse in many societies, particularly in the United States, could well be an expression of people's bewilderment concerning their family life. By saying so, I am certainly not espousing the neo-conservative argument that blames feminism, or sexual liberation, for the plight of children. I am pinpointing a fundamental issue in our society that must be addressed without ideological prejudice: children are being massively neglected, as documented by social scientists and journalists.[154] The solution is not an impossible return to an obsolete, and oppressive, patriarchal family. The reconstruction of the family under egalitarian relations, and the responsibility of public institutions in securing material and psychological support for children, are possible ways to alter the course toward mass destruction of the human psyche that is implicit in the currently unsettling life of millions of children.

Body identity: the (re)construction of sexuality

There is a sexual revolution in the making, but not the one announced, and sought, by the 1960s/1970s' social movements, although they have been important factors in inducing the really existing sexual revolution. *It is characterized by the de-linking of marriage, family, heterosexuality, and sexual expression* (or desire, as I call it). These four factors, linked under modern patriarchalism for the past two centuries, are now in the process of autonomization, as a number of observations reported in this chapter seem to show. As Giddens writes:

> Heterosexual marriage superficially appears to retain its central position in the social order. In reality, it has been largely undermined by the

153   Shapiro et al. (1995).
154   Susser (1996).

rise of the pure relationship and plastic sexuality. If orthodox marriage is not yet widely seen as just one life-style among others, as in fact it has become, this is partly the result of the complicated mixture of attraction and repulsion which the psychic development of each sex creates with regard to the other... Some marriages may still be contracted, or sustained, mainly for the sake of producing, or bringing up, children. Yet... most heterosexual marriages (and many homosexual liaisons) which do not approximate to the pure relationship are likely to evolve in two directions if they do not lapse into codependence. One is a version of a companionate marriage. The level of sexual involvement of the spouses with each other is low, but some degree of equality and mutual sympathy is built into the relationship.... The other form is where marriage is used as a home base for both partners who have only a slight emotional investment in one another.[155]

In both cases, sexuality is de-linked from marriage. This was indeed the case for most women throughout history,[156] but the affirmation of women's sexuality, of homosexuality for both men and women, and of elective sexuality, are inducing an increasing distance between people's desire and their families. However, this does not translate into sexual liberation, but, for the majority of the population, scared by the consequences of infidelity (for which men now also have to pay), and, in the 1980s and 1990s, by the AIDS epidemic, the consequence is sexual poverty, if not misery. This is at least what can be inferred from the comprehensive, empirical survey of sexual behavior in America, conducted in 1992 on a representative national sample.[157] Some 35.5 percent of men reported having sex a few times a month, and another 27.4 percent a few times a year or not at all. For women, respective percentages were 37.2 percent and 29.7 percent. Only 7.7 percent of men and 6.7 percent of women reported having sex four or more times per week, and even in the 18–24 age group (the most sexually active), the percentage of high frequency was 12.4 percent both for men and women. High activity rates (over four times a week) are slightly lower for married couples than for the population at large (7.3 percent for men, 6.6 percent for women). These data also confirm the gender gap in reported orgasms: 75 percent of sexual encounters for men, only 29 percent for women, although the gap is narrower in reporting "pleasure."[158] The number of sex partners in the last 12 months shows a limited range of sexual partnerships for the overwhelming majority

155   Giddens (1992: 154–5).
156   Buss (1994).
157   Laumann et al. (1994).
158   Laumann et al. (1994: 116).

of the population: 66.7 percent of men and 74.7 percent of women had only one partner; and 9.9 percent and 13.6 percent respectively, had none. So, there was no widespread sexual revolution in America in the early 1990s.

Yet, beneath the surface of sexual tranquility, the rich database of this University of Chicago study reveals trends toward an increasing autonomy of sexual expression, particularly among the younger age groups. For instance, there has been a steady decrease over the past four decades in the age of first intercourse: in spite of AIDS, teenagers are more sexually active than ever. Secondly, cohabitation before marriage has become the norm rather than the exception. Adults increasingly tend to form sexual partnerships outside marriage. About half of these cohabitations end within a year, 40 percent of them being transformed into marriages, 50 percent of which will end up in divorce, two-thirds of which will end up in remarriage, whose likelihood of divorce is even greater than the average for all marriages. It is this drying up of desire by successive efforts to link it up to living arrangements that seems to characterize turn-of-millennium America.

On the other hand, "consumerist sexuality" appears on the rise, although the indications here are rather indirect. Laumann et al. analyze their sample in terms of sexual normative orientations following the classic distinction between traditional sexuality (procreational), relational (companionship), and recreational (oriented toward sexual enjoyment). They also isolate a "libertarian-recreational" type that seems closer to the images of pop-sexual liberation or, in Giddens's terms, "plastic sexuality." When analyzing their sample by major regions in America, they found that 25.5 percent of their sample in New England, and 22.2 percent in the Pacific region, could be included under such a "libertarian-recreational" category: this is about one-quarter of the population in some of the most culturally trend-setting areas of America.

A meaningful indicator of increasing sexual autonomy, as a pleasure-oriented activity, is the practice of oral sex which, I remind you, is catalogued as sodomy, and explicitly prohibited by law in 24 American states, albeit under conditions of doubtful enforcement. Figure 4.14 displays the occurrence of oral sex by cohort, by which is meant the percentages of women and men who have experienced either cunnilingus or fellatio in their lifetime by birth cohort. Laumann et al., commenting on these findings, assert that:

> The overall trend reveals what we might call a rapid change in sexual techniques if not a revolution. The difference in lifetime experience of

Men

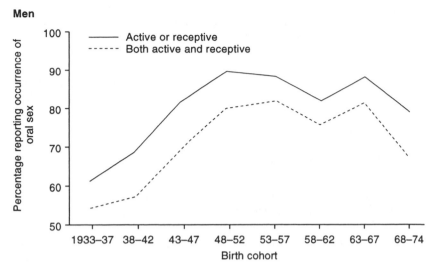

Women

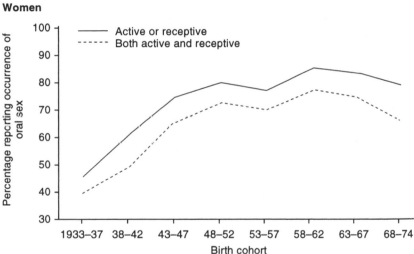

Figure 4.14 Lifetime occurrence of oral sex, by cohort: men and
women
Source: Laumann et al. (1994)

oral sex between respondents born between 1933 and 1942 and those
born after 1943 is dramatic. The proportion of men experiencing oral
sex in their lifetime increases from 62 percent of those born between
1933–37 to 90 percent of those born between 1948–52 ... The timing of
sexual techniques appears to have been responsive to cultural changes in
the late 1950s, changes that peaked in the mid to late 1960s, *when they*

approached saturation level of the population. The lower rates among the youngest groups in our survey are not necessarily evidence of decline in oral sex; these groups simply have not yet engaged in sexual relationships in which oral sex has become likely if not normative.[159]

Incidentally, between 75 and 80 percent of women in the latest cohorts also experienced oral sex, and in the younger groups their occurrence is higher than for men. Laumann et al. also report widespread incidence of auto-eroticism (associated with high levels of partnered sexual activity), and of masturbation, hardly a novel technique, but that seems to involve two-thirds of men, and over 40 percent of women.

Thus, if instead of reading sexual behavior under the norm of heterosexual, repetitive partnership, we take a more "perverse" approach to it, the data reveal a different story, a story of consumerism, experimentation, and eroticism in the process of deserting conjugal bedrooms, and still searching for new modes of expression, while watching out for AIDS. Since these new patterns of behavior are more visible among younger groups, and in trend-setting cities, I feel safe to predict that, if, when, and where the AIDS epidemic comes under control, there will be one, two, three, many Sodoms, emerging from fantasies freed by the crisis of patriarchalism, and excited by the culture of narcissism. Under such conditions, as Giddens proposes, sexuality becomes the property of the individual.[160] Where Foucault saw the extension of apparatuses of power into the sexually constructed/construed subject, Giddens sees, and I concur, the fight between power and identity in the battleground of the body.[161] It is not necessarily a liberating struggle, because desire often emerges from transgression, so that a "sexually liberated society" becomes simply a supermarket of personal fantasies, in which individuals will consume each other rather than produce themselves. However, by assuming the body as identity principle, away from the institutions of patriarchalism, the multiplicity of sexual expressions empowers the individual in the arduous (re)construction of her/his personality.[162]

159   Laumann et al. (1994: 103–4); my italics.
160   Giddens (1992: 175).
161   Giddens (1992: 31).
162   Grosz (1995).

Flexible personalities in a post-patriarchal world

New generations are being socialized out of the traditional pattern of the patriarchal family, and are being exposed from an early age to the need to cope with different settings, and different adult roles. In sociological terms, the new process of socialization downplays to some extent the institutional norms of the patriarchal family and diversifies the roles within the family. In their insightful exploration of this matter, Hage and Powers propose that, as an outcome of such processes, new personalities emerge, more complex, less secure, yet more capable of adapting to changing roles in social contexts, as adaptive mechanisms are triggered by new experiences at an early age.[163] The increasing individualization of relationships within the family tends to emphasize the importance of personal demands beyond the rules of institutions. Thus, sexuality becomes, at the level of social values, a personal need that does not necessarily have to be channeled and institutionalized within the family. With the majority of the adult population, and one-third of children, living outside the boundaries of the traditional nuclear family, and with both proportions growing, the construction of desire increasingly operates on interpersonal relationships outside the lineage of trad-itional family context: it becomes an expression of the self. The socialization of teenagers under these new cultural patterns leads to a higher degree of sexual freedom than that of previous generations, including those in the liberated sixties, in spite of the menace of the AIDS epidemic.

Thus, the revolt of women against their condition, induced and allowed by their massive entry into the informational labor force, and the social movements of sexual identity have called into question the patriarchal nuclear family. This crisis has taken the form of a growing separation between the different dimensions that were previously held together in the same institution: interpersonal relationships between the two members of the couple; the working life of each member of the household; the economic association between members of the household; the performance of domestic work; the raising of children; sexuality; emotional support. The difficulty of coping with all these roles at the same time, once they are not fixed any longer in a formal, institutionalized structure, such as the patriarchal family, explains the difficulty of maintaining stable social relationships within the

163   Hage and Powers (1992).

family-based household. For families to survive, new institutionalized forms of social relationships, in accordance with transformed relationships between genders, will have to emerge.

At the same time, technological change in biological reproduction has allowed the possibility of disassociating the reproduction of the species from the social and personal functions of the family. The possibilities of *in vitro* fertilization, of sperm banks, of surrogate mothers, of genetically engineered babies, open up a whole area of social experimentation that society will try to control and repress as much as possible because of its potential threat to our moral and legal foundations. Yet, the fact that women can have children on their own without having to even know the father, or that men, even after their death, can use surrogate mothers to have their children, severs the fundamental relationship between biology and society in the reproduction of the human species, thus separating socialization from parenting. Under these historical conditions, families, and people's living arrangements, are being redefined in terms still unclear.

Because family and sexuality are fundamental determinants of personality systems, the calling into question of known family structures, and the coming into the open of personally projected sexuality, bring about the possibility of new types of personality that we are just beginning to perceive. Hage and Powers consider that the key ability to respond to current changes in society at the individual level is the ability to engage in "role redefinition," what they consider to be the "pivotal micro-process of postindustrial society."[164] While I concur with this most insightful analysis, I will add a complementary hypothesis to understand emerging personality systems. Daring to remain loyal to my psychoanalytical inclination, I would advance the idea that the open recognition of individual desire, as insinuated in the emerging culture of our society, would lead to such an aberration as the institutionalization of desire. Because desire is often associated with transgression, the recognition of sexuality outside the family would lead to extreme social strain. This is because as long as transgression consisted merely in expressing sexuality outside the family boundaries, society could easily cope with it, by channeling it through coded situations and organized contexts, such as prostitution, earmarked homosexuality, or condoned sexual harassment: this was Foucault's world of sexuality as normalization. Things are different now. If the patriarchal family is not there to be betrayed any longer, the transgression will have to be an individual act against society. The bumper

164   Hage and Powers (1992).

function of the family is lost. This opens the way to the expression of desire in the form of non-instrumental violence. As welcome as it can be as a liberating development, the breakdown of the patriarchal family (the only one existing historically) is indeed giving way simultaneously to the normalization of sexuality (porno movies in prime-time television), and to the spread of senseless violence in society through the back alleys of wild desire, that is, perversion.

Liberation from the family confronts the self with its own inflicted oppression. The escape to freedom in the open, networked society will lead to individual anxiety and social violence, until new forms of coexistence and shared responsibility are found that bring together women, men, and children in a reconstructed, egalitarian family better suited to free women, informed children, and uncertain men.

The End of Patriarchalism?

The continuing struggles in and around patriarchalism do not allow a clear forecasting of the historical horizon. Let me again repeat that there is no predetermined directionality in history. We are not marching through the triumphant avenues of our liberation, and, when we feel so, we had better watch out to see where these shining paths ultimately lead. Life muddles through life and, as we know, is full of surprises. A fundamentalist restoration, bringing patriarchalism back under the protection of divine law, may well reverse the process of the undermining of the patriarchal family, unwillingly induced by informational capitalism, and willingly pursued by cultural social movements. The homophobic backlash may undo the recognition of homosexual rights, as shown by the overwhelming vote by the US Congress in July 1996 to declare heterosexuality a requisite for legal marriage. And, around the world, patriarchalism is still alive and well, in spite of the symptoms of crisis that I have tried to emphasize in this chapter. However, the very vehemence of the reactions in defense of patriarchalism, as in the religious fundamentalist movements thriving in many countries, is a sign of the intensity of the anti-patriarchal challenges. Values that were supposed to be eternal, natural, indeed divine, must now be asserted by force, thus retrenching in their last defensive bastion, and losing legitimacy in people's minds.

The ability or inability of feminist and sexual identity social movements to institutionalize their values will essentially depend on their relationship to the state, the last resort apparatus of patriarchalism throughout history. However, the extraordinary demands placed upon the state by social movements, attacking institutions of domination at their root, emerge at the very moment when the state seems to be itself in the midst of a structural crisis, brought about by the contradiction between the globalization of its future and the identification of its past.

5

Globalization, Identification, and the State: A Powerless State or a Network State?

"What is specific to the capitalist state," wrote Nicos Poulantzas in 1978, "is that it absorbs social time and space, sets up the matrices of time and space, and monopolizes the organization of time and space that become, by the action of the state, networks of domination and power. This is how the modern nation is the product of the state."[1] Not any longer. State control over space and time is increasingly bypassed by global flows of capital, goods, services, technology, communication, and information. The state's capture of historical time through its appropriation of tradition and the (re)construction of national identity is challenged by plural identities as defined by autonomous subjects. The state's attempt to reassert its power in the global arena by developing supranational institutions further undermines its sovereignty. And the state's effort to restore legitimacy by decentralizing administrative power to regional and local levels reinforces centrifugal tendencies by bringing citizens closer to government but increasing their aloofness toward the nation-state. Thus, while global capitalism thrives, and nationalist ideologies explode all over the world, the nation-state, as historically created in the modern age, seems to be losing power, although, and this is essential, *not its influence*.[2] In this chapter

1 Poulantzas (1978: 109); my translation.
2 Tilly (1975); Giddens (1985); Held (1991, 1993); Sklair (1991); Camilleri and Falk (1992); Guehenno (1993); Horsman and Marshall (1994); Touraine (1994); Calderon et al. (1996); Habermas (1998); Nye and Donahue (2000); Keohane (2002); Calderon (2003).

I shall explain why, and elaborate on the potential consequences of this fundamental development.

The growing challenge to state sovereignty around the world seems to originate in the inability of the modern nation-state to navigate the uncharted, stormy waters between the power of global networks and the challenge of singular identities.[3] However, the very existence of these challenges has triggered a number of strategic responses from the nation-state. These responses are shaped by the power relationships existing in and around political institutions. Thus, what we observe in the early years of the twenty-first century is simultaneously the crisis of the nation-state of the modern age and the return of the state under new organizational forms, new procedures of power-making, and new principles of legitimacy. This is the argument that will be presented in this chapter.

Globalization and the State

The instrumental capacity of the nation-state is decisively undermined by the globalization of core economic activities, by the globalization of media and electronic communication, by the globalization of crime, by the globalization of social protest, and by the globalization of insurgency in the form of transborder terrorism.[4] I have analyzed social protests and violent insurgency against globalization in the

3   The analysis of the crisis of the nation-state presupposes a definition, and a theory, of the nation-state. But since my work in this matter builds on already developed sociological theories, from various sources, I will refer the reader to the definition of Anthony Giddens in *The Nation-state and Violence* (1985: 121): "The nation-state, which exists in a complex of other nation-states, is a set of institutional forms of governance, maintaining an administrative monopoly over a territory with demarcated boundaries (borders), its rule being sanctioned by law, and direct control of the means of internal and external violence." Yet, as Giddens writes, "only in modern nation-states can the state apparatus generally lay successful claim to the monopoly of the means of violence, and only in such states does the administrative scope of the state apparatus correspond directly with territorial boundaries about which that claim is made" (p. 18). Indeed, as he argues, "a nation-state is a bordered power-container, the pre-eminent power-container of the modern era" (p. 120). So, what happens, and how should we conceptualize that state, when borders break down, and when containers are becoming contained themselves? My investigation starts, in theoretical continuity, from where the nation-state, as conceptualized by Giddens, appears to be superseded by historical transformation.

4   For a definition and an analysis of globalization, as I understand it, see volume I, chapter 2. For a salutary critique of simplistic views on globalization, see Hirst and Thompson (1996). It has been often argued that globalization is not a new phenomenon, and has occurred in different historical periods, particularly with the expansion of capitalism at the end of the nineteenth century. It may be so, although I am not convinced that the new infrastructure based on information technology does not introduce a qualitative social and economic change, by enabling global processes to operate in real time. But I have no real quarrel with this argument: it does not concern my inquiry. I am trying to analyze, and explain, our society at the turn of the millennium, in its variety of cultural, economic, and political contexts. So, my intellectual contribution should

preceding chapters. Here I will focus on other global challenges to the nation-state.

The transnational core of national economies

The interdependence of financial markets and currency markets around the world, operating as a unit in real time, links up national currencies. The constant exchange between dollars, yens, and euros forces systemic coordination between these currencies, as the only measure able to keep some degree of stability in the currency market, and thus in global investment and trade. All other currencies in the world have become linked, for all practical purposes, to this triangle of wealth. If the exchange rate is systemically interdependent, so are, or will be, monetary policies. And if monetary policies are somehow harmonized at a supranational level, so are, or will be, prime interest rates, and, ultimately, budgetary policies. It follows that individual nation-states are losing and will lose control over fundamental elements of their economic policies.[5] In fact, this was already the experience of developing countries in the 1980s, and of European countries during the early 1990s. Barbara Stallings has shown how economic policies in developing countries were shaped during the 1980s by international pressures, as international financial institutions and private banks moved to stabilize developing economies as a prerequisite to international investment and trade.[6] In the European Union, the European Central Bank determines monetary policy and prime interest rates, so that the budgetary autonomy of nation-states is limited to the allocation of their resources between different items of the budget within the parameters of macroeconomic equilibrium imposed by the independent monetary authority and monitored by the European Commission. The UK and Sweden, even though they still have their own currency, are in fact dependent on the overall monetary policy of

---

be discussed on its own ground, concerning contemporary processes as observed and theorized in the three volumes of this work. Undoubtedly, scholarly thinking would greatly benefit from comparative historical study, contrasting current processes of interaction between technology, the globalization of the economy and communications, politics, and political institutions with past experience of a similar transformation. I am hopeful that such an effort will be undertaken by colleagues, primarily by historians, and I will be more than happy to rectify my general theoretical statements on the basis of the implications of such research. For the time being, the few attempts I have seen in this direction pay insufficient attention, in my opinion, to the radically new processes in technology, finance, production, communications, and politics, so that while they may be right on the historical record, it is unclear why the present is just a repetition of past experience, beyond the rather pedestrian view that there is nothing new under the sun.

5   Moreau Deffarges (1993); Orstrom Moller (1995); Cohen (1996); Frankel (2000); Aglietta (2002); Wyplosz (2002).
6   Stallings (1992).

the European Union, and their joining of the euro zone is simply a matter of political timing.

Japanese economic policy is essentially determined by the relationship between the trade balance and the exchange rate with the United States. As for the United States, the most self-sufficient economy, it could only remain so in spite of a substantial trade deficit from the 1980s by financing increased government spending through borrowing, to a large extent from foreign capital. While fast growth of the new economy in the 1990s transformed the substantial budget deficit that followed this borrowing into a budget surplus under Clinton, in 2002–3 the situation changed. The economic downturn, the military and security effort, and the tax breaks of a conservative administration induced a new budgetary imbalance, making America again directly dependent on borrowing capital to offset its twin deficits in foreign trade and the federal budget. It can be argued that the degree of freedom of US governments' economic policy has been drastically reduced since the 1990s, with their budget policy caught between automatic entitlements inherited from the past and high capital mobility experienced in the present, and probably increasing in the future.[7]

Furthermore, global financial markets are largely out of the control of any individual government, including the United States. Financial valuation of currencies and securities in these global markets is influenced by information turbulences of various origins, interacting in the global networks of information and valuation, as I documented in volume I, chapter 2. Therefore, national economic policies become highly constrained by loosely regulated, barely controlled financial markets, thus curtailing governments' autonomy in economic policy.[8]

The growing difficulty of government control over the economy is accentuated by the transnationalization of production, not just under the impact of multinational corporations, but mainly through the production and trade networks in which these corporations are integrated.[9] There follows a declining capacity of governments to ensure, in their territories, the productive basis for generating revenue. As companies and wealthy individuals alike find fiscal havens around the world, and as accounting of value added in an international production system becomes increasingly cumbersome, a new fiscal crisis of the state arises, as the expression of a contradiction between the internationalization of investment, production, and consumption, on the one hand, and the national basis of taxation

7   Chesnais (1994); Nunnenkamp et al. (1994).
8   Hutton and Giddens (2000).
9   Buckley (1994).

systems, on the other.[10] Is it an accident that the two wealthiest countries in the world, in *per capita* terms, are Luxembourg and Switzerland? It may well be that one of the last stands of the nation-state is being fought in cyber-accounting space, between dutiful tax inspectors and sophisticated transnational lawyers.

A statistical appraisal of the new fiscal crisis of the state in the global economy

At this point in the analysis, it may be helpful to look at the evolution of government finances in the period of stepped-up globalization of national economies between 1980 and the early 1990s. To limit the complexity of the analysis, I have selected six countries: the three largest market economies (US, Japan, Germany); the most open of the large European economies (the UK); another European country, Spain, which, while being the eighth largest market economy in the world, is at a lower level of economic/technological development than the G-8 countries; and one major economy of the newly industrialized world, India. On the basis of statistics compiled and elaborated by Sandra Moog, tables 5.1 and 5.2 have been constructed to provide an overview of some indicators of government finance and economic activity, related to the process of the internationalization of economies. I will not comment in detail. Rather, I will use these tables to expand and specify the argument on globalization and the state as presented in the preceding pages.

Let us first examine the group of four countries (US, UK, Germany, and Spain) that seem to behave, in very broad terms, along similar lines, albeit with differences that I shall emphasize. Government expenditures increased for the period under consideration to reach a level between one-quarter and more than 40 percent of GDP. Government jobs decreased everywhere. The share of government consumption decreased in the three major countries, while increasing in Spain. The share of government capital formation increased in the US and declined in Germany. Central government's tax revenue decreased in the US, while increasing in the other countries, substantially in Spain. Government deficit increased, and substantially so in the US and Germany. Government debt decreased in the UK, although it still represented about 34 percent of GDP, and dramatically increased in Spain, Germany, and the US, where in 1992 it represented 52.2 percent of GDP. The financing of government deficits led the four countries to increase, in some cases substantially, dependency on

10   Guehenno (1993).

Table 5.1 Internationalization of the economy and public finance: rates of change, 1980–93 (and 1993 ratios, unless otherwise indicated)

	United States	United Kingdom	Germany	Japan	Spain	India
Gov. foreign debt/GDP %	104.2 (9.8)	31.8 (5.8/1992)	538.5 (16.6)	0.0 (0.3/1991)	1,066.7 (10.5)	−25.3 (5.9)
Gov. foreign debt/currency reserves %	20.1 (998.6)	44.7 (168.1/1992)	325.3 (p) (368.4) (p)	9.9 (12.2/1991)	674.5 (121.6)	−16.5 (149.4)
Gov. foreign debt/exports %	133.0 (134.0)	50.5 (32.2/1992)	590.8 (75.3)	9.5 (2.3/1990)	795.5 (79.7)	−55.6 (70.7)
Gov. foreign debt/gov. expenditures %	92.2 (41.7)	17.4 (13.5/1992)	423.5 (p) (44.5) (p)	—	586.8 (36.4)	−40.7 (35.4)
Gov. net foreign borrowing/gov. expenditures %	203.0 (6.12)	787.5 (14.2/1992)	223.4 (15.2)	—	—	10.3 (4.3)
Direct foreign investment abroad/domestic investment %	52.8 (5.5)	44.4 (17.9)	52.2 (3.5)	57.1 (1.1)	183.3 (2.8)	—
Inflow of direct foreign investment/domestic investment %	−35.5 (2.0)	−8.9 (10.2)	−50.0 (0.1)	—	236.7 (8.6)	—

(p) indicates preliminary data.

Note: For figures and details about sources and methods of calculation, please see the Methodological Appendix.

Sources: Compiled and elaborated by Sandra Moog from the following sources: *Government Finance Statistics Yearbook*, vol. 18 (Washington DC: IMF, 1994); *International Financial Statistics Yearbook*, vol. 48 (Washington DC: IMF, 1995); *The Europa World Yearbook* (London: Europa Publications, 1982, 1985, 1995); *National Accounts: Detailed Tables, 1980–1992*, vol. 2 (Paris: OECD, 1994); *OECD Economic Outlook*, vol. 58 (Paris: OECD, 1995); *World Tables, 1994* (The World Bank, Baltimore: The Johns Hopkins University Press, 1994)

Table 5.2 Government role in the economy and public finance: rates of change, 1980–92 (and 1992 ratios, unless otherwise indicated)

	United States	United Kingdom	Germany	Japan	Spain	India
Gov. expenditures/GDP %	9.1 (24.0)	13.1 (43.2)	19.7 (36.4)	—	49.4 (25.1)	29.3 (p) (17.2) (p)
Budgetary central gov. tax revenue/GDP %	−15.6 (10.8)	8.0 (27.0)	11.6 (p) (13.5) (p)	18.2 (13.0/1990)	64.2 (17.4/1991)	17.3 (p) (11.2) (p)
Gov. budget deficit/GDP %	42.9 (4.0)	8.7 (5.0)	44.4 (2.6)	−78.6 (1.5/1990)	16.2 (4.3)	−20.0 (p) (5.2) (p)
Gov. debt/GDP %	91.9 (52.2)	−26.0 (34.1)	78.1 (28.5)	30.1 (53.2/1990)	160.8 (39.9)	28.2 (p) (52.8) (p)
Gov. employment/total employment %	−4.7 (16.2)	−3.1 (22.2)	−0.6 (16.4)	−20.9 (7.2)	—	—
Gov. capital formation/gross fixed capital formation %	21.2 (16.0)	—	−7.0 (27.9)	—	—	—
Gov. consumption/private consumption %	−6.9 (27.2)	−2.7 (34.5)	−8.1 (32.7)	66.3 (16.3)	33.8 (26.9)	40.2 (18.5)

(p) indicates preliminary data.

Note: For figures and details about sources and methods of calculation, please see the Methodological Appendix.

Sources: Compiled and elaborated by Sandra Moog from the following sources: *Government Finance Statistics Yearbook*, vol. 18 (Washington DC: IMF, 1994); *International Financial Statistics Yearbook*, vol. 48 (Washington DC: IMF, 1995); *The Europa World Yearbook* (London: Europa Publications, 1982, 1985, 1995); *National Accounts: Detailed Tables, 1980–1992*, vol. 2 (Paris: OECD, 1994); *OECD Economic Outlook*, vol. 58 (Paris: OECD, 1995); *World Tables, 1994* (The World Bank, Baltimore: The Johns Hopkins University Press, 1994)

foreign debt and foreign net lending. The ratios of government foreign debt and government net borrowing on GDP, central banks' currency reserves, government expenditures, and countries' exports show, in general terms, *the increasing dependence of governments on global capital markets for the period under consideration.* Thus, for the United States, between 1980 and 1993, government foreign debt as a percentage of GDP more than doubled; as a percentage of currency reserves, it increased by 20 percent and, in 1993, represented almost ten times the level of total currency reserves; as a percentage of exports, it increased by 133 percent; and as a percentage of government expenditures, it almost doubled, to reach a level of 41.7 percent of total expenditures. As for the US government's net foreign borrowing, it grew in these 14 years by a staggering 456 percent, increasing by 203 percent its ratio to government expenditure, to reach a level equivalent to 6 percent of government expenditure. Since US direct foreign investment abroad, as a proportion of domestic investment, increased by 52.8 percent, while inflow of direct foreign investment, also as a proportion of US domestic investment, decreased by 35.5 percent, it can be argued that the US federal government became largely dependent on global capital markets and foreign lending.

The story is somewhat different for the UK, Germany, and Spain, but trends are similar. It is important to notice that, while the UK seems to be less dependent, Germany increased its dependency on foreign capital much faster than the US, as shown by several indicators: government foreign debt over GDP (538.5 percent increase), over currency reserves (325.3 percent increase), and over exports (590.8 percent increase). The German government's net foreign borrowing in 1993 reached a level representing over 15 percent of government expenditure, and its foreign debt is the equivalent of 44.5 percent of government expenditure, in both cases a higher percentage than those for the US. Thus, in spite of a strong export performance in the 1980s, Germany, unlike Japan, substantially increased the international dependence of its national state.

Interestingly enough, India, while increasing government expenditure, consumption, and indebtedness, seems to be much less dependent on foreign debt: indeed, all its indicators of financial dependency show negative growth for the period, with the exception of the ratio of government foreign borrowing on government expenditure, still kept at a modest level. A sizable increase in the share of tax revenue in GDP is only part of the explanation, the main one being the substantial acceleration of economic growth in India during these years. I should emphasize, however, that while the rate of change of indicators of the government's financial dependency in India has been negative over the period, the level of dependency remained very high (government foreign debt represented over 70 percent of exports, and almost 150 percent of currency reserves).

As is often the case, Japan is different. The Japanese government was not affected by foreign borrowing during the 1980s. Its budget deficit over GDP was by far the lowest, and it substantially declined during the period 1980–93. On the other hand, government consumption increased, government debt also increased, and Japan was as high as America in the ratio of government debt to GDP (over 50 percent). These observations indicate that the Japanese government's finances relied, rather, on domestic borrowing. This also reflected the greater competitiveness of the Japanese economy at that time, and the considerable trade and balance of payments surplus accumulated by the country in the 1980s. So, the Japanese state is much more autonomous than other states *vis-à-vis* the rest of the world, but the Japanese economy is much more dependent on trade performance, since Japanese capital finances its government with the proceeds of its competitiveness. So, what appears to be an exception to the rule of government dependency, and increasing government deficit, is not. Japanese corporations took on the world economy, and their competitiveness financed the state, whose consumption grew much faster than in any other of the countries studied. The Japanese state displays a second-order financial dependency on the movements of the international economy, via its borrowing from Japanese banks financed by their *keiretsu*.

Three major trends can be underlined with regard to the arguments presented in this chapter:

1   In spite of a particular state's disengagement in the economy, particularly in terms of direct employment and regulation, there is a substantial economic role for the state that requires additional financing besides taxation, thus increasing the financial liability of the state, with the exception of the UK (see figure 5.1).
2   Government borrowing, with the major exception of Japan, is increasingly dependent on foreign lending, to an extent that already overwhelms central banks' currency reserves, and overshadows export performance. This reflects the broader phenomenon of an increasing gap between the faster growth of global financial markets in relation to the growth of global trade.
3   The Japanese state succeeded for some time in establishing a measure of fiscal autonomy *vis-à-vis* foreign capital. However, it did so on the basis of domestic borrowing, financed with Japanese

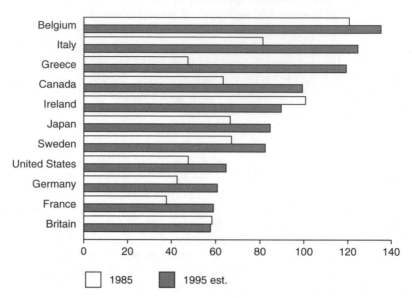

Figure 5.1   General government gross financial liabilities (% of GDP)
Source: OECD, elaborated by *The Economist* (January 20, 1996)

corporations' earnings from protectionism and export performance; so that the Japanese economy, and the Japanese state, have
become addicted to trade surpluses and the recycling of profits on
Japanese soil. This state of affairs led to the Japanese "bubble
economy" of the late 1980s, and, subsequently, when the bubble
burst, to the recession of the early 1990s, and to the stagnation of
the 1990s

Overall, the intertwining of national economies, and the dependency
of government finance on global markets and foreign lending, have
created the conditions for an international fiscal crisis of the nation-
state, including the wealthiest and most powerful nation-states.

Globalization and the welfare state

The globalization of production and investment also threatens the
welfare state, a key element in the policies of the nation-state in the
past half-century, and probably the main building block of its legitimacy in industrialized countries.[11] This is because it becomes increasingly contradictory for firms to operate in globalized, integrated

11   Wilensky (1975); Janowitz (1976); Navarro (1994, 1995); Castells (1996).

markets, while experiencing major cost differentials in social benefits, as well as distinct levels of regulation between countries. This happens not only between North and South, but between different OECD countries, as well: for example, social benefits-related labor costs are much lower in the US than in Germany (see figure 5.2). But what is a comparative advantage of US location *vis-à-vis* Germany becomes a disadvantage *vis-à-vis* Mexico, after the implementation of the NAFTA Treaty. Since firms, because of information technology, can locate in many different sites and still link up to global production networks and markets (see volume I, chapter 6), there follows a downward spiral of social costs competition.

The limits to such "negative competitiveness" in the past have been twofold: on the one hand, the productivity and quality lag between countries protected workers from advanced economies *vis-à-vis* less-developed competitors; on the other hand, domestic pressure induced protectionism, so as to increase the price of imports, via tariffs, to a level where the comparative advantage of external sourcing would disappear. Both limits are withering away. The World Trade Organization is setting up a watch dog system to detect and penalize barriers to free trade. While the politics of international trade condition the actual impact of such controls, it would seem that, unless there is a

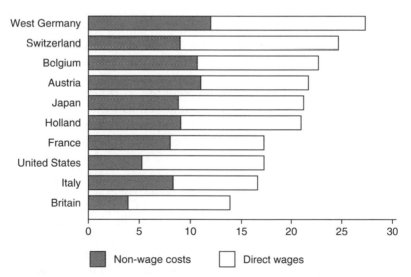

Figure 5.2 Labor costs in manufacturing, 1994 ($ per hour)
Source: Swedish Employers' Federation, elaborated by *The Economist* (January 27, 1996)

dramatic reversal in the process of global economic integration, blatant, large-scale protectionism could become increasingly subject to retaliation from other countries. As for the quality and productivity lag, Harley Shaiken's study of American automobile factories in Mexico has shown the rapid catch-up of Mexican workers' productivity, which equalled that of American workers in about 18 months. Similar processes have been observed in Asia.[12] And (Europeans should be reminded) American labor productivity is still the highest in the world, so canceling a potential European competitiveness differential that could still allow for a generous welfare state.

In an economy whose core markets for capital, goods, and services are increasingly integrated on a global scale, there seems to be little room for vastly different welfare states, with relatively similar levels of labor productivity and production quality. Only a global social contract (reducing the gap, without necessarily equalizing social and working conditions), linked to international tariff agreements, could avoid the demise of the most generous welfare states. Yet, because in the new liberalized, networked, global economy such a far-reaching social contract is unlikely, welfare states are being downsized to the lowest common denominator that keeps spiraling downwards.[13]

The crisis of the welfare state means that a fundamental component of the legitimacy and stability of the nation-state fades away, not only in Europe but throughout the world, from middle-class welfare states in Chile and Mexico to the remnants of statist welfare states in Russia, China, and India, or to the urban welfare state induced in the United States by the social struggles of the 1960s. As Habermas writes: "The economic problems of welfare societies can be explained on the grounds of a structural change in the world economic system which we call globalization. This change reduces the space of action of the nation-states so drastically that the possibilities of action left to them are not sufficient to withstand the undesirable impacts of transnational markets."[14]

There is, however, a somewhat more complex relationship between productivity, competitiveness, and the welfare state, emerging in the knowledge-based economy. As our study of the Finnish model of the information society shows, Finland was able, in the second half of the 1990s, to become the most competitive economy in the world and to increase its productivity faster than the United States, while preserving its comprehensive welfare state.[15] Furthermore, the

12   Shaiken (1990); Rodgers (1994).
13   Sengenberger and Campbell (1994); Navarro (1995, 2002); Castells (1996).
14   Habermas (1998/2000: 730); my translation.
15   Castells and Himanen (2002).

welfare state was a key factor in inducing productivity growth in Finland by providing the human resource base for the advanced knowledge economy, in terms of education, health, cultural development, innovation capacity, and social stability. However, Finland (as other countries in Europe, such as The Netherlands) proceeded to reform the welfare state, reducing some of its bureaucratic features. In addition, Finland, and other countries, made an agreement with the labor unions to increase flexibility in the labor market in exchange for the preservation of the safety net by the government. These countries also set up a connection between the welfare state and the economy by fostering higher education, and R&D investment, in close cooperation with business. Therefore, the Finnish welfare state of the twenty-first century is not exactly the traditional Scandinavian welfare state, but it retains the fundamental principle of comprehensive social protection for all citizens.

Thus, what we observe is the emergence of two sharply contrasting models: one, the American knowledge economy model, using the massive import of highly skilled labor (over 200,000 engineers and scientists per year in the 1990s) as a source of productivity and innovation; the other, the Finnish, and to some extent Northern European, model of investing in home-grown, human capital, and improving standards of living that strengthen the social sources of productivity in the new, knowledge-based economy. In both cases, what is clear is that the welfare state, in order to survive in a globalized, interdependent economy, needs to be connected to productivity growth to create a virtuous circle by a feedback loop between social investment and economic growth. On the other hand, the decline of human capital formation makes economies either non-competitive (because of lower productivity) or dependent on immigrant skilled labor.

In sum, if productivity increases in a given economy are small, its welfare state cannot sustain competitive pressures in the global context. It is only by raising productivity and the quality of production on the basis of knowledge and information processing that advanced economies can step up their competitiveness and afford higher standards of living. The specific forms of human capital formation to sustain the knowledge economy determine the model of development of each economy.[16] The more a society relies on mobility of capital and immigration to produce knowledge labor, the less the role of the state. On the other hand, reliance on the welfare state and strategic development policies aimed at increasing productivity and

16 Carnoy (2000).

competitiveness requires a more active role for the state. This is, however, a new form of state intervention that refers, on the one hand, to the link between the welfare of society and the generation of wealth in the economy, and, on the other hand, to the capacity of the state to position its economy in the global network of competition and cooperation. Therefore, the economic role of the state continues to be significant, but what emerges is a very different kind of welfare state, and a very different kind of competitive strategy, both based on the capacity to generate and apply knowledge and information, by using different means. The state survives by connecting the nation to the global context, and adjusting domestic policies to the imperatives of global competitive pressures. However, this adjustment proceeds along different lines of action, depending on the culture, institutions, and politics of each society.[17]

Thus, the nation-state is increasingly powerless in controlling monetary policy, deciding its budget, organizing production and trade, collecting its corporate taxes, and fulfilling its commitments to provide social benefits, unless it assures the competitiveness of its economy in the global context. It has lost most of its sovereign economic power, although it still has some regulatory capacity and relative control over its subjects. Yet it retains its capacity as a strategic actor to act upon the conditions that underlie the performance of its economy. This requires that the state becomes interdependent within a broader network of economic processes out of its control.

Global communication networks, local audiences, uncertain regulators

The prospects for national regulation and control are not much better in another decisive area of state power: media and communication. Control of information and entertainment, and, through them, of opinions and images has historically been the anchoring tool of state power, to be perfected in the age of mass media.[18] In this realm, the nation-state confronts three major, interrelated challenges: globalization and the interlocking of ownership; the flexibility and pervasiveness of technology; and the autonomy and diversity of the media (see volume I, chapter 5). In fact, it has already surrendered to them in most countries.[19]

---

17   Castells (2004).
18   Mattelart (1991).
19   Blumenfield (1994); Brenner (1994); Chong (1994); Graf (1995).

Until the early 1980s, with the major exception of the United States, most television in the world was government-controlled, and radios and newspapers were under the severe potential constraint of government good will, even in democratic countries. Even in the United States, the Federal Communications Commission exercised close control over electronic media, not always exempt from special interest biases,[20] and the three major television networks monopolized 90 percent of the audience, framing, if not shaping, public opinion. Everything changed in a decade.[21] The change was technology-driven. The diversification of communication modes, the link-up of all media in a digital hypertext, opening the way for interactive multimedia, and the inability to control satellites beaming across borders or computer-mediated communication over the telephone line, blew up the traditional lines of regulatory defense. The explosion of telecommunications, and the development of cable, provided the vehicles for unprecedented broadcasting power. Business saw the trend and seized the opportunity. Mega-mergers took place, and capital was mobilized around the world to take position in the media industry, an industry that could link up power in the economic, cultural, and political spheres.[22] Pressure was brought to bear on national governments during the 1980s under various forms:[23] public, or published, opinion, yearning for freedom and diversity in the media; buy-outs of national media in difficulty; syndication of columnists writing the apology of unfettered communication; promises of political complacency, if not support, to almost everyone in power or with the chance to be in the near future; and, not least, personal benefits for those officials who were consenting adults. Symbolic politics, assimilating the liberalization of the media to technological modernization, played a major role in tilting elite opinion in favor of the new media system.[24]

There is hardly any country, outside China, Singapore, and the Islamic fundamentalist world, in which the institutional and business structure of the media did not experience a dramatic turnaround between the mid-1980s and the mid-1990s.[25] Television and radio were privatized on a large scale, and those government networks that remained often became indistinguishable from private television since

20   Cohen (1986).
21   Doyle (1992); Irving et al. (1994); Negroponte (1995); Scott et al. (1995); Campo Vidal (1996); Norris (2000b).
22   MacDonald (1990); Volkmer (1999); Croteau and Hoynes (2001).
23   Gerbner et al. (1993); Campo Vidal (1996); Croteau and Hoynes (2000).
24   Vedel and Dutton (1990).
25   MacDonald (1990); Doyle (1992); Perez-Tabernero et al. (1993); Dentsu Institute for Human Studies (1994); Schiller (1999).

they were submitted to the discipline of audience ratings and/or advertising revenues.[26] Newspapers became concentrated in major consortiums, often with the backing of financial groups. And, most importantly, media business went global, with capital, talent, technology, and corporate ownership spinning all over the world, away from the reach of nation-states.

It does not entirely follow that states have no stake in the media. Governments still control important media, own stock, and have means of influence in a vast array of the media world. And business is careful not to antagonize the gatekeepers of potential markets: when Murdoch's Star Channel was chastised by the Chinese government for its liberal views on Chinese politics, Star obliged with newly found restraint, canceling the BBC's news service from the channel's Chinese programming, and investing in an on-line edition of the *People's Daily*. But, if governments still have influence over the media, they have lost much of their power, except for those media under the direct control of authoritarian states. Moreover, the media need to build their independence as a key ingredient of their credibility – not only *vis-à-vis* public opinion, but with regard to the plurality of power-holders and advertisers, since the advertising industry is the economic foundation of the media business. If a given medium becomes predominantly attached to an explicit political option or systematically represses certain kinds of information, it will restrict its audience to a relatively small segment, will hardly be able to make a profit in the marketplace, and will not appeal to the interests of a plurality of constituencies. On the other hand, the more a medium is independent, broad, and credible, the more it attracts information, sellers and buyers from a wide spectrum. Independence and professionalism are not only rewarding ideologies for the media: they translate into good business, including, sometimes, the possibility of selling this independence at a higher price when the occasion arises.

Once the media are acknowledged in their independence, once the nation-state acquiesces to this quality as an essential proof of its democratic character, the circle is closed: any attempt to curtail the media's liberty will become politically costly, since the citizenry, not necessarily picky concerning the accuracy of news, jealously defends the privilege of receiving information from sources that are not submitted to the state. This is why even authoritarian states are losing the battle over media in the information age. The ability of information, and images, to diffuse via satellite, video-cassette, and the Internet has dramatically expanded, so that news black-outs are increasingly

26   Perez-Tabernero et al. (1993).

ineffective in the main urban centers of authoritarian countries, precisely those places where the educated, alternative elites live.[27] Furthermore, since governments all over the world want also to "go global," and global media are their accessing tool, governments often enter into negotiation for two-way communication systems that, even when proceeding slowly and cautiously, ultimately undermine their hold on communication.

In a movement parallel to globalization of the media, there has also been, in many countries, thanks to new communication technologies, such as cost-sharing satellite transmission, an extraordinary growth of local media, particularly for radio and cable television.[28] Most of these local media, which often share programming, have established a strong connection to specific, popular audiences, bypassing the standardized views of the mass media. So doing, they escape the traditional channels of control (be it direct or indirect) that nation-states have set up *vis-à-vis* television networks and major newspapers. The growing political autonomy of local and regional media, using flexible communication technologies, is as important a trend as the globalization of the media in shaping public attitudes. Furthermore, the two trends converge in many instances, with global media corporations buying into niche markets, on the condition of accepting the specificity of audiences built around local and national media.[29] Besides, globalization of media communication does not necessarily mean cultural dominance by Western media, although this is generally the case in the early twenty-first century. The growing influence of Al Jazeera (the Arab-language, international television network created by the emirate of Qtar) illustrates the fact that all cultures and political interests seek to influence and shape information and public opinion in the world at large: this is the return flow from the local to the global. The new pattern of interaction between media and the state is characterized by the tension between globalization and identification, as demonstrated by Anshu Chatterjee in her doctoral dissertation on the customized globalization of Indian media in the 1990s.[30]

Computer-mediated communication is also escaping the control of the nation-state, ushering in a new era of extra-territorial communication.[31] Most governments seem to be terrified at the prospect. In January 1996, the French Minister of Information Technology

27 Ho and Zaheer (2000); Price (2002); Qiu and Chan (2003).
28 Croteau and Hoynes (2000).
29 Levin (1987); Abramson et al. (1988); Scheer (1994); Spragen (1995); Fallows (1996); Chatterjee (2002); Volkmer (2003).
30 Chatterjee (2002).
31 Kahn (1994); *Financial Technology International Bulletin* (1995); Kuttner (1995); Ubois (1995); Mansell (2002).

announced the intention of his government to propose to the European Union a series of measures to ban free access to the Internet. The event that prompted this scheme of technological censorship from the country that spurred revolutionary ideals of liberty in Europe, as well as Minitel, was Mitterrand's last battle. After his death, a book was published by his doctor revealing that Mitterrand had had prostate cancer for all the 14 years of his presidency. The book was banned in France, at the request of Mitterrand's family, but everybody could read it on the Net. The fury of the French government went far beyond this particular issue. There was a clear understanding that government's or court's decisions over information could no longer be implemented. And the control of information has been, long before the information age, the foundation of state power.[32] Similar initiatives came, around the same time, from the Chinese, German, and American governments, on a variety of issues ranging from financial and political information in China to child pornography in the United States.[33]

At the heart of the matter was the question of transborder information flows that make it difficult to prosecute the source of information even if it can be detected. It is still under debate whether it is technically possible to cut access to the Internet without shutting off a whole country from the network. It would seem that *ex post facto* censorship and penalties, and self-operated screening devices, are easier than the jamming of communication. But even if external screening measures become effective, they will shrink the network, thus undermining access to much useful information and diminishing the extent and scope of interactivity. Furthermore, to be able to shrink the Net selectively, all countries connected to it will have to agree on the topics they want to see banned, and then set up a joint monitoring system that will certainly be challenged as unconstitutional in democratic countries. Indeed, in the United States, in June 1996, a federal judicial panel in Pennsylvania declared unconstitutional most of the new federal law intended to regulate pornographic material diffused over the Net. In a forceful decision, the three judges wrote: "Just as the strength of the Internet is chaos, so the strength of our liberty depends upon the chaos and cacophony of the unfettered speech the First Amendment protects."[34] Thus, for the years to come, nation-states will be struggling to control information circulating in globally interconnected telecommunication networks. I bet it is a lost battle. And with this eventual defeat will come the loss of a corner-

32   Couch (1990).
33   Berman and Weitzner (1995); Faison (1996); Lewis (1996a).
34   Cited by Lewis (1996b).

stone of state power.[35] Altogether, the globalization/localization of media and electronic communication is tantamount to the de-nationalization and de-statization of information, the two trends being inseparable for the time being.

A lawless world?

The globalization of crime further subverts the nation-state, profoundly transforming processes of governance, and actually paralyzing the state in many instances. This is a crucial trend which is as easily acknowledged as promptly ignored in its consequences.[36] A whole chapter (in volume III, chapter 3) analyzes what is one of the most relevant trends of our world, and a distinctive one in respect of other periods, but it is necessary, at this point in the argument, to include such a critical trend in our understanding of the current crisis of the nation-state. What is new is not the pervasiveness of crime and its impact on politics. What is new is the global linkage of organized crime, its conditioning of international relations, both economic and political, because of the scale and dynamism of the criminal economy. What is new is the deep penetration, and eventual destabilization, of national states in a variety of contexts under the influence of transnational crime.

While drug traffic is the most significant industrial sector in the new criminal economy, all kinds of illicit traffics come together in this shadow system that extends its reach and power over the world: weapons, technology, radioactive materials, art treasures, human beings, human organs, killers for hire, and smuggling of every profitable item from anywhere to anywhere are connected through the mother of all crimes – money laundering. Without it, the criminal economy would neither be global nor very profitable. And, through money laundering, the criminal economy is connected to the global financial markets, of which it is a sizable component, and a relentless source of speculation. According to the United Nations Conference on the Global Criminal Economy held in Naples in October 1994,[37] a reasonable estimate would put the figure for capital from illegal sources being laundered in the global financial system at about US$ 750 billion a year. These capital flows need to be processed with greater mobility and flexibility than those originating from any

---

35   Castells (2001).
36   Arrieta et al. (1991); Roth and Frey (1992); Smith (1993); Lodato (1994); Sterling (1994); Golden (1995); Handelman (1995); Johnson (1995); WuDunn (1996); Gootenberg (1999).
37   United Nations, Economic and Social Council (1994).

other industry, since it is their constant swirling that makes them able to avoid tracking by law-enforcement agencies.

The impact of these trends on national states occurs along three main lines:

1   In many instances, the entire structure of the state, often including the highest levels of power, is penetrated by criminal networks, either through corruption, threats, or illegal political financing, thus creating havoc in the conduct of public affairs.

2   International relations between nation-states, in many countries, come to be dependent, in various degrees, on the handling or mishandling of cooperation in the fight against the criminal economy. The typical case until now has been that of relationships between the United States and some Latin American countries (Colombia, Bolivia, Mexico, Paraguay, Panama), but it is becoming a broader phenomenon, as the criminal economy diversifies (for instance, Germany's concern with Russian *Mafiya*-originated traffic in radioactive materials; or the Russian government's worries about the increasing involvement of the Sicilian Mafia and of Colombian cartels with the Russian *Mafiya*).

3   The growing importance of financial flows of criminal origin as a key element in stimulating or destabilizing entire national economies, so that economic policy cannot be properly conducted in many countries and areas without including into the picture this highly unpredictable factor.

It used to be that national governments deeply affected by the wheelings and dealings of the criminal economy were a handful of usual suspects, such as Italy or Colombia. Not any more. The importance of the phenomenon, its global reach, the size of its wealth and influence, and its entrenched connection with international finance, make criminal linkages to political corruption a frequent feature in major countries. For instance, the Japanese *Yakuza* has recently internationalized its connections. And the open, and less open, links of the *Yakuza* with Japanese government leaders are well known, to the point that the Ministry of Construction was considered, over a long period, to be the way to exchange government contracts in public works for generous contributions from *Yakuza*-sponsored businesses to the Liberal Democratic party – a system not too dissimilar to that of Italian Christian Democracy's *Mezzogiorno* development programs in relation to the Mafia. Or, when in 1996 a series of bank crises rocked Japan, resulting in unpaid loans for hundreds of billions of dollars, serious suspicions arose on the role of *Yakuza* in forcing bank managers to grant these loans, including the killing of two bankers.[38]

In another context, the suspected penetration of internationally connected Russian criminal organizations in various spheres of government of one of the world's most powerful states, including the armed forces, is a worrisome development. And the chain of political scandals that shook governments all over the world in the 1990s (a topic that I shall analyze in chapter 6) is not unrelated, in many instances, to the continuing power struggle between the structures of global crime and the structures of nation-states. Furthermore, even major governments, which think they are relatively immune to penetration by crime in their higher levels, do suffer the aftershocks of criminal political maneuvering. For instance, when in 1994–5 the Mexican economy crumbled, in spite of massive US lending, because of a political crisis partly prompted by the penetration of drug traffickers in the highest levels of the Mexican ruling party, the dollar went down sharply, and the German mark skyrocketed in the currency markets, destabilizing the European monetary system because of investors' fears that the US government deficit would balloon in the effort to lift Mexico out of its potential crash. In this entangled whirlwind of crime, capital, and power, there is no safe place. Or, for that matter, no safe national institutions.

Thus, globalization, in its different dimensions, undermines the autonomy and decision-making power of the nation-state. And this happens at the very moment when the exercise of state power in the international area is also subject to the constraints of multilateralism in defense, foreign policy, and global public policies, such as environmental policy.

The Nation-state in the Age of Multilateralism

The post-Cold War period is characterized by increasing multilateral interdependence between nation-states, although this is a contradictory process rather than a gradual evolution.[39] Structural multilateralism is a function, primarily, of three factors: the dissolution or loosening of the military blocs built around the two superpowers; the dramatic impact of new technologies on warfare; and the social perception of the global character of major challenges to humankind

---

38 WuDunn (1996).
39 Baylis and Rengger (1992); McGrew et al. (1992); Falk (1995); Orstrom Moller (1995); Alonso Zaldivar (1996); Keohane and Nye (2000).

because of increased knowledge and information, and because of the rise of a global civic consciousness, as in the case of environmental security.

With the disappearance of the Soviet Union, and regardless of possible future tensions between Russia, China, and NATO, the major mechanism for the stabilization of strategic links for most nation-states around the two superpowers disappeared as well.[40] While NATO continues to be organized around a US-led Western alliance, its functions were redefined in the second half of the 1990s toward the fulfillment of security tasks on behalf of a broad consortium of Western nations, in association, whenever possible, with the United Nations, yet under the unchallenged leadership of the only superpower, the United States. The new notion of global, collective security,[41] which emerged for the first time with the Gulf War to face the common threat to the oil supply from the Middle East, involved a symbiotic relationship between the most capable military forces (the US and UK professional armies), the financiers of operations (Japan, Germany, the Arab princes, in the first place), and the rhetorical statements on behalf of the civilized world. The deliberate attempt by this US-based alliance to involve Russia in joint operations, as was the case in Bosnia, was indicative of the transformation of military alliances toward joint policing of a shaky world order against potential unpredictable threats to the system. The new security system is being built, primarily, against outer barbarians, whose names change over time, as the axis of evil designated by George W. Bush in 2001 displays a variable geometry according to the vagaries of US foreign policy.[42] So doing, nation-states, including the most powerful, are enmeshed in a web of interests and negotiations that reshapes itself into a different format for each issue to be tackled or each enemy to be confronted.[43]

The muddling through of a foreign policy with variable geometry translates into the growing inability of any state to act on its own in the international arena. As Joseph Nye writes: "To achieve what they want, most countries, including the United States, find that they have to coordinate their activities. Unilateral action simply cannot produce the right results on what are inherently multilateral issues."[44] Indeed, the global character of the main issues concerning humankind, be it global warming, global environmental crises, global epidemics, global

40   Alonso Zaldivar (1996); McGrew (1992b).
41   McGrew (1992a); Mokhtari (1994).
42   Rosenau (1990); Berdal (1993); Guehenno (1993); Castells and Serra (2003).
43   Keohane (2002).
44   Nye (2002: 105).

crime, global financial instability, or global terror, places foreign policy, in principle, in a multilateral framework.[45] However, the trend toward multilateralism is being counteracted by the effort by some states to remain sovereign and to use their power to shape multilateralism around their unilateral interests.

The main challenge to multilateralism comes from the United States, particularly in the aftermath of September 11[46] because the United States is the only military superpower, as well as the second largest economic area in the world, and still the main center of knowledge production and technological innovation. American unilateralism, manifested in environmental policy, in trade negotiations, and, above all, in war making, introduces a fundamental contradiction in the international system. While the issues are interdependent, their management is disrupted by the deliberate continuation of US unilateralism, imposing its "hard power" even at the price of depleting its "soft power" (made up of cultural influence), and ultimately destabilizing the multilateral interactions on which the equilibrium of the world depends. As this is a key question for our analysis of the transformation of the state in the context of globalization, I will discuss it below, after reviewing some additional factors that are essential components of the transformation of inter-state relationships.

Rapid changes in military technology are also undermining the capability of the nation-state, other than the United States, to stand alone.[47] Warfare is now essentially dependent upon electronics and communications technology, as demonstrated by the Gulf War, the Balkans war, the Afghan war, and the war in Iraq. The massive devastation that can be inflicted from a distance, through missile launches and air strikes, can cripple a sizable army in a few hours, particularly if its defenses are made blind by electronic counter-measures, and if targets have been identified by satellite and processed by computers thousands of kilometers away to direct actual fire in this invisible war. Conventional warfare is, as it always was, technologically dependent. The difference in the current period is, on the one hand, the speed of technological change, which makes weapons obsolete in a short time span.[48] This forces the continuous upgrading of weapons systems if armies are supposed to really fight other armies, instead of controlling their own people, as is still the case for much of humankind. Low-tech armies are not armies at all, but disguised police forces.

45   Frankel (1988); McGrew et al. (1992); Jacquet et al. (2002).
46   Castells and Serra (2003).
47   McInnes (1992).
48   McInnes and Sheffield (1988); Grier (1995); Arquilla and Rondfeldt (2001).

On the other hand, the character of new military technology requires a professional army in which personnel is equipped with advanced knowledge to manipulate semi-automated weaponry, and communication systems. This gives an advantage to countries with an advanced technological level, regardless of the size of their armed forces, as the cases of Israel and Singapore illustrate. Because of the essential role of technology, nation-states still wanting to assert their capacity to exercise violence become permanently dependent on technological suppliers, not just of hardware, but of human resources. This dependency, however, has to be placed in the context of a growing diversification of conventional war weapons, as countries industrialize and technology diffuses.[49] Thus, Brazil and Israel can be efficient suppliers of advanced warfare equipment. France, the UK, Germany, Italy, and China have increased their role, together with the United States and Russia, as suppliers of the world's armies.

An increasingly complex pattern of cooperation and competition emerges, with China buying advanced fighters from Russia and communications technology from the United States, and France selling missiles to whoever wants to buy them, with after-sale services for training and maintenance included. Furthermore, illegal global markets for weapons, for any kind of weapons, have proliferated, making possible the widespread diffusion of whatever technology becomes available, from "Stingers" to "Patriots," from nerve gas to electronic jamming devices. It follows that, unlike in other historical periods, no single state is self-sufficient in the production of warfare equipment, with the essential exception of the United States (since Russia is now technologically dependent in microelectronics and communications). Because nation-states cannot control sources for the supply of state-of-the-art equipment, they are permanently dependent, in the potential exercise of their war-making power, not on the US, but on diverse, global supply networks. The fact that the United States is technologically self-sufficient gives the United States the title of being the only true superpower.

Technological evolution adds a new twist in international relations to the dialectics between multilateralism and unilateralism. Industrialization of new areas of the world, diffusion of scientific and technological knowledge, and illegal trade in everything have pushed, and are pushing, toward proliferation of nuclear, chemical, and biological warfare capabilities.[50] Thus, while nation-states are increasingly dependent on cutting-edge technology in conventional warfare, they

49 McGrew (1992b).
50 McGrew (1992b); Kaldor (1999).

may nevertheless have access to what I would call "veto technologies," that is, weapons of mass destruction that by their existence can deter a more powerful state from winning. The global "terror equilibrium" is in the process of being decentralized to many local "terror equilibria." This trend forces, on the one hand, major powers to undertake concerted, multilateral action to prevent the control of these weapons by new countries, political forces, or terrorist groups. On the other hand, once some countries come, anyway, into the possession of these weapons, the global security system is compelled to intervene and assist in balancing powers of destruction in each area of the world to prevent dangerous local confrontations.[51] There follows a complex, entangled web of different levels of destructive power, controlling each other with ad hoc agreements, and negotiated processes of disarmament and disengagement. In such a web no nation-state, not even the United States, is free any longer, since a miscalculation, or an excess in exercising superior power, could trigger a nuclear, or bacteriological, local holocaust. Humankind will live for a long time with the monsters of destruction we have created, either for mass, standardized annihilation, or miniaturized for customized carnage. Under such circumstances, the most fundamental task of nation-states (and not just for the superpowers as in the Cold War period) has become to limit the actual exercise of their own military power, thus weakening their original *raison d'être*.

Nation-states also confront the limits of their legitimacy, and thus ultimately of their power, regarding the global management of the planet's environment.[52] Science and technology are producing, because of increased computing capacity, unprecedented new knowledge on the degradation of nature, and on its consequences for our species. In a related development, as shown in chapter 3, the environmental movement has raised ecological consciousness in societies around the world, putting increasing pressure on the responsibility of governments to halt the path toward catastrophe. Yet, individual nation-states are powerless, on their own, to act on issues such as global warming, the ozone layer, the deforestation of the planet, the pollution of water reserves, the depletion of life in the oceans, and the like. Efforts for states to come together take, more often than not, the form of international shows and solemn rhetoric, rather than actual implementation of joint action programs. Lipschutz and Coca write, in concluding their global survey on concerted environmental policies:

51 Daniel and Hayes (1995); Nye (2002).
52 Rowlands (1992); Vogler (1992); Morin and Kern (1993); Wapner (1995); Hempel (1996); Bureau et al. (2002).

The possibility of an hegemonic direction or the emergence of a central coordinating authority seem remote with respect to environmental matters. And the likelihood of effective multilateral coordination seems small, as well, because of major uncertainties about the costs and benefits of environmental protection and management. To these barriers and conditions we would add a number of factors that stem from the nature of the state itself: the fundamental incapacity of governments to control the destructive processes involved, the scarcity of effective policy levers, and the importance of key resource-extraction (and hence environmental destruction) for key state-society alliances.[53]

This is not necessarily because of ignorance or ill-faith on the part of governments, but because each nation-state continues to act on behalf of its own interests, or of the interests of the constituencies it values most.[54] The studies conducted by Nuria Castells, with Peter Nijkamp, and with Jeroe Van de Berg, on the negotiation and implementation of international environmental agreements demonstrate how the interests of states, and particularly those of the states that come first to the definition of environmental policy, shape the agenda for the latecomers.[55] So doing, multilateralism becomes a forum of debate and a negotiating arena, rather than a tool for exercising collective responsibility. Following a Habermasian logic of "crisis displacement," "the fundamental and global environmental-economic contradiction," as Hay puts it, "becomes displaced to the level of the nation-state."[56] This structurally induced stubbornness of nation-states to give priority to their specific interests over the management of global public goods[57] paradoxically leads to their weakening as viable political institutions. This is because citizens around the world realize the incapacity of these rather expensive and cumbersome apparatuses to deal with the major issues challenging humankind. Thus, to overcome their growing irrelevance, nation-states increasingly band together, shifting gears toward a new supranational order of governance.

Global Governance and Networks of Nation-states

"If one wants a shorthand explanation for the renewed momentum of European integration in the mid-1980s," as Streeck and Schmitter write, "one would probably account for it as the result of an align-

53 Lipschutz and Coca (1993: 332).
54 Castells, N. (1999).
55 Nijkamp and Castells, N. (2001); Van de Berg and Castells, N. (2003).
56 Hay (1994: 87).
57 Severino and Tubiana (2002).

ment between two broad interests – that of large European firms struggling to overcome perceived competitive advantages in relation to Japanese and US capital and that of state elites seeking to restore at least part of the political sovereignty they had gradually lost at the national level as a result of growing international interdependence."[58] On both counts, for business interests and political interests, what was sought for was not supranationality, but the reconstruction of nation-based state power at a higher level, at a level where some degree of control of global flows of wealth, information, and power could be exercised. The formation of the European Union (as I will argue in volume III) was not a process of building the European federal state of the future, but the construction of a political cartel, the Brussels cartel, in which European nation-states can still carve out, collectively, some level of sovereignty from the new global disorder, and then distribute the benefits among its members, under endlessly negotiated rules. This is why, rather than ushering in the era of supranationality and global governance, we are witnessing the emergence of the super nation-state, that is of a state expressing, in a variable geometry, the aggregate interests of its constituent members.[59]

A similar argument can be extrapolated to the plurality of international institutions that share the management of the economy, of security, of development, of the environment.[60] The World Trade Organization has been set up to make free trade compatible with trade restrictions in a non-disruptive mechanism of control and negotiation. The United Nations in the past decade has tried to establish its new, double role as a legitimate police force on behalf of peace and human rights, and as a world media center, staging global conferences every six months on the headlines of humankind: environment, population, social exclusion, women, cities, and the like. The G-8 countries club has appointed itself as the supervisor of the global economy, instructing the International Monetary Fund and the World Bank to keep financial markets and currencies under discipline, both globally and locally. Post-Cold War NATO has lost its status as the nucleus of a credible military force to police the new world disorder, but the US and the UK have rebuilt this global police capacity on an ad hoc basis around their military might, extending their surveillance and intervention networks to every corner of the world. NAFTA is tightening up the economic integration of the Western hemisphere, with the

---

58   Streeck and Schmitter (1991: 148).
59   Orstrom Moller (1995).
60   Berdal (1993); Rochester (1993); Bachr and Gordenker (1994); Dunaher (1994); Falk (1995); Kraus and Knight (1995); Oversight of IMF/World Bank (1995); Jacquet et al. (2002).

incorporation of Chile belying its Northern label. MERCOSUR, on the other hand, is asserting South America's independence by increasingly trading with Europe rather than with the United States. Various Pacific international cooperation institutions are trying to build the commonality of economic interests, bridging over the historical mistrust between major players in the Asian Pacific (Japan, China, Korea, Russia). Countries around the world are using old institutions, such as ASEAN or the Organization of African Unity, or even post-colonial institutions, such as the British Commonwealth, or the French cooperation system, as platforms for joint ventures toward a diversity of goals that could hardly be reached by individual nation-states.

Most assessments of this growing process of internationalization of state policies seem to doubt the feasibility of global governance as fully shared sovereignty, in spite of this notion's powerful rationale. Rather, global governance is usually considered as the negotiated convergence of national governments' interests and policies.[61] Nation-states, and their elites, are too jealous of their privileges to surrender sovereignty, except under the promise of tangible returns. In addition, according to opinion polls, it is highly unlikely, in the foreseeable future, that the majority of citizens in any country would accept full integration in a supranational, federal state.[62] The US experience of federal nation building is so historically specific that, in spite of its forceful appeal, it can hardly be a model for twenty-first century federalists in other areas of the world.

Furthermore, the growing incapacity of states to tackle the global problems that make an impact on public opinion (from the fate of whales to the torture of dissidents around the world) leads civil societies to take into their own hands the responsibilities of global citizenship.[63] Thus, Amnesty International, Greenpeace, *Médecins sans frontières*, Oxfam, and so many other humanitarian non-governmental organizations have become a major force in the international arena since the 1990s, often attracting more funding, performing more effectively, and receiving greater legitimacy than government-sponsored international efforts. The "privatization" of global humanitarianism is gradually undermining one of the last rationales for the necessity of the nation-state.[64]

In sum, what we are witnessing is, at the same time, the irreversible sharing of sovereignty in the management of major economic, environmental, and security issues, and, on the other hand, the entrench-

---

61 United Nations Commission on Global Governance (1995).
62 Orstrom Moller (1995).
63 Anheier et al. (2001).
64 Guehenno (1993); Rubert de Ventos (1994); Falk (1995); Anheier et al. (2001).

ment of nation-states as the basic components of this entangled web of political institutions.[65] However, the outcome of such a process is not the reinforcement of nation-states, but the systemic erosion of their power in exchange for their durability. This is, first of all, because the processes of relentless conflict, alliance, and negotiation make international institutions rather ineffective, so that most of their political energy is spent in the process, rather than in the product. This seriously slows down the intervening capacity of states, unable to act by themselves, yet paralyzed when trying to act collectively. Moreover, international institutions, partly to escape from such a paralysis, partly because of the inherent logic of any large bureaucracy, tend to take on a life on their own. So doing, they define their mandate in ways that tend to supersede the power of their constituent states, instituting a *de facto* global bureaucracy. For instance, it is essentially wrong, as leftist critics often argue, that the International Monetary Fund is an agent of American imperialism or, for that matter, of any imperialism. It is an agent of itself, fundamentally moved by the ideology of neoclassical economic orthodoxy, and by the conviction of being the bulwark of measure and rationality in a dangerous world built on irrational expectations. The cold-bloodedness I have personally witnessed of IMF technocrats' behavior in helping to destroy Russian society in the critical moments of transition in 1992–95 had nothing to do with capitalist domination. It was, as in Africa, as in Latin America, a deep-seated, honest, ideological commitment to teach financial rationality to the people of the world, as the only serious ground to build a new society. Claiming victory in the Cold War for free-wheeling capitalism (a historical affront to the harsh combats of social democracy against Soviet communism), IMF experts do not act under the guidance of governments who appoint them, or of citizens who pay them, but as self-righteous surgeons skillfully removing the remnants of political controls over market forces.

Joseph Stiglitz, the 2001 Nobel Prizewinner in economics, and former chief economist of the World Bank, has provided a documented, thoroughly argued analysis of the ideological bias of IMF policies, and of its responsibility in aggravating global economic crises in the 1990s, thus imposing unnecessary hardship on millions of people around the world.[66] It is true nonetheless that the IMF's capacity to translate its economic ideology into economic policy imposed on many countries derives from the service that these policies

65   Jacquet et al. (2002).
66   Stiglitz (2002).

provide to the interests of multinational corporations, international banks, and major Western nations, particularly the United States. It is not an accident that the economic thinking common to most economic reforms undertaken in the past decade has been labeled "the Washington consensus," a reference to the location of both the IMF/World Bank headquarters and of the US government. It is this consensus that has been decisively challenged by citizens all over the world, who feel the full impact of these global institutions on their lives, bypassing their obsolete nation-states (see chapter 2). The grassroots reaction against unilateral domination by the IMF and international economic institutions translates into a new political situation in the world, particularly in Latin America. Indeed, in the early years of this century, several elections, and social movements, from Brazil and Argentina to Ecuador and Peru, seemed to signal the end of the ideological hegemony of neoliberalism.[67]

Thus, the growing role played by international institutions and supranational consortia in world policies cannot be equated to the demise of the nation-state. But the price paid by nation-states for their survival as nodes of states' networks is that of their decreasing sovereignty.

Identities, Local Governments, and the Deconstruction of the Nation-state

On December 25, 1632, the Count-Duke of Olivares wrote to his king, Philip IV:

> The most important business in your Monarchy is for Your Majesty to make yourself King of Spain; I mean, Sir, that Your Majesty should not be content with being King of Portugal, Aragon, Valencia, and Count of Barcelona, but should work and secretly scheme to reduce these kingdoms of which Spain is composed to the style and laws of Castile, with no differentiation in the form of frontiers, custom posts, the power to convoke the Cortes of Castile, Aragon and Portugal wherever it seems desirable, and the unrestricted appointment of ministers of different nations both here and there... And if Your Majesty achieves this, you will be the most powerful prince in the world.[68]

The king acted on this advice, thus inducing a process that ultimately led to the Revolt of the Reapers in Catalonia, the revolt against the

67   Calderon (2003).
68   Cited by Elliott and de la Pena (1978: 95); translation by Elliott.

salt tax in the Basque Country, and the rebellion and eventual independence of Portugal. At the same time, he also built, in the process, the foundations of the modern, centralized, Spanish nation-state, albeit in such a precarious condition that it prompted almost three centuries of uprisings, repressions, civil wars, terrorism, and institutional instability.[69] Although the Spanish state, until 1977, represented an extreme situation of imposed homogeneity, most modern nation-states, and particularly the French revolutionary state, have been built on the denial of the historical/cultural identities of its constituents to the benefit of that identity that better suited the interests of the dominant social groups at the origins of the state. As argued in chapter 1, the state, not the nation (defined either culturally or territorially, or both), created the nation-state *in the modern age*.[70] Once a nation became established, under the territorial control of a given state, the sharing of history did induce social and cultural bonds, as well as economic and political interests, among its members. Yet, the uneven representation of social interests, cultures, and territories in the nation-state skewed national institutions toward the interests of originating elites and their geometry of alliances, thus opening the way for institutional crises when subdued identities, historically rooted or ideologically revived, were able to mobilize for a renegotiation of the historical national contract.[71]

The structure of the nation-state is territorially differentiated, and this territorial differentiation, with its sharing, and not sharing, of powers, expresses alliances and oppositions between social interests, cultures, regions, and nationalities that compose the state. As I elaborated elsewhere,[72] the territorial differentiation of state institutions explains to a large extent the apparent mystery of why states are often ruled on behalf of the interests of a minority while not necessarily relying on repression. Subordinate social groups, and cultural, national, regional minorities, do have access to power at lower levels of the state, in the territories in which they live. Thus, a complex geometry emerges in the relationship between the state, social classes, social groups, and identities present in civil society. In each community and in each region, the social alliances and their political expression are specific, corresponding to the existing local/regional power relationships, the history of the territory, and its specific economic structure.

69   Alonso Zaldivar and Castells (1992).
70   Norman (1940); Halperin Donghi (1969); Tilly (1975); Gellner (1983); Giddens (1985); Rubert de Ventos (1994).
71   Hobsbawm (1990): Blas Guerrero (1994).
72   Castells (1981).

This differentiation of power alliances according to various regions and communities is an essential mechanism for keeping in balance, overall, the interests of various elites which jointly benefit from the policies of the state, albeit in different proportions, in different dimensions, and in different territories.[73] Local and regional notables trade power in their territory for their allegiance to structures of dominance at the national level, where interests of national or global elites are more powerful. Local notables are intermediaries between local societies and the national state: they are, at the same time, political brokers and local bosses. Since agreements reached between social actors at the level of local government do not often correspond to the political alliances established between various social interests at the national level, the local system of power does not develop easily along strict party lines, even in the European situation of party-dominated democracies. Local and regional social alliances are frequently ad hoc arrangements, organized around local leadership. Thus, local and regional governments are, at the same time, the manifestation of decentralized state power, the closest point of contact between the state and civil society, and the expression of cultural identities which, while hegemonic in a given territory, are sparsely included in the ruling elites of the nation-state.[74]

I have argued, in chapter 1, that the increasing diversification and fragmentation of social interests in the network society result in their aggregation under the form of (re)constructed identities. Thus, a plurality of identities forwards to the nation-state the claims, demands, and challenges of civil society. The growing inability of the nation-state to respond *simultaneously* to this vast array of demands induces what Habermas called a "legitimation crisis,"[75] or, in Richard Sennett's analysis, the "fall of public man,"[76] the figure that is the foundation of democratic citizenship. To overcome such a legitimation crisis, states decentralize some of their power to local and regional political institutions. This movement results from two convergent trends. On the one hand, because of the territorial differentiation of state institutions, regional and national minority identities find their easiest expression at local and regional levels. On the other hand, national governments tend to focus on managing the strategic challenges posed by the globalization of wealth, communication, and power; thus they let lower levels of governance take responsibility for

73   Dulong (1978); Tarrow (1978); Garcia de Cortazar (2001); Caminal (2002).
74   Gremion (1976); Ferraresi and Kemeny (1977); Rokkan and Urwin (1982); Borja (1988); Ziccardi (1995); Borja and Castells (1997).
75   Habermas (1973).
76   Sennett (1978).

linking up with society by managing the issues of everyday life, in order to rebuild legitimacy through decentralization. However, once this decentralization of power occurs, local and regional governments may seize the initiative on behalf of their populations, and may engage in developmental strategies *vis-à-vis* the global system, eventually coming into competition with their own parent states.

These trends are apparent all over the world. Pippa Norris has analyzed the self-definition of people in terms of their territorial identity on the basis of her elaboration of the data of the World Values Survey in 1990–91 and 1995–97.[77] She shows that, by and large, the hypothesis of the rise of cosmopolitanism, understood as the feeling of being citizens of the world, in the age of globalization is not supported by the evidence. Only 15 percent of the people surveyed feel close to their continent or to the world as their primary identity. Furthermore, only 2 percent are pure cosmopolitans; that is, those who indicate exclusively a continental/world identity. Some 38 percent of those surveyed consider the nation to be their primary source of territorial identity, but the most widely diffused primary territorial identity is local/regional; that is, chosen in the first place by 47 percent of the people surveyed. In the younger generations there is a higher proportion of those who feel citizens of the world, up to 21 percent for the youngest cohort. But even for this age group, 44 percent of those interviewed chose their region or locality as their primary territorial identity.[78] The local/regional identity is particularly strong in south-western Europe (64 percent selected local/regional as their primary identity, the largest frequency in the world), and in north-western Europe (62 percent), while in North America (41 percent) and the Middle East (39 percent) it ranks the lowest. Indeed, for these two regions, the nation appears to be the primary source of territorial identity (43 percent and 49 percent). Pure localists/regionalists, that is those who identify only with their locality or region, represent about 20 percent of the people interviewed, a figure ten times greater than the pure cosmopolitans. There is, however, a trend toward increasing cosmopolitanism among the younger, more educated, and more affluent groups of the population, but this trend is overwhelmed by the persistence of localities, regions, and, to a lesser extent, nations, as the primary sources of territorial identity in the minds of most people, and particularly of those left out of the benefits of globalization.

The attachment of people around the world to their spatial and cultural environment bears considerable weight in the politics

77 Norris (2000a).
78 In this survey, territorial identity based on nationalities under an umbrella nation-state, such as Catalonia or Quebec, are included as regional identity.

and institutions of each country. Thus, in the United States, the growing distrust of federal government goes hand in hand with a revival of local and state governments as sites of public attention. Indeed, according to opinion polls in the mid-1990s,[79] this re-localization of government offers the most immediate avenue for the re-legitimation of politics, be it in the form of ultra-conservative populism, as in the "county rights" movement, or the born-again Republican party, building its hegemony on attacking the federal government.[80]

In the European Union, while substantial areas of sovereignty have been transferred to Brussels, responsibility for many matters of everyday life has been shifted to regional and local governments, including, in most countries, education, social policy, culture, housing, environment, and urban amenities.[81] Furthermore, cities and regions across Europe have gathered together in institutional networks that bypass national states, and constitute one of the most formidable lobbies, acting simultaneously on European institutions and on their respective national governments. In addition, cities and regions actively engage in direct negotiations with multinational corporations, and have become the most important agents of economic development policies, since national governments are limited in their actions by EU regulations.[82]

In Latin America, the restructuring of public policy to overcome the crisis of the 1980s gave new impetus to municipal and state governments, whose role had been traditionally overshadowed by dependency on the national government, with the important exception of Brazil. Local, provincial, and state governments in Mexico, in Brazil, in Bolivia, in Ecuador, in Argentina, in Chile, benefited, in the 1980s and 1990s, from decentralization of power and resources, and undertook a number of social and economic reforms which are transforming Latin America's institutional geography. So doing, not only did they share power with the nation-state, but, most importantly, they created the basis for a new political legitimacy in favor of the local state.[83]

China is experiencing a similar fundamental transformation, with Shanghai and Guandong controlling the main avenues of access to the global economy, and many cities and provinces around the country organizing their own linkages to the new market system. While

---

79   Roper Center of Public Opinion and Polling (1995).
80   Balz and Brownstein (1996).
81   Orstrom Moller (1995).
82   Borja et al. (1992); Goldsmith (1993); Graham (1995).
83   Ziccardi (1991, 1995); Laserna (1992).

Beijing seems to be keeping political control with an iron hand, in fact the power of the Chinese Communist party relies on a delicate balance of power-sharing and wealth distribution between national, provincial, and local elites. This central/provincial/local arrangement of the Chinese state in the process of primitive accumulation may well be the key mechanism in ensuring an orderly transition from statism to capitalism.[84] A similar situation can be observed in post-Communist Russia. The balance of power between Moscow and local and regional elites has been critical for the relative stability of the Russian state in the midst of a chaotic economy, as in the sharing of power and profits between the federal government and the "oil generals" in Western Siberia; or between Moscow elites and local elites in both European Russia and in the Far East.[85] On the other hand, when demands of national identity were not duly acknowledged, and eventually mishandled, as in Chechnya, the ensuing war was largely responsible for derailing the course of the Russian transition.[86]

Thus, from the glory of Barcelona to the agony of Grozny, territorial identity and local/regional governments have become decisive forces in the fate of citizens, in the relationships between state and society, and in the reshaping of nation-states. A survey of comparative evidence on political decentralization seems to support the popular saying according to which national governments in the information age are too small to handle global forces, yet too big to manage people's lives.[87]

The Identification of the State

The selective institutionalization of identity in the state has a very important, indirect effect on the overall dynamics of state and society. Namely, not all identities are able to find refuge in the institutions of local and regional governments. In fact, one of the functions of territorial differentiation of the state is to keep the principle of universal equality, while organizing its application as segregated inequality. Separate and unequal from the norm that underlies, for instance, the strong local autonomy of American local government.[88] The concentration of poor people and ethnic minorities in America's central cities or in French *banlieues* tends to confine social problems

---

84 Cheung (1994); Li (1995); Hsing (1996).
85 Kiselyova and Castells (1997); Castells and Kiselyova (2000).
86 Khazanov (1995); Bonnell and Breslauer (2001).
87 Borja and Castells (1997).
88 Blakely and Goldsmith (1993).

spatially, while decreasing the level of available public resources precisely by retaining local autonomy. Local/regional autonomy reinforces territorially dominant elites and identities, while depriving those social groups who are either not represented in these autonomous government institutions or, else, are ghettoized and isolated.[89]

Under such conditions, two different processes may take place. On the one hand, identities that tend to be inclusive use their control of regional institutions to broaden the social and demographic basis of their identity. On the other hand, local societies retrenched in a defensive position build their autonomous institutions as mechanisms of exclusion. An example of the first process is democratic Catalonia: it is run by Catalans and in Catalan, but on the basis of assimilation of immigrants from the rest of Spain, since Catalan women have been traditionally giving birth below the replacement rate. Thus, in 2002, a survey of a representative sample of the Catalan population found that only 58.5 percent of people older than 29 years were born in Catalonia, in contrast to 92.6 percent of those between 15 and 29 years of age.[90] The process of cultural integration and social assimilation for immigrants from southern Spain has been relatively smooth, so that their children become culturally Catalan and fully bilingual (see chapter 1), although it remains to be seen what happens with the new immigrants from developing countries. What is important in this example is to observe how a given cultural/national identity, to be Catalan, uses the control of the local/regional state to survive as an identity, both by reinforcing its bargaining position *vis-à-vis* the Spanish nation-state, and by using its hold on the regional/local institutions to integrate non-Catalans, thus producing them as Catalans, and reproducing Catalonia through surrogate families.

A totally different situation arises when identities and interests dominating in local institutions reject the notion of integration, as in ethnically divided communities. More often than not, the rejection of official culture is answered by the excluded building pride in their excluded identity, as in many Latino communities in American cities, or with the young *beurs* of French North African ghettos.[91] These excluded ethnic minorities do not aim at the local state but call upon the national state in order to see their rights acknowledged, and their interests defended, above and against local/state governments, as in the case of American minorities requesting "affirmative action" programs to make up for centuries of institutional and social discrimination. However, the nation-state, in order to survive its legitimation

89   Smith (1991).
90   Castells et al. (2002).
91   Sanchez Jankowski (1991); Wieviorka (1993); Hagedorn (1998)

crisis *vis-à-vis* the "majority," increasingly shifts power and resources to local and regional governments. In so doing, it becomes less and less able to equalize the interests of various identities and social groups represented in the nation-state at large. Thus, mounting social pressures threaten the equilibrium of the whole nation. The nation-state's growing inability to respond to such pressures, because of the decentralization of its power, further de-legitimizes its protective and representative role *vis-à-vis* discriminated minorities. Subsequently, these minorities seek refuge in their local communities, in non-governmental structures of self-reliance.[92] Thus, what started as a process of re-legitimizing the state by shifting power from national to local level, may end up deepening the legitimation crisis of the nation-state, and the tribalization of society in communities built around primary identities, as shown in chapter 1.

At the limit, when the nation-state does not represent a powerful identity, or does not provide room for a coalition of social interests that empower themselves under a (re)constructed identity, a social/political force defined by a particular identity (ethnic, territorial, religious) may take over the state, to make it the exclusive expression of such an identity. This is the process of formation of fundamentalist states, such as the Islamic Republic of Iran, or the institutions of American governance proposed by the Christian Coalition in the 1990s, or else the rise of Hindu fundamentalism in the governments of India, both at the federal level and at the level of key states, such as Gujarat.[93]

At first glance, it would seem that fundamentalism gives a new, and powerful, breath to the nation-state, in an updated historical version. Yet it is, in fact, the deepest manifestation of the demise of the nation-state. As explained in chapter 1, the expression of Islam is not, and cannot be, the nation-state (a secular institution), but the *umma*, the community of believers. The *umma* is, by definition, transnational, and should reach out to the entire universe. This is also the case with the Catholic Church, a transnational, fundamentalist movement seeking to convert the entire planet to the only true God, using when possible the support of any state. Under this perspective, a fundamentalist state is not a nation-state, both in its relationship to the world and in its relationship to the society living in the national territory. *Vis-à-vis* the world, the fundamentalist state has to maneuver, in alliance with other believers' apparatuses, states or not, toward the expansion of the faith, toward the molding of institutions, national, international, and local, around the principles

---

92   Wacquant (1994); Trend (1996).
93   Jambar (2002).

of the faith: the fundamentalist project is a global theocracy, not a national, religious state. *Vis-à-vis* a territorially defined society, the fundamentalist state does not aim at representing the interests of all citizens, and of all identities present in the territory, but aims at helping those citizens, in their various identities, to find the truth of God, the only truth. Therefore, the fundamentalist state, while unleashing the last wave of states' absolute power, does so, in fact, by negating the legitimacy and durability of the nation-state.

Thus, the current death dance between identities, nations, and states, leaves, on the one hand, historically emptied nation-states, drifting on the high seas of global flows of power; on the other hand, fundamental identities, retrenched in their communities or mobilized toward the uncompromising capture of an embattled nation-state; in between, the local state strives to rebuild legitimacy and instrumentality by navigating transnational networks and integrating local civil societies.

The Return of the State

How could the state be powerless in the global age and in the network society? Aren't we witnessing, instead, a surge of violence and repression throughout the world? Isn't privacy facing the greatest dangers in human history because of the pervasiveness of new information technologies? Didn't Big Brother arrive, as Orwell predicted, around 1984? How could the state be powerless when mastering a formidable technological capacity, and controlling an unprecedented stock of information?[94] Furthermore, isn't the global war on global terror and the unilateral assertion of sovereign superpower by the United States, in the early years of the twenty-first century, a striking manifestation of the return of the nation-state as the primary site of power? These are fundamental questions that require careful consideration. I will take them in sequential order.

The state, violence, and surveillance: from Big Brother to little sisters

These essential, and usual, questions mix contradictory evidence with confused theory. Yet their treatment is central in the understanding of the crisis of the state. First of all, the Big Brother imagery must be empirically dismissed, as it refers to the connection between our

94 Burnham (1983); Lyon (1994, 2001).

societies and the Orwellian prophecy. Indeed, George Orwell could well have been right, *vis-à-vis* the object of his prophecy, Stalinism, not the liberal, capitalist state, if political history and technology had followed a different trajectory in the past half-century, something that was certainly within the realm of possibility. But statism disintegrated in contact with new information technologies, instead of being capable of mastering them (see volume III); and new information technologies unleashed the power of networking and decentralization, actually undermining the centralizing logic of one-way instructions and vertical, bureaucratic surveillance (see volume I). Our societies are not orderly prisons, but disorderly jungles.

However, new, powerful information technologies might indeed be put to the service of surveillance, control, and repression by state apparatuses (police, tax collection, censorship, suppression of political dissidence, and the like). But so might they be used for citizens to enhance their control over the state, by rightfully accessing information in public data banks, by interacting with their political representatives on-line, by watching live political sessions, and eventually commenting live on them.[95] Also, new technologies may enable citizens to videotape events, so providing visual evidence of abuses, as in the case of the global environmental organizations that distribute video power to local groups around the world to report on environmental crimes, thus putting pressure on the ecological culprits.

What the power of technology does is to extraordinarily amplify the trends rooted in social structure and institutions: oppressive societies may be more so with the new surveillance tools, while democratic, participatory societies may enhance their openness and representativeness by further distributing political power with the power of technology. Thus, the direct impact of new information technologies on power and the state is an empirical matter, on which the record is mixed. But, a deeper, more fundamental trend is at work, actually undermining the nation-state's power: the increasing diffusion of both surveillance capacity and the potential for violence outside the institutions of the state and beyond the borders of the nation.

Reports of the growing threat to privacy concern less the state as such than business organizations and private information networks, or public bureaucracies following their own logic as apparatuses, rather than acting on behalf of the government. States, throughout history, have collected information on their subjects, very often by rudimentary but effective brutal means. Certainly, computers

95   Anthes (1993); Betts (1995); Gleason (1995).

qualitatively changed the ability to cross-refer information, combining social security, health, ID cards, residence, and employment information. But with the limited exception of Anglo-Saxon countries, rooted in a libertarian tradition (currently under threat), people around the world, from democratic Switzerland to Communist China, have spent their lives dependent on files of information of residence, work, and on every domain of their relationship to government. On the other hand, if it is true that police work has been facilitated by new technologies, it has also become extraordinarily complicated by the similar, and sometimes superior, sophistication of organized crime in using new technologies (for instance, interfering with police communications, linking up electronically, accessing computer records and so on).

The real issue is somewhere else: it is in the gathering of information on individuals by business firms, and organizations of all kinds, and in the creation of a market for this information. The credit card, more than the ID card, is giving away privacy. This is the instrument through which people's lives can be profiled, analyzed, and targeted for marketing (or blackmailing) purposes. And the notion of the credit card as life in the public record must be extended to a variety of business offerings, from frequent flyer programs to consumer services of every possible type, and to membership of miscellaneous associations. *Rather than an oppressive "Big Brother," it is a myriad of well-wishing "little sisters," relating to each one of us on a personal basis because they know who we are, who have invaded all realms of life.* What computers do, indeed, is to make possible the gathering, processing, and using for specific purposes of a mass of individualized information, so that our name can be printed, or the offering personalized, or an offer mailed out, or beamed in, to millions of individuals. Or, in a telling illustration of new technological logic, the V-chip allows households to program censorship according to a system of codes that will also be implanted in the television signals emitted from the stations. So doing, it decentralizes surveillance rather than centralizing control.

David Lyon, in his insightful books on the matter, has insisted on the critical development of this extension of surveillance way beyond the boundaries of the state.[96] What he calls "the electronic eye" is indeed a surveillance "society," rather than a "surveillance state." This is, after all, the heart of Foucault's theory of micro-powers, although he confused many of his superficial readers by calling "the state" what, in his own view, is in fact "the system"; that is, the network

96   Lyon (1994, 2003).

of sources of power in various domains of social life, including the power in the family. If, in the Weberian tradition, we restrict the concept of the state to the set of institutions holding the legitimate monopoly of the means of violence, and by nation-state the territorial delimitation of such a power,[97] it would seem that we are witnessing in fact the diffusion of the power of surveillance and of violence (symbolic or physical) into society at large.

This trend is even more apparent in the new relationship between state and media. Given the growing financial and legal independence of the media, increased technological capacity puts into the hands of the media the ability to spy on the state, and to do so on behalf of society and/or of specific interest groups (see chapter 6). When, in 1991, a Spanish radio station recorded the conversation over cellular 'phones of two socialist officials, the broadcasting of their very critical remarks about the socialist Prime Minister triggered a political crisis. Or when Prince Charles and his friend indulged over the 'phone in postmodern elaborations on Tampax and related matters, the tabloid printing of these conversations shook the British Crown. To be sure, media revelations, or gossip, have always been a threat to the state, and a defense of citizens. But new technologies, and the new media system, have exponentially increased the vulnerability of the state to the media, thus to business, and to society at large. In historically relative terms, today's state is more surveilled than surveillant.

Furthermore, while the nation-state retains the capacity for violence,[98] it is losing its monopoly because its main challengers are taking the form of, either, transnational networks of terrorism, or, communal groups resorting to suicidal violence. In the first case, the global character of terrorism (political, criminal, or both), and of their supplier networks in information, weapons, and finance, requires a systemic cooperation between nation-states' police, so that the operating unit is an increasingly transnational police force.[99] In the second case, when communal groups, or local gangs, renounce their membership of the nation-state, the state becomes increasingly vulnerable to violence rooted in the social structure of its society, as if states were to be permanently engaged in fighting a guerrilla war.[100] Hence the contradiction the state faces: if it does not use violence, it fades away as a state; if it uses it, on a quasi-permanent basis, a substantial part of its resources and legitimacy will disappear because it would imply an endless state of emergency. So, the state can only proceed with such a

97   Giddens (1985).
98   Tilly (1995).
99   Fooner (1989).
100 Wieviorka (1988).

durable violence when and if the survival of the nation, or of the nation-state, is at stake. Because of the increasing reluctance of societies to support a lasting use of violence, except in extreme situations, the difficulty for the state in actually resorting to violence on a scale large enough to be effective leads to its diminishing ability to do so frequently, and thus to the gradual loss of its privilege as holding the means of violence. However, when an emergency situation arises, the state falls back on its historical routine as the repository of violence and the guardian of security, with its means of power dramatically enhanced by information and communication technologies.

Thus, the capacity for surveillance is diffused in society, the monopoly of violence is challenged by transnational, non-state networks, and the ability to repress rebellion is eroded by endemic communalism and tribalism. While the nation-state still looks imposing in its shiny uniform, and people's bodies and souls are still routinely tortured around the world, information flows bypass, and sometimes overwhelm, the state; terrorist wars criss-cross national boundaries; and communal turfs exhaust the law-and-order patrol. The state still relies on violence and surveillance, but it does not hold the monopoly on them any longer; nor can it exercise them from its national enclosure.

It is to respond to these challenges that the network state appears on the historical stage. I have analyzed in the preceding pages the logic and workings of the network state. I must add here the observation of the return of the state in the form of the American superpower.

American unilateralism and the new geopolitics

The collapse of the Soviet Union left the United States as the only military superpower in the world. The American government used its favorable position to shape the world according to its national interests. Reflecting upon the historical record, I doubt whether any other superpower would have done otherwise. The United States imposed its views on global economic policies, using the two main levers of global economic governance, the G-8 meetings and the IMF. As Stiglitz writes, referring to Russia, but implying a broader policy orientation: "The IMF is a political institution. . . . IMF policies were closely related to the political viewpoints of the Clinton administration."[101] Nonetheless, given the global character of the issues to be tackled, during the 1990s the United States joined the world trend toward a multilateral system of international management, albeit

101   Stiglitz (2002: 222).

under the form of asymmetrical multilateralism; that is, keeping a de facto power of veto on common policies.

The position changed under the Bush administration, even before September 11. The US established itself, in the words of Javier Solana, as the last sovereign nation-state. At the time that countries around the world were engaging in building institutions of global governance to address global issues and to manage global public goods, the US government retained its unilateral attitude, in areas as diverse as the environment (particularly with its refusal to ratify the Kyoto protocol), humanitarian causes (declining to sign the treaty banning antipersonnel mines), or global justice (refusal to accept the jurisdiction of the International Criminal Court).[102]

Yet the United States, in spite of its military might, the size and dynamism of its economy, and its technological superiority, is enmeshed in a web of economic, political, cultural, and environmental interactions that make it interdependent with the world, an argument that Joseph Nye has developed from the perspective of the national interests of the United States.[103] Indeed, the notion of an "American" economy is misleading in the age of global production networks and interdependent financial markets. American multinational corporations are organized in global networks of production and management, and a substantial share of American economic activity and employment depends on investment and trade from foreign companies. American science and technology rely largely on foreign talent: foreign students account for over 50 percent of PhDs in science and engineering granted by American universities, and most of them stay in the United States to work. High-technology industries could not have grown in the 1990s without the import of over 200,000 engineers and scientists per year. And, in the past decade, over one-third of new firms created in Silicon Valley were headed by a Chinese or Indian engineer, to which should be added numerous other firms led by executives from other nationalities.[104]

Global security for the United States, from crime to drugs to terrorism, continues to be dependent on the cooperation of governments around the world. And what Nye and others label "soft power" (that is, power projected through cultural/ideological influence) depends on the ability of American cultural products to mix with other cultures without being imposed by coercion. This is why, in spite of the one-sided policy perspective of the US administration, during the 1990s there was an underlying trend toward the practice of

102   Jacquet et al. (2002); Serra (2003).
103   Nye (2002).
104   Saxenian (2003).

shared governance.[105] Sharing does not mean the absence of power relationships. Global governance by the network state is still a process marked by asymmetrical relationships, not all nodes are equal, and each agent still pursues its own interest, rather than the common good. But in the face of economic crises, political conflicts, and social protests arising from the process of globalization, a practice of de facto, tentative global governance was muddling through around 2001.

Then, September 11 changed everything: less because of the challenge of the terrorist threat, as serious as it is, than because of the qualitative shift in the policy of the United States. Given the weight and influence of the American state in the international system, its new course of policy, foreign and domestic, changed the political management of the world at large. Why was this so? What are the tenets of this new unilateralism? And what are its observable consequences?

The reason why America reacted in terms of the absolute priority given to its national security is that for the first time in its young history it felt vulnerable. The new form of enemy was far more insidious, and difficult to counter, than the Soviet Union or, for that matter, any other national power that could be matched, and ultimately vanquished, by American technological and economic resources. Furthermore, American people felt personally threatened, by an invisible menace, whose shadowy profile fed collective paranoia, exactly what the terrorists intended to accomplish. From this collective feeling of insecurity rose the political support for the security policy. National security became the paramount concern in the country and the overarching principle for the government, both in domestic and foreign affairs. Based on these premises, a conservative political team, which had been advocating unilateralism in foreign policy, and full exercise of American power long before September 11, was able to impose its views. Richard Perle was the organic intellectual of this team, Wolfowitz the strategist, Rumsfeld the operative, and Cheney the political figurehead. President Bush, seeing the defense of the United States as his moral duty and his political trump card, fully assumed this strategy that reflected the views of the pro-Israeli lobby in foreign policy, aligned on Sharon's position of the uncompromising defense of the West against the dangers of an unruly world in the Middle East and beyond.

The components of this strategy can be summarized as follows. First, to shield the United States, against missiles through technology,

105   Keohane (2002).

and against individual terrorism through a comprehensive homeland security system that involves the monitoring of foreigners, and the granting of extensive powers of surveillance to federal agencies, consolidated in a new Homeland Security Department. Second, to act decisively against any base of terrorist attacks, both to suppress the danger and to intimidate countries that could harbor terrorists in the future. The war in Afghanistan was the first expression of this policy. Third, to take preventive action against any potential source of development of weapons of mass destruction that cannot be tamed by direct influence. This led to the war in Iraq, but it also potentially extends to all countries that could be considered part of the so-called "axis of evil" (North Korea, Iran, and a long list of possible suspects, depending on the areas of US foreign policy and of the geopolitics of future terrorism). Fourth, to engage in a relentless, global war against global terrorist networks. Fifth, as an interesting byproduct, to assert American interests, and the interests of global capitalism, in key strategic areas of the world. This includes tightening up control over resources of oil and gas, which partly explains the interest in seizing Iraq, and the use of Afghanistan as a controlled route for the pipelines from Central Asia. Sixth, support for Israel, regardless of Israeli policies, at all costs, both for domestic and geopolitical reasons. Seventh, to use economic protectionism and environmental unilateralism when necessary to safeguard American economic interests. Eighth, to maintain the sovereignty of the American nation-state. This implies, in an interdependent world made up of global networks, asserting American interests in the exchanges taking place in these networks.

If this political project has a strong internal coherence, and is likely to receive the support of American public opinion in the short term, how feasible is it? And what are its consequences for the world at large, and therefore for the evolution of the state in the network society? Since my purpose in these pages is strictly analytical, and since one of the principles of this book is not to venture into predictions, I will not speculate on future developments. But I will introduce into the argument the results of my observation of the first stage of the implementation of this policy in 2001–3.

The security policy of the Bush/Cheney administration is predicated on three principles. New military technologies, and their quasi-monopoly by the US armed forces, make it possible to overwhelm any enemy in a short time, and with minimal American cost. Even considering the need to engage troops on the ground, and suffer some losses, the new military strategy is based on the ability to fight quick wars with professional armies, with most people back home not suffering the consequences of war, and staying mobilized behind the patriotism of their defenders, dying for a just cause. This kind of war allows the US to finally overcome the limits imposed by public sentiment in the last period of the Vietnam War – limits that were lifted with the Gulf War, and even more so with the wars in Afghanistan and Iraq.[106]

Second, a permanent emergency situation in the homeland, similar to the one practiced in Israel, will minimize the risk of terrorist attacks on US soil. Furthermore, the eventuality of such attacks will feed the support of the American people for the priority given to safety and security, so that, counting on this support, and on American power, in the long run the world will be made a safer place. After all, in the view of US conservative think tanks, American will has already buried, in just half a century, German Nazism, Japanese imperialism, and Soviet Communism, emerging stronger from each challenge.

The third principle is a moral–ethical one. Conservative American political leaders are convinced that they are saving the world along with America, and that some countries (particularly in Europe) are either irresponsible or cynical free-riders. In any case, in the words of Richard Perle: irrelevant. In this context, America should assume its responsibility and leadership without hesitation. Other powers are more respected, Russia and China particularly. To them, the United States offers a deal: help the defense of the US in this difficult period, and they will be given a relevant place in the world being redesigned, a world of global governance under the hegemony of the United States, a global network state built around the interests of the last sovereign nation-state.

The coherence of this strategy must be confronted as to its feasibility. In 2001–3, the first phase of its implementation took place without major challenge. The Taliban regime was obliterated in a few weeks with minimal US losses, Afghanistan became an American protectorate, hundreds of prisoners were taken into custody without international supervision, no terrorist acts took place in the US, or in any other Western nation, with the major exception of the Chechen attack on a Moscow theater. A global coalition against terror was formed around the United States, in part because of the outpouring of sincere solidarity that many countries felt for the victims of the barbarous attacks of September 11. The Patriot Act and the Homeland Security Act received overwhelming, bipartisan support in the US Congress, and while there was a significant movement of protest

106   Kaldor (1999).

against the war in Iraq, the majority of American public opinion continued to support the preventive strike against Iraq even in the absence of support from the United Nations. Furthermore, the direct control of Iraq, with the second largest oil reserves in the world, freed the hands of the US to deal more conclusively with the shadowy relationship between the Arab elites and *al-Qaeda*. Of course, the war with Iraq was a turning point, ushering in a new geopolitical era.

The Iraq War and its aftermath

From the military standpoint, the 2003 war in Iraq was a stunning demonstration of the technological superiority of the US armed forces, and their British allies. In three weeks, an admittedly weakened Iraqi army and militia were annihilated or disbanded, with scant resistance in Baghdad – and none in the North against a small contingent of special forces and Kurd guerrillas. The key, of course, was overwhelming air power which made any front-line resistance impossible. But even more important were the effective communication networks linking up in real time a multiplicity of attacking units, from special forces on foot to fighter planes and B52 bombers, and to fast-moving armored battalions provided with superior electronic gear.

The two-decade long effort in developing new military technology and strategy to overcome the limitations of the Vietnam War finally paid off. American forces are now in a condition to destroy any conventional army in the world with proportionally very small losses of their own. Naturally, fighting Iraq after years of embargo is easier than Iran, and much easier that any major country that could become an adversary in the long-term future. Yet the essence of the statement still applies: as the conquest of the American West was highly facilitated by the superiority of the Winchester rifle over arrows and bows, conventional wars in the twenty-first century will be determined by the kind of technologies that are today almost exclusively in the hands of the US and Israel – and the new US military policy is predicated on the continuation of this technological effort to keep the political–military edge.

Under such conditions, only terrorism and guerrilla war can confront the United States militarily. Both imply a readiness to die for the cause, which was obviously absent in the case of Iraq, beyond a small core of the thugs of the dictator. But even in the case of the Taliban, more ideologically motivated, their determination was not enough to match American technological might. So, here we are in the historical moment of the implementation of "instant war," as analyzed in volume I (chapter 7) of this trilogy. Not that violence can be limited to a few days or weeks or months – indeed, it is very likely that this kind of "instant war" may trigger multiple forms of violence for long periods of time. Yet it does mean that war in the traditional terms of conventional wars between armies can be limited to a quick, extraordinarily violent assault in which the balance of power is pre-determined by technology (particularly communications technology), equipment (particularly air power), and the human ability to use it (dependent on accurate intelligence and professional military personnel).

American performance in managing information to shape public opinion in the Iraq War also improved over their performance in the first Gulf War. This was, of course, the critical error in managing the Vietnam War, which was ultimately lost in the campuses and homes of America. In the first Gulf War, the open manipulation of information, and the news black-out, hid the war, and limited the damage in terms of visions of death and destruction, but it could not offer a positive spin to the story. In the Iraq campaign, there was a skillful mixture of embedded journalism (amounting to accepted censorship), and threats to the personal safety of independently reporting journalists (resulting in the death of 20 journalists, in most cases killed by US/British fire, and in the limited ability to report for many others). This policy of shaping public opinion in favor of the war was particularly effective in the US, where there were few alternative sources of audiovisual information to the mainstream American media that had, by and large, accepted embedded journalism. In Europe, and in the world at large, broadcasting from Al Jazeera, Abu Dhabi Television, and a number of European networks provided a much more diversified source of information. Yet there was an obvious priority given to shaping public opinion about the war in the United States, and, in this case, the Bush administration won the propaganda war, another critical success in preparing the country for the pursuit of the new security policy.

Building on the victory in Iraq, the Bush administration reasserted its geopolitical design of defensive control of the world through pre-emptive strikes or the threat of them. Immediate threats and warnings to Syria and Iran came within hours of the control of Baghdad. The crisis with North Korea went into an acute phase. And President Bush included in his victory speech on board the *Abraham Lincoln* the commitment to continue the global war on terrorism and to destroy any person, organization, or country that could be associated with terrorism against the United States – or (my words) suspected of it. Thus, the most apparent consequence of the war in Iraq was the confirmation of the possibilities and success of unilateralism based on technological–military superiority.

Yet, the Bush administration knows that the world is somewhat more complex, and particularly so the Middle East. So, a new "road map" for the creation of a Palestinian state and peace between Israel and the Palestinians was proposed in the immediate aftermath of the war. Nevertheless, Israel did not seem to be ready to relent in its punitive operations or in giving up illegally occupied territory, and the Palestinian extremists, particularly Hamas (the fundamentalist organization originally supported by the Israeli secret services to weaken Arafat), appeared to continue their practice of indiscriminate terrorism. So, the predicament of the US/British policy of imposing a settlement on the basis of the weakening of the Arabs runs against historical experience or recent political evidence.

Furthermore, the occupation of Iraq projected a threatening shadow over the stability of the Middle East and of the world. Indeed, the historical reason for the support of Saddam Hussein by the US and by the West (including a personal visit by Rumsfeld in 1983 to arm Iraq against Iran) was to use his secular regime as a bulwark against the spread of Islamism, and particularly against Shiite militancy, since Shiites constitute over 60 percent of the Iraqi population. Now, we seem to be back to the first square of this complicated puzzle. The first wave of popular expression in Iraq after the fall of Saddam was mainly organized around two main themes: a rejection of the American presence in Iraq, and support for Islam, both in its Shiite and its Sunni forms. To this should be added a pro-American stand by the Kurds in the North, signaling a potentially explosive contradiction, as the Kurds are in search of independence, and they are the main worry of Turkey, a country in which an Islamic party is in government, and which needs to appease an overwhelmingly anti-American public opinion. The refusal of the US to relinquish power to the United Nations in post-war Iraq highlighted its determined unilateralism, but also left the US, and its allies, alone in confronting the extraordinary turmoil that may arise in Iraq and in the region at large in the wake of a lengthy occupation without international support and local institutional basis.

Perhaps the most lasting impact of the Iraq War will be the calling into question of the international system of governance built in the aftermath of World War II, centered around the United Nations. The bypassing of the UN, as the majority of the Security Council resisted the US unilateral decision, and the creation of a "coalition of the willing" around US foreign policy design, created a new geopolitical situation. In all areas of the world, the US started to build specific coalitions around its interests, as in the time of the Cold War, but this time without a counterbalancing power, and without the ideological justification of resisting Soviet expansionism. The first victim was the European Union, where France and Germany began to build an autonomous defense and security policy after Rumsfeld made the distinction official between the "old Europe" and the "new Europe," and after the US engaged in retaliatory policies against France. Yet, the "new Europe" included countries such as Spain in which public opinion was 90 percent against the policy of its government, so that the pro-Bush stand of the Spanish government was uncertain. Indeed, if we look at public opinion in Europe during the Iraq War and its aftermath (which, in democracy, is a good indicator of political trends in the next election), the "new Europe" could be reduced to the UK (since the Tory alternative to Blair would also be pro-American), to Denmark, and to the newcomers from Eastern Europe, which are structurally pro-American because of their historical fears. Not enough to tilt the European Union towards the US, but enough to disrupt and decisively weaken the EU as an autonomous political actor in the international scene.

Similarly, in Latin America, US unilateralism, expressed in retaliation against Mexico because of Fox's independent position on the war, was creating a major rift with a country deeply enmeshed with the US; it was provoking a distance in relations with Chile and Brazil; it was destabilizing Venezuela and Bolivia; it was intensifying the war in Colombia; and, at the time of writing, it was moving toward a dangerous confrontation with Cuba, using the window of opportunity provided by an erratic Castro metamorphosed into a bloody, aging dictator. In Asia, North Korea decided to take the initiative in the confrontation before its turn would come, declaring possession of operational nuclear weapons, and forcing China and South Korea to come to its rescue, eventually as guarantors of its security. But also provoking nationalist calls in Japan to build a nuclear self-defense. And, of course, around the Islamic world, bin Laden's ideology and tactics appeared to be vindicated, as no other form of confrontation could be effective against the US and Israel. The probability of terrorism against the US and the West, in increasingly vicious forms, seemed to have been increased, not decreased, by the war in Iraq. Its likely occurrence will feed into the US policy of global war on terror, thus inducing a worldwide spiral of violence and destabilization. And this is happening at an historical juncture when the world has become fully interdependent, but is losing the institutions and processes of global governance that were a work in progress in the last years of the twentieth century.

The consequences of American unilateralism

The observable consequences of American geopolitical unilateralism are considerable. First of all, there is significant erosion of the so-called "soft power" in most areas of the world. While Hollywood movies and rock music continue to be influential, because they are a critical part of global culture, opinion polls show a growing uneasiness about America, since people have some difficulty in differentiating between the US government and the people who vote for it. This uneasiness becomes open hostility in Islamic countries, in Latin America, and Africa. In Europe, both West and East, people are still attracted by America, but there is resentment against unilateral American policy in the majority of public opinion. The growing obstacles to immigration and to study in America are also curtailing a key channel of American influence in the world. The spread of new technologies to other countries (e.g. in mobile telephony and wireless Internet) is reducing the technological lead of the US over the rest of the world, and countries are more reluctant to be locked into American sources of technology. In other words, the full exercise of "hard power" over an extended period of time, even under the conditions of a global terrorist threat, is seriously undermining American "soft power" because of the modalities of the exercise of its military power.

Second, on the domestic front, the Orwellian prediction has received, for the first time, some hints of fulfillment in the United States under the new information agency set up by the Homeland Security Act. This is precisely because, for the first time, "Big Brother" was given the authorization to build a surveillance system on the basis of "little sisters." This means the possibility of compiling a database on the social security number of each person living in the United States, integrating all electronic records in the same file, including commercial records, and private transactions, as well as any records from electronic surveillance. Although the existence of an independent judiciary and the protection of the constitution provide a line of defense against an overzealous security administration, it is clear that the United States has entered a period of recession of civil liberties. The psychological dimension of this shrinking freedom is even more important than individual cases of the abuse of human rights. It is the feeling of suspicion, of control, of guarding against the intrusion of people's own government that erodes the last bond of legitimacy between citizens and the state, leaving the state in its role as policeman and protector of personal safety, its oldest role in history. Also, its most dangerous manifestation.

Thirdly, perhaps the most lasting consequences of American unilateralism are being observed precisely in the area whose imbalances it
was intended to address: geopolitical security. In this regard, three
trends are apparent in early 2003. The unilateral policy of preventive
strikes as a way of enforcing security creates incentives for any
country wishing to preserve its autonomy (or its autonomous surren-
dering of sovereignty) to arm itself before falling into the blacklist of
the superpower. In the extreme case, North Korea clearly took advantage of the window of opportunity created by the US focus on Iraq to
step up its nuclear program, either as a means of deterrence or as a
major bargaining chip toward its internationally guaranteed security.
Iran, another member of the Bushian "axis of evil," in a more discreet
manner, increased its nuclear program with the help of Russia and
China. North Korea and Pakistan cooperated in military technology,
exchanging Korean missile technology and parts for Pakistani nuclear
technology and components. Other countries, with lesser capabilities
or more modest ambitions, may engage in bacteriological warfare
capability, easier to conceal until the moment comes to use it as a
deterrent. In fact, it was too late for Iraq, but for the world at large,
the policy of pre-emptive strike builds a powerful incentive to pre-
empt the pre-emption.

The US rationale for the policy of prevention is that intelligence
services will be able to detect any new developments, and act before
new capabilities are added. However, given the blatant failure of US
intelligence services to prevent amateur terrorists from blowing up
New York, it is unlikely that they could systematically eradicate
proliferation in a timely manner. Furthermore, there is already
widespread diffusion of weapons of mass destruction in countries
that are not under the firm control of the United States. This is the
case, of course, for Russia, China, and India, besides France and
the UK, in addition to Israel, which is under control only to some extent.
But it is also the case for Pakistan, where control of the pro-American
command of the army is rather loose. In other words, unilaterally
imposed, asymmetrical disarmament of weapons of mass destruction
is leading to the growing proliferation of such weapons. Attempts at
correcting mistakes of control and surveillance by a series of pre-
emptive strikes bring the world to a state of systemic instability.

On the other hand, while *al-Qaeda* and other terrorist networks
have suffered devastating losses in the first period of the global war
against terror, they have not been eradicated, and similar networks
seem to spring up from various conflicts, in the absence of any
treatment of the issues at the source of these conflicts, politically,
culturally, and economically. In a context of shared global govern-

ance, the one-sided policy of policing the world simply exacerbates these conflicts, as the endless Israeli–Palestinian war has tragically demonstrated. Thus, the war on terror feeds the terrorist war, in a spiral of destruction that adds to global instability.

Furthermore, the integration of the United Nations and other institutions of global governance into a system dominated by American unilateralism is gradually destroying the legitimacy and efficiency of the only instruments available for the management of global issues and global common goods.[107] This is because, if the United Nations follows the initiatives of the United States, without much control over the outcome, it appears to be purely a legitimizing instance of US domination. If, instead, the UN tries to restrain the American superpower it may lose its capacity to stabilize global conflicts – starting with the military capacity that is largely dependent on US logistical support. To be sure, Kofi Annan tried to steer a middle course of integrating the US in a system of multilateral consultation, helped by the voice of moderation in the US administration, Colin Powell. Yet, the margin for maneuver was very narrow when this sensible approach had to face the strategic views and messianic will of the unilateralists in the Bush administration.

So, the return of the nation-state, in its most traditional manifestation, as the holder of the monopoly of violence, took place in defiance of historical logic. It ran against the structural trends evolving toward a new world of global networks. This world requires a system of global governance, gradually implemented by the emerging forms and processes of the network state, not the re-enacting of the empires of the past. Yet history is not structurally pre-determined. It is created and lived by human agency. The return of the state was the result of an historical coincidence. The coming into the US presidency of a conservative foreign policy team around an inexperienced president, elected by the minority vote of an electorate comprising just over a half of American voters, in a contested election decided in favor of the president by a 5 to 4 vote of the American Supreme Court. Yet, in spite of this weak basis of political legitimacy, September 11 provided the opportunity to this small, but decisive group of politicians to change the course of history, by inducing the return of the last would-be sovereign state in a world and at a time made up of interdependent networks. Thus, instead of a network state learning to enact global governance, we are witnessing the unfolding contradiction between the last imperial hurrah and the first truly interdependent world.

107   Castells and Serra (2003).

The Crisis of the Nation-state, the Network State, and the Theory of the State

In his seminal article on democracy, the nation-state, and the global system, David Held summarized his analysis by writing that

> the international order today is characterized by both the persistence of the sovereign state system and the development of plural authority structures. The objections to such a hybrid system are severe. It is open to question whether it offers any solutions to the fundamental problems of modern political thought which have been preoccupied by, among other things, the rationale and basis of order and toleration, of democracy and accountability, and of legitimate rule.[108]

Although he goes on to offer his own optimistic proposal for re-legitimizing the state in its postnational reincarnation, the powerful arguments against continuing state sovereignty that he puts forward in the preceding pages explain his hesitant concluding line: "There are good reasons for being optimistic about the results – and pessimistic."[109] In this context, I am not sure what "optimistic" and "pessimistic" mean. I have no particular sympathy for modern nation-states that have eagerly mobilized their people for reciprocal mass slaughter in the bloodiest century of human history – the twentieth century.[110] But this is a matter of opinion. *What really matters is that the new power system is characterized*, and I agree with David Held on this, *by the plurality of sources of authority (and, I would add, of power), the nation-state being just one of these sources*. This, in fact, seems to have been the historical rule, rather than the exception. As Spruyt argues, the modern nation-state had a number of "competitors" (city-states, trading pacts, empires),[111] as well, I would add, as military and diplomatic alliances, which did not disappear, but coexisted with the nation-state throughout its development in the modern age. However, what seems to be emerging now, for the reasons presented in this chapter, is the de-centering of the nation-state within the realm of shared sovereignty that characterizes the current world's political scene, albeit with the major contradiction introduced, as I argued above, by the American attempt at sovereign unilateralism.

108   Held (1991: 161).
109   Held (1991: 167).
110   Tilly (1995).
111   Spruyt (1994).

Hirst and Thompson, whose vigorous critique of simplistic views on globalization emphasizes the continuing relevance of nation-states, acknowledge, nonetheless, the state's new role:

> The emerging forms of governance of international markets and other economic processes involve the major national governments but in a new role: states come to function less as "sovereign" entities and more as components of an international "polity". The central functions of the nation-state will become those of providing legitimacy for and ensuring the accountability of supranational and subnational governance mechanisms.[112]

Furthermore, in addition to its complex relationship to miscellaneous expressions of political power/representation, the nation-state is increasingly submitted to a more subtle, and more troubling, competition from sources of power that are undefined, and, sometimes, indefinable. These are networks of capital, production, communication, crime, international institutions, supranational military apparatuses, non-governmental organizations, transnational religions, movements of public opinion, and social movements of all kinds, including terrorist movements. And below the state, there are communities, tribes, localities, cults, and gangs.

So, while nation-states continue to exist, and they will continue to do so in the foreseeable future, they are, and will increasingly be, *nodes of a broader network of power.* They will often be confronted by other flows of power in the network, which directly contradict the exercise of their authority, as happens nowadays to central banks whenever they have the illusion of countering global markets' runs against a given currency. Or, for that matter, when nation-states, alone or together, decide to eradicate drug production, traffic, or consumption, a battle repeatedly lost over the past two decades everywhere – except in Singapore (with all the implications of this remark). Nation-states have lost their sovereignty because the very concept of sovereignty, since Bodin, implies that it is not possible to lose sovereignty "a little bit": this was precisely the traditional *casus belli.* Nation-states may retain decision-making capacity, but, having become part of a network of powers and counterpowers, they are dependent on a broader system of enacting authority and influence from multiple sources. This statement, which I believe to be consistent with the observations and elaborations presented in this chapter, has serious consequences for the theory and practice of the state.

---

112   Hirst and Thompson (1996: 171).

The theory of the state has been dominated, for decades, by the debate between institutionalism, pluralism, and instrumentalism in their different versions.[113] Institutionalists, in the Weberian tradition, have emphasized the autonomy of state institutions, following the inner logic of an historically given state once the winds of history planted its seeds in a territory that became its national basis. Pluralists explain the structure and evolution of the state as the outcome of a variety of influences in the endless (re)formation of the state, according to the dynamics of a plural civil society, in a constant enacting of the constitutional process.

Instrumentalists, Marxists or historicists, see the state as the expression of social actors pursuing their interests and achieving domination, be it without challenge within the state ("the executive committee of the bourgeoisie"), or as the unstable result of struggles, alliances, and compromise. But, as Giddens, Guehenno, and Held argue, in all schools of thought, *the relationship between state and society, and thus the theory of the state, is considered in the context of the nation, and has the nation-state as its frame of reference*. What happens when, in Held's formulation, the "national community" is not any more the "relevant community" as such a frame of reference?[114] How can we think of non-national, diversified social interests represented in, or fighting for, the state? The whole world? But the unit relevant for capital flows is not the same as that for labor, for social movements, or for cultural identities. How can interests and values expressed, globally and locally, in a variable geometry, be linked up in the structure and policies of the nation-state?

Thus, *from the point of view of theory*, we must reconstruct the categories to understand power relationships without presupposing the necessary intersection between nation and the state; that is, separating identity from instrumentality. New power relationships, beyond the powerless nation-state, must be understood as the capacity to control global instrumental networks on the basis of specific identities, or, seen from the perspective of global networks, to subdue any identity in the fulfillment of transnational instrumental goals. The control of the nation-state, one way or the other, becomes just one means among others to assert power; that is, the capacity to impose a given will/interest/value, regardless of consensus. The theory of power, in this context, supersedes the theory of the state, as I shall elaborate in the Conclusion to this volume.

---

113   Carnoy (1984); Carnoy and Castells (2001).
114   Held (1991: 142–3).

Thus, the theory of the state must be recast to comprehend the practice of the network state in the context of what Habermas conceptualizes as the postnational constellation. The key issue is that power relationships, while not being confined to the state, continue to be the essence of the practice of the state, in all its forms. Therefore, while life in the networks raises matters of coordination and compatibility between the institutions and actors that are the nodes of each network, we must also account for the manifestation of power relationships in this new organizational environment.

To understand the dynamics of the state we must place it in its relationship to society. In addition, in my own conceptualization, this relationship has to be specified to include the territorial differentiation of the state at different levels: national, regional, and local, as I argued above. Each territorial level of the state expresses the alliance of specific social interests and values that, together, constitute what Gramsci called "the power bloc," underlying the actual power institutionalized in the state.[115] This power bloc does not necessarily have to include the social actors that hold power in society. In fact, in contemporary societies, the interests and values that are dominant in society are represented by professional politicians. We know that they are representative of these interests because of the way in which they act in the political institutions, relating to the political constituencies that support them with votes and with financial and organizational means for their campaigns. True, there are always exceptions, such as Berlusconi accessing power on behalf of his own business interests, using the power of his own media. But, even in such cases, what made his access to government possible is the power bloc of economic interests and social values that clustered around his political coalition. Political leaders are institutional entrepreneurs who bet their fate on certain products (symbolic themes, policy decisions), and certain markets (constituencies).

This power bloc is not monolithic: it is the result of a complex pattern of social alliances and compromises that may sometimes include social interests or values that are not dominant in society (e.g. labor or environmentalists), but play a subordinate role in the alliance in exchange for advancing some elements of their specific agenda. The complex, but necessary concept to introduce here, in order to understand the dynamics of the state, is the territorial differentiation of the relationship between the power bloc and the state, in the terms already presented in this chapter. The power bloc at the national level is not reproduced at the level of each locality or region.

115   Gramsci (1975); Buci-Glucksman (1978); Carnoy and Castells (2001).

Even if the political actors sometimes belong to the same party, they may actually represent different interests and values than those supported by the party at the national level.

This concept of the territorial differentiation of the state in its relationship to the power bloc allows us to consider this relationship at a higher level of complexity in the networks of governance constituted above the nation-state. In the same way that the local state expresses, at the same time, local power relationships and the power institutionalized at the national level of the state, the nation-state inserted into the global network state represents the specific power bloc of its national society, while being subordinated to the overarching logic of the interests expressed in the global power bloc – a more complex and changing reality.

Nevertheless, the state, at any level, does not express exclusively and directly the interests and values of the power bloc. This is because the state has its own interests, and its own historical inertia: its administrative elite holds to its own interests and values. Also, state institutions have been historically produced as crystallizations of power blocs and social struggles in the specific evolution of each state, and bear the marks of a conflictive process. Furthermore, in contrast to the instrumentalist approach to the state, to understand the complexity of state policy we need to take into account the dialectics between domination and legitimation, and between development and redistribution. Let me elaborate on this analytical proposition.

States are organizations (systems of means oriented toward certain goals) whose performance is shaped by the interests and values that have institutionalized their domination in the historical process. But states also aim at representing the interests of their subjects, so legitimizing their capacity to manage their lives. Thus, the right balance between domination and legitimation determines the political stability of state institutions, usually through political actors alternating in government, within the limits of ensuring the domination of the structural interests institutionalized in the state (e.g. the domination of market relationships in a state built around the principles of capitalism). Even in non-democratic regimes, the principle of legitimation must be present in the practice of the state, at least for a segment of society, or for some shared values (e.g. the defense of the nation as a symbolic community). On the other hand, for the state to have access to resources on which its existence depends, it also performs a key role in fostering development and regulating redistribution. The process of development refers to the growth of the material wealth of society through an increase in productivity. Redistribution refers to the allocation of resources among different groups, organizations, and institutions, following the values and interests established in these institutions and enforced by the state.

This simple analytical model sees the state as the institutional system that mediates and manages the dual relationship between domination and legitimation, and between development and redistribution, under the influence of conflicts and negotiations between different social actors. This set of relationships is territorially differentiated, so that each state institution in each locality or region expresses at the same time the dynamics of the local and regional society (including the national and transnational interests actually present in the locality or region), as well as the overall set of relationships present in the nation-state. The hierarchy of authority between the nation-state and the local state ensures the domination in the last resort of the national set of relationships between the power bloc and the state, over the local configuration of the power bloc.

The variable geometry of the state, constructed around the positioning of various power blocs in the four processes of domination, legitimation, development, and redistribution, continues to work at the supranational level in the practice of global governance. When the state links up with other states, or fragments of states, or associations of states, in the network state, this mediation between the four terms of the relationship between state and society does not disappear, it is redefined. Each individual state has to perform these four functions in relation to its own society. This performance, however, is dependent on what the state does *vis-à-vis* the nodes of the overall network, from which resources are obtained, and thanks to whom, domination is ensured. Therefore, the actual practice of the network state is characterized by the tension between three processes that are intertwined in the policies of the state: how individual states relate to their constituencies, by representing their weighted interests in the network state; how they ensure the balance and power of the network state to which they belong, as this network state provides the operational platform that ensures the efficiency of the state in a globalized system; and how they advance their own specific interests *vis-à-vis* other states in their shared network.

The state must continue to perform the four different functions I have proposed, in this three-dimensional political space. This is what constitutes the reality of global governance. As Jacquet et al. explain, we think in terms of governance as indicating the act of governing without government. The process of governance is formal and informal at the same time, it relates to procedures, and mutual understanding, more than to legislation, but it also induces a body of shared legislation, and institutions. It is, in the last resort, "an apparatus of production of public norms and interventions," or else, in Pascal Lamy's definition, "the ensemble of transactions by which collective rules are elaborated, decided, legitimated, implemented, and controlled."[116]

However, in my view, we still have to conceptualize how power relationships operate in this process of global governance. We must account for the operation of power relationships within the state, between states and their societies, and between states in their shared network. The analysis of power relationships in this context can only proceed empirically, referring to specific policies and specific forms of networking. The usefulness of the conceptual framework proposed above must be judged in the practice of such an analysis.

What we can say, though, is that the political decision-making system founded on the network state is characterized by higher orders of complexity and uncertainty. Therefore, political strategies enacted by the state increase their relative autonomy *vis-à-vis* the interests that they are supposed to represent. Agency prevails over structure. Nevertheless, the structure (the global network society) determines the parameters framing the field of action for strategic actors. This is expressed, for instance, by the concept of common goods that environmental economists have proposed to emphasize the common interest of, among other matters, preserving the planet from an irreversible process of long-term global warming.[117] Or, else, preventing global epidemics, AIDS, SARS, and others.

We could use a similar perspective in other domains, for instance, in the regulation of global financial markets, to preserve the common good of financial stability and predictability of investment. Or to preserve the world from global crime or global terror. Or to preserve peace. Or to eradicate hunger. Or to ensure respect for global human rights. However, I have deliberately broadened the meaning of common public goods to illustrate that the interpretation of what is a common good may be biased toward specific interests. In other words, the definition of what exactly constitutes a public good, which becomes the shared goal of a network state, is in itself a power relationship. When we say that the fight against global terrorism is a common good, does it mean that Palestinians (or Colombian guerrillas) must refrain from any violent act regardless of their condition of oppression? When we affirm the universality of human rights does it mean that all transgressions should be punished by the inter-

116   Cited by Jacquet et al. (2002: 13).
117   Severino and Tubiana (2002).

national community? And who is the international community? This is the point I want to make: defining global governance goals in the absence of legitimate global government institutions depends on power relationships expressed in the network state.

This asymmetrical complexity of the network state introduces maximum distance between domination and legitimation in the practice of each state. To ensure the prevalence of its specific interests, and of the dominant interests it represents in its own society, the state can hardly refer to the representation of its constituency at large. It must assume the interests of the overall network state, and therefore it must respect the domination of the most powerful interests in this network, as a condition of being a node in it. On the other hand, within the network state, there are alliances formed to impose conditions on other nodes in the network. For instance, environmental conservation, a clear common good, is often used by the rich, developed states to justify their protectionism, in spite of the supposedly common rules for free trade for all WTO members. Another example: in the view of multinational corporations, largely shared by the G-8 states, intellectual property rights are a key factor in the development of the knowledge economy, but at the same time, their strict enforcement becomes a major obstacle for the redistribution of wealth in the planet. In another instance of power relationships: if the United States unilaterally imposes its military strategy to ensure the domination of its national interests, as well as its legitimation on its own people, it decreases its legitimacy *vis-à-vis* other states in the network. It also jeopardizes the legitimacy of these states in their own societies, and ultimately may threaten the stability of the fragile network state built over time to share governance in a global world managed by nation-states.

Thus, ultimately, the stability of the network state depends on assuming the loss of individual sovereignty for every node of the network, including the most dominant of these nodes. The affirmation of sovereign rights by some node(s), as an ad hoc amendment to the informal constitution of the network state, is ultimately contradictory to the existence of the network state. The crisis of the network state would then develop into a crisis of global governance itself, as individual nation-states would again retrench into the defense of their specific interests, to be negotiated case by case, and context by context, with other states and political actors.

It is an open question whether a globalized world can be governed by a disparate collection of national interests. This is why several respected political theorists, with Jürgen Habermas and Ulrich Beck at the forefront of this debate, consider the transition of our society to a cosmopolitan system of government indispensable, starting, as the most feasible step, with a European federal state. Such a cosmopolitan government is not a world government. A cosmopolitan government, in Ulrich Beck's terms, is a different kind of state.[118] As he says, paradoxically, in order to fulfill their national interests, nation-states must de-nationalize, and internationalize. So doing, they break the mold of the nation-state based on the assimilation of sovereignty and autonomy. In his view, if sovereignty is understood as the capacity of a given country to influence the problems of the world on behalf of its citizens, then it is only by engaging in international cooperation, by networking, that states can actually become sovereigns in the global, risk society. Therefore, actual sovereignty can only be accrued by losing autonomy. The institutionalization of the network state in a cosmopolitan form of government could then be a form of collective assertion of sovereignty at the price of reducing autonomy.

However, as both Habermas and Beck acknowledge, this cosmopolitan system of governance could only be the result of the rise of a cosmopolitan culture in civil societies around the world. Habermas writes: "The change of perspective from 'international relations' to a world domestic policy cannot be expected from the governments unless people reward this transformation of consciousness."[119] Public opinion data, in Europe as elsewhere, point in the opposite direction, starting with the widespread reluctance of Europeans to surrender national sovereignty. American unilateralism runs directly counter to this vision of bringing together a globalized economy, environment, and society with a cosmopolitan consciousness, and a cosmopolitan government. Indeed, what we observe in the early twenty-first century is the growing disjunction between the globalization of issues, the self-identification of people, and the affirmation of national interests in the reluctantly shared ground of the informal network state.

Conclusion: The King of the Universe, Sun Tzu, and the Crisis of Democracy

In sum, the actual operating unit of political management in a globalized world is a network state formed by nation-states, international institutions, associations of nation-states, regional and local governments, and non-governmental organizations. It is this network state

118   Beck (2003).
119   Habermas (1998/2001: 145).

that negotiates, manages, and decides global, national, and local issues. This network state expresses power relationships between its different components, and within the power blocs underlying each level of the state. Not all the nodes of the network are equal, and their interests diverge, coalesce, or conflict, depending on issues and contexts. Moreover, under some circumstances, one of the components of the network (e.g. the American state in the early twenty-first century) may decide to impose its interests on the whole network, using its superior organizational capacity. While it is unlikely that it can prevail systematically (if it does the network would be replaced by a global chain of command), its unilateral logic destabilizes the delicate balance of cooperation and competition on which the network state is based. Ultimately, unilateralism breaks the network state into different networks and introduces a confrontational logic between these networks. Therefore, in analytical terms, the reality of the state in the network society requires an understanding of both networking and domination, the practice of shared global governance and the new forms of war-making.

So, will the nation-state wither as far as historical practice is concerned? In answer to this question, Martin Carnoy issues a resounding no.[120] He argues, and I concur with him, that national competitiveness is still a function of national policies, and the attractiveness of economies to foreign multinationals is a function of local economic conditions; that multinationals depend heavily on their home states for direct or indirect protection; and that national human–capital policies are essential for the productivity of economic units located in a national territory. Supporting this argument, Hirst and Thompson show that, if in addition to the relationship between multinational corporations and the state, we include the wide range of policies through which nation-states can use their regulatory powers to ease or block movements of capital, labor, information, and commodities, it is clear that, at this point in history, the fading away of the nation-state is a fallacy.[121]

However, in the past decade, nation-states have been transformed from sovereign subjects into strategic actors, playing their interests, and the interests they are supposed to represent, in a global system of interaction, in a condition of systemically shared sovereignty. They marshal considerable influence, but they exercise their power in a network of interaction with supranational macro-forces and subnational micro-processes. Furthermore, when acting strategically in the international arena, they are submitted to tremendous internal stress. On the one hand, to foster the productivity and

---

120 Carnoy (1993: 88).
121 Hirst and Thompson (1996).

competitiveness of their economies they must ally themselves closely with global economic interests, and abide by global rules favorable to capital flows, while their societies are being asked to wait patiently for the trickled down benefits of corporate ingenuity. Also, to be good citizens of a multilateral world order, nation-states have to cooperate with each other, accept the pecking order of geopolitics, and contribute dutifully to subdue renegade nations and agents of potential disorder, regardless of the actual feelings of their usually parochial citizens. Yet, on the other hand, nation-states survive beyond historical inertia because of the defensive communalism of nations and people in their territories, hanging onto their last refuge in order not to be pulled away by the whirlwind of global flows. Thus, the more states emphasize communalism, the less effective they become as co-agents of a global system of shared power. However, the more they triumph in the planetary scene, in close partnership with the agents of globalization, the less they represent their national constituencies. When they give exclusive priority to their national interests, as is the case with the American superpower, they destabilize the networks on which they ultimately depend for their survival and well-being. Politics, almost everywhere in the world, is dominated by this fundamental contradiction.

Thus, it may well be that nation-states are reaching the status of Saint-Exupéry's King of the Universe, fully in control of ordering the sun to rise every day. From the East. Unless they force a new sunrise from the West, from a nuclear blast. But, at the same time, while losing sovereignty, states, in all their forms, emerge as major intervening players, in a purely strategic world, such as the one informing Sun Tzu's war treatise 2,500 years ago:

> It is the business of a general to be quiet and thus ensure secrecy; upright and just, and thus maintain order. He must be able to mystify his officers and men by false reports and appearances, and thus keep them in total ignorance. By altering his arrangements and changing his plans he keeps the enemy without definite knowledge. By shifting his camp and taking circuitous routes, he prevents the enemy from anticipating his purpose. At the critical moment the leader of an army acts like one who has climbed up a height and then kicks away the ladder behind him.[122]

This is how states can still be victorious, and regain a share of their power, on the condition of "kicking away" the ladder of their nations, thus ushering in the crisis of democracy.

---

122   Sun Tzu (c.505–496 BC, 1988: 131–3).

6

Informational Politics and the Crisis of Democracy

Introduction: The Politics of Society

Power used to be in the hands of princes, oligarchies, and ruling elites; it was defined as the capacity to impose one's will on others, modifying their behavior. This image of power does not fit with our reality any longer. Power is everywhere and nowhere: it is in mass production, in financial flows, in lifestyles, in the hospital, in the school, in television, in images, in messages, in technologies... Since the world of objects escapes to our will, our identity is no longer defined by what we do but by what we are, thus making our societies somewhat closer to the experience of so-called traditional societies, searching for balance rather than for progress. Such is the central question to which political thought and action must respond: how to restore a link between the excessively open space of the economy, and the excessively closed, and fragmented world of cultures?... The fundamental matter is not seizing power, but to recreate society, to invent politics anew, to avoid the blind conflict between open markets and closed communities, to overcome the breaking down of societies where the distance increases between the included and the excluded, those in and those out.
Alain Touraine, *Lettre à Lionel*, pp. 36–8, 42; my translation

The blurring of boundaries of the nation-state confuses the definition of citizenship. The absence of a clear situs of power dilutes social control and diffuses political challenges. The rise of communalism, in its different forms, weakens the principle of political sharing on which democratic politics is based. The growing inability of the state to control capital flows and ensure social security diminishes its relevance for the average citizen. The emphasis on local institutions of governance increases the distance between mechanisms of political control and management of global problems. The voiding of the social contract between capital, labor, and the state, sends everybody home to fight for their individual interests, counting exclusively on their own forces. As Guehenno writes:

> Liberal democracy was based on two postulates, currently called into question: the existence of a political sphere, the site of social consensus and general interest; and the existence of actors provided with their own energy, who exercised their rights, and manifested their powers, even before society constituted them as autonomous subjects. Nowadays, instead of autonomous subjects, there are only ephemeral situations, which serve as support to provisional alliances supported by capacities mobilized for each occasion. Instead of a political space, the site of collective solidarity, there are just dominant perceptions, as ephemeral as the interests that manipulate them. There is simultaneous atomization and homogenization. A society that is endlessly fragmented, without memory and without solidarity, a society that recovers its unity only in the succession of images that the media return to every week. It is a society without citizens, and ultimately, a non-society. This crisis is not – as Europeans would like in the hope of escaping from it – the crisis of a particular model, the American model. The United States certainly pushes to the extreme the logic of confrontation of interests that dissolves the idea of a common interest; and the management of collective perceptions reaches in America a degree of sophistication without parallel in Europe. Yet, extreme cases help us to understand average situations, and the American crisis reveals our future.[1]

The transformation of politics, and of democratic processes, in the network society is even deeper than presented in these analyses. Because, to the processes cited above, I shall add, as a major factor inducing this transformation, the direct consequences of new information technologies on the political debate and power-seeking strategies. This technological dimension interacts with the broader trends characteristic of the network society, and with the communal reactions to the dominant processes emerging from this social structure. But it adds a powerful twist to this transformation, inducing what I call *informational politics*. Thus, while Bobbio is correct in pinpointing the persistent differences between political right and political left throughout the world (basically because of their sharply divergent

---

1   Guehenno (1993: 46); my translation.

concern with social equality),[2] right, left, and center must process their projects and strategies through a similar technological medium if they wish to reach society, so securing the support of enough citizens to win access to the state. I contend that this technological sharing induces new rules of the game that, in the context of the social, cultural, and political transformations presented in this book, dramatically affect the substance of politics. The key point is that electronic media (including not only television and radio, but all forms of communication, such as newspapers and the Internet) have become the privileged space of politics.[3] Not that all politics can be reduced to images, sounds, or symbolic manipulation. But, without it, there is no chance of winning or exercising power. Thus, everybody ends up playing the same game, although not in the same way or with the same purpose.

For the sake of clarity, let me warn the reader, from the outset of this analysis, against two simplistic, erroneous versions of the thesis according to which electronic media dominate politics. On the one hand, it is sometimes argued that the media impose their political choices on public opinion. This is not so, because, as I will elaborate below, the media are extremely diverse. Their linkages to politics and ideology are highly complex, and indirect, albeit with obvious exceptions whose frequency depends on countries, periods, and specific media. In fact, in many cases, media campaigns may support the public against the political establishment, as was the case in America during the Watergate crisis, or in 1990s' Italy, when most of the media supported the judicial anti corruption drive against both traditional political parties, and against Berlusconi, in spite of Berlusconi's ownership of the three private national television channels. On the other hand, public opinion is often considered to be a passive recipient of messages, easily open to manipulation. Again, this is belied by the empirical record. As I argued in volume I, chapter 5, there is a two-way process of interaction between the media and their audience concerning the actual impact of messages, which are twisted, appropriated, and occasionally subverted by the audience. In the American context, the analysis by Page and Shapiro of citizens' attitudes toward policy issues in a long-term perspective shows the independence and common sense of collective public opinion in most circumstances.[4] Overall, the media are rooted in society, and their interaction with the political process is highly undetermined, depending on context, the strategies of political actors, and specific interaction between an array of social, cultural, and political features.

2   Bobbio (1994).
3   Volkmer (1999, 2003).
4   Page and Shapiro (1992); Norris (2000b).

By pinpointing the critical role of electronic media in contemporary politics, I am saying something different. I am saying that, because of the convergent effects of the crisis of traditional political systems and of the dramatically increased pervasiveness of the new media, political communication and information are essentially captured in the space of the media. Outside the sphere of the media there is only political marginality. What happens in this media-dominated political space is not determined by the media: it is an open social and political process. But the logic, and organization, of electronic media frame and structure politics. I shall argue, on the basis of evidence, and with the help of a number of cross-cultural examples, that this framing of politics by their capture in the space of the media (a trend characteristic of the information age) impacts not only elections, but political organization, decision-making, and governance, ultimately modifying the nature of the relationship between state and society. And because current political systems are still based in organizational forms and political strategies of the industrial era, they have become politically obsolete, and their autonomy is being denied by the flows of information on which they depend. This is a fundamental source of the crisis of democracy in the information age.

To explore its contours, I will use data and examples from various countries. The United States is the democracy that first reached this technological stage, in a very open, unstructured political system, and thus it better manifests the broader trend. However, I certainly reject the idea that the "American model" will have to be followed by other countries in the world. Nothing is more specifically rooted in history than political institutions and political actors. Yet, in the same way that democratic habits and procedures, originating in England, America, and France, diffused around the world in the past two centuries, I would argue that informational politics, as it is practiced in the United States (for example, the dominance of television, computerized political marketing, instant polling as an instrument of political navigation, character assassination as political strategy and so on) is a good indicator of the times to come, with all due cultural/ institutional translations. To broaden the scope of my analysis, I will be discussing, as well, examples of political processes in the UK, Russia, Spain, Italy, Japan, and, in an effort to reach out to new democracies in less-developed countries, I shall focus on the case of Bolivia. On the basis of these observations, I shall try to link up processes of social, institutional, and technological transformation at the roots of the crisis of democracy in the network society. In conclusion, I shall explore the potential for new forms of "informational democracy."

Media as the Space of Politics in the Information Age

Politics and the media: the citizens' connection

I shall state my argument before elaborating it empirically. In the context of democratic politics, access to state institutions depends on the ability to mobilize a majority of votes from citizens. In contemporary societies people receive their information, and form their political opinion, essentially through the media, and fundamentally from television (tables 6.1 and 6.2). Furthermore, at least in the United States, television is the most credible source of news, and its credibility has increased over time (figure 6.1). Thus, to act on people's minds, and wills, conflicting political options, embodied in parties and candidates, use the media as their fundamental vehicle of communication, influence, and persuasion. So doing, as long as the media are relatively autonomous from political power, political actors have to abide by the rules, technology, and interests of the media. The media frame politics.[5] And because governance is dependent on re-election, or election to a higher office, governance itself becomes dependent on the daily assessment of the potential impact of government decisions on public opinion, as measured by opinion polls, focus groups,

Table 6.1 Sources of news in the US, 1993–2002 (%)

Date	Television	News-papers	Radio	Magazines	Internet	Other
January 1993	83	52	17	5	n.a.	1
January 1994	83	51	15	10	n.a.	5
September 1995	82	63	20	10	n.a.	1
January 1996	88	61	25	8	n.a.	2
January 1999	82	42	18	4	6	2
October 1999	80	48	19	5	11	2
February 2001	76	40	16	4	10	2
September 2001	74	45	18	6	13	1
January 2002	82	42	21	3	14	2

Note: The question asked was: "How have you been getting most of your news about national and international issues? From television, from newspapers, from radio, from magazines, or from the Internet?" (two responses permitted).
Source: Pew Research Center for the People and the Press Surveys (various years)

5 Edwards and Wood (1999); Croteau and Hoynes (2000: 229–6); Miller and Krosnick (2000); White et al. (2002).

Table 6.2   Sources of political information of residents of
Cochabamba, Bolivia, 1996

Source of information	% declaring main source of information	% expressing preference for source
Newspapers	32.0	8.7
Radio	43.3	15.7
Television	51.7	46.0
Other	4.7	–

Source: Survey of Information Sources of Cochabamba Residents, Centro de
Estudios de la Realidad Economica y Social, Cochabamba, 1996

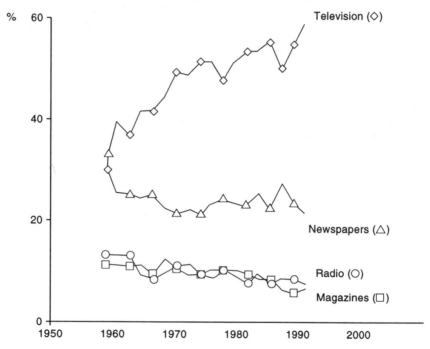

Figure 6.1   Credibility of news source in US, 1959–91
Source: Roper Organization, *America's Watching: Public Attitudes toward Television*
(New York, 1991)

and image analyses. Furthermore, in a world increasingly saturated by
information, the most effective messages are the most simple, and the
most ambivalent, so that they leave room for people's own projections.
Images fit best into this characterization. Audiovisual media are the
primary feeders of people's minds, as they relate to public affairs.

But who are the media? What is the source of their political autonomy? And how do they frame politics? In democratic societies, mainstream media are, essentially, business groups, increasingly concentrated and globally interconnected, although they are, at the same time, highly diversified and geared toward segmented markets (see chapter 5, and volume I, chapter 5). Government-owned television and radio have come close to the behavior of private media groups in the past decade, in order to be able to survive global competition, and have become equally dependent on audience ratings.[6] Audience ratings are essential because the main source of income in the media business is advertising.[7] Performance in audience ratings requires an appealing medium, and, in the case of news, credibility. Without credibility, news is worthless, either in terms of money or power. Credibility requires relative distance *vis-à-vis* specific political options, within the parameters of mainstream political and moral values. Furthermore, only from a credible position of independence can this independence be parlayed occasionally into an open, opportunistic political endorsement, or into a hidden financial deal in exchange for support by diffusing or suppressing information.

The autonomy of the media, rooted in their business interests, also fits well with the ideology of the profession, and with the legitimacy and self-respect of journalists. They report, do not take sides. Information is paramount, news analysis must be documented, opinion must be regulated, and detachment is the rule. This double bind of independence, as corporations and as professionals, is reinforced by the fact that the media world is submitted to relentless competition, even if it is increasingly oligopolistic competition.[8] Any breach in credibility for a given TV network or newspaper, and the competition will take audience (market) share away. Thus, on the one hand, the media must be close to politics and government, close enough to access information, to benefit from regulation, and, in many countries, to receive considerable subsidies. On the other hand, they must be neutral enough and distant enough to maintain their credibility, so being the intermediaries between citizens and parties in the production and consumption of information flows and images, at the roots of public opinion formation, voting, and political decision-making.

Once politics is captured in the space of the media, political actors themselves close the field of media politics by organizing political action primarily around the media: for instance, by leaking information to

6   Perez-Tabernero et al. (1993).
7   MacDonald (1990).
8   Volkmer (2003).

advance a given personal or political agenda. This leads, inevitably, to counter-leaks, so making the media the battleground in which political forces and personalities, as well as pressure groups, try to undermine each other, to collect the benefits in opinion polls, in the polling booths, in parliamentary votes, and in government decisions.

Naturally, media politics does not preclude other forms of political activity. Grassroots campaigns have proved their vitality in recent years, as shown by the Christian Coalition in the United States, the Green party in Germany, or the Workers party in Brazil. Mass gatherings and street demonstrations are still essential rituals in Spanish, French, Italian, and Mexican political campaigns. And candidates must still travel, appear, shake hands, go to meetings, kiss children (but carefully), address students, policemen, and every possible ethnic group. Yet, with the exception of fundraising activities, the main target of these various forms of person-to-person politics is to stage the persona, or the message, in the media, be it prime-time TV news, a radio talk show, or a featured article in an influential newspaper. In Spanish political campaigns (and I suppose in other countries as well), leading candidates speaking at a public meeting are warned by a red light in their micro when there is live TV coverage (for one or two minutes), so that he/she switches automatically to a pre-programmed sound bite on a topic of choice, regardless of what he/she was saying to the live audience. In American elections, town meetings, school children's gatherings, stops along a candidate's bus, train, or plane route, are arranged in accordance with times and sites of potential media coverage. Cheerers and jeerers are on stage to provide the chance for interesting footage.

However, let me repeat again: to say that the media are the space of politics does not mean that television dictates what people decide, or that the ability to spend money on TV advertising or to manipulate images is, by itself, an overwhelming factor. All countries, and particularly the United States, are full of examples in which a television advertising barrage was not enough to elect a candidate, or a mediocre media performance did not preclude a candidate from winning (although examples also abound of the enhancing impact of TV presence in launching, and sustaining, a politician; for example, Ronald Reagan and Ross Perot in the United States, Felipe Gonzalez in Spain, Berlusconi in Italy, Jirinovsky in Russia in 1993, Aoshima in Tokyo in 1995, the late Pim Fortuyn in The Netherlands in 2002). In 1990s' Brazil, Collor de Mello was elected president out of nowhere because of his masterful television performance, but people took to the streets to force his resignation once it became clear that he was a crook pillaging the state. Three years later, Fernando Henrique Cardoso, not unskillful on TV, but obviously disliking media gimmicks, was elected president because, as Finance Minister, he was able to subdue hyperinflation for the first time in decades, although the support of O *Globo Televisao* for his candidacy did help. And in 2002, Lula, the Brazilian left-wing leader, was elected president by a landslide vote, in spite of general support for his opponent by the mainstream media.

Neither television nor other media determine political outcomes by themselves, precisely because media politics is a contradictory realm, where different actors and strategies are played out, with diverse skills, and with various outcomes, sometimes resulting in unexpected conse-quences. *Mediacracy* is not contradictory to democracy because it is as plural and competitive as the political system is. That is, not much. Furthermore, if we consider the previous system, of a party-dominated democracy, where party organizations, largely insulated from the majority of citizens, entirely decided political programs and candidates, it is arguable which system provides for broader citizen input, at least once we had passed the mythical times of communal town meetings.

Yet, *the critical matter is that, without an active presence in the media, political proposals or candidates do not stand a chance of gathering broad support.* Media politics is not all politics, but all politics must go through the media to affect decision-making. So doing, *politics is fundamentally framed, in its substance, organization, process, and leadership, by the inherent logic of the media system, particularly by the new electronic media.* As for how exactly this framing occurs it will help to refer to the actual evolution of media politics, starting with the American experience of the past three decades.

Show politics and political marketing: the American model

The transformation of American politics in the last decades of the twentieth century resulted from three interconnected processes: (a) the decline of political parties, and of their role in selecting candi-dates; (b) the emergence of a complex media system, anchored in television, but with an increasing diversity of flexible media, electron-ically interconnected; and (c) the development of political marketing, with constant opinion polling, feedback systems between polling and politicking, media spinning, computerized direct mailing and 'phone banks, and real time adjustments of candidates and issues to the format that could win.[9]

9 Abramson et al. (1988); Patterson (1993); Roberts and McCombs (1994); Balz and Brown-stein (1996).

Although the transformation of the American political system has deep roots in social and cultural trends, the most direct manifestation of these transformations were the electoral reforms of the McGovern–Frazer Committee in response to the 1968 Democratic National Convention where the party apparatus chose Humphrey as a presidential candidate over the more popular Eugene McCarthy. Under the new system delegates to the convention were elected, in their vast majority, through direct primaries among presidential contenders.[10] Thus, while in the 1950s 40 percent of the delegates were chosen by this method, in the 1990s the proportion reached 80 percent.[11] In addition, a series of campaign finance reforms have forced candidates to rely more on their fundraising skills, and direct contacts with society, and much less on party support. Interest groups and citizens at large have pushed party organizations to the backstage of American politics.[12] Both trends have extraordinarily reinforced the role of the media: they have become the privileged intermediaries between candidates and the public, decisively influencing presidential primaries, as well as congressional and gubernatorial elections. And, because media advertising and media-oriented campaigning are very expensive, candidates have to rely on the support of private donors and political action committees external to the party system.[13]

The political role of the media has evolved considerably in the past three decades, both technologically and organizationally. Experts consider that the turning point in the relationship between media, polls, and politics was John Kennedy's campaign in 1960.[14] Not only did Kennedy base his campaign for the first time on polling and television strategy, but his victory was largely credited to his televised debate with Nixon (the first of the genre), which he dominated, while the radio audience of the same debate selected Nixon as the winner.[15] Subsequently, television became the agenda-setting device of American politics. While influential newspapers, such as *The New York Times* or *The Washington Post*, are critical sources of investigative reporting, and of opinion trends, only events that are played out on television reach an audience large enough to set, or reverse, a trend in public opinion. Thus, television, newspapers, and radio work as a system, with newspapers often reporting an event, and elaborating on it, television digesting it and diffusing it to a broad audience, and

10   Patterson (1993: 30–3).
11   Ansolabehere et al. (1993: 75).
12   Magleby and Nelson (1990).
13   Garber (1984, 1996); Gunlicks (1993).
14   Jacobs and Shapiro (1995).
15   Ansolabehere et al. (1993: 73).

radio talk shows providing the opportunity for citizen interaction, and for customized, partisan debate on the issues raised by television.[16]

The increasingly central political role of television has induced two major features. On the one hand, political spending on television has skyrocketed: in the early 1960s, about 9 percent of the budgets of national political campaigns were spent on TV advertising, while in the 1990s, the proportion was about 25 percent of much larger budgets; in 1990, an estimated $203 million went on airtime political advertising;[17] and in 1994, $350 million were spent on television political advertising.[18] The figure for the 1996 elections was over $800 million, and in 2000 reached well over 1 billion. On the other hand, political spinning by advisers to political candidates has become an essential factor in political campaigning, as well as in obtaining support, or opposition, for government decisions. What really matters is not so much the event that is originally reported but the debate around it, how it is debated, by whom it is debated, and for how long it is debated. Victory, not explanation or clarification, becomes the critical matter. For instance, in 1993–94, after months of acrimonious debate on Clinton's health plan reform proposal, which occupied extensive media attention, polls indicated that the large majority of Americans were confused and unsure about the content of the proposal, and about the substance of criticisms aimed at the plan. Never mind. What the barrage of media controversy, fed by insurance companies, medical associations, and the pharmaceutical industry, succeeded in doing was to kill the proposal even before it came before Congress for a vote, let alone was discussed by the citizenry.[19] Media have become the main political arena.

Technology has transformed the political role of the media, not only by its effects on the media themselves, but by linking up the media system in real time with political marketing.[20] Starting in the late 1960s, the introduction of computers in the tabulation of polls led to the emergence of "strategic polling," testing different political strategies on targeted groups of potential voters, so as to modify the strategy, the form, and even the substance of the message as the campaign develops.[21] In the next two decades pollsters such as Patrick Caddell, Peter Hart, and Robert Teeter, decisively influenced

16 Friedland (1996).
17 Ansolabehere et al. (1993: 89).
18 Freeman (1994).
19 Fallows (1996).
20 D. West (1993).
21 Moore (1992: 128–9).

campaign strategy, and became key intermediaries between candidates, citizens, and the media. Together with image makers and political advertisers, they built campaigns, platforms, issues, and personas by feeding back opinion trends into media reports and vice versa.[22] As technology accelerated media reporting, and increased the speed and flexibility of information systems, feedback effects, and spins, became daily activities, so that in most high political offices, starting with the White House, communication strategists meet every day early in the morning to monitor the pulse of the nation, being ready to intervene in real time, even changing messages and schedules between morning and afternoon, depending on reporting in the main sources (CNN, TV networks, leading morning newspapers).[23]

The fact that the media themselves are able to break the news any time, through uninterrupted reporting, means that communication warriors must be constantly on the alert, actually codifying and translating any political decision into the language of media politics, and measuring effects by polls and focus groups. Pollsters and image makers have become decisive political actors, able to make, and unmake, presidents, senators, congressmen, and governors, by blending information technology, mediology, political savvy, and cocky wizardry. And when they are mistaken, in their polls for instance, they are still influential because their mistakes change political trends, as in the 1996 New Hampshire Republican primary, in which polls' errors undermined Forbes's performance by measuring his votes against mistaken upward predictions of polls in previous days.[24]

As the media diversified and decentralized their scope in the 1990s, their grasp on political attitudes and behavior became ever more comprehensive.[25] Local cable television and radio talk shows customized audiences and allowed politicians to better target their message, while interest groups and ideological constituencies were more able to forward their arguments without the cautious filter of mainstream media. VCRs became essential tools in distributing packaged video messages in town meetings and private homes through direct mailing. Around the clock coverage by C-Span and CNN allowed for instant delivery of politically packaged news and information. In one instance, Republican leader Newt Gingrich was able to televise (by C-Span) a passionate, anti-liberal speech on the Congress floor, with no fear of stirring hostile reactions since, beyond the cameras' reach, the room was empty. Narrowcasting of messages to certain areas or

22   Mayer (1994).
23   Fallows (1996).
24   Mundy (1996).
25   Garber (1996); Hacker (1996).

social groups, through local stations, is fragmenting national politics, and undermining the influence of TV networks, yet embracing an even greater share of political expressions in the universe of electronic media. Additionally, the Internet has become the vehicle for campaign propaganda, the forum for controlled debate, and the means of linking up with supporters.[26] Often, television programs, or ads, refer to an Internet address where information or the development of arguments can be found, while computer-mediated communication picks up on media events, or on televised political advertising, to set up an electronic hook for concerned citizens.

By incorporating politics into their electronic space, the media decisively frame process, messages, and outcomes, regardless of the actual purpose or effectiveness of specific messages. Not that the medium is the message, because political options do differ, and the differences matter. But, by entering the media space, political projects, and politicians, are shaped in particular ways.[27] In which ways?

To understand the framing of politics by the logic of the media, we must refer to *the overarching principles governing news media: the race for audience ratings, in competition with entertainment; the necessary detachment from politics in order to induce credibility.* These translate into traditional assumptions in news coverage, as identified by Gitlin: "News concern the event, not the underlying condition; the person, not the group; conflict, not consensus; the fact that 'advances the story', not the one that explains it."[28] Only "bad news," relating to conflict, drama, unlawful deals, or objectionable behavior, is interesting news. Since news is increasingly framed to parallel (and compete with) entertainment shows, or sports events, so is its logic. It requires drama, suspense, conflict, rivalries, greed, deception, winners and losers, and, if possible, sex and violence. Following the pace, and language, of sports casting, "horse race politics" is reported as an endless game of ambitions, maneuvers, strategies, and counter-strategies, with the help of insider confidences and constant opinion polling from the media themselves. The media provide decreasing attention to what politicians have to say: the average soundbite shrank from 42 seconds in 1968 to less than 10 in 1992.[29] The media's detached attitude turns into cynicism when literally everything is interpreted as a pure strategic game. News reporting provides the basis for these analyses, but they are consider-

26   Klinenberg and Perrin (1996); Dutton (1999); Docter et al. (1999); Norris (2000b); Castells (2001); Kamarck and Nye (2002).
27   Patterson (1993); Balz and Brownstein (1996); Fallows (1996).
28   Gitlin (1980: 28).
29   Patterson (1993: 74).

ably reinforced by pundit shows (such as CNN's *Crossfire*), which are built around sharply opposing, impolite, vociferous commentators, who, of course, smile and shake hands at the end, thus underscoring that everything is a show. On the other hand, as James Fallows argues, the fast-paced, punchy, summary assessments of politics by increasingly popular television pundits directly impact the coverage of events in the TV news, and in newspapers.[30] In other words, media statements about politics become political events by themselves, with weekly announcements of winners and losers in the political race. As Sandra Moog writes:

> News stories are tending to devolve into mere discussions of public reactions to recent news coverage. Who are the winners and the losers, whose popularity ratings have crept up and whose have dropped, as a result of political events of the last month, last week, or last day. Frequent public opinion polling by news agencies makes this kind of hyper-reflexivity possible, by providing supposedly objective grounding for journalists' speculations about the impacts of political actions and the journalistic reactions to those actions, on the public's assessment of different politicians.[31]

An additional, and powerful, framing of political news reporting is the personalization of events.[32] Politicians, not politics, are the actors of the drama. And because they may change their programmatic proposals, while navigating the political waters, what remains in the minds of most people is personal motivation, and personal images, as the source of politics. Thus, questions of character come to the forefront of the political agenda, as the messenger becomes the message.

The framing of political news expands into the framing of politics itself, as strategists play in and with the media to influence voters. Thus, because only bad news is news, political advertising concentrates on negative messages, aimed at destroying the opponent's proposals, while advancing one's own program in very general terms. Indeed, experiments show that negative messages are much more likely to be retained, and to influence political opinion.[33] Furthermore, because politics is personalized in a world of image-making and soap operas, character assassination becomes the most potent weapon.[34] Political projects, government proposals, and political

30 Fallows (1996).
31 Moog (1996: 20).
32 Ansolabehere et al. (1993); Fallows (1996).
33 Ansolabehere and Iyengar (1994).
34 Garramone et al. (1990); Fallows (1996).

careers can be undermined or even destroyed with the revelation of improper behavior (Nixon's Watergate inaugurated the new era); with the exposure of private life departing from strict moral standards, and of the cover-up of information (Bill Clinton); or with the accumulation of various accusations, rumors, insinuations, relayed one after another in the media, as soon as the impact of one allegation starts fading away (Hillary Clinton, Felipe Gonzalez). In some cases, unproven allegations lead to dramatic personal consequences, such as the suicide of the targeted politician (for example, French Socialist Minister of Finance Pierre Beregovoy in 1993). Therefore, the monitoring of personal attacks on a daily basis, and counter-attacking, or threatening to, with similar allegations, becomes a fundamental part of political life. Indeed, in the 1992 presidential campaign Clinton's advisers forced Republicans to downplay their focus on Clinton's extramarital affair by threatening to elaborate on Bush's alleged involvement with a former assistant at the White House: they had found another Jennifer.[35] Communication strategists and spokepersons are at the center of informational politics.

The increasing restriction of media exposure to the content of political proposals (except in segmented media away from a mass audience; for example, public television or newspapers' lengthy special reports) leads to an extreme simplification of political messages. Complex political platforms are scrutinized to select a few key issues that will be highlighted, for a broad audience, in dichotomous terms: pro-life or pro-choice; gay rights or gay-bashing; social security and budget deficit versus balanced budget and dismantling of Medicaid. Referendum politics mimics television game shows, with the electoral buzzer announcing winners and losers, and pre-electoral bells (polls) sounding warnings. Images, coded messages, and horse-race politics between heroes and villains (they switch roles periodically), in a world of faked passions, hidden ambitions, and back-stabbing: such is American politics as framed in and by the electronic media, thus transformed into political real virtuality, determining access to the state. Could this "American model" be the forebear of a broader political trend, characterizing the information age?

Is European politics being "Americanized"?

No and yes. No, because European political systems rely much more extensively on political parties, with a long, established tradition, and considerable roots in their specific history, culture, and society. No,

35 Swan (1992).

because national cultures matter, and what is admissible in America would be inadmissible in most of Europe, and would actually backfire on the would-be aggressor: for instance, it was a known fact in French political circles that late President Mitterrand had a long-lasting, extramarital relationship, from which he had a daughter. It was never used against him, in spite of his many enemies, and, if it had been used, most citizens would have found it disgraceful to interfere with the privacy of the president. (UK media occupy an intermediate position between America and most of Europe concerning respect for political leaders' private lives.) Also, until the late 1980s, most of European television was controlled by government, so that political access to television was regulated, and paid advertising is still forbidden. Even if this restraint on European television has changed with the liberalization and privatization of television networks, there are still substantial differences both in the media and in their relationship to political systems between America and in Europe.[36]

On the other hand, while candidates and programs are selected and decided by parties, the media have become as important in Europe as in America in deciding the outcome of political bids.[37] The media (and particularly television) are the fundamental source of political information and opinion for people, and the main attributes of informational politics, as identified in America, characterize European politics as well: simplification of the message, professional advertising and polling as political tools, personalization of options, negativism as a predominant strategy, the leaking of damaging information as a political weapon, image-making and spin control as essential mechanisms in seizing power, and in keeping it. Let us briefly review some comparative evidence.

In the UK, television was the main source of political news for 58 percent of people in the 1980s: it increased to 80 percent in the 1990s,[38] with newspapers being the main source for the other 20 percent. However, paid TV advertising is illegal in Britain, and parties are given free broadcasts both during campaign times, and out of them. Yet, deregulation, privatization, and multiplication of sources of televised information have driven audiences away from formal political advertising, and toward political reporting.[39] Commentary on parties' advertising in regular programs becomes more influential than the advertising itself. For instance, in 1992, the Labour party used an election broadcast to feature Jennifer, a young girl who had to

36   Siune and Truetzschler (1992); Kaid and Holtz-Bacha (1995).
37   Guehenno (1993); Kaid and Holtz-Bacha (1995).
38   Moog (1996).
39   Berry (1992).

wait a year for an ear operation because of the crisis in the health service. When her identity (to be kept anonymous) was revealed, the real issue became the inability of Labour to keep information confidential, thus undermining its ability to be trusted in government.[40] Negative advertising, particularly from the Tories, became a focus of the 1992 campaign, and played a role in the Conservative victory.[41]

Reliance on instant polling, targeted mailing, the use of professional advertising and public relations firms, events and speeches oriented toward image-making and soundbites, slick professional advertisements using actors and photo montages, focus on image rather than on policy, are now the staple of British politics as much as they are in America.[42] Personalization of politics has a long tradition in Britain, with leaders as forceful as Winston Churchill, Harold Wilson, and Margaret Thatcher. However, the new wave of personalization does not relate to historic, charismatic leaders, but to anyone applying for the Prime Minister's job. Thus, in 1987, Labour focused its campaign on a "young and glamorous" couple, Neil and Glenys Kinnock, and ran as its main party election broadcast (PEB), a televised biography titled *Kinnock*, produced by Hugh Hudson, the director of *Chariots of Fire*.[43] In 1992, two out of five Conservative PEBs focused on John Major (*Major – The Journey*, produced by Schlesinger, the director of *Midnight Cowboy*, depicting Major's rise from working-class Brixton).[44] Personalization leads to character assassination as political strategy, and such was the case as well in recent British politics: in the 1992 campaign, Kinnock was attacked in the Tory tabloid press (with the stories then being picked up by television news), with attacks ranging from alleged Mafia connections to his private life (the so-called "Boyo affair"). Paddy Ashdown, the Liberal Democrat leader, was publicly attacked with regard to his sex life. And while Axford et al. suggest that, after the 1992 election, the British media appeared ready to restrain themselves in the use of "dirty tricks," this new-found discipline does not seem to have spared the Royal Family.[45] In 2002, the prestige of Tony Blair, still at the height of his power, was tainted by a tabloid press campaign on the allegedly murky business deals of his wife.

The advent of Russian democracy has meant also the introduction of American-style, television-oriented political campaigns since the

40 Scammell and Semetko (1995).
41 Berry (1992); Scammell and Semetko (1995).
42 Axford et al. (1992); Philo (1993); Franklin (1994).
43 Philo (1993: 411).
44 Scammell and Semetko (1995: 35).
45 Axford et al. (1992).

parliamentary elections of December 1993.[46] In the decisive 1996 Russian presidential elections, Yeltsin was able to regain control of the electorate, in danger of turning to Zyuganov out of desperation, in the last weeks of the campaign, by launching a media barrage, and by using, for the first time in Russia, computerized direct mailing, targeted polling, and segmented propaganda. Yeltsin's campaign combined old and new strategies of media use, but, in both approaches, television was the focus. On the one hand, government and private television channels aligned themselves with Yeltsin, and used news and programming as vehicles of anti-Communist propaganda, including the broadcasting of several films on the horrors of Stalinism in the week before the vote. On the other hand, Yeltsin's political advertising was carefully designed. A political consulting company, "Niccolò M" (M for Machiavelli), played a major role in designing a media strategy in which Yeltsin would appear on regular television news while TV political advertising would focus on real people (I know one of them) who would explain their support for Yeltsin. The spots ended with the words "I believe, I love, I hope," followed by Yeltsin's signature, his only presence in the advertisement. Yekaterina Yegorova, director of "Niccolò M," understood that, in her own words: "The idea behind his absence is that Yeltsin, as president, appears so often on the screen [in the regular news] that if he were on commercials as well, people would get sick of him."[47] Thus, "absent personalization," by combining different forms of media messages, becomes a new, subtle strategy in a world saturated by audiovisual propaganda.

Some California Republican consultants also played an advisory role on political technology in the Yeltsin campaign (albeit to a much lesser extent than they claimed), as well as a variety of media and political advisers, propelling Russia into informational politics even before it had time to become an information society. It worked: out-financed, outpowered, and outsmarted, the Communists relied on large-scale grassroots organizing, too primitive a medium to counter the alliance of television, radio, and major newspapers that rallied around Yeltsin. Although other factors played a role in the Russian election (rejection of Communism, fear of disorder, electoral demagoguery, skillful last-minute presidential decisions, particularly about Chechnya, the incorporation of Lebed in the Yeltsin administration before the second round of the election), the old and new systems of politics were measured up, and the result was a one-sided Yeltsin victory, after badly trailing in the polls four months earlier. In order

46 Hughes (1994); White et al. (2002).
47 *Moscow Times* (1996: 1).

to pay for this very expensive campaign, Yeltsin needed the financing of the Russian oligarchs, who received in exchange a stock of controlling shares in some of the most valuable assets being privatized by the Russian state.

Spain's young democracy also learned quickly the new trade of informational politics.[48] In the 1982 general election, the skillful use of media and personalization, around the figure of an extraordinary leader, Felipe Gonzalez, led the Socialists (PSOE) to an unprecedented electoral landslide. Subsequently, in 1986 and 1989, Gonzalez's Socialists were twice re-elected with an absolute majority, and even won in 1985 a national referendum to join NATO, in the most difficult conditions. In addition to the Socialist policy's own merits, three major factors contributed to overwhelming political domination by the Socialist party in the 1980s: the charismatic personality of Felipe Gonzalez, and his powerful presence in the media, particularly on television, whether in face-to-face debates, journalists' interviews, or televised political events; the technological sophistication of Socialist political strategists, who, for the first time in Spain, used focus groups, constant polling, image analysis/design, and targeting of issues in time and space, in a coherent, sustained strategy of political propaganda that did not stop after the election day; and the government monopoly on television, giving a clear edge to the government, until relentless criticism by the opposition on television coverage, as well as Gonzalez's democratic convictions, led to the liberalization and partial privatization of television in the 1990s.

On the other hand, it was the losing of the battle in the media in the 1990s that first eroded the Socialist government in Spain in 1993, and later brought a center-right government into power in 1996. I will elaborate, in the following section, on scandal politics and the politics of corruption as an essential strategy of informational politics, again using, among other cases, this most revealing contemporary Spanish example. But it is important to underline, while discussing the possible extrapolation of American-style politics to Europe, that contemporary Spain had nothing to learn from America concerning techniques of media politicking, character assassination, and feedback loops between polling, broadcasting, and play acting.

Although in a less dramatic manner (after all, Spain is a high-drama country), politics in most European democracies has come to be dominated by similar processes. Thus, observers in France rebelled against "*télécratie*,"[49] while others emphasize the coming of "virtual

48   Alonso Zaldivar and Castells (1992).
49   *Esprit* (1994: 3–4).

democracy."[50] The sudden rise to power of Berlusconi in Italy was directly linked to the new role played by the media in Italian politics.[51] Comparative analyses of other European countries in the 1990s[52] describe a complex, transitional situation of media dominating the diffusion of information, while parties are unequipped, underfinanced, and strictly regulated, thus finding it hard to adapt to the new technological environment. The outcome seems to be that, on the one hand, political parties keep, by and large, their autonomy *vis-à-vis* the media, with the support of the state. On the other hand, because of the restricted access of parties to the media, people increasingly form their political opinions from sources external to the political system, thus accentuating the distance between parties and citizens.[53] Thus, while institutions, culture, and history make European politics highly specific, technology, globalization, and the network society incite political actors and institutions to engage in technology-driven, informational politics. I contend that this is a new, historical trend, affecting, by successive waves, the entire world, albeit under specific historical conditions that introduce substantial variations in political competition, and in the conduct of politics. Bolivia provides an exceptional opportunity to test this hypothesis.

Bolivia's electronic populism: compadre *Palenque* and the coming of Jach'a Uru[54]

If we had to select the most likely country in the world to resist the globalization of culture, and to assert grassroots politics, Bolivia would be an obvious candidate. Its Indian identity is extremely present in the collective memory of its population (even if 67 percent consider themselves *mestizos*), and Aymara and Quechua are widely spoken. Nationalism is the paramount ideology of all political parties. Since the 1952 revolution, Bolivian miners and peasant unions have been among the most conscious, organized, and militant social actors in Latin America. The main nationalist-populist party, the *Movi-*

---

50 Scheer (1994).
51 Di Marco (1994); Santoni Rugiu (1994); Walter (1994).
52 Kaid and Holtz-Bacha (1995).
53 Di Marco (1993).
54 I am indebted, for their help in the elaboration of this section on Bolivian media politics, to Fernando Calderon in La Paz, and to Roberto Laserna in Cochabamba. The analysis is based on the following studies by Bolivian researchers: Mesa (1986); Archondo (1991); Contreras Basnipeiro (1991); Saravia and Sandoval (1991); Laserna (1992); Albo (1993); Mayorga (1993); Perez Iribarne (1993a, b); Ardaya and Verdesoto (1994); Calderon and Laserna (1994); Bilbao La Vieja Diaz et al. (1996); Szmukler (1996).

miento Nacionalista Revolucionario (MNR), has been in and out of power for the past four decades, and is still holding the presidency in 2003, with the support of left nationalists of the *Movimiento Bolivia Libre*, and of the Katarist (indigenist) movement. Social tensions and political militancy in the country prompted frequent military coups, not always disliked by the US Embassy, until the open participation of the high ranks of the army in drug traffic in the late 1970s, and the change of policy under Carter, modified the US attitude, facilitating the restoration of stable democracy in 1982, with a left coalition coming to power.

Since then, while social tensions did heighten, because of the structural adjustment policies introduced by the MNR in 1985 (later to be followed by other governments), democracy seems solidly established. A most lively political struggle developed, with parties being formed, split, and reformed, and the most unlikely political alliances being forged to achieve state power. Thus, social mobilization and democratic politics were, and are, alive and well in Bolivia, apparently leaving little room for the transformation of the political scene by an Andean brand of informational politics. And yet, since 1989, the politics of La Paz–El Alto (the Bolivian capital and its periphery of popular settlements) has been dominated by a political movement built around Carlos Palenque, a former folk musician of humble origin, who became a radio and television show host, then the owner of a media network (RTP, *Radio Television Popular*), and finally leader of *Conciencia de Patria* (Condepa), founded on September 21, 1988, in Tihuanaco, the ancient capital of the Aymara world. Although the story may sound familiar to those aware of the old tradition of Latin American populism, it is in fact unusual, complex, and revealing.

Palenque's saga started in 1968 when, around his folk group, *Los Caminantes*, he created a radio program that gradually incorporated direct contact with the audience, using popular language, including a mixture of Spanish and Aymara, which made it easier for people from poor urban strata to communicate without being intimidated by the formalism of the medium. In 1978, he started a television show, where he offered a platform for people to voice their complaints. He introduced himself as the *compadre* of his audience, and he also referred to his interlocutors as *compadres* and *comadres*, thus leveling the field of communication, and introducing a reference to a fundamental communality, rooted in the Aymara and Catholic traditions.[55] In

---

55 *Compadre* and *comadre* are terms signifying membership in the community. They bring together elements of Aymara tradition and of Catholic celebration (e.g godfathers and godmothers for christened children). As such, *compadres* and *comadres* are expected to understand, to contribute, to share, and to assume reciprocity.

1980, he succeeded in buying Radio Metropolitana, and later on Canal 4, a television station in La Paz. They soon became the most listened-to media in the La Paz area, and they remain so: indeed, 25 percent of the radio audience declared that they listen exclusively to Metropolitana.

Five elements are critical in Palenque's communication strategy. The first is the personalization of the shows, with forceful *compadres* and *comadres* representing various constituencies, such as *comadre* Remedios Loza, a common woman (*mujer de pollera*), a human type never before seen on television, in spite of being the very image of La Paz's popular families; or *compadre* Paco, closer to the middle class; or his own wife, Monica Medina de Palenque, a former flamenco ballet dancer, assuming the role of the bottom-line, wise woman. The personalization of interaction with the audience does not stop with live shows, but extends to much of the programming. For instance, while Canal 4 broadcasts the same Latin American soap operas that capture attention throughout the entire Spanish-speaking world, *compadre* Palenque and his team personally comment on the events and drama of various episodes, and engage with their audience in relating the soap opera's story to the daily lives of *paceos*. Secondly, is the targeting of women, particularly of lower-class women, and the prominent presence of women in the programs. Thirdly, there is a direct connection to people's concerns, and joys, with programs such as *People's Saturdays* broadcast live with the participation of hundreds of people from urban locations; or *The People's Tribune*, in which people denounce live the abuses to which they are subjected by whoever. Fourthly, there is a willingness to listen to people's complaints, providing an ear open to the laments arising from the painful integration of rural and Indian life in the sprawling urban periphery of La Paz. And, fifthly, is the religious reference, legitimizing hope as God's will, with the promise of the coming of *Jach'a Uru*, the day when, according to the Aymara tradition, all suffering will come to an end.

However, Palenque's path to prominence was not a smooth one. Because of his criticism of authorities, under the pretext of a radio interview with a leading drug trafficker, RTP media network was twice closed by the government, in June and November 1988. But mass protests, and a decision by the Supreme Court, reopened it months later. Palenque answered by creating a party (Condepa), and running for president. In the first election in which it participated, in May 1989, Condepa became the fourth largest national party, and the first party in the capital. In the municipal elections, it won the mayoralty of El Alto (fourth largest urban area of Bolivia), and entered into the municipal council of La Paz. In the next municipal election,

Monica Medina de Palenque became the mayor of La Paz, a post she kept until 1996. Condepa is also present in the National Congress: among other deputies, *comadre* Remedios played a leading role in pushing legislation for Bolivian women. In spite of its populism, Condepa did not develop a confrontational attitude toward various governments. In 1989 its votes helped to elect in the Congress President Jaime Paz Zamora, in spite of his third place in the popular vote. And when a new MNR President, Sanchez de Losada, was elected in 1993, Condepa, while not participating in government, cooperated with the government in several legislative initiatives.[56]

The success of *compadre* Palenque did not take place in a social vacuum. He had a pointed message, not just a medium, which seemed to fit well with the actual experience of the urban masses in La Paz. He appealed to the cultural identity of La Paz's recent immigrants, by the use of language, by the emphasis on Aymara traditions, by the reference to folk and religion. Against policies of economic adjustment and integration in the global economy, he exposed the daily suffering of displaced workers and urban poor, the abuses imposed upon them under the pretext of economic rationality. *Compadre* Palenque became the voice of the voiceless. Using the media as platform, but linking up with local institutions where Condepa was present, Palenque ran a number of social programs, one of the most successful being geared toward helping industrial workers displaced by economic restructuring and privatization.

Refusing the categorical imperative of globalization, *compadre* Palenque proposed (albeit in rather vague terms) a model of "endogenous development," based on Bolivia's own resources, and counting on the communal spirit of its people. Thus, Condepa's influence is not just a media manipulation: its themes refer to the actual suffering of people in La Paz, and its language directly communicates with the cultural and local identity of popular strata in La Paz and El Alto (to the point that the movement remains by and large local, authorizing some analysts to speak of a "metropolitan *ayllu*").[57] However, without the power of the media, and without a perceptive communication strategy, mixing entertainment radio and television with a space for public complaints and the building of charismatic trust between the leaders and the audience, Condepa would have been reduced to a minor role, as happened to other populist movements in Bolivia, such as Max Fernandez's *Unidad*

56 In 1997 *compadre* Palenque experienced a marital crisis that ended in divorce from his wife, the ex-Mayor of La Paz. Shortly after his divorce, Carlos Palenque died from a heart attack. His movement went on, led by *comadre* Remedios.

57 *Ayllu* is the traditional form of a territorial/cultural community in the Aymara tradition.

Civica Solidaridad. Indeed, in 1996, Bolivians trust the media more than they trust their political representatives (table 6.3).

So, media politics does not have to be the monopoly of influential interest groups, or of established political parties using the power of technology to perfect the technology of power. As the example of *compadre* Palenque seems to indicate, identity-based communalism, and poor people's movements, sometimes under the form of religious millennialism, can access the political mainstream by using the media. By so doing, they force other political actors to play a similar game (as in Bolivia in the 1990s), thus contributing to the gradual enclosing of politics in the media space, albeit with specific characteristics fitting the Bolivian cultural tradition, economic condition, and political dynamics.

Furthermore, in spite of the communal orientation of Condepa, we find in the experience of *compadre* Palenque a series of features not dissimilar to the broader trends of informational politics, as described above: the extreme personalization of leadership; the simplification of messages in dichotomous terms, good and evil; the pre-eminence of moral and religious judgments in framing public and personal life; the decisive importance of electronically broadcast language, images, and symbols in mobilizing consciousness and deciding politics; the volatility of public mood, lost in the feeling of a world spinning out of control; the difficulty of fitting these new political expressions into traditional political categories (to the point that some Bolivian analysts refer to the emergence of "informal politics," parallel to the "informal economy");[58] and, ultimately, we also find, among these

Table 6.3 Opinion of Bolivian citizens on which institutions represent their interests

Institution	% of favorable opinion
Congress of Deputies	3.5
Any political party	3.4
President	3.3
Mayor	6.9
Neighborhood committee	11.3
Labor union	12.6
Mass media	23.4

Note: Answers to the question: "Do you feel that the following institutions represent your interests?" (percentage over total of polled citizens; national representative sample).
Source: Collective Author (1996)

58   Ardaya and Verdesoto (1994).

compadres and *comadres*, a dependence on their financial ability to support media politics, thus creating a feedback loop (or a vicious circle) between power, media, and money. While the "resurrection of a metropolitan *ayllu*"[59] shows the limits to globalization, it is by inhabiting the space of media flows that traditional cultures and popular interests assert their power. So doing, they survive, but they transform themselves at the same time, entering a new world of sounds and images, of electronically modulated *charangos*, environmentally preserved condors, and television scripted *Jach'a Uru*.

Informational Politics in Action: The Politics of Scandal[60]

In the past decade, political systems have been shaken all over the world, and political leaders have been destroyed, in a relentless succession of scandals. In some cases, political parties solidly entrenched in power for about half a century have collapsed, taking with them in their demise the political regime they had shaped in their interest. Among important examples of this evolution are: the Italian Christian Democrats, which literally disintegrated in the 1990s; the German Christian Democrats, whose respected leader, Helmut Kohl was forced to resign after admitting accepting illegal financing of his party, prompting the decline of the Conservative party after a long period of unchallenged hegemony; Japan's Liberal Democratic Party, which was split and lost the government, for the first time, in 1993, although the party as such survived, and still governs in coalition or in minority; and India's Congress Party, which, after governing the largest democracy in the world for 44 years of the more than 48 years since Independence, suffered a humiliating defeat, to the benefit of Hindu nationalists in the 1996 elections, after a major scandal

---

59 Archondo (1991).

60 This section is partly based on a reading of mainstream newspapers and magazines from different countries, as well as on personal knowledge of some events. I consider it unnecessary to provide detailed references for facts that are public knowledge. An international overview of political scandals is Longman (1990) *Political Scandals and Causes Célèbres since 1945*. A major scholarly, comparative volume on the topic is Heidenheimer et al. (1989). Historical accounts of American political scandals can be found in Fackler and Lin (1995), and Ross (1988). A recent account of congressional scandals in America is in Balz and Brownstein (1996: 27ff). An annotated bibliography on American political corruption is Johansen (1990). Additional sources used in this section are: King (1984); Markovits and Silverstein (1988a); Bellers (1989); Ebbinghausen and Neckel (1989); Bouissou (1991); Morris (1991); Sabato (1991); Barker (1992); CQ *Researcher* (1992); Meny (1992); Phillips (1992); Swan (1992); Tranfaglia (1992); Barber (1993); Buckler (1993); DeLeon (1993); Grubbe (1993); Roman (1993); *Esprit* (1994); Gumbel (1994); Walter (1994); Arlacchi (1995); Fackler and Lin (1995); Garcia Cotarelo (1995); Johnson (1995); Sechi (1995); Thompson (1995).

involving Congress leader Narasimha Rao, seemingly putting an end to a political system built around the uncontested domination of Nehru's successors.

President Clinton survived a deliberate impeachment attempt as a result of his public lies concerning his scandalous sexual affair. His troubled second term opened the way for the election of George W. Bush in a bitterly contested election, ultimately decided by the US Supreme Court by 5 votes to 4. With the exception of Scandinavian democracies, and a few other small countries, I cannot think of any country in North America, Latin America, Western and Eastern Europe, Asia, or Africa, where major political scandals, with significant, and sometimes dramatic, consequences, have not exploded in recent years.[61]

In a few instances, scandals referred to the personal morality of a leader (usually a man improperly driven by sexuality or drunkenness). But, in most cases, the matter was political corruption, that is, in Carl Friedrich's definition: "Whenever a powerholder who is charged with doing certain things, i.e., who is a responsible functionary or office-holder, is by monetary or other rewards not legally provided for, induced to take actions which favor whoever provides the rewards and thereby does damage to the public and its interests."[62] In some cases, government officials simply took the money, without even needing to run with it. Or so they believed. From South Korea's President Roh to Brazil's President Collor de Mello, and from some members of Russia's military, or of the United States Congress, to some high-ranking members of the Spanish and French Socialist administrations, wave after wave of corruption-related political scandals have become the main staple of public life throughout the world in the 1990s and into the twenty-first century.

Why is this so? Are our political systems the most corrupt in history? I doubt it. Use and abuse of power for personal benefit is one of those features that would qualify as "human nature," if such an entity were to exist.[63] This is precisely one of the reasons why democracy was invented, and became the most sought after, if not ideal, form of governance. Behind the scenes, in situations of the control of information by the state, political elites, in ancient times as in recent years, went happily into establishing their personalized tax system on subjects and interest groups, the main differences being in the degree

61 Heidenheimer et al. (1989); Longman (1990); Garment (1991); CQ Researcher (1992); Meny (1992); Grubbe (1993); Roman (1993); Gumbel (1994); Walter (1994); D. F. Thompson (1995); J. Thompson (2000); Rose-Ackerman (1999).
62 Friedrich (1966: 74).
63 Leys (1989).

of arbitrariness in bribing, and in the variable dysfunctionality of hidden contributions for the conduct of public affairs. Thus, a first observation points to the fact that the denunciation of corruption could precisely be a good indicator of a democratic society, and of the freedom of the press.[64]

For instance, Spain under the dictatorship of Franco suffered from direct pillage of the country by the dictator's entourage, starting with Mrs Franco's notorious visits to jewelry stores whose owners never dared to send the bill to his excellency. No serious observer would assert that political corruption in Spain was more pervasive during the 1980s' Socialist governments than under Franco.[65] And yet, while, during the dictatorship, corruption was mainly a matter of gossip among reliable friends, political life in 1990s' Spanish democracy was entirely shaped by revelations, and allegations, of government corruption and unlawful behavior. Furthermore, in long-established democracies, with freedom of the press, such as the United States, the occurrence of political corruption, as reported in the press, goes up and down, with no clear long-term trend, as can be observed in figure 6.2, elaborated by Fackler and Lin for the past hundred years.[66] There is, however, a most spectacular surge of reporting on political corruption around the time of Nixon's Watergate, precisely the event that struck the imagination of both journalists and politicians with the possibility of bringing down the most powerful political office on earth, by obtaining and diffusing damaging information.

The historical study by King on political corruption in nineteenth-century Britain[67] shows the pervasiveness of the phenomenon, prompting the 1867 Reform Act to curtail such practices, as democracy made progress. And Bouissou reports that in 1890 the Japanese press denounced widespread electoral fraud, with the newspaper *Asahi* writing that "whoever buys his election will be for sale once elected."[68] Moreover, in a most insightful analysis, Barker has shown that, when unlawful actions by politicians do not provide enough ammunition to discredit them, other types of behavior (for example, improper sex) become the raw material for political scandal.[69] Thus, using the Longman international series of political scandals,[70] he calculated that the proportion of unlawful and not unlawful political scandals for all countries (73 : 27) was relatively close to the

64   Markovits and Silverstein (1988).
65   Alonso Zaldivar and Castells (1992).
66   Fackler and Lin (1995).
67   King (1989).
68   Bouissou (1991: 84).
69   Barker (1992).
70   Longman (1990).

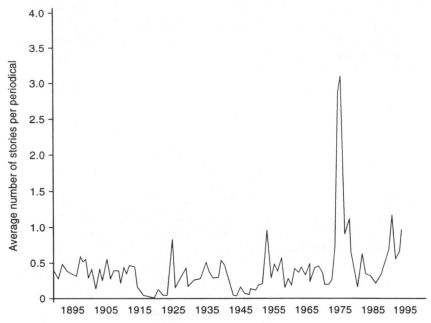

Figure 6.2   Average number of corruption stories per periodical
in US, 1890–1992
Source: Fackler and Lin (1995)

proportion in the US or France, but very different in the UK (41 : 59), so that sex and espionage became in Britain the functional equivalent of graft and bribery in other countries.

Since 1995 a well-respected NGO, Transparency International, elaborates a corruption index by country that allows us to compare countries with each other as well as the evolution of corruption (that is, political corruption) in each country. On the one hand, the reports elaborated by Transparency International show the widespread existence of political corruption throughout the world, including most Western democracies. On the other hand, there is no general upward trend that can be detected for the period in which comparable data have been collected; that is, between 1995 and 2002. For instance, the US (number 16 in the ranking of the less corrupt, together with Israel) remained stable; Japan and the UK improved slightly; Germany and France became less clean, while Italy and Spain became less dirty. In other words, there does not seem to be an increase in political corruption either at the world level or in individual countries. Corruption, and its perception, goes up and down as a result of a number of circumstances related, fundamentally, to the strength of public institutions and to the level of welfare in society: it is no surprise that the Scandinavian democracies still occupy the top of the scale of clean government. On the other hand, the poorer a country is and the weaker the legitimacy of the institutions of the state, the higher the danger of corruption. Thus, concerning the political process, corruption *per se* seems to be less significant than scandals (that is, corruption or wrongdoing revealed) and their political impact.[71]

So, why now? If it is unlikely that corruption is at an historical high point, why does it explode all over the media, and why does it so devastatingly affect political systems and political actors at the turn of this century? There are a number of structural factors, and macropolitical trends, which have weakened political systems, making them more vulnerable to the turmoil created in public opinion. Political competition, and the struggle to influence the center of the electorate's political spectrum, have downplayed ideological contrasts, as parties/coalitions, having secured their hard-core supporters, strive to steal adversaries' themes and positions as much as possible. There follows a blurring of political positions, and the tendency by citizens to be more sensitive to the reliability of parties and candidates than to their professed positions on issues. Personalization of politics also focuses attention on leaders, and on their character, thus opening the way for attacks on precisely those qualities as a form of winning votes.

The rise of a potent global criminal economy has penetrated state institutions in many countries, often at the highest levels of government, thus providing ammunition for scandal-making, and also using information to blackmail politicians into submission. Geopolitical factors also play a role: thus, the Italian and Japanese political systems, organized around the Christian Democratic and the Liberal Democratic parties respectively, were set up in the aftermath of World War II, with considerable help and influence from the US, to establish a bulwark against communism in two democracies that were critical in the Cold War context, and where communist and socialist parties were strong.[72] The long-standing, well-known connections of some leading Christian Democrats with the Mafia,[73] and of some Liberal Democrat leaders with the *Yakuza*,[74] were not an obstacle to the unrelenting support of international and domestic forces for these parties, as long as their replacement was an excessively risky operation. In the

71   Lowi (1988); Hodess (2001).
72   Johnson (1995).
73   Tranfaglia (1992). In 2002, an Italian court convicted Andreotti, the towering figure of the Italian Christian Democrats for over three decades, of contributing to the murder of a journalist who had reported on his possible cooperation with the Mafia. The verdict is still on appeal at the time of writing.
74   Bouissou (1991); Johnson (1995).

post-Cold War environment, each party is left to itself, to the movements of each country's political market; discipline inside the parties becomes less strict because fierce competition can be better afforded in the absence of an external enemy. Guehenno has also suggested that, in a world of fading nation-states and uncertain ideological commitments, the rewards for being in office are no longer distinct from those offered in society at large, that is, ultimately, money, as the key to personal or organizational projects, from enjoying life to providing for the family, or helping humanitarian causes.[75]

All these factors seem to contribute to making political systems vulnerable to corruption. But there is something else, something that, in my view, changes the nature of political systems in contemporary societies. As Thompson writes: "Scandals are struggles over symbolic power in which reputation and trust are at stake,"[76] and, in the information age, symbolic power – that is, the capacity to shape people's minds – is the fundamental source of power. Thus, *I contend that scandal politics is the weapon of choice for struggle and competition in informational politics*. The argument goes like this. Politics has been, by and large, enclosed in the space of the media. The media have become more powerful than ever, technologically, financially, and politically. Their global reach and networking allow them to escape from strict political controls. Their capacity for investigative reporting and their relative autonomy *vis-à-vis* political power make them the main source of information and opinion for society at large. Parties and candidates must act in and through the media to reach society. Not that the media are the Fourth Power: they are, instead, the ground for power struggles. Media politics is an increasingly expensive operation, made even more expensive by the whole paraphernalia of informational politics: polling, advertising, marketing, analyzing, image-making, and information processing. Current institutional systems of political financing are not up to the task. Political actors are chronically underfinanced, and the gap between necessary expenses and legal revenues has grown exponentially, and continues to grow.[77] Thus, after exhausting all legal sources, personal contributions, and business deals, parties and politicians often resort to the only real source of money: under the table contributions from business and interest groups, obviously in exchange for government decisions in favor of these interests.[78] *This is the matrix of systemic political corruption, from which develops a shadow network of front businesses and intermediaries.*

75   Guehenno (1993).
76   Thompson (2000: 244).
77   Weinberg (1991); Freeman (1994); Pattie et al. (1995).
78   Meny (1992).

Once corruption becomes widespread, and after a few people add their personal take to the channels of political funding, everybody in politics, and in the media, knows (or thinks he/she knows) that, if one looks closely, and long enough, damaging information can be found on almost anyone. Thus, the hunt begins: by political advisers to prepare ammunition to attack or to defend; by journalists to fulfill their job as investigative reporters, finding material to boost their audience and their sales; by freelancers, and crooks, to find information that can be used in potential blackmail, or for sale to interested parties. In fact, most of the damaging material published by the media is leaked by political actors themselves, or by associated business interests. Finally, once the market of damaging political information is created, if there is not enough clear-cut material, then allegations, insinuations, and even fabrications, may come in, depending, of course, on the individual ethics of politicians, journalists, and the media. Indeed, the strategy in scandal politics does not necessarily aim at an instant blow on the basis of one scandal. It is the relentless flow of various scandals of different kinds, and with different levels of likelihood, from solid information on a minor incident to shaky allegations on a major issue, that weave the thread with which political ambitions are finally strangled, and political dreams subdued – unless a deal is made, thus feeding back into the system. What counts is the final impact upon public opinion, by the accumulation of many different touches.[79] As in the old Russian saying: "I cannot remember if she stole a coat, or if a coat was stolen from her."

The superior stage of scandal politics is the judicial or parliamentary investigation, leading to indictments, and, with increasing frequency, to imprisonment of political leaders.[80] Judges, prosecutors, and investigative committee members enter into a symbiotic relationship with the media. They protect the media (ensuring their independence), and often feed them with calculated leaks. In exchange, they are protected by the media, they become media heroes, and sometimes successful politicians with the support of the media. Together, they fight for democracy and clean government, they control the excesses of politicians, and, ultimately, they seize power away from the political process, diffusing it into society. While doing so, they may also delegitimize parties, politicians, politics, and, ultimately, democracy in its current incarnation.[81]

79 Barker (1992); CQ Researcher (1992).
80 Garment (1991); Garcia Cotarelo (1995); Thompson (1995).
81 Bellers (1989); Arlachi (1995); Garcia Cotarelo (1995); Fallows (1996); Thompson (2000); Adsera et al. (2001).

The politics of scandal, as practiced in the 1990s against the governing Spanish Socialist party, offers an interesting illustration of this analysis. After the 1989 Socialist victory in the Spanish general election (the third in a row), a behind-the-scenes coalition of interest groups decided it was time to check the uncontested domination of the Socialists in Spain's political life, a domination that could be foreseen going into the twenty-first century.[82] Explosive political files were leaked, discovered, manipulated, or invented, and published in the press. Because of self-restraint by the main Spanish newspapers (*El Pais, El Periodico, La Vanguardia*) most of the potential anti-Socialist "scandals" were first published in *El Mundo*, a professionally sophisticated newspaper created in 1990. From there, weekly tabloids and radio talk show pundits (mainly from the Catholic Church-owned radio network) would hammer the audience until the rest of the media, including television, echoed the news. Scandals started to be revealed in January 1990 with information on the brother of the then vice-president of the government selling his assumed political influence to various businessmen. Although the wrongdoings of this little crook were not of great significance, and the courts cleared the vice-president of any impropriety, the "affair" occupied the political headlines of the Spanish media for almost two years, actually prompting the resignation of the vice-president, the influential number two of the Socialist party, who refused to condemn his brother publicly.

As soon as this scandal started to fizzle out, a new media campaign started, focusing on illegal financing of the Socialist party, after a party accountant defected and gave information to the media, apparently as a result of a personal vendetta. A judicial investigation was opened, leading to the indictment of some Socialist leaders. When, in spite of all these accusations, the Socialist party still retained enough seats to form a government in the 1993 elections, scandal politics accelerated its tempo in the Spanish media and judicial scene: the Governor of the Bank of Spain was suspected of insider trading, and confessed to tax fraud; the first civilian director of the legendary Guardia Civil was caught requesting bribes, fled the country, was arrested in Bangkok, and returned to a Spanish prison, in a sequence that fell between the thriller and the burlesque; more seriously, a resentful officer of the Spanish military intelligence leaked papers showing unlawful eavesdropping on Spanish leaders, including the king; and, to complete the disintegration of public morale, former special agents of the Spanish police, incarcerated for organizing

82   Cacho (1994); Garcia Cotarelo (1995); *Temas* (1995).

assassinations in the "dirty war" carried on in the 1980s against Basque terrorists (emulating Thatcher's tactics against the IRA), turned their coats against the government, and involved the Minister of the Interior, and several high-ranking officials in the conspiracy. Of paramount importance in this political process was the attitude of the Spanish judges, who earnestly pursued the slightest possibility of embarrassing the Socialist party. Felipe Gonzalez executed what was considered a brilliant maneuver by recruiting the most famous of these zealous judges as an independent deputy on the Socialist ticket in the 1993 election, and appointing him to a high post in the Ministry of Justice. It was a disaster: whether because the post was not high enough (the Socialist version) or because the judge was disappointed by what he saw (his version), he quit the government, and engaged in a most militant prosecution against any potential wrongdoing from the highest levels of the Socialist government. After parliamentary and judicial investigations were opened, some leading to indictments, others fizzling out because of lack of substance, political scandals became the daily headlines of the Spanish media for about five years, literally paralyzing the action of government, destroying a number of political and business figures, and shaking up the most potent political force in Spain. The Socialists were eventually defeated in 1996, and again in 2000.

Why and how this judicial/media anti-Socialist barrage happened in Spain is a complex matter that has not been brought fully to public light as yet, although some of the participants in the conspiracy stated publicly that the conspiracy as described above indeed took place. There was, in any case, a combination of several factors reinforcing each other: the illegal financing of the Socialist party, which involved several members of its leadership in setting up a network of shadow businesses; the actual corruption, and unlawful actions, of several high-ranking members of the Socialist administration, and of many local Socialist bosses; the exasperation of some groups against the government (some fringe businessmen, including a financial tycoon whose property was expropriated by the Socialists; some ultra-conservative forces; probably some elements of the integrist wing of the Catholic Church; some special interests; disaffected journalists who felt marginalized by Socialist power); the internal in-fighting in the Socialist party, with several leaders leaking information against each other to undermine the credibility of their rivals in the eyes of Felipe Gonzalez, the undisputed leader above the fray; the fight between two major financial groups, one of them representing traditional Spanish finance, close to the economic team of the Socialist government, the other organized around an outsider trying to make inroads into the system, and attempting alliances with some Socialist factions against others; a battle between media groups, jockeying for control of the new media system in Spain; personal vendettas, as, for example, the one by the editor of the most militantly anti-Socialist newspaper, convinced that he had lost his job as a result of government pressures; and a more complex, diffused opinion in the media world, and in other circles of Spanish life, according to which Socialist dominance was excessive, and the arrogance of some Socialist leaders intolerable, so that informed social elites should react and expose the true face of the Socialists to a seduced electorate which, in its majority, kept voting Socialist in four consecutive elections.

Thus, ultimately, and regardless of personal motivation or specific business interests, the media asserted their power collectively, and, in alliance with the judiciary, made sure that the Spanish political class, including the conservatives (*Partido Popular*), learned the lesson for the future. While it is indisputable that there was unlawful behavior and a significant level of corruption in the Socialist administration and in the Socialist party, what really matters for our analytical purpose is the use of scandal politics in and by the media as the fundamental weapon utilized by political actors, business interests, and social groups to fight one another. So doing, they transformed Spanish politics forever by making it dependent upon the media. The main lesson learned by the victorious conservative party was that media control was crucial for staying in power. Thus, the Aznar government in 1996–2004, besides controlling the government-owned television networks, used the telephone company to buy one of the two private television networks, and won decisive influence over the other one. It also engaged in blacklisting prominent independent journalists to make sure they would not have access to the TV networks, and brought relentless legal and financial pressure to bear on the media groups that were not under their influence. Media policy became the essential political medium to keep the conservatives in power in a country that opinion polls show to be situated on the center–left of the political spectrum.

What is characteristic of scandal politics is that all political actors practicing it become entrapped by the system, often reversing roles: today's hunter is tomorrow's game. A case in point is the political adventure of Berlusconi in Italy. The facts are known: he parlayed his control of all three private TV networks into mounting a devastating campaign against the corrupt Italian political system.[83] Then, he created, in three months, an ad hoc "party" (*Forza Italia!*, named

83   Walter (1994).

after the fans' rallying cry for the Italian national football team), and, in alliance with the neo-Fascist party and the Northern League, won the 1994 general election and became Prime Minister. Control of government gave him, theoretically, authority over the three other, government-owned, TV networks. Yet, the autonomy of the media, and of journalists, was strongly asserted. In spite of his overwhelming presence in the media business (in newspapers and magazines, as well as in television), as soon as Berlusconi became Prime Minister, the judiciary and the media, again together, launched an all-out assault on Berlusconi's financial frauds and bribery schemes, undermining his business, bringing some of his associates to justice, indicting Berlusconi himself, and ultimately damaging his image in such a way that parliament censured his government. Then, in 1996 the electorate rejected Berlusconi, electing instead *Il Ulivo*'s center–left coalition, whose main component, the ex-Communist, now Socialist, *Partito Democratico di Sinistra*, had not yet been in the national government, and thus had saved its reputation. Nevertheless, Berlusconi's media empire was again instrumental in seizing the opportunity provided by the splits and quarrels among the Italian left, and leading *"il Cavaliere"* anew to the government, in alliance with the ex-Fascist party and the xenophobic Northern League, in 2001. Berlusconi then used his control of the parliament in attempting to subdue the two bastions of the independence of civil society: the judiciary and the media. Nonetheless, at the time of writing, in 2003, he is again in the midst of judicial prosecution, with one of his main collaborators convicted of the bribery of judges, and Berlusconi himself under suspicion of illegal dealings. And so this modern version of *commedia dell'arte* goes on.

The extremely important lesson of this development in Italian politics is that overwhelming business influence in the media is not tantamount to political control in informational politics. The media system, with its symbiotic linkages to the judiciary and prosecutorial institutions of democracy, sets its own pace, and receives signals from the whole spectrum of the political system, to transform them into sales and influence, regardless of the origin and destination of political impacts. However, in this complex relationship, political forces also have their cards to play: acting on the media by legal means, and building their own defense against the judiciary by manipulating the legal system (voting for their own immunity). So doing, politicians seek to reinstate their lost autonomy *vis-à-vis* the mechanisms of symbolic power. However, they can only do so by reducing the autonomy of the media *vis-à-vis* the state, thus provoking their lack of credibility and ultimately inviting society to find alternative forms of expression and communication, for instance via the Internet.

So, the political system becomes engulfed in the endless turbulence of media reporting, leaking, counter-leaking, and scandal-making. To be sure, some daring political strategists try to ride the tiger, by positioning themselves in the media business, by making alliances, by targeting and timing informational strikes. This is exactly what Berlusconi tried, failing in the first attempt, but succeeding later, and maybe ultimately failing. However, observation of the international scene seems to indicate that the likely fate of most of these new creatures, half-politicians / half-media tycoons, could be similar to the fate of those financial speculators who pretended to know how to navigate in the unpredictable, global financial markets. In scandal politics, as in other domains of the network society, the power of flows overwhelms the flows of power.

The Crisis of Democracy

Let us bring together the various threads we have identified concerning the transformation of the nation-state, and of the political process in contemporary societies. When woven into an historical framework, they reveal the crisis of democracy as we have known it in the past century [84]

The nation-state, defining the domain, procedures, and object of citizenship, has lost much of its sovereignty, undermined by the dynamics of global flows and trans-organizational networks of wealth, information, and power. Particularly critical for its legitimacy crisis is the state's decreasing ability to fulfill its commitments as a welfare state because of the integration of production and consumption in a globally interdependent system, and the related process of capitalist restructuring. Indeed, the welfare state, in its different manifestations, depending on the history of each society, was a critical source of political legitimacy in the reconstitution of government institutions after the Great Depression of 1930s and World War II.[85] The rejection of Keynesianism, and the decline of the labor movement, may accentuate the demise of the sovereign nation-state because of the weakening of its legitimacy.

The (re)construction of political meaning on the basis of specific identities fundamentally challenges the very concept of citizenship. The state could only shift the source of its legitimacy from representing people's will and providing for their well-being, to asserting collective identity, by

84 Minc (1993); Guehenno (1993); Patterson (1993); Ginsborg (1994); Touraine (1995b); Katznelson (1996); Weisberg (1996); Nye et al. (1997); Pharr and Putnam (2000); Calderon (2003); Inglehart (2003).
85 Navarro (1995).

identifying itself with communalism to the exclusion of other values and of minorities' identities. This is indeed the source of the fundamentalist, nationalist, ethnic, territorial, or religious states, which seem to emerge from the current political crises of legitimacy. I contend that they cannot, and will not, sustain democracy (that is, liberal democracy) because the very principles of representation between the two systems (national citizenship, singular identity) are contradictory.

To the crisis of legitimacy of the nation-state we must add the crisis of credibility of the political system, based on open competition between political parties. Captured in the media arena, reduced to personalized leadership, dependent on technologically sophisticated manipulation, pushed into unlawful financing, driven by and toward scandal politics, the party system has lost its appeal and trustworthiness, and, for all practical purposes, is a bureaucratic remainder deprived of public confidence.[86]

As a result of these three convergent and interacting processes, public opinion, and citizens' individual and collective expressions, display a growing and fundamental disaffection *vis-à-vis* parties, politicians, and professional politics. Thus, in the United States, according to a Times Mirror Center survey in September 1994: "Thousands of interviews with American voters this summer find no clear direction in the public's political thinking other than frustration with the current system and an eager responsiveness to alternative political solutions and appeals."[87] In 1994, 82 percent of respondents to a national Harris Poll did not think that the government represented their interests (against 72 percent in 1980), and 72 percent considered that in fact the government represented interest groups (with 68 percent identifying these groups as business interests); along the same lines, a 1995 Roper Poll found that 68 percent of respondents thought that there were not many differences between Republicans and Democrats, and 82 percent wished that a new party could be created.[88] In 1998, 39 percent of people in California, and in the United States, thought that "Quite a few people in government are crooked," and 70 percent in California and 63 percent in the US believed that "Government is run by a few big interests." Some 54 percent in California and 60 percent in the US agreed with the statement that "Public officials don't care what people like me think."[89]

Let us examine some political opinion polls on a comparative basis for the past decade. The World Values Survey, conducted by the University

86 D. M. West (1993); Anderson and Comiller (1994); Mouffe (1995); Navarro (1995); Salvati (1995); Balz and Brownstein (1996); Wattenberg (1996); Dupin (2002).
87 Quoted by Balz and Brownstein (1996: 28).
88 Cited by Navarro (1995: 55).
89 Baldassare (2000).

of Michigan's Institute of Social Research, under the direction of Ronald Inglehart, is one of the best sources to analyze political opinion worldwide.[90] Using these and other data we have elaborated figures 6.3–6.5 which display the level and evolution of public attitudes toward the government and the political system for selected countries. In all these countries, over two-thirds of citizens have little or no confidence in political parties. Figure 6.5 displays the answers to a classic question of political surveys: the proportion of citizens who think "their country is run by a few big interests looking out for themselves." In 1997–2001, in all the countries considered, over 53 percent of people interviewed held this view, including 63.2 percent in the United States, and 72.5 percent in Finland, usually considered a model of democracy.

Other surveys, conducted at the world level, find similar trends of political dissatisfaction. The 1999 Gallup International Millennium Survey conducted for the United Nations Millennium Assembly found that 62.1 percent of the 57,000 people interviewed in 60 countries believed that their countries were not governed by the will of the people. When asked to select a term that would better describe their perception of the government, their main choices were "corrupt" and "bureaucratic". The survey claims to be representative of the views of 1.25 billion people (see figure 6.6).[91]

In 2002, Gallup conducted a similar survey, this time commissioned by the World Economic Forum, interviewing 36,000 people across 47 countries in six continents, considered to be representative of 1.4 billion citizens. Again, over two-thirds of citizens believed that their countries were not governed by the will of the people, and this view was held by 52 percent of citizens in North America and by 61 percent of citizens in the European Union (see figure 6.7). The same survey found little or no trust in the ability of parliament to operate in society's best interest among 51 percent of citizens in the world at large, with this view held by 59 percent of people in the European Union. However, in this instance, North America ranked better, with only 22 percent of citizens expressing such a view.

When asked about the institutions able to operate in society's best interests, the armed forces, NGOs, educational institutions, the United Nations, religious institutions, police, and health institutions come at the top, enjoying the confidence of the majority of citizens. While, on the other hand, global companies, and parliaments, were trusted by a minority of citizens, with governments in the middle of the scale of trust (see figure 6.8).[92]

90   Inglehart (2003); Nevitte (2003).
91   Gallup International Millennium Survey (1999).
92   Gallup International Millennium Survey (2002).

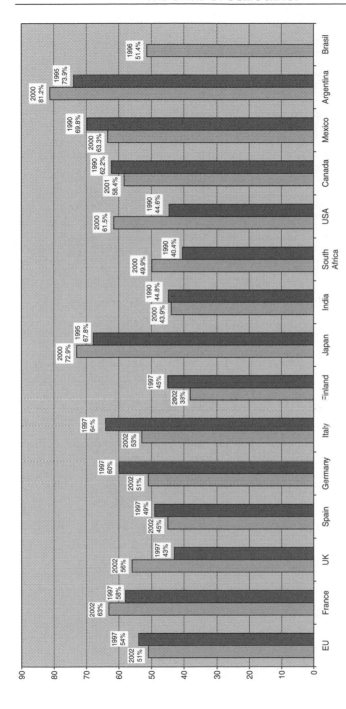

Figure 6.3 Percentage of citizens expressing not very much or no confidence in government for selected countries (year and percentage indicated in figure).

Sources: Nevitte (2003: 387–412); *Eurobarometer* 1997 and 2002 (France, UK, Spain, Germany, Italy, and Finland)

Elaborated by Esteve Ollé

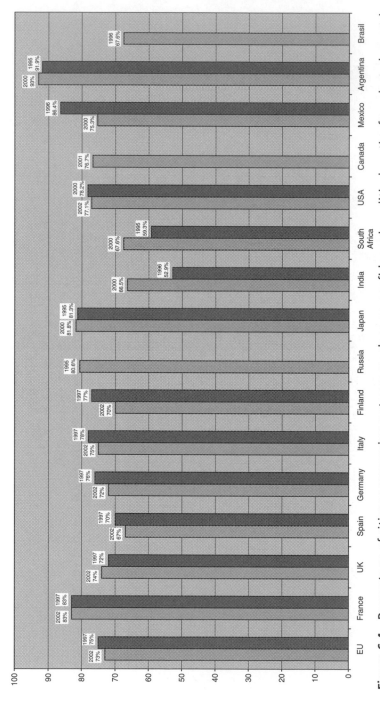

Figure 6.4 Percentage of citizens expressing not very much or no confidence in political parties for selected countries (year and percentage indicated in figure).

Sources: Nevitte (2003: 387–412); *Eurobarometer* 1997 and 2002 (France, UK, Spain, Germany, Italy, and Finland) Elaborated by Esteve Ollé

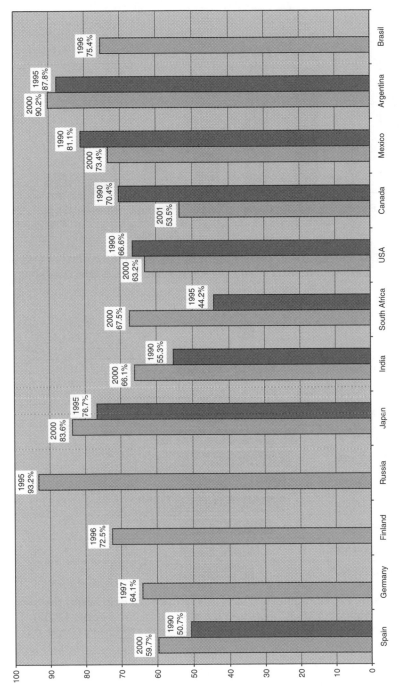

Figure 6.5 Percentage of people in selected countries expressing the view that their country is run by a few big interests looking out for themselves (year and percentage indicated in figure).

Sources: Nevitte (2003: 387–412) Elaborated by Esteve Ollé

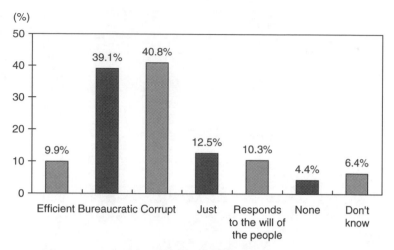

Figure 6.6 Perception of government by citizens of 60 countries (1999)
Source: Gallup International Millennium Survey (1999) Compiled by Esteve Ollé

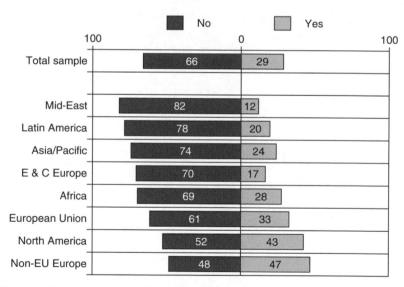

Figure 6.7 Percentage of citizens in 47 countries expressing the view
that their country is governed by the will of the people (2002)
Source: Gallup International Millennium Survey (2002) Compiled by Esteve Ollé

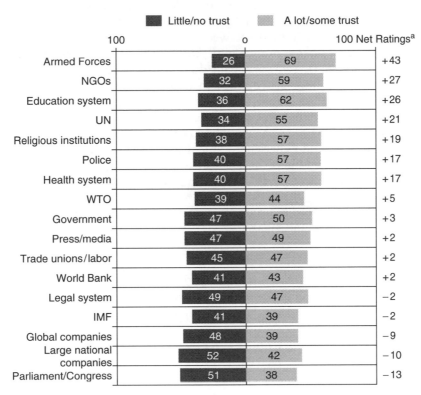

Figure 6.8 Trust in institutions to operate in society's best interest (2002)

[a]Net rating = % trust minus % distrust.

Source: Gallup International Millennium Survey (2002)

Compiled by Esteve Ollé

However, this skepticism toward mainstream parties and politics does not necessarily mean that people do not vote any longer, or that they do not care about democracy. For that matter, in much of the world, democracy has been attained only recently after a tremendous effort, conquered with blood, sweat, and tears, so that people are not easily ready to give up hope. Indeed, when people perceive the chance of meaningful political action, they mobilize enthusiastically, as they did around the election of Lula to the presidency of Brazil in 2002. Even in veteran democracies, where the rituals of free elections have been practiced for two hundred years (except for half of the population, i.e. women), political participation goes up and down. People do not vote much in the United States (51.2 percent in the 2000 presidential election, 49 percent in 1996, 54 percent in 1992, 51 percent in 1984, down from 68 percent in 1968), but participation rates are consistently high (between 65 percent and 80 percent) in Italy, Spain, Germany, France until 2002, and most European countries (see table 6.4). Yet, Europeans do not trust their politicians more than Americans do.[93] It would seem that individualism, rather than political disaffection, accounts for American exceptionalism.[94]

There are, nevertheless, powerful expressions of growing political alienation worldwide, as people observe the state's incapacity to solve their problems, and experience cynical instrumentalism from professional politicians. One of these expressions is the increasing support for a variety of "third party" forces, and for regional parties, since, in

Table 6.4 Turnout in national elections: recent figures compared to rates for the 1970s and 1980s (%)

| | 1970s–1980s | | 1990s | | |
	Average turnout	Turnout range	1990s (1st election)	1990s (2nd election)	2000s
United States	55.2	52.8–57.1	55.9 (1992)	49.0 (1996)	51.2 (2000)
Japan	71.2	67.9–74.6	67.3 (1993)	59.6 (1996)	62.5 (2000)
Germany	88.6	84.3–91.1	79.1 (1994)	80.2 (1998)	79.1 (2002)
France (1st ballot)	82.2	81.1–84.2	78.4 (1995)		71.6 (2002)
United Kingdom	74.8	72.2–78.9	75.8 (1992)	71.4 (1997)	59.2 (2001)
Spain	73.9	70.6–77.0	77.3 (1993)	77.4 (1996)	68.7 (2000)
Italy	91.4	89.0–93.2	86.4 (1992)	86.0 (1994) 82.7 (1996)	81.2 (2001)

Note: US and France figures are for presidential elections; all others are for lower house of parliament. Voting in Italy is compulsory.
Sources: 1970s and 1980s: *The International Almanac of Electoral History* (rev. 3rd edn, Thomas T. Mackie and Richard Rose, Washington, DC: Macmillan Press, 1991); recent elections: *The Statesman's Yearbook 1994–1995, 1995–1996* and *1997–1998* (ed. Brian Hunter, New York: St Martin's Press, 1994, 1995, 1997), *1998–1999, 2003* (ed. Barry Turner, London: Macmillan, 1998, 2002); *The Societies of Europe: Elections in Western Europe since 1815* (Daniele Caramani, London: Macmillan, 2000); www.elysee.fr (Présidence de la République official website, France).
Compiled by Sandra Moog and Esteve Ollé

93 *Eurobarometer* (various years); Castells et al. (2002); Dupin (2002); Gallup International Millennium Survey (2002).
94 Lipset (1996).

most political systems, the final showdown to seize national executive power takes place between two candidates, representing two broad coalitions. Thus, voting for someone else becomes a protest vote against the overall political system, and maybe the attempt to help build a different alternative, often on a local or regional basis. Esteve Ollé, Sandra Moog, and I have built an index of voting for mainstream parties for some major democracies in different continents, measuring its evolution at several points in time in the 1980s, 1990s, and 2002.[95]

As shown in figure 6.9, the overall trend seems to confirm the declining proportion of the vote for mainstream parties up to the mid-1990s. However, political systems are living systems: when confronted with a crisis they reconfigure to increase their capacity to integrate pressures from their citizens. This is what happened in the democracies analyzed here. In Italy, in 1994, the old political system, dominated by the Christian Democrats and their allies, collapsed, delegitimized by corruption, patronage, and inefficiency. As discussed above, a political entrepreneur and media tycoon, Berlusconi, built a different political coalition, won election in the short run, and built a new power basis for the dominant interest groups in the longer run. Thus, his coalition was an outsider before the 1994 election, but became a mainstream political actor after 1994. In Germany, the decline of the mainstream vote laid open the way to government for the main expression of political challenge in society, the Green party. Thus, after its entry to the government in the aftermath of the 1998 election, mainstream parties (now including the newly respectable Greens) reversed the trend of decline. Japan, where the long-term dominance of the LDP went into a catastrophic downturn in 1993, also succeeded in reinventing a conservative coalition, by bringing together various spin-offs from the old LDP, all with a new look, a new discourse, and some new leaders. In Spain, the decline of the socialists in the mainstream was compensated by the ability of the Conservative party to absorb a number of conservative regional parties. This, combined with the mobilization of the electorate against the perceived corruption of the Socialists, and the abstention of a proportion of Socialist voters, increased the percentage vote for mainstream parties, although it remained at a lower level than in 1982. In the US, the disappearance of the Ross Perot phenomenon brought the system back to normal – that is, the strong bipartisan control of national politics – at the price of a low level of electoral turnout. The UK, also a political system institutionally locked into a bipartisan

95   For sources, definitions, and methods of calculation, see the Methodological Appendix.

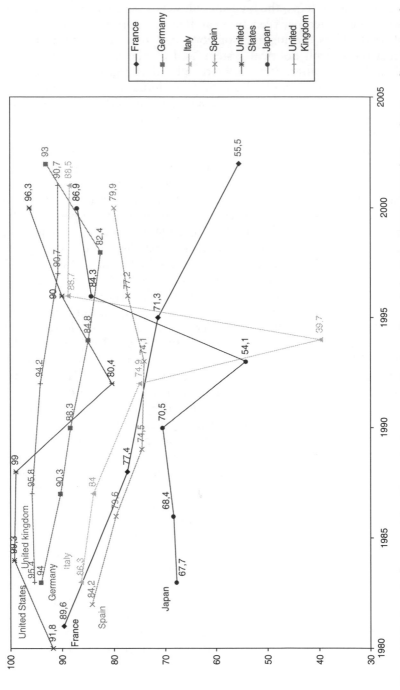

Figure 6.9 Level of support for the mainstream parties in national elections, 1980–2002 (US and France figures are for presidential elections; all others are returns for lower house of parliament).

Sources: see Methodological Appendix for figures and sources Compiled and elaborated by Esteve Ollé.

monopoly of power, followed a slight decline in the vote for main-stream parties, which declined from 95.4 percent in 1983 to 90.7 percent in 2001. France, on the other hand, failed to incorporate the anti-establishment vote into the political mainstream, in spite of the Socialist-led government alliance with Communists and Greens. As a result, the protest vote in the presidential elections in 2002 placed the Fascist candidate in the second position in the first round, as the left disintegrated, and the trend toward disaffection with mainstream parties reached a level of 45 percent of the voters making their choices outside the mainstream.

In sum, we perceive a trend of discontent *vis-à-vis* mainstream parties that leads to political crises in the system of institutional integration, in spite of the built-in mechanisms to keep the system under the control of established parties. When these controls do not work any longer, the system opens itself up to new components, thus channeling the political pressure. However, with each reconfigur-ation, the risk of further disaffection increases if the protests that began the crisis are not addressed. When and if citizens feel frustrated, they turn to non-institutional forms of politics. This is what the important comparative analysis of Inglehart and Catterberg shows. Using data from the World Values Survey, they measured empirical indicators of elite-challenging action, outside the institutional system, showing their increase over the past decade for 17 established democ-racies.[96] On the other hand, in the new democracies, in Latin America or in Eastern Europe, after the change of regime, and once people experience democracy, there is a decline in political action during the years immediately following regime change, prompting what they label a post-honeymoon decline in democratic support.

These observations point to a general conclusion: there is, world-wide, an increasing tension between political participation, social demands, and the responsiveness of democratic institutions. The con-crete expressions of this tension vary in each country, depending on level of development, political institutions, and the political cycle of the country. Yet the general trend is the erosion of the capacity of the democratic political system to process social demands and value changes. While most people do not see any alternative to democracy as a system of government, a growing majority of citizens do not feel that democracy will help them very much in addressing the issues that confront them in their daily lives.

As a consequence of these developments, we do not witness, in general terms, people's withdrawal from the political scene, but the

96   Inglehart and Catterberg (2003).

penetration of the political system by symbolic politics, single-issue mobilizations, localism, referendum politics, and, above all, ad hoc support for personalized leadership. With political parties fading away, it is the time of saviors. This introduces systemic unpredictability. It could turn out to be the regeneration of politics, as was expected in Brazil under Lula in 2003. Or, it could end up in a demagogic flare up, disintegrating political institutions, jeopardizing world stability, or launching a new assault on reason. Or, still, it could favor the return of a democratic, authoritarian state seizing the opportunity of global insecurity to assert itself as the last resort for safety, as some tendencies seem to indicate in the United States in 2003.

Whatever the future, what the observation of the present seems to indicate is that, under different forms, and through the variety of processes I have outlined in this and previous chapters, we are witnessing the fragmentation of the state, the unpredictability of the political system, and politics focused on single issues. Political freedom may still exist, as people will continue to fight for it. But political democracy, as conceived by the liberal revolutions of the eighteenth century, and as diffused throughout the world in the twentieth century, has become an empty shell. Not that it was just "formal democracy": democracy lives out of these very "forms," such as secret, universal suffrage, and respect of civil liberties.[97] But the new institutional, cultural, and technological conditions of democratic exercise have made the existing party system, and the current regime of competitive politics, obsolete as adequate mechanisms of political representation in the network society. People know it, and feel it, but they also know, in their collective memory, how important it is to prevent tyrants from occupying the vanishing space of democratic politics. Citizens are still citizens but they are uncertain of which city, and of whose city.

Conclusion: Reconstructing Democracy?

These are alarming words, indeed. It would be tempting at this point to seize the opportunity to lecture you on my personal model of informational democracy. Do not worry. For reasons that I will present in the general conclusion to this book (in volume III), I have forbidden myself normative prescriptions, and political admonition. However, in strict fairness to political hope, I will conclude by com-

97   Katznelson (1996).

menting on potential paths of democratic reconstruction, *as they manifest themselves in the observed practice of societies at the turn of the millennium*, regardless of my personal views on their merits. Since, fortunately, embryos of new democratic politics are numerous, and diverse around the world, I will restrain my commentary to three trends that I consider particularly relevant for the future of informational politics.

The first one is the re-creation of the local state. In many societies around the world, local democracy, for reasons exposed in chapter 5, appears to be flourishing, at least in terms relative to national political democracy. This is particularly true when regional and local governments cooperate with each other, and when they extend their reach to neighborhood decentralization and citizen participation. When electronic means (computer-mediated communication or local radio and television stations) are added to expand participation and consultation by citizens (for example, in Barcelona, Stockholm, Lyon, or Bologna) new technologies contribute to enhanced participation in local government. Experiences of local self-management, as the one in Porto Alegre, show the possibility of reconstructing links of political representation to *share* (if not control) the challenges of economic globalization and political unpredictability. There are obvious limits to this localism since it accentuates the fragmentation of the nation-state. But, strictly in terms of observation, the most powerful trends legitimizing democracy are taking place, worldwide, at the local level.[98]

A second perspective often discussed in the literature,[99] and in the media,[100] is the opportunity offered by electronic communication to enhance political participation and horizontal communication among citizens. Indeed, on-line information access and computer-mediated communication facilitate the diffusion and retrieval of information, and offer possibilities for interaction and debate in an autonomous, electronic forum, bypassing the control of the media. Indicative referendums on a variety of issues may provide a useful tool, when used carefully without yielding to the oversimplified frame of referendum politics. More importantly, citizens could form, and are forming, their own political and ideological constellations, circumventing established political structures, thus creating a flexible, adaptable political field.

98   Cooke (1994); Graham (1995); Ziccardi (1995); Borja and Castells (1997).
99   Ganley (1991); Castells (2001).
100   *The Economist* (1995a).

However, serious criticism may be addressed, and indeed has been addressed, to the prospects of electronic democracy.[101] On the one hand, should this form of democratic politics emerge as an important instrument of debate, representation, and decision, it would certainly institutionalize a form of "Athenian democracy," both nationally and internationally. That is, while a relatively small, educated, and affluent elite in a few countries and cities would have access to an extraordinary tool of information and political participation, actually enhancing citizenship, the uneducated, switched-off masses of the world, and of the country, would remain excluded from the new democratic core, as were slaves and barbarians at the outset of democracy in classical Greece. On the other hand, the volatility of the medium could induce an accentuation of "show politics," with the flaring up of fashions, and myths, once the rationalizing power of parties and institutions was bypassed by the flows of suddenly convergent and divergent political moods. In other words, on-line politics could push the individualization of politics, and of society, to a point where integration, consensus, and institution building would become dangerously difficult to reach.

To explore the matter, my students in the graduate seminar on Sociology of the Information Society at Berkeley proceeded with some on-line observation of the Internet in the spring of 1996. The results of their analysis reveal some interesting trends. Thus, Klinenberg and Perrin observed that, in the 1996 American presidential Republican primaries, Internet usage played an important role in diffusing information about the candidates (Dole), as well as in reaching out for support (Buchanan), and contributions (all candidates).[102] Yet the channels of communication were monitored and tightly controlled, thus becoming, in fact, one-way communication systems, more powerful and flexible than television, but not more open to citizen participation. This could change in the future, but it seems that the logic of informational politics restrains openness of the system, since candidates must control the messages in their networks, so as not to be made responsible for positions or statements that are prejudicial or out of touch with the electorate. Tight political control and electronic openness seem to be mutually exclusive in the present system. Thus, as long as political parties and organized campaigns control the political procedure, electronic citizen participation will take a back seat in informational politics, as it refers to formal elections and decision-making.

101   High Level Experts Group (1996).
102   Klinenberg and Perrin (1996).

However, Steve Bartz, on the environmental movement, and Matthew Zook, on the American militia movement, found a process of empowerment for grassroots groups using the Internet as an instrument of information, communication, and organization.[103] Moreover, the analysis presented in chapter 2 on the anti-globalization movement shows how the Internet can contribute to enhance the autonomy of citizens to organize and mobilize around issues that are not properly processed in the institutional system. It appears that it is in the realm of symbolic politics, and in the development of issue-oriented mobilizations by groups and individuals outside the mainstream political system, that new electronic communication may have the most dramatic effects. The impact of such developments on democracy is unclear. On the one hand, allowing issue mobilization to bypass formal politics may undermine even further the institutions of democracy. On the other hand, if political representation and decision-making could find a linkage with these new sources of inputs from concerned citizens, without yielding to a technologically savvy elite, a new kind of civil society could be reconstructed, thus allowing for electronic grassrooting of democracy.

The development of symbolic politics, and of political mobilization around "non-political"causes, electronically or otherwise, is the third trend that could be in the process of reconstructing democracy in the network society. Humanitarian causes, such as the ones supported by Amnesty International, *Médecins sans frontières*, Greenpeace, Oxfam, Food First, and thousands and thousands of both local and global, activist groups and non-governmental organizations around the world, are the most powerful proactive, mobilizing factor in informational politics.[104] These mobilizations develop around issues that receive a wide consensus, and that are not necessarily aligned with one or other political party. Indeed, in terms of official position, most political parties apparently support most of these causes. And most humanitarian organizations abstain from supporting a given political party, except on specific issues at specific times. Most of these mobilizations are in between social movements and political actions, since they address themselves to citizens, asking people to put pressure on public institutions or private firms that can make a difference on the particular matter targeted by the mobilization. In other instances, they do appeal to people's solidarity directly. Ultimately, their horizon is to act on the political process; that is, to influence the management of society by the representatives of society. But they do not necessarily,

103   Bartz (1996); Zook (1996).
104   Guehenno (1993).

and in fact not frequently, use the channels of political representation and decision-making, for instance by electing their candidates to office. These forms of political mobilization, which could be defined as issue-oriented, non-partisan politics, seem to win increasing legitimacy in all societies, and to condition the rules and outcomes of formal political competition. They re-legitimize the concern with public affairs in people's minds and lives. They do so by introducing new political processes, and new political issues, thus furthering the crisis of classic liberal democracy while fostering the emergence of the yet to be discovered, informational democracy.

Conclusion: Social Change in the Network Society

At the dawn of the information age, a crisis of legitimacy is voiding of meaning and function the institutions of the industrial era. Bypassed by global networks of wealth, power, and information, the modern nation-state has lost much of its sovereignty. By trying to intervene strategically in the global scene, the state loses the capacity to represent its territorially rooted constituencies. In a world in which multilateralism is the rule, the separation between nations and states, between the politics of representation and the politics of intervention, disorganizes the political accounting unit on which liberal democracy was built and came to be exercised in the past two centuries. The privatization of public agencies and the attack on the welfare state, while relieving societies of some bureaucratic burden, worsen living conditions for the majority of citizens, break the historic social contract between capital, labor, and the state, and remove much of the social safety net, the nuts and bolts of legitimate government for the common people.

Torn by the internationalization of finance and production, unable to adapt to the networking of firms and the individualization of work, and challenged by the degendering of employment, the labor movement is weakened as a major source of social cohesion and workers' representation. It does not disappear, but it becomes, primarily, a political agent integrated into the realm of public institutions. Mainstream churches, practicing a form of secularized religion dependent either on the state or on the market, lose much of their capacity to enforce behavior in exchange for providing solace, and selling heavenly real estate. The challenge to patriarchalism, and the crisis of the patriarchal family, disturb the orderly sequence of transmitting cultural codes from generation to generation, and shake the foundations of personal security, thus forcing men, women, and children to find new ways of living. Political ideologies that emanate from industrial institutions and organizations, from nation-state-based democratic liberalism to labor-based socialism, find themselves deprived of actual meaning in the new social context. Therefore, they lose their appeal, and, trying to survive, they engage in a series of endless adaptations, running behind the new society, like dusty flags of forgotten wars.

As a result of these convergent processes, the *sources* of what I call in chapter 1 *legitimizing identities* are drained away. The institutions and organizations of civil society that were constructed around the democratic state, and around the social contract between capital and labor, have become, by and large, empty shells, decreasingly able to relate to people's lives and values in most societies. It is indeed a tragic irony that when most countries in the world finally fought their way to access the institutions of liberal democracy (in my view, the foundation of all political democracy), these institutions are so distant from the structure and processes that really matter that they appear to most people as a sarcastic grimace on the new face of history. At the turn of the millennium, the king and the queen, the state and civil society, are both naked, and their children-citizens are wandering around a variety of foster homes.

The dissolution of shared identities, which is tantamount to the dissolution of society as a meaningful social system, may well be the state of affairs in our time. Nothing says that new identities have to emerge, new social movements have to re-create society, and new institutions will be rebuilt toward the *lendemains qui chantent*. At first sight, we are witnessing the emergence of a world exclusively made of markets, networks, individuals, and strategic organizations, apparently governed by patterns of "rational expectations" (the new, influential economic theory), except when these "rational individuals" suddenly shoot their neighbor, rape a little girl, or spread nerve gas in the subway. No need for identities in this new world: basic instincts, power drives, self-centered strategic calculations, and, at the macro-social level, "the clear features of a barbarian nomadic dynamic, of a Dionysian element threatening to inundate all borders and rendering international political-legal and civilizational norms problematic."[1] A world whose counterpoint could be, as we are seeing already in a number of countries, a nationalist reassertion by the remnants of state structures, abandoning any pretension to legitimacy, and clawing

1   Panarin (1994: 37).

back from history to the principle of power for the sake of power, sometimes wrapping it in nationalist rhetoric. In the landscapes we have crossed in the first two volumes of this trilogy, we have perceived the seeds of a society whose *Weltanschauung* would split between the old logic of *Macht* and a new logic of *Selbstanschauung*.[2]

However, we have also observed the emergence of powerful resistance identities, which retrench in communal heavens, and refuse to be flushed away by global flows and radical individualism. They build their communes around the traditional values of God, nation, and the family, and they secure the enclosures of their encampments with ethnic emblems and territorial defenses. Resistance identities are not limited to traditional values. They can also be built by, and around, proactive social movements, which choose to establish their autonomy in their communal resistance as long as they are not powerful enough to mount an assault on the oppressive institutions they oppose. This is, by and large, the case of the women's movement, building women's spaces where a new anti-patriarchal consciousness may rise; and it is certainly the case of the sexual liberation movements, whose spaces of freedom, from bars to neighborhoods, are essential devices of self-recognition. Even the environmental movement, whose ultimate horizon is cosmological, more often than not starts in the backyards and communities around the world, protecting spaces before engaging in the conquest of time.

Thus, resistance identities are as pervasive in the network society as are the individualistic projects resulting from the dissolution of former legitimizing identities that used to constitute the civil society of the industrial era. However these identities resist, they barely communicate. They do not communicate with the state, except to struggle and negotiate on behalf of their specific interests/values. They rarely communicate with each other because they are built around sharply distinct principles, defining an "in" and an "out." And because the communal logic is the key to their survival, individual self-definitions are not welcome. Thus, on the one hand, the dominant, global elites inhabiting the space of flows tend to consist of identity-less individuals ("citizens of the world"); while, on the other hand, people resisting economic, cultural, and political disfranchisement tend to be attracted to communal identity.

We should, then, add another layer to the social dynamics of the network society. Together with state apparatuses, global networks, and self-centered individuals, there are also communes formed

2 *Macht* = strong power; *Weltanschauung* = culture-centered view of the world; *Selbstanschauung* (proposed neologism) = self-centered view of the world.

around *resistance identity*. However, all these elements do not glue together, their logic excludes each other, and their coexistence is unlikely to be peaceful.

The key issue becomes then the emergence of *project identities* (see chapter 1), potentially able to reconstruct a new civil society of sorts, and, eventually, a new state. On this matter, I will not be prescriptive or prophetic, but, rather, I will elaborate on the provisional results of my observation of social movements and political processes. My analysis does not preclude the possibility that social movements quite different from those considered here may have a major role in constituting future society. But, at the dawn of the twenty-first century, I have not detected their signals.

New *project identities* do not seem to emerge from former identities of civil society of the industrial era, but from a development of current *resistance identities*. There are, I believe, theoretical reasons, as well as empirical arguments, for such a trajectory in the formation of new historical subjects. But, before proposing some ideas on the matter, let me clarify how project identities may emerge from the resistance identities we have observed.

The fact that a commune is built around a resistance identity does not mean that it will likely evolve toward building a project identity. It may well remain as a defensive commune. Or else, it may become an interest group, and join the logic of generalized bargaining, the dominant logic of the network society. Yet, in other cases, resistance identities may generate project identities, aiming at the transformation of society as a whole, in continuity with the values of communal resistance to dominant interests enacted by global flows of capital, power, and information.

Religious communes may develop into religious fundamentalist movements aimed at re-moralizing society, re-establishing godly, eternal values, and embracing the whole world, or at least the nearby neighborhood, in a community of believers, thus founding a new society.

The trajectory of nationalism in the information age is more undetermined, according to observation of recent experience. On the one hand, it can lead to retrenchment into a reconstructed nation-state, re-legitimizing it on behalf of the nation, rather than of the state. On the other hand, it may supersede the modern nation-state, by affirming nations beyond the state, and building multilateral networks of political institutions in a variable geometry of shared sovereignty.

Ethnicity, while being an essential ingredient of both oppression and liberation, seems to be usually framed in support of other communal identities (religious, national, territorial), rather than inducing either resistance or new projects by itself.

Territorial identity is at the root of the worldwide surge of local and regional governments as significant actors in both representation and intervention, better suited to adapt to the endless variation of global flows. The reinvention of the city-state is a salient characteristic of this new age of globalization, as it was related to the rise of a trading, international economy at the origin of the modern age.

Women's communes, and the spaces of freedom of sexual identity, project themselves into society at large by undermining patriarchalism, and by reconstructing the family on a new, egalitarian basis that implies the degendering of social institutions, in opposition to patriarchal capitalism and to the patriarchal state.

Environmentalism shifts from the defense of one's environment, health, and well-being to the ecological project of integrating humankind and nature, on the basis of the socio-biological identity of the species, assuming humankind's cosmological meaning.

These identity projects emerge from communal resistance rather than from the reconstruction of institutions of civil society, because the crisis of these institutions, and the emergence of resistance identities, originate precisely from the new characteristics of the network society that undermine the former and induce the latter. Namely, globalization, capitalist restructuring, organizational networking, the culture of real virtuality, and the primacy of technology for the sake of technology, the key features of social structure in the information age, are the very sources of crisis of the state and civil society as constituted in the industrial era. They are also the forces against which communal resistance is organized, with new identity projects potentially emerging around these resistances. Resistance and projects contradict the dominant logic of the network society by engaging in defensive and offensive struggles around three foundational realms of this new social structure: space, time, and technology.

The communes of resistance defend their space, their places, against the placeless logic of the space of flows characterizing social domination in the information age (volume I, chapter 6). They claim their historic memory, and/or affirm the permanence of their values, against the dissolution of history in timeless time, and the celebration of the ephemeral in the culture of real virtuality (volume I, chapter 7). They use information technology for people's horizontal communication, and communal prayer, while rejecting the new idolatry of technology, and preserving transcendent values against the deconstructing logic of self-regulating computer networks.

Ecologists affirm the control of uses of space on behalf of both people and nature against the a-natural, abstract logic of the space of flows. They advance the cosmological vision of glacial time, integrating the human species into its evolving environment, and reject the annihilation of time by de-sequencing, a logic embedded in timeless time (volume I, chapter 7). And they support the use of science and technology for life, while opposing the domination of life by science and technology.

Feminists and sexual identity movements affirm the control of their most immediate spaces, their bodies, over their disembodiment in the space of flows, influenced by patriarchalism, where reconstructed images of the woman, and fetishes of sexuality, dissolve their humanity and deny their identity. They also fight for the control of their time, as the timeless logic of the network society piles up roles and functions over women without adapting their new lives to new timing; so that alienated timing becomes the most concrete expression of the chores of being a liberated woman in a non-liberated social organization. Women and sexual identity movements also aim at using technology to enhance their rights (for instance, their reproductive rights, and the right to control their bodies), against the patriarchal uses of science and technology, as expressed in the submission of women to arbitrary medical rituals and prejudices; or in the temporary lack of will of some scientific institutions in fighting AIDS so long as it was considered to be a homosexual disease. At the moment when humankind reaches the technological frontier of social control over the biological reproduction of the species, a fundamental battle is being fought between bodies as autonomous identities and bodies as social artifacts. This is why identity politics starts with our bodies.

Thus, the dominant logic of the network society triggers its own challenges, in the form of communal resistance identities, and of project identities potentially emerging from these spaces, *under conditions and through processes that are specific to each institutional and cultural context*. The resulting contradictory dynamics is at the heart of the historical process through which a new social structure, and the flesh and blood of our societies, are being constituted. Where is power in this social structure? And what is power under these historical conditions?

Power, as argued, and to some extent shown, in this and in volume I of this trilogy, is no longer concentrated in institutions (the state), organizations (capitalist firms), or symbolic controllers (corporate media, churches). It is diffused in global networks of wealth, power, information, and images, which circulate and transmute in a system of variable geometry and dematerialized geography. Yet it does not disappear. *Power still rules society; it still shapes, and dominates, us.* Not only because apparatuses of different kinds can still discipline bodies and silence minds. This form of power is, at the same time, eternal, and fading away. It is eternal because humans are, and will be, predators. But, in its current form of existence, it is fading away: the exercise of this kind of power is increasingly ineffective for the interests that it is supposed to serve. States can shoot, but because the profile of their enemies, and the whereabouts of their challengers, are increasingly unclear, they tend to shoot randomly, with the probability that they may shoot themselves in the process.

The new power lies in the codes of information and in the images of representation around which societies organize their institutions, and people build their lives, and decide their behavior. The sites of this power are people's minds. This is why power in the information age is at the same time identifiable and diffused. We know what it is, yet we cannot seize it because power is a function of an endless battle around the cultural codes of society. Whoever, or whatever, wins the battle of people's minds will rule, because mighty, rigid apparatuses will not be a match, in any reasonable timespan, for the minds mobilized around the power of flexible, alternative networks. But victories may be ephemeral, since the turbulence of information flows will keep codes in a constant swirl. This is why identities are so important, and ultimately, so powerful in this ever-changing power structure – because they build interests, values, and projects, around experience, and refuse to dissolve by establishing a specific connection between nature, history, geography, and culture. Identities anchor power in some areas of the social structure, and build from there their resistance or their offensives in the informational struggle about the cultural codes constructing behavior and, thus, new institutions.

Under these conditions, who are the subjects of the information age? We already know, or at least I suggest we know, the sources from which they are likely to emerge. I would also add that I think we know from where they are not likely to develop. For instance, the labor movement seems to be historically superseded. Not that it will entirely disappear (although it is dwindling down in much of the world), or that it has lost all relevance. In fact, labor unions are influential political actors in many countries. And in many instances they are the main, or the only, tools for workers to defend themselves against the abuses of capital and of the state. Yet, because of the structural features and historical processes that I have tried to convey in the first two volumes of this trilogy, the labor movement does not seem fit to generate by itself and from itself a project identity able to reconstruct social control and to rebuild social institutions in the information age. Labor militants will undoubtedly be a part of new, transformative social dynamics. I am less sure that labor unions will.

Political parties have also exhausted their potential as autonomous agents of social change, caught into the logic of informational politics, and with their main platform, the institutions of the nation-state, having lost much of its relevance. They are still, however, essential instruments in processing the demands of society, spearheaded by social movements, into the realms of national, international, and supranational polities. Indeed, while social movements will have to provide the new codes under which societies may be re-thought, and re-established, political parties of some kind (maybe under new, informational incarnations) are still crucial agencies in institutionalizing social transformation. They are influential brokers rather than powerful innovators.

Thus, social movements emerging from communal resistance to globalization, capitalist restructuring, organizational networking, uncontrolled informationalism, and patriarchalism – that is, for the time being, ecologists, feminists, religious fundamentalists, nationalists, localists, and the vast democratic movement that emerges as the coalition for global justice against capitalist globalization – are the potential subjects of the information age. In what forms will they express themselves? My analysis here is necessarily more speculative, although I feel obliged to suggest some hypotheses, as grounded as possible on the observations reported in this volume.

The agencies voicing identity projects aimed at changing cultural codes must be symbol mobilizers. They ought to act on the culture of real virtuality that frames communication in the network society, subverting it on behalf of alternative values, and introducing codes emerging from autonomous identity projects. I have observed two main sorts of such potential agencies. The first I will call *the Prophets*. They are symbolic personalities whose role is not that of charismatic leaders, or of shrewd strategists, but to give a face (or a mask) to a symbolic insurgency, so that they speak on behalf of the insurgents. Thus, voiceless insurgents have a voice, and their identity may enter the realm of symbolic struggles, and stand a chance of seizing power – in people's minds. This is, of course, the case of Subcomandante Marcos, Mexico's *Zapatistas* leader. But also of *compadre* Palenque in La Paz–El Alto. Or of Asahara, the guru of the murderous Japanese cult. Or, to emphasize the diversity of expression of such potential oracles, the case of the Catalan nationalist leader, Jordi Pujol, whose moderation, rationality, and strategic wit often hide his patient determination to insert *Catalunya* as a nation among other European nations, speaking on its behalf, and reconstructing a Carolingian identity for *Catalunya*. He may be the voice of a new, original, stateless brand of nationalism in informational Europe.

In another, different example, ecological consciousness is often represented by popular rock singers, such as Sting in his campaign to save Amazonia; or by movie stars, such as Brigitte Bardot, engaging in a crusade on behalf of animal rights. A different kind of prophet could be the neo-luddite Unabomber in America, linking up the anarchist tradition to the violent defense of essential nature against the evils of technology. In the Islamic or Christian fundamentalist movements, a number of religious leaders assume a similar leading role by interpreting the holy texts, thus restating God's truth in the hope it will reach, and touch, the minds and souls of would-be believers. When religious fundamentalism clashes violently with the dominant logic of the global system, messianic leaders emerge, as is the case with bin Laden. Human rights movements are also often dependent on the agency of symbolic, uncompromising personalities, as is the case in the tradition of Russian dissidents, historically represented by Sakharov, and exemplified in the 1990s by Sergei Kovalov.

I deliberately choose to mix the genres in my examples to indicate that there are "good" and "bad" prophets, depending on individual preferences, including my own. But they are all prophets in the sense that they declare the path, affirm the values, and act as symbol senders, becoming a symbol in themselves, so that the message is inseparable from the messenger. Historical transitions, often made in the midst of crumbling institutions and exhausted political forms, have always been a time for prophets. And it should be even more so in the transition to the information age; that is, a social structure organized around information flows and symbol manipulation.

However, the second and *main agency* detected in our journey across the lands inhabited by social movements, is a *networking, decentered form of organization and intervention, characteristic of the new social movements*, mirroring, and counteracting, the networking logic of domination in the informational society. This is clearly the case for the environmental movement, built around national and international networks of decentralized activity. But I have also shown this to be the case for women's movements, insurgents against the global order, religious fundamentalist movements, and the anti-globalization movement. These networks do more than organizing activity and sharing information. *They are the actual producers, and distributors, of cultural codes.* Not only over the Net, but also in their multiple forms of exchange and interaction. Their impact on society rarely stems from a concerted strategy, masterminded by a center. Their most successful campaigns, their most striking initiatives, often result from "turbulences" in the interactive network of multilayered communication – as in the production of a "green culture" by a universal forum of putting together experiences of preserving nature and surviving capitalism at the same time. Or in the demise of patriarchalism resulting from the exchange of women's experiences in women's groups, women's magazines, women's bookstores, women's films, women's clinics, and women's networks of support in raising children. Or, else, in the demise of the cultural hegemony of neo-liberal ideology.

It is this decentered, subtle character of *networks of social change* that makes it so difficult to perceive, and identify, new identity projects coming into being. Because our historical vision has become so used to orderly battalions, colorful banners, and scripted proclamations of social change, we are at a loss when confronted with the subtle pervasiveness of incremental changes of symbols processed through multiform networks, away from the halls of power. It is in these back alleys of society, whether in alternative electronic networks or in grassrooted networks of communal resistance, that I have sensed the embryos of a new society, labored in the fields of history by the power of identity.

To be continued.

Methodological Appendix

Appendix for Tables 5.1 and 5.2

The ratios and rates of change in tables 5.1 and 5.2 were calculated using data from a number of different statistical sources. The tables below have been organized in order to show the actual figures used in the calculations, as well as the ratios and rates of change that were calculated using these data. In those rows in which the original data are presented, sources have been indicated in the far right-hand column, using the following abbreviations:

GFSY = *Government Finance Statistics Yearbook*, vol. 18 (Washington, DC: IMF, 1988, 1990, 1994)

IFSY = *International Financial Statistics Yearbook*, vol. 48 (Washington, DC: IMF, 1995)

EWY = *The Europa World Yearbook* (London: Europa Publications, 1982, 1985, 1995)

OECDNA = *National Accounts: Detailed Tables, 1980–1992*, vol. 2 (Paris: OECD, 1994)

WT = *World Tables, 1994* (The World Bank, Baltimore, MD: The Johns Hopkins University Press, 1994)

The tables are arranged alphabetically by country. For each country, table 5.1A provides data, calculations, and sources for table 5.1, and table 5.2A provides information for table 5.2.

Listed below are a few definitions and explanations of our calculations. Full definitions of all categories included in these tables, and descriptions of the original sources of data and methods of calculation, can be found in the appendices of the source materials.

Exchange rates	=	period averages of market exchange rates and official exchange rates.
Currency reserves	=	reserves, other than gold, at national valuation.
Exports	=	merchandise exports, f.o.b.
Foreign debt	=	distinguished from domestic debt according to the residence of the lender, where possible, and otherwise, according to the currency in which the debt instruments are denominated.
Domestic investment	=	calculated by multiplying each country's figures in the IFSY's "Investment as Percent of GDP" world table by that country's GDP. Investment comprises Gross Fixed Capital Formation and Increase in Stocks.

A (p) following a figure indicates that it is a preliminary figure.
An (f) indicates a final figure.
An * indicates that there is a change in methods of calculation in relation to previous years' figures.

Tables 5.1 and 5.2 and these appendices have been compiled and elaborated by Sandra Moog.

Germany: Table 5.1A Internationalization of the economy and public finance (in billions of deutschmarks, unless otherwise indicated)

	1980	1991	1992	1993	1994	Rate of change 1980–93 (%)	Source
Average exchange rate (DM per US $)	1.8177	1.6595	1.5617	1.6533	1.6228		IFSY'95
GDP (DM)	1,470.0	2,647.6	2,813.0	2,853.7	2,977.7		IFSY'95
(1990 DM)	(1,942.4)	(2,548.6)	(2,593.5)	(2,549.5)	(2,608.3)		IFSY'95
Gov. foreign debt	38.05	243.21	311.73*	472.87(p)			IFSY'95
Gov. foreign debt/GDP (%)	2.6	9.2	28.5	16.6		538.5	
Gov. net foreign borrowing	20.84	45.05	68.52*	161.14(p)			
Total currency reserves minus gold (in millions of US $)	48,592	63,001	90,967	77,640	77,363		IFSY'95
Total currency reserves minus gold (in billions of DM)	88.33	104.55	121.25	128.36	125.54		
Gov. foreign debt/ currency reserves (%)	43.1	232.6	257.1	368.4		325.3(p)	
Exports	350.33	665.81	658.47	628.39	677.81		IFSY'95
Gov. foreign debt/ exports (%)	10.9	36.5	47.3	75.3		590.8	
Gov. expenditures	447.54	860.74	1,022.95*	1,062.38(p)			IFSY'95

Gov. foreign debt/gov. expenditures (%)	8.5	28.3	30.5	44.5		423.5(p)	
Gov. net foreign borrowing/ expenditures (%)	4.7	5.2	6.7	15.2		223.4	
Domestic investment (gr. fixed cap. form. + increases in stocks)	367.73	680.43	706.06	684.89	738.47		IFSY'95
Direct foreign investment abroad (in billions of US $)	4.7	23.72	19.67	14.48	14.65		IFSY'95
Direct foreign investment abroad (in billions of DM)	8.54	39.36	30.72	23.94	23.77		
Direct foreign investment abroad/domestic investment (%)	2.3	5.8	4.4	3.5	3.2	52.2	
Inflow foreign direct investment (in billions of US $)	0.33	4.07	2.44	0.32	−3.02		IFSY'95
Inflow foreign direct investment (in billions of DM)	0.60	6.75	3.81	0.53	−4.90		
Inflow foreign direct investment/domestic investment (%)	0.2	1.0	0.5	0.1	−0.7	−50.0	

Germany: Table 5.2A Government role in the economy and public finance (in billions of deutschmarks, unless otherwise indicated)

	1980	1991	1992	1993	1994	Rate of change 1980–92 (%)	Source
GDP	1,470.9	2,647.6	2,813.0	2,853.7	2,977.7		IFSY'95
Gov. expenditures	447.54	860.74	1,022.95*	1,062.38(p)			IFSY'95
Gov. expenditure/GDP (%)	30.4	32.5	36.4	37.2(p)		19.7	
Tax revenue (budgetary central gov.)	177.54	351.74	378.82(p)*				GFSY'90,'94
Tax revenue/GDP (%)	12.1	13.3	13.5(p)			11.6(p)	
Gov. budget deficit	−26.91	−62.29	−73.10*	−75.56(p)			IFSY'95
Gov. budget deficit/GDP (%)	1.8	2.3	2.6	2.6		44.4	
Gov. debt	235.77	680.81	801.57	902.52(p)			IFSY'95
Gov. debt/GDP (%)	16.0	25.7	28.5	31.6		78.1	
Gov. employment (employees in thousands)	3,929	4,307	4,340				OECDNA'92
Total employment	23,818	26,183	26,432				OECDNA'92

Gov. employment/ total employment (%)	16.5	16.5	16.4			−0.6	IFSY'95
Gov. consump.	298.0	466.5	502.9	508.5	520.2		IFSY'95
Private consump.	837.0	1,448.8	1,536.3	1,588.9	1,644.5		IFSY'95
Gov. consump./ private consump. (%)	35.6	32.2	32.7	32.0	31.6	−8.1	
Gov. capital expenditures	101.52	175.92	197.72	199.51			EWY'85,'95
Gross fixed capital formation	337.98	652.07	709.22	705.71			EWY'85,'95
Gov. capital expenditures/ gross fixed capital formation (%)	30.0	27.0	27.9	28.3		−7.0	

India: Table 5.1A Internationalization of the economy and public finance (in billions of rupees, unless otherwise indicated)

	1980	1991	1992	1993	1994	Rate of change 1980–93 (%)	Source
Average exchange rate (rupees per US $)	8.659	22.724	25.918	30.493	31.374		IFSY'95
GDP (rupees) (1990 rupees)	1,360.1 (3,031.6)	6,160.6 (5,381.3)	7,028.3 (5,629.1)	7,863.6 (5,824.6)			IFSY'95
Gov. foreign debt	107.6	369.5	412.2(p)	464.5(f)			IFSY'95
Gov. foreign debt/ GDP (%)	7.9	6.0	5.3(p)	5.9(f)		−25.3	
Gov. net foreign borrowing	7.0	54.2	46.8	55.8			
Total currency reserves minus gold (in millions of US $)	6,944	3,627	5,757	10,199	19,698		IFSY'95
Total currency reserves minus gold (in billions of rupees)	60.13	82.42	149.21	311.00	618.01		
Gov. foreign debt/ currency reserves (%)	178.9	448.3	276.3(p)	149.4(f)		−16.5	

Exports	67.52	401.23	508.71	656.89	785.94		IFSY'95
Gov. foreign debt/exports (%)	159.4	92.1	81.0(p)	70.7(f)		−55.6	IFSY'95
Gov. expenditures	180.3	1,050.5	1,209.6(p)	1,310.7(f)			IFSY'95
Gov. foreign debt/gov. expenditures (%)	59.7	35.2	34.1(p)	35.4(f)		−40.7	
Gov. net foreign borrowing/ expenditures (%)	3.9	5.2	3.9	4.3		10.3	
Domestic Investment (gr. fixed cap. form. + increases in stocks)	284.26	1,410.78	1,637.59	1,674.95			IFSY'95

India: Table 5.2A Government role in the economy and public finance (in billions of rupees, unless otherwise indicated)

	1980	1991	1992	1993	1994	Rate of change 1980–92 (%)	Source
GDP	1,360.1	6,160.6	7,028.3	7,863.6			IFSY'95
Gov. expenditures	180.3	1,050.5	1,209.6(p)	1,310.7(f)			IFSY'95
Gov. expenditures/ GDP (%)	13.3	17.1	17.2(p)	16.7(f)		29.3(p)	
Tax revenue (consolidated central gov.)	132.7	673.6	787.8(p)	848.7(f)			GFSY'90,'94
Tax revenue/ GDP (%)	9.8	10.9	11.2(p)	10.8(f)		17.3(p)	
Gov. budget deficit	−88.6	−358.2	−366.5(p)	−372.0			IFSY'95
Gov. budget deficit / GDP (%)	6.5	5.8	5.2(p)	4.7		−20.0(p)	
Gov. debt	561.0	3,312.0	3,714.0(p)	4,136.6(f)			IFSY'95
Gov. debt/GDP (%)	41.2	53.8	52.8(p)	52.6		28.2(p)	

Gov. consump.	130.8	694.6	785.9	910.5		IFSY'95
Private consump.	992.9	3,848.0	4,245.6	4,795.9		IFSY'95
Gov. consump./ private consump. (%)	13.2	18.1	18.5	19.0	40.2	
Gross fixed capital formation	262.8	1,367.8	1,511.8	1,643.8		EWY'85,'95

Japan: Table 5.1A Internationalization of the economy and public finance (in billions of yen, unless otherwise indicated)

	1980	1991	1992	1993	1994	Rate of change 1980–93 (%)	Source
Average exchange rate (yen per US $)	226.74	134.71	126.65	111.20	102.21		IFSY'95
GDP (yen) (1990 yen)	240,176 (271,500)	451,297 (422,720)	463,145 (428,210)	465,972	469,240		IFSY'95 (WT'94)
Gov. foreign debt	621	1,186 ('90)					IFSY'95
Gov. foreign debt/ GDP (%)	0.3	0.3				0.0('90)	
Total currency reserves minus gold (in millions of US $)	24,636	72,059	71,623	98,524	125,860		IFSY'95
Total currency reserves minus gold (in billions of yen)	5,586	9,707.1	9,071.1	10,956	12,864		
Gov. foreign debt/ currency reserves (%)	11.1	12.2				9.9('90)	
Exports	29,382	42,359	43,011	40,200	40,470		IFSY'95
Gov. foreign debt/ exports (%)	2.1	2.3('90)				9.5('90)	
Gov. expenditures	44,137						IFSY'95
Gov. foreign debt/ gov. expenditures	1.4						

Domestic investment (gr. fixed cap. form. + increases in stocks)	77,337	146,672	144,038	139,326	135,610		IFSY'95
Direct foreign investment abroad (in billions of US $)	2.39	30.74	17.24	13.74	17.97		IFSY'95
Direct foreign investment abroad (in billions of yen)	541.91	4,140.99	2,183.45	1,527.89	1,836.71		
Direct foreign investment abroad/ domestic investment (%)	0.7	2.8	1.5	1.1	1.4	57.1	
Inflow foreign direct investment (in billions of US $)	0.28	1.37	2.72	0.10	0.89		IFSY'95
Inflow foreign direct investment (in billions of yen)	63.49	184.55	344.49	11.12	90.97		
Inflow foreign direct investment/ domestic investment (%)	0.08	0.13	0.23	0.01	0.07	(erratic)	

Japan: Table 5.2A: Government role in the economy and public finance (in billions of yen, unless otherwise indicated)

	1980	1991	1992	1993	1994	Rate of change 1980–92 (%)	Source
GDP	240,176	451,297	463,145	465,972	469,240		IFSY'95
Gov. expenditures	44,137						IFSY'95
Gov. expenditures/ GDP (%)	0.18						
Tax revenue (budgetary central gov.)	26,392	58,730('90)					GFSY'90,'94
Tax revenue/GDP (%)	11.0	13.0('90)				18.2('90)	
Gov. budget deficit	16,872	6,781('90)					IFSY'95
Gov. budget deficit/ GDP (%)	7.0	1.5				−78.6('90)	
Gov. debt	98,149	239,932('90)					IFSY'95
Gov. debt/GDP (%)	40.9	53.2('90)				30.1('90)	
Gov. employment (employees in thousands)	43,070	54,185	55,381				OECDNA'92
Total employment	3,911	3,960	3,975				OECDNA'92

Gov. employment/total employment (%)	9.1	7.3	7.2			−20.9	
Gov. consump.	23,568	41,232	43,258	44,666	46,108		IFSY'95
Private consump.	240,176	255,084	264,824	270,919	277,677		IFSY'95
Gov. consump./private consump. (%)	9.8	16.2	16.3	16.5	16.6	66.3	
Gross fixed capital formation	75,420	143,429	142,999	141,322			EWY'85,'95

Spain: Table 5.1A Internationalization of the economy and public finance (in billions of pesetas, unless otherwise indicated)

	1980	1991	1992	1993	1994	Rate of change 1980–93 (%)	Source
Average exchange rate (pesetas per US $)	71.70	103.91	102.38	127.26	133.96		IFSY'95
GDP (psts) (1990 psts)	15,168 (37,305)	54,901 (51,269)	59,002 (51,625)	60,904 (51,054)	64,673 (52,064)		IFSY'95
Gov. foreign debt	133.6	2,968.8	3,259.9	6,364.6	5,893.0		IFSY'95
Gov. foreign debt/GDP (%)	0.9	5.4	5.5	10.5	9.1	1,066.7	
Gov. net foreign borrowing		1,775.0	124.2	2,712.9	462.4		
Total currency reserves minus gold (in millions of US $)	11,863	65,822	45,504	41,045	41,569		IFSY'95
Total currency reserves minus gold (in billions of pesetas)	850.60	6,839.56	4,658.70	5,233.39	5,568.58		
Gov. foreign debt/currency reserves (%)	15.7	43.4	70.0	121.6	105.8	674.5	
Exports	1,493.2	6,225.7	6,605.7	7,982.3	9,795.2		IFSY'95
Gov. foreign debt/exports (%)	8.9	47.7	49.3	79.7	60.2	795.5	
Gov. expenditures	2,522.7	13,102.1	14,835.5	17,503.0	17,034.0		IFSY'95

Gov. foreign debt/gov. expenditures (%)	5.3	22.7	22.0	36.4	34.6	586.8	
Gov. net foreign borrowing/gov. expenditures (%)		13.5	0.9	15.5	2.7		
Domestic investment (gr. fixed cap. form. + increases in stocks)	3,518.98	13,505.65	13,393.45	12,119.90	12,740.85		IFSY'95
Direct foreign investment abroad (in millions of US $)	311	4,442	2,192	2,652	4,170		IFSY'95
Direct foreign investment abroad (in billions of pesetas)	22.30	461.57	224.42	337.49	558.61		
Direct foreign investment abroad/domestic investment (%)	0.6	3.4	1.7	2.8	4.4	183.3	
Inflow foreign direct investment (in millions of US $)	1,493	12,493	13,276	8,144	9,700		IFSY'95
Inflow foreign direct investment (in billions of pesetas)	107.05	1,298.15	1,359.20	1,306.41	1,299.41		
Inflow foreign direct investment/domestic investment (%)	3.0	9.6	10.1	8.6	10.2	236.7	

Spain: Table 5.2A Government role in the economy and public finance (in billions of pesetas, unless otherwise indicated)

	1980	1991	1992	1993	1994	Rate of change 1980–92 (%)	Source
GDP	15,168	54,901	59,002	60,904	64,673		IFSY'95
Gov. expenditures	2,552.7	13,102.1	14,835.5	17,503.0	17,034.0		IFSY'95
Gov. expenditures/ GDP (%)	16.8	23.9	25.1	28.7	26.3	49.4	
Tax revenue (budgetary central gov.)	1,602.4	9,530.6					GFSY'90,'94
Tax revenue/GDP (%)	10.6	17.4				64.2('91)	
Gov. budget deficit	−555.8	−1,758.0	−2.523.5	−4,221.4	−4,943.9		IFSY'95
Gov. budget deficit/ GDP (%)	3.7	3.2	4.3	6.9	7.6	16.2	
Gov. debt	2,316.7	20,837.3	23,552.7	28,708.9	34,448.0		IFSY'95
Gov. debt/GDP (%)	15.3	38.0	39.9	47.1	53.3	160.8	
Gov. employment (employees, in thousands)		2,041	2,084				OECDNA'92
Total employment		9,789	9,616				OECDNA'92

Gov. employment/ total employment (%)		20.8	21.7				
Gov. consump.	2,008	8,882	10,027	10,669	10,992		IFSY'95
Private consump.	9,992	34,244	37,220	38,511	40,854		IFSY'95
Gov. consump./ private consump. (%)	20.1	25.9	26.9	27.7	26.9	33.8	
Gross fixed capital formation	3,368	13,041	12,859	12,040	12,709		IFSY'95

United Kingdom: Table 5.1A Internationalization of the economy and public finance (in billions of pounds sterling, unless otherwise indicated)

	1980	1991	1992	1993	1994	Rate of change 1980–93 (%)	Source
Average exchange rate (pounds per US $)	0.4299	0.5652	0.5664	0.6658	0.6529		IFSY'95
GDP (pounds) (1990 pounds)	231.7 (423.49)	575.32 (540.31)	597.24 (537.45)	630.71 (549.59)	668.87 (570.72)		IFSY'95
Gov. foreign debt	10.14	28.45	34.89				IFSY'95
Gov. foreign debt/ GDP (%)	4.4	4.9	5.8			31.8('92)	
Gov. net foreign borrowing	1.43	5.50	4.71				
Total currency reserves minus gold (in billions of US $)	20.65	41.89	36.64	36.78	41.01		IFSY'95
Total currency reserves minus gold (in billions of pounds)	8.73	23.68	20.75	24.49	26.78		
Gov. foreign debt/ currency reserves (%)	116.2	120.1	168.1			44.7('92)	
Exports	47.36	104.88	108.51	120.94	133.03		IFSY'95
Gov. foreign debt/ exports (%)	21.4	27.1	32.2			50.5('92)	

						GSFY'90,'94
Gov. expenditures	88.48	229.15	257.89			
Gov. foreign debt/ gov. expenditures (%)	11.5	12.4	13.5		17.4('92)	
Gov. net foreign borrowing/ expenditures (%)	1.6	18.3	14.2		787.5('92)	
Domestic investment (gr. fixed cap. form. + increases in stocks)	38.94	92.63	91.97	95.24	103.67	IFSY'95
Direct foreign investment abroad (in millions of US $)	11.23	16.40	19.35	25.64	29.95	IFSY'95
Direct foreign investment abroad (in millions of pounds)	4.83	9.27	10.96	17.07	19.55	
Direct foreign investment abroad/ domestic investment (%)	12.4	10.0	11.9	17.9	18.9	44.4
Inflow foreign direct investment (in millions of US $)	10.12	16.06	16.49	14.56	10.94	IFSY'95
Inflow foreign direct investment (in millions of pounds)	4.35	9.08	9.34	9.69	7.14	
Inflow foreign direct investment/domestic investment (%)	11.2	9.8	10.2	10.2	6.9	−8.9

United Kingdom: Table 5.2A Government role in the economy and public finance (in billions of pounds sterling, unless otherwise indicated)

	1980	1991	1992	1993	1994	Rate of change 1980–92 (%)	Source
GDP (pounds) (1990 pounds)	231.7 (423.49)	575.32 (540.31)	597.24 (537.45)	630.71 (549.59)	668.87 (570.72)		IFSY'95
Gov. expenditures	88.48	229.15	257.89				GSFY'90,'94
Gov. expenditures/GDP (%)	38.2	39.8	43.2			13.1	
Tax revenue (budgetary central gov.)	58.04	159.87	161.21				GSFY'90,'94
Tax revenue/GDP (%)	25.0	27.8	27.0			8.0	
Gov. budget deficit	–10.73	–5.69	–30.0				IFSY'95
Gov. budget deficit/GDP (%)	4.6	1.0	5.0			8.7	
Gov. debt	106.75	189.65	203.51				IFSY'95
Gov. debt/GDP (%)	46.1	33.0	34.1			–26.0	
Gov. employment (employees in thousands)	5,349	5,129	4,915				OECDNA'92
Total employment	23,314	22,559	22,138				OECDNA'92

Gov. employment/ total employment (%)	22.9	22.7	22.2			-3.1	
Gov. consump.	49.98	124.11	131.88	137.97	144.08		IFSY'95
Private consump.	138.56	364.97	381.72	405.46	428.08		IFSY'95
Gov. consump./ private consump. (%)	36.1	34.0	34.5	34.0		-2.7	
Gov. capital expenditures		20.23	20.08	19.64			EWY'95
Gov. fixed capital formation		41.79	45.99	49.56			EWY'95
Gov. capital expenditures/gross fixed capital formation (%)	48.4	43.7	39.6				EWY'95

United States: Table 5.1A Internationalization of the economy and public finance (in billions of dollars, unless otherwise indicated)

	1980	1991	1992	1993	1994	Rate of change 1980–93 (%)	Source
GDP ($) (1990 $)	2,708.1 (4,275.6)	5,722.9 (5,458.3)	6,020.2 (5,673.5)	6,343.3 (5,813.2)	6,738.4 (6,050.4)		IFSY'95
Gov. foreign debt	129.7	491.7	549.7	622.6			IFSY'95
Gov. foreign debt/ GDP (%)	4.8	8.6	9.1	9.8		104.2	
Gov. net foreign borrowing	0.2	68.8	57.6	91.4			IFSY'95
Total currency reserves minus gold	15.60	66.66	60.27	62.35	63.28		IFSY'95
Gov. foreign debt/ currency reserves (%)	831.4	737.6	912.1	998.6		20.1	
Exports	225.57	421.73	448.16	464.77	512.52		IFSY'95
Gov. foreign debt/ exports (%)	57.5	116.6	122.7	134.0		133.0	
Gov. expenditures	596.6	1,429.1	1,445.1	1,492.4			IFSY'95
Gov. foreign debt/ gov. expenditures (%)	21.7	34.4	38.0	41.7		92.2	

Gov. net foreign borrowing/gov. expenditures (%)	0.03	4.8	4.0	6.12		203.0	IFSY'95
Domestic investment (gr. fixed cap. form. + increases in stocks)	541.62	875.60	939.15	1,052.99	1,246.60		
Direct foreign investment abroad	19.23	31.30	41.01	57.87	58.44		IFSY'95
Direct foreign investment abroad/domestic investment (%)	3.6	3.6	4.4	5.5	4.7	52.8	
Inflow foreign direct investment	16.93	26.09	9.89	21.37	60.07		IFSY'95
Inflow foreign direct investment/domestic investment (%)	3.1	3.0	1.1	2.0	4.8	-35.5	

United States: Table 5.2A Government role in the economy and public finance (in billions of dollars, unless otherwise indicated)

	1980	1991	1992	1993	1994	Rate of change 1980–92 (%)	Source
GDP	2,708.1	5,722.9	6,020.2	6,343.3	6,738.4		IFSY'95
Gov. expenditures	596.6	1,429.1	1,445.1	1,492.4			IFSY'95
Gov. expenditures/ GDP (%)	22.0	25.0	24.0	23.5		9.1	
Tax revenue (budgetary central gov.)	346.83	635.54	651.00	706.79			GFSY'88, '94
Tax revenue/ GDP (%)	12.8	11.1	10.8	11.1		−15.6	
Gov. budget deficit	−76.2	−272.5	−289.3	−254.1			IFSY'95
Gov. budget deficit/ GDP (%)	2.8	4.8	4.0			42.9	
Gov. debt	737.7	2,845.0	3,142.4	3,391.9			IFSY'95
Gov. debt/GDP (%)	27.2	49.7	52.2	53.5		91.9	
Gov. employment (employees in thousands)	14,890	16,893	16,799				OECDNA'92
Total employment	87,401	103,499	103,637				OECDNA'92

Gov. employment/ total employment (%)	17.0	16.3	16.2			−4.7	
Gov. consump. & investment	507.1	1,099.3	1,125.3	1,148.4	1,175.3		IFSY'95
Private consump.	1,748.1	3,906.4	4,136.9	4,378.2	4,628.4		IFSY'95
Gov. consump./ private consump. (%)	29.0	28.1	27.2	26.2	25.4	−6.9	
Gov. capital formation	72.7	139.6	150.6	155.1	160.8		IFSY'95
Gross fixed capital formation	549.8	876.5	938.9	1,037.1	1,193.7		IFSY'95
Gov. capital formation/gross fixed capital formation (%)	13.2	15.9	16.0	15.0	13.5	21.2	

Appendix for Figure 6.9: Level of Support for Mainstream Parties in National Elections, 1980–2002

The percentages in figure 6.9 have been calculated using the electoral returns for elections to the lower house of parliament, except in the cases of the United States and France, in which returns for presidential elections were used. Parties were considered to be mainstream if they had served in government or had been the main opposition party before the specific moment of the election. Once a party has accomplished these conditions, we consider it mainstream for the rest of the years. Parties' clear splits and coalitions were considered to have the same background as their original parties.

For sources, see the last row of the table for each country below. All data come from the following sources:

EWY   =   *Europa World Yearbook* (London: Europa Publications, 1982–2002)

SY   =   *Statesman's Yearbook* (ed. Brian Hunter, New York: St Martin's Press, 1994–1995, 1995–1996)

Elysee   =   www.elysee.fr (statistics in French from the Présidence de la République official website)

FRO   =   www.bundeswahlleiter.de (statistics in German from the Federal Returning Officer website)

Soumu   =   www.soumu.go.jp (statistics in Japanese from the Ministry of Public Management, Home Affairs, Posts and Telecommunications of Japan official website)

Congreso   =   www.congreso.es (statistics in Spanish from the Congreso de los Diputados official website).

All figures in tables are percentages.

France First round votes for presidential elections

	1981 (1st ballot)	1988 (1st ballot)	1995 (1st ballot)	2002 (1st ballot)
Mainstream parties				
Jacques Chirac (RPR)	18.0	20.0	20.8	19.9
Other RPR			18.6	
Liberal Democracy (DL)				3.9
UDF	28.3	16.5		6.8
François Mitterrand (PS)	25.8	34.1		
Lionel Jospin (PS)			23.3	16.2
MRG	2.2			
Communists (PCF)	15.3	6.8	8.6	3.4
Greens				5.3
Other parties				
Workers Struggle (LO)	2.3	2.0	5.3	5.7
LCR				4.3
Other extreme left	1.1	2.5		8.1
Jean-Marie Le Pen (FN)		14.4	15.0	16.9
Other extreme right	3.0		5.0	3.5
Greens		3.8	3.3	
Other ecologists	3.9			1.9
Others				4.2
Total vote for mainstream parties	**89.6**	**77.4**	**71.3**	**55.5**
Source	Elysee	Elysee	Elysee	Elysee

Germany Votes for Bundestag

	1983	1987	1990	1994	1998	2002
Mainstream parties						
CDU/CSU	48.8	44.2	43.8	41.5	35.2	38.5
Social Democratic Party (SPD)	38.2	37.0	33.5	36.4	40.9	38.5
Free Democrats (FDP)	7.0	9.1	11.0	6.9	6.3	7.4
Greens (+ Alliance '90 in 1990, 1994, 1998, 2002)						8.6
Other parties						
Communists (DKP)	0.2					
Party of Dem. Soc. (PDS) (former Com. Party of GDR)			2.4	4.4	5.1	4.0
Republican Party			1.2	1.9	1.8	0.6
Nat. Dem. Party (NDP)	0.2	0.6				
Greens (+ Alliance '90 in 1990, 1994, 1998, 2002)	5.6	8.3	5.0	7.3	6.7	
Ecological Dem. Party (ODP)		0.3				
Women's Party		0.2				
Others		0.3	2.1	1.7	4.0	2.4
Total vote for mainstream parties	**94.0**	**90.3**	**88.3**	**84.8**	**82.4**	**93.0**
Source	EWY-84	EWY-88	EWY-92	EWY-95	EWY-99	FRO

Italy Votes for Chamber of Deputies

	1983	1987	1992	1994	1996[a]	2001[a]
Mainstream parties						
Republicans (PRI)	5.1	3.7	4.4			
Liberals (PLI)	2.9	2.1	2.8			
Christian Democrats (DC)	32.9	34.3	29.7			
Italian People's Party (PPI)				11.1	6.8	
Christian Democratic Center, United Christian Democrats					5.8	3.2
Social Democrats (PSDI)	4.1	3.0	2.7			
Socialists (PSI)	11.4	14.3	13.6	2.2		
Communist Party (PCI)	29.9	26.6				1.7
Dem. Party of the Left (PDS) (formerly communists)			16.1	20.4	21.1	16.6
Refounded communists (formerly communists)			5.6	6.0	8.6	5.0
Forza Italia!					20.6	29.4
Northern League					10.1	3.9
Alleanza Nationalle					15.7	12.0
Girasole (Verdi + Italian Democratic Socialists)						2.2
Margherita (PPI + RI + Union of Demo. for Europe)						14.5
Other parties						
Forza Italia!				21.0		
Alleanza Nationalle				13.5		
Rinnovamento Italiano (RI)					4.3	
Italian Social Movement (MSI)	6.8	5.9	5.4			
Proletarian Dem.	1.5	1.7				
Radicals (PR)	2.2	2.6				
Regional parties						
Northern League			8.7	8.4		
Sudtiroler Volkspartei	0.5					
La Rete			1.9	1.9		

Italy contd

	1983	1987	1992	1994	1996[a]	2001[a]
Patto Segni				4.6		
Alleanza Democratica				1.2		
New Italian Socialist Party						0.9
Lista di Pietro						3.9
European Democracy						2.4
Lista Bonino						2.3
Social Movement of the Tricolour Flame						0.4
Greens		2.5	2.8	2.7	2.5	
Others	2.7	3.3	6.3	7.0	4.5	1.6
Total vote for mainstream parties	**86.3**	**84.0**	**74.9**	**39.7**	**88.7**	**88.5**
Source		EWY-84	EWY-88	SY-94–5	EWY-95	EWY-97 EWY-02

[a] Figures refer to seats elected by proportional representation.

Japan Votes for House of Representatives

	1983	1986	1990	1993	1996[a]	2000[a]
Mainstream parties						
Liberal Dem. (LDP)	45.8	49.4	46.1	36.6	32.8	28.3
New Lib. Club (NLC)	2.4	1.8				
(rejoins LDP in '86)						
Sakigake				2.1	1.1	
Socialists (JSP)	19.5	17.2	24.4	15.4	6.4	9.4
(becomes Soc. Dem.						
Party of Japan in 1991)						
New Frontier Party					28.0	
(Komeito + JNP + JRP						
+ DSP + SDL, integrates						
into DPJ after 1998)						
Democratic Party					16.0	25.2
of Japan (DPJ)						
New Komeito						13.0
Liberal Party						11.0
Other parties						
Dem. Soc. Party (DSP)	7.3	6.5	4.8	3.5		
Progressive Party			0.4			
Komeito	10.1	9.4	8.0	8.1		
(New Komeito						
after 1998)						
Japan New Party (JNP)				8.1		
Soc. Dem. Fed. (SDF)	0.7	0.8	0.9	0./		
(+ Un. Soc.						
Dem. P. in '93)						
Communists (JCP)	9.3	8.8	8.0	7.7	13.1	11.2
Japan Renewal Party				10.1		
Independent	4.9	5.8	7.3	6.9		
Others	0.1	0.2	0.1	0.2	2.6	1.9
Total vote for	**67.7**	**68.4**	**70.5**	**54.1**	**84.3**	**86.9**
mainstream parties						
Source	EWY-86	EWY-88	EWY-90	EWY-95	Soumu	Soumu

[a] Figures refer to seats elected by proportional representation.

Spain Votes for Congress of Deputies

	1982	1986	1989	1993	1996	2000
Mainstream Spain-wide parties						
ADP + PDP (+ PL in '88 = CP)	26.5	26.1				
Popular Party (AP → PP in 1989)			26.5	35.0	39.2	45.2
Union de Centro Dem. (UCD)	6.5					
Social and Democratic Center (CDS)	2.9	9.2	8.0			
Spanish Workers' Socialist Party (PSOE)	48.3	44.3	40.0	39.1	38.0	34.7
Mainstream regionalist and nationalist parties						
Basque Nationalist Party (PNV)	1.9	1.5	1.2	1.3	1.3	1.6
Convergence and Union (CiU)	3.7	5.0	5.0	5.0	4.6	4.3
Other parties						
Span. Communist Party (PCE)	3.3					
United Left (IU)		3.8	8.0	8.1	9.5	5.5
Other regionalist and nationalist parties	2.9	3.6	5.4	5.3	5.3	5.5
Others	4.1	6.3	6.1	6.0	2.2	3.2
Total vote for mainstream Spain-wide parties	**84.2**	**79.6**	**74.5**	**74.1**	**77.2**	**79.9**
Source	Congreso	Congreso	Congreso	Congreso	Congreso	Congreso

United Kingdom Votes for House of Commons

	1983	1987	1992	1997	2001
Mainstream UK-wide parties					
Conservatives	42.4	42.3	41.9	30.7	31.7
Liberals (+ Soc. Dem.)	25.4	22.6	17.9	16.8	18.3
Labour Party	27.6	30.9	34.4	43.2	40.7
Mainstream regionalist and nationalist parties					
Scottish National Party	1.1	1.3	1.9	2.0	1.8
Ulster Popular Unionist Party	0.1				
Ulster Unionist Party	0.8			0.8	0.8
Dem. Unionist Party	0.5			0.3	0.7
(All 3)		1.2	1.2		
Plaid Cymru (Welsh Nationalist Party)	0.4	0.4	0.5	0.5	0.7
Other parties					
Soc. and Dem. Lab. Party	0.4	0.5	0.5	0.6	0.6
Sinn Fein	0.3	0.3		0.4	0.7
Others	1.0	0.5	1.8	4.7	4.0
Total vote for mainstream UK-wide parties	**95.4**	**95.8**	**94.2**	**90.7**	**90.7**
Source	EWY-86	EWY-90	EWY-95	EWY-98	EWY-02

United States Popular vote for President

	1980	1984	1988	1992	1996	2000
Mainstream parties						
Democrats	41.0	40.5	45.6	42.9	49.2	48.4
Republicans	50.8	58.8	53.4	37.5	40.7	47.9
Others						
John Anderson	6.6					
Ross Perot				18.9	8.4	
Ralph Nader						2.7
Others	1.6	0.7	1.0	0.8	1.7	1.0
Total vote for mainstream parties	**91.8**	**99.3**	**99.0**	**80.4**	**89.9**	**96.3**
Source	EWY-81	EWY-88	EWY-90	EWY-94	EWY-97	EWY-02

Summary of Contents of Volumes I and III

Throughout this second volume of *The Information Age: Economy, Society, and Culture*, reference has been made to the themes presented in volumes I and III of this work. An outline of their contents is given below:

Volume I: *The Rise of the Network Society*

Prologue: The Net and the Self
1 The Information Technology Revolution
2 The New Economy: Informationalism, Globalization, Networking
3 The Network Enterprise: The Culture, Institutions, and Organizations of the Informational Economy
4 The Transformation of Work and Employment: Networkers, Jobless, and Flex-timers
5 The Culture of Real Virtuality: The Integration of Electronic Communication, the End of the Mass Audience, and the Rise of Interactive Networks
6 The Space of Flows
7 The Edge of Forever: Timeless Time
Conclusion: The Network Society

Volume III: *End of Millennium*

References

Abdel Majed, Nash'at Hamid (2001) "Al-Afghan Al-Arab, Muhawalah lil-Ta'rif" (www.islamonline.net/arabic/famous/2001/1o/article2-b.shtml).

Abelove, Henry, Barale, Michele Aina, and Halperin, David M. (eds) (1993) *The Lesbian and Gay Studies Reader*. New York: Routledge.

Abramson, Jeffrey B., Artertone, F. Christopher, and Orren, Cary R. (1988) *The Electronic Commonwealth: The Impact of New Media Technologies in Democratic Politics*. New York: Basic Books.

Adler, Margot (1979) *Drawing Down the Moon: Witches, Druids, Goddess-worshippers, and Other Pagans in America Today*. Boston: Beacon.

Adsera, Alicia, Boix, Carles, and Payne, Mark (2001) "Are you being served? Political accountability and quality of government," revised, unpublished version of a paper presented at the Performance of Democracies Workshop, Harvard University, Department of Government, Cambridge, MA, October 25, 2000.

Aglietta, Michel (2002) *La monnaie entre violence et confiance*. Paris: O. Jacob.

Aguirre, Pedro et al. (1995) *Una reforma electoral para la democracia. Argumentos para el consenso*. Mexico: Instituto de Estudios para la transicion democratica.

Akhmatova, Anna (1985) *Selected Poems*, trans. D. M. Thomas. London: Penguin.

Al-Azmeh, Aziz (1993) *Islams and Modernities*. London: Verso.

Alberdi, Ines (ed.) (1995) *Informe sobre la situacion de la familia en Espana*. Madrid: Ministerio de Asuntos Sociales.

Albo, Xavier (1993) *Y de Kataristas a MNRistas? La soprendente y audaz alianza entre Aymaras y neoliberales en Bolivia*. La Paz: CEDOIN-UNITAS.

Alexander, Herbert E. (1992) *Financing Politics: Money, Elections, and Political Reform*. Washington, DC: CQ Press.

Al-Hayat (2001) Sunday October 21, issue no. 14098.

Allen, Thomas B. (1987) *Guardian of the Wild: The Story of the National Wildlife Federation, 1936–1986*. Bloomington, IN: Indiana University Press.

Alley, Kelly D. et al. (1995) "The historical transformation of a grassroots environmental group," *Human Organization*, 54 (4): 410–16.

Alonso Zaldivar, Carlos (1996) *Variaciones sobre un mundo en cambio*. Madrid: Alianza Editorial.

——and Castells, Manuel (1992) *Espana fin de siglo*. Madrid: Alianza Editorial.

Al-Sayyad, Nezar and Castells, Manuel (eds) (2002) *Muslim Europe or Euro-Islam? Politics, Culture, and Citizenship in the Age of Globalization*. New York: Lexington Books.

Al-Zhawahiri, Muhammad Rabi (1999) *Al-Hasad al-Murr: al-Ikhwan al-Muslimun fi sittin aman*. Amman, Jordan: Dar al-Bayariq.

Ammerman, Nancy (1987) *Bible Believers: Fundamentalists in the Modern World*. New Brunswick, NJ: Rutgers University Press.

Anderson, Benedict (1983) *Imagined Communities: Reflections on the Origin and Spread of Nationalism*. London: Verso (2nd edn, 1991).

Anderson, P. and Comiller, P. (eds) (1994) *Mapping the West European Left*. London: Verso.

Anheier, Helmut, Glasius, Marlies, and Kaldor, Mary (eds) (2001) *Global Civil Society 2001*. Oxford: Oxford University Press.

Ansolabehere, Stephen and Iyengar, Shanto (1994) "Riding the wave and claiming ownership over issues: the joint effects of advertising and news coverage in campaigns," *Public Opinion Quarterly*, 58: 335–57.

——et al. (1993) *The Media Game: American Politics in the Television Age*. New York: Macmillan.

Anthes, Gary H. (1993) "Government ties to Internet expand citizens' access to data," *Computerworld*, 27 (34): 77.

Anti-Defamation League (1994) *Armed and Dangerous*. New York: Anti-Defamation League of B'nai B'rith.

——(1995) *Special Report: Paranoia as Patriotism: Far-right Influence on the Militia Movement*. New York: Anti-Defamation League of B'nai B'rith.

Aoyama, Yoshinobu (1991) *Riso Shakai: kyosanto sengen kara shinri'e* [*The Ideal Society: From Communist Manifesto to Truth*]. Tokyo: AUM Press.

Appiah, Kwame Anthony and Gates, Henry Louis, Jr (eds) (1995) *Identities*. Chicago: University of Chicago Press.

Archondo, Rafael (1991) *Compadres al microfono: la resurreccion metropolitana del ayllu*. La Paz: Hisbol.

Ardaya, Gloria and Verdesoto, Luis (1994) *Racionalidades democraticas en construccion*. La Paz: ILDIS.

Arlachi, Pino (1995) "The Mafia, Cosa Nostra, and Italian institutions," in Sechi (ed.), pp. 153–63.

Armond, Paul (1995) "Militia of Montana meeting at the Maltby Community Center," *World Wide Web*, MOM site, February 11.

Armstrong, David (1995) "Cyberhoax!," *Columbia Journalism Review*, September/October.

Arquilla, John and Rondfeldt, David (1993) "Cyberwar is coming!," *Comparative Strategy*, 12 (2): 141–65.

—— and —— (2001) *Networks and Netwars*. Santa Monica, CA: Rand Corporation.

Arrieta, Carlos G., et al. (1991) *Narcotrafico en Colombia: Dimensiones politicas, economicas, juridicas e internacionales*. Bogota: Tercer Mundo Editores.

Asahara, Shoko (1994) *Metsubo no Hi* [*The Doomsday*]. Tokyo: AUM Press.

—— (1995) *Hi Izuru Kuni Wazawai Chikashi* [*Disasters Come Close to the Nation as the Rising Sun*]. Tokyo: AUM Press.

Astrachan, Anthony (1986) *How Men Feel: Their Response to Women's Demands for Equality and Power*. Garden City, NY: Anchor Press/Doubleday.

Athanasiou, Tom (1996) *Divided Planet: The Ecology of Rich and Poor*. Boston: Little, Brown.

Aust, Stefan and Schnibben, Cordt (eds) (2002) *11 de Septiembre: Historia de un ataque terrorista* (Spanish trans. of original 2002 German edn).

Awakening (1995) Special issue, no. 158–161, Taipei (Chinese language).

Axford, Barrie, et al. (1992) "Image management, stunts, and dirty tricks: the marketing of political brands in television campaigns," *Media, Culture, and Society*, 14 (4): 637–51.

Azevedo, Milton (ed.) (1991) *Contemporary Catalonia in Spain and Europe*. Berkeley, CA: University of California, Gaspar de Portola Catalonian Studies Program.

Bachr, Peter R. and Gordenker, Leon (1994) *The UN in the 1990s.* New York: St Martin's Press.

Badie, Bertrand (1992) *L'état importe: essai sur l'occidentalisation de l'ordre politique.* Paris: Fayard.

Bakhash, Shaul (1990) "The Islamic Republic of Iran, 1979–1989," *Middle East Focus,* 12 (3): 8–12, 27.

Baldassare, Mark (2000) *California in the New Millennium: The Changing Social and Political Landscape.* Berkeley, CA: University of California Press.

Balta, Paul (ed.) (1991) *Islam: Civilisations et sociétés.* Paris: Editions du Rocher.

Balz, Dan and Brownstein, Ronald (1996) *Storming the Gates: Protest Politics and the Republican Revival.* Boston: Little, Brown.

Barber, Benjamin R. (1993) "Letter from America, September 1993: the rise of Clinton, the fall of democrats, the scandal of the media," *Government and Opposition,* 28 (4): 433–43.

——(1995) *Jihad vs. McWorld.* New York: Basic Books.

Barker, Anthony (1992) *The Upturned Stone: Political Scandals in Twenty Democracies and their Investigation Process.* Colchester: University of Essex, Essex Papers in Politics and Government.

Barnett, Bernice McNair (1995) "Black women's collectivist movement organizations: their struggles during the 'doldrums'," in Ferree and Martin (eds), pp. 199–222.

Barone, Michael and Ujifusa, Grant (1995) *The Almanac of American Politics 1996.* Washington, DC: National Journal.

Barron, Bruce and Shupe, Anson (1992) "Reasons for growing popularity of Christian reconstructionism: the determination to attain dominion," in Misztal and Shupe (eds), pp. 83–96.

Bartholet, E. (1990) *Family Bonds, Adoption and the Politics of Parenting.* New York: Houghton Mifflin.

Bartz, Steve (1996) "Environmental organizations and evolving information technologies," Berkeley, CA: University of California, Department of Sociology, unpublished seminar paper for SOC 290.2, May.

Baylis, John and Rengger, N. J. (eds) (1992) *Dilemmas of World Politics: International Issues in a Changing World.* Oxford: Clarendon Press.

Beccalli, Bianca (1994) "The modern women's movement in Italy," *New Left Review,* 204, March/April: 86–112.

Beck, Ulrich (2003) "Las instituciones de gobernanza mundial en la sociedad global de riesgo," in Castells and Serra (eds), pp. 53–66.

Bellah, Robert N., Sullivan, William M., Swidler, Ann, and Tipton, Steven M. (1985) *Habits of the Heart: Individualism and*

Commitment in American Life. Berkeley, CA: University of California Press (cited in the Perennial Library edition from Harper and Row, New York, 1986).

Bellers, Jurgen (ed.) (1989) *Politische Korruption.* Munster: Lit.

Bennett, David H. (1995) *The Party of Fear: The American Far Right from Nativism to the Militia Movement.* New York: Vintage Books.

Bennett, William J. (1994) *The Index of Leading Cultural Indicators: Facts and Figures on the State of American Society.* New York: Touchstone.

Berdal, Mats R. (1993) *Whither UN Peacekeeping?: An Analysis of the Changing Military Requirements of UN Peacekeeping with Proposals for its Enhancement.* London: Brassey's for International Institute of Strategic Studies.

Bergen, Peter L. (2001) *Holy War, Inc.: Inside the Secret World of Osama bin Laden.* New York: The Free Press.

Berins Collier, Ruth (1992) *The Contradictory Alliance: State–Labor Relationships and Regime Changes in Mexico.* Berkeley, CA: University of California, International and Area Studies.

Berlet, Chips and Lyons, Matthew N. (1995) "Militia nation," *The Progressive,* June.

Berman, Jerry and Weitzner, Daniel J. (1995) "Abundance and user control: renewing the democratic heart of the First Amendment in the age of interactive media," *Yale Law Journal,* 104 (7): 1619–37.

Bernard, Jessie (1987) *The Female World from a Global Perspective.* Bloomington, IN: Indiana University Press.

Berry, Sebastian (1992) "Party strategy and the media: the failure of Labour's 1991 election campaign," *Parliamentary Affairs,* 45 (4): 565–81.

Betts, Mitch (1995) "The politicizing of cyberspace," *Computerworld,* 29 (3): 20.

Bilbao La Vieja Diaz, Antonio, Perez de Rada, Ernesto and Asturizaga, Ramiro (1996) "CONDEPA movimiento patriotico," La Paz: Naciones Unidas/CIDES, unpublished research monograph.

Birnbaum, Lucia Chiavola (1986) *Liberazione della donna: Feminism in Italy.* Middletown, CT: Wesleyan University Press.

Black, Gordon S. and Black, Benjamin D. (1994) *The Politics of American Discontent: How a New Party Can Make Democracy Work Again.* New York: John Wiley and Sons.

Blakely, Edward and Goldsmith, William (1993) *Separate Societies: Poverty and Inequality in American Cities.* Philadelphia: Temple University Press.

Blas Guerrero, Andres (1994) *Nacionalismos y naciones en Europa*. Madrid: Alianza Editorial.

Blossfeld, Hans-Peter (ed.) (1995) *The New Role of Women: Family Formation in Modern Societies*. Boulder, CO: Westview Press.

Blum, Linda (1991) *Between Feminism and Labor: The Politics of the Comparable Worth Movement*. Berkeley, CA: University of California Press.

Blumberg, Rae Lesser, Rakowski, Cathy A., Tinker, Irene, and Monteon, Michael (eds) (1995) *EnGENDERing Wealth and Wellbeing*. Boulder, CO: Westview Press.

Blumenfield, Seth D. (1994) "Developing the global information infrastructure," *Federal Communications Law Journal*, 47 (2): 193–6.

Blumstein, Philip and Schwartz, Pepper (1983) *American Couples: Money, Work, Sex*. New York: William Morrow.

Boardmann, Robert (1994) *Post-socialist World Orders: Russia, China, and the UN System*. New York: St Martin's Press.

Bobbio, Norberto (1994) *Destra e sinistra: ragioni e significati di una distinzione politica*. Roma: Donzelli Editore.

Bonnell, Victoria and Breslauer, George (eds) (2001) *Russia at the End of the Twentieth Century*. Boulder, CO: Westview Press.

Borja, Jordi (1988) *Estado y ciudad*. Barcelona: Promociones y Publicaciones Universitarias.

——and Castells, Manuel (1997) *Local and Global: The Management of Cities in the Information Age*. London: Earthscan.

——, et al. (1992) *Estrategias de desarrollo e internacionalizacion de las ciudades europeas: las redes de ciudades*. Barcelona: Consultores Europeos Asociados, Research Report.

Bouissou, Jean-Marie (1991) "Corruption à la Japonaise," *L'Histoire*, 142, March: 84–7.

Bramwell, Anna (1989) *Ecology in the 20th Century: A History*. New Haven, CT: Yale University Press.

——(1994) *The Fading of the Greens: The Decline of Environmental Politics in the West*. New Haven, CT: Yale University Press.

Brenner, Daniel (1994) "In search of the multimedia grail," *Federal Communications Law Journal*, 47 (2): 197–203.

Brisard, Jean-Charles and Dasquie, Guillaume (2002) *Forbidden Truth: US–Taliban Secret Oil Diplomacy and the Failed Hunt for Bin Laden*. New York: Thunderer's Mouth Press / Nation Books.

Broadcasting and Cable (1995) "Top of the week," May.

Brown, Helen (1992) *Women Organising*. London: Routledge.

Brown, Michael (1993) "Earth worship or black magic?," *The Amicus Journal*, 14 (4): 32–4.

Brubaker, Timothy H. (ed.) (1993) *Family Relations: Challenges for the Future*. Newbury Park, CA: Sage.

Bruce, Judith, Lloyd, Cynthia B., and Leonard, Ann (1995) *Families in Focus: New Perspectives of Mothers, Fathers, and Children*. New York: Population Council.

Brulle, Robert J. (1996) "Environmental discourse and social movement organizations: a historical and rhetorical perspective on the development of US environmental organizations," *Sociological Inquiry*, 66 (1): 58–83.

Buci-Glucksman, Christine (1978) *Gramsci et l'état*. Paris: Grasset.

Buckler, Steve (1993) *Dirty Hands: The Problem of Political Morality*. Brookfield: Averbury.

Buckley, Peter (ed.) (1994) *Cooperative Forms of Transnational Corporation Activity*. London: Routledge.

Buechler, Steven M. (1990) *Women's Movement in the United States*. Brunswick, NJ: Rutgers University Press.

Bull, Hedley (1977) *The Anarchical Society*. London: Macmillan.

Bureau, Dominique, et al. (2002) "Gouvernance mondiale et environnement," in Jacquet et al. (eds), pp. 449–62.

Burgat, Francois and Dowell, William (1993) *The Islamic Movement in North Africa*. Austin, Tex.: University of Texas Center for Middle Eastern Studies.

Burnham, David (1983) *The Rise of the Computer State*. New York: Vintage.

Business Week (1995a) "The future of money," June 12.

—— (1995b) "Hot money," March 20.

—— (1995c) "Mexico: Salinas is fast becoming a dirty word," December 25: 54–5.

—— (1995d) "The new populism," March.

—— (1995e) "Power to the states," August: 49–56.

Buss, David M. (1994) *The Evolution of Desire: Strategies of Human Mating*. New York: Basic Books.

Butler, Judith (1990) *Gender Trouble: Feminism and the Subversion of Identity*. New York: Routledge.

Cabre, Anna (1990) "Es compatible la proteccion de la familia con la liberacion de la mujer?," in Instituto de la Mujer (ed.), *Mujer y Demografia*. Madrid: Ministerio de Asuntos Sociales.

—— and Domingo, Antonio (1992) "La Europa despues de Maastrich: reflexiones desde la demografia," *Revista de Economia*, 13: 63–9.

Cacho, Jesus (1994) *MC: un intruso en el laberinto de los elegidos*. Madrid: Temas de hoy.

Caipora Women's Group (1993) *Women in Brazil*. London: Latin American Bureau.

Calabrese, Andrew and Borchert, Mark (1996) "Prospects for electronic democracy in the United States: rethinking communication and social policy," *Media, Culture, and Society*, 18: 249–68.

Calderon, Fernando (1995) *Movimientos sociales y politica*. Mexico: Siglo XXI.

——(ed.) (2003) *Es sostenible la globalización en America Latina?* Mexico: Fondo de Cultura Economica.

——and Laserna, Roberto (1994) *Paradojas de la modernidad*. La Paz: Fundacion Milenio.

——, et al. (1996) *Esa esquiva modernidad: desarrollo, ciudadania y cultura en America Latina y el Caribe*. Caracas: Nueva Sociedad/ UNESCO.

Calhoun, Craig (ed.) (1994) *Social Theory and the Politics of Identity*. Oxford: Blackwell.

Camilleri, J. A. and Falk, K. (1992) *The End of Sovereignty*. Aldershot: Edward Elgar.

Caminal, Miquel (2002) *El federalismo pluralista: del federalismo nacional al federalismo plurinacional*. Barcelona: Paidos.

Campbell, B. (1992) "Feminist politics after Thatcher," in H. Hinds et al. (eds), *Working Out: New Directions for Women's Studies*, pp. 13–17. London: Taylor and Francis.

Campbell, Colin and Rockman, Bert A. (eds) (1995) *The Clinton Presidency: First Appraisals*. Chatham, NJ: Chatham House.

Campo Vidal, Manuel (1996) *La transicion audiovisual*. Barcelona: B Ediciones.

Cardoso de Leite, Ruth (1983) "Movimientos sociais urbanos: balanco critico," in *Sociedade e politica no Brasil pos-64*. São Paulo: Brasiliense.

——(2002) Intervention in the seminar on "America Latina en la Era de la Informacion," organized in Santa Cruz, Bolivia, March (notes taken in seminar by author).

Carnoy, Martin (1984) *The State and Political Theory*. Princeton, NJ: Princeton University Press.

——(1993) "Multinationals in a changing world economy: whither the nation-state?," in Carnoy et al., pp. 45–96.

——(1994) *Faded Dreams: The Politics and Economics of Race in America*. New York: Cambridge University Press.

——(2000) *Sustaining the New Economy: Work, Family and Community in the Information Age*. Cambridge, MA: Harvard University Press.

—— and Castells, Manuel (2001) "Globalization, the knowledge society, and the network state: Poulantzas at the millenium," *Global Networks*, 1 (1): 1–8.

——, Castells, Manuel, Cohen, Stephen S., and Cardoso, Fernando H. (1993) *The New Global Economy in the Information Age*. University Park, PA: Penn State University Press.

Carre, Olivier (1984) *Mystique et politique: Lecture révolutionnaire du Coran par Sayyed Qtub*. Paris: Editions du Cerf-Presses de la Fondation Nationale des Sciences Politiques.

Carrere d'Encausse, Helene (1987) *Le grand défi: Bolcheviks et nations, 1917–1930*. Paris: Flammarion.

—— (1993) *The End of the Soviet Empire: The Triumph of Nations*. New York: Basic Books (original French edn 1991).

Castells, Manuel (1981) "Local government, urban crisis, and political change," in *Political Power and Social Theory: A Research Annual*, vol. 2, pp. 1–20. Greenwich, CT: JAI Press.

—— (1983) *The City and the Grassroots: A Cross-cultural Theory of Urban Social Movements*. Berkeley, CA: University of California Press.

—— (1992a) "Four Asian tigers with a dragon head: a comparative analysis of the state, economy, and society in the Asian Pacific rim," in Richard Appelbaum and Jeffrey Henderson (eds), *States and Development in the Asian Pacific Rim*, pp. 33–70. Newbury Park, CA: Sage.

—— (1992b) *La nueva revolucion rusa*. Madrid: Sistema.

—— (1992c) "Las redes sociales del SIDA," keynote address delivered at the Social Sciences Symposium, World Congress on AIDS research, Madrid, May 1992.

—— (1996) "El futuro del estado del bienestar en la sociedad informacional," *Sistema*, 131, March: 35–53.

—— (2001) *The Internet Galaxy*. Oxford: Oxford University Press.

—— (2004) *Comparative Studies on the Network Society*. London: Edward Elgar.

—— and Himanen, Pekka (2002) *The Information Society and the Welfare Sate: The Finnish Model*. Oxford: Oxford University Press.

—— and Kiselyova, Emma (2000) "Russian federalism and Siberian regionalism, 1990–2000," *City*, 4 (2): 175–98.

—— and Murphy, Karen (1982) "Cultural identity and urban structure: the spatial organization of San Francisco's gay community," in Norman I. Fainstein and Susan S. Fainstein (eds), *Urban Policy under Capitalism*, Urban Affairs Annual Reviews, vol. 22, pp. 237–60. Beverly Hills, CA: Sage.

—— and Serra, Narcis (eds) (2003) *Guerra y paz en el siglo XXI: una perspectiva europea*. Barcelona: Tusquets.

——, Yazawa, Shujiro, and Kiselyova, Emma (1996) "Insurgents against the global order: a comparative analysis of the Zapatistas in Mexico, the American Militia and Japan's Aum Shinrikyo," *Berkeley Journal of Sociology*, 40: 21–60.

——, et al. (2002) "La societat xarxa a Catalunya," research monograph of the Internet Interdisciplinary Unit, Universitat Oberta de Catalunya, published on line (www.uoc.edu).

Castells, Nuria (1999) "International environmental agreements: institutional innovation in European transboundary air pollution policies," unpublished doctoral dissertation, Economics Department, Free University of Amsterdam, Amsterdam.

Chatterjee, Anshu (2002) "Global media and cultural identity: the globalization and identification of Indian television, 1985–2002," unpublished PhD thesis in Asian Studies, University of California, Berkeley, CA.

Chatterjee, Partha (1993) *The Nation and its Fragments: Colonial and Postcolonial Histories*. Princeton, NJ: Princeton University Press.

Chesnais, François (1994) *La mondialisation du capital*. Paris: Syros.

Cheung, Peter T. Y. (1994) "Relations between the central government and Guandong," in Y. M. Yeung and David K. Y. Chu (eds), *Guandong: Survey of a Province Undergoing Rapid Change*, pp. 19–51. Hong Kong: The Chinese University Press.

Chiriboga, Manuel (2003) "Sociedad civil global: movimientos indigenas y el Internet," in Calderon (ed.).

Cho, Lee-Jay and Yada, Moto (eds) (1994) *Tradition and Change in the Asian Family*. Honolulu: University of Hawaii Press.

Chodorow, Nancy (1978) *The Reproduction of Mothering: Psychoanalysis and the Sociology of Gender*. Berkeley, CA: University of California Press.

—— (1989) *Feminism and Psychoanalytical Theory*. New Haven, CT: Yale University Press.

—— (1994) *Femininities, Masculinities, Sexualities: Freud and Beyond*. Lexington, KY: University Press of Kentucky.

Chong, Rachelle (1994) "Trends in communication and other musings on our future," *Federal Communications Law Journal*, 47 (2): 213–19.

Choueri, Youssef M. (1993) *Il fondamentalismo islamico: Origine storiche e basi sociali*. Bologna: Il Mulino.

Coalition for Human Dignity (1995) *Against the New World Order: The American Militia Movement*. Portland, Oregon: Coalition for Human Dignity Publications.

Coates, Thomas J., et al. (1988) *Changes in Sex Behavior of Gay and Bisexual Men since the Beginning of the AIDS Epidemics*. San Francisco: University of California, Center for AIDS Prevention Studies.

Cobble, Dorothy S. (ed.) (1993) *Women and Unions: Forging a Partnership*. New York: International Labour Review Press.

Cockburn, Alexander (2000) *5 Days that Shook the World: Seattle and Beyond*. London: Verso.

Cohen, Jeffrey E. (1986) "The dynamics of the 'revolving door' on the FCC," *American Journal of Political Science*, 30 (4).

Cohen, Roger (1996) "Global forces batter politics," *The New York Times*, Sunday November 17, s. 4: 1–4.

Cohen, Stephen (1993) "Geo-economics: lessons from America's mistakes," in Carnoy et al., pp. 97–148.

Coleman, Marilyn and Ganong, Lawrence H. (1993) "Families and marital disruption," in Brubaker (ed.), pp. 112–28.

Coleman, William E., Jr and Coleman, William E., Sr (1993) *A Rhetoric of the People: The German Greens and the New Politics*. Westport, CT: Praeger.

Collective Author (1996) *La seguridad humana en Bolivia: percepciones politicas, sociales y economicas de los bolivianos de hoy*. La Paz: PRONAGOB-PNUD-ULDIS.

Collier, George A. (1995) *Restructuring Ethnicity in Chiapas and the World*. Stanford University, Department of Anthropology, Research Paper (published in Spanish in Nash et al. (eds), pp. 7–20).

—— and Lowery Quaratiello, Elizabeth (1994) *Basta! Land and the Zapatista Rebellion in Chiapas*. Oakland, CA: Food First Books.

Conquest, Robert (ed.) (1967) *Soviet Nationalities Policy in Practice*. New York: Praeger.

Contreras Basnipeiro, Adalid (1991) "Medios multiples, pocas voces: inventario de los medios de comunicacion de masas en Bolivia," *Revista UNITAS*, pp. 61–105.

Cook, Maria Elena, et al. (eds) (1994) *The Politics of Economic Restructuring: State–Society Relations and Regime Change in Mexico*. La Jolla: University of California at San Diego, Center of US–Mexican Studies.

Cooke, Philip (1994) *The Cooperative Advantage of Regions*. Cardiff: University of Wales, Centre for Advanced Studies.

Cooper, Jerry (1995) *The Militia and the National Guard in America since Colonial Times: A Research Guide*. Westport, CT: Greenwood Press.

Cooper, Marc (1995) "Montana's mother of all militias," *The Nation*, May 22.

Corn, David (1995) "Playing with fire," *The Nation*, May 15.

Costain, W. Douglas and Costain, Anne N. (1992) "The political strategies of social movements: a comparison of the women's and environmental movements," *Congress and the Presidency*, 19 (1): 1–27.

Cott, Nancy (1989) "What's in a name? The limits of 'social feminism'; or, expanding the vocabulary of women's history," *Journal of American History*, 76: 809–29.

Couch, Carl J. (1990) "Mass communications and state structures," *The Social Science Journal*, 27, (2): 111–28.

CQ Researcher (1992) Special Issue: "Politicians and privacy," 2 (15), April 17.

Croteau, David and Hoynes, William (2000) *Media/Society: Industries, Images, and Audiences*, 2nd edn. Thousand Oaks, CA: Pine Forge Press.

—— and —— (2001) *The Business of Media: Corporate Media and the Public Interest*. Thousand Oaks, CA: Pine Forge Press.

Dalton, Russell J. (1994) *The Green Rainbow: Environmental Groups in Western Europe*. New Haven, CT: Yale University Press.

—— and Kuechler, Manfred (1990) *Challenging the Political Order: New Social and Political Movements in Western Democracies*. Cambridge: Polity Press.

Danaher, Kevin and Burbach, Roger (2001) *Globalize This! The Battle against the World Trade Organization and Corporate Rule*. Philadelphia: Common Courage Press.

Daniel, Donald and Hayes, Bradd (eds) (1995) *Beyond Traditional Peacekeeping*. New York: St Martin's Press.

Davidson, Osha Grey (1993) *Under Fire: The NRA and the Battle for Gun Control*. New York: Henry Holt.

Davis, John (ed.) (1991) *The Earth First! Reader*. Salt Lake City: Peregrine Smith Books.

Dees, Morris and Corcoran, James (1996) *Gathering Storm: America's Militia Network*. New York: Harper-Collins.

Dekmejian, R. Hrair (1995) *Islam in Revolution: Fundamentalism in the Arab World*. Syracuse, NY: Syracuse University Press.

Delcroix, Catherine (1995) "Algériennes et Égyptiennes: enjeux et sujets de sociétés en crise," in Dubet and Wieviorka (eds), pp. 257–72.

DeLeon, Peter (1993) *Thinking about Political Corruption*. Armonk, NY: M.E. Sharpe.

Delphy, Christine (ed.) (1984) *Particularisme et universalisme*. Paris: Nouvelles Questions Feministes, n. 17/17/18.

D'Emilio, John (1980/1993) "Capitalism and gay identity," in Abelove et al. (eds), pp. 467–76.

—— (1983) *Sexual Politics, Sexual Communities: The Making of a Homosexual Minority in the United States, 1940–1970*. Chicago: University of Chicago Press.

DeMont, John (1991) "Frontline fighters," *Mclean's*, 104 (50): 46–7.

Dentsu Institute for Human Studies (1994) *Media in Japan*. Tokyo: DataFlow International.

Deutsch, Karl (1953) *Nationalism and Social Communication: An Inquiry into the Foundations of Nationality* (consulted in the 1966 edn, Cambridge, MA: MIT Press).

De Vos, Susan (1995) *Household Composition in Latin America*. New York: Plenum Press.

Diamond, Irene and Orenstein, Gloria (1990) *Reweaving the World: The Emergence of Ecofeminism*. San Francisco: Sierra Club Books.

Diani, Mario (1995) *Green Networks: A Structural Analysis of the Italian Environmental Movement*. Edinburgh: Edinburgh University Press.

Dickens, Peter (1990) "Science, social science and environmental issues: ecological movements as the recovery of human nature," paper prepared for the meeting of the British Association for the Advancement of Science, University of Swansea, August.

Dietz, Thomas and Kalof, Linda (1992) "Environmentalism among nation-states," *Social Indicators Research*, 26: 353–66.

Di Marco, Sabina (1993) "Se la televisione guarda a sinistra," *Ponte*, 49 (7): 869–78.

—— (1994) "La televisione, la politica e il cavaliere," *Ponte*, 50 (2): 9–11.

Dionne, E. J. (1996) *They Only Look Dead: Why Progressives Will Dominate the Next Political Era*. New York: Simon and Schuster.

Dobson, Andrew (1990) *Green Political Thought: An Introduction*. London: Unwin Hyman.

—— (ed.) (1991) *The Green Reader: Essays toward a Sustainable Society*. San Francisco: Mercury House.

Docter, Sharon, Dutton, William H., and Elberse, Anita (1999) "An American democracy network: factors shaping the future of on-line political campaigns," in Stephen Coleman et al. (eds), *Parliament in the Age of the Internet*, pp. 173–90. Oxford: Oxford University Press.

Doyle, Marc (1992) *The Future of Television: A Global Overview of Programming, Advertising, Technology and Growth*. Lincolnwood, IL: NTC Business Books.

Drew, Christopher (1995) "Japanese sect tried to buy US arms technology, Senator says," *The New York Times*, October 31: A5.

Dubet, François, and Wieviorka, Michel (eds) (1995) *Penser le sujet*. Paris: Fayard.

Duffy, Ann and Pupo, Norene (eds) (1992) *Part-time Paradox: Connecting Gender, Work and Family*. Toronto: The Canadian Publishers.

Dulong, Rene (1978) *Les regions, l'état et la société locale*. Paris: Presses Universitaires de France.

Dunaher, Kevin (ed.) (1994) *50 Years is Enough: The Case against the World Bank and the IMF*. Boston, MA: South End Press.

Dupin, Eric (2002) *Sortir la gauche de coma*. Paris: Flammarion.

Dutton, William H. (1999) *Society on the Line: Information Politics in the Digital Age*. New York: Oxford University Press.

Ebbinghausen, Rolf and Neckel, Sighard (eds) (1989) *Anatomie des politischen Skandals*. Frankfurt: Suhrkamp.

The Economist (1994) "Feeling for the future: special survey of television," February 12.

—— (1995a) "The future of democracy," June 17: 13–14.

—— (1995b) "The Mexican connection," December 26: 39–40.

—— (1995c) "Mexico: the long haul," August 26: 17–19.

—— (1996) "Satellite TV in Asia: a little local interference," February 3.

Edwards, George C. and Wood, B. Dan (1999) "Who influences whom? The President, Congress, and the media," *The American Political Science Review*, 93 (2): 327–44.

Ehrenreich, Barbara (1983) *The Hearts of Men: American Dreams and the Flight from Commitment*. Garden City, NY: Anchor Press/ Doubleday.

Eisenstein, Zillah R. (1981/1993) *The Radical Future of Liberal Feminism*. Boston, MA: Northeastern University Press.

Ejercito Zapatista de Liberacion Nacional (1994) *Documentos y comunicados*. Mexico: Ediciones Era (with preface by Antonio Garcia de Leon, and chronicles by Elena Poniatowska and Carlos Monsivais).

—— /Subcomandante Marcos (1995) *Chiapas: del dolor a la esperanza*. Madrid: Los libros de la catarata.

Eley, Geoff, and Suny, Ronald Grigor (eds) (1996) *Becoming National: A Reader*. New York: Oxford University Press.

Elliott, J.H. and de la Pena, J.F. (1978) *Memoriales y cartas del Conde-Duque de Olivares*. Madrid: Alfaguara.

Epstein, Barbara (1991) *Political Protest and Cultural Revolution: Nonviolent Direct Action in the 1970s and 1980s*. Berkeley, CA: University of California Press.

—— (1995) "Grassroots environmentalism and strategies for social change," *New Political Science*, 32: 1–24.

Ergas, Yasmine (1985) *Nelle maglie della politica: femminismo, instituzione e politiche sociale nell'Italia degli anni settanta*. Milan: Feltrinelli.

Espinosa, Maria and Useche, Helena (1992) *Abriendo camino: historias de mujeres*. Bogota: FUNDAC.

Esposito, John L. (1990) *The Iranian Revolution: Its Global Impact*. Miami: Florida International University Press.

Esprit (1994) "Editorial: face à la télécratie," 5: 3–4.

Etzioni, Amitai (1993) *The Spirit of Community: Rights, Responsibilities, and the Communitarian Agenda*. New York: Crown.

Evans, Sara (1979) *Personal Politics: The Roots of Women's Liberation in Civil Rights Movement and the New Left*. New York: Knopf.

Eyerman, Ron and Jamison, Andrew (1989) "Environmental knowledge as an organizational weapon: the case of Greenpeace," *Social Science Information*, 28 (1): 99–119.

Fackler, Tim and Lin, Tse-Min (1995) "Political corruption and presidential elections, 1929–1992," *The Journal of Politics*, 57 (4): 971–93.

Faison, Seth (1996) "Chinese cruise Internet, wary of watchdogs," *The New York Times*, February 5, p. A1.

Falk, Richard (1995) *On Humane Governance: Towards a New Global Politics*. University Park, PA: Pennsylvania State University Press.

Fallows, James (1996) *Breaking the News: How the Media Undermine American Democracy*. New York: Pantheon.

Faludi, Susan (1991) *Backlash: The Undeclared War on American Women*. New York: Crown.

Farnsworth Riche, Martha (1996) "How America is changing – the view from the Census Bureau, 1995," in *The World Almanac and Book of Facts*, 1996: 382–3.

Fassin, Didier (1996) "Exclusions, underclass, marginalidad: figures contemporaines de la pauvreté urbaine en France, aux États-Unis et en Amérique Latine," *Revue Française de Sociologie*, 37: 37–75.

Ferraresi, Franco and Kemeny, Pietro (1977) *Classi sociali e politica urbana*. Rome: Officina Edizioni.

Ferrater Mora, Josep (1960) *Les formes de la vida catalana*. Barcelona: Editorial Selecta.

Ferree, Myra Marx and Hess, Beth B. (1994) *Controversy and Coalition: The New Feminist Movement across Three Decades of Change*. New York: Maxwell Macmillan.

—— and Martin, Patricia Yancey (eds) (1995) *Feminist Organizations: Harvest of the Women's Movement*. Philadelphia: Temple University Press.

Ferrer i Girones, F. (1985) *La persecucio politica de la llengua catalana*. Barcelona: Edicions 62.

Financial Technology International Bulletin (1995) "A lawless frontier," 12 (12): 10.

Fischer, Claude S. (1982) *To Dwell among Friends: Personal Networks in Town and City*. Chicago: University of Chicago Press.

——, et al. (1995) *Inequality by Design*. Princeton, NJ: Princeton University Press.

Fisher, Robert and Kling, Joseph (eds) (1993) *Mobilizing the Community: Local Politics in the Era of the Global City*. Thousand Oaks, CA: Sage.

Fitzpatrick, Mary Anne and Vangelisti, Anita L. (eds) (1995) *Explaining Family Interactions*. Thousand Oaks, CA: Sage.

Fooner, Michael (1989) *Interpol: Issues in World Crime and International Criminal Justice*. New York: Plenum Press.

Foucault, Michel (1976) *La volonté de savoir: histoire de la sexualité*, vol. I. Paris: Gallimard.

—— (1984a) *L'usage des plaisirs: histoire de la sexualité*, vol. II. Paris: NRF.

—— (1984b) *Le souci de soi: histoire de la sexualité*, vol. III. Paris: NRF.

Frankel, J. (1988) *International Relations in a Changing World*. Oxford: Oxford University Press.

—— (2000) "Globalization of the economy,' in Nye and Donahue (eds), pp. 45–71.

Frankland, E. Gene (1995) "The rise, fall, and recovery of Die Grunen," in Richardson and Rootes (eds), pp. 23–44.

Franklin, Bob (1994) *Packaging Politics: Political Communications in Britain's Media Democracy*. London: Edward Arnold.

Franquet, Rosa and Larregola, Gemma (eds) (1999) *Comunicar a l'era digital*. Barcelona: Societat Catalana de Comunicacio.

Freeman, Michael (1994) "Polls set spending record," *Mediaweek*, 4 (44): 6.

Friedland, Lewis A. (1996) "Electronic democracy and the new citizenship," *Media, Culture, and Society*, 18: 185–211.

Friedrich, Carl J. (1966) "Political pathology," *Political Quarterly*, 37: 74.

Fujita, Shoichi (1995) *AUM Shinrikyo Jiken* [*The Incidents of AUM Shinrikyo*]. Tokyo: Asahi-Shinbunsha.

Funk, Nanette and Mueller, Magda (eds) (1993) *Gender Politics and Post-Communism: Reflections from Eastern Europe and the Former Soviet Union.* New York: Routledge.

Fuss, Diana (1989) *Essentially Speaking: Feminism, Nature, and Difference.* London: Routledge.

Galdon, Gemma (2002) *Mundo S. A. Voces contra la globalizacion.* Barcelona: La Tempestad.

Gallup International Millennium Survey (1999) Downloaded from the website (http://www.gallup-international.com/survey5.htm).

—— (2002) Voice of the People Survey conducted by Gallup International and Environics International for the World Economic Forum. Downloaded from the website (www.voice-of-the-people.net/ContentFiles/docs/VOP_Trust_Survey.pdf).

Gallup Poll Monthly (1995) April, 355: 2.

Ganley, Gladys G. (1991) "Power to the people via personal electronic media," *The Washington Quarterly,* Spring: 5–22.

Gans, Herbert J. (1995) *The War against the Poor: The Underclass and Anti-poverty Policy.* New York: Basic Books.

Garaudy, Roger (1990) *Integrismes.* Paris: Belfont.

Garber, Doris A. (1984) *Mass Media in American Politics,* 2nd edn. Washington, DC: CQ Press.

—— (1996) "The new media and politics – what does the future hold?," *Political Science and Politics,* 29 (1): 33–6.

Garcia de Cortazar, Fernando (ed.) (2001) *El estado de las autonomias en el siglo XXI: cierre o apertura indefinida.* Madrid: Fundación para el Análisis y los Estudios Sociales.

Garcia Cotarelo, Ramon (1995) *La conspiracion.* Barcelona: Ediciones B.

Garcia de Leon, Antonio (1985) *Resistencia y utopia: memorial de agravios y cronica de revueltas y profecias acaecidas en la provincia de Chiapas durante los ultimos quinientos anos de su historia,* vol. 2. Mexico: Ediciones Era.

Garcia-Ramon, Maria Dolors and Nogue-Font, Joan (1994) "Nationalism and geography in Catalonia," in Hooson (ed.), pp. 197–211.

Garment, Suzanne (1991) *Scandal: The Culture of Mistrust in American Politics.* New York: New York Times Books.

Garramone, Gina M., et al. (1990) "Effects of negative political advertising on the political process," *Journal of Broadcasting and Electronic Media,* 34 (3): 299–311.

Gates, Henry Louis, Jr (1996) "Parable of the talents," in Gates and West (eds), pp. 1–52.

—— and West, Cornel (eds) (1996) *The Future of the Race.* New York: Alfred Knopf.

Gelb, Joyce and Lief-Palley, Marian (eds) (1994) *Women of Japan and Korea: Continuity and Change*. Philadelphia: Temple University Press.

Gellner, Ernest (1983) *Nations and Nationalism*. Ithaca, NY: Cornell University Press (originally published by Blackwell, Oxford).

Gerami, Shahin (1996) *Women and Fundamentalism: Islam and Christianity*. New York: Garland.

Gerbner, George, Mowlana, Hamid, and Nordenstreng, Kaarle (eds) (1993) *The Global Media Debate: Its Rise, Fall, and Renewal*. Norwood, NJ: Ablex.

Giddens, Anthony (1985) *A Contemporary Critique of Historical Materialism*, vol. II: *The Nation-state and Violence*. Berkeley, CA: University of California Press.

——(1991) *Modernity and Self-identity: Self and Society in the Late Modern Age*. Cambridge: Polity Press.

——(1992) *The Transformation of Intimacy: Sexuality, Love and Eroticism in Modern Societies*. Stanford, CA: Stanford University Press.

Gil, Jorge, et al. (1993) "La red de poder mexicana: el caso de Miguel Aleman," *Revista Mexicana de Sociologia*, 3/95: 103–20.

Ginsborg, Paul (ed.) (1994) *Stato dell'Italia*. Milan: Il Saggiatore.

Giroux, Henry A. (1996) *Fugitive Cultures: Race, Violence and Youth*. New York: Routledge.

Gitlin, Todd (1980) *The Whole World is Watching: Mass Media in the Making and Unmaking of the New Left*. Berkeley, CA: University of California Press.

Gleason, Nancy (1995) "Freenets: cities open the electronic door," *Government Finance Review*, 11 (4): 54–5.

Godard, Francis (ed.) (1996) *Villes*, Special issue of *Le Courrier du CNRS*. Paris: Centre National de la Recherche Scientique.

Gohn, Maria da Gloria (1991) *Movimientos sociais e luta pela moradia*. São Paulo: Edicoes Loyola.

Golden, Tim (1995) "A cocaine trail in Mexico points to official corruption," *The New York Times*, April 19: 1, 8.

Goldsmith, M. (1993) "The Europeanisation of local government," *Urban Studies*, 30: 683–99.

Gole, Nilufer (1995) "L'émergence du sujet islamique," in Dubet and Wieviorka (eds), pp. 221–34.

Gonsioreck, J. C. and Weinrich, J. D. (1991) *Homosexuality: Research Implications for Public Policy*. Newbury Park, CA: Sage.

Goode, William J. (1993) *World Changes in Divorce Patterns*. New Haven, CT: Yale University Press.

Gootenberg, Paul (1999) *Cocaine: Global Histories*. London: Routledge.

Gottlieb, Robert (1993) *Forcing the Spring: The Transformation of the American Environmental Movement*. Washington, DC: Island Press.

Graf, James E. (1995) "Global information infrastructure first principles," *Telecommunications*, 29 (1): 72–3.

Graham, Stephen (1995) "From urban competition to urban collaboration? The development of interurban telematic networks," *Environment and Planning C: Government and Policy*, 13: 503–24.

Gramsci, Antonio (1975) *Quaderni del carcere*. Turin: Einaudi.

Granberg, A. (1993) "The national and regional commodity markets in the USSR: trends and contradictions in the transition period," *Papers in Regional Science*, 72: 1.

—— and Spehl, H. (1989) *Regionale Wirtschaftspolitik in der UdSSR und der BRD*, Report to the Fourth Soviet–West German Seminar on Regional Development, Kiev, 1–10 October 1989.

Greenberg, Stanley B. (1995) *Middle Class Dreams: The Politics of Power of the New American Majority*. New York: Times Books.

Gremion, Pierre (1976) *Le pouvoir périphérique*. Paris: Seuil.

Grier, Peter (1995) "Preparing for the 21st century information war," *Government Executive*, 28 (8): 130–2.

Griffin, Gabriele (ed.) (1995) *Feminist Activism in the 1990s*. London: Francis and Taylor.

——, et al. (eds) (1994) *Stirring It: Challenges for Feminism*. London: Francis and Taylor.

Grosz, Elizabeth (1995) *Space, Time, and Perversion*. London: Routledge.

Grubbe, Peter (1993) *Selbstbedienungsladen: vom Verfall der Demokratischen Moral*. Wuppertal: Hammer.

Guehenno, Jean Marie (1993) *La fin de la démocratie*. Paris: Flammarion. (Read in the Spanish translation, Barcelona: Paidos, 1995; quotations are my own translation into English.)

Gumbel, Andrew (1994) "French deception," *New Statesman and Society*, 7, 328: 24.

Gunaratna, Rohan (2002) *Inside al-Qaeda: Global Network of Terror*. New York: Columbia University Press.

Gunlicks, Arthur B. (ed.) (1993) *Campaign and Party Finance in North America and Western Europe*. Boulder, CO.: Westview Press.

Habermas, Jurgen (1973) *Legitimation Crisis*. Boston: Beacon Press.

—— (1998) *Die postnationale Konstellation*. Frankfurt: Suhrkamp (quoted from the Spanish translation, Barcelona, Paidos, 2000).

Hacker, Kenneth L. (1996) "Missing links and the evolution of electronic democratization," *Media, Culture, and Society*, 18: 213–323.

Hadden, Jeffrey and Shupe, Hanson (1989) *Fundamentalism and Secularization Reconsidered*. New York: Paragon House.

Hage, Jerald, and Powers, Charles (1992) *Postindustrial Lives: Roles and Relationships in the 21st Century*. London: Sage.

Hagedorn, John M. (1998) *People and Folks: Gangs, Crime, and the Underclass in a Rustbelt City*, 2nd edn. Chicago: Lakeview Press.

Halperin, David M., Winkler, John J. and Zeitlin, Froma I. (eds) (1990) *Before Sexuality: The Construction of Erotic Experience in the Ancient Greek World*. Princeton, NJ: Princeton University Press.

Halperin Donghi, Tulio (1969) *Historia contemporanea de America Latina*. Madrid: Alianza Editorial.

Handelman, Stephen (1995) *Comrade Criminal: Russia's New Mafiya*. New Haven, CT: Yale University Press.

Hay, Colin (1994) "Environmental security and state legitimacy," *Capitalism, Nature, Socialism*, 1: 83–98.

Heard, Alex (1995) "The road to Oklahoma City," *The New Republic*, May 15.

Heidenheimer, Arnold J., Johnston, Michael, and LeVine, Victor T. (eds) (1989) *Political Corruption: A Handbook*. New Brunswick, NJ: Transaction.

Held, David (1991) "Democracy, the nation-state and the global system," *Economy and Society*, 20 (2): 138–72.

—— (ed.) (1993) *Prospects for Democracy*. Cambridge: Polity Press.

Heller, Karen S. (1992) "Silence equals death: discourses on AIDS and identity in the gay press, 1981–1986," unpublished PhD dissertation, San Francisco: University of California.

Helvarg, David (1995) "The anti-enviro connection," *The Nation*, May 22.

Hempel, Lamont C. (1996) *Environmental Governance: The Global Challenge*. Washington, DC: Island Press.

Herek, Gregory M. and Greene, Beverly (eds) (1995) *HIV, Identity and Community: The HIV Epidemics*. Thousand Oaks, CA: Sage.

Hernandez Navarro, Luis (1995) *Chiapas: la guerra y la paz*. Mexico: ADN Editores.

Hester, Marianne, Kelly, Liz, and Radford, Jill (1995) *Women, Violence, and Male Power: Feminist Activism, Research and Practice*. Philadelphia: Open University Press.

Hicks, L. Edward (1994) *Sometimes in the Wrong, but Never in Doubt: George S. Benson and the Education of the New Religious Right.* Knoxville: University of Tennessee Press.

High Level Experts Group (1996) *The Information Society in Europe.* Report to the European Commission, Brussels: Commission of the European Union.

Himmelfarb, Gertrude (1995) *The De-moralization of Society: From Victorian Virtues to Modern Values.* New York: Alfred Knopf.

Hiro, Dilip (1989) *Holy Wars: The Rise of Islamic Fundamentalism.* New York: Routledge.

Hirst, Paul and Thompson, Grahame (1996) *Globalization in Question: The International Economy and the Possibilities of Governance.* Cambridge: Polity Press.

Hiskett, Mervyn (1992) *Some to Mecca Turn to Pray: Islamic Values in the Modern World.* St Albans: Claridge Press.

Ho, K. C. and Zaheer, Barber (2000) *Sites of Resistance: Charting the Alternative and Marginal Websites in Singapore.* Singapore: National University of Singapore.

Hobsbawm, Eric J. (1990) *Nations and Nationalism since 1780.* Cambridge: Cambridge University Press.

——(1992) *Naciones y nacionalismo desde 1780.* Barcelona: Critica (expanded and updated version of original 1990 English publication).

——(1994) *The Age of Extremes: A History of the World, 1914–1991.* New York: Pantheon Books.

Hochschild, Jennifer L. (1995) *Facing up to the American Dream: Race, Class, and the Soul of the Nation.* Princeton, NJ: Princeton University Press.

Hodess, Robin (ed.), with Banfield, Jessie and Wolfe, Toby (2001) "Global corruption report," Transparency International (downloaded from the Internet).

Holliman, Jonathan (1990) "Environmentalism with a global scope," *Japan Quarterly,* July–September: 284–90.

hooks, bell (1989) *Talking Back: Thinking Feminist, Thinking Black.* Boston, MA: South End Press.

——(1990) *Yearning: Race, Gender, and Cultural Politics.* Boston, MA: South End Press.

——(1993) *Sisters of the Yaw: Black Women and Self-recovery.* Boston, MA: South End Press.

Hooson, David (1994a) "Ex-Soviet identities and the return of geography," in Hooson (ed.), pp. 134–40.

——(ed.) (1994b) *Geography and National Identity.* Oxford: Blackwell.

Horsman, M. and Marshall, A. (1994) *After the Nation State*. New York: Harper-Collins.

Horton, Tom (1991) "The green giant," *Rolling Stone*, September 5: 43–112.

Hsia, Chu-joe (1996) Personal communication.

Hsing, You-tien (1996) *Making Capitalism in China: The Taiwan Connection*. New York: Oxford University Press.

Hughes, James (1994) "The 'Americanization' of Russian politics: Russia's first television election, December 1993," *The Journal of Communist Studies and Transition Politics*, 10 (2): 125–50.

Hulsberg, Werner (1988) *The German Greens: A Social and Political Profile*. London: Verso.

Hunter, Robert (1979) *Warriors of the Rainbow: A Chronicle of the Greenpeace Movement*. New York: Holt, Rinehart and Winston.

——(1994) "Issues, candidate image and priming: the use of private polls in Kennedy's 1960 presidential campaign," *American Political Science Review*, 88 (3): 527–40.

Hutton, Will and Giddens, Anthony (eds) (2000) *On the Edge: Living with Global Capitalism*. London: Jonathan Cape.

Inglehart, Ronald (ed.) (2003) *Mass Values and Social Change: Findings from the Values Surveys*. Leiden: Brill Academic.

——and Catterberg, Gabriela (2003) "Trends in political action: the developmental trend and the post-honeymoon decline," *International Journal of Comparative Sociology*, Spring.

Inoguchi, Takashi (1993) "Japanese politics in transition: a theoretical review," *Government and Opposition*, 28 (4): 443–55.

Irigaray, Luce (1977/1985) *Ce sexe qui n'en est pas un*. Read in the English translation, *This Sex Which is Not One*, trans. Catherine Porter with Carolyn Burke (1985). Ithaca, NY: Cornell University Press.

——(1984/1993) *Éthique de la difference sexuelle*. Read in the English translation, *An Ethics of Sexual Difference*, trans. Carolyn Burke and Gillian C. Gill (1993). Ithaca, NY: Cornell University Press.

Irving, Larry et al. (1994) "Steps towards a global information infrastructure," *Federal Communications Law Journal*, 47 (2): 271–9.

Ivins, Molly (1995) "Fertilizer of hate," *The Progressive*, June.

Jacobs, Lawrence R. and Shapiro, Robert Y. (1995) "The rise of presidential polling: the Nixon White House in historical perspective," *Public Opinion Quarterly*, 59: 163–95.

Jacquard, Roland (2002) *In the Name of Osama bin Laden: Global Terrorism and the bin Laden Brotherhood*. Durham, NC: Duke

University Press (updated translation from the 2001 French edition, Paris: Jean Picollec Editeur).

Jacquet, Pierre, Pisani-Ferry, Jean, and Tubiana, Laurence (eds) (2002) *Gouvernance mondiale*. Paris: Conseil d'Analyse Economique, La Documentation Française.

Jambar, Avni (2002) "Globalization, identity, and the state: religious fundamentalism and urban riots in Ahmedabad," Berkeley, CA: University of California, unpublished research seminar paper for CP 229.

Janowitz, Morris (1976) *Social Control of the Welfare State*. Chicago: University of Chicago Press.

Jaquette, Jane S. (ed.) (1994) *The Women's Movement in Latin America: Participation and Democracy*. Boulder, CO: Westview Press.

Jarrett-Macauley, Delia (ed.) (1996) *Reconstructing Womanhood, Reconstructing Feminism: Writings on Black Women*. London: Routledge.

Jelen, Ted (ed.) (1989) *Religion and Political Behavior in America*. New York: Praeger.

—— (1991) *The Political Mobilization of Religious Belief*. New York: Praeger.

Johansen, Elaine R. (1990) *Political Corruption: Scope and Resources: An Annotated Bibliography*. New York: Garland.

Johnson, Chalmers (1982) *MITI and the Japanese Miracle*. Stanford, Stanford University Press.

—— (1995) *Japan: Who Governs? The Rise of the Developmental State*. New York: W. W. Norton.

Johnston, R. J, Knight, David, and Kofman, Eleanore (eds) (1988) *Nationalism, Self-determination, and Political Geography*. London: Croom Helm.

Jordan, June (1995) "In the land of white supremacy," *The Progressive*, June.

Judge, David, Stokes, Gerry, and Wolman, Hall (1995) *Theories of Urban Politics*. Thousand Oaks, CA: Sage.

Juergensmeyer, Mark (1993) *The New Cold War? Religious Fundamentalism Confronts the Secular State*. Berkeley, CA: University of California Press.

—— (2000) *Terror in the Mind of God: The Global Rise of Religious Violence*. Berkeley, CA: University of California Press.

Juris, Jeff (2003) "Transnational activism and the cultural logic of networking," unpublished PhD thesis, University of California, Berkeley, CA.

Jutglar, Antoni (1966) *Els burgesos catalans*. Barcelona: Fontanella.

Kahn, Robert E. (1994) "The role of government in the evolution of the Internet," *Communications of the ACM*, 37 (8): 15–19.

Kahne, Hilda and Giele, Janet Z. (eds) (1992) *Women's Work and Women's Lives: The Continuing Struggle Worldwide*. Boulder, CO: Westview Press.

Kaid, Lynda Lee and Holtz-Bacha, Christina (eds) (1995) *Political Advertising in Western Democracies*. Thousand Oaks, CA: Sage.

Kaldor, Mary (1999/2001) *New and Old Wars: Organized Violence in a Global Era*. Read in Spanish translation, Barcelona: Tusquets (2001).

Kamarck, Elaine Ciulla and Nye, Joseph, Jr (2002) *Governance.com: Democracy in the Information Age*. Washington, DC: Brookings Institution Press.

Kaminiecki, Sheldon (ed.) (1993) *Environmental Politics in the International Arena: Movements, Parties, Organizations, Policy*. Albany, NY: State University of New York Press.

Kanagy, Conrad L., et al. (1994) "Surging environmentalisms: changing public opinion or changing publics," *Social Science Quarterly*, 75 (4): 804–19.

Katznelson, Ira (1996) *Liberalism's Crooked Circle: Letters to Adam Michnik*. Princeton, NJ: Princeton University Press.

Kazin, Michael (1995) *The Populist Persuasion: An American History*. New York: Basic Books.

Keating, Michael (1995) *Nations against the State: The New Politics of Nationalism in Quebec, Catalonia, and Scotland*. New York: St Martin's Press.

Keen, Sam (1991) *Fire in the Belly: On Being a Man*. New York: Bantam Books.

Kelly, Petra (1994) *Thinking Green: Essays on Environmentalism, Feminism, and Nonviolence*. Berkeley, CA: Parallax Press.

Keohane, Robert O. (2002) *Power and Governance in a Partially Globalized World*. London: Routledge.

—— and Nye, Joseph (2000) "Introduction," in Nye and Donahue (eds), pp. 1–44.

Kepel, Gilles (1995) "Entre société et communauté: les musulmans au Royaume-Uni et au France aujourd'hui," in Dubet and Wieviorka (eds), pp. 273–88.

—— (2002) *Jihad: The Trail of Political Islam*. Cambridge, MA: Harvard University Press (updated American edition of the original 2000 edition).

Khazanov, Anatoly M. (1995) *After the USSR: Ethnicity, Nationalism, and Politics in the Commonwealth of Independent States*. Madison: University of Wisconsin Press.

Khosrokhavar, Farhad (1995) "Le quasi-individu: de la néo-communauté à la nécro-communauté," in Dubet and Wieviorka (eds), pp. 235–56.

Khoury, Philip and Kostiner, Joseph (eds) (1990) *Tribes and State Formation in the Middle East.* Berkeley, CA: University of California Press.

Kim, Marlene (1993) "Comments," in Cobble (ed.), pp. 85–92.

King, Anthony (1984) "Sex, money and power: political scandals in Britain and the United States," Colchester, University of Essex, Essex Papers in Politics and Government.

King, Joseph P. (1989) "Socioeconomic development and corrupt campaign practices in England," in Heidenheimer et al. (eds), pp. 233–50.

Kiselyova, Emma and Castells, Manuel (1997) *The New Russian Federalism in Siberia and the Far East.* Berkeley, CA: University of California, Center for Eastern European and Slavic Studies/ Center for German and European Studies, Research Paper.

Klanwatch/Militia Task Force (KMTF) (1996) *False Patriots. The Threat from Antigovernment Extremists.* Montgomery, Alabama: Southern Poverty Law Center.

Klein, Naomi and Levy, Debra Ann (2002) *Fences and Windows: Dispatches from the Front Line of the Globalization Debate.* New York: Picador.

Klinenberg, Eric and Perrin, Andrew (1996) "Symbolic politics in the Information Age: the 1996 presidential campaign in cyberspace," Berkeley, CA: University of California, Department of Sociology, Research Paper for Soc 290.2, unpublished.

Kolodny, Annette (1984) *The Land before Her: Fantasy and Experience of the American Frontiers, 1630–1860.* Chapel Hill, NC: University of North Carolina Press.

Kozlov, Viktor (1988) *The Peoples of the Soviet Union.* Bloomington, IN: Indiana University Press.

Kraus, K. and Knight, A. (1995) *State, Society, and the UN System: Changing Perspectives on Multilateralism.* New York: United Nations University Press.

Kuppers, Gary (ed.) (1994) *Companeras: Voices from the Latin American Women's Movement.* London: Latin American Bureau.

Kuttner, Robert (1995) "The net as free-market utopia? Think again," *Business Week,* September 4: 24.

Lamberts-Bendroth, Margaret (1993) *Fundamentalism and Gender: 1875 to Present.* New Haven, CT: Yale University Press.

Langguth, Gerd (1984) *The Green Factor in German Politics: From Protest Movement to Political Party.* Boulder, CO: Westview Press.

Lasch, Christopher (1980) *The Culture of Narcissism*. London: Abacus.

Laserna, Roberto (1992) *Productores de democracia: actores sociales y procesos politicos*. Cochabamba: Centro de Estudios de la Realidad Economica y Social.

Lash, Scott and Urry, John (1994) *Economies of Signs and Space*. London: Sage.

Laumann, Edward O., et al. (1994) *The Social Organization of Sexuality: Sexual Practices in the United States*. Chicago: University of Chicago Press.

L'Avenc: Revista d'Historia (1996) Special issue: "Catalunya-Espanya," 200, February.

Lavrakas, Paul J., et al. (eds) (1995) *Presidential Polls and the New Media*. Boulder, CO: Westview Press.

Lawrence, Bruce B. (1989) *Defenders of God: The Fundamentalist Revolt against the Modern Age*. Columbia, SC: University of South Carolina Press.

Lawton, Kim A. (1989) "Whatever happened to the Religious Right?," *Christianity Today*, December 15: 44.

Leal, Jesus, et al. (1996) *Familia y vivienda en Espana*. Madrid: Universidad Autonoma de Madrid, Instituto de Sociologia, Research Report.

Lechner, Frank J. (1991) "Religion, law, and global order," in Robertson and Garrett (eds), pp. 263–80.

Lesthaeghe, R. (1995) "The second demographic transition in Western countries: an interpretation," in Mason and Jensen (eds), pp. 17–62.

Levin, Murray B. (1987) *Talk Radio and the American Dream*. Lexington, MA: Heath.

Levine, Martin (1979) "Gay ghetto," in Martin Levine (ed.), *Gay Men*. New York: Harper and Row.

Lewis, Bernard (1988) *The Political Language of Islam*. Chicago: University of Chicago Press.

Lewis, Peter H. (1996a) "Judge temporarily blocks law that bars indecency on Internet," *The New York Times*, February 16: C1–C16.

——(1996b) "Judges turn back law to regulate Internet decency," *The New York Times*, June 13: A1.

Leys, Colin (1989) "What is the problem about corruption?," in Heidenheimer et al. (eds), pp. 51–66.

L'Histoire (1993) Special dossier "Argent, politique et corruption: 1789–1993," May, 166: 48ff.

Li, Zhilan (1995) "Shanghai, Guandong ruheyu zhongyang zhouxuan [How did Shanghai and Guandong negotiate with the central government?]," *The Nineties Monthly*, December, 311: 36–9.

Lienesch, Michael (1993) *Redeeming America: Piety and Politics in the New Christian Right*. Chapel Hill, NC: University of North Carolina Press.

Lipschutz, Ronnie D. and Coca, Ken (1993) "The implications of global ecological interdependence," in Ronnie D. Lipschutz and Ken Coca (eds), *The State and Social Power in Global Environmental Politics*. New York: Columbia University Press.

Lipset, Seymour M. (1996) *American Exceptionalism: A Double-edged Sword*. New York: Norton.

—— and Raab, Earl (1978) *The Politics of Unreason: Right-wing Extremism in America, 1790–1970*. New York: Harper and Row.

Lloyd, Gary A. and Kuselewickz, J. (eds.) (1995) *HIV Disease: Lesbians, Gays, and the Social Services*. New York: Haworth Press.

Lodato, Saverio (1994) *Quindici anni di Mafia*. Milan: Biblioteca Universale Rizzoli.

Longman (1990) *Political Scandals and Causes Célèbres since 1945*. London: Longman's International Reference Compendium.

Lowi, Theodore J. (1988) "Foreword," in Markovits and Silverstein (eds), pp. vii–xii.

Luecke, Hanna (1993) *Islamischer Fundamentalismus: Rueckfall ins Mittelalter oder Wegbereiter der Moderne?* Berlin: Klaus Schwarz Verlag.

Lyday, Corbin (ed.) (1994) *Ethnicity, Federalism and Democratic Transition in Russia: A Conference Report*. Report of a Conference sponsored by the Berkeley–Stanford Program in Soviet and Post-Soviet Studies held at Berkeley on November 11–17, 1993.

Lyon, David (1994) *The Electronic Eye: The Rise of Surveillance Society*. Cambridge: Polity Press.

—— (2001) "Surveillance after September 11," *Sociological Review Online*, 6 (3) (www.socresonline.org.uk/6/3/lyon/html).

—— (ed.) (2003) *Surveillance as Social Sorting: Privacy, Risk, and Digital Discrimination*. London: Routledge.

MacDonald, Greg (1990) *The Emergence of Multimedia Conglomerates*. Geneva: ILO, Multinational Enterprises Program, working paper 70.

McDonogh, Gary W. (ed.) (1986) *Conflict in Catalonia*. Gainsville: University of Florida Press.

McGrew, Anthony G. (1992a) "Global politics in a transitional era," in McGrew et al. (eds), pp. 312–30.

—— (1992b) "Military technology and the dynamics of global militarization," in McGrew et al. (eds), pp. 83–117.

—— Lewis, Paul G., et al. (1992) *Global Politics: Globalization and the Nation State*. Cambridge: Polity Press.

McInnes, Colin (1992) "Technology and modern warfare," in Baylis and Rengger (eds), pp. 130–58.

—— and Sheffield, G. D. (eds) (1988) *Warfare in the 20th Century: Theory and Practice*. London: Unwin Hyman.

McLaughlin, Andrew (1993) *Regarding Nature: Industrialism and Deep Ecology*. Albany, NY: State University of New York Press.

Macy, Joanna (1991) *World as Lover, World as Self*. Berkeley, CA: Parallax Press.

Magleby, David B. and Nelson, Candice J. (1990) *The Money Chase: Congressional Campaign Finance Reform*. Washington, DC: Brookings Institution.

Maheu, Louis (1995) "Les mouvements sociaux: plaidoyer pour une sociologie de l'ambivalence," in Dubet and Wieviorka (eds), pp. 313–34.

Mainichi Shinbun (1995), May 1.

Manes, Christopher (1990) *Green Rage: Radical Environmentalism and the Unmaking of Civilization*. Boston, MA: Little, Brown.

Mansbridge, Jane (1995) "What is the feminist movement?," in Ferree and Martin (eds), pp. 27–34.

Mansell, Robin (ed.) (2002) *Inside the Communication Revolution: Evolving Patterns of Social and Technical Interaction*. Oxford: Oxford University Press.

Markovits, Andrei S. and Silverstein, Mark (eds) (1988a) *The Politics of Scandal: Power and Process in Liberal Democracies*. New York: Holmes and Meier.

—— and —— (1988b) "Power and process in liberal democracies," in Markovits and Silverstein (eds), pp. 15–37.

Marquez, Enrique (1995) *Por que perdio Camacho*. Mexico: Oceano.

Marsden, George M. (1980) *Fundamentalism and American Culture: The Shaping of the 20th Century Evangelicalism, 1870–1925*. New York: Oxford University Press.

Martinez Torres, Maria Elena (1994) "The Zapatista rebellion and identity," Berkeley, CA: University of California, Program of Latin American Studies, research paper (unpublished).

—— (1996) "Networking global civil society: the Zapatista movement. The first informational guerrilla," Berkeley, CA: University of California, unpublished seminar paper for CP 229.

Marty, Martin E. (1988) "Fundamentalism as a social phenomenon," *Bulletin of the American Academy of Arts and Sciences*, 42: 15–29.

——and Appleby, Scott (eds) (1991) *Fundamentalisms Observed.* Chicago: University of Chicago Press.

Masnick, George, S. and Ardle, Nancy M. (1994) *Revised US Households Projections: New Methods and New Assumptions.* Cambridge, MA: Harvard University, Graduate School of Design/ John F. Kennedy School of Government, Joint Center for Housing Studies, Working Papers Series.

——and Kim, Joshua M. (1995) *The Decline of Demand: Housing's Next Generation.* Cambridge, MA: Harvard University, Joint Center for Housing Studies, Working Papers Series.

Mason, Karen O. and Jensen, An-Magritt (eds) (1995) *Gender and Family Change in Industrialized Countries.* New York: Oxford University Press.

Mass, Lawrence (1990) *Dialogues of the Sexual Revolution.* New York: Haworth Press.

Massolo, Alejandra (1992) *Por amor y coraje: Mujeres en movimientos urbanos de la Ciudad de Mexico.* Mexico: El Colegio de Mexico.

Mattelart, Armand (1991) *La communication-monde: histoire des ideés et des stratégies.* Paris: La Découverte.

Matthews, Nancy A. (1989) "Surmounting a legacy: the expansion of racial diversity in a local anti-rape movement," *Gender and Society,* 3: 519–33.

Maxwell, Joe and Tapia, Andres (1995) "Guns and Bibles," *Christianity Today,* 39 (7): 34.

Mayer, William G. (1994) "The polls – poll trends: the rise of the new media," *Public Opinion Quarterly,* 58: 124–46.

Mayorga, Fernando (1993) *Discurso y politica en Bolivia.* La Paz, ILDIS-CERES.

Mejia Barquera, Fernando et al. (1985) *Televisa: el quinto poder.* Mexico: Claves Latinoamericanas.

Melchett, Peter (1995) "The fruits of passion," *New Statesman and Society,* April 28: 37–8.

Melucci, Alberto (1995) "Individualisation et globalisation: au-delà de la modernité?," in Dubet and Wieviorka (eds), pp. 433–48.

Meny, Yves (1992) *La corruption de la Republique.* Paris: Fayard.

Merchant, Carolyn (1980) *The Death of Nature: Women, Ecology, and the Scientific Revolution.* New York: Harper and Row.

Mesa, Carlos D. (1986) "Como se fabrica un presidente," in *Cuarto Intermedio,* pp. 4–23.

Meyer, David S., Whittier, Nancy, and Robnett, Belinda (eds) (2002) *Social Movements: Identity, Culture and the State.* New York: Oxford University Press.

Michelson, William (1985) *From Sun to Sun: Daily Obligations and Community Structure in the Lives of Employed Women and their Families*. Totowa, NJ: Rowman and Allanheld.

Mikulsky, D.V. (1992) *Ideologicheskaya kontseptsiya Islamskoi partii vozrozhdeniya* [*Ideological Concept of Islamic Revival Party*]. Moscow: Gorbachev-Fund.

Miller, Joanne M. and Krosnick, Jon A. (2000) "News media impact on the ingredients of presidential evaluations: politically knowledgeable citizens are guided by a trusted source," *American Journal of Political Science*, 44 (2): 301–15.

Minc, Alain (1993) *Le nouveau Moyen Âge*. Paris: Gallimard.

Misztal, Bronislaw and Shupe, Anson (1992a) "Making sense of the global revival of fundamentalism," in Bronislaw and Shupe (eds), pp. 3–9.

—— and —— (eds) (1992b) *Religion and Politics in Comparative Perspective: Revival of Religious Fundamentalism in East and West*. Westport, CT.: Praeger.

Mitchell, Juliet (1966) "Women: the longest revolution," *New Left Review*, 40, November/December.

Miyadai, Shinji (1995) *Owarinaki Nichijo of Ikiro* [*Live in Endless Everyday Life*]. Tokyo: Chikuma-Shobo.

Moen, Matthew C. (1992) *The Transformation of the Christian Right*. Tuscaloosa: University of Alabama Press.

—— and Gustafson, Lowell S. (eds) (1992) *The Religious Challenge to the State*. Philadelphia: Temple University Press.

Mokhtari, Fariborz (ed.) (1994) *Peacemaking, Peacekeeping and Coalition Warfare: The Future of the UN*. Washington, DC: National Defense University.

Monereo, Manuel and Riera, Miguel (2002) *Porto Alegre: otro mundo es posible*. Barcelona: El Viejo Top.

Monnier, Alain and de Guibert-Lantoine, Catherine (1993) "La conjoncture démographique: l'Europe et les pays développés d'outre-mer," *Population*, 48 (4): 1043–67.

Moog, Sandra (1995) "To the root: the mobilization of the culture concept in the development of radical environmental thought," Berkeley, CA: University of California, Department of Anthropology, unpublished seminar paper for Anthro. 250X.

—— (1996) "Electronic media and informational politics in America," Berkeley, CA: University of California, Department of Sociology, unpublished research paper for Soc 290.2.

Moore, David W. (1992) *The Superpollsters: How They Measure and Manipulate Public Opinion in America*. New York: Four Walls Eight Windows.

Moreau Deffarges, Philippe (1993) *La mondialisation: vers la fin des frontières?* Paris: Dunod.

Moreno Toscano, Alejandra (1996) *Turbulencia politica: causas y razones del 94.* Mexico: Oceano.

Morgen, Sandra (1988) "The dream of diversity, the dilemmas of difference: race and class contradictions in a feminist health clinic," in J. Sole (ed.), *Anthropology for the Nineties.* New York: Free Press.

Morin, Edgar and Kern, Anne B. (1993) *Terre-Patrie.* Paris: Seuil.

Morris, Stephen D. (1991) *Corruption and Politics in Contemporary Mexico.* Tuscaloosa: University of Alabama Press.

Moscow Times (1996), "Style beats substance in ad campaigns," May 30: 1.

Moser, Leo (1985) *The Chinese Mosaic: The Peoples and Provinces of China.* London: Westview Press.

Mouffe, Chantal (1995) "The end of politics and the rise of the radical right," *Dissent*, Fall: 488.

Mundy, Alicia (1996) "Taking a poll on polls," *Media Week*, 6 (8): 17–20.

Murray, Charles and Herrnstein, Richard (1994) *The Bell Curve: Intelligence and Class Structure in American Life.* New York: Free Press.

Nair, Sami (1996) "La crisis argelina," in *Claves*, April: 14–17.

Nakazawa, Shinichi, et al. (1995) "AUM Jiken to wa Nandatta no ka [Was AUM an incident?]," in *Kokoku Hihyo*, June.

Nash, June, et al. (eds) (1995) *La explosion de comunidades en Chiapas.* Copenhagen: International Working Group on Indian Affairs, Document IWGIA no. 16.

The Nation (1995) "Editorial," May 15.

Navarro, Vicente (1994) *The Politics of Health Policy: The US Reforms, 1980–1994.* Oxford: Blackwell.

—— (1995) "Gobernabilidad, desigualdad y estado del bienestar. La situacion en Estados Unidos y su relevancia para Europa," unpublished paper delivered at the International Symposium on Governability, Inequality, and Social Policies, organized by the Institut d'Estudis Socials Avancats, Barcelona, November 23–25.

—— (ed.) (2002) *The Political Economy of Social Inequalities.* Amityville, NY: Baywood.

Negri, Toni, et al. (2002) *On Fire: The Battle of Genoa and the Anti-capitalist Movement.* One/Off Press.

Negroponte, Nicholas (1995) *Being Digital.* New York: Alfred Knopf.

Nevitte, Neil (2003) "Authority orientations and political support: a cross-national analysis of satisfaction with governments and democracy," in Inglehart (ed.), pp. 387–412.

The New Republic (1995a) "An American darkness," May 15.

—— (1995b) "TRB from Washington," May 15.

The New York Times (1995) "Where cotton's king, trouble reigns," October 9: A6.

The New York Times Sunday (1995a) "The rich: a special issue," November 19.

—— (1995b) "The unending search for demons in the American imagination," July 23: 7.

Nijkamp, Peter and Castells, Nuria (2001) "Transboundary environmental problems in the EU: lessons from air pollution policies," *Journal of Environmental Law and Policy*, 4: 501–17.

Norman, E. Herbert (1940) *Japan's Emergence as a Modern State: Political and Economic Problems of the Meiji Period*. New York: Institute of Pacific Relations.

Norris, Pippa (2000a) "Global governance and cosmopolitan citizens," in Nye and Donahue (eds), pp. 155–77.

—— (2000b) *A Virtuous Circle: Political Communications in Post-industrial Societies*. Cambridge: Cambridge University Press.

Nunnenkamp, Peter, et al. (1994) *Globalisation of Production and Markets*. Tubingen: Kieler Studien, J.C.B. Mohr.

Nye, Joseph S. (2002) *The Paradox of American Power*. Oxford: Oxford University Press.

—— and Donahue, John D. (eds) (2000) *Governance in a Globalizing World*. Washington, DC: Brookings Institution.

——, Zelikow, Philip, and King, David (eds) (1997) *Why People Don't Trust Government*. Cambridge, MA: Harvard University Press.

O'Brien, Robert, Scholte, Anne Marie, Aart, Jan, and Williams, Mary (2000) *Contesting Global Governance: Multilateral Economic Institutions and Global Social Movements*. Cambridge: Cambridge University Press.

OECD (1993–95) *Employment Outlook*. Paris: OECD.

—— (1994a) *The OECD Jobs Study*. Paris: OECD.

—— (1994b) *Women and Structural Change: New Perspectives*. Paris: OECD.

—— (1995) *Labour Force Statistics*. Paris: OECD.

Offen, Karen (1988) "Defining feminism: a comparative historical approach," *Signs*, 14 (11): 119–57.

Ohama, Itsuro (1995) "AUM toiu Danso [AUM as an attempt to disconnect themselves from history]," in *Seiron*, July.

Orr, Robert M. (1995) "Home-grown terrorism plagues both the US and Japan," *Tokyo Business*, July.

Orstrom Moller, J. (1995) *The Future European Model: Economic Internationalization and Cultural Decentralization*. Westport, CT.: Praeger.

Osawa, Masachi (1995) "AUM wa Naze Sarin ni Hashitakka [Why did AUM use sarin]?," in *Gendai*, October.

Ostertag, Bob (1991) "Greenpeace takes over the world," *Mother Jones*, March–April: 32–87.

Oumlil, Ali (1992) *Islam et état national*. Casablanca: Editions Le Fennec.

Oversight of the IMF and the World Bank (1995) *A Meeting of a Multinational Group of Parliamentarians Involved in Oversight of the IMF and the World Bank*. Washington, DC: US Government Printing Office.

Pagano, Michael A. and Bowman, Ann O'M. (1995) "The state of American federalism, 1994–95," *Publius: The Journal of Federalism*, 25 (3): 1–21.

Page, Benjamin I. and Shapiro, Robert Y. (1992) *The Rational Public: Fifty Years of Trends in Americans' Policy Preferences*. Chicago: University of Chicago Press.

Panarin, Alexander S. (1994) "Rossia v evrazii: geopolitisichie vyzovy i tsivilizatsionnye otvety", *Voprosy filosofii*, 12: 19–31 (read from *Russian Social Science Review: A Journal of Translations*, May–June 1996: 35–53).

Pardo, Mary (1995) "Doing it for the kids: Mexican American community activists, border feminists?," in Ferree and Martin (eds), pp. 356–71.

Partido Revolucionario Institucional (1994) *La reforma del PRI y el cambio democratico en Mexico*. Mexico: Editorial Limusa.

Patterson, T. E. (1993) *Out of Order: How the Decline of the Political Parties and the Growing Power of the News Media Undermine the American Way of Electing Presidents*. New York: Alfred Knopf.

Pattie, Charles, et al. (1995) "Winning the local vote: the effectiveness of constituency campaign spending in Great Britain, 1983–1992," *American Political Science Review*, 89 (4): 969–85.

Perez-Argote, Alfonso (ed.) (1989) *Sociologia del nacionalismo*. Vitoria: Argitarapen Zerbitzua Euskal Herriko Unibertsitatea.

Perez Fernandez del Castillo, German, et al. (1995) *La voz de los votos: un analisis critico de las elecciones de 1994*. Mexico: Miguel Angel Porrua Grupo Editorial.

Perez Iribarne, Eduardo (1993a) *La opinion publica al poder*. La Paz: Empresa Encuestas y Estudios.

—— (1993b) "La television imposible," *Fe y Pueblo*, 3: 67–84.

Perez-Tabernero, Alfonso, et al. (1993) *Concentracion de la comunicacion en Europa: empresa comercial e interes publico*. Barcelona: Generalitat de Catalunya, Centre d'Investigacio de la Comunicacio.

Pharr, Susan and Putnam, Robert (eds) (2000) *Disaffected Democracies: What's Troubling the Trilateral Countries?* Princeton, NJ: Princeton University Press.

Phillips, Andrew (1992) "Pocketbook politics: Britain's Tories face a tough fight against Labour Party rivals in an April election," *Maclean's*, 105 (12): 22–5.

Philo, Greg (1993) "Political advertising, popular belief and the 1992 British general election," *Media, Culture, and Society*, 15 (3): 407–18.

Pi, Ramon (ed.) (1996) *Jordi Pujol: Cataluna, Espana*. Madrid: Espasa Hoy.

Pinelli, Antonella (1995) "Women's condition, low fertility, and emerging union patterns in Europe," in Mason and Jensen (eds), pp. 82–104.

Pipes, Richard (1954) *The Formation of the Soviet Union: Communism and Nationalism, 1917–23*. Cambridge, MA: Harvard University Press.

Piscatori, James (1986) *Islam in a World of Nation-states*. Cambridge: Cambridge University Press.

Pi-Sunyer, Oriol (1991) "Catalan politics and Spanish democracy: the matter of cultural sovereignty," in Azevedo (ed.), pp. 1–20.

Plant, Judith (1991) "Ecofeminism," in Dobson (ed.), pp. 100–4.

Po, Lan-chih (1996) "Feminism, identity, and women's movements: theoretical debates and a case study in Taiwan," Berkeley, CA: University of California, Department of City and Regional Planning, unpublished research paper.

Poguntke, Thomas (1993) *Alternative Politics: The German Green Party*. Edinburgh: Edinburgh University Press.

Pollith, Katha (1995) "Subject to debate," *The Nation*, 260 (22): 784.

Porrit, Jonathan (1994) *Seeing Green: The Politics of Ecology Explained*. Oxford: Blackwell.

Portes, Alejandro, et al. (eds.) (1989) *The Informal Economy*. Baltimore, MD: The Johns Hopkins University Press.

Poulantzas, Nicos (1978) *L'état, le pouvoir, le socialisme*. Paris: Presses Universitaires de France – Politiques.

Prat de la Riba, Enric (1906) *La nacionalitat catalana*. Barcelona: Edicions 62, republished in 1978.

Price, Monroe E. (2002) *Media and Sovereignty: The Global Information Revolution and its Challenge to State Power*. Cambridge, MA: MIT Press.

Price, Vincent and Hsu, Mei-Ling (1992) "Public opinion about AIDS policies: the role of misinformation and attitudes towards homosexuals," *Public Opinion Quarterly*, 56 (1).

The Progressive (1995) "The far right is upon us," June.

Puiggene i Riera, Ariadna, et al. (1991) "Official language policies in contemporary Catalonia," in Azevedo (ed.), pp. 30–49.

Putnam, Robert (1995) "Bowling alone: America's declining social capital," *Journal of Democracy*, 6 (1): 65–78.

Qiu, Jack Linchuan and Chan, Joseph Man (2003) "China Internet studies: a review of the field," in Monroe Price and Helen Nissembaum (eds), *The Academy and the Internet: New Directions in Information Scholarship*. London: Sage.

Qtub, Sayyid (n.d./1970s) *Maalim fi al-Tariq*. Cairo: Dar al-Shuruq.

Rashid, Ahmed (2001) *Taliban: Islam, Oil and the New Game in Central Asia*, 2nd edn. London: I. B. Tauris.

Reigot, Betty Polisar and Spina, Rita K. (1996) *Beyond the Traditional Family: Voices of Diversity*. New York: Springer Verlag.

Rich, Adrienne (1980/1993) "Compulsory heterosexuality and lesbian existence," in Abelove et al. (eds), pp. 227–54.

Richardson, Dick and Rootes, Chris (eds) (1995) *The Green Challenge: The Development of Green Parties in Europe*. London: Routledge.

Riechmann, Jorge and Fernandez Buey, Francisco (1994) *Redes que dan libertad: introduccion a los nuevos movimientos sociales*. Barcelona: Paidos.

Riesebrodt, Martin (1993) *Pious Passion: The Emergence of Modern Fundamentalism in the United States and Iran*. Berkeley, CA: University of California Press.

Roberts, Marilyn and McCombs, Maxwell (1994) "Agenda setting and political advertising: origins of the news agenda," *Political Communication*, 11: 249–62.

Robertson, Roland and Garrett, William R. (eds) (1991) *Religion and Global Order*. New York: Paragon House.

Rochester, J. Martin (1993) *Waiting for the Millennium: The UN and the Future of World Order*. Columbia, SC: University of South Carolina Press.

Rodgers, Gerry (ed.) (1994) *Workers, Institutions and Economic Growth in Asia*. Geneva: International Institute of Labour Studies.

Rojas, Rosa (1995) *Chiapas: la paz violenta*. Mexico: Ediciones La Jornada.

Rokkan, Stein and Urwin, Derek W. (eds) (1982) *The Politics of Territorial Identity*. London: Sage.

Roman, Joel (1993) "La gauche, le pouvoir, les médias: à propos du suicide de Pierre Beregovoy," *Esprit*, 6: 143–6.

Rondfeldt, David (1995) "The battle for the mind of Mexico," electronically published in June 1995 at RAND Corporation home page (http://www.eco.utexas.edu/homepages/faculty/cleaver/chiapas95/netawars).

Roper Center of Public Opinion and Polling (1995) "How much government, at what level? Change and persistence in American ideas," *The Public Perspective*, 6 (3).

Rose-Ackerman, Susan (1999) *Corruption and Government: Causes, Consequences and Reform*. New York: Cambridge University Press.

Rosenau, J. (1990) *Turbulence in World Politics*. London: Harvester Wheatsheaf.

Ross, Loretta J. (1995) "Saying it with a gun," *The Progressive*, June.

Ross, Shelley (1988) *Fall from Grace: Sex, Scandal, and Corruption in American Politics from 1702 to present*. New York: Ballantine.

Roth, Jurgen and Frey, Marc (1992) *Die Verbrecher Holding: das vereinte Europa im Griff der Mafia*. Piper and Co. (read in the Spanish translation, Madrid: Anaya/Mario Muchnik, 1995).

Rovira i Virgili, A. (1988) *Catalunya: Espanya*. Barcelona: Edicions de la Magrana (originally published in 1912).

Rowbotham, Sheila (1974) *Hidden from History: Rediscovering Women in History from the 17th Century to the Present*. New York: Pantheon Books.

——(1989) *The Past is Before Us: Feminism and Action since the 1960s*. London: Pandora.

——(1992) *Women in Movement: Feminism and Social Action*. New York: Routledge.

Rowlands, Ian H. (1992) "Environmental issues and world politics," in Baylis and Rengger (eds), pp. 287–309.

Rubert de Ventos, Xavier (1994) *Nacionalismos: el laberinto de la identidad*. Madrid: Espasa-Calpe.

Rubin, Rose M. and Riney, Rose (1994) *Working Wives and Dual-earner Families*. Westport, CT: Praeger.

Ruiz-Cabanas, Miguel (1993) "La campana permanente de Mexico: costos, beneficios y consecuencia," in Smith (ed.), pp. 207–20.

Rupp, Leila J. and Taylor, Verta (1987) *Survival in the Doldrums: The American Women's Rights Movement, 1945 to the 1960s*. New York: Oxford University Press.

Sabato, Larry J. (1991) *Feeding Frenzy: How Attack Journalism has Transformed American Politics*. New York: Free Press.

Saboulin, Michel and Thave, Suzanne (1993) "La vie en couple marié: un modèle qui s'affaiblit," in INSEE, *La société française: données sociales*. Paris: INSEE.

Said, Edward W. (1979) *Orientalism*. New York: Vintage Books.

Salaff, Janet (1981) *Working Daughters of Hong Kong*. Cambridge: Cambridge University Press.

—— (1988) *State and Family in Singapore: Restructuring a Developing Society*. Ithaca, NY: Cornell University Press.

—— (1992) "Women, family and the state in Hong Kong, Taiwan and Singapore," in Richard Appelbaum and Jeffrey Henderson (eds), *States and Development in the Asian Pacific Rim*. Newbury Park, CA: Sage.

Salmin, A. M. (1992) *SNG: Sostoyanie i perspektivy razvitiya*. Moscow: Gorbachev Fund.

Salrach, Josep M. (1996) "Catalunya, Castella i Espanya vistes per si mateixes a l'edad mitjana," *L'Avenc*, 200: 30–7.

Saltzman-Chafetz, Janet (1995) "Chicken or egg? A theory of relationship between feminist movements and family change," in Mason and Jensen (eds), pp. 63–81.

Salvati, Michele (1995) "Italy's fateful choices," *New Left Review*, 213: 79–96.

Sanchez, Magaly and Pedrazzini, Yves (1996) *Los malandros: la culture de l'urgence chez les jeunes des quartiers populaires de Caracas*. Paris: Fondation Humanisme et Développement.

Sanchez Jankowski, Martin (1991) *Islands in the Street: Gangs and American Urban Society*. Berkeley, CA: University of California Press.

Santoni Rugiu, Antonio (1994) "La bisciopedagogia," *Ponte*, 50 (2): 20–5.

Saravia, Joaquin and Sandoval, Godofredo (1991) *Jach'a Uru: la esperanza de un pueblo?* La Paz: CEP-ILDIS.

Savigear, Peter (1992) "The United States: superpower in decline?," in Baylis and Rengger (eds), pp. 334–53.

Saxenian, Anna Lee (2003) *Global Networks of Immigrant Entrepreneurs in High Technology Industries*. Cambridge: Cambridge University Press.

Scammell, Margaret and Semetko, Holli A. (1995) "Political advertising on television: the British experience," in Kaid and Holtz-Bacha (eds), pp. 19–43.

Scanlan, J. (ed.) (1990) *Surviving the Blues: Growing up in the Thatcher Decade*. London: Virago.

Scarce, Rik (1990) *Eco-warriors: Understanding the Radical Environmental Movement*. Chicago: Noble Press.

Schaeffer, Francis (1982) *Time for Anger: The Myth of Neutrality.* Westchester, IL: Crossway Books.

Scharf, Thomas (1994) *The German Greens: Challenging the Consensus.* Oxford: Berg.

Scheer, Leo (1994) *La democratie virtuelle.* Paris: Flammarion.

Scheff, Thomas (1994) "Emotions and identity: a theory of ethnic nationalism," in Calhoun (ed.), pp. 277–303.

Schiller, Dan (1999) *Digital Capitalism: Networking the Global Market System.* Cambridge, MA: MIT Press.

Schlesinger, Philip (1991) "Media, the political order and national identity," *Media, Culture, and Society,* 13: 297–308.

Schneir, Miriam (ed.) (1994) *Feminism in our Time: The Essential Writings, World War II to the Present.* New York: Vintage Books.

Scott, Allen (1995) *From Silicon Valley to Hollywood: Growth and Development of the Multimedia Industry in California.* Los Angeles, UCLA's Lewis Center for Regional Policy Studies, Working Paper no. 13, November.

Scott, Beardsley, et al. (1995) "The great European multimedia gamble," *McKinsey Quarterly,* 3: 142–61.

Sechi, Salvatore (ed.) (1995) *Deconstructing Italy: Italy in the Nineties.* Berkeley, CA: University of California, International and Area Studies, Research Series.

Sengenberger, Werner and Campbell, Duncan (eds) (1994) *Creating Economic Opportunities: The Role of Labour Standards in Industrial Restructuring.* Geneva: ILO, International Institute of Labour Studies.

Sennett, Richard (1978) *The Fall of Public Man.* New York: Vintage Books.

—— (1980) *Authority.* New York: Alfred Knopf.

Serra, Narcis (2003) "Europa y el nuevo sistema internacional," in Castells and Serra (eds), pp. 179–200.

Servon, Lisa and Castells, Manuel (1996) *The Feminist City: A Plural Blueprint.* Berkeley, CA: University of California, Institute of Urban and Regional Development, Working Paper.

Severino, Jean-Michel and Tubiana, Laurence (2002) 'La question des biens publics globaux," in Jacquet et al. (eds), pp. 349–74.

Shabecoff, Philip (1993) *A Fierce Green Fire: The American Environmental Movement.* New York: Hill and Wang.

Shaiken, Harley (1990) *Mexico in the Global Economy: High Technology and Work Organization in Export Industries.* La Jolla, CA: University of California at San Diego, Center for US–Mexican Studies.

Shapiro, Jerrold L., et al, (eds) (1995) *Becoming a Father: Contemporary Social, Developmental, and Clinical Perspectives.* New York: Springer Verlag.

Sheps, Sheldon (1995) "Militia – history and law FAQ", *World Wide Web,* September.

Shimazono, Susumu (1995) *AUM Shinrikyo no Kiseki* [*Trajectory of AUM Shinrikyo*]. Tokyo: Iwanami-Shoten.

Simpson, John H. (1992) "Fundamentalism in America revisited: the fading of modernity as a source of symbolic capital," in Misztal and Shupe (eds), pp. 10–27.

Singh, Tejpal (1982) *The Soviet Federal State: Theory, Formation, and Development.* New Delhi: Sterling.

Sisk, Timothy D. (1992) *Islam and Democracy: Religion, Politics, and Power in the Middle East.* Washington, DC: United States Institute of Peace Press.

Siune, Karen and Truetzschler, Wolfgang (eds) (1992) *Dynamics of Media Politics: Broadcast and Electronic Media in Western Europe.* London: Sage.

Sklair, Leslie (1991) *The Sociology of the Global System.* London: Harvester/Wheatsheaf.

Slezkine, Yuri (1994) "The USSR as a communal apartment, or how a Socialist state promoted ethnic particularism," *Slavic Review,* 53 (2): 414–52.

Smith, Anthony D. (1986) *The Ethnic Origins of Nations.* Oxford: Blackwell.

——(1989) "The origins of nations," *Ethnic and Racial Studies,* 12 (3): 340–67 (quoted from Eley and Suny (eds) (1996), p. 125).

Smith, Michael P. (1991) *City, State and Market: The Political Economy of Urban Society.* Oxford: Blackwell.

Smith, Peter H. (ed.) (1993) *El combate a las drogas en America.* Mexico: Fondo de Cultura Economica.

Sole-Tura, Jordi (1967) *Catalanisme i revolucio burgesa: la sintesi de Prat de la Riba.* Barcelona: Edicions 62.

Spalter-Roth, Roberta and Schreiber, Ronnee (1995) "Outsider issues and insider tactics: strategic tensions in the women's policy network during the 1980s," in Ferree and Martin (eds), pp. 105–27.

Spence, Jonathan D. (1996) *God's Chinese Son: The Taiping Heavenly Kingdom of Hong Xiuquan.* New York: Norton.

Spitz, Glenna (1988) "Women's employment and family relations: a review," *Journal of Marriage and the Family,* 50: 595–618.

Spivak, Gayatri Chakravorty (1990) *The Postcolonial Critique: Interviews, Strategies, Dialogues,* ed. Sarah Harasym. New York: Routledge.

Spragen, William C. (1995) *Electronic Magazines: Soft News Programs on Network Television*. Westport, CT: Praeger.

Spretnak, Charlene (ed.) (1982) *The Politics of Women's Spirituality: Essays on the Rise of Spiritual Power within the Women's Movement*. New York: Anchor.

Spruyt, Hendrik (1994) *The Sovereign State and its Competitors*. Princeton, NJ: Princeton University Press.

Stacey, Judith (1990) *Brave New Families: Stories of Domestic Upheaval in Late Twentieth Century America*. New York: Basic Books.

Staggenborg, Susan (1991) *The Pro-choice Movement*. New York: Oxford University Press.

Stallings, Barbara (1992) "International influence on economic policy: debt, stabilization, and structural reform," in Stephan Haggard and Robert Kaufman (eds), *The Politics of Economic Adjustment*, pp. 41–88. Princeton, NJ: Princeton University Press.

Standing, Guy (1990) "Global feminization through flexible labor," *World Development*, 17 (7): 1077–96.

Stanley, Harold W. and Niemi, Richard G. (1992) *Vital Statistics on American Politics*, 3rd edn. Washington, DC: CQ Press.

Starhawk (2002) *Webs of Power: Notes from the Global Uprising*. Gabriola Island, BC: New Society Publishers.

Starovoytova, Galina (1994) "Lecture at the Center for Slavic and East European Studies," University of California at Berkeley, February 23.

Stebelsky, Igor (1994) "National identity of Ukraine," in Hooson (ed.), pp. 233–48.

Sterling, Claire (1994) *Thieves' World: The Threat of the New Global Network of Organized Crime*. New York: Simon and Schuster.

Stern, Kenneth S. (1996) *A Force upon the Plain: The American Militia Movement and the Politics of Hate*. New York: Simon and Schuster.

Stevens, Mark (1995) "Big boys will be cow boys," *The New York Times Sunday Magazine*, November 19: 72–9.

Stiglitz, Joseph (2002) *Globalization and its Discontents*. New York: W. W. Norton (quoted in the Catalan translation, Barcelona: Editorial Empuries).

Streeck, Wolfgang and Schmitter, Philippe C. (1991) "From national corporatism to transnational pluralism: organized interests in the single European market," *Politics and Society*, 19 (2): 133–63.

Strobel, Margaret (1995) "Organizational learning in the Chicago Women's Liberation Union," in Ferree and Martin (eds), pp. 145–64.

Summers, Lawrence (1995) "Ten lessons to learn," *The Economist*, December 23: 46–8.

Sun Tzu (c.505–496 BC) *On the Art of War*, trans. with critical notes by Lionel Giles. Singapore: Graham Brash, 1988 (first published in English in 1910).

Suny, Ronald Grigor (1993) *The Revenge of the Past: Nationalism, Revolution, and the Collapse of the Soviet Union*. Stanford, CA: Stanford University Press.

Susser, Ida (1982) *Norman Street: Poverty and Politics in an Urban Neighborhood*. New York: Oxford University Press.

—— (1991) "The separation of mothers and children," in John Mollenkopf and Manuel Castells (eds), *Dual City: Restructuring New York*, pp. 207–24. New York: Russell Sage.

—— (1996) "The construction of poverty and homelessness in US cities," *Annual Reviews of Anthropology*, 25: 411–35.

—— (1997) "The flexible woman: re-gendering labor in the informational society," *Critique of Anthropology*.

Swan, Jon (1992) "Jennifer," *Columbia Journalism Review*, 31 (4): 36.

Szasz, Andrew (1994) *EcoPopulism: Toxic Waste and the Movement for Environmental Justice*. Minneapolis, MN: University of Minnesota Press.

Szmukler, Monica (1996) *Politicas urbanas y democracia: la ciudad de La Paz entre 1985 y 1995*. Santiago de Chile: ILADES.

Tanaka, Martin (1995) "La participacion politica de los sectores populares en America Latina," *Revista Mexicana de Sociologia*, 3: 41–65.

Tarrow, Sydney (1978) *Between Center and Periphery*. New Haven, CT: Yale University Press.

Tello Diaz, Carlos (1995) *La rebelion de las canadas*. Mexico: Cal y Arena.

Temas (1995) Special issue "Prensa y poder," 5: 18–50.

Thompson, Dennis F. (1995) *Ethics in Congress: From Individual to Institutional Corruption*. Washington, DC: Brookings Institution.

Thompson, John B. (2000) *Political Scandal: Power and Visibility in the Media Age*. Cambridge: Polity Press.

Thurman, Joseph E. and Trah, Gabriele (1990) "Part-time work in international perspective," *International Labour Review*, 129 (1): 23–40.

Thurow, Lester (1992) *Head to Head: The Coming Economic Battle between Japan, Europe, and the United States*. New York: Morrow.

Tibi, Bassam (1988) *The Crisis of Modern Islam: A Pre-industrial Culture in the Scientific-technological Age*. Salt Lake City: Utah University Press.

—— (1992a) *Die fundamentalische Herausforderung: der Islam und die Weltpolitik*. Munich: Beck Press.

—— (1992b) *Religious Fundamentalism and Ethnicity in the Crisis of the Nation-state in the Middle-East: Superordinate Islamic and Pan-Arabic Identities and Subordinate Ethnic and Sectarian Identities*. Berkeley, CA: University of California, Center for German and European Studies, working paper.

Tilly, Charles (ed.) (1975) *The Formation of Nation States in Western Europe*. Ann Arbor: University of Michigan Press.

—— (1995) "State-incited violence, 1900–1999," *Political Power and Social Theory*, 9: 161–79.

Time (1995) "Hell raiser: a Huey Long for the '90s: Pat Buchanan wields the most lethal weapon in Campaign 96: scapegoat politics," November 6.

Tirado, Ricardo and Luna, Matilde (1995) "El Consejo Coordinador Empresarial de Mexico: de la unidad contra el reformismo a la unidad para el Tratado de Libre Comercio (1975–1993)," *Revista Mexicana de Sociologia*, 4: 27–60.

Toner, Robin (1996) "Coming home from the revolution," *The New York Times*, Sunday November 10, s. 4: 1.

Tonry, Michael (1995) *Malign Neglect: Race, Crime, and Punishment in America*. New York: Oxford University Press.

Touraine, Alain (1965) *Sociologie de l'action*. Paris: Seuil.

—— (1966) *La conscience ouvrière*. Paris: Seuil.

—— (1988) *La parole et le sang: politique et société en Amérique Latine*. Paris: Odile Jacob.

—— (1992) *Critique de la modernité*. Paris: Fayard.

—— (1994) *Qu'est-ce que la démocratie?* Paris: Fayard.

—— (1995a) "La formation du sujet," in Dubet and Wieviorka (eds), pp. 21–46.

—— (1995b) *Lettre à Lionel, Michel, Jacques, Martine, Bernard, Dominique ... et vous*. Paris: Fayard.

——, et al. (1996) *Le grand refus: reflexions sur la grève de décembre 1995*. Paris: Fayard.

Tranfaglia, Nicola (1992) *Mafia, Politica e Affari, 1943–91*. Rome: Laterza.

Trejo Delarbre, Raul (1994a) *Chiapas: la comunicacion enmascarada. Los medios y el pasamontanas*. Mexico: Diana.

—— (ed.)(1994b) *Chiapas: La guerra de las ideas*. Mexico: Diana.

Trend, David (ed.) (1996) *Radical Democracy: Identity, Citizenship, and the State*. London: Routledge.

Trias, Eugenio (1996) "Entrevista: el modelo catalan puede ser muy util para Europa," *El Mundo*, June 30: 32.

Tsuya, Noriko O. and Mason, Karen O. (1995) "Changing gender roles and below-replacement fertility in Japan," in Mason and Jensen (eds), pp. 139–67.

Twinning, David T. (1993) *The New Eurasia: A Guide to the Republics of the Former Soviet Union*. Westport, CT: Praeger.

Ubois, Jeff (1995) "Legitimate government has its limits," *Midrange Systems*, 8 (22): 28.

United Nations (1970–1995) *Demographic Yearbook*, various years. New York: United Nations.

—— (1995) *Women in a Changing Global Economy: 1994 World Survey on the Role of Women in Development*. New York: United Nations.

United Nations Commission on Global Governance (1995) *Report of the Commission*. New York: United Nations.

United Nations Economic and Social Council (1994) "Problems and dangers posed by organized transnational crime in the various regions of the world," unpublished background document for World Ministerial Conference on Organized Transnational Crime, Naples, November 21–23.

US Bureau of the Census (1994) *Diverse Living Arrangements of Children*. Washington, DC: US Bureau of the Census.

—— (1996) *Composition of American Households*. Washington, DC: Department of Commerce, Bureau of the Census.

US Department of Commerce, Economics and Statistics Administration, Bureau of the Census, Current Population Reports, Washington, DC: Bureau of the Census:

—— (1989) *Singleness in America: Single Parents and their Children. Married-couple Families with their Children.*

—— (1991) *Population Profile of the United States, 1991*, Series P23, no. 173.

—— (1992a) *Households, Families, and Children: A 30-year Perspective*, P23–181.

—— (1992b) *When Households Continue, Discontinue, and Form* by Donald J. Hernandez, P23, no. 179.

—— (1992c) *Marriage, Divorce, and Remarriage in the 1990s*, by Arthur J. Norton and Louisa F. Miller, P23–180.

—— (1992d) *Population Trends in the 1980s*, P–23, no. 175.

Vajrayana Sacca (1994), August, no. 1. Tokyo: Aum Press.

Valdes, Teresa and Gomariz, Enrique (1993) *Mujeres latinoamericanas en cifras*. Madrid: Ministerio de Asuntos Sociales, Instituto de la Mujer.

Van de Berg, Jeroe and Castells, Nuria (2003) "International coordination of environmental policies and multilateral environmental agreements," in K. J. Button and D. A. Henschen (eds), *Handbook of Transportation and Environment*. Amsterdam: Elsevier.

Vedel, Thierry and Dutton, William H. (1990) "New media politics: shaping cable television policy in France," *Media, Culture, and Society*, 12 (4): 491–524.

Vicens Vives, Jaume (1959) *Historia social y economica de Espana y America*. Barcelona: Ariel.

——and Llorens, Montserrat (1958) *Industrials i Politics del Segle XIX*. Barcelona: Editorial Teide.

Vilar, Pierre (1964) *Catalunya dins l'Espanya Moderna*. Barcelona: Edicions 62.

——(ed.) (1987–90) *Historia de Catalunya*, 8 vols. Barcelona: Edicions 62.

Vogler, John (1992) "Regimes and the global commons: space, atmosphere and oceans," in McGrew et al. (eds), pp. 118–37.

Volkmer, Ingrid (1999) *News in the Global Sphere: A Study of CNN and its Impact on Global Communication*. Luton: Luton University Press.

——(2003) "The global network society and the global public sphere," *Journal of Development*, 46: 9–16.

Wacquant, Loïc J. D. (1994) "The new urban color line: the state and fate of the ghetto in postfordist America," in Calhoun (ed.), pp. 231–76.

Walter, David (1994) "Winner takes all: the incredible rise – and could it be fall – of Silvio Berlusconi," *Contents*, 23, (4/5): 18–24.

Walton, John and Seddon, David (1994) *Free Markets and Food Riots: The Politics of Global Adjustment*. Oxford: Blackwell.

Wapner, Paul (1995) "Politics beyond the state: environmental activism and world civic politics," *World Politics*, April: 311–40.

——(1996) *Environmental Activism and World Civic Politics*. Albany, NY: State University of New York Press.

Wattenberg, Martin (1996) *The Decline of American Political Parties: 1952–1994*. Cambridge, MA: Cambridge University Press.

Weinberg, Steve (1991) "Following the money," *Columbia Journalism Review*, 30 (2): 49–51.

Weisberg, Jacob (1996) *In Defense of Government: The Fall and Rise of Public Trust*. New York: Scribner.

Wellman, Barry (1979) "The community question," *American Journal of Sociology*, 84: 1201–31.

Welton, Neva and Wolf, Linda (2001) *Global Uprising: Confronting the Tyrannies of the 21st Century. Stories from a Generation of Activists*. Gabriola Island, BC: New Society Publishers.

WEPIN Store (1995) "Michigan Militia T-shirt," *World Wide Web*, West El Paso Information Network.

West, Cornel (1993) *Race Matters*. Boston: Beacon Press.

——(1996) "Black strivings in a twilight civilization," in Gates and West (eds), pp. 53–112.

West, Darrell M. (1993) *Air Wars: Television Advertising in Election Campaigns, 1952–1992*. Washington, DC: CQ Press.

Whisker, James B. (1992) *The Militia*. Lewiston, NY: E. Mellen Press.

White, Stephen, McAllister, Ian, and Oates, Sarah (2002) "Was it Russian public television that won it?," *Press/Politics*, 7 (2): 17–33.

Whittier, Nancy (1995) *Feminist Generations: The Persistence of the Radical Women's Movement*. Philadelphia: Temple University Press.

Wideman, Daniel J. and Preston, Rohan B. (eds) (1995) *Soulfires: Young Black Men on Love and Violence*. New York: Penguin.

Wiesenthal, Helmut (1993) *Realism in Green Politics: Social Movements and Ecological Reform in Germany*, ed. John Ferris. Manchester: Manchester University Press.

Wieviorka, Michel (1988) *Sociétés et terrorisme*. Paris: Fayard.

——(1993) *La démocratie à l'épreuve: nationalisme, populisme, ethnicité*. Paris: La Decouverte.

Wilcox, Clyde (1992) *God's Warriors: The Christian Right in 20th Century America*. Baltimore, MD: The Johns Hopkins University Press.

Wilensky, Harold (1975) *The Welfare State and Equality: Structural and Ideological Roots of Public Expenditures*. Berkeley, CA: University of California Press.

Williams, Lance and Winokour, Scott (1995) "Militia extremists defend their views," *San Francisco Examiner*, April 23.

Wilson, William Julius (1987) *The Truly Disadvantaged: The Inner City, the Underclass, and Public Policy*. Chicago: University of Chicago Press.

Winerip, Michael (1996) "An American place: the paramilitary movement. Ohio case typifies the tensions between Militia groups and law," *The New York Times*, June 23: A1.

Wittig, Monique (1992) *The Straight Mind*. Boston: Beacon Press.

Woldenberg, Jose (1995) *Violencia y politica*. Mexico: Cal y Arena.

Woodward, Bob (1994) *The Agenda: Inside the Clinton White House*. New York: Simon and Schuster.

World Almanac Books (1996) *The World Almanac of Books and Facts, 1996*. New York: Funk and Wagnalls.

WuDunn, Sheryl (1996) "Uproar over a debt crisis: does Japan's mob bear part of the blame?," *The New York Times*, February 14: C1.

Wyplosz, Charles (2002) "L'économie en avance sur les institutions," in Jacquet et al. (eds), pp. 301–12.

Yazawa, Shujiro (1997) *Japanese Social Movements since World War II*. Boston, MA: Beacon Press.

Yoshino, Kosaku (1992) *Cultural Nationalism in Contemporary Japan*. London: Routledge.

Zaller, John and Hunt, Mark (1994) "The rise and fall of candidate Perot: unmediated versus mediated politics, part I," *Political Communication*, 11: 357–90.

Zaretsky, Eli (1994) "Identity theory, identity politics: psychoanalysis, marxism, post-structuralism," in Calhoun (ed.), pp. 198–215.

Zeskind, Leonard (1986) *The Christian Identity Movement: Analyzing its Theological Rationalization for Racist and Anti-semitic Violence*. Atlanta, GA: National Council of the Churches of the Christ in the USA, Center for Democratic Renewal.

Ziccardi, Alicia (ed.) (1991) *Ciudades y gobiernos locales en la America Latina de los noventa*. Mexico: Miguel Angel Porrua Grupo Editorial.

—— (ed.) (1995) *La tarea de gobernar: gobiernos locales y demandas ciudadanas*. Mexico: Miguel Angel Porrua Grupo Editorial.

Ziegler, Jean (2002) *Les nouveaux maîtres du monde et ceux qui leur résistent*. Paris: Fayard.

Zisk, Betty H. (1992) *The Politics of Transformation: Local Activism in the Peace and Environmental Movements*. Westport, CT: Praeger.

Zook, Matthew (1996) "The unorganized militia network: conspiracies, computers, and community," Berkeley, CA: University of California, Department of Sociology, unpublished seminar paper for SOC 290.2.

Index